D1609675

Financial Markets

The Accumulation and Allocation of Wealth

McGraw-Hill Series in Finance

Professor Charles A. D'Ambrosio
University of Washington
Consulting Editor

Financial Markets

The Accumulation and Allocation of Wealth

Second Edition

Roland I. Robinson
Professor of Finance, Emeritus
Michigan State University

Dwayne Wrightsman
Professor of Economics
The Whittemore School of Business
and Economics
University of New Hampshire

McGraw-Hill Book Company

New York   St. Louis   San Francisco   Auckland   Bogotá   Hamburg
Johannesburg   London   Madrid   Mexico   Montreal   New Delhi   Panama
Paris   São Paulo   Singapore   Sydney   Tokyo   Toronto

Library of Congress Cataloging in Publication Data

Robinson, Roland I
    Financial markets.

    (McGraw-Hill series in finance)
    Bibliography: p.
    Includes index.

    1. Finance—United States. 2. Money market—United States. 3.   Capital
market—United States. I. Wrightsman, Dwayne, joint author. II. Title.
HG181.R59 1980   332.4   79-21955
ISBN 0-07-053274-5

FINANCIAL MARKETS: The Accumulation and Allocation of Wealth

34567890 FGFG 8987654321

This book was set in Times Roman by The Total Book (ECU/BD). The editor was
Bonnie E. Lieberman; the designer was Caliber Design Planning; the production supervisor
was Richard A. Ausburn.
Fairfield Graphics was printer and binder.

contents

part TWO
Money Markets

part THREE
Capital Markets

preface

This book is appropriate for anyone who wants to learn about financial markets, but it is designed especially as a textbook for courses in financial markets and institutions. The financial markets course has become an important adjunct to the financial management course in the business school curriculum. This is because good microfinancial decision making goes hand in glove with a good knowledge of the macrofinancial environment. The financial markets course is also an important extension to the traditional money and banking course offered by economics departments. It is widely recognized that money is just one among many financial assets and that banks compete with other types of financial intermediaries. This book covers the whole spectrum of financial markets and the sectors that participate in them. Considerable attention is paid, however, to the special role of commercial banks and the Federal Reserve in the money markets.

The expository format of this book follows that of the 1974 and 1964 editions (the 1964 edition being entitled *Money and Capital Markets*). It is written for business and economics students who have had some exposure to the principles of economics. The book is neither a descriptive how-to-succeed-in-business book nor is it a theoretical economics text; rather, it strives for a balance of description and analysis. The analysis is intended to encourage a maximum of understanding with a minimum of technical or formal apparatus. The book is written from the perspective that the whats, hows, and whys of finance go together inextricably. Business students and economics majors should feel equally at home in reading this book.

The book is divided into five parts. The first covers the basic economic forces operating in financial markets generally. This part analyzes how the level and structure of market interest rates serve to determine the wealth accumulation and allocation decisions of individual units and how these decisions, taken collectively, feed back to determine the level and structure of interest rates in the market. With this overview of the entire system, the book turns to the specifics of financial markets. Part two of the book examines the money markets, which are markets for different short-term securities. Part three covers the capital markets, which include the markets for stocks and bonds, mortgages, and long-term government securities. The fourth part of the book focuses on the international dimensions of financial markets. Increasingly, U.S. corporations have sought international markets despite the uncertainty of foreign exchange rates and other barriers to foreign trade and finance. The fifth and final section of the book deals with public policies toward financial markets and institutions. This part looks at government policies designed to stabilize and regulate the financial market system.

This edition of the book has been revised extensively and includes much new material. Two new chapters—one on the theory of interest (see Chapter 3) and another on stock market research (see Chapter 18) have been added. The coverage of international finance has been expanded from one chapter to two. The material on the Federal Reserve and its influence in financial markets has been completely rewritten. The introductory chapter has been changed to focus attention on the functions of financial markets. The money market chapters have been reorganized. So have the chapters on financial market performance; these are now organized within a government policy framework. Every chapter in the book has been revised, updated, and (we hope) improved. For example, almost every chapter now has some treatment of the role of expected inflation and the role of inflation uncertainty, as the forces of inflation have invaded nearly every nook and cranny of the financial market system.

This edition also has some pedagogical improvements. Bibliographies have now been placed at the ends of the chapters; this gives the reader much easier access to related readings. End-of-chapter questions, problems, and projects have also been added. For teachers, a new instructor's manual has been prepared. And for adopting teachers, an annual supplement with updated statistics and references to new materials is being offered. This annual supplement is designed to ease the lives of busy teachers and to improve the quality of material available to students.

The authors gratefully acknowledge William Handorf, George Washington University; Kenneth Locke, University of Missouri; Kelly Price, Michigan State University; Peter Rose, Texas A&M University; and Samual Taddesse, Federal Reserve Bank of N.Y., for reading the manuscript.

A textbook with so many details cannot possibly appear without errors. No matter how diligent the search, some mistakes or oversights will inevitably elude the authors, editors, reviewers, and others who deal with the material in the publication process. Readers are urged to call any detected errors to the attention of the authors. Comments and constructive criticisms will be greatly appreciated.

ROLAND I. ROBINSON

DWAYNE WRIGHTSMAN

Financial Markets

The Accumulation and Allocation of Wealth

part one

The Economic Logic of Financial Markets

chapter 1
Functions of Financial Markets

Markets are among the greatest of social inventions. Without markets, life would be brutish, short, and unrewarding. Most of us lack the skills, tastes, time, and endurance to struggle through a life of total self-sufficiency. Romantic illusions aside, living only off what we could produce with our own labor would be dreary and risky. One would have no time for pleasure or relaxation after an exhausting day of scrounging for food, making clothes, and building shelter, all done by hand and with tools made by hand.

The beauty of markets is that we can separate the decision of how we want to make a living from the decision of how we want to live. In the parlance of economics this means that one's production decisions can be separated from one's consumption decisions. A person who loves to produce sour pickles but prefers to consume candy bars can trade with another person who loves to make candy but prefers to eat sour pickles. This barter, however, will take place only if there is a coincidence of wants. Money, another great social invention, solves the exchange problem by serving as a medium for multisided exchange.

The ultimate function of product markets, aided by money, is to increase income and the standard of living. People are free to specialize in work where they have a comparative advantage, so that everyone's income is higher than it would be otherwise. Alternatively, people can specialize in work that is intrinsically satisfying, to increase psychic income. People are fortunate when these two specializations lead to the same work.

Money is not only an efficient medium of exchange between producers and consumers, it also facilitates borrowing and lending. One who does not want to consume today can lend to one who does, and when the loan is later repaid, the lender will have even more to consume. Functioning as the medium of debt transactions gives a time dimension to money. This is the point at which financial markets become important.

Financial markets permit each economic unit to separate the decision to save out of income from the decision to invest in capital goods. Lending in the financial markets makes it possible for a person to save without having to invest in capital goods. Borrowing in the market makes it possible to finance investment in capital goods without having to save out of income. Since financial markets are the subject of this book, we shall have much to say about the subject. It is well to stress, however, that when borrowing and lending transactions originate we have reached a stage of society at which there must be a system of law that governs such transactions. Lenders must be able to lend with some confidence that both custom and law will be on their side when it comes time to collect. Furthermore, the fact that the amount paid back is larger than the amount borrowed—that there is *interest* involved in the transaction—gives rise to a strong incentive for borrowers to use borrowed money productively.

The borrowing of money for productive purposes makes it possible for society to accumulate more wealth and enjoy a higher standard of living in the long run than would be possible if financial markets did not exist. In this sense, the function of financial markets runs parallel to that of product markets: Both help to increase society's standard of living.

THE ACCUMULATION OF WEALTH

Wealth is the reservoir of all past net saving embodied (one could say "invested") in those enduring objects or skills that make us more productive and fulfilled. Wealth increases with production and decreases with consumption. The improvement of land, the training of labor, the production of plant and equipment, and the stockpiling of goods, all add to the amount of wealth. The depletion of resources, the obsolescence of skills, the depreciation of capital goods, and the drawing down of inventories, all subtract from wealth. In order for wealth to increase on a net basis, society must consume less than it earns; it must *save*. But society must *invest* what it saves. Just as production and income are two sides of the same coin, so are investment and saving. Either way you look at it, wealth can accumulate only by the sacrifice of current consumption, thereby reducing the current standard of living below its current potential. The payoff, however, is a higher standard of living in the long run.

In free societies, saving and investment are voluntary acts. People freely choose to give up a little consumption now for a lot more consumption later. The fact that some nations freely save, invest, and accumulate wealth at much lower rates than other nations does not necessarily mean that the former are populated by greedy, shortsighted people. Rather, the rate of wealth accumulation often reflects the stage of development of a nation's economic and financial system. Income is so meager and financial markets so rudimentary in poor nations that wealth has little opportunity to grow.

Let us consider the wealth accumulation process in a rudimentary economy that has no financial markets. In such an economy, each person has to be financially self-sufficient. No one can invest in the means of production without financing it out of his or her own saving; and no one can save without a simultaneous act of real investment. Every opportunity to invest is dependent upon the individual's ability to save. Likewise, the desire to save is constrained by the individual's opportunities to invest. So what happens? Individuals who want to invest more than they can possibly save are forced to cut back on their investment. And those who want to save more than their investment opportunities allow are forced to cut back on saving. As a result, very little of either gets done.

Financial markets make it possible for acts of saving and investment to be separated (in the same way that product markets make it possible to separate production decisions from consumption decisions). Financial markets make it possible for some members of society to save, while others may assume responsibility for real investment operations. The separation of the acts of saving and investment serves to increase both saving and investment and hence the wealth and growth of the economy. Individuals who want to save but not invest (in a real sense) can do so by lending in financial markets. Others who want to invest but not save can do so by borrowing in financial markets. Financial markets increase the availability of financial capital by tapping the savings potential of noninvesting individuals. Thus, a major function of financial markets is to provide a link between saving and investment, thereby facilitating the creation of new wealth.

The existence of financial markets does not mean that individual financial behavior is totally unconstrained, nor does it negate the equality of saving and investment in the aggregate. The boundaries and limits of financial behavior can be demonstrated by some very simple equations. The starting point is that of the balance sheet equation:

$$\text{Assets} \equiv \text{liabilities} + \text{net worth}$$

This equation can be expanded to the form:

$$\text{Real assets } (RA) + \text{financial assets } (FA) \equiv \text{liabilities } (L; \text{ all financial}) \\ + \text{net worth } (NW)$$

Real assets represent the cumulation of real items such as plant and equipment, inventories, houses, and human capital. Financial assets are the cumulation of securities and all other types of IOUs held *against others* who owe them. Liabilities are just the opposite; they represent cumulated debt *to others*. Net worth can be viewed as a cumulation of all past saving.

The balance sheet, which is a statement at a point in time, can be converted into a statement of changes over time:

$$\Delta RA + \Delta FA \equiv \Delta L + \Delta NW$$

The terms on the left-hand side of this equation represent uses of funds; those on the right-hand side, sources of funds. By interpreting each term we obtain the following identity:

$$\text{Investment} + \text{lending} \equiv \text{borrowing} + \text{saving}$$

Real assets grow through investment. Financial assets build up through lending. Liabilities increase with borrowing. And net worth accumulates through saving. But these acts are constrained: The total of investment and lending is always equal to the total of borrowing and saving. This identity is necessarily true of the financial behavior of each economic unit. It also holds in the aggregate.

There is one important difference, however, between individual and aggregate financial behavior. In the aggregate, total lending must equal total borrowing since they are two ways of looking at the same thing. They can therefore be canceled in the equation above, leaving us with the familiar result that total saving equals total investment. Similarly, total net worth is measured by total real assets. Financial froth cannot and should not obscure the basic fact that society is not richer except as is expressed in some form of real wealth. Real wealth does not exclude intangibles such as human skills, but it does exclude the paper claims created by lending and borrowing transactions.

The equality of saving and investment in the aggregate does not apply to individual economic entities. Households, businesses, governments, and other entities are constrained only to the extent that the two uses of funds (investment and lending) must equal the two sources (borrowing and saving). Saving and investment are rarely equal for individual entities. The average household saves more than it invests by lending more than it borrows. Some households (particularly those buying new houses and new consumer durables such as automobiles) invest more than they save and therefore borrow more than they lend. Businesses and governments are generally net borrowers. Business investment in plant and equipment and inventories is usually greater than business saving from retained earnings. Governments, especially the federal government, have a tendency to tax less than they spend so they must borrow to cover negative saving.

Each person (or corporation or governmental unit) may feel free to make saving and investment decisions, but they are not really as free as they think. The different individual decisions of participants in the market must be balanced. If everyone decided to invest more than they saved, then everyone would need to borrow, but no one could, because there would be no lenders. Fortunately, the balancing process is facilitated through the movement of interest rates toward an equilibrium. The interest-rate price of lending and borrowing transactions adjusts rapidly so that those who want to borrow can find willing lenders and vice versa. If everyone wanted to borrow, the rate of interest would quickly rise to such a high level that enough participants would change their minds and decide to lend instead. The fact that the rate of interest adjusts freely and impersonally in the market means that market participants can behave as if their decisions are independent of each other. The rate of interest is the "invisible hand" that coordinates financial behavior in financial markets. Its role in financial markets is no different from any other price in any other market.

The development of markets to bring those who want to save and lend together with those who want to borrow and invest is an important step toward financial development. However, direct face-to-face dealing between ultimate net savers and ultimate net investors is often not practical. "Securities brokers" are needed when face-to-face transacting is too costly. "Financial intermediaries" are needed to resolve differences between the needs of savers and the needs of those who invest. Even if saver-lender and borrower-investor can agree on an interest rate, they will conclude their transaction only if they can further agree on all other terms such as maturity, collateral, method of redemption, etc. Such agreement can be exceedingly difficult. Most savers prefer to keep their savings liquid by lending short-term. Investment, on the other hand, is usually long-term; it is usually financed through long-term borrowing. Obviously, a single market connecting such lenders with such borrowers cannot work to mutual advantage. This, then, suggests the development of differentiated markets: one for short-term lending and one for long-term borrowing. But who will borrow in the former? And who will lend in the latter? The problem is solved by the development of different types of financial intermediaries. Institutions such as commercial banks, savings banks, and savings and loan associations are quite willing to borrow short-term from individual savers and to put these borrowings to work by lending them on a longer-term basis to home buyers, businesses, governments, and other borrowers.

The presence of many various financial intermediaries in an economy indicates that the economy is in an advanced stage of financial development. With intermediaries, the choices of uses and sources of funds available to the decision maker is expanded:

$$\begin{array}{c} & \text{lending} & \text{lending} \\ \text{Investment} + & \text{to ultimate} + & \text{to financial} & \equiv \\ & \text{borrowers} & \text{intermediaries} \end{array}$$

$$\begin{array}{c} \text{borrowing} & \text{borrowing} \\ \text{from financial} + & \text{from ultimate} + \text{saving} \\ \text{intermediaries} & \text{lenders} \end{array}$$

The three uses of funds on the left-hand side of the equation, along with the three sources on the right-hand side, are related to the three channels through which funds flow from saving to investment. One channel is "internal finance" through which one's own saving is used for one's own real investment. A second channel is "direct external finance" through which funds are loaned directly from those who save to those who invest. The third channel is "indirect external finance" through which saving flows from ultimate lenders to financial intermediaries, and then from intermediaries to ultimate borrowers. By increasing the options for using and securing funds, the potential develops for more saving, more investment, and a greater rate of wealth accumulation.

The choice that is thus put before both borrowers and lenders reveals one of several distinctions that we shall observe in our study of financial markets: the distinction between the market for "primary" credit instruments (issued by ultimate borrowers) and the market for "indirect" credit instruments (issued by financial intermediaries). Duplication exists, of course, since the lending and borrowing of financial intermediaries cancels out in a literal sense. This cancellation, however, should not and does not belittle the importance of financial intermediaries. These intermediaries have made it practical for many more persons to employ their savings safely and profitably than would have been possible in a system only of borrowing and lending between ultimate savers and ultimate investors.

Another distinction within financial markets is between "negotiated" and "open" financial markets. When transactions are not standardized, as in a primitive society, every transaction involving credit has to be personally negotiated. However, the appearance of large borrowers who could break their borrowings down into smaller but homogeneous units (such as thousand-dollar bonds in a million-dollar bond issue) created the potential for open markets. An open market is one in which the unit of transactions is well known and does not need to be negotiated each time it changes hands. Open market securities can be offered for bidding by many buyers. In addition, when the unit of transaction is very similar, even if not identical, something like an open market readily develops. High-grade corporate bonds are not all alike, but they are similar enough that an open market in corporate bonds in general can be said to exist.

An open market system is very beneficial for capital formation. When a large corporation needs hundreds of millions of dollars to finance plant and equipment, it can offer small-denomination securities on the open market to tap the savings of tens of thousands of relatively small investors.

The opportunity for an ultimate borrower to secure credit by selling securities in the open market exists only in highly developed financial economies. An open market must be open to all qualified participants. The number of buyers and sellers must be large enough that interest rates are determined impersonally by the forces of supply and demand. Open market rates must be known to all market participants so that uniform securities are traded at uniform prices.

Negotiated markets, by way of contrast, include all those transactions between a single lender and a single borrower, or among a small number of parties. Between them the terms of a loan are personally bargained. This includes the interest rate, although negotiated rates are almost always in line with rates in the open market. As to who borrows in which type of market, the open market is open only to those borrowers of large size and with known credit standing (General Motors or the U.S. Treasury, for example). The rest of us can do no better than to negotiate for credit. The lending side of the open market is much less discriminating. Anyone can buy securities in the open market provided one can pay the cash involved.

Maturity is the characteristic used to distinguish open money market instruments from open capital market securities. Short-term credit contracts are generally included in what is known as the "money market"; the longer-term debt contracts and equities are "capital market" instruments. The maturity limit of one year is sometimes used as a device for distinguishing between the two markets, but this line of division is artificial at best. Maturity is relative, not absolute. In many ways it can be argued that a one-day maturity differs more from a one-year maturity than the latter does from a twenty-year maturity.

Another way of distinguishing between money market and capital market securities is by purpose of offering. Offerings of capital market securities are generally associated with investment expenditures and the accumulation of real wealth. Bonds and stocks are issued by corporations for the presumed purpose of raising money to pay for corporate investment in plant and equipment. A net increase in home mortgages in the mortgage market is usually associated with residential construction expenditures. Municipal bonds are offered when local authorities need capital funds to finance school construction and other public investments. Transactions in the money market, on the other hand, generally involve no change in real investment and saving. Rather, the money market system provides a mechanism for managing cash positions when cash is temporarily excessive or deficient. We shall discuss this "liquidity adjustment" function later in this chapter.

By definition, the instruments traded in the capital markets share the common characteristic of being long-term. Other than this, these instruments are considerably differentiated. U.S. government securities differ from all other long-term debt instruments in that they are protected against the risk of default of interest and principal. The federal government can always keep its promises to pay interest and return principal through its powers to tax income and print money. State and local government securities are differentiated by the exemption of interest earned on them from income subject to federal taxes. Corporate equities differ from corporate debt instruments by their noncontractual nature. The dividends paid on equities are neither fixed in amount nor promised in terms of payment. Dividends are paid at the discretion of corporate boards of directors, varying roughly with corporate profits. Equities also have no predetermined maturity dates; they live on with the life of the corporation. All debt instruments have specific dates of maturity, but the range of maturities is quite broad. The differences in risk, tax status, and period to maturity account for most of the observed differences between yields quoted in the long-term credit markets.

The proliferation of financial markets necessarily involves a proliferation of market interest rates: a differentiated rate for each differentiated market. The job of these interest rates is to guide the lending and borrowing decisions of all participants across all markets and to coordinate these decisions so that the amount that lenders want to lend in each market is equal to the amount that borrowers want to borrow. The decision to lend or borrow in any given market depends not only on the interest rate associated with that market, but also on those interest rates associated with markets providing lending and borrowing alternatives. Moreover, the interest rate in any given market is determined not only by the amount of lending and borrowing in that market, but also by the amounts of lending and borrowing in all related markets. Because financial markets are clearly interrelated, the only meaningful way to understand them is to think in complex terms of general equilibrium analysis.

The proliferation of financial markets also adds to the complexity of making decisions. The greater the number of markets in which to lend or borrow, the greater the number of interest rates to watch and the greater the number of lending and borrowing alternatives to consider. Even though constrained by the necessary equality of uses and sources of funds, the number of possible decision sets can be endless. Nevertheless, greater choice is preferable to less choice. One can always elect not to take advantage of an available choice, but one can never elect to take advantage of an unavailable choice.

The wealth accumulation function of the financial market system should now be clear. The more developed (and complex) the system, the greater the opportunity for individuals and society to increase wealth and thereby raise the long-run standard of living. Financial development means that savers have many more choices for putting savings to work and that those specializing in investment have many more choices for financing investment. The countries with the most fully developed financial market systems also have the highest standards of living. This association is no proof that cause and effect runs from financial development to economic welfare, but it is certainly suggestive.

THE ALLOCATION OF WEALTH

The accumulation of wealth is necessary if a society is to improve its lot and to make cultural advances possible. Another condition required is that the wealth accumulated by savers be allocated to productive and timely purposes. A society that uses savings to build pyramids as tombs for vain kings may create employment, but it does not improve its lot very much. A basic test of the social utility of financial markets, therefore, is their success in allocating wealth in such a way as to benefit society.

Financial transactions in which some parties save and lend while others borrow and invest (in real assets) are transactions that add to both the stock of financial assets and to the stock of real wealth in the economy. Not all financial transactions lead to this result, however. Financial assets can be created without net saving and investment taking place. If Mr. Profligate borrows to indulge his taste for luxurious living and Mr. Pinchpenny is willing to save and lend him the wherewithal for this fling, a debt contract will have been created without any net saving. Mr. Pinchpenny has saved, but Mr. Profligate has done quite the opposite: He has dissaved. This somewhat trivial illustration has a parallel in the financing of government deficits. The federal government is one of the biggest borrowers in financial markets. The money that it borrows is not used to pay for investment in the conventional sense but is used instead to pay for the government's "consumption" in excess of its "income" from taxes. In this case, the creation of government debt adds little to real wealth because the private saving of those who lend to the government tends to be cancelled by the government's dissaving.

The allocative function of financial markets does not stop with the handling of newly saved funds; it is also operative when investors shift the compositions of their portfolios. In this process, they sell off already outstanding financial claims and the financial claims that they purchase in replacement may not be newly issued, but may have already been outstanding and are being sold by some other investor. Such transactions are "secondary" market transactions. This is in contrast to "primary" market transactions that involve the sale of new securities to finance the formation of capital goods or to finance other real expenditures.

Secondary market transactions have no effect on either the creation of new real wealth or the creation of new financial assets. The stock markets (the New York Stock Exchange, for example) are a good case in point. Millions of individuals and institutions transact in these markets, switching back and forth among issues of different corporations. When John Doe buys Xerox stock, he does not get new securities from Xerox but instead gets Xerox stock already outstanding and in the hands of some willing seller. Similarly, Xerox does not get any funds with which to finance capital outlays; the money goes to the seller. He or she, in turn, will likely reinvest in some other stock already outstanding. The stock, bond, and other security exchanges are the "used car lots" of the financial markets; they are true secondary markets. Trading in them adds no new wealth, real or financial.

The actions of the numerous individual buyers and sellers in the secondary markets produce signals in the form of prices that indicate a market consensus of relative values. These values, or prices, feed back into the "primary" market, or market for new issues. Unlike new and used cars, new and used securities are nearly perfect substitutes. Prices determined in the secondary market have a powerful influence as to prices that can be expected from the purchase and sale of new issues. Secondary markets provide valuable pricing information to society. Without these markets, ultimate savers and investors would have to make lending and borrowing decisions in the dark.

The role of the secondary market system extends well beyond its support of the primary market system. Indeed, it plays a starring role in that function of financial markets concerned with the allocation of wealth. Every wealth holder must decide not only how much to add to existing wealth (the wealth accumulation decision), but must also decide how existing wealth is to be allocated among alternative assets (the wealth allocation decision). Net worth, which is the measure of an individual's wealth, must be apportioned between real assets and net financial assets (financial assets minus liabilities). The latter, which are indirect claims on real assets, must, in turn, be apportioned among the thousands of available securities and debt instruments traded in the market. The wealth allocation decision is often made in conjunction with the decision to accumulate, but the two decisions do not have to go together. The wealth allocation problem would still exist even if saving, investment, and primary market activity were to cease.

The main function of secondary financial markets is to enable individuals and institutions to allocate and reallocate their financial asset holdings at any time. An individual naturally does not want to be trapped into any given holding of securities; neither does a person want to be stopped from buying a security that is not presently being issued in the primary market. With secondary markets, one can buy and sell any security at any time.

The prices of securities traded in the market bear heavily on the wealth allocation process. They guide individuals in their portfolio selection decisions and coordinate these decisions so that everyone is able to satisfy his or her demand for particular securities at any given time. The pricing mechanism ensures that buyers in the secondary market can find sellers and vice versa.

The trading of a security in the market indicates that buyer and seller are reallocating their financial assets in opposite directions: The buyer seeks a larger position in the security, the seller seeks to unload. This, combined with the fact that the buyer pays the same market price that the seller receives (ignoring commissions), indicates that the market price is not the sole guiding force in making portfolio or wealth allocation decisions. The very fact of trading indicates that buyer and seller do not agree with the market that the market price is a correct measure of the security's value.

Evaluation of a security involves weighing the expected rate of return from holding the security against the risk that the expected rate of return will not be realized. Using the conventional present-value formula, the expected rate of return is calculated from: (1) what you think the market price of the security will be at some point in the future, (2) what you think it will return in interest or dividends in the interim, and (3) what price you have to pay for it now in the market. Except for this last element, which is given, any disagreement as to the other elements will naturally lead to disagreement about the security's value. All that is needed to effect a trade in the market is a belief (the buyer's) that the security is underpriced combined with the opposite belief (the seller's) that it is overpriced.

Market price, however, is always the correct measure of value in terms of its market-clearing function. It always adjusts to equilibrate the volume of desired purchases and sales. It always seeks a level at which the amount outstanding of a security is willingly held. Market price reflects the market's consensus of its intrinsic value. In this sense, the price is always right.

In making a portfolio selection decision, the wealth allocator needs to assess the expected rate of return and the risk of return on each portfolio under consideration. This assessment of portfolio risk and return is not just a simple matter of adding up the risk and return of all the securities in the portfolio. If the portfolio is suitably diversified, the risk of the whole portfolio will be less than the risk of the sum of the portfolio's parts. Diversification makes it possible to earn a target expected return at less risk, or a higher expected return for a target level of risk, than is possible in the absence of diversification. Moreover, this risk-reducing advantage increases the more the portfolio is diversified, especially among securities whose returns are not highly correlated. A highly developed financial system of secondary markets is absolutely essential to realize the full benefits of portfolio diversification. These markets give wealth holders the opportunity to spread their holdings over the greatest number and variety of financial assets.

LIQUIDITY ADJUSTMENT

A major dimension of the wealth allocation process is the adjustment of liquidity. Liquidity measures the nearness of a financial asset to cash, which itself is a financial asset differing from all others in that only cash is used as a medium of exchange. The liquidity of a given financial asset is gauged by the ability to convert the asset into cash at any time without taking a loss. Cash, of course, is itself perfectly liquid. All other financial assets have varying degrees of liquidity. Marketable securities can be converted into cash at any time by selling them in the open secondary markets, but there is no guarantee against loss. Debt instruments can be redeemed for face value at maturity (provided that they do not default), but maturity comes at only one particular time.

Of all the financial assets traded in financial markets, the instruments of the open money market are the most liquid (other than cash itself). Money market instruments are marketable, have little risk of default, and have such short maturities that their market values are quite stable relative to the instruments traded in the capital markets. Indeed, the money market can be said to owe its name to the fact that the instruments traded in it are about as good as money itself.

Money is the universal medium of exchange. It flows in from receipts and flows out with disbursements. Cash balances build up during those periods when receipts exceed disbursements, and they are drawn down when the opposite occurs. An important reason for allocating some part of financial wealth to the holding of cash is to bridge the gap between receipts and outlays.

Holding cash is costly, however. Cash in the form of currency and demand deposits pays no interest. The law currently prevents it. Consequently, wealth held in this form bears an opportunity cost of the interest that could be earned if earning assets were held instead. This opportunity cost factor is a strong inducement to hold as little cash as possible. But this course of action can be equally costly in terms of the risks of running out of cash. At best, no cash means no more spending. At worst, it can lead to bankruptcy.

By allocating a portion of wealth to the holding of money market instruments, the wealth allocator is able to reduce the risk of keeping a low cash balance and, at the same time, avoid the cost of foregoing interest. These liquid instruments can be converted into instant cash as the need arises. All that is entailed is a telephone call to a broker, the payment of the broker's fee, and the possibility of having to take a relatively small capital loss.

The advantage of holding money market instruments in place of cash is, of course, the money market interest rates that these instruments pay. On the average, these rates are less than capital market rates because the latter tend to command a premium that compensates for the lack of liquidity of capital market instruments. At times, however, the interest rates on short-term maturities are considerably higher than they are for longer-term maturities. (The relation between yield and maturity is one of the most complex but fascinating relations in the study of financial markets.)

The switching back and forth between cash holdings and holdings of money market instruments, as the need for cash changes, is the major way in which the money markets are used for adjusting liquidity. But it is not the only way. These instruments represent short-term debts of the borrowers who place and sell them originally in the market, and this borrowing is often done for the same purpose, that is, to secure needed cash until cash flow turns around. When cash flow does turn around, the borrower can then use the cash to retire debts.

The money market works because the parties in the market have temporary needs for cash at different times. When borrowers sell money market instruments, they need cash. And they get it from those lenders (buyers) who, at the time, have excess cash. Then, when the latter need cash, they can cash in the instruments with the borrowers, or, if the instruments are yet to mature, they can resell them in the secondary market to others with excess cash. In short, the money market allocates the existing supply of cash to those who, at any point in time, need it the most. Two qualifications are in order, however. The open money market is very impersonal; it measures need by the willingness and ability to pay the going rate of interest. The central open money market is also a wholesale market; it deals in transactions of $100,000 and up.

THE SPECIAL ROLE OF MONEY

Money is at the heart of finance; maybe even at the heart of economics. For exchange of goods and services it is without parallel. When people are cut off from a money system (as in prisoner-of-war camps) they quickly reinvent it (by using cigarettes for example). In financial markets, money serves a special role of vast importance. Money is the substance that lenders lend and borrowers borrow. The debt contracts exchanged for money are themselves written, expressed, and valued in terms of money. The obligation to pay interest and return principal is a monetary obligation.

When borrowers go into debt and borrow money, they end up, strangely enough, borrowing debt. Money in the form of paper currency is itself a debt of the government and the central banking authority: Most of the paper currency in the United States is in the form of Federal Reserve Notes, which are debt instruments of the twelve Federal Reserve banks. Checking account money, also, is debt: Most of it is in the form of demand deposits, which are claims against commercial banks.

Money, however, is both much more and much less than ordinary debt. It is a special kind of debt in that it is the only kind used as the medium of exchange.

Money is lacking, however, in some of the usual characteristics of ordinary debt. By law, currency and demand deposits currently pay no interest. Moreover, money never comes due, yet it can be redeemed at any time. Demand deposits can be converted into Federal Reserve Notes at commercial banks upon demand. In turn, Federal Reserve Notes can be redeemed at Federal Reserve banks at any time, although all that one would get back would be more Federal Reserve Notes (with different serial numbers).

Because money is the medium of exchange, its demand is nearly universal. There are no simple rules governing the holding of money, but we do know that the demand for money falls as interest rates—which are the opportunity costs of holding money—rise. We also know that the demand for money rises as individuals and organizations have greater incomes and expenditures. The revolution in communications and electronic funds transfer systems has helped transactors, however, to economize on their money holdings.

Because of its medium of exchange function, money plays a key role in the determination of things that really matter to people, things like employment, income, and the price level. The rate of price-level inflation is always to some extent a product of the growth rate of the money supply. The unemployment rate and the rate of real economic growth are also affected by the monetary growth rate, particularly in the short run. Interest rates, too, are influenced by how fast the money supply grows, but here the relation is subject to much controversy. Keynesian economists believe that monetary expansion leads to lower interest rates. Monetarist economists believe just the opposite: They argue that an increase in the growth rate of the money supply produces an about equal increase in the expected rate of inflation, which, in turn, produces an about equal increase in the market (or nominal) rate of interest. Whichever way the effect of money on interest, the element of expected inflation invades nearly every nook and cranny of financial market analysis.

Finally, money plays a special role in financial markets in that its supply is both the object and subject of social control. Unlike ordinary debt, which is supplied by considerations such as the cost and profitability of using borrowed funds, money is supplied in terms of its likely effects on the overall economy. The authority for managing the supply of money rests within the Federal Reserve System. The exercise of this authority is called monetary policy. Through various techniques, principally through "open market operations," the "Fed" is able to directly control the supply of its own monetary debt to the economy. To the extent that this "high-powered" money supply is held by the commercial banking system and used to support a "multiple expansion" of its own demand deposit debt, the Fed has indirect management over the entire money supply.

The Fed's control of the money supply is far from perfect, however, because the money supply process is very complex and indirect, involving many intervening private decisions. These private decisions are the very same wealth accumulation and wealth allocation decisions discussed earlier in this chapter. Monetary policy is designed to stabilize the overall economy, but its direct impact is felt most keenly in the financial markets.

PURPOSE AND PERSPECTIVE OF THIS BOOK

The primary purpose of this book is to deepen the reader's understanding of the system of financial markets. These markets play an important role in the workings of the overall economy. One cannot really understand how the economy works without an understanding of the financial side of the economy. Most elementary economics books stress the real side of the economy and give short shrift to the financial side. One purpose of this book, therefore, is to fill a knowledge gap in the reader's understanding of the economy in general.

An equally important reason for understanding the financial market system is to prepare one's self for a career in financial management. The study of financial markets complements specialized subjects in finance such as business finance and money and banking. These specialized aspects of finance do not exist in a vacuum. Each is a subset of the larger financial system. Understanding the whole system of financial markets is a necessary step to the in depth study of any one of its parts.

What is the best way to gain an understanding of financial markets? The answer depends on the kind of understanding sought. On the one hand, a descriptive approach is appropriate for those who want to understand *what* financial markets are and *how* they operate. On the other hand, an analytical approach is useful if one wants to understand *why* financial markets and their participants behave the way they do.

The approach of this book is to strike a balance between description and analysis. The purpose is to impart a *general* understanding of financial markets. The book is written from the perspective that the whats, hows, and whys of finance go together inextricably. In the chapters to follow, analysis is interwoven with description as much as possible. As such, most of the analysis is informal and nontechnical, but it is nevertheless there.

PROJECTS AND QUESTIONS

1. Using library resources, write a research report that describes and analyzes the financial market system of some underdeveloped country. Comment on how the results of your research lead you to accept or reject the hypothesis that greater financial development would significantly raise the country's standard of living.

2. The central open money market is a wholesale market open only to very rich persons, large businesses, banks, governments, and other large organizations. At the retail level, however, the market is indirectly open to all of us. Explain how, and provide examples.

3. What is the current size of the United States money supply? Does your answer imply some operational definition of money? If so, what? If not so,

why not? Why is the definition of money an important issue in the conduct of monetary policy?

BIBLIOGRAPHY

Dougall, H.E., and J.E. Gaumnitz: *Capital Markets and Institutions,* Prentice-Hall, Englewood Cliffs, N. J., 1975.

Gurley, J.G., and E.S. Shaw: *Money in a Theory of Finance,* Brookings, Washington, D.C., 1960.

Henning, C.N., W. Pigott, and R.H. Scott: *Financial Markets and the Economy,* Prentice-Hall, Englewood Cliffs, N. J., 1978.

McKinnon, R.I.: *Money and Capital in Economic Development,* Brookings, Washington, D.C., 1973.

Moore, B.J.: *An Introduction to the Theory of Finance,* The Free Press, New York, 1968.

Polakoff, M.E. et al.: *Financial Institutions and Markets,* Houghton Mifflin, Boston, 1970.

Smith, P.F.: *Economics of Financial Institutions and Markets,* Irwin, Homewood, Ill., 1971.

Van Horne, J.C.: *Financial Market Rates and Flows,* Prentice-Hall, Englewood Cliffs, N. J., 1978.

chapter 2
Economic Determinants of Saving and Investment

Without saving and investment, financial markets would not exist. Saving is necessary in order to provide a pool of funds for lending. And, unless saving is completely washed out by dissaving, real investment is necessary to give reason for borrowing. Much borrowing is done to finance personal consumption, but most borrowing is used to finance large-ticket investment goods. Thus, while lending and borrowing behavior is the main focal point in our study of financial markets, saving and investment behavior is the basic foundation upon which the financial market system is built.

Even the most pragmatic of financial market practitioners reverts to economic fundamentals rather quickly in accounting for current developments in these markets. Bankers explain the levels of their deposits in terms of the saving done by and the cash holdings of their customers. When accounting for movements of bank loans, they tend to look behind their customers' affairs into such matters as inventory accumulation, other working capital needs, capital expenditure plans, and the state of their cash flow.

Investment bankers often base forecasts of the state of capital markets partly on the volume of new issues scheduled for sale in the market—the so-called visible supply. Even so, they quickly look behind visible supply to more fundamental factors such as the level of expected capital expenditures, the volume of capital expenditures now being made on an unfunded basis that will later require funding, and similar factors. When looking at the demand for securities in the capital markets, they examine the rate at which various institutional investors will be accumulating funds. But, back of that, they are aware of the basic importance of ultimate saving.

The present chapter is organized into four major sections. The first section examines the essential factors behind investment and saving. The second section takes a deeper look into investment behavior, exploring various theories of the determination of investment, including the role of interest. The third section does the same thing for saving behavior. The fourth, and final, section examines the process of reaching an equilibrium between total saving and total investment in the economy.

INVESTMENT OPPORTUNITIES AND TIME PREFERENCES

Why do economic entities save? Why do they invest? How do they determine how much to save and to invest? These questions have stimulated much economic thought. Answers vary, but a good starting point for discussion is the simple but elegant theory of Irving Fisher (1930). We shall begin with his ideas.

Fisher reasoned that saving-investment behavior is influenced by "investment opportunities" that increase the standard of living in the long run, the cost of undertaking such opportunities being some sacrifice of consumption in the immediate short run. Since people prefer more consumption to less, they are induced to take advantage of investment opportunities that have high rates of return. In fact, all investment opportunities whose rates of return are positive potentially fulfill the preference for more consumption to less. To illustrate, suppose you have a $200 income; that you can spend it all on consumption goods in the present period (and invest nothing), or you can use half for consumption now and invest the other half in capital goods. If the rate of return on your investment is 15 percent per period, you will then be able to liquidate your investment next period for $115 and use it, if you wish, for consumption next period. Altogether, you will be able to consume $15 more of consumption goods over the two periods than would have been the case without the investment. The investment opportunity satisfies your preference for more consumption to less. But will you take it? Maybe, maybe not, for investment opportunities are only half the story.

Fisher reasoned that behavior is also influenced by "time preferences" that are biased toward an impatience to consume. He argued that people generally prefer to consume a little more now and a little less later than to pattern it the other way around. Ask yourself: Would you rather take one dollar out of next year's income to have and spend now, or would you rather forgo one dollar out of this year's income to have and spend next year? (Base your answer on assuming no interest.) If you are like most people, you would prefer to spend the dollar this year instead of next. This is called positive time value of money, meaning that a dollar today is worth more than a dollar tomorrow.

Impatience to consume works as a brake on investment. The greater the preference for current consumption over future consumption, the less it pays to invest. The actual investment decision is governed by both the impatience to consume and the opportunity to invest. Let us return to our previous illustration. If your decision was to invest half your $200 income in order to take advantage of the 15 percent rate of return, it means that the opportunity more than outweighed your impatience. Your personal time value of money on the $100 must be less than 15 percent. On the other hand, if you decided to reject the investment, your impatience must outweigh the opportunity, and your time value must be greater than 15 percent.

In a modern economy, a person can allocate current income between current consumption and investment in any proportions that opportunities and the monetary unit of account permit. Still, the basic forces of opportunity and impatience govern this allocation. People who are patient and have good investment opportunities invest relatively great proportions of their incomes. People who are impatient (either by nature or by necessity) and lack opportunities do little or no investing.

The decision to invest carries with it the need to plan the investment's financing. In financially undeveloped countries, the financing method is limited: Investment can only be paid for out of income that is not consumed, that is, through saving. In this case, the investment decision and the decision to save are the same. The decision rests simply on equating the incremental rate of return on investment with the incremental time value of money, subject to the condition that the amount invested and the amount saved are equal. Table 2-1 assists to illustrate this principle. Given the opportunities and preferences in Table 2-1, the rational decision involves saving and investing $300 out of income. Any other decision fails to maximize utility.

In financially more developed nations, the acts of investment and saving can be (and usually are) separated. Investment is not tied to saving because a person can finance investment alternatively through borrowing. Similarly, saving is not governed solely by investment because saving can be employed

TABLE 2-1

Hypothetical Schedules of Opportunities and Preferences Facing a Saver-Investor

Investment This Year	Value of Investment Next Year	Average Rate of Return on Investment	Incremental Rate of Return on Investment
$100	$140	40%	40%
200	270	35	30
300	390	30	20
400	500	25	10

Current Saving (Consumption Foregone This Year)	Consumption Next Year Equivalent in Utility	Average Time Value of Money	Incremental Time Value of Money
$100	$110	10%	10%
200	225	12.5	15
300	345	15	20
400	470	17.5	25

NOTE: The time value of money associated with each level of saving is constant only if all other factors (including income and wealth) are held constant.

alternatively by lending. How, then, are investment and saving determined? Investment is determined by relating the incremental rate of return on investment to the interest-rate cost of borrowing. It will pay to invest up to the point where the incremental rate of return no longer exceeds the rate of interest. And saving is determined by relating the incremental time value of money with the interest rate on lending. It pays to save up to the point where the interest rate no longer exceeds the incremental time value of money. Since the rate that borrowers pay is the same as lenders receive, the saving and investment decisions again rest on equating the incremental rate of investment return with the incremental time value of money, subject now to the condition that both are equal to the market rate of interest.

When lending and borrowing are possible, the amount one saves will almost always be different from the amount of one's investment. Again, refer to Table 2-1. If the market rate of interest is 10 percent, it will pay to invest up to $400, and to save $100, the $300 difference having to be covered through borrowing.

With financial markets, economic entities use their investment opportunities, their subjective time preferences, and the given market rate of interest to determine simultaneously their quantities of saving, investment, lending, and borrowing. This is the central idea of Fisher's theory. The emphasis is on the rate of interest. Investment is stimulated by lower interest rates (and discouraged by higher rates). But it is influenced by other factors as well. Saving, too, is influenced by other factors. Indeed, as we shall discover later in this chapter, economists are not even sure about the direction of the interest rate's effect on saving. Thus our task is to explore in still greater detail the economic determinants of investment and saving.

DETERMINANTS OF INVESTMENT

Investment is not homogeneous. The various categories of investment have unique characteristics requiring fairly specialized analysis. For example, purely economic factors play a larger role in the determination of private investment than they do in the determination of public (government) investment. Even in those rare instances where public investment decisions are based on formal cost-benefit analysis, the costs and benefits are often more external than internal, as much social as economic, and they are difficult to measure. For these reasons, we will focus our discussion in this section on the determination of private investment.

"Fixed business investment" in plant and equipment is the dominant form of private investment. It is well suited for economic analysis; in fact, a whole body of literature known as "capital budgeting" covers this type of investment. "Inventory investment," by comparison, is so short-lived and volatile that the standard capital budgeting techniques apply with considerably less force. Businesses do nevertheless consider a number of economic factors in making inventory decisions. Households are less likely than businesses to scrutinize their capital expenditures on purely economic grounds. "Residential construction" is sensitive to the mortgage rate of interest and to other economic conditions, but the decision to buy a new home is motivated in large part by psychological forces. The same applies to household expenditures on "consumer durables." Purchases of new cars, television sets, and other durables are often made without much financial planning or economic forethought.

Fixed Business Investment

Approximately one-tenth of expenditures on the gross national product (GNP) are made by the private business sector for plant and equipment. Most of this gross investment is for capital to replace old capital that has depreciated; the rest is for net additions to capital, or net investment. Replacement expenditures, though large, are relatively stable because they are closely aligned to depreciation schedules. Net investment, on the other hand, is more volatile; it responds to changing economic conditions. Our concern in this section will be to examine the economic determinants of net business investment. These determinants are identified in Figure 2-1.

figure 2-1   Determinants of Investment.

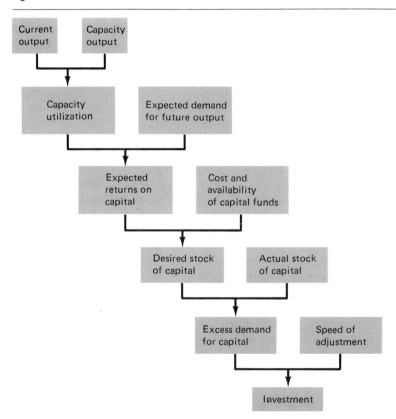

The direct determinants of investment are the desired stock of capital goods, the actual stock of capital goods, and the speed by which the actual stock is adjusted to the desired stock. For example, if the desired stock of capital is eighteen machines and the actual stock is twelve, total net additions to machines will be six in order to adjust supply to demand. If it takes a year to make a full adjustment, annual net investment will be six machines. If a year is required to make half the desired adjustment, investment will be three machines; if the adjustment is one-third, investment will be two; and so on. The more that desired capital exceeds actual capital, the greater the rate of investment. On the other hand, the longer the adjustment process, the lower the rate of investment. The adjustment period stretches out over time because it takes time to produce and finance business structures and complicated equipment.

The indirect determinants of business investment are those factors that determine the desired stock of capital, the actual stock of capital, and the time structure of the investment process. The latter is largely determined by technologically induced lags and financial constraints, but it is not completely time-inelastic. Business decision makers have some discretion over how fast they adjust actual to desired capital. It may be technologically possible to build a plant in six months, but the parties involved may decide to stretch it over a couple of years. A business may be slow to adjust its actual capital to that desired because of uncertainty. Uncertainty may make the firm more hesitant, more sluggish to change its stock of capital, even if other factors indicate that a change is in order. Some suggestive evidence that this is the case was recently reported by Birch and Siebert (March 1976). Most econometric studies of investment tend, however, to assume simply that the speed by which actual capital is adjusted to the desired level is a constant.

In theory, adjustment is made only when the desired stock of capital is out of equilibrium with the actual stock of capital. The actual stock of capital is, of course, predetermined; it is already in existence. Our interest thus focuses on the desired stock of capital. The demand for capital is very sensitive to economic variables. This sensitivity carries over to investment, which is sensitive for the same reasons. In fact, if the speed of adjustment is assumed constant, investment is a constant proportion of the difference between the desired capital stock and the actual (predetermined) capital stock. The economic variables that determine desired capital therefore determine investment. What, then, are these variables?

One of the oldest theories of investment is the "accelerator principle." This theory, in its crude version, holds that the stock of capital needed varies proportionately with the amount of output produced. Thus, if output doubles, twice as much capital is required. If output does not change, additional capital is not required. As for net investment, it will accelerate during periods of rising output, only to fall off completely after output reaches a new plateau. Obviously, this version of the theory is rigid and mechanical, standing mute on the question of the returns, costs, and profitability of investment. Studies do indicate that current output is a statistically significant determinant of investment.[1] This finding, however, does not disregard the profitability aspect of investment. When output increases, existing capacity may become strained, and marginal and unit costs may begin to rise sharply. When this happens, it usually pays to add to capacity. Such additional investment enables the firm to achieve economies of scale, to lower its costs, and, consequently, to earn greater returns on capital.

When existing capacity is fully used, there is a strong incentive to add to capacity. On the other hand, operations at a level considerably below capacity discourage further capital expenditures. The existence of some unused capacity does not necessarily mean that actual capital is greater than desired. Most operations can always squeeze out more output with given capital, but they may do so at extremely high marginal costs. When this happens, it may be cheaper in the long run to add to existing capital facilities. In short, desired capital may exceed actual capital even though the actual capital is not operating at "full" capacity.

Surprising as it might seem, the concept of capacity is not a settled statistical question. For the purpose of relating capacity to expected business investment, the principal point to bear in mind is that of costs. As long as unit variable costs do not increase faster than unit fixed costs are reduced by increased output, capacity has not been reached. Even after marginal costs start rising gently, it is not clear that plant capacity is being approached. But at some point optimum plant usage is reached and pressure for more plant is felt.

Despite measurement problems, capacity utilization is a pretty good indication of excess demand for capital. The demand for capital can be taken as a derived demand for output. Similarly, the supply of capital can be viewed as fixing the supply of output, or at least a least-cost supply of output. When the demand for output exceeds this least-cost supply of output, it implies that the demand for capital exceeds the supply of capital. But it also shows up as high capacity utilization.

There are other reasons why capacity utilization indicates demand for capital and, therefore, investment. Profit-maximizing businesses add to capital to produce more output only if they expect to earn a rate of return on capital greater than the cost of capital funds. Operations near capacity usually imply profits adequate to justify sizable capital expenditures. Lenders view high capacity utilization as a favorable sign, and financing is usually easily arranged by those using existing capacity fully.

If these arguments have a familiar ring, they should. To a large extent, capacity utilization is just another way of looking at current output. In the short run, capacity output is fixed, so the utilization of this fixed capacity is solely a matter of how much is being produced. Consequently, capacity utilization has about the same bearing on investment as does output. In fact, econometricians who study investment behavior treat output and capacity utilization as if they were virtually interchangeable determinants.

A closely related, but more modern theory of investment is the "permanent

[1]See Jorgenson (December 1971) for a review.

demand" theory associated with Robert Eisner (June 1967). According to Eisner, the decision to invest rests more on the relation between existing capacity and expected (permanent) demand for future output than on the relation between capacity and current output. When the demand for current output pushes capacity to the limit, the firm will expand capacity only if it expects this demand to continue permanently into the future. If the current high rate of demand is viewed as only transitory, then the firm will not be induced to expand capacity. The rationale is to minimize expected losses: Temporary undercapacity is less costly than permanent overcapacity.

Other theories of the determination of investment focus on the cost and availability of capital funds used to finance investment. Neoclassical economists have long therorized that the cost of capital funds is a crucial determinant of the demand for capital and investment. The cost of capital funds is the discount rate used by a firm to capitalize expected outlays and returns associated with investment. The capitalized value is called "net present value." The more that net present value exceeds zero, the more profitable the investment. Since net present value varies inversely with the cost of capital, so should investment.

The firm calculates its percentage cost of capital as a weighted average of the costs of the debt and equity funds in its capital structure. The cost of debt is the interest rate that the firm must pay its creditors. The cost of equity is the rate of return required by the firm's owners. Since owners assume more risk than creditors, the cost of equity exceeds the cost of debt by a risk premium. Both costs increase, however, as the proportion of debt in the capital structure increases.

As fine as the cost-of-capital concept is in theory, many firms have difficulty measuring it in practice. For such firms, one alternative is to solve for the discount rate that makes the present value of returns on an investment equal to the present value of the outlays for the investment. This rate is called the "internal rate of return" on investment. A firm can calculate the internal rate of return for each of its investment opportunities and accept each investment where the rate of return is acceptably high. Acceptability, however, must rest eventually on comparing returns to costs. When market interest rates rise and funds become more expensive, the "acceptable" rate of return on investment is likewise increased. The firm will still take advantage of lucrative investment opportunities, but it will be under pressure to scrap those opportunities having only marginally attractive returns. Thus, whether the firm uses either the net present value method or the internal rate of return method of evaluating fixed investment opportunities, the amount expended for plant and equipment should vary inversely with the cost of capital funds. Since the cost of capital is determined *externally* in the financial markets, this view has come to be known as the "external cost of capital" theory.

A vastly different approach is taken by proponents of the "internal availability of capital" theory. According to this theory, investment is determined primarily by the amount of funds generated internally through the retention of profits. In the crude version of this theory, retained earnings are regarded as an extremely low-cost source of funds for financing net investment. However, once these funds have been committed, additional investment can be financed only by turning to investors in the market who charge prohibitively high prices for the use of their money. Consequently, investment is thought to be both stimulated and constrained by the availability of internal funds.

The key issue between the two theories hinges on the cost of internal funds relative to the cost of external financing. The internal availability theory focuses on the behavior of corporate managers who may see little or no cost to retaining the earnings that are already on the books (thanks to their decisions). The external cost theory focuses on the behavior of the corporation's stockholders. To the stockholders, retained earnings bear a substantial opportunity cost equal to the rate of return on equity in the market. This return could be earned if the earnings were not retained but paid out instead in the form of dividends. The question is: Do managers manage for themselves, or do they act in the best interests of stockholders? This issue has been debated for years without resolve.

Empirical research on the sensitivity of investment to cost and availability variables has shed little light on the issue. Before the 1960s, there was virtually no evidence from econometric studies that the cost of capital exerts a significant influence on fixed business investment. These early studies suffered, however, from a number of econometric problems, one of them being inappropriate specification of the cost of capital, another being unclear identification of cause and effect. Research in the 1960s and 1970s suggests that the cost of capital funds is a significant determinant, but its role, relative to liquidity, internal cash flow, and related availability measures, is still an unsettled issue.[2]

Inventory Investment

Inventory investment is more volatile than fixed investment. The accelerator principle bears even more clearly on inventory levels. The firm's demand for inventory is inextricably tied to the flow of output that the firm expects to produce and sell. As output increases, the stock of inventory needed increases. Inventories vary less than proportionately with production and sales owing to order quantity and other economies associated with inventory control methods. Investment, however, is still volatile. As sales reach a peak, inventory investment can quickly turn into inventory disinvestment.

Inventory stocks also vary positively with the degree of unexpected sales variation. Most firms keep buffer (safety) stocks of inventory to meet unexpected demand. It is usually more profitable to carry a positive buffer stock to meet some unexpected demand than it is to carry no buffer in order to hold down handling, storage, and capital costs. The costs of handling, storing, and financing inventories are not without significance, however. Were it not for these carrying costs, a firm would have no reason to limit the amount of inventory carried. It would carry inventory sufficient to meet any level of demand, expected and unexpected. The fact that firms do run out of items

---

[2]Research by Jorgenson and Siebert (September 1968) indicates that the cost of capital is a dominant determinant of investment. Their results have been challenged, however, by Elliott (March 1973).

indicates that the costs of carrying inventory are calculated into the inventory decision.

Inventories can also fluctuate with expected price changes of raw materials. Some firms purchase and stockpile materials when they believe that prices are going to be higher in the future. This is a gamble, however, that must be weighed against the costs of storing and financing such stockpiles.

Inventory investment, like any investment, must be financed. Capital costs are involved. Whether the appropriate cost of funds for financing inventory is a short-term interest rate or a weighted-average cost of long-term debt and equity is a matter for debate. What is clear is that inventory investment should vary inversely with the cost of funds used to finance it, other factors remaining the same.

Empirical evidence on inventory investment reveals that inventories relate closely to sales. The response of inventory investment to interest rates and other measures of capital costs, however, has been less clear.[3] This has been surprising because inventory is capital, and capital has a cost. Either the art of inventory control has not conformed to theoretical norms or the econometric studies have generally failed to detect a true cost-of-capital effect. Our guess is the latter. The most recent evidence, though meager, has been supportive of the latter. P.W. Kuznets (1964) has found that inventories respond significantly to interest rates, and J.M. Joyce (October 1973) has found a significant response to various measures of the firm's overall cost of capital.

Residential Construction

Investment in new housing is determined by a complex of demand factors and supply factors. The demand for housing in general (as distinct from new housing) is shaped by such factors as population, household size, and family formation. People must have shelter. However, they do have choices. They can choose between new houses and old, between single and multifamily dwellings, between mansions and shacks, between owning and renting. Prices, rents, incomes, and tastes help to determine these choices. When new houses are selling at prices that compare favorably to prices of existing structures and to rents, the demand for new houses is strong. Such is often the case in a growing community that has a housing shortage. When prices are high relative to incomes, demand weakens for new single-family dwellings, but it may increase for multifamily units. In recent years, incomes have not kept up with prices of new houses. The result has been that a large proportion of new housing starts has been in multifamily dwellings. More people are living in apartments and condominiums. Trailers, too, are becoming a way of life for millions, and this raises an interesting question: Should trailer manufacturing be counted in housing starts? If not, are we making a social judgment that trailers are inferior to houses constructed from the ground up? What about prefabs? Are they better than trailers but worse than "regular" houses?

---

[3]See Lovell (1964) for a review of the empirical determinants of inventory investment.

The cost and availability of credit are important determinants of new housing demand. Residential construction makes somewhat greater demands on the capital markets than does business plant and equipment investment, even though the latter accounts for a much greater dollar volume of expenditures. With new houses selling at prices that are three, four, or more times a family's annual income, most buyers have no choice but to borrow as much as possible, usually in the form of a mortgage. The loan-to-value ratio varies, but usually it is in the range of 60 to 90 percent. If credit were not available, the housing market would collapse.

The demand for housing and the concomitant demand for mortgage credit are very sensitive to the mortgage rate of interest. Empirical evidence indicates that the demand for mortgage credit is highly elastic with respect to the mortgage rate. Ordinarily, the mortgage rate is the device for rationing credit to finance new homes; its economic function is to clear the market for mortgage funds. High rates tend to stifle the demand for mortgages and, therefore, for housing; low rates do just the opposite. The reason why home buyers are sensitive to mortgage rates is that an increase in the mortgage rate by a single percentage point can easily raise total interest payments by several thousand dollars over the life of the mortgage.

The availability of mortgage credit can affect housing demand during periods of market disequilibrium. Sometimes the mortgage rate fails to clear the market for mortgages. In the late 1960s, many prospective homeowners were prevented from buying houses because they could not get credit. They were willing to pay the going mortgage rates of 7½ to 9 percent, but the credit was not there. (In terms of clearing the market, the rates were not high enough.) The suppliers of mortgage credit, chiefly savings and loan associations, mutual savings banks, life insurance companies, and commercial banks, decided to ration the limited supply of mortgage funds on nonprice bases. This usually took the form of increasing the amount of the down payment and shortening the mortgage credit period. Some prospective buyers could not meet the required down payments, others had insufficient incomes to make the larger monthly installments caused by shortening the credit period. Still others who could meet all the financial requirements were refused credit because of no previous credit record or economic standing in the community. Limited credit was rationed by lenders to the wealthy and the lucky.

The effect of mortgage credit availability was mostly temporary, however, as are most disequilibrium situations. In the mid-1970s, the mortgage market was more nearly clearing. Although mortgage rates remained high, the demand for mortgage credit (at these rates) was being more nearly met. New housing, however, was in the doldrums. Real factors seemed to be responsible. Personal incomes failed to keep up with prices of houses, which, in turn, were trying to keep up with construction costs.

Construction costs are important determinants of the supply of new housing. The costs of labor and materials have risen dramatically in recent years. Contractors are caught in a squeeze. If they pass these costs on in the form of higher prices, demand falls and they lose some of their market. If they do not raise prices, they cannot cover their costs and are forced to curtail operations. Either way, investment in residential construction suffers.

Other determinants of new housing supply include inventories of new homes and vacancies in existing structures. When these go up, new housing tends to go down. Credit also influences supply. Contractors and developers have to finance their in-process inventories of houses. This factor can be a major determinant of housing starts when credit is tight. High interest rates for construction loans can slow down a developer considerably.

Numerous empirical studies have attempted to explain the level and cyclical movements of expenditures on residential construction. These studies have covered all the determinants discussed above plus others.[4] The different studies do not agree on the specifics, but there is consensus that both real and financial market variables influence investment in new housing. The secular trend of residential construction is largely guided by real factors, but cyclical variations from the trend are due largely to financial conditions.

Investment in residential construction is quite volatile. Housing starts are subject to sizable cyclical fluctuations. Moreover, the short cycle in housing tends to be countercyclical to the rest of the economy. Residential construction has typically risen sharply when general activity was reaching a trough. Declines in building activity have tended to take hold well in advance of peaks in the general business cycle.

Jack Guttentag (June 1961) and W.W. Alberts (June 1962) were among the first of many economists to link this countercyclical behavior to countercyclical movements in the supply of mortgage credit. In an expanding economy, the total demand for credit tends to run ahead of the total supply of credit. Credit becomes "tight" and interest rates rise. The feedback effect of tight credit conditions on general expenditures is to dampen economic activity somewhat, but not by enough to reverse its generally upward course. Housing, however, is an exception. The supply of mortgage credit has typically become so short during general expansion that housing starts have actually fallen while other kinds of production have continued to rise. For various reasons, tight credit has a tendency to become concentrated and compounded in the mortgage market.

One reason for this is the "disintermediation" process. The inability of savings institutions to raise their rates on savings deposits when open market interest rates are rising serves to facilitate a flow of funds out of these intermediaries and into the open market. This would have little effect on the mortgage market were it not for the fact that savings and loan associations and mutual savings banks, and to a lesser extent life insurance companies and commercial banks, invest heavily and disproportionately in the mortgage market. Consequently, a dollar of savings taken out of one of these intermediaries is apt to be a dollar taken out of the mortgage market. The supply of mortgage credit is therefore reduced.

---

[4]See Fair (May 1972) and Meltzer (June 1974) for reviews of some of these studies. One of the most complete studies of housing investment and the mortgage market is presented in Gramlich and Jaffee (1972).

But this is not the end of the story. Financial intermediaries are apt to reduce their investments in mortgages by more than the funds lost through disintermediation. Mortgage rates of interest do not rise or fall as far or as fast as other rates of interest. When interest rates are rising, mortgage rates tend to lag behind. Profit-motivated commercial banks and other intermediaries can therefore increase return by switching out of mortgages and into other forms of investment. The supply of mortgage credit is thus further reduced.

Why are mortgage rate movements slow and small? For one thing, mortgage rates are frequently in disequilibrium, held back by such interferences as legal rate ceilings on federally underwritten mortgage loans and state usury ceilings in the conventional mortgage market.[5] For another, equilibrium mortgage rates are stable relative to other market rates because mortgage borrowers are more sensitive to mortgage rates than borrowers usually are to interest rates in general. With a highly elastic demand curve for mortgage funds, mortgage rates may change little relative to other market rates even if there is a large shift in the supply of mortgage funds.

The upshot of this discussion is that the housing market appears to be uniquely susceptible and vulnerable to changes in financial market conditions in general, and to mortgage market conditions in particular. This is the conventional wisdom. However, not all economists agree. Allan Meltzer (June 1974) has argued that the housing market is not beholden to the mortgage market. In his view, the demand for housing is not constrained by the supply of mortgage credit since investment in new housing can be financed with alternative sources of credit; neither is the demand for mortgage credit solely derived from the demand for housing since mortgage credit can be used to finance alternative investments in real assets. For Meltzer, investment in general is affected by capital costs in general; housing is not a special case.

Consumer Durables

Purchases of new cars, appliances, and other consumer durables are difficult to classify. Because these durables can depreciate so fast, a case can be made for classifying them as consumption expenditures; yet there are good reasons to treat them as investment. First, durables themselves are not consumed; only the services they provide are consumed. An automobile produces transportation. A washing machine and dryer produce laundry service. Second, consumer durables are durable in the same sense as business equipment. In fact, when Hertz and Avis buy cars, and when the local laundromat buys washers and dryers, these same items are classified as business equipment. Third, expenditures on consumer durables are highly volatile, not as volatile as inventory investment, but almost. If consumer durables were truly consumption goods, one would expect their demand to be a stable function of consumer

[5]The effects of state usury ceilings have been studied by Robins (March 1974) and Ostas (June 1976). Both studies conclude that these ceilings substantially reduce the supply of mortgage credit during tight money periods.

income. Purchases of durables do vary with income, but the relation is not nearly as close as it is between nondurables and income.

Why are purchases of consumer durables so volatile relative to the gross national product and income? If durables are not consumption goods, but capital goods, we would expect investment in durables to be determined in the same general way as investment in business equipment; that is, we would expect investment in durables to be determined by adjusting discrepancies between desired and actual stocks of durables. The level of income would directly affect the desired stock of durables, which, in turn, would affect net investment in durables only if different from the actual stock. Investment in durables would thus be determined more by changes in income than by the level of income.

Empirical research supports this view.[6] The stock of durables is more closely related to the level of income than is investment in durables (changes in the stock). Income is not the only determinant, however. Interest rates and other costs and returns on capital affect the stock of durable goods demanded. M.J. Hamburger (December 1967) and A.C. Hess (February 1973) have found that the stock of durables demanded varies inversely with interest rates. Moreover, they have found the demand to be relatively elastic. Thus, the evidence suggests that expenditures on consumer durables are determined by the same general forces that determine business investment.

DETERMINANTS OF SAVING

The factors that account for saving by individuals form a complex of many elements. Although considerable research has been devoted to assessing the various incentives for saving, the results are inconclusive. The traditional view that people save for their old age has some validity, but it is not the whole story. People also save for large-unit or "lumpy" expenditures. Other incentives also seem to be at work. It is clear that some cultural backgrounds encourage saving and others do not. The Puritan tradition that encouraged thrift may have had something to do with the early rapid development of this country, particularly those parts of it most under that influence. A low saving rate hampers many underdeveloped nations.

Saving for large-unit expenditures explains an interesting point about the saving process. The gross volume of saving is constantly being offset by a varying amount of spending from saved funds, or dissaving. Studies suggest that fluctuations in dissaving account for more of the irregularity in net saving than changes in gross saving.

Whatever the reasons for saving, the level of saving is influenced by economic conditions. This section examines a number of leading theories of saving. A flow diagram of some of the major determinants of saving is shown in Figure 2-2.

The assumption of classical economists was that the rate of interest has a

[6]See, for example, Harberger (1960).

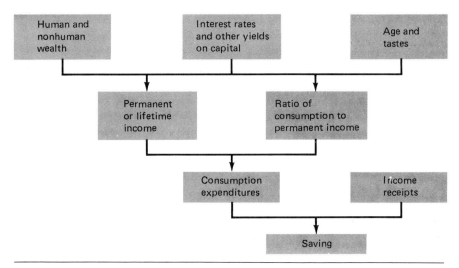

figure 2-2   Some Determinants of Saving.

significant influence on individual saving and on saving in the aggregate. A low interest rate was thought to curb saving; a high rate to encourage it. This notion persisted for more than a century.

The influential ideas of John M. Keynes (1936) and the monumental study of saving by Raymond Goldsmith (1955, 1956) were instrumental in convincing economists that income, not interest rates, is the principal determinant of saving. Keynes hypothesized that both saving and the ratio of saving to income vary directly with income. Budget studies of individual and individual household saving behavior have tended to support this hypothesis. Low-income families and individuals save proportionately less of their incomes than high-income individuals and families do. A large portion of saving is done by a relatively small number of upper-income families.

While the concentration of saving in upper-income groups seems to be well established empirically, one logical problem remains. For many years the United States (along with other countries) has enjoyed a considerable increase in income. If higher-income groups save more than lower-income groups, an increase in average income shifts people up the income scale. If they save the proportion of income characteristic of this new income level, aggregate saving should increase not only absolutely but proportionately. Aggregate statistics, however, indicate that this has not proved to be the case. As near as can be estimated, the proportion of income now saved is about the same as it was a generation ago or two generations ago.

Long-term estimates made by Goldsmith and published in his study of saving suggested that the saving rate has increased slightly when equity in consumer durables is counted as saving; but that if these durables are excluded, the saving rate appears to have actually dwindled slightly. Since this definitional issue could be decided either way with almost equal logic, a rough generalization of "no change" is probably not too far from the truth.

This absence of secular increase in the saving ratio has stimulated a great deal of speculation. Some interesting and plausible hypotheses have been developed in an effort to reconcile the facts.

One such hypothesis relies on the wealth effect. Here the position is taken that the aggregate saving-income ratio *does* increase over time with increases in current aggregate income, *all other things held constant*. But all other things are not constant. Wealth, for example, grows with income, and the effect of increases in wealth is to decrease the saving ratio: Growing wealth decreases the need to save out of current income. Thus, with the wealth effect working in the opposite direction from the income effect, the two effects may cancel out, leaving the saving ratio intact as both income and wealth increase.[7]

Although saving bears a close relation to income over the long run, it is quite erratic in the short run. Goldsmith found the ratio of aggregate annual saving to annual income to be about one-eighth on the average, with no upward or downward trend but with considerable cyclical fluctuations around the average. Others have found that the fluctuations are even more severe when the saving ratio is computed from quarterly data.

A widely accepted explanation for an unstable ratio of current saving to current income is provided by the "permanent income" hypothesis. This hypothesis has several forms, but the best known is one developed by Milton Friedman (1957). The basic argument is that spending and saving decisions are guided by a long-run view of income rather than income of the moment. What one family spends and saves on, say, Tuesday has little or no bearing to income received on Tuesday. (Payday might be Friday.) The same applies to weekly, monthly, quarterly, and even annual flows of receipts and expenditures, though with diminishing force. Accordingly, the permanent income hypothesis contends that consumption depends on a more permanent notion of income, that is, income normalized from past experiences or future expectations or both. Friedman has found that the ratio of consumption to permanent income is more stable than it is to current measured income.

The permanent income hypothesis can explain much of the erratic nature of saving during the business cycle. When current income falls below permanent income, consumption stays tied to permanent income, and saving out of current income drops (by roughly the amount of the drop in current income). The ratio of current saving to current income also drops (since the numerator and denominator fall by the same amount). The opposite happens when current income rises above permanent income.

Although the permanent income hypothesis goes a long way toward explaining saving and consumption behavior, it does not tell the whole story. One of the latest developments in the theory of saving behavior has been to judge the effects of uncertainty of income. Juster and Taylor (May 1975) have found that saving varies positively with real-income uncertainty. As people

[7]See Tobin (1951).

become less certain about their expected future real incomes, they apparently insure themselves by saving more.

A major source of real-income uncertainty is thought to be uncertainty regarding the price level and the rate of inflation. Moreover, inflation uncertainty is thought to influence saving behavior independently of its effect working through real-income uncertainty. For example, Deaton (December 1977) has found evidence to support the hypothesis that the ratio of saving to income varies directly with unexpected inflation.[8]

Another development in the study of saving has been to reopen the issue of the effect of the interest rate on saving. Actually, there are several effects. One effect is the substitution effect. When the interest rate drops, the return on saving (in terms of future consumption) drops relative to the cost of saving (present consumption foregone). Rational individuals can be expected to do some substitution, out of saving and future consumption, into present consumption. Thus the substitution effect implies that saving varies positively with the rate of interest. A second effect, the interest-income effect, implies an inverse relation (for most people). With a lower interest rate, future interest income on current saving declines. Less optimistic prospects of future income can be expected to bring cuts in current consumption. For given current incomes, this means higher saving. This effect is reversed, however, if an individual borrows more than he or she lends. A third effect, the capital-value effect, reinforces the substitution effect (again, for most people). With this effect, a decrease in the interest rate increases the present market value of the person's existing holdings of financial and other assets. The present market value increases owing to capitalizing future returns on existing assets at a lower rate. Being wealthier, a person will consume more and save less out of current income. This effect is reversed, however, if a person owes more than he or she owns.

When these three effects are combined, the net effect of interest on saving is difficult to discern. The only case where the effect is totally unambiguous is the case of a net debtor who has positive net worth. For such a person, saving varies positively with the interest rate. The average household, however, is in a net creditor position with positive net worth. For the entire household sector, saving will vary positively with the interest rate if the combined substitution and capital-value effects outweigh the interest-income effect. The evidence on this matter is somewhat mixed.[9] Our reading of this evidence is that household

---

[8]Economists are becoming increasingly aware that all types of behavior respond to both the expected and the unexpected (deviations or variations from the expected). Much current research is being devoted to studying the effects of uncertainty on various types of economic behavior, saving being one.

[9]Studies by Wright (September 1967, 1969), Boskin (April 1978) and others suggest that saving varies positively with interest rates. Weber (September 1970, December 1975) has reached the opposite conclusion. Weber's results, however, have been described by Ferber (December 1973) as requiring "a number of heroic assumptions."

saving does have some net positive response to interest-rate movements, but that this response is relatively inelastic.

EQUILIBRIUM OF SAVING AND INVESTMENT

We have examined the most important determinants of saving and investment behavior. These determinants apply to how individual economic entities behave. For the most part, they also apply to the determination of saving and investment in the aggregate. What is true for the parts is usually, though not necessarily, true for the whole.

We have also seen in the first section of this chapter that individual entities can invest and save by different amounts when borrowing and lending opportunities are available. This uncoupling of saving and investment exists for the individual, but not for the whole economy. Aggregate investment is always equal to aggregate saving. This confuses some people, since the group in society that does most of the saving (households) is different from the group that carries on most of the investment (business corporations). Moreover, the two groups save and invest for different reasons.

The equality is not really difficult to understand. If investors want to invest more than savers want to save, investors will actually invest less than intended, and savers will save more than intended. Actual saving must equal actual investment because saving is unconsumed income and investment is unconsumed production. Since total income and total production constitute an identity, so do saving and investment. But again, this does not necessarily mean that desired investment equals desired saving.

The amount savers wish to save has an effect on investment; likewise, the amount investors wish to invest affects saving. Suppose desired investment is greater than desired saving. What happens? In this case, producers underestimate consumption expenditures in their production planning. The producers will divide production between what they want to invest and what they expect consumers to consume. However, as consumers attempt to consume more than producers planned for, the producers will find their inventories falling to levels below what is desired. This unexpected decrease in inventory constitutes unintended disinvestment. Thus actual investment is less than intended investment. From the consumers' point of view, they find they cannot consume as much as they would like because consumer goods production and inventory carryovers of consumer goods are deficient. With actual consumption less than intended, actual saving is more than intended. Putting the two together, the unintended disinvestment and the unintended saving make actual investment equal to actual saving, even though desired investment is greater than desired saving (see Figure 2-3, Panel A).

The above situation is not lasting because economic forces tend to bring desired investment and desired saving into equality. Although actual saving and investment are always equal, equality of desired saving and investment constitutes equilibrium. The mechanics of the equilibrating process are quite

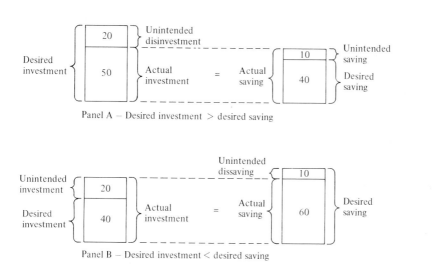

Panel A — Desired investment > desired saving

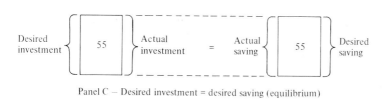

Panel B — Desired investment < desired saving

Panel C — Desired investment = desired saving (equilibrium)

figure 2-3   Relations between Saving and Investment.

simple. Producers will respond to the unintended drop in inventories by producing more. This creates more income out of which more saving is desired. Desired saving thus increases over its previous position. At the same time, the short supply of desired saving (relative to investment demand) will bring pressure to bear on the financial markets. Interest rates and other capital costs will tend to rise, which, in turn, will cut the amount of desired investment. Desired investment thus decreases from its previous position. Putting the two together, desired saving increases and desired investment decreases until equality is reached. At this point, the real side of the economy is in equilibrium (see Figure 2-3, Panel C).

To sum up, if desired saving and investment are unequal, market forces will bring appropriate changes in income and the rate of interest, thereby changing desired saving and investment to a position of equality. But all the while actual saving and investment will have been equal. The line of causation between desired saving and investment is in both directions: Saving influences investment through an interest-rate effect; investment affects saving through an income effect.

Does the interaction of aggregate saving and aggregate investment determine the rate of interest? Classical economists thought so, but, as we shall discover in the next chapter, there is considerably more to determining the interest rate than saving and investment alone.

PROJECTS AND QUESTIONS

1. Study Table 2-1. Why does the incremental rate of return on investment decrease as investment increases? Why does the incremental time value of money increase as saving increases? Is the hypothetical saver-investor better off with financial markets than he or she would be without them? How much better off? (Assume a market rate of interest of 10 percent.) How do you explain this result? Is financial development good for economic welfare? Why?
2. Using published data from the national income accounts, find the annual amounts of "net national product" and "net private domestic investment" over a recent ten-year period. After examining your net national product and net investment figures, demonstrate that the figures either do or do not agree with the acceleration principle.
3. Write a short library-research paper on the following subject: "The Net Present Value and Internal Rate of Return Methods of Capital Budgeting." Include in your paper how the cost of capital funds influences investment expenditures under each of the two methods.

BIBLIOGRAPHY

Alberts, W.W.: "Business Cycles, Residential Construction Cycles, and the Mortgage Market," *Journal of Political Economy*, June 1962, pp. 263–281.

Ando, A., and F. Modigliani: "The Life Cycle Hypothesis of Saving," *American Economic Review*, March 1963, pp. 55–84.

Birch, E.M., and C.D. Siebert: "Uncertainty, Permanent Demand, and Investment Behavior," *American Economic Review*, March 1976, pp. 15–27.

Boskin, M.J.: "Taxation, Saving, and the Rate of Interest," *Journal of Political Economy*, April 1978, pp. S3–S27.

Deaton, A.: "Involuntary Saving through Unanticipated Inflation," *American Economic Review*, December 1977, pp. 899–910.

Eisner, R.: "A Permanent Income Theory for Investment: Some Empirical Explorations," *American Economic Review*, June 1967, pp. 363–390.

Elliott, J.W.: "Theories of Corporate Investment Behavior Revisited," *American Economic Review*, March 1973, pp. 195–207.

Fair, R.C.: "Disequilibrium in Housing Models," *Journal of Finance,* May 1972, pp. 207–221.

Ferber, R.: "Consumer Economics, A Survey," *Journal of Economic Literature,* December 1973, pp. 1303–1342.

Fisher, I.: *The Theory of Interest,* Macmillan, New York, 1930.

Friedman, M.: *A Theory of the Consumption Function,* Princeton University Press, Princeton, N. J., 1957.

Goldsmith, R.W.: *A Study of Saving in the United States,* Princeton University Press, Princeton, N. J., 1955 and 1956 (three volumes).

Gramlich, E.M., and D.M. Jaffee, eds.: *Savings Deposits, Mortgages, and Housing,* Heath, Lexington, Mass., 1972.

Guttentag, J.M.: "The Short Cycle in Residential Construction, 1946–1959," *American Economic Review,* June 1961, pp. 275–298.

Hamburger, M.J.: "Interest Rates and the Demand for Consumer Durable Goods," *American Economic Review,* December 1967, pp. 1131–1153.

Harberger, A.C., ed.: *The Demand for Durable Goods,* University of Chicago Press, Chicago, 1960.

Hess, A.C.: "Household Demand for Durable Goods: The Influences of Rates of Return and Wealth," *Review of Economics and Statistics,* February 1973, pp. 9–15.

Hirshleifer, J.: "On the Theory of Optimal Investment Decision," *Journal of Political Economy,* August 1958.

Jorgenson, D.W.: "The Theory of Investment Behavior," in *Determinants of Investment Behavior,* National Bureau of Economic Research, New York, 1967.

————, and C.D. Siebert: "A Comparison of Alternative Theories of Corporate Investment Behavior," *American Economic Review,* September 1968, pp. 681–712.

————: "Econometric Studies of Investment Behavior: A Survey," *Journal of Economic Literature,* December 1971, pp. 1111–1147.

Joyce, J.M.: "Cost of Capital and Inventory Investment: Further Evidence," *Southern Economic Journal,* October 1973, pp. 323–329.

Juster, F. T., and L.D. Taylor: "Towards a Theory of Saving Behavior," *American Economic Review,* May 1975, pp. 203–209.

Keynes, J.M.: *The General Theory of Employment, Interest, and Money,* Harcourt, Brace, New York, 1936.

Kuh, E.: "Theory and Institutions in the Study of Investment Behavior," *American Economic Review,* May 1963, pp. 260–268.

Kuznets, P.W.: "Financial Determinants of Manufacturing Inventory Behavior," *Yale Economic Essays,* 1964, pp. 331–369.

Lovell, M.C.: "Determinants of Inventory Investment," in *Models of Income Determination,* Princeton University Press, Princeton, N. J., 1964.

Meltzer, A.H.: "Credit Availability and Economic Decisions: Some Evidence from the Mortgage and Housing Markets," *Journal of Finance,* June 1974, pp. 763–777.

Ostas, J.R.: "Effects of Usury Ceilings in the Mortgage Market," *Journal of Finance,* June 1976, pp. 821–834.

Robins, P.K.: "The Effects of State Usury Ceilings on Single Family Homebuilding," *Journal of Finance,* March 1974, pp. 227–235.

Solomon, E., ed.: *The Management of Corporate Capital,* The Free Press, New York, 1959.

Smith, P.F.: *Economics of Financial Institutions and Markets,* Irwin, Homewood, Ill., 1971, chap. 1.

Sparks, G.: "An Econometric Analysis of the Role of Financial Intermediaries in Postwar Residential Building Cycles," in *Determinants of Investment Behavior,* National Bureau of Economic Research, New York, 1967.

Tobin, J.: "Relative Income, Absolute Income, and Saving," in *Money, Trade and Economic Growth: Essays in Honor of John Henry Williams,* New York, 1951.

Weber, W.E.: "The Effect of Interest Rates on Aggregate Consumption," *American Economic Review,* September 1970, pp. 591–600.

————: "Interest Rates, Inflation, and Consumer Expenditures," *American Economic Review,* December 1975, pp. 843–858.

Wright, C.: "Some Evidence on the Interest Elasticity of Consumption," *American Economic Review,* September 1967, pp. 850–854.

————: "Saving and the Rate of Interest," in *The Taxation of Income from Capital,* Brookings, Washington, D.C., 1969.

chapter 3
Lending, Borrowing, and the Rate of Interest

The rate of interest is the cost of borrowing and the return on lending. The interest rate influences the amount of funds that borrowers are willing to borrow, and the amount that lenders are willing to lend. But cause and effect work both ways. Borrowing and lending influence the interest rate. Unless the amount that borrowers want to borrow is equal to the amount that lenders want to lend, the interest rate will be out of equilibrium. The equating of total desired borrowing with total desired lending is a necessary condition for determining the equilibrium interest rate. It is not a sufficient condition, however. Additionally, total desired saving (private and public) must be equal to total desired investment, and total demand for money must be equal to the total money supply.

Once in equilibrium, the interest rate does not remain constant. In fact, interest rates are constantly changing, seeking new equilibrium positions. Various factors serve to shift the schedules for lending and borrowing, saving and investment, and the demand for and supply of money. These factors include, among other things, autonomous investment, government spending, and monetary policy. In recent times, inflationary expectations have played a dominant role in shaping interest rate movements.

This chapter explores the above facets in considerable detail. Our primary concern will be to explain the overall level of interest rates and movements in this level over time. (We will not explain relative interest rates—the relation of one interest rate to another—as that is the subject for Chapter 7.) We will also be concerned in this chapter with calculating the rate of interest using the present value formula. Knowledge of mathematical relations between dollar values and percentage rates is crucial to understanding this book. Such knowledge is also useful for coping with personal financial problems.

THE INFLUENCE OF INTEREST ON LENDING AND BORROWING

When economic units invest more than they save (or, alternatively, spend more than they earn), they cover their deficits by borrowing. When economic units save more than they invest (earn more than they spend), they use their surpluses by lending. Even that saving that takes the form of holding larger cash balances is a form of lending since cash is a claim against the banking system or the government. In any given period, deficit units seeking to borrow exist side by side with surplus units seeking to lend. All units cannot be deficit units at the same time, for there would be nobody with funds to lend. Likewise, all units cannot be surplus units, for then, there would be nobody to borrow their funds.

In modern economies, surplus units and deficit units are easy to identify. Households are typically surplus units; they save more than they invest and therefore have funds left over for lending. Of course, there are exceptions. College-aged and young-married households often spend more than they earn. The pattern is repeated when children are born and the first home is purchased. It can show up again during retirement. But over a whole lifetime, most households have a surplus of funds to lend. Surpluses are particularly characteristic of empty-nest couples working at peak pay in their careers. Aggregatively, the household sector is consistently a surplus sector, supplying the lion's share of loanable funds to the financial markets.

Business and government are the primary deficit sectors. Business corporations do save through retained earnings, but this is ordinarily insufficient to cover profit-motivated expenditures on plant, equipment, and inventories. The need for external financing varies, but net issues of debt and equity instruments by the business sector are almost always on the plus side.[1]

Governments, at all levels, are accustomed to running deficits. There are many reasons for this. Pressures from liberals and bureaucrats to spend more, and from conservatives and taxpayers to tax less, are partly responsible. Legislators are motivated by the electoral process. They often include expenditures in their budgets that they think will satisfy their constituents. But there are economic reasons as well. At the federal level, deficit spending is considered to be a measure of fiscal policy designed to stimulate the economy. At the state and local level, borrowing is frequently used as a legitimate means of financing large, sporadic expenditures on highways, schools, and other public projects. Financing such expenditures on a current-tax basis would make poor economic sense.

The one sector that is neither, consistently, a surplus sector nor a deficit sector, in the domestic economy, is the "rest of the world." The foreign sector is a net lender of funds in some periods and a net borrower in others. The

---

[1]The issuance of equity instruments (stocks) is not borrowing in a legal sense, but it is in a financial sense because it represents corporate "borrowing" of funds from owners. Stocks are nonfixed claims against corporations.

reasons have to do with balance of payments and other considerations that are covered in Part Four of this book.

Surplus and deficit units and sectors are affected by the rate of interest and other factors. As the interest rate rises, surplus units respond by lending more, while deficit units borrow less. The opposite occurs when the interest rate falls. This is to be expected since the interest rate is the return on lending and the cost of borrowing.

Decisions to change the quantity of borrowing and/or lending, in response to a change in the rate of interest, imply decisions to change the quantity of investment and/or saving. For every economic unit, deficit or surplus, real investment I plus lending L is equal to borrowing B plus saving S. Or, as expressed previously in Chapter 1:

$$I + L \equiv B + S$$

If the interest rate rises, an economic unit will respond by lending more and/or borrowing less. But, constrained by the equation above, the unit must also respond by investing less and/or saving more. It makes sense that investment would fall. We learned from the previous chapter that investment varies inversely with the interest rate. We also learned that saving varies positively with the interest rate, provided that a negative interest-income effect does not dominate saving behavior. But even if this effect should dominate, causing saving to vary inversely with the interest rate, an economic unit could still lend more and borrow less, at a higher interest rate, as long as investment decreases more than saving. Since theory and research confirm that saving is less sensitive to interest rates than is investment, the indicated influence of interest on lending and borrowing is perfectly consistent with Chapter 2's interest theory of saving and investment.

DETERMINATION OF THE RATE OF INTEREST

Lending and borrowing are the transactions that take place in the financial markets. Aggregate lending represents the supply-of-funds side of the market, aggregate borrowing the demand side. The price of funds in the market is the rate of interest. The interest rate is the price factor that brings the supply of and demand for funds into equilibrium. If supply exceeds demand—that is, if desired lending is greater than desired borrowing—the interest rate is above its equilibrium and market forces will cause it to fall. On the other hand, if demand is greater than supply—that is, if intended borrowing exceeds intended lending—the interest rate is too low and will tend to rise. The relations between lending, borrowing, and the rate of interest are depicted in Figure 3-1.

Aggregate lending is shown in Figure 3-1 as responding positively with the interest rate, while aggregate borrowing varies inversely. The aggregates, of course, are summations of individual lending and borrowing behavior. Since

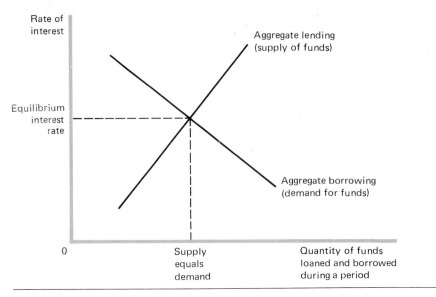

figure 3-1 The Market for Funds.

the amount of lending by each lender in the market varies directly with the interest rate, so does lending by all lenders. The same applies to borrowing. Total borrowing varies inversely with the interest rate because that sums up the behavior of each borrower in the market.

The Neoclassical Loanable Funds Theory

The notion that the interest rate is determined by the flow of funds supplied and demanded is the basis of the neoclassical loanable funds theory of interest. Figure 3-1 is an incomplete sketch, however, of this theory. To complete the theory, we need to define the supply of loanable funds in terms of its component sources, and the demand in terms of component uses. When we do this, we will find that saving is the primary source of funds that are loaned, and that investment is the primary use of borrowed funds. We will also find other component sources and uses. Money, for example, plays an important role in the loanable funds theory. When the public hoards more cash (created by the banking system), this amounts to lending to the banking system (or, alternatively, borrowing by the banking system). This lending (hoarding) and borrowing (money creation) has to be subtracted from total lending and borrowing to arrive at the supply of and demand for loanable funds because interest on money is controlled by the government. The loanable funds theory is, after all, a theory of the free market rate of interest. This is another reason why Figure 3-1 is an oversimplification.

The component uses and sources of loanable funds demanded and supplied can be derived using simple algebra. To facilitate the algebraic operations, we will use the following notation:

I = total investment (all private)

S = total saving

S_p = saving by the private sector

S_g = saving by the government sector (taxes minus government spending)

B = total borrowing

LFD = borrowing at free market rate of interest (the flow of loanable funds demanded)

ΔMS = borrowing by the banking system (change in the stock of money supplied)

L = total lending

LFS = lending at free market rate of interest (the flow of loanable funds supplied)

ΔMD = lending to the banking system (change in the stock of money demanded, i.e., hoarding)

We are already familiar with the accounting concept that uses of funds are equal to sources of funds. We have expressed this identity several times previously by saying that investment plus lending equals borrowing plus saving:

$$I + L \equiv B + S \qquad (1)$$

Identity (1) can be expanded by defining lending, borrowing, and saving in terms of their respective components:

$$L \equiv LFS + \Delta MD \qquad (2)$$

$$B \equiv LFD + \Delta MS \qquad (3)$$

$$S \equiv S_p + S_g \qquad (4)$$

When Identities (2), (3), and (4) are substituted into Identity (1), we get an expanded identity of uses and sources:

$$I + LFS + \Delta MD \equiv LFD + \Delta MS + S_p + S_g \qquad (5)$$

In *equilibrium*, the demand for loanable funds must equal the supply of loanable funds:

$$LFD = LFS \qquad (6)$$

More specifically, equilibrium requires that the uses of the demand for loanable funds be equal to the sources of the supply of loanable funds. This specification of the equilibrium condition is completed by solving Equations (5) and (6), and rearranging terms:

$$I - S_g = S_p + (\Delta MS - \Delta MD) \qquad (7)$$

Equation (7) includes the components of the demand for loanable funds on the left-hand side, and the components of supply on the right-hand side. The demand for loanable funds is derived from the demand for private investment, plus the government deficit.[2] The supply of loanable funds is derived from the supply of private saving, plus any change in the stock of money supplied by the banking system that is not willingly hoarded by the public.

The workings of the loanable funds market are depicted in Figure 3-2. Figure 3-2 is basically the same as Figure 3-1 except that the supply and demand schedules are now defined in terms of their component parts. The downward-sloping demand schedule reflects the inverse response of investment to the interest rate. The upward-sloping supply schedule is more difficult to explain. As we have learned, the response of saving to the interest rate is unclear. The shape of the supply schedule must therefore reflect the response of changes in the money stock to the interest rate.

Changes in the stock of money *supplied* do vary *directly* with the interest rate. When the interest rate rises, the banking system is induced to increase its demand-deposit liabilities in order to acquire more earning assets. When the interest rate falls, the banking system contracts its assets and deposit liabilities. (The process of deposit expansion and contraction is described in Chapter 10.)

Changes in the stock of money *demanded*, on the other hand, vary *inversely* with the interest rate. The interest rate is the opportunity cost of holding money. When the interest rate rises, people are induced to cut back on their cash balances. When it falls, they add to cash balances. Thus, the behavior of

[2] The negative of taxes minus government spending is government spending minus taxes. In other words, the negative of government saving is the government deficit.

figure 3-2 The Loanable Funds Market.

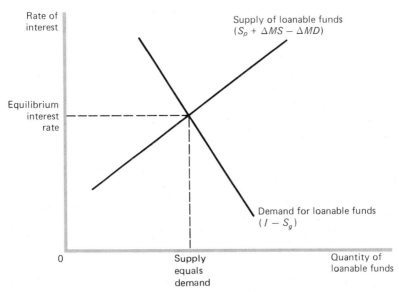

the money-demanding public, together with that of the money-supplying banking system, explains why the supply of loanable funds varies directly with the rate of interest. This is just a roundabout way of saying, however, that lenders will do more free market lending at higher interest rates, and less at lower rates.

The Keynesian Liquidity Preference Theory

An alternative theory of interest rate determination is the Keynesian liquidity preference theory. This theory differs from the neoclassical loanable funds theory in three important regards. First, it focuses on the supply of and demand for money as the principle determinants of the interest rate. It is more purely a monetary theory of interest. Second, it analyzes the interest rate in terms of the stock of money supplied and demanded, whereas the loanable funds theory analyzes the flow of changes in the money stock. Third, it focuses on the determination of the "nominal" rate of interest, whereas the neoclassical theory is primarily concerned with "real" rates and quantities. This difference is important, as we shall see later in this chapter, in analyzing the effect of inflation on the interest rate.

The basic elements of the liquidity preference theory are straightforward. Keynes reasoned that the rate of interest is determined in the first instance by the interaction of the supply of and demand for the money stock. The demand for holding money varies inversely with the interest rate, because of assetholders' preferences for liquidity. Money is the most liquid of all assets. People prefer to hold it over other assets if the sacrifice of returns, which could be earned by holding other assets, is sufficiently small. Such is the case at extremely low interest rates. At higher interest rates, however, the sacrifice becomes larger, inducing assetholders to do some switching out of cash balances and into earning assets. Consequently, people will hold less money at high interest rates, and more at low rates.

The stock of money supplied by the banking system—more specifically, by the commercial banking system—varies directly with the interest rate. Commercial banks are private, profit-seeking businesses. They, too, want to hold more earning assets when interest rates are high. The financing of these assets is through expansion of demand and time deposit debt. Since these deposits constitute the largest part of the money stock, the stock of money supplied varies directly with the interest rate.

The stock of money supplied is also influenced by the monetary policies of the central bank. If the commercial banking system is expanding the money supply "too fast" or "too slowly," the central bank will exercise tools of policy designed to control the growth of money. In this sense, the supply of money is not a free-market variable that responds to interest rates. Instead, it is a policy-controlled variable (see Chapter 11).

In equilibrium, the demand for money must equal the supply of money. The interest rate is the primary equilibrating variable. When the demand for money is greater than the supply of money, money becomes scarce and the interest rate rises. As the rate increases, the quantity of money demanded decreases.

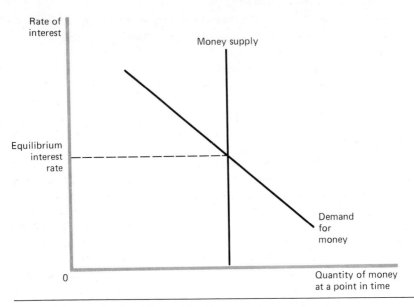

figure 3-3 Supply of and Demand for Money.

This process continues until the quantity demanded no longer exceeds supply. On the other hand, when the supply of money is greater than demand, money is overly abundant and the interest rate falls. As the rate decreases, the quantity of money demanded increases until it equals the quantity supplied. At this point, the interest rate is at its equilibrium level. This is shown in Figure 3-3.

Partial versus General Equilibrium

Which theory is correct: The loanable funds theory? Or the liquidity preference theory? Is the interest rate determined by the flow of loanable funds supplied and demanded? Or by the stock of money supplied and demanded? Actually, the interest rate is not fully determined by the logic of either theory. Both theories are partial equilibrium theories. Equilibrium in the loanable funds market is a necessary condition for determining the interest rate, but it is not a sufficient condition. The same applies to the supply of and demand for money. Let us see why.

Full equilibrium requires equality of all relevant supply and demand schedules, that all uses and sources of funds be at their desired levels. This means that the supply of loanable funds must be equal to the demand for loanable funds, that the supply of money must be equal to the demand for money, and that the desired level of saving must be equal to the desired level of investment.

Equilibrium in any one market does not guarantee, by itself, equilibrium in other markets. Suppose the market for loanable funds is in equilibrium, that the amount that lenders want to lend at the free market rate of interest is equal to the amount that borrowers want to borrow at the free rate. Suppose, however, that the increase in the stock of money demanded is greater than the increase in the stock of money supplied. In this case, the amount of desired total lending (in the free market plus to the banking system) is greater than the amount of desired total borrowing (free market plus bank borrowing). Since financial planning is constrained by the condition that investment plus total lending must be equal to saving plus total borrowing, the excess of desired total lending over desired total borrowing implies an excess of desired saving over desired investment.

Thus, even though the loanable funds market is in partial equilibrium, the interest rate is not yet fully determined. The excess of desired saving over desired investment exerts a *downward* pressure on the interest rate (as argued in the last section of the previous chapter). The excess of desired hoarding over desired money creation implies that the stock of money demanded exceeds the stock of money supplied.[3] This shortage exerts an *upward* pressure on the interest rate (as argued in the previous section of this chapter). Since the two pressures oppose each other, it is unclear whether the interest rate will rise or fall, but it will not come to rest until all relevant market forces are in equilibrium.[4]

Of the various theories of interest, the loanable funds theory is probably the best suited for handling a full equilibrium analysis. Saving and investment and money creation and hoarding are the component sources and uses of the supply of and demand for loanable funds. If we require that each component source be equal to its counterpart use—that is, that desired saving be equal to desired investment, and that desired money creation be equal to desired hoarding—we are then closer to a full determination of the interest rate. Moreover, when each component part of loanable funds is in equilibrium, the loanable funds market, itself, is automatically in equilibrium, the whole being the sum of the parts.

CHANGES IN THE RATE OF INTEREST

One of the most striking characteristics of interest rates is their extreme variability. The range of fluctuations for short-term interest rates is particularly great. (The range of movements in short-term interest rates may be noted in Figure 3-4.) Although long-term interest rates are less volatile than are short-term rates, both series tend to move up and down together. It is a well-known fact that all interest rates are highly correlated with each other, and

---

[3]If we assume that the stock of money supplied and demanded was initially in equilibrium, a change in the stock of money demanded that is larger than the change in the stock of money supplied means that the stock of money demanded will become larger than the stock of money supplied.
[4]The excess supply of saving and the excess demand for money can both be reduced by a decrease in aggregate income. Since income is also an equilibrating variable, it will tend to fall. Lower income will be associated with a higher or lower interest rate, depending on the direction of the income effect in the loanable funds market.

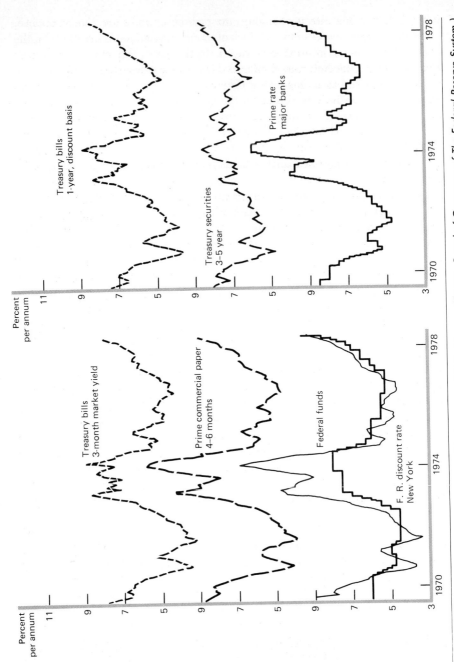

figure 3-4 Short-Term Interest Rates. Monthly Averages of Daily Figures. *(Source: Board of Governors of The Federal Reserve System.)*

50

that when any one rate is changing, most all other rates are changing in the same direction.

In recent years, interest rate movements have been closely related to changes in the expected rate of inflation. Inflationary expectations play such an important role in explaining interest rates that we will devote the next section of this chapter entirely to this factor. In this section, we shall analyze interest rate changes that are caused by factors other than expected inflation. To simplify our analysis, we shall assume that the price level is expected to remain perfectly stable. This way we can avoid the problem of having to distinguish between nominal and real interest rates and nominal and real quantities of loanable funds.

The interest rate changes whenever there is a shift in the supply schedule or in the demand schedule for loanable funds. When the supply schedule shifts to the right, the interest rate falls; when supply shifts to the left, it rises. When the demand schedule shifts to the right, the interest rate rises; when demand shifts to the left, it falls. (The reader can verify this by mentally shifting the schedules in Figure 3-2.) Changes in the rate of interest are thus caused by those factors capable of shifting the supply of and/or the demand for loanable funds.

A major shift variable is the internal rate of return expected on investment in capital goods. When expected returns on capital increase, firms invest more. This increase in investment, in turn, increases the demand for loanable funds and causes the interest rate to rise. Expected returns on capital are not directly observable, but they can be measured indirectly by looking at factors that bear closely upon them. Capacity utilization is one such factor. The return on capital varies directly with capacity utilization. Consequently, so does the interest rate.

Another shift factor is aggregate income. Income affects supply, demand, and the interest rate in several ways. One way is through the demand for money. The demand for money varies directly with income: When income increases, the demand for money increases. This produces a shortage of money and an increase in hoarding. By either the liquidity preference or loanable funds theory, the interest rate should rise. This effect is offset, however, by another effect working through desired saving. When income increases, so does saving. The latter increases the supply of loanable funds; consequently, the interest rate should fall. Since increased hoarding decreases the supply of loanable funds, while increased saving increases it, the net effect on the supply side of the market could be either way theoretically.

The effect of income on the demand side of the market is equally ambiguous. Growing income stimulates investment (via the acceleration principle), but sustained high-level income requires no net investment once the stock of capital is built up. The depreciation of capital, however, is related to the level of income. To the extent that replacement investment is partly financed through borrowing in the loanable funds market, the interest rate should increase as income increases. On the other hand, an increase in income raises tax revenues and lowers the government deficit. This decreases the government's demand for loanable funds, thus exerting a downward pressure on the interest rate. Since business borrowing and government borrowing respond by changing in opposite directions, the net effect of a change in income on the demand side of the market is theoretically unclear.

The effect of income on the government deficit, just described, assumes a passive fiscal policy. But tax rates and government expenditures are not constants. An active fiscal policy requires that tax rates be cut and expenditures raised as measures to stimulate a depressed economy.

Changes in tax rates and government expenditures are shift factors on the demand side of the loanable funds market. When tax rates are cut, or expenditures increased, the size of the government deficit becomes larger. This increases the government's demand for loanable funds. As a consequence, the interest rate rises. The government is less prone to use fiscal policy to slow down an overheated economy. Politically, it is more difficult to cut government expenditures and raise tax rates. But when these measures are taken, the effect is to lower the interest rate.

The usual cure for overexpansion is monetary policy. Contractionary monetary policy is indicated when the monetary authorities use their powers to reduce the rate of growth of the money supply. This factor serves to shift the supply side of the loanable funds market. When the increase in the money supply is made smaller, the supply of loanable funds decreases, and the interest rate rises. Expansionary monetary policy, on the other hand, is indicated by larger increases in the money supply. This increases the supply of loanable funds and, consequently, lowers the interest rate.

This effect of the money supply on the interest rate is called "the liquidity effect," deriving its name from the Keynesian liquidity preference theory. In Keynesian economics, the interest rate is the key variable that makes the quantity of money demanded come into equilibrium with the supply of money. Since the quantity of money demanded varies inversely with the interest rate, it follows from the logic of supply and demand analysis that the interest rate varies inversely with the supply of money.

Or does it? In monetarist economics, monetary expansion ultimately leads to higher, not lower, interest rates. Monetarists believe that price inflation is the result of money supply inflation. They believe that an increase in the rate of growth of the money supply causes people to *expect* an increase in the rate of growth of the price level. This expectation, in turn, results in a higher market rate of interest (for reasons explained in the next section). Sooner or later, this expectations effect is thought to more than offset the liquidity effect, so that the net effect is to raise the interest rate. Although Keynesians disagree that the liquidity effect of monetary policy is dominated, they do agree with monetarists that inflationary expectations play an important role in determining interest rate movements.

THE NOMINAL INTEREST RATE, THE REAL INTEREST RATE, AND EXPECTED INFLATION

A rational lender or borrower would never dream of entering into a loan contract without considering the effect of expected inflation. Interest payments and the return of principal are contracted in nominal dollar amounts. But these amounts depreciate in real purchasing power in a world of inflation. When prices rise 6 percent a year, dollars are worth 6 percent less each year in real value. Unless lenders and borrowers consider this factor, lenders will receive (and borrowers will pay) 6 percent less in real interest than would be the case if prices were not rising. Ignoring inflation hurts lenders and helps borrowers.

Irving Fisher was the first American economist to clearly distinguish between the nominal and expected real rates of interest and to incorporate this distinction into the body of economic theory. As a neoclassical economist, Fisher argued that real lending and real borrowing depend on the expected real rate of interest, not the nominal rate, despite the fact that loan contracts are stated (and markets are quoted) in terms of nominal rates. The rational lender or borrower need not despair, however. The difference between the nominal rate of interest and the expected real rate of interest is, quite simply, the expected rate of inflation.

How is this so?

Suppose you make a loan of $100 for a year at 10 percent nominal interest. At the end of the year you will get back $110 (assuming the borrower keeps his or her promise). But if you expect inflation to be 6 percent next year, you will need $106 back at the end of the year just to break even in terms of expected purchasing power. Only the remaining $4 represents a net expected real return, which is about 4 percent on the original $100.[5] This relation is the same on the borrowing side. If you borrow $100 for a year at 10 percent, paying back $110 at the end of the year, only $4 represents an expected real cost. The other $106 merely gives back to the lender the same expected purchasing power that you borrowed in the first place.

As the expected rate of inflation changes, the difference (or spread) between the nominal interest rate and the expected real rate changes by the same amount. The spread might be changed in two extreme ways, however. At one extreme, an increase in expected inflation might be met with an identical increase in the nominal interest rate, with no change in the expected real rate. At the other extreme, the expected real interest rate might decrease by the amount of the increase in expected inflation, with no change in the nominal rate.

Fisher, himself, emphasized the former extreme. He argued that the real rate is determined by real factors, that is, by real saving and investment and real lending and borrowing. Moreover, he argued that inflation has no lasting effect on these real magnitudes. Consequently, the only long-run effect of an increase in expected inflation is to increase the nominal rate of interest, leaving the expected real rate intact.

Keynes, on the other hand, emphasized the opposite extreme. He maintained (in his liquidity preference theory) that the nominal interest rate is determined by the nominal supply of and demand for money. He reasoned, further, that an increase in inflation will not be passed on to the nominal

[5]It is slightly less than 4 percent because the remaining $4 a year from now is also depreciated by inflation.

interest rate because a higher nominal rate reduces the nominal demand for money. Since this would violate the equilibrium condition of demand equaling supply, the nominal rate will not change. What will change, according to Keynes, is the real rate. It will decrease by the amount of the increase in inflation.[6]

Neither of these extreme positions is entirely correct. The Keynesian position, as described, is reached through partial equilibrium analysis. In full equilibrium, interest rates and other prices must clear all markets, not the supply of and demand for money alone. However, Keynes' focus on the relation of interest to money does offer some useful insights. From his analysis we can demonstrate that inflation does affect certain real magnitudes, including the real rate of interest. As a consequence, the Fisherian position is not entirely valid, at least in the short run.

The *real* cost of holding money is the *nominal* rate of interest. When you hold money, you lose purchasing power owing to price inflation, and you forego purchasing power in terms of real interest that could be earned if earning assets were held instead. These two real costs add up to the nominal rate. Now suppose that there is an increase in the expected rate of inflation. If, as Fisher argued, this increase is added to the nominal interest rate, the real cost of holding money will increase. This, in turn, will decrease the real demand for holding money. Consequently, real money balances will be dishoarded and the supply of real loanable funds will increase. The end result will be a decrease in the expected real rate of interest. Note, however, that the real rate will not decrease unless the nominal rate increases. Moreover, the nominal rate will not rise by the full amount of the increase in expected inflation since part of the increase is absorbed by a drop in the expected real rate. Our analysis suggests, therefore, that an increase in expected inflation will lead to both an increase in the nominal interest rate and a decrease in the expected real rate.

What do the facts reveal?

Even the most casual observer will have noticed that market interest rates are much higher during periods of rapidly rising prices than they are during periods of relatively stable prices. In the 1973–1974 period, when the inflation rate increased to double digits, interest rates in the market shot up to levels higher than most people had ever experienced. This was particularly true of short-term rates. Then, in the 1975–1976 period, as the inflation rate crept slowly downward (to about 6 percent), so did the level of market rates. But the decline was short-lived. By the end of 1978, inflation and short-term interest rates were again at double-digit levels.

The observed covariation between interest rates and actual inflation is interesting. But it cannot be used to test the effect of expected inflation. The nominal interest rate is agreed to by lenders and borrowers based on what they expect inflation to be before the fact, not on what inflation actually turns out to be after the fact. Since lenders and borrowers are not, unfortunately, blessed

---

[6]See LeRoy (May 1973) for a good exposition of the contrast between the Keynesian position and the Fisherian position.

with perfect foresight, actual inflation does not measure expected inflation. The response of market rates to expected inflation can be estimated only if we have a good measure of expected inflation.

Various methods have been used for measuring the expected rate of inflation. One method has been to take the average of expectations expressed in surveys of "experts." Joseph Livingston, a respected financial columnist, has conducted such surveys twice yearly since 1946. The survey method is good in that it measures expectations directly, but the method also suffers in that the expectations of those polled represent a biased estimate of the overall level of expectations in the market.

Another method of measuring expected inflation has been to use a weighted average of past inflation rates as a proxy. This method assumes that expectations are formed "adaptively" on the basis of past experience. The adaptive expectations method is widely used, but it has its problems. Is the past a good guide to the future? How many past inflation rates are relevant? How much weight should be given to each past rate being weighted?

Still another method is to use the current growth rate of the money supply as an indicator of expected inflation. This method assumes that expectations are formed "rationally" on the basis of the most relevant and currently available information. Accordingly, the expected rate of inflation is thought to be indicated more closely by current monetary conditions than by past rates of inflation and past monetary conditions.[7]

Whichever method is used for measuring expected inflation, the evidence from econometric studies has tended to lend support to Irving Fisher's views. Changes in expected inflation are associated with lagged changes (of nearly equal size) in the nominal rate of interest.[8] It is possible, however, that this statistical association is to some extent a coincidental response to other factors affecting both inflation and market interest rates. It is probable, moreover, that the statistical measures of expected inflation are biased, that they do not reflect true expectations. Finally, we know of at least one study in which the statistical results suggest that the market rate of interest does *not* adjust fully for changes in expected inflation.[9] Thus, we cannot rule out the possibility that the

[7]If expected inflation adjusts to changing monetary conditions without any substantial lag, the money supply has an ambiguous overall effect on the rate of interest. Monetary change will be simultaneously associated with both a positive expectations effect and a negative liquidity effect. However, if expected inflation adjusts sluggishly to changing conditions, then the interest rate should vary negatively with concurrent changes in the money supply, and positively with past inflation experience caused by past monetary conditions. See Jackson (September 1976) for an example of an econometric forecast of the rate of interest in which the current money supply and the average of past inflation rates both appear as independent variables.

[8]Results of studies that employ past inflation data vary widely with respect to the length of time it takes for the nominal rate to adjust to expected inflation. Yohe and Karnosky (December 1969) found that the period of adjustment is short. Sargent (May 1972) concluded that the adjustment takes a very long time. See Pyle (August 1972) and Gibson (December 1972) for studies employing expectations based on the survey method. Finally, see Fama (June 1975) for a study that concludes that the nominal interest rate is the best predictor of actual inflation. Fama's results are consistent with Fisher's notion that the nominal interest rate adjusts fully for changes in expected inflation.

[9]See Benjamin M. Friedman (June 1978).

expected real interest rate *is* affected by expected inflation, as Keynes and others have argued.

While we have much to learn about the effect of the level of expected inflation on interest rates, we have even more to learn about the effect of the uncertainty that surrounds this level. Expectations rarely if ever come true. Forecasting inflation is a very risky business.

Inflation uncertainty carries over to real-interest-rate uncertainty. The more uncertain a person is about future inflation, the more uncertain he or she will be about the real rate of interest. Theoretically, an increase in uncertainty about the real interest rate can be expected to decrease both the supply of and the demand for real loanable funds, if we assume that both lenders and borrowers are averse to risk. However, if lenders are more averse to risk than borrowers (a reasonable assumption?), supply should fall relative to demand, and the expected real rate should rise. But this conclusion is only speculative.

Inflation uncertainty also carries over to real-income uncertainty. The more uncertain a person is about future inflation, the more uncertain that person will be about his or her real income from wages, interest, etc. As we learned in the previous chapter, an increase in real-income uncertainty leads to an increase in real saving. Since an increase in real saving increases the supply of real loanable funds, the expected real rate of interest should drop.

Inflation uncertainty probably also carries over to other variables that affect the real interest rate. We cannot be sure what the overall direction of the inflation-uncertainty effect is when all the channels (real-interest-rate uncertainty, real-income uncertainty, etc.) are netted out. We also do not know much about the interrelation of the level of expected inflation and the degree of uncertainty surrounding it. Does inflation uncertainty increase as expected inflation rises? Or is it independent? If dependent, how do expected inflation and inflation uncertainty jointly affect interest rates? We have much to learn.

THE MATHEMATICS OF INTEREST

Most people understand the concept of interest but do not know how interest rates are actually calculated. This is because loan contracts are usually mysterious, and often complex. Some contracts are so simple and straightforward that the interest rate is easy to figure, but most are sufficiently complex that the interest rate cannot be calculated intuitively or simply. Some more common loan arrangements are shown in Table 3-1. Of those shown, the simple-interest, single-payment loan is the only arrangement in which the interest rate is intuitively obvious to most people.[10]

---

[10]Before reading on, try calculating (in your own way) the interest rate on each of the loan arrangements shown in Table 3-1. Your answers can then be compared to the mathematically correct answers calculated below.

TABLE 3-1

Illustrations of Common Loan Arrangements

Type of Loan Arrangement	Present Value of the Loan	Future Returns of Interest and Principal ($)				
		Year 1	Year 2	Year 3	Year 4	Beyond
Simple-interest, single-payment	$100	$121	0	0	0	0
Compound interest, single-payment	100	0	$144	0	0	0
Amortized (installment)	100	$57.62	$57.62	0	0	0
Coupon bond	100	$5	$5	$5	$105	0

Fortunately, the interest rate can be calculated for any type of loan arrangement by using the "present value formula":

$$\begin{matrix} \text{Present} \\ \text{value} \\ \text{of a} \\ \text{loan} \end{matrix} = \frac{\begin{matrix}\text{return of} \\ \text{interest \&} \\ \text{principal in} \\ \text{year one}\end{matrix}}{(1+i)^1} + \frac{\begin{matrix}\text{return of} \\ \text{interest \&} \\ \text{principal in} \\ \text{year two}\end{matrix}}{(1+i)^2} + \cdots + \frac{\begin{matrix}\text{return of} \\ \text{interest \&} \\ \text{principal in} \\ n\text{th year}\end{matrix}}{(1+i)^n}$$

The i in the formula is the annual interest rate. It can be calculated by plugging in the present value of the loan and the future returns of interest and principal.

The interest rate for the simple-interest, single-payment loan (in Table 3-1) is 21 percent. Most people would know this without consciously using the present value formula. Nevertheless, this answer is confirmed by the formula:

$$\$100 = \frac{\$121}{(1.21)^1}$$

Simple-interest, single-payment loans are common. Most people have entered into such a loan, at one time or another, with a friend or relative.

The interest rate for the compound-interest, single-payment loan (in Table 3-1) is 20 percent.[11] Again, the answer is confirmed by the present value formula:

$$\$100 = \frac{\$144}{(1.20)^2}$$

At a 20 percent rate, the $100 is worth $120 after one year; and when the $120 is reinvested at 20 percent, it is worth $144 after the second year. Four dollars

[11] If you calculated it at 22 percent, you forgot to compound the interest.

of the $144 represents interest on the interest. This is what compound interest is all about.

Unfortunately, the present value formula is a complex equation. Except for very simple loans, it is impossible to solve for the interest rate using elementary algebra. For this reason, banks and other lenders of funds use present-value tables in which interest rates (already calculated) can be looked up. Another way to solve for interest rates is to use a pocket calculator. Most of the newer electronic calculators are programmed to do present value and interest rate problems.

The interest rate for the amortized (installment) loan (in Table 3-1) is 10 percent. We can verify this by the present value formula:

$$\$100 = \frac{\$57.62}{(1.10)^1} + \frac{\$57.62}{(1.10)^2}$$

We can also verify it by working out the mechanics of such a loan. If the interest rate is 10 percent, then $10 of the $57.62 (first installment) will be an interest payment, and the remaining $47.62 will be return of principal. This will leave $52.38 of principal remaining at the end of the first year. The second installment of $57.62 will consist of $5.24 of interest (10 percent of the remaining principal) and the remaining principal of $52.38.

Amortized loans are very common. Most mortgage loans and auto loans are amortized. The size of payment is the same every period (usually monthly). But the composition of the payment is always changing. At the beginning of the loan, most of the installment consists of interest; very little represents return of principal. At the end of the loan, the situation is reversed.

The interest rate for the coupon bond (in Table 3-1) is 5 percent, as verified by the present value formula:

$$\$100 = \frac{\$5}{(1.05)^1} + \frac{\$5}{(1.05)^2} + \frac{\$5}{(1.05)^3} + \frac{\$105}{(1.05)^4}$$

The interest on the coupon bond is paid out periodically as it accrues.[12] The expression "clipping coupons" has literally meant trading in coupons (attached to the bonds) for interest (stated on the coupon). Thus the $5 of return in each of the first three years is interest pure and simple ($5 is 5 percent of $100). The $105 returned in the fourth year also includes $5 of interest; the remaining $100 is the return of principal upon maturity. Most bonds traded in the market have the pattern of returns characterized by the coupon bond arrangement. Interest is paid along the way, and principal is returned at maturity.

Now let us pose a question: What will be the value of the coupon bond (in Table 3-1) after two years pass by? This is a tricky question because there are

[12]Semiannual payments are typical. Our illustration uses annual payments in order to simplify the mathematics.

two ways of specifying value and two corresponding ways of specifying the interest rate. One measure of value is "face value." It is called face value because it actually appears on the face of the bond instrument. The face value is the principal that is returned when the bond matures. The corresponding interest rate is the "coupon rate." It, too, is stated in the instrument. Since the face value and the coupon rate appear on the bond, they do not change with time. They remain fixed throughout the life of the bond. In two years, the face value of the bond will still be $100, the coupon rate will still be 5 percent, and the bond will continue to pay fixed periodic interest of $5 (which is the product of the coupon rate and the face value).

The other measure of value is the "market value." It is the price the buyer pays (or seller receives) in the market. Bonds can be traded in the secondary market after they have been issued and before they mature. Buyers can enter the market and buy bonds that were issued at an earlier time. Sellers can use the market to sell bonds that are not ready to mature.

The market value of a bond is not fixed. It depends upon the corresponding "market rate" of interest, which, as we have learned, is very volatile. If, in two years, the market rate is 5 percent, then the market value of the bond will be $100. This we can confirm from the present value formula:

$$\$100 = \frac{\$5}{(1.05)^1} + \frac{\$105}{(1.05)^2}$$

Note that we are talking about the present two years from now. In two years the bond will have only two more years to go before it matures. The market value will be different if the market rate is different. If, two years hence, the market rate is 6 percent, the market value, two years hence, will be:

$$\$98.17 = \frac{\$5}{(1.06)^1} + \frac{\$105}{(1.06)^2}$$

If, instead, the market rate is 4 percent, then the market value will be:

$$\$101.89 = \frac{\$5}{(1.04)^1} + \frac{\$105}{(1.04)^2}$$

There is no further need to keep on repeating this experiment. We are now in a position to list four very important conclusions:

1. The market value of a bond is equal to the face value of a bond when the market rate of interest is equal to the coupon rate of interest.
2. The market value of a bond is less than the face value of a bond when the market rate of interest is greater than the coupon rate of interest.
3. The market value of a bond is greater than the face value of a bond when the market rate of interest is less than the coupon rate of interest.
4. The market value of a bond varies inversely with the market rate of interest. When market rates rise, bond prices fall. And when market rates fall, bond prices rise.

All four conclusions follow logically from the exercises conducted above. They exemplify some of the most important principles of finance. The fourth one is particularly important. The inverse relation between market value and market yield applies not only to bonds, but to all securities traded in the market.

We will close by posing one final question: What will be the market value of the coupon bond (in Table 3-1) three years hence? In three years, the bond will only be one year away from maturity. If, three years hence, the market rate is 5 percent (the same as the coupon rate), the market value will then be $100. If, in three years, the market rate is 6 percent, then the market value will be:

$$\$99.06 = \frac{\$105}{(1.06)}$$

If 4 percent, then:

$$\$100.96 = \frac{\$105}{(1.04)}$$

When these market values are compared to the market values that were calculated above, when the bond was two years away from maturity, we see that they are now closer to face value. Indeed, as a bond approaches maturity, market value will approach face value. At maturity, market value equals face value, regardless of the market rate of interest. This phenomenon gives us two more important principles of finance to add to the list:

5. The longer the maturity of a debt instrument, the further its market value will be from face value for any given market interest rate different from the face rate.
6. The longer the maturity of a debt instrument, the more its market value will change for any given change in the market interest rate.

The market facts clearly indicate that market values of long-term debt instruments are more unstable than they are for short-term instruments. This is despite the fact that short-term interest rates are less stable than long-term rates.

PROJECTS AND QUESTIONS

1. Is it possible for the loanable funds theory and the liquidity preference theory to predict opposite changes in the rate of interest? If so, which theory gives us the more reliable prediction? Explain your answers.

2. Is it possible for a market rate of interest to be less than the expected rate of inflation? Is it possible for a market rate of interest to be less than zero? Explain your answers.
3. There is a fairly close time-series relationship between ex post real interest rates and measures of industrial capacity utilization. How can this relationship be explained?
4. Check interest rate changes in long-term government bonds during the most recent year. Does interest rate theory help you explain such changes in rates as took place?
5. Write a short essay on the "truth" contained in the federal "truth-in-lending" laws.

BIBLIOGRAPHY

Bomberger, W.A., and G.E. Makinen: "The Fisher Effect: Graphical Treatment and Some Econometric Implications," *Journal of Finance,* June 1977, pp. 719–733.

Conard, J.W.: *An Introduction to the Theory of Interest,* University of California Press, Berkeley, 1959.

Fama, E.F.: "Short-Term Interest Rates as Predictors of Inflation," *American Economic Review,* June 1975, pp. 269–282.

Fisher, I.: *The Theory of Interest,* Macmillan, New York, 1930.

Friedman, B.M.: "Who Puts the Inflation Premium into Nominal Interest Rates?" *Journal of Finance,* June 1978, pp. 833–845.

Gibson, W.E.: "Interest Rates and Inflationary Expectations: New Evidence," *American Economic Review,* December 1972, pp. 854–865.

Henning, C.N., W. Pigott, and R.H. Scott: *Financial Markets and the Economy,* Prentice-Hall, Englewood Cliffs, N. J., 1978. chap. 12.

Jackson, W.D.: "Federal Deficits, Inflation, and Monetary Growth: Can They Predict Interest Rates?" *Federal Reserve Bank of Richmond Economic Review,* September/October 1976, pp. 13–25.

Lahiri, K.: "Inflationary Expectations: Their Formation and Interest Rate Effects," *American Economic Review,* March 1976, pp. 124–131.

LeRoy, S.F.: "Interest Rates and the Inflation Premium," *Federal Reserve Bank of Kansas City Monthly Review,* May 1973, pp. 11–18.

Levi, M.D., and J.H. Makin: "Anticipated Inflation and Interest Rates," *American Economic Review,* December 1978, pp. 801–812.

Lutz, F.A.: *The Theory of Interest,* Aldine, Chicago, 1968.

Mundell, R.A.: "Inflation and Real Interest," *Journal of Political Economy,* June 1963, pp. 280–283.

Polakoff, M.E. et al.: *Financial Institutions and Markets,* Houghton Mifflin, Boston, 1970, chap. 3 especially.

Pyle, D.H.: "Observed Price Expectations and Interest Rates," *Review of Economics and Statistics,* August 1972, pp. 275–280.

Sargent, T.J.: "Anticipated Inflation and the Nominal Rate of Interest," *Quarterly Journal of Economics,* May 1972, pp. 212–225.

Smith, P.F.: *Economics of Financial Institutions and Markets,* Irwin, Homewood, Ill., 1971, chap. 14.

Yohe, W.P., and D.S. Karnosky: "Interest Rates and Price Level Changes," *Federal Reserve Bank of St. Louis Review,* December 1969, pp. 19–36.

chapter 4
Financial Institutions: Intermediaries between Ultimate Lenders and Ultimate Borrowers

The flow of funds from saving to investment can take three routes. One route is "internal finance." The farmer or the merchant who cuts back on consumption expenditures out of given income in order to remodel the barn or the store is engaging in internal (or self-) finance. He or she is performing a simultaneous act of saving and investment. In a world of complete self-finance, everyone's own saving is channeled into everyone's own investment. Everyone is financially self-sufficient. No one runs a deficit or a surplus. Financial markets are unnecessary; they do not exist. Neither do financial intermediaries. Obviously, such a world represents only the most rudimentary economy.

A second route is "direct external finance." The college student who borrows from his or her parents to finance investment in education is an example. The loan is a direct connection between the student doing the investment and the parents doing the saving to finance the investment. In a world of direct external finance, funds flow directly from those who save to those who invest. Those who save have surpluses to lend. Those who invest have deficits that are financed by borrowing directly from surplus units. The borrowing and lending require the existence of financial markets. Financial intermediaries, however, are not required in this world of direct finance.

Financial intermediaries play a role only in the third route: "indirect external finance." This route is the most circuitous of the three. In a world of indirect finance, funds flow from surplus units to intermediaries, and then from intermediaries to deficit units. A financial intermediary is just that; it intermediates between ultimate lenders (surplus units) and ultimate borrowers (deficit units). Intermediaries borrow from surplus units, and with these funds, they lend to deficit units. An intermediary, itself, is neither a surplus unit nor a deficit unit. It neither saves nor invests (in any important way). It only borrows and lends. But neither is an intermediary self-sufficient. It cannot survive without surplus units to supply funds and deficit units to demand them.

In our modern economy, indirect external finance is the most important route by which funds flow from saving to investment. All business corporations require external financing. Even those corporations that have no legal debt on their books do finance externally by "borrowing" from their stockholders. And who are these stockholders? To a large (and growing) extent they are intermediaries such as pension funds, mutual funds, and insurance companies. These same institutions hold much of the corporate sector's bonded indebtedness too. And when corporations borrow on a short-term basis, it is usually from commercial banks. The business sector relies very heavily on indirect external finance, though certainly not exclusively.

By definition, all government deficits are financed externally. Most government debt is held by financial intermediaries, particularly by the central bank and commercial banks. This is more true of federal debt than the debt of state and local governments. Many wealthy individuals buy municipal bonds for tax purposes, but, for the same reason, so do commercial banks and casualty insurance companies.

The external financing of housing is usually indirect. The vast majority of first mortgages are held by savings and loan associations, mutual savings banks, commercial banks, and life insurance companies. Consumer credit, too, usually flows indirectly through intermediaries. Consumers borrow from commercial banks, credit unions, and personal finance companies. Consumption is also financed by borrowing from retailers, but these retailers, in turn, are usually forced to finance consumer credit by borrowing from commercial banks and sales finance companies.

The point is that we live essentially in a world of indirect external finance. Internal and direct external finance are present and important, but indirect finance dominates. For this reason, this chapter focuses on the role and behavior of the various financial institutions that intermediate between surplus and deficit units.[1]

THE RATIONALE FOR FINANCIAL INTERMEDIATION

Financial intermediaries are run much like businesses. All intermediaries must at least try to cover their costs, and many attempt to earn profits in addition. The way they do this is to pay lower interest rates on funds borrowed from surplus units than the rates charged on loans to deficit units. The difference between the rate charged and the rate paid is the spread. The product of this spread and the volume of funds borrowed and loaned is the operating income out of which labor costs, overhead, and other expenses are paid. Income remaining, if any, is profit. The spread cannot be made too large, otherwise volume will fall too much. Financial intermediaries can use marginal-cost, marginal-revenue analysis to determine the best spread, if they have some

---

[1]The present chapter does not cover investment banks and security dealers. These institutions are discussed in Part Three. Another omission of this chapter is that it does not cover market structure and government regulation aspects of financial institutions. These aspects are discussed in Chapter 22.

monopoly power. In the presence of strong competition, however, the spread is determined by market forces.

Since ultimate-lending surplus units receive lower interest rates from intermediaries than ultimate-borrowing deficit units are charged, it would seem that surplus and deficit units could mutually improve their positions by cutting out the middleman and dealing directly with each other. This is true as far as interest rates are concerned, but not for other credit characteristics. Ultimate borrowers, such as corporations, often need to borrow on a long-term basis in order to finance fixed investment, such as plant and equipment. They also have other special financing requirements. Savers, on the other hand, usually prefer to keep their savings liquid and safe. They need both liquidity to convert savings into cash, without loss, when the need arises, and stable growth of savings for long-term purposes. If ultimate lenders and borrowers dealt directly and exclusively with each other, they would have to unduly compromise their divergent needs in order to strike a bargain. The purpose of financial intermediaries is to meet the separate needs of both savers and borrowers. Intermediaries are willing and able to meet the long-term and other special financing requirements of deficit units. At the same time, they provide surplus units with the opportunity to keep their savings liquid and safe.

Since the liabilities of deficit units are not safe enough for most savers, it seems strange that the liabilities of intermediaries should be so safe, particularly since the latter claims are issued by intermediaries in order to finance the unsafe claims issued by deficit units. On the face of it, it would seem that the safety feature promised to savers by intermediaries is an illusion. But it is not. Intermediaries create safety through a "liability transformation effect" and through an "asset transformation effect."[2]

The liability transformation effect is best illustrated by the operations of savings and loan associations. These intermediaries secure funds from savers by offering savings accounts. Savings accounts are highly liquid. They can be converted into cash for full value at any time. Savings and loan associations employ funds, on the other hand, by making mortgage loans. (Over 80 percent of the assets of savings and loan associations are in mortgages.) Mortgages are long-term instruments, usually running ten, twenty, or thirty years in duration. They turn over slowly. They are not liquid in any sense of the word. The liquidity of savings accounts is obviously not provided by the mortgage assets of savings and loan associations. Instead, these intermediaries transform their own liabilities into long-term or permanent sources of funds (from their point of view) without impairing liquidity (from their depositors' point of view). This "magic" is achieved through the law of large numbers. A savings and loan association will have thousands of depositors. Each time an individual depositor withdraws from his or her account, the savings and loan association does not have to sell off a mortgage (possibly at a big loss) in order to make good on the account. Instead, it will be secure with the knowledge that there is a high

---

[2] These effects are described alternatively as "transmutation" effects. See Moore (1968) and Smith (1978).

probability of some other individual making a deposit at the same time the withdrawal is made. By the law of large numbers, the aggregate of savings accounts of many depositors is more stable and predictable than the savings account of the individual depositor. This quality enables a savings and loan association to meet the liquidity needs of depositors without having to keep its own assets liquid. However, as extra measures of precaution, a savings and loan association will keep some assets liquid and will space the maturities of its mortgage holdings. It should be noted that the phenomenon of liability transformation applies not only to savings and loan associations but to financial intermediaries generally.

There is more to keeping savings safe than liquidity alone. Those who save for retirement and other far-off purposes are not all that interested in short-run liquidity. Rather, they seek a high rate of return on their savings, with a minimum of risk. The asset transformation effect of intermediation gives most savers a chance to obtain a high return with less risk than would be possible in the absence of intermediaries. A good example is the mutual fund. Mutual funds offer savers an indirect way of acquiring corporate stocks. Rates of return on corporate equities are higher, over long periods of time, than rates of return on other financial assets. But stock returns are also more risky. Dividends are not promised. Stock prices are highly volatile. Healthy capital gains are realized at times, but so are capital losses. There is no way a saver can avoid this risk completely, but a small saver can reduce risk substantially (without impairing return) by buying shares of a mutual fund. A mutual fund is able to transform its asset holdings of individually risky stocks into a less risky, diversified portfolio. Diversification reduces risk. When one portfolio company performs poorly, chances are the shares of some other portfolio company will be doing well. Portfolios of many stocks thus have more stable rates of return than do individual stocks (a phenomenon we shall explore in considerable detail in Chapter 6). Wealthy savers, of course, can diversify on their own. Most savers, however, lack sufficient funds to diversify efficiently and effectively other than through a financial intermediary. The benefits of asset transformation through efficient diversification are offered by mutual funds, pension funds, life insurance companies, and intermediaries generally. Moreover, diversification applies not only to stocks, but to bonds, mortgages, and other assets as well.

In addition to liquidity and safety, intermediaries provide savers with expertise, economies of scale, and other advantages that most savers cannot provide for themselves. It takes trained personnel to evaluate credit, make loans, analyze securities, deal with Wall Street and corporate financial officers, and manage portfolios. The typical saver does not have this expertise, but the saver is expert enough to go to a financial intermediary that does. In addition to expertise, financial intermediaries enable the saver to share the fixed costs of administering loans, managing securities, transacting in the market, etc., with other savers. One intermediary, acting in behalf of many savers, can perform these functions at a much lower cost than that which would accrue to many savers acting independently. By saving at a financial institution, the ultimate-lending surplus unit is indirectly able to lend in the open capital markets with expertise and economy.

The emergence of financial intermediaries has been a key factor in the growth of the economy. Most savers prefer to keep their savings safe and therefore find claims against financial intermediaries to be more attractive than stocks, bonds, and other capital market securities. Savers thus save more than they would without financial intermediation. At the same time, those who invest borrow more and expend more than they would without intermediation. Financial intermediaries are visible, centralized, and offer credit in sufficient quantity and on favorable terms. In short, the lending needs of savers are different from the borrowing needs of deficit units, so intermediaries come between them and meet the needs of both. The result is more saving, more investment, and a faster rate of economic growth.

HOW INDIVIDUALS EMPLOY THEIR SAVINGS

A basic factor in determining how individuals employ their savings is the relationship between individuals' needs and the services that the different forms of savings provide. When individuals want convenience and liquidity above all other considerations, they hold money. Some use paper currency for this purpose. The commonly used form of money, however, is demand deposits. Individuals who want some interest return and who, while willing to forego complete assurance of liquidity, wish to enjoy a high degree of it may choose a savings account in a commercial bank, a savings and loan association, a mutual savings bank, or a credit union. Increasingly, these institutions are offering accounts that combine the services of checking accounts and savings accounts.

Insurance against death and other risks does not, strictly speaking, require savings. Term insurance, for example, is pure life insurance. It has no savings value; it only "pays off" in the event of death. Most life insurance policies are whole-life, however. These policies offer both insurance protection at death and savings value during one's life. Whole-life premiums are larger than term premiums because part of the former is saving. The insured party can recoup this saving at any time by cashing in the policy. The future value of saving through life insurance depends on the rate of return that the insurer assumes can be earned on the insured's savings.

Life insurance is also involved with another type of saving: that for retirement income. Annuities and insured pension plans involve a large volume of saving. The distribution of benefits is subject to a risk-pooling element in that these plans undertake to pay a regular income to participants no matter how long they live. Thus the amount collected varies with length of life and fits into the insurance category logically.

Noninsured pension plans (funds administered by banks and other trustees) are also a very popular way of providing for retirement needs. Some of these plans are in the form of fixed annuities and are thus like insurance plans. Some, however, are variable annuities: The income payments received at retirement are determined by the financial investment performance of the funds. Since these funds are heavily invested in common stocks over a long period of time, large realized capital gains can provide for handsome retirement incomes.

Mutual funds represent another outlet for savings (as we have learned). By buying into a mutual fund, the saver is indirectly buying into a portfolio of corporate stocks. Mutual funds offer returns tied to the performance of the stock market plus built-in, risk-reducing diversification for individuals who lack the financial resources for do-it-yourself diversification. In short, they provide a relatively safe although indirect way of playing the stock market.

All the above forms of saving are done through financial intermediaries: commercial banks, savings banks, savings and loan associations, insurance companies, pension funds, mutual funds, etc. Aside from this, the principal way in which individuals employ their savings is in the purchase of corporate equities (stocks) or in the purchase of homes. Owned homes provide housing as well as being a direct means for channeling saving into investment. The purchase of corporate stocks already outstanding does not directly affect real investment, but it does bypass financial intermediation. Moreover, corporate equities represent the one financial market area in which holdings of individuals exceed holdings by institutions. For some individuals, buying stock offers the hope of large and quick returns. Others diversify and hold, wanting nothing more than long-run returns that grow with the economy and keep pace with inflation.

One form of saving usually performs more than one service, while a given service usually is provided by more than one form of saving. The latter point is important because it means that savers have a choice of outlets through which to employ their savings. The allocation of savings among competing outlets is partly determined by relative interest rates. A good example is substitution between the different kinds of savings accounts. During the 1950s, a number of individuals withdrew savings from accounts at commercial banks and placed them with savings and loan associations in order to take advantage of higher interest rates. Then, during the 1960s, a reverse flow took place as commercial banks closed the interest-rate gap. Also, in the late 1960s there was a general shift of savings out of money, savings accounts, and other liquid assets into open-market securities where rates were much higher. Individuals do not automatically shift their savings from one form to another, but when movements in interest-rate differentials are sizable, as they have been in the last fifteen years, many do not hestitate to move their savings around. The basic consideration is that of weighing risk versus expected return. Ordinarily, most individual savers stick to savings accounts rather than open-market securities because the greater expected return on securities is not worth the extra risk of holding them. However, when the return differential becomes large enough some savers shift into securities because the extra return more than compensates for the extra risk.

Other factors that determine the employment of savings are the wealth, the income, and the age of the saver. These three elements are interrelated. Income and wealth usually go together, but not perfectly. At the beginning of a career, income rises much more rapidly than wealth. Many young families have reasonably good incomes, but the expenses of setting up house and having children leave little or no saving for accumulating wealth. When the children grow up and are on their own, wealth then usually begins to rise faster than income. Peak income is frequently reached at an earlier age than peak wealth. At the age of retirement, income falls sharply, but wealth continues to grow as long as the earnings on wealth more than cover current expenditures.

Once a minimum threshold of income and wealth is obtained, individuals of relatively low income and wealth tend to allocate a relatively large share of saving to building up equity in home ownership. This is probably mainly a function of age. Homes are usually purchased during the child-bearing and child-rearing ages. After the children leave home and the mortgage is paid off, relatively little saving is for housing. This comes, of course, at a time when income and wealth are usually still growing. Saving through life insurance follows the same pattern. Insurance is needed more by young families than by older couples. When the children are on their own and the parents become more secure financially, the need for life insurance drops dramatically.

After home ownership and life insurance, saving for eventual retirement is apparently the next priority item for most households. The proportion of income saved for this purpose often keeps on growing up to and even through the early years of retirement. Equity in pension funds and other retirement plans is an increasing proportion of wealth as wealth increases, at least for most individuals. Very wealthy individuals, however, often elect to place their saving more directly in corporate equities, municipal bonds, and real investment assets. It is well known that high-income and wealthy individuals keep a relatively large proportion of their savings in investment assets.

People of all ages and from every economic status keep part of their savings in liquid form. Those of high income and wealth hold more demand deposits and savings accounts than do those of less income and wealth, but it is not clear whether the proportion of total wealth allocated to liquid assets changes with the amount of total wealth. The demand for liquid assets is a very personal thing. It varies from individual to individual, independently of income, wealth, or age.

From the above, it is clear that the demand for claims against financial intermediaries is extensive. The demand for liquidity is satisfied by checking and savings accounts offered by banks and other thrift institutions. Insurance, with an element of saving, is demanded from life insurance companies. Saving for retirement is satisfied through the institution of pension funds. At one time or another, all savers come into touch with nearly all kinds of financial intermediaries.

FINANCIAL INVESTMENT POLICIES OF DIFFERENT FINANCIAL INSTITUTIONS

Specialized institutions tend to have specialized policies for financial investment in the capital markets. The specialization itself constrains the intermediary's available investment alternatives. A commercial bank, for example, specializes in providing fixed-amount demand obligations to individuals. A person with a $100 checking account (demand deposit) can get exactly $100 in legal tender currency whenever he or she demands it. For the commercial bank, this limits the kinds of financial assets appropriate for investment. The bank must assure itself of adequate liquidity and security of principal by keeping cash reserves plus secondary reserves of high-grade, short-term, fixed-obligation securities. A variable-annuity pension plan, on the other hand, specializes in providing late-conversion liabilities of unfixed amounts. It is hoped that the amounts will be large and keep pace with inflation. The pension fund seeks capital growth by investing heavily in common stocks. The assets of a commercial bank are inappropriate for a pension fund, and vice versa. Specialized institutions are therefore constrained in their financial investments by the general principle of employing assets that are appropriately geared to the kind of liabilities to be protected or discharged.

The principle of gearing assets to liabilities is obviated to some extent by the liability transformation and the asset transformation effects discussed previously. Savings and loan associations, for example, do not invest in mortgages in order to gear their assets to their savings-account liabilities. Instead, mortgages are held by savings and loan associations because of the liability transformation effect, custom and tradition, and laws and regulations.

Laws and regulations serve to constrain the various intermediaries. Each type of institution is highly regulated. Commercial banks, for one, are regulated by state and federal authorities. Commercial banks with federal charters (national banks) fall under the jurisdiction of three federal authorities: the Federal Reserve, the Treasury Department, and the Federal Deposit Insurance Corporation. Other types of financial institutions are perhaps not so heavily regulated, but all are subject to tighter financial regulation than are organizations in the nonfinancial sector. One aspect of financial regulation is the drawing up of authorized investments or legal lists. Another aspect circumscribes the percentages or proportions of the asset mix: Some institutions are subject to minimum constraints on certain assets and maximum constraints on others. Often, these regulations governing financial policy merely enforce or reinforce the general principle of gearing assets to liabilities.

Beyond regulation, tax law is the major legal consideration given to financial policy. Tax law makes certain types of investments more profitable after taxes to certain types of intermediaries than to others. For example, the tax exemption of interest on municipal bonds makes these securities more profitable after taxes to those intermediaries that pay corporate taxes than to those that pay little or no taxes.

Another constraint on financial policy is size and location. For example, a small savings and loan association located in a rural area has neither the financial resources nor contacts to finance an office building in the city. On the other hand, a large insurance company may choose not to service a large number of small mortgages if large-denomination mortgages are available.

Subject to self-imposed legal and practical constraints, financial investment policy is determined by striking a balance between the two opposing forces of expected return on assets and the risk of asset loss. Financial intermediaries, like most lenders, seek high expected returns and low risk. An intermediary can maximize its expected rate of return on assets by holding nothing but the highest yielding loans and securities, but this also tends to maximize risk. On the other hand, it can minimize risk by holding nothing but cash and short-term liquid assets, but this tends to minimize return. Because risk and expected return go together, it is impossible to maximize expected return and to minimize risk simultaneously. The optimal allocation between different financial assets is therefore a consideration of weighing risk versus return. The theoretical relation between risk and expected return and the general principles governing asset choices under conditions of risk are explored in much greater detail in Chapter 6. One lesson of that chapter is that different financial investors hold different mixes of financial assets because of differences in risk tolerance. This lesson certainly applies to financial intermediaries. Different intermediaries have different asset structures because of differences in risk tolerance and exposure.

Commercial Banks

Approximately 40 percent of total funds flowing through all financial intermediaries flow through commercial banks. No other category of intermediaries comes even close to this proportion. Commercial banks channel their own funds into all the money and capital markets except the stock market. They also provide trust-account services for other people's money, much of which is invested in the stock market. Unlike other intermediaries in the private sector, commercial banks play a special role in the monetary system. Their deposit liabilities constitute the largest part of the money supply. Commercial banks are so important and pervasive that we shall devote Chapter 10 entirely to their role and financial behavior. Our discussion in this chapter will therefore be brief relative to their importance.

The commercial banking *system*, subject to special control by the Federal Reserve System because of its monetary nature, creates its own funds on the basis of the reserves created for it by the Federal Reserve. Since the amount of money is believed to be important in determining price levels and economic activity, this governmental control is accepted as a part of our financial system.

Individual commercial banks do not have any special way of creating their own holdings of funds. They must compete with other commercial banks for them; something that amounts to competing for the scarce and limited supply of reserve funds created by the Federal Reserve. The customers of a commercial bank bring to it the funds it needs for its operations. This fact accounts for one principle that governs the employment of commercial bank funds: They must meet the basic service needs of customers to continue to enjoy their patronage. The basic thing customers want is ready access to their deposits without question and without delay. Banks use some portion of the funds that they acquire for liquidity purposes. These funds are not the required reserves (which tend to be a frozen and quite illiquid asset because they are required) but rather excess reserves and secondary reserves. The ways in which secondary reserves are invested include U.S. government securities and private short-term paper traded in the open money markets. U.S. government securities are highly liquid. However, to the extent that they are held as collateral for backing government deposit accounts, they, too, tend to be somewhat frozen. Large money market banks are less prone to use secondary-reserve assets for meeting their liquidity needs. Instead, they borrow in the money markets as the need arises. This method can be very costly, however, when money market interest rates shoot up, as they often do.

Another principle is that banks be prepared to lend to good customers when the customers want loan accommodations. A "good" customer is naturally a creditworthy one with enough net worth, liquidity, and earning power to make his or her business attractive. Yet another attribute of good customers is that they ordinarily keep good deposit balances with the bank during times when they are both in and out of debt. The satisfaction of customers' credit needs is a two-way street. The customer receives a necessary service, but the bank earns its bread and butter in the process. Interest on loans is the primary source of income and profit for commercial banks.

Commercial banks have to be both liquid and profitable. Unfortunately, assets that are liquid (reserves) are not profitable, while those that are profitable (loans) are not liquid. The task of bank asset management is to strike a balance between the two. Modern portfolio theory views this balancing as a problem of maximizing utility. According to this theory, a bank will allocate assets in such a way that the marginal utility of return from investing an additional dollar in earning assets is equal to the marginal utility of risk avoidance from investing an additional dollar in nonearning cash reserves.

A simpler solution to the problem was provided by Robinson (1962). He suggested that the liquidity objective may take priority over the interest income objective. Accordingly, the first job of bank asset management would be to ensure adequate liquidity by building up sufficient reserves. After this priority is met, the bank's next job would be to accommodate customers' loan demands. Still another view was taken by Hodgman (1963). He felt it was wrong to view the problem as a matter of allocating given total assets. He argued that total assets can be increased if a bank concentrates on making loans to depositor customers who will leave part of the money at the bank (either voluntarily or through the imposition of a compensating balance requirement). Accordingly, a bank may be able to increase income with little sacrifice in liquidity if it specializes in loaning to its depositor customers. There is a problem, however, with this approach. If all banks try to keep their reserves intact, one bank may not lose reserves to other banks, but neither will it gain reserves from other banks. However, the approach is merited in that it tends to reduce uncertainty and strengthen bank-customer relations.

Loans, like reserves, can assume different forms. At one time, short-term business loans were the dominant use of bank funds. These loans continue to occupy a special place in banking, but this type of credit fails to exhaust available funds in most banks; most are extended into wider lending activities (see Table 4-1). One extension takes the form of greater maturity. Business "term loans," a form of intermediate-maturity credit, accommodate businesses in a way not available through short-term credit. In addition, banks lend to consumers in a substantial way. This has been done indirectly through lending to consumer-financing concerns such as small loan companies and sales finance companies, but more is done directly. Banks also lend to farmers and to many others, including churches, universities, and other nonprofit enterprises.

Aside from liquid assets and loans, commercial banks purchase mainly tax-exempt state and local government securities. These securities are favored by commercial banks because they are one of the few financial intermediaries fully exposed to the corporate income tax. Commercial banks buy corporate bonds only when after-tax yields on them are particularly attractive. Usually, the term loan has seemed a better deal that the corporate bond, partly because it could be used to attract or hold deposits.

Commercial banks are legally prohibited from investing financially in corporate equities. Stocks are too risky to meet the safety standards required for bank assets. Banks do invest in the stock market for their personal trust and pension fund accounts. But these trusts and funds are kept separate from the banks' own assets.

Commercial bank asset management of the funds secured from time deposits deserves separate mention. The competition for these funds is primarily with savings and loan associations and mutual savings banks, and it might be expected that the policies followed would be familiar—investment in real estate mortgages.

TABLE 4-1
Financial Assets of Commercial Banks

Financial Assets	Year-end Outstandings (billions of dollars)		
	1955	1965	1975
Cash reserves	$ 21.7	$ 23.3	$ 43.7
Private short-term securities	1.3	3.6	10.2
U.S. government securities	64.5	65.3	119.0
State and local obligations	12.7	38.7	102.0
Mortgages	20.8	49.3	134.8
Corporate bonds	1.8	1.1	8.1
Commercial credit	42.2	104.9	257.3
Consumer credit	13.2	35.7	90.3
Security credit	5.0	8.5	14.3
Miscellaneous	1.7	6.0	42.6
Total financial assets	$185.0	$336.4	$822.3

SOURCE: Adapted from *Flow of Funds Accounts 1946–1975*, Board of Governors of the Federal Reserve System, December 1976.

To some extent this is true. The legal regulation of national bank investment in real estate mortgages is indeed tied to the amount of time deposits they hold. Nevertheless, commercial banks have not been as active in this form of investment as the other savings institutions have. Commercial banks originate many mortgages and keep some in their own portfolios, but they also pass such mortgages along to trust department funds and in some cases even to other institutional investors.

The basic consideration is one of taxes. Under most circumstances a commercial bank can secure a better after-tax return from a tax-exempt security than from a mortgage. Although tax-exempt securities do not have exceptional qualities of liquidity, they are undoubtedly better than mortgages in this regard. In addition, they are more economical to purchase and to service.

Mutual Savings Banks

Mutual savings banks are much more specialized than commercial banks. Their original purpose was to encourage thrift among working-class people, that is, to provide an easy and safe way for the "average" person to save. The savings banks, in turn, were to invest these savings in the capital markets in such a way as to guarantee security of principal and interest. Savings banks experimented with several forms of financial investment, but they settled on mortgages as their primary investment medium (see Table 4-2).

The turnover of deposits at mutual savings banks used to be slow, and balance sheet totals in most individual mutual savings banks were usually sufficiently stable that liquidity requirements were low. However, because of conservatism, mutual savings banks tended to maintain more than adequate liquidity reserves. Part of these reserves were a holdover from World War II, when loan demand was so weak that they could find an outlet for funds only in

TABLE 4-2
Financial Assets of Mutual Savings Banks

Financial Assets	Year-end Outstandings (billions of dollars)		
	1955	1965	1975
Cash reserves	$ 1.0	$ 1.0	$ 2.3
Private short-term securities	.1	.3	2.2
U.S. government securities	8.6	6.3	10.9
State and local obligations	.6	.3	1.5
Mortgages	17.5	44.6	77.2
Corporate bonds	2.6	2.9	17.5
Corporate stocks	1.0	2.3	4.4
Other financial assets	.3	1.3	5.0
Total financial assets	$ 31.7	$ 59.1	$121.1

SOURCE: Adapted from *Flow of Funds Accounts 1946–1975*, Board of Governors of the Federal Reserve System, December 1976.

U.S. government securities. After the war, loan demand picked up. During the 1950s and 1960s, mutual savings banks were putting almost all added funds into mortgages. By the late 1960s, mortgages constituted about 75 percent of savings bank assets.

Since the areas in which savings banks operate, mainly the slower-growing Eastern and New England states, have not generated enough mortgages, the banks have had to devise new methods for acquiring mortgages or to use the service of mortgage bankers located in states of higher loan demand. Mutual savings banks acquire all classes of mortgages—Federal Housing Administration (FHA), Veterans Administration (VA), and conventional—and their rates are usually competitive. Their terms (down payments and loan periods) tend to be slightly more conservative than those of savings and loan associations, about equal to those of insurance companies, and a bit more liberal than those of commercial banks. Mutual savings banks make commercial and multifamily mortgage loans as well as mortgage loans on single-family homes.

Two developments in the 1970s served to alter the composition of assets of mutual savings banks. One was a severe drop in housing starts and, consequently, a decrease in demand for mortgage credit. During the first half of the 1970s, mortgage lending could not keep up with the funds flowing into mutual savings banks. The banks were forced to find other outlets such as lower-yielding corporate bonds. (Bonds usually take up the slack when mortgage demand is low, and they are run off when mortgage demand picks up.) The other development was the introduction of the "negotiable order of withdrawal," or NOW account. This development made savings accounts at mutual savings banks in New England transferable by check. In effect, these savings accounts became checking accounts that pay interest. Since the turnover of deposits subject to check is faster than it is for nonnegotiable deposits, the mutual savings banks offering NOW accounts found themselves needing more liquidity. As a result, their investment in short-term, open-market securities rose considerably.

Although mutual savings banks are authorized to invest in corporate equities to a limited extent, they have not shown much interest. The proportion of assets in corporate stocks has been small—below 4 percent. As mutual associations, savings banks are not taxed at the full corporate income tax rate. Consequently, their demand for tax-exempt state and local government securities has been very little—even less than it has been for equities.

Savings and Loan Associations

Savings and loan associations were originally introduced for the purpose of making mortgage credit available to persons who sought home ownership but who lacked access to banks and other sources of credit. Loans were made to members from savings of other members. The associations grew up with the westward expansion of the country. Many towns in the Middle and Far West were built with building-and-loan money. Today there is little functional difference between savings and loan associations and mutual savings banks.

Both these institutions secure funds by issuing savings accounts and both use funds by acquiring mortgages.

The investment policies of savings and loan associations are simple: They maintain liquidity and use almost all remaining funds to acquire mortgages (see Table 4-3). Liquidity, without undue loss of income, is provided by investment in U.S. government securities.

The savings and loan associations tend to prefer conventional mortgages on in-state, single-family homes, but many of them have acquired VA mortgages as a matter of service to the veterans in their local areas. Because of early opposition to the federal government program of mortgage insurance, these associations seldom acquire FHA mortgages. The down payments and loan periods on conventional mortgages granted by savings and loan associations are typically rather more liberal than those granted by either commercial banks or life insurance companies on similar mortgage loans. On the other hand, mortgage rates charged by savings and loan associations are usually higher than rates charged by other institutions. This is partly a function of acquiring riskier mortgages, but it is also linked to the fact that the associations have tended to pay higher rates of interest on savings accounts. Higher rates on savings, location in fast-growing areas, and effective advertising and promotion help to explain the rapid growth in assets of savings and loan associations.

The housing and mortgage market slump of the 1970s had less of an impact on savings and loan associations than it did on mutual savings banks. Even so, many savings and loan associations found themselves with some excess funds. These funds, however, did not sit idle. They were invested in, and shifted among, the highest-yielding money market instruments. Between 1967 and 1975, savings and loan associations increased their holdings of private short-term paper from next to nothing to over $5 billion. This sum was not large by capital market standards, but it was quite large for the money market, considering its source.

TABLE 4-3
Financial Assets of Savings and Loan Associations

Financial Assets	Year-end Outstandings (billions of dollars)		
	1955	1965	1975
Cash reserves	$ 1.4	$ 2.9	$ 8.1
Private short-term securities	.0	.0	5.3
U.S. government securities	2.4	8.2	22.6
State and local obligations	.0	.0	1.1
Mortgages	31.4	110.3	278.7
Other financial assets	2.4	8.3	22.6
Total financial assets	$ 37.6	$129.6	$338.4

SOURCE: Adapted from *Flow of Funds Accounts 1946–1975,* Board of Governors of the Federal Reserve System, December 1976.

Credit Unions

Credit unions are similar to mutual savings banks and to savings and loan associations inasmuch as all three are thrift institutions. All three secure funds through the offering of savings accounts. But that is where the similarity ends. A credit union is uniquely a nonprofit cooperative association of people with a common bond, accepting deposits from its members and making consumer loans to them. As nonprofit associations, credit unions pay no federal income taxes. The smaller credit unions depend on their members to provide volunteer labor. Deposits and loans are for members only. Members are required to have a common bond such as a common employer, a common labor union, a common church, or a common neighborhood. If a person meets this requirement, he or she may join the credit union by making and keeping a small deposit account at the credit union.

Credit unions were first organized to provide urban factory workers with an opportunity to borrow money at reasonable interest. Most commercial banks were reluctant to extend consumer credit to the lower-middle class, and interest rates charged by small loan companies (personal finance companies) have always been very high. The credit union has thus filled the gap between commercial banks and personal finance companies in the consumer credit field. The interest rate charged on loans has tended to be equal to or less for members than they could get anywhere else. Defaults on loans have been surprisingly low.

The success of credit union lending to members reflects the common bond and sense of loyalty shared by members. Many borrowing members honor their credit unions by becoming major depositors in later years. This way there is always a pool of funds for younger, newer members to borrow at reasonable interest. The interest rate paid on savings accounts at credit unions is actually relatively high—6 to 7 percent in most cases. The reason that credit unions can pay relatively high rates on members' savings and charge relatively low rates on members' borrowings is because of volunteer labor, low overhead, and the absence of the profit motive.

Not all the assets of credit unions are tied up in loans to members (see Table 4-4). A minimum level of liquid assets must be kept due to the deposit nature of credit union liabilities. Beyond this minimum, credit unions build up their holdings of U.S. government securities and other liquid assets when loan demand is down.

In the aggregate, credit unions are still far behind other thrift institutions in total assets. But their asset growth rate has been the highest of all the thrifts in recent periods. There are many reasons for this growth. One has been the introduction in some credit unions of the "share draft." This instrument is essentially the same as the NOW account offered by mutual savings banks; it is a combined savings-checking account. With the opportunity to do all one's "banking" under one roof, and given the loyalty that members have toward their credit unions, some observers are forecasting that credit unions will become tough competition for commercial banks and the other thrift institutions in the not-too-distant future.

TABLE 4-4
Financial Assets of Credit Unions

Financial Assets	Year-end Outstandings (billions of dollars)		
	1955	1965	1975
Cash reserves	$ .9	$ 2.8	$ 5.0
U.S. government securities	.1	.3	5.0
Mortgages	.2	.6	1.6
Consumer credit	1.7	7.3	25.4
Total financial assets	$ 2.9	$11.0	$37.0

SOURCE: Adapted from *Flow of Funds Accounts 1946–1975*, Board of Governors of the Federal Reserve System, December 1976.

Life Insurance Companies

The primary mission of life insurance companies is to insure against loss of life. The element of saving and investment associated with life insurance is incidental to this primary mission. The actuarial liabilities of life insurance companies are very long-term and highly predictable—in large numbers, human life expectancy can be quite accurately calculated. Life insurance policies give their holders cash surrender values that equal or approach the holders' equity share of policy reserves. Experience shows that this right of surrender is exercised mostly in predictable degrees. The stability, predictability, and slow turnover of policyholder equity contribute to a relatively low demand for liquid assets by life insurance companies.

Life insurance policies also give their holders the right to borrow against equity. Policy loans are a contractual right in cash value policies at an interest rate specified in the policy. These loans are not nearly as predictable as surrenders. Studies indicate that policy loans are sensitive to interest rates in the market. Schott (June 1971), for example, found that the dramatic rise in policy loans that occurred in 1966, and again in 1969, could be explained almost entirely by the high market interest rates of those years. With most policy loans costing 5 percent at the time, many sophisticated policyholders were able to reap substantial profits by borrowing against their policies and investing in the market at much higher rates.

Since market rates are so unstable, the volume of policy loans is also unstable. This factor contributes positively to the demand for liquidity by life insurance companies. In recent times, this demand has been satisfied by investing in private short-term securities. Still, investment in liquid assets is only a very small proportion of total investment. Most investment is in long-term assets (see Table 4-5).

Life insurance companies must act prudently, and this carries over to their financial investment policies. The need to safeguard principal restrains life insurance companies from investing in high-risk, high-return securities. Within the safety-of-principal constraint, life insurance companies seek good returns

TABLE 4-5
Financial Assets of Life Insurance Companies

Financial Assets	Year-end Outstandings (billions of dollars)		
	1955	1965	1975
Cash reserves	$ 1.3	$ 1.5	$ 1.9
Private short-term securities	.0	.3	4.8
U.S. government securities	8.6	5.3	6.2
State and local obligations	2.0	3.5	4.5
Mortgages	29.4	60.0	89.4
Corporate bonds	37.1	61.0	105.5
Corporate stocks	3.6	9.1	28.1
Other financial assets	5.8	13.4	39.5
Total financial assets	$ 87.8	$154.2	$279.9

SOURCE: Adapted from *Flow of Funds Accounts 1946–1975,* Board of Governors of the Federal Reserve System, December 1976.

on their investments. High-grade corporate bonds and mortgages offer both good returns and capital stability. The life insurance companies' distaste for defaults rules out low-grade corporate bonds. Ninety percent of life insurance company holdings of corporate bonds are in bonds of Baa quality or better. The companies' taste for returns rules out U.S. government bonds. High-grade corporates outyield Treasury bonds without imposing excess extra risk. Coming out of World War II, life insurance companies held large amounts of Treasury bonds, but these holdings have been gradually liquidated.

Long-term lending to business is the most important use of the funds of life insurance companies. At one time, life insurance companies were important buyers of corporate bonds in the open market, and small life insurance companies still make such purchases; but the companies learned to make direct placement loans and found they could make loans at higher rates in this way. Private placements have also been instrumental in enabling life insurance companies to make forward commitments of funds. In this way, life insurance companies make financial investment decisions prior to the actual employment of funds. The forward commitment gives the insurance company the advantage of knowing in advance what the interest rate will be on the employment of funds. But it requires the insurance company to forecast its funds flows accurately, otherwise it will find itself being over- or undercommitted. Pesando (September 1974) found that the flow of funds through life insurance companies is quite sensitive to market interest rates. His finding implies that life insurance companies must forecast interest rates in order to plan both the price and the quantity of forward commitments.

Mortgages are also an important life insurance investment outlet. Because most life insurance companies are rather large, they are not in a good position to acquire mortgages directly; most of them use the services of mortgage bankers to do this. Exceptions exist; one very big life insurance company developed an extensive system of regional offices for the granting of mortgage loans. Life insurance mortgage acquisitions include all the major types: FHA and VA as well as conventional. Their down payments and loan periods on conventional mortgages are fairly conservative, but their rates are competitive. They also buy or make commercial and rental property mortgage loans.

The investment policies of life insurance companies have been rather closely regulated by law. These regulations have sometimes limited access to investment outlets that some life insurance companies would have otherwise used. In some cases, however, the limits have been extended with the result that few companies take advantage of them; e.g., life insurance companies have not fully exercised the authority they have to invest in real estate.

To some extent the legal regulation is more qualitative than quantitative; life insurance companies are required to buy securities on "approved" lists or to observe the "prudent man" rule in making such purchases. Few life insurance companies in modern times have had any desire to breach the reasonable elements in such standards, but it cannot be said that the standards have always been wholly reasonable. The preference for direct placements may have been induced by the fact that life insurance companies were more confident of their ability to judge investment quality and to write protective features into their loan agreements than they were of the standards of rating used by the supervisory authorities.

Because the federal income tax rule applying to life insurance companies is complicated and has been frequently amended, these companies have had a varying role in buying tax-exempt securities. In some periods they have bought them, but the practice varies from company to company. On the average, investment in tax-exempt bonds has been only about one-twentieth of the investment in corporate bonds.

Life insurance company investment in corporate stocks has been a growing proportion of total investment. This investment in equities has been due largely to the rapid growth of variable-annuity, retirement-plan policies sold by life insurance companies. As we shall see in the following section on pension fund investment, stocks play an important role in investing for retirement. Stocks are not ideal assets, however, for protecting against death. Death-payment liabilities on regular life insurance policies are in predetermined, fixed amounts. Since the asset values of common stocks are not fixed in any way, stocks do not meet the test of gearing assets to fixed liabilities. The laws covering life insurance company investment recognize this by limiting the proportion of assets that may be held in corporate stocks, particularly common stocks.

Private Pension Funds

The typical pension fund is a group retirement plan covering the employees of a business establishment or other organization. During an employee's working years, contributions are made into the fund, where they are invested.

Upon retirement, payments are made out of the fund. The employee's equity in the pension fund usually depends on the amount of contributions made on the employee's behalf and on the investment performance of the contributions. Saving through a pension fund is automatic; the employer deducts contributions before making up the payroll.

A pension fund may be either insured or trusteed. An insured pension fund is a plan funded through a group annuity policy with a life insurance company. A trusteed pension fund is a plan funded through a trust arrangement, usually with the trust department of a large commercial bank. (The assets of these pension trusts are the direct property of the fund itself; they are not included as part of the assets of commercial banks.) The assets of private pension trusts are more than twice the size of assets accumulated through insured pension plans.

The growth of private pension funds has been one of the striking financial developments of recent years. Pension plans were not at all common before World War II (although a number of excellent plans were in operation long before that). Since then almost all large companies have established such plans. In the attraction and retention of able officers and employees, they have become a virtual necessity. The establishment of social security and the general demand for personal financial security that grew out of adverse experience of many individuals in the Great Depression also added to this popular demand. Tax exemption also has stimulated the growth of these funds. Employer contributions to the funds, as well as income earned on the funds, are exempt from the federal income tax.

Pension plans have proved to be very costly. As time has gone on, employers have borne a larger share of the total cost. High earnings are therefore demanded of the investors of these funds. Since pension benefits are often tied to salary levels near the date of retirement, the potential liabilities of these funds are very much a function of the price level. Higher price levels increase the liability of these funds greatly. Those paying the bill have thus put another demand on the investment process: price level protection. Only one demand is really absent: liquidity. The dating of liabilities is so easily forecast that virtually no liquidity is needed in the operation of these funds.

Faced with these demands, private pension funds have invested heavily in corporate stocks and to a lesser extent in corporate bonds (see Table 4-6). The rationale for investing so heavily in corporate stocks has been the old notion that equities provide price-level protection, i.e., that stock prices rise with the consumer price index. Bonds, on the other hand, have not been viewed as a good hedge against inflation since their values are fixed upon maturity. Their role in pension fund investment has been to provide certainty, regularity, and downside protection of income and capital value.

In the mid-1970s, some of the old notions about proper investment of pension fund assets were called into question. Consumer prices had risen dramatically over a period stretching back to the Vietnam war escalation during the mid-1960s. Stock prices, however, did not keep up. In fact, most of them fell most of the time. Meanwhile, scientific papers presented at the December 1975 meetings of the American Finance Association reported negative correla-

TABLE 4-6
Financial Assets of Private Pension Trusts

Financial Assets	Year-end Outstandings (billions of dollars)		
	1955	1965	1975
Cash reserves	$ .4	$ .9	$ 3.9
U.S. government securities	3.0	3.0	10.8
Mortgages	.3	3.4	2.4
Corporate bonds	7.9	22.7	37.8
Corporate stocks	6.1	40.8	88.6
Other financial assets	.7	2.9	5.5
Total financial assets	$ 18.3	$ 73.6	$148.9

SOURCE: Adapted from *Flow of Funds Accounts 1946–1975*, Board of Governors of the Federal Reserve System, December 1976.

tions between consumer prices and stock prices. Can it be that stocks are not good hedges against inflation? If so, where does that leave pension fund investment?

In the authors' view, stocks do not hedge against inflation *in the short run* when the rate of inflation is rising. A rising rate of inflation causes investors to require a rising nominal rate of return on investment in order to safeguard their real rate of return. The nominal rate of return on a share of common stock can be measured (approximately) by the ratio of the earnings of the share to the price of the share in the market. Even if earnings inflate along with consumer prices, rising inflation will cause the earnings-price ratio to increase as well, so that the price of stock cannot keep up with earnings and consumer prices. In fact, if the whole ratio increases by a larger percentage than the numerator, the denominator must fall. In this case, the price of stock will fall as consumer prices rise. In the short run, this sometimes does happen.

Nevertheless, stocks perform much better against inflation in the long run when the average rate of inflation (even if very high) is not expected to change. In the long run, the earnings-price ratio has a stable average. The average will be high if average inflation is high, and low if inflation is low, but as long as inflation has a stable average (whether high or low), the earnings-price ratio will likewise have a stable average. This means that if the numerator (earnings) of the ratio grows with consumer prices, so must the denominator (price). In this case, stock prices should rise along with consumer prices. Thus, we believe that stocks are a relatively good hedge against inflation *in the long run* (when changes in inflation average out to zero). We have not tested this hypothesis, however.

Since pension fund investment is essentially long-run, stocks should be very suitable assets for pension funds. Historically, the average rate of return on common stocks has been higher than the average rate of return on bonds (and on other securities) over very long periods of time. It may be true that inflation impairs the real rate of return on stocks, but so it does also with real rates on all other securities. Thus, the expected real rate of return on common stocks should be higher than expected real rates on alternative investments in securities.

This does not mean, however, that stocks should completely dominate the assets of pension funds. Clearly, this would be too risky. The beneficiaries of pension funds need considerable downside protection if, unfortunately, they should happen to retire during one of those recurring short-run periods of low and falling stock prices. Such downside protection is provided by bonds and other debt instruments that can be redeemed at maturity for full face value. Moreover, to the extent that nominal interest rates on debt instruments include an inflation premium that turns out to be accurate, debt instruments also provide a hedge against inflation.

Governmental Pension Funds

Unlike the private pension funds, public pension systems have often been subject to detailed regulations and rules for the investment of their funds. Many have been relieved from the less rational and more inhibiting rules, but some are still rather restricted. As is true of private pension funds, they have little need for liquidity. Public pension plans tend to require somewhat larger relative contributions from employees and relatively less from the employing governments; even so, the larger part of the burden is still on the employing governmental units. The social security and civil service plans of the federal government are, without material exception, invested in the securities of that government. With fixed benefits (not dependent on fund earnings), this only means that part of the federal share of contributions is concealed.

In the past, pension funds of state and local governments were often limited to investment in the securities of those bodies or in U.S. government securities. Lack of financial experience of the trustees was often cited as the reason for this severe limitation. But a more compelling reason might have been to enlarge the market for state and local government securities. In recent years these rules have been much liberalized. Pension funds of public authorities now are investing mainly in corporate bonds and stocks (see Table 4-7). Bonds are all acquired in the public open market; direct placements are quite rare. At present, state and local government pension funds are among the leading buyers of newly offered corporate bonds.

Investment in stocks is a relatively recent phenomenon. It is an attempt to remedy a former inconsistency between public pension promises and public pension laws. The laws prohibited investment in stocks, but stocks were the only securities that could have delivered the promised benefits: retirement incomes tied indirectly to increases in productivity and the cost of living. While stockholdings have been increased, they are still far below those for private pension funds. In 1975, the private funds held 60 percent of their assets in stocks, and 25 percent in bonds. For state and local government funds, the percentages were reversed.

TABLE 4-7
Financial Assets of State and Local Government Employee Retirement Funds

Financial Assets	Year-end Outstandings (billions of dollars)		
	1955	1965	1975
Cash reserves	$ .2	$ .3	$ 1.7
U.S. government securities	4.7	7.6	6.8
State and local obligations	2.7	2.6	2.5
Mortgages	.3	3.7	8.3
Corporate bonds	2.7	17.2	60.9
Corporate stocks	.2	2.5	25.8
Total financial assets	$ 10.8	$ 34.0	$106.0

SOURCE: Adapted from *Flow of Funds Accounts 1946–1975*. Board of Governors of the Federal Reserve System, December 1976.

Investment Companies

Investment companies are pure financial intermediaries that secure funds by issuing and selling their own securities to surplus units and use funds by buying securities issued by deficit units. Generally, the securities (or shares) of investment companies that are sold to surplus units are not fixed obligations; rather their value varies with the market value of the securities purchased by the investment companies. The primary function of investment companies is to meet the need for diversification. The small saver is able to diversify through the investment company medium by pooling his or her savings with other small savers. A large pool of funds for financial investment is necessary in order to spread risks. This diversification (or asset transformation effect) reduces risk for the small saver without impairing the saver's expected rate of return.

There are many kinds of investment companies. The most common is the open-end fund, usually referred to as a "mutual fund." Mutual funds secure funds by selling their own shares to individuals and they utilize funds by acquiring corporate shares and other capital market securities (see Table 4-8). The volume of mutual fund shares outstanding is determined solely by the demand of the buying public. Mutual funds issue and sell new shares whenever buyers want them, and they redeem old shares whenever buyers want to sell them back. The price or value of mutual fund shares is determined by the market value of the mutual fund's assets.

The assets of mutual funds vary according to the type of fund. "Growth funds" are invested solely in common stocks that pay low dividends but are expected to have exceptionally high yields in terms of capital gains. "Income funds" are invested in corporate bonds and those stocks that pay high, regular dividends. "Balanced funds" fall in between; they are less risky and lower yielding (on the average) than growth funds, but their expected return and risk are greater than for income funds. Another type of mutual fund is the

TABLE 4-8
Financial Assets of Mutual Funds

Financial Assets	Year-end Outstandings (billions of dollars)		
	1955	1965	1975
Cash reserves	$ .1	$ .5	$ 1.2
Private short-term securities	.1	.5	1.5
U.S. government securities	.3	.8	1.1
Corporate bonds	.5	2.6	4.8
Corporate stocks	6.9	30.9	33.7
Total financial assets	$ 7.8	$35.2	$42.2

SOURCE: Adapted from *Flow of Funds Accounts 1946–1975,* Board of Governors of the Federal Reserve System, December 1976.

tax-exempt income fund for high tax-bracket individuals seeking to spread the risks of holding municipal bonds.

The intermediating role of mutual funds is premised on two considerations. One is the ability to diversify. Small investors cannot sufficiently diversify on their own, but they can spread their risks by buying a mutual fund, which is essentially a diversified portfolio in a single package. The second consideration is management expertise. There is a presumption that professional mutual fund managers have the skill and financial acumen to select the highest-yielding stocks for a given level of risk. Studies have shown, however, that mutual funds do not consistently perform any better than diversified portfolios whose stocks are selected at random. In short, mutual funds do offer the advantage of diversification, but it is doubtful that they have an advantage of *superior* diversification.

A variant of the mutual fund is the "money market fund." Money market funds provide ordinary savers with access to the open money markets just as mutual funds open up capital market opportunities. Money market funds came into full bloom in 1974 when short-term, open-market interest rates were twice as high as allowable interest rates on regular savings accounts at thrift institutions. Ordinary savers, frustrated by this disparity and unable to afford large-denomination, open-market paper, were a ready market for money market funds to tap. Unlike the static regulated interest on savings accounts, the interest on shares of money market funds, in essence, slides up and down with interest rates in the open market. Money market funds were an instant success. Their fortune, however, is tied to money market rates. They can sell shares only during periods when short-term, open-market interest rates are above the interest rates paid on regular savings accounts.

Another type of investment company is the "real estate investment trust" (REIT). Unlike open-end funds, the REIT is a type of closed-end investment company. Shares are issued and sold at the discretion of the REIT. They cannot be redeemed, but they can be sold in the secondary market. The REIT emerged in the 1960s when savers were seeking inflation-proof investments. By specializing in real estate equities and ventures, the REIT promised some hope of beating inflation. In the early-to-mid-1970s, the REITs were in financial difficulty. Many of them had taken on too many ventures in which the expected return was clearly not commensurate with the amount of risk involved. Since then, however, the REITs have made a pretty good comeback as prime real estate equity has hedged very well against inflation.

The closed-end fund is the oldest type of investment company. However, the number of closed-end funds that invest in stocks and bonds is much smaller than the number of open-end funds. Market prices for various kinds of closed-end funds, traded over the counter, are reported weekly in *The Wall Street Journal*. In addition, about a dozen closed-end bond funds are traded on the New York Stock Exchange.

Finance Companies

As lenders of short-term and intermediate-term credit to consumers and businesses, finance companies compete directly with commercial banks. Many borrowers can choose between these two intermediaries to meet their shorter-term credit needs. There is some degree of market segmentation, however. The success of finance companies in the consumer credit and commercial credit fields owes, partly, to the ability of these companies to service the needs of relatively high-risk borrowers. Commercial banks prefer to keep their loans safe; most of their commercial credit, for example, goes to prime and near-prime borrowers. Finance companies, on the other hand, are more willing to lend to anyone (at a price, of course). Small loan companies, for example, are in the business of lending to consumers whose credit standings are marginal.[3]

To some extent, finance companies are second-stage intermediaries. Large amounts of the funds loaned by finance companies are funds that are borrowed by finance companies from commercial banks. Indirectly, then, commercial banks lend to ultimate borrowers of marginal credit worth. The risks are assumed and the profits are taken, however, by the finance companies layered between the banks and the borrowers. Finance companies also procure funds in very large amounts by issuing long-term bonds and short-term paper (in about equal amounts). Most of the buyers of these securities are banks, businesses, and other organizations. Very little personal saving gets placed directly with finance companies.

Property and Liability Insurance Companies

Strictly speaking, companies that insure against fire, automobile accidents, goods damaged in transit, broken contracts, and casualties of all types, are not intermediaries because their "policy payables" are contingent. Their payables are not paid unless a fire or other casualty actually occurs. From the saver's

---

[3]However, see Boczar (March 1978) for some evidence that the consumer credit market is only partially segmented as between banks and finance companies.

point of view, the purchase of property and liability insurance does not build up net worth. The purchaser is a creditor of sorts, but he or she can collect only if something of equal or better worth is destroyed.

Because accidents, casualties, and disasters are not all that predictable, property and liability insurance companies must have reserves of funds to cover large claims and settlements if and when they occur. These funds are invested in stocks and bonds, particularly tax-exempt bonds. Like commercial banks, but unlike most other financial intermediaries, property and liability insurance corporations are subject to the full federal tax rate on corporate income. For this reason, these insurance corporations invest heavily in the tax-exempt obligations of state and local governments. About 15 percent of all tax-exempt bonds are held by property and liability insurance companies. Compared to other financial intermediaries, this investment is second only to commercial banks. The investment in tax-exempt bonds is volatile, however. Unless a company has income to report, there is no tax advantage to holding tax-exempt bonds. Companies that suffer underwriting losses tend to reduce their holdings of tax-exempt securities, only to build them up again when profits are good.

CONVERGING EVOLVEMENT OF DEPOSIT-TYPE INTERMEDIARIES

The lines of demarcation between financial intermediaries and their activities are far from constant. This chapter has described the structure of financial intermediation that existed in the late 1970s. It does not describe how things will be in the future. Over time, new intermediaries emerge; old ones change with the times, or else they drop out of the picture.

The money market fund is a case in point. It was popularized in 1974 as the way for an ordinary saver to invest at high interest in the money market. However, by 1978, banks and thrift institutions were offering their customers $10,000-denomination, six-month, money market certificates. These money market certificates (MMCs) pay money market interest rates and therefore compete with money market funds. Moreover, MMCs can be purchased at your local bank. Thus, if and when MMCs become offered in small denominations, the money market fund could disappear from the scene.

The modern finance company has diversified and now performs services that were separate activities of specialized finance companies ten or twenty years ago. The same was true of property and liability insurance companies. Each company may have started out with a specialty line, but the larger surviving companies are usually full-line companies. A return to specialization does not seem likely at this time, but it could happen. History is filled with examples of institutions that have been forced, by competition, regulation, or technology, to cut back on their activities.

Life insurance companies have shifted their activities. Their shift in emphasis from fixed to variable annuities allowed them to make great inroads into the pension fund business during the 1960s and 1970s. Life insurance companies also went into the mutual fund business, packaging mutual fund opportunities with term insurance policies. Mutual funds, themselves, were a thriving business during the general bull-market period between 1949 and 1968. But the mutual funds learned too late how to cope with the prolonged bearish conditions that followed. Unless they change with the times, they will be a diminishing force among financial intermediaries. Pension funds, too, will have to seek new investment strategies to safeguard against excessive capital losses.

The most significant change in activities in recent times, however, has been with the deposit-type intermediaries: commercial banks, mutual savings banks, savings and loan associations, and credit unions. As a group, these institutions handle more than 60 percent of the total flow of funds through financial intermediaries. They have long competed with each other for funds by offering interest-bearing deposits called savings accounts. While savings accounts were about the only source of funds for the nonbank thrift institutions, commercial banks procured most of their funds through the offering of non-interest-bearing demand deposits (checking-account money). This was true before the 1960s.

During the 1960s, commercial banks went after the savings account market. Because of curbs on demand deposit expansion by monetary policy, commercial banks had found that they were not able to supply customers with funds as adequately as the nonbank thrifts, nor were they growing as rapidly. Convinced that demand deposit growth would continue to be curbed, they set about competing more actively for savings account funds. Increased competition occurred for all forms of savings deposits, from ordinary passbook accounts to certificates of deposit. Commercial banks also introduced the "negotiable certificate of deposit," or NCD. The NCD was not only negotiable—it could be traded in the open secondary market—but it was exempted from interest rate ceilings and could therefore pay the market rate. This financial innovation was an immediate success. By the end of the decade, commercial banks had greatly improved their positions relative to savings and loan associations and other nonbank thrifts.

Meanwhile, a number of government-sponsored reports were published, urging a convergence in scope and activities of all deposit-type intermediaries. If commercial banks could offer both checking accounts and savings accounts, why restrict the nonbank thrifts to savings accounts only? Why not change the law to allow them to offer checking accounts as well? Such a broadening of the powers (and responsibilities) of nonbank thrift institutions was recommended in the 1961 Report of the Commission on Money and Credit, the 1963 Heller Report, the 1971 Report of the Hunt Commission, and the 1975 Study of Financial Institutions and the Nation's Economy. These studies and reports had little political clout, however. The Financial Institutions Act of 1976, which would have given demand deposit powers to all thrifts, was defeated.

But this did not deter the nonbank thrift institutions from competing against commercial banks for the demand deposit market. Working within existing federal statutes, and lobbying (often successfully) for changes in statutes at the state level, the thrifts made remarkable progress toward homogeneity with banks. In 1970, a mutual savings bank in Massachusetts invented and promoted the "negotiable order of withdrawal," or NOW account. This account, while legally defined as a savings account transferable by draft (check), could just as well have been defined as a demand deposit paying interest. But that would not have been legal. Savings banks are not empowered to offer demand deposits. Moreover, demand deposits cannot pay interest by federal law. Semantics aside, the NOW account is a checking account, and because it pays interest, it has become very popular in New England and other states where it has been legalized. The NOW account is currently widely offered not only by mutual savings banks and other nonbank thrifts located in these states, but by competing commercial banks as well. In addition, many credit unions offer "share drafts," which are also savings accounts transferable by check. Still another innovation is the automatic transfer service (ATS) between savings and checking (demand deposit) accounts. This service (introduced in 1978) allows one to keep funds in a savings account at a commercial bank with the bank providing automatic transfer to a checking account whenever a check is written.

The check is a device for transferring funds (deposited at an institution) from the depositer to the payee without the inconvenience of having to make a withdrawal or cash conversion. All of us who have checking accounts appreciate this convenience. But transfer by check is not the only way of making a convenient "third-party payment." Funds can also be transferred electronically through the use of computers. Commercial banks were the early developers of "electronic funds transfer systems," or EFTS. The banks foresaw the probability that transfer-by-computer would eventually replace transfer-by-check. They did not envision, however, that the transfers would be in anything other than their own demand deposits. Nevertheless, in 1974, a savings and loan association in Nebraska started making its savings accounts transferable electronically by use of computers. Soon thereafter, other savings and loan associations followed suit.

These recent developments of third-party payments by nonbank thrift institutions clearly indicate the demise of commerical bank demand deposits as a unique medium of exchange. The laws governing demand deposits are already outmoded. And so is the practice of giving demand deposits special recognition in defining and measuring the nation's money supply. The deposit liabilities of banks and thrift institutions have become increasingly identical. Time will tell whether or not this convergence will spread to the asset side of the balance sheet. Our guess is that it will.

PROJECTS AND QUESTIONS

1. Most of the external equity financing by corporations is through sale of shares to individual stockholders. Is this clear case of "direct external finance" an exception to the rule that the "lending" needs of surplus units are different from the "borrowing" needs of deficit units? If so, what is the rationale for intermediaries that invest in stocks? If not so, why do so

many individuals elect to own stocks directly rather than indirectly through the medium of an intermediating fund?

2. Compare the asset management policies practiced at a local financial institution (ask for financial statements) with the asset management policies taught in a book on the subject (see bibliography). Your financial statement analysis will be more instructive if you do your book research first.

3. What effect would the lifting of interest rate ceilings on deposit accounts at deposit institutions have on the borrowing rates charged by these institutions? Defend your answer with the tools of economic analysis.

4. Prepare a case for (or against) the liberalization of laws that would allow nonbank deposit institutions to have the same borrowing and lending powers as commercial banks.

BIBLIOGRAPHY

Bensten, G.: "Savings Banking and the Public Interest," *Journal of Money, Credit, and Banking,* February 1972, pp. 136–226.

Bishop, G.A.: *Capital Formation Through Life Insurance,* Irwin, Homewood, Ill., 1976.

Boczar, G.E.: "Competition Between Banks and Finance Companies," *Journal of Finance,* March 1978, pp. 245–258.

Bodie, Z.: "Common Stocks as a Hedge Against Inflation," *Journal of Finance,* May 1976, pp. 459–470.

Brockschmidt, P.: "Credit Union Growth in Perspective," *Federal Reserve Bank of Kansas City Monthly Review,* February 1977, pp. 3–13.

Cole, R.H., ed.: *Consumer and Commercial Credit Management,* Irwin, Homewood, Ill., 1972.

Crockett, J., and I. Friend: "Consumer Investment Behavior," in *Determinants of Investment Behavior,* National Bureau of Economic Research, New York, 1967.

Crosse, H.D., and G.A. Hempel: *Management Policies for Commercial Banks,* Prentice-Hall, Englewood Cliffs, N. J., 1973.

Ferretti, A.P., ed.: *Investment Company Portfolio Management,* Irwin, Homewood, Ill., 1970.

"Finance Companies: An Era of Change," *Banker's Monthly,* July 1975, pp. 24–28.

Flannery, M.J.: "Credit Unions as Consumer Lenders in the United States," *New England Economic Review,* July/August 1974, pp. 3–12.

Friend, I., ed.: *Study of the Savings and Loan Industry,* Federal Home Loan Bank Board, Washington, D.C., 1970 (four volumes).

——, M. Blume, and J. Crockett: *Mutual Funds and Other Instituional Investors: A New Perspective,* McGraw-Hill, New York, 1970.

Gardner, E.B., ed.: *Pension Fund Investment Management,* Irwin, Homewood, Ill., 1969.

Gibson, K.: "The Early History and Initial Impact of NOW Accounts," *New England Economic Review,* January/February 1975, pp. 17–26.

Goldsmith, R.W.: *A Study of Saving in the United States,* Princeton University Press, Princeton, N. J., 1955 and 1956 (three volumes).

————: *Financial Intermediaries in the American Economy Since 1900,* Princeton University Press, Princeton, N. J., 1958.

Grebler, L.: *The Future of Thrift Institutions,* Joint Savings and Mutual Savings Banks Exchange Groups, Danville, Ill., 1969.

Gurley, J.C., and E.S. Shaw: *Money in a Theory of Finance,* Brookings, Washington, D.C., 1960.

Hempel, G.H., and J.B. Yawitz: *Financial Management of Financial Institutions,* Prentice-Hall, Englewood Cliffs, N. J., 1977.

Hendershott, P.H., and R.C. Lemmon: "The Financial Behavior of Households: Some Empirical Estimates," *Journal of Finance,* June 1975, pp. 733–759.

Hodgman, D.R.: *Commercial Bank Loan and Investment Policy,* University of Illinois, Champaign, Ill., 1963.

Howell, P.L.: "Common Stocks and Pension Fund Investing," *Harvard Business Review,* November/December 1958, pp. 92–106.

Jessup, P.F., ed.: *Innovations in Bank Management,* Holt, Rinehart and Winston, New York, 1969.

Jones, L.D.: *Investment Policies of Life Insurance Companies,* Harvard Business School, Boston, 1968.

Jones, S.B., ed.: *Property and Liability Insurance Investment Management,* Irwin, Homewood, Ill., 1971.

Kasriel, P.L.: "New Six-Month Money Market Certificates—Explanations and Implications," *Federal Reserve Bank of Chicago Economic Perspectives,* July/August 1978, pp. 3–7.

Light, J.S.: "Increasing Competition Between Financial Institutions," *Federal Reserve Bank of Chicago Economic Perspectives,* May/June 1977, pp. 23–31.

Lovati, J.M.: "The Growing Similarity Among Financial Institutions," *Federal Reserve Bank of St. Louis Review,* October 1977, pp. 2–11.

Moore, B.J.: *An Introduction to the Theory of Finance,* The Free Press, New York, 1968.

Nadler, P.S.: *Commercial Banking in the Economy,* Random House, New York, 1973.

Nichols, D.A.: "Inflation and Stock Prices: Discussion," *Journal of Finance,* May 1976, pp. 483–487.

O'Brien, J.M.: "The Household as a Saver," *Federal Reserve Bank of Philadelphia Business Review,* June 1971, pp. 14–23.

Pesando, J.E.: "The Interest Sensitivity of the Flow of Funds Through Life Insurance Companies: An Econometric Analysis," *Journal of Finance,* September 1974, pp. 1105–1121.

Reed, E.W. et al.: *Commercial Banking,* Prentice-Hall, Englewood Cliffs, N. J., 1976.

Robinson, R.I.: *The Management of Bank Funds,* McGraw-Hill, New York, 1962.

————: "The Hunt Commission Report: A Search for Politically Feasible Solutions to the Problems of Financial Structure," *Journal of Finance,* September 1972, pp. 765–777.

————: "REIT's: The Risks of Financial Innovation," *The MGIC Newsletter,* February 1977.

Schott, F.H.: "Disintermediation Through Policy Loans at Life Insurance Companies," *Journal of Finance,* June 1971, pp. 719–729.

Schulkin, P.A.: "Real Estate Investment Trusts: A New Financial Intermediary," *New England Economic Review,* November/December 1970, pp. 2–14.

Smith, P.F.: *Money and Financial Intermediation,* Prentice-Hall, Englewood Cliffs, N. J., 1978, chap. 9 especially.

Teck, A.: *Mutual Savings Banks and Savings and Loan Associations: Aspects of Growth,* Columbia University Press, New York, 1968.

Welfling, W.: *Mutual Savings Banks: The Evolution of a Financial Intermediary,* Case Western Reserve University Press, Cleveland, 1968.

Winningham, S.: "Automatic Transfers and Monetary Policy," *Federal Reserve Bank of Kansas City Economic Review,* November 1978, pp. 18–27.

Wood, O.G.: *Commercial Banking,* D. Van Nostrand, New York, 1978.

chapter 5
Flow of Funds in Financial Markets

We have learned from Chapters 3 and 4 that there are three types of economic units in the financial system: (1) surplus units, (2) deficit units, and (3) financial intermediaries. Surplus units save more than they invest and therefore lend more than they borrow. Deficit units invest more than they save and consequently borrow more than they lend. Surplus units can lend directly to borrowing deficit units, but more often than not, funds flow indirectly from surplus units to deficit units via financial intermediaries. The latter neither save nor invest, in any significant sense, but they make it easier for surplus units to save and for deficit units to finance investment. These patterns of saving, investment, lending, and borrowing (direct and indirect) are illustrated in Table 5-1. The broken lines to the right of the numbers illustrated indicate that uses and sources of funds must be equal for each sector, while those to the left indicate that one sector's lending to another must be equal to the other's borrowing from that sector. Uses and sources of funds are interconnected and they must balance.

The purpose of this chapter is to present the flow-of-funds system of financial accounts for the nation. The flow-of-funds accounts (prepared by the Federal Reserve Board of Governors) provide real-world data for the various types of financial behavior discussed in the last three chapters. These accounts play the same role in financial market analysis as do the national income accounts in macroeconomic analysis. The accounts lend quantitative substance and give empirical meaning to the various concepts and categories of behavior. They tell us what has actually happened in the past. They provide data for conducting empirical tests of theories. They suggest empirical relationships that are useful for forecasting what will happen in the future. In short, the accounts allow us to bridge the gap between abstract analysis and concrete events.

TABLE 5-1
**Uses and Sources of Funds Statements Illustrated for the Three
Types of Sectors**

DEFICIT UNIT SECTOR

Uses of funds:
    Investment   85

Sources of funds:
    Saving   25
    Net borrowing from surplus units   10
    Net borrowing from financial intermediaries   50
                                          85

FINANCIAL INTERMEDIARY SECTOR

Uses of funds:
    Net lending to deficit units   50

Sources of Funds:
    Net borrowing from surplus units   50

SURPLUS UNIT SECTOR

Uses of funds:
    Net lending to financial intermediaries   50
    Net lending to deficit units   10
    Investment   40
                            100

Sources of funds:
    Saving   100

The basic structure and format of the flow-of-funds system of accounts is captured in Table 5-2. This table contains the same information as Table 5-1. It indicates the same equalities: Each sector's uses of funds equals that sector's sources of funds; aggregate saving equals aggregate investment; total lending to deficit units equals total borrowing from surplus units; and lending to intermediaries equals borrowing from intermediaries.

The only difference between Table 5-2 and Table 5-1 is the format. The format of Table 5-2 has been the basic format used in the Federal Reserve's system of accounts. It is a matrix format with the columns showing uses and sources by sector and the rows showing uses and sources by transaction category or type of financial behavior. Beyond this, however, Table 5-2 bears little resemblance to the Federal Reserve's matrix of the flow of funds. First, the numbers in Table 5-2 have been made up for illustrative purposes; they are not the real-world quantities reported in the actual accounts. Second, the breakdown of transaction categories in Table 5-2 has been greatly oversimpli-

TABLE 5-2
Alternative Format of Uses and Sources of Funds by Sector

Transaction Category	Sector							
	Surplus Units		Deficit Units		Financial Intermediaries		All Sectors	
	Use	Source	Use	Source	Use	Source	Use	Source
Saving		100		25				125
Investment	40		85				125	
Lending to deficit units	10				50		60	
Borrowing from surplus units				10		50		60
Lending to and borrowing from intermediaries	50			50			50	50
All categories	100	100	85	85	50	50	235	235

fied. The number and variety of categories in the official accounts is much more detailed and complex owing to the complex nature of our financial system. Third, the sectoring in Table 5-2 is contrived to fit the conceptual distinctions between surplus units, deficit units, and financial intermediaries. The official accounts include many more sectors classified by type of constituency: households, business, government, banks, etc. The result of so much detail in the official flow-of-funds accounts is that the uninitiated can become lost in a sea of numbers. We will therefore proceed slowly with the logic and structure of the accounts before presenting the matrix itself.

Once the flow-of-funds accounts have been presented, the chapter will continue with some discussions of using the accounts. We will find that the accounts are useful for quantifying supply and demand participation by different sectors in each of the major financial markets. We will also discuss how the accounts are used for forecasting interest rates and for building econometric models of the financial economy. Finally, we will follow this discussion with an actual illustration of the forecasting process.

Our first task, however, is to learn to understand the accounts themselves.

THE BREAKDOWN OF TRANSACTIONS IN FLOW-OF-FUNDS ACCOUNTING

The flow-of-funds system of social accounting starts out with the analysis of a single time period, in practice a quarter or a year. Within this period the financial economy is cross-classified by types of transactions and by sectors. Transactions of each sector are summed into statements of the uses of funds and

TABLE 5-3
Transaction Categories in the Flow-of-Funds Accounts

I. Real uses and sources

    A. Saving

    B. Investment
        1. Consumer durables
        2. Residential construction
        3. Plant and equipment
        4. Inventory change
        5. Mineral rights

II. Financial uses and sources

    A. Monetary claims
        1. Official foreign exchange
        2. Treasury currency
        3. Demand deposits and currency
        4. Time deposits at commercial banks
        5. Interbank claims

    B. Claims against nonbank financial intermediaries
        1. Savings accounts at savings institutions
        2. Life insurance reserves
        3. Pension fund reserves

    C. Corporate equities

    D. Credit market instruments
        1. U.S. Treasury securities
        2. Federal agency securities
        3. State and local government securities
        4. Corporate bonds
        5. Mortgages
        6. Consumer credit
        7. Bank loans
        8. Private short-term paper (money market instruments)
        9. Other loans

    E. Other credit
        1. Security credit
        2. Trade credit
        3. Taxes payable

    F. Equity in noncorporate business

    G. Miscellaneous

the sources of funds. These uses and sources are classified according to type of financial transaction. The sources and uses for the various sectors are then summed for the economy as a whole.

The transactions within the flow-of-funds accounts are categorized by type of use or source of funds. They are first divided between uses and sources that relate to real investment and saving and those financial uses and sources that relate to lending and borrowing. Real investment and financial investment (lending) are the two broad categories of uses of funds; saving and borrowing the two broad categories of sources.

Since financial investment and borrowing take many forms, the financial investment and borrowing categories are further subdivided by type. For example, financial investment in corporate bonds is separated from financial investment in savings accounts. Similarly, borrowing in the form of issuing corporate bonds is separated from borrowing through real estate mortgages. There are about as many subdivisions as there are different financial markets. Table 5-3 presents the categories and subcategories of transactions included in the flow-of-funds accounts. Some of the categories are self-explanatory, but others may seem unfamiliar. If so, the reader may wish to consult the Federal Reserve Board's *Introduction to Flow of Funds Accounts* (1975) for precise definitions.

The use of a financial market classification of transaction categories allows for a balancing of the uses and sources of funds within each market. For every borrower in a given financial market there is a lender; a source of funds for one individual is a use of funds for another. Borrowing transactions (sources of funds) must equal lending transactions (uses of funds) for each transaction category.

Financial transactions within each transaction category appear as either uses of funds or as sources of funds. Financial investment is clearly a use of funds, borrowing is clearly a source. But what are transactions such as financial disinvestment and debt repayment? The uses and sources of funds figures that appear in the flow-of-funds accounts are usually netted. Financial disinvestment transactions are subtracted from financial investment transactions in arriving at financial uses of funds. Similarly, debt repayment transactions are subtracted from borrowing transactions in figuring sources of funds. The result of this netting is to conceal a great many financial transactions. It also has the effect of allowing for negative entries into the accounts. For example, if corporations retire more old bonds than they sell new bonds over a given period, the accounts will show a negative source of funds in the corporate bond transaction category. The accounts will also show a negative use of funds as corporate bond holders will have experienced net disinvestment.

SECTORING FLOW-OF-FUNDS TRANSACTIONS

The economy as a whole is a complex entity. The detail that might be included if many sectors were used is almost endless. The practical necessities of statistics and analysis, however, limit the number of these sectors. In practice

TABLE 5-4
Sectors in the Flow-of-Funds Accounts

I. Private domestic nonfinancial sectors
    A. Households
        1. Households
        2. Personal trusts
        3. Nonprofit organizations

    B. Business
        1. Corporate business
        2. Farm business
        3. Nonfarm noncorporate business

II. Government sectors

    A. State and local governments

    B. U.S. government

III. Financial sectors

    A. Public
        1. Federally sponsored credit agencies
        2. Monetary authorities (central banks)

    B. Commercial banking
        1. Commercial banks
        2. Domestic affiliates of commercial banks
        3. Edge Act corporations and agencies of foreign banks
        4. Banks in U.S. possessions

    C. Private nonbank finance
        1. Savings and loan associations
        2. Mutual savings banks
        3. Credit unions
        4. Life insurance companies
        5. Private pension funds
        6. State and local government employee retirement funds
        7. Other insurance companies
        8. Finance companies
        9. Real estate investment trusts
        10. Open-end investment companies (mutual funds)
        11. Money market funds
        12. Security brokers and dealers

IV. Rest of the world (foreign sector)

the sectors usually shown separately are individuals, business, government, financial institutions themselves, and "the rest of the world." Some further subcategories are used in the Federal Reserve flow-of-funds system, such as, under business, corporate and noncorporate business, and, under government, the federal, state, and local levels. Table 5-4 gives an outline of the sectors and subsectors covered in the flow-of-funds accounts. Of these sectors, the household sector is the primary surplus-unit sector, and the business and government sectors are the primary deficit-unit sectors. The financial sectors comprise the various financial intermediaries.

The logic for appropriate sectoring is that of combining those segments that are similar in their motives, operations, legal constraints, and other behavior-explaining factors. If we have homogeneous categories, what is true of a category can be safely imputed to the individual units within a category. However, logic and practice cannot always be squared, and some odd companions are lumped together. For example, nonprofit units are included with individuals in the published flow-of-funds accounts. Availability of raw data sometimes accounts for such strange combinations. Sometimes a small sector is included with the least illogical larger sector to avoid cluttering up the accounts with too much detail.

COMBINING TRANSACTIONS AND SECTORS IN A USE-SOURCE MATRIX

The uses and sources of funds by transaction categories can be combined with the uses and sources of funds by sectors to form a matrix or a table. The Federal Reserve publishes such flow-of-funds tables, listing sectors across the top and transaction categories down the left-hand side. Each number inside the table is a use or source of funds that, reading up, identifies the sector and, reading to the left, identifies the transaction category. Each sector column of uses and sources of funds gives a reading of the involvement of that sector in the different financial markets. Each transaction category row of uses and sources of funds gives a reading of the involvement of the different sectors in that transaction category or financial market category.

The detailed breakdown of sectors and transaction categories gives rise to a matrix with an overwhelming number of columns, rows, and cells. Table 5-5 shows the Federal Reserve Board's matrix of the flow-of-funds accounts for the year 1978. As imposing as the table appears, the reader can take some small comfort that it is a *summary* table. (The Federal Reserve Board publishes supplementary materials that include more more detail.)

If we bear in mind that the logic of Table 5-5 is the same as in Table 5-2, the easiest way to begin to understand the table is to focus on individual cell numbers in the matrix. Each number is expressed in billions of dollars. Reading to the left, one can identify the category of transaction. Reading up, one can then identify the sector involved and whether the item is a use or source of funds. To illustrate, let us examine the first cell in the first row. Reading to the left, the amount represents an act of saving. Reading up, we find that this

TABLE 5-5
Summary of Flow-of-Funds Accounts for the Year 1978
(Billions of dollars)

Transaction category	Private Domestic Nonfinancial Sectors								Rest of the world		U.S. government	
Sector	Households		Business		State & local governments		Total					
	U	S	U	S	U	S	U	S	U	S	U	S
1 Gross saving		**335.4**		**190.1**		**11.8**		**537.4**		**24.8**		**-36.6**
2 Capital consumption		177.6		173.5				351.1				
3 Net saving (1-2)		157.8		16.6		11.8		186.2		24.8		-36.6
4 Gross investment (5+11)	**353.9**		**175.6**		**4.7**		**534.2**		**13.0**		**-36.0**	
5 Pvt. capital expenditures	295.5		242.1				537.6				-2.0	
6 Consumer durables	197.6						197.6					
7 Residential construction	92.0		14.9				106.9					
8 Plant and equipment	5.9		209.5				215.4					
9 Inventory change			15.7				15.7				-2.0	
10 Mineral rights			2.0				2.0					
11 Net financial investment (12-13)	**58.4**		**-66.5**		**4.7**		**-3.3**		**13.0**		**-34.0**	
12 Financial uses	223.7		79.7		30.6		334.0		59.6		28.7	
13 Financial sources		**165.3**		**146.2**		**25.9**		**337.4**		**46.5**		**62.6**
14 Gold & off. fgn. exchange									1.3	.2	-2.6	
15 Treasury currency												.5
16 Demand deposits & currency	14.5		3.6		-1.6		16.4		1.1		6.9	
17 Private domestic	14.5		3.6		-1.6		16.4		1.1			
18 Foreign									1.1			
19 U.S. government											6.9	
20 Time and savings accounts	111.5		-1.4		7.8		117.8		1.5		-.1	

		1	2	3	4	5	6	7	8	9	10	11	12
21	At commercial banks	50.2		-1.4		7.8		56.5		1.5		-.1	
22	At savings institutions	61.3						61.3					
23	Life insurance reserves	9.0						9.0					.3
24	Pension fund reserves	60.6						60.6					6.9
25	Interbank claims												
26	Corporate equities	-3.6			2.6			-3.6	2.6	1.8	-.5	18.3	53.7
27	Credit mkt. instruments	56.1	161.3	8.3	121.3	23.3	24.9	87.7	307.5	33.5	26.2		
28	U.S. Treasury securities	11.9		-7.2		17.1		21.9		27.5		7.7	55.1
29	Federal agency securities	6.5		.7		4.1		11.3					-1.3
30	State & local govt. secur.	7.5		.2	3.2	1.1	26.5	8.8	29.6				
31	Corporate & foreign bonds	-.9			20.1			-.9	20.1	1.1	4.3	-.2	-.1
32	Mortgages	14.6	101.6		43.5	1.0		15.6	145.1				
33	Consumer credit		50.5	3.2				3.2	50.5				
34	Bank loans N.E.C.		5.6		31.5				37.1		12.0		
35	Pvt. short-term paper	16.5		11.3	4.9		-1.5	27.8	4.9	4.9	6.6		
36	Other loans		3.6		18.2				20.2		3.3	10.7	
37	Security credit	1.4	1.9					1.4	1.9	-	-		
38	Trade credit		1.4	53.7	48.8		1.0	53.7	51.2	2.4	-.4	1.8	1.5
39	Taxes payable				1.8	1.2		1.2	1.8			2.9	
40	Equity in noncorp. bus.	-32.2			-32.2			-32.2	-32.2	18.0	21.0		
41	Miscellaneous	6.4	.8	15.6	3.8			22.0	4.6	11.8		1.4	-.3
42	Sector discrepancies (1-4)	-18.5		14.5		7.1		3.1				-.6	

continued on following page

TABLE 5-5 (continued)
Summary of Flow-of-Funds Accounts for the Year 1978
(Billions of dollars)

Transaction category	Financial Sectors										All sectors		Discr.	Natl. saving and investment
	Total		Sponsored agencies and mortgage pools		Monetary authority		Commercial banking		Pvt. nonbank finance					
	U	S	U	S	U	S	U	S	U	S	U	S	U	
1 Gross saving	**15.6**			**1.0**		**.5**		**4.0**		**10.1**		**541.2**		**516.4**
2 Capital consumption		6.0						2.7		3.3		357.2		357.2
3 Net saving (1–2)		9.6		1.0		.5		1.3		6.8		184.1		159.2
4 Gross investment (5+11)	**20.6**		**.5**		**.5**		**10.0**		**9.6**		**531.9**		**9.3**	**529.1**
5 Pvt. capital expenditures	6.5						4.6		2.0		542.1		-.9	542.1
6 Consumer durables											197.6			197.6
7 Residential construction	-.1								-.1		106.8			106.8
8 Plant and equipment	6.6						4.6		2.1		222.0			222.0
9 Inventory change											15.7			15.7
10 Mineral rights														
11 Net financial investment (12–13)	**14.1**		**.5**		**.5**		**5.4**		**7.7**		**-10.2**		**10.2**	**-13.0**
12 Financial uses	**403.7**		**44.0**		**13.2**		**151.2**		**195.3**		**826.0**		**10.2**	**46.5**
13 Financial sources		**389.6**		**43.5**		**12.7**		**145.7**		**187.7**		**836.1**		**59.6**
14 Gold & off. fgn. exchange	1.5				1.5						.2	.2	*	
15 Treasury currency	.6				.6						.6	.5		
16 Demand deposits & currency	2.4	26.0	.1			6.3	.3	19.7	2.0		26.7	26.0	-.8	
17 Private domestic	2.4	18.3	.1			9.3	.3	9.0	2.0		18.8	18.3	-.5	
18 Foreign		1.1				.1		1.0			1.1	1.1		
19 U.S. government		6.6				-3.0		9.7			6.9	6.6	-.3	
20 Time and savings accounts	5.9	125.2						65.9		59.4	125.2	125.2		

102

#	Label	1	2	3	4	5	6	7	8	9	10	11	12	13
21	At commercial banks	7.9	65.9							65.9	7.9		65.9	65.9	
22	At savings institutions	-1.9	59.4								-1.9	59.4	59.4	59.4	
23	Life insurance reserves		8.7									8.7	9.0	9.0	
24	Pension fund reserves		53.7									53.7	60.6	60.6	
25	Interbank claims	22.7	22.7			3.6	5.9	19.1	16.8				22.7	22.7	
26	Corporate equities	4.9	1.1					–	.2		4.9	.8	3.1	3.1	
27	Credit mkt. instruments	340.6	92.7	44.0	39.0	7.0		119.2	12.3		170.4	41.4	480.1	480.1	
28	U.S. Treasury securities	5.7		.5		7.7		-5.5			3.0		55.1	55.1	
29	Federal agency securities	18.7	39.0	*	39.0	-.4		6.3			12.8		37.7	37.7	
30	State & local govt. secur.	20.8						8.4			12.4		29.6	29.6	
31	Corporate & foreign bonds	31.9	7.7					-.3	.2		32.2	7.5	32.1	32.1	
32	Mortgages	130.4	.9	28.7				34.4			67.4	.9	145.9	145.9	
33	Consumer credit	47.3						26.9			20.4		50.5	50.5	
34	Bank loans N.E.C.	50.2	1.2	.2		–		50.2	12.1			1.2	50.2	50.2	
35	Pvt. short-term paper	10.1	31.3					-1.3			11.6	19.3	42.8	42.8	
36	Other loans	25.3	12.5	14.6	—	-.4		–			10.7	12.5	36.1	36.1	
37	Security credit	.2	-.2					-1.6			1.8	-.2	1.7	1.7	
38	Trade credit	1.3									1.3		59.1	52.3	-6.8
39	Taxes payable		1.7						.3			1.4	4.2	3.6	-.6
40	Equity in noncorp. bus.			-.2	4.5	.5	.5						-32.2	-32.2	
41	Miscellaneous	23.7	58.0					14.2	30.6		9.1	22.4	65.1	83.4	18.3
42	Sector discrepancies (1-4)	-5.0		.5		–		-6.0			.5		9.3	9.3	-12.7

saving was a source of funds for the household sector. Another illustration: Suppose we want to find out how many billions of dollars commercial banks invested in state and local government securities. In this case we need to go to the sector column for commercial banks and to the transaction row for state and local government securities. The answer is found by going down the column until we reach the row, or by going across the row until the column is reached.

Once the meaning of individual cells is understood, the whole matrix can then be viewed as a complete and interlocking set of accounts. Uses and sources of funds balance in two dimensions. They balance vertically for each sector. And they balance horizontally for each transaction or market category. Note, however, that this balancing is achieved in the table by including a row and a column for discrepancies. These discrepancies are statistical in nature; they point out the fact that the numbers in the table are not true values, but merely estimates.

COMBINING TRANSACTIONS AND SECTORS IN AN ASSET-LIABILITY MATRIX

Uses and sources of funds are flows between two points in time. These flows are additions or subtractions (if negative) to financial assets and liabilities. Assets and liabilities, on the other hand, are amounts outstanding—stocks—that exist at a point in time. Stocks are essentially cumulated flows. The relation between stocks and flows is encountered throughout economic analysis: "savings" is a stock, "saving" a flow; "capital" is a stock, "investment" a flow; "liabilities" is a stock, "borrowing" a flow; and so forth.

The use-source matrix of Table 5-5 shows the funds flows that occurred between December 31, 1977 and December 31, 1978. However, it does not show the amounts outstanding, or stocks, that existed at the beginning or end of this period. For this we need an asset-liability matrix. Fortunately, the Federal Reserve Board publishes asset-liability tables that complement its use-source tables. The asset-liability table has a structure similar to that of the use-source table: Sectors are listed across the top; financial-instrument categories are down the side. The numbers in the asset-liability table are what make the difference: Assets and liabilities (both stocks) replace uses and sources (both flows).

The Federal Reserve Board's summary matrix of financial assets and liabilities for December 31, 1978 is shown in Table 5-6. Each sector-column shows the various financial assets and liabilities of that sector. Each financial-instrument–category-row now reveals the amounts owned or owed by the various sectors across the given category. The asset-liability matrix is an interlocking set of accounts, but, unlike the use-source matrix, it is not complete. Because real assets and net worth are excluded, assets and liabilities do not balance vertically by sector. However, they do balance horizontally: Across any given category, the amounts owned by creditor sectors equal the amounts owed by debtor sectors. However, the column for discrepancies indicates that the estimates do not always balance.

RELATIONS BETWEEN THE USE-SOURCE MATRIX AND THE ASSET-LIABILITY MATRIX

Since stocks are cumulated flows, the numbers in the annual use-source table should resemble the differences in the numbers between the end-of-year and beginning-of-year asset-liability tables. Alternatively, the numbers in the end-of-year asset-liability table should resemble the sums of the numbers in the beginning-of-year asset-liability table and the yearly use-source table. Unfortunately, reconciliation of the two kinds of tables is not practical. Valuation and other problems prevent us from fully equating uses and sources with *changes* in assets and liabilities.

The major obstacle to integrating the flow-of-funds accounts with the asset-liability accounts is the valuation problem. Financial assets and liabilities can change between two points in time without any financial investment and borrowing if there is a change in the prices at which financial instruments are valued. Corporate shares, for example, are measured in the Federal Reserve accounts at market value. A change in the price level of corporate shares effects a change in the value of shares outstanding even if the number of shares remains constant. In a rising market, the recorded change in corporate equities outstanding is larger than the recorded investment in equities. Similarly, the change in equities outstanding understates actual investment during a declining market. This valuation problem and other technical considerations complicate reconciliations between the Federal Reserve's use-source tables and its asset-liability tables.

Aside from these problems, a stock-flow relation does exist between the asset-liability accounts and the use-source accounts. Financial assets and liabilities reflect cumulated uses and sources of funds, and current uses and sources of funds effect changes in financial assets and liabilities. Both types of accounts, asset-liability and use-source, are useful for discerning the behavior of individual transacting sectors and individual financial markets. Examination of one type alone can leave a distorted impression of financial behavior.

An instructive exercise is to compare the percentage composition of each sector's uses and sources of funds with the percentage composition of its financial assets and liabilities. Discrepancies between flow and stock compositions indicate divergences between short-run and long-run financial behavior. The composition of any year's flows tends to reflect short-run behavior, while the composition of assets and liabilities outstanding (cumulated flows) provides a more accurate reading of long-run behavior. Short-run behavior, even for a period as long as a year, is pretty erratic. Consequently, there are few periods during which the flow of funds in the use-source matrix follows a typical pattern.

Another instructive exercise is to compare the dollar amounts of flows and stocks associated with each financial market or transaction category. Often the markets that are large in terms of amounts outstanding are also large in terms of funds flows. But there are exceptions. For example, new issues of corporate shares during a quarter or a year are usually a small fraction of the value of

TABLE 5-6

Financial assets and liabilities, December 31, 1978
(billions of dollars)

Transaction category	Private Domestic Nonfinancial Sectors								Rest of the world		U.S. government	
	Households		Business		State & local governments		Total					
	A	L	A	L	A	L	A	L	A	L	A	L
1 Total financial assets	3374.3		810.0		206.3		4390.7		408.4		185.2	
2 Total liabilities		1209.7		1476.4		305.9		2992.1		402.3		719.7
3 Gold									37.6		*	
4 S.D.R.'s									9.7	1.0	1.6	
5 I.M.F. position											1.1	
6 Official foreign exchange										4.4	2.8	
7 Treasury currency												10.7
8 Demand deposits and currency	218.9		78.0		12.4		309.4		19.5		21.5	
9 Private domestic	218.9		78.0		12.4		309.4				21.5	
10 U.S. government									19.5			
11 Foreign												
12 Time and savings accounts	1103.9		27.8		65.0		1196.6		22.0		.8	
13 At commercial banks	479.0		27.8		65.0		571.8		22.0		.8	
14 At savings institutions	624.8						624.8					
15 Life insurance reserves	188.6						188.6					8.7

	1	2	3	4	5	6	7	8	9	10	11	12
16 Pension fund reserves	530.1						530.1					59.8
17 Interbank claims									42.7			
18 Corporate equities	791.9						791.9					
19 Credit market instruments	473.1	1164.3	97.5	1119.1	117.1	291.6	687.7	2575.1	168.1	157.2	127.4	626.2
20 U.S. treasury securities	139.5		2.6		70.4		212.6		137.1			619.2
21 Federal agency securities	33.3		3.5		22.0		58.9				23.8	6.2
22 State & local govt. secur.	89.4		3.7	15.8	9.0	285.2	102.1	301.0	10.6	43.2		
23 Corporate & foreign bonds	63.2			318.3			63.2	318.3				
24 Mortgages	106.0	762.3		392.7	15.6		121.6	1155.0			10.1	.8
25 Consumer credit		339.9	43.6				43.6	339.9				
26 Bank loans N.E.C.		22.7		251.2				274.0		41.9		
27 Open-market paper	41.6		44.1	25.1			85.8	25.1	20.3	26.6		
28 Other loans		39.3		116.1		6.5		161.9		45.4	93.5	
29 Security credit	8.8	22.2					8.8	22.2	-	-		
30 Trade credit		13.2	354.4	295.6		14.2	354.4	323.1	19.0	12.9	7.9	14.2
31 Taxes payable				22.3	11.8		11.8	22.3			13.0	
32 Miscellaneous	59.0	10.1	252.3	39.4			311.3	49.5	89.8	226.8	9.2	*

continued on following page

TABLE 5-6 (continued)

Transaction category	Financial Sectors										All sectors		Floats and discrepancies
	Total		Sponsored agencies and mortgage pools		Monetary authority		Commercial banking		Pvt. nonbank finance				
	A	L	A	L	A	L	A	L	A	L	A	L	A
1 Total financial assets	3427.6		219.4		156.2		1218.0		1834.0		8411.9		47.4
2 Total liabilities		3259.1		216.0		156.2		1153.6		1733.2		7373.1	
3 Gold	11.7				11.7						49.3	11.2	
4 S.D.R.'s	*				*						1.0	1.0	
5 I.M.F. position	1.6				1.6						4.4	4.4	
6 Official foreign exchange	13.1				13.1						13.1	10.7	-2.5
7 Treasury currency	22.3		.4	.4									
8 Demand deposits and currency	22.3	401.7				104.3	1.5	297.5	20.4		372.7	401.7	29.0
9 Private domestic		360.8				99.1	1.5	261.7	20.4		331.7	360.8	29.1
10 U.S. government		21.5				4.5		17.0			21.5	21.5	-.1
11 Foreign		19.5				.7		18.8			19.5	19.5	
12 Time and savings accounts	24.1	1243.6						616.6	24.1	627.0	1243.6	1243.6	
13 At commercial banks	21.9	616.6						616.6	21.9		616.6	616.6	
14 At savings institutions	2.2	627.0							2.2	627.0	627.0	627.0	
15 Life insurance reserves		179.9								179.9	188.6	188.6	

Item	(1)	(2)	(3)	(4)	(5)	(6)	(7)	(8)	(9)	(10)	(11)	(12)	(13)	No.
Pension fund reserves		470.4								470.4	530.1	530.1		16
Interbank claims	99.9	99.9			7.7	46.7	92.2	53.2		43.8	99.9	99.9		17
Corporate equities	234.8	43.8					1.2	43.3	233.6	195.6	1069.5	43.8		18
Credit market instruments	2811.7	436.4	217.3	197.5	119.2		1008.3	43.3	1466.9		3794.8	3794.8		19
U.S. treasury securities	269.4	197.5	1.5		110.6		97.2		60.2		619.2	619.2		20
Federal agency securities	121.0		.1	197.5	8.0		43.1		69.8		203.7	203.7		21
State & local govt. secur.	198.9						123.5		75.4		301.0	301.0		22
Corporate & foreign bonds	348.7	61.0					7.6	5.9	341.1	55.1	422.5	422.5		23
Mortgages	1037.3	13.3	158.8				213.3		665.2	13.3	1169.0	1169.0		24
Consumer credit	296.4						167.2		129.1		339.9	339.9		25
Bank loans N.E.C.	343.4	27.5			—		343.4			27.5	343.4	343.4		26
Open-market paper	50.1	104.4	3.8				13.0	37.4	32.7	67.0	156.2	156.2		27
Other loans	146.4	32.7	53.1	—	.6		—		93.3	32.7	239.9	239.9		28
Security credit	38.5	25.1					20.8		17.8	25.1	47.3	47.3		29
Trade credit	11.3									11.3	392.6	350.2	−42.4	30
Taxes payable		5.4								4.5	24.8	27.7	2.9	31
Miscellaneous	158.7	352.9	1.7	18.5	3.0	5.2	94.0	142.2	59.9	187.0	568.9	629.2	60.3	32

shares outstanding. Since outstanding issues swamp new issues, prices of corporate shares are largely determined by the supply of and demand for outstanding issues. An opposite case is the market for foreign exchange. Public authorities keep minimal balances of foreign exchange. Relative to other categories in the asset-liability matrix, the official foreign exchange account is extremely small. Annual changes in this account are proportionately large, however. In contrast to the stock market, foreign exchange prices respond sharply to newly injected flows of supply and demand.

QUANTITIES OF SUPPLY AND DEMAND IN MONEY AND CAPITAL MARKETS

One of the most valuable aspects of the flow-of-funds accounts is that they provide empirical data for quantifying the supply and demand sides of financial markets. Most of the rows in the use-source and asset-liability tables represent financial markets that will be individually analyzed in considerable detail in Parts Two and Three of this book. The flow-of-funds accounts give us a base of data on the amounts by which each sector supplies or demands funds in each market. For individual capital markets, the accounts indicate which sectors are the primary participating sectors, and those that are not. Thus, when we analyze the capital markets (in Part Three), we can concentrate on the behavior of the principal participating sectors.

The accounts are less useful for providing supply and demand data for the money markets. Instruments of the open money markets include federal funds, repurchase agreements, Eurodollars, commercial paper, bankers' acceptances, negotiable certificates of deposit, Treasury bills, and short-term federal agency securities. These instruments do not appear explicitly as transaction categories in the flow-of-funds system of accounts. Rather, they tend to be grouped in and scattered among some fairly disparate categories in the matrix. The transaction category called "private short-term paper" includes commercial paper, bankers' acceptances, and part (but not all) of the markets for federal funds and repurchase agreements. Treasury bills are included in the "U.S. Treasury securities" category, but this category also includes long-term Treasury securities. The same is true for the "federal agency securities" category. It includes both short-term and long-term agency securities. Negotiable certificates of deposit are included under "time and savings accounts at commercial banks," but this category also includes nonnegotiable certificates and ordinary savings accounts as well. In short, the flow-of-funds accounts do not lend themselves well to discerning quantities for the open money markets.

There are several related reasons for this. One is that money market information is more difficult to obtain and compile than capital market data. Another is that most money market activity tends to cancel out over a relatively short period of time. An economic entity usually invests in money market instruments when it has excess cash and disinvests when cash is needed. Since this cycle repeats itself many times a year, net flows over a year, or even over a quarter, are insubstantial compared to net capital market flows. Another reason is the design of the flow-of-funds accounts themselves. The Federal Reserve Board has been slow to include specific money market transactions in its flow-of-funds accounts partly because these transactions do not relate as well as capital market transactions to such real magnitudes as saving, investment, income, and expenditures. The function of the open money markets is not so much the "accumulation of wealth" function as it is a means for adjusting liquidity.

Nevertheless, by scrutinizing all the flow-of-funds accounts and supplementary materials available from the Federal Reserve Board, and by sometimes reading between the lines, it is possible to discern some rough estimates of supply and demand quantities for a few of the various money markets. We will report some of these figures in Part Two when we analyze money market behavior.

Fortunately, the major transaction categories in the flow-of-funds accounts are named after the major capital market instruments: federal government securities (U.S. Treasury and federal agency), state and local government securities, mortgages, corporate bonds, and corporate equities (corporate stocks). These instruments are distinctly long-term instruments, with the exception of federal government securities which have become increasingly short-term. Moreover, the names of these capital markets instruments tell us the names of the borrowing sectors. The federal government is on the demand-for-funds side of the market for federal government securities. State and local governments demand funds as the issuers of state and local government securities. Corporate bonds and stocks are the instruments issued by corporations as demanders of capital market funds. The mortgage market is the one capital market that does not identify the demanders of funds in its name. Instead, this market is named after its function to finance real estate. The household sector is on the demand-for-funds side of the home mortgage market but so is that part of the corporate sector in the housing business. The mortgage market is also used by unincorporated businesses and small corporations seeking funds to finance business real estate.

The sectors on the supply-of-funds side of each capital market are not indicated by the name of the market. They are, however, easily identified in the flow-of-funds accounts. Supplying funds shows up as a use of funds in the use-source matrix (and as an asset in the asset-liability matrix). Thus, the quantity of funds supplied by each sector in a market is found by reading horizontally across the corresponding row in the matrix.

Virtually every sector supplies funds in the market for federal government securities. But some sectors dominate. The largest amounts of the federal debt are held by the central banking system (the monetary authority), the commercial banking system, the foreign sector, and the household sector. The central bank holds Treasury bills and other short-term Treasury securities in connection with its open market operations (see Chapter 11). The same securities serve as collateral and provide a measure of liquidity for commercial banks (see Chapter 10). Foreign banks and other authorities hold these securities in connection with balance of payments and international liquidity considerations (see Part Four). These elements and others of the supply-of-funds side of the market for federal government securities are joined with the government's demand for funds in Chapter 13, which analyzes the market as a whole.

Three sectors stand out on the supply-of-funds side of the market for state and local government securities. More than 90 percent of these securities are held by commercial banks, wealthy individuals, and property and casualty insurance companies. The tax-exempt status of interest on state and local obligations makes these securities particularly attractive to institutions and individuals in relatively high tax brackets. This important capital market is analyzed in Chapter 14.

The supply of mortgage credit is mainly from financial intermediaries, with savings and loan associations, commercial banks, life insurance companies, and mutual savings banks doing most of the lending. Households and federal credit agencies are also important suppliers of mortgage credit. Many households hold "second mortgages" and "purchase-money sales contracts" on the homes of other households. Mortgage credit from federal credit agencies is a relatively recent phenomenon. Federal participation in the mortgage market has been widely criticized for its practices, but in theory it serves the laudable purpose of smoothing and expanding the overall flow of mortgage credit. The mortgage market is one of the more complicated and complex of the capital markets, particularly on the supply-of-funds side. These complications and complexities are covered in Chapter 15.

The most important sectors on the supply-of-funds side of the corporate bond market are life insurance companies, pension funds (public and private), and households. Together, these sectors hold just under 90 percent of all corporate bonds outstanding. A large portion of the bonds acquired by insurance companies and pension funds originate through the mechanism of direct or private placement. Interest rates on such private placements are negotiated directly between corporate borrower and institutional lender. Household acquisitions of bonds, on the other hand, are through the open market. The market for corporate bonds and other forms of long-term business debt is analyzed in Chapter 16.

The supply-of-funds side of the corporate stock market is dominated by households, pension funds, and mutual funds. Together they hold over 90 percent of all stocks outstanding. This is the one capital market in which the household sector is the leading sector supplying funds. However, the proportion of stocks held by institutional investors, particularly by pension funds, has been growing. Supply, demand, and other characteristics of this well-known but fast-changing market are explored in Chapters 17 and 18.

ANALYTICAL USES OF THE FLOW-OF-FUNDS ACCOUNTS

The flow-of-funds accounts, as we have seen, are quite complex and comprehensive. They reveal a multiplicity of financial markets. Rather than one market for loanable funds and one rate of interest to be determined, there are many markets and many rates (one for each market). For each market there is a supply schedule and a demand schedule for funds and an interest rate that brings supply and demand into equilibrium. The same principles apply in the many-markets case as in the single-market case. There is a problem, however, of market interrelations. Supply and demand in one market depend not only on the interest rate in that market but on interest rates in other markets. Moreover, the interest rate in one market depends not only on supply and demand in that market but on supply and demand in other markets. These complex interrelations make analysis of the flow-of-funds accounts difficult but not impossible.

One of the oldest paradoxes in economic analysis is that one cannot explain one phenomenon without "explaining everything else." In any equilibrium system this is true, whether it be the system of price markets for commodities, an electrical circuit, the solar system, or financial markets. The flow-of-funds system is also an equilibrium system. The actual uses and sources of funds figures that appear in the flow-of-funds accounts are not necessarily equilibrium quantities, but they are quantities that reflect a process of balancing supply and demand simultaneously in the various financial markets.

Practical analysts of various sectors of the financial markets recognize this truth intuitively. An investment banker in the state and local government security market would not dream of trying to analyze or forecast events in this market without bringing in the money markets and other capital markets. The flow-of-funds system allows this to be done formally with a minimum of sweat.

The two principal analytical uses of flow-of-funds are interest-rate forecasting and financial econometric model building. These two uses are not mutually exclusive. Some forecasters use econometric models and some econometricians use models for forecasting. Generally, however, interest-rate forecasting is done by practical analysts who feel there is more to forecasting than solving a constricted set of simultaneous equations. On the other hand, econometric model building is usually done by academically oriented economists who see their work in a broader context than that of mere forecasting; they are often more interested in "explaining why" than in "forecasting what."

Practical analysts use the flow-of-funds framework in arriving at interest-rate forecasts. Some of the better-known forecasts are the ones prepared by the Bankers Trust Company, the Life Insurance Association of America, and Salomon Brothers. The basic procedure used in these forecasts is that of iteration, or successive approximation. The first step in the iterative procedure is to make a forecast of the GNP and its major components: consumer, business, and government expenditures. Expenditure forecasts are then translated into forecasts for the demand for funds. For example, the demand for residential construction is translated into a demand for residential mortgage funds. The same thing is done on the supply-of-funds side of the market. Forecasts of saving are converted into supply-of-funds estimates. Trends in the behavior of financial intermediaries also enter into the supply-of-funds estimates. After much thought and manipulation, a quantity of demand for funds and a quantity of supply of funds are estimated for each of the different capital markets. These first-round estimates are also based on some assumption of interest rates, since interest rates affect both the supply of and demand for funds.

After the first estimates of supply and demand have been made, the forecaster usually finds that supply and demand do not balance when put into flow-of-funds matrix form. The lack of balance itself then becomes evidence as to the nature of likely future developments. An excess of borrowing plans over lending plans suggests higher interest rates and a shortage of funds. A shortage of funds in one market and a surplus of funds in another suggest that relative interest rates may change even if the overall level remains unchanged.

The second round of successive approximations involves interest-rate revisions and hence supply of and demand for funds revisions. Even after the second round it is unlikely that the quantities will balance, because the quantities in each market are influenced by the whole spectrum of interest rates and each interest rate is affected by more than one financial market. Thus the iterative procedure is continued until all interest rates and all supply and demand quantities are consistent and reasonable. The final approximation of interest rates is the one that is expected to ensure equality of uses and sources of funds for each financial market or transaction category and for each transacting sector. Of course, different forecasters come up with different interest-rate forecasts. Very few forecasters are able to come close to the mark most of the time, and even the very best are way off target occasionally.

The iterative procedure used by practical analysts for forecasting interest rates involves working with behavioral relations. Quantities supplied and demanded are related to interest rates, and interest rates are related to supply and demand. Practical analysts usually have a feel for these interrelations based on personal experiences in the capital markets; they may or may not take the step of formulating an explicit set of equations, and even if they do, they may or may not estimate the parameters of the equations statistically.

The mark of financial econometric model building is to specify the behavioral relations, market constraints, and market-clearing conditions in the form of a system of simultaneous equations. Observed flow-of-funds quantities and observed interest rates are used as data for estimating the parameters of the equations. These parameters provide a statistical measure of the response of demand and supply to interest rates and the response of interest rates to demand and supply.

The overall purpose of a financial econometric model is to explain financial market behavior—past, present, and future. Explaining the future is called prediction, but it is important to note that econometric models are capable of making any number of predictions, depending upon the assumed values of the exogenous variables fed into the model. For example, an assumption that the federal deficit will be $20 billion leads to one prediction of future interest rates and funds flows, while an assumption that the deficit will be $25 billion leads to another prediction. A good economist never states categorically that future variables will be such and such; rather, he or she is always careful to qualify predictions with assumptions. This applies to all kinds of forecasting, real as well as financial.

FORECASTING INTEREST RATES: A NUMERICAL ILLUSTRATION

On the notion that nothing explains quite so well as an example, let us trace through the process of forecasting interest rates with a numerical illustration. Let us imagine a relatively unencumbered financial economy that has only *five* sectors:

1. households
2. business
3. government
4. banking system
5. nonbank finance

Let us further simplify by supposing that this elementary economy has only *six* transaction categories:

1. saving
2. investment
3. demand deposit money (debt of banking system)
4. savings accounts (debt of nonbank finance)
5. bonds (debt of business and government)
6. mortgages (debt of households)

(Saving and investment are real transactions. The remaining four represent categories of financial transactions and financial markets.) Let us assume, finally, that the interest rates on demand deposit money and on savings accounts are fixed by the government. (Money pays no interest rate if you wish.) This leaves but *two market-determined interest rates:*

1. the interest rate on bonds
2. the interest rate on mortgages

Now, how can we forecast the changes in store for these two market interest rates?

The first step in the process is to obtain saving and investment quantities from a forecast of the Gross National Product accounts. Suppose the forecast is that given in Table 5-7. By subtracting consumption expenditures from disposable income, we obtain *household saving of 90*. The retained earnings forecast gives us *business saving of 20*. And, by subtracting government spending from taxes, we obtain *government saving of −10*. (Being negative, it represents a deficit for the government.) On the investment side, the residential construction forecast gives us *household investment of 20;* and the plant and equipment forecast, *business investment of 80*. These amounts of saving and investment can now be used to plug into the flow-of-funds matrix for our hypothetical economy. (This is done in Table 5-8, which is the completed first-round matrix based on this step and the ones to follow.)

The second step in the forecasting process is to estimate the amounts of

TABLE 5-7

Forecast of Gross National Product by Expenditure and Income Components

EXPENDITURES ON THE GROSS NATIONAL PRODUCT:

Consumption expenditures	640
Residential construction expenditures	20
Plant and equipment expenditures	80
Government expenditures	60
Total Gross National Product	800

INCOME FROM THE GROSS NATIONAL PRODUCT:

Retained earnings	20
Taxes	50
Disposable income	730
Total Gross National Product	800

desired borrowing by deficit units and the amounts of desired lending by surplus units. Let us start with the *household sector*. Suppose from past experience that buyers of new houses run deficits that require them to borrow an amount equal to half their investment in new housing. This means that they will need *mortgage credit of 10*. The household sector as a whole, however, is a surplus sector. It lends more than it borrows. Let us suppose that its usual lending pattern is 37.5 percent in demand deposits, 37.5 percent in savings accounts, and 25 percent in bonds. Given its total sources of funds (90 from saving and 10 from mortgage borrowing), and given that a use of 20 is forecasted for investment, the remaining funds of 80 will be allocated as follows: acquisition of *demand deposits of 30*, acquisition of *savings accounts of 30,* and acquisition of *bonds of 20*. (These amounts for household borrowing and lending are also shown in Table 5-8.)

Turning to the *business sector,* we find it needs to borrow to cover its deficit between investment and saving. Moreover, we would expect that the sector will need additional working cash balances to complement its expansion in plant and equipment. If the cash-to-fixed-assets ratio has averaged 1 to 19 in the past, the forecast of business fixed investment of 80 implies a forecast of increasing *demand deposits by 5*. With total forecasted uses of funds of 85 (80 for real investment and 5 for increasing cash), and with a source of 20 forecasted for saving, the business sector will need to borrow 65. Thus, we can forecast an issue of *bonds of 65* as the balancing source of funds for the business sector. (This source and the use of 5 to increase demand deposits are shown in Table 5-8.)

Turning, finally, to the *government sector,* we see it will have to borrow to cover its deficit between spending and taxes. With government spending forecasted at 60, and taxes at 50, we can forecast an issue of *bonds of 10* by this sector. (This source of funds is also entered into Table 5-8.)

The third step in the forecasting process is to estimate the uses and sources of funds for the financial intermediary sectors. The nonbank finance sector receives funds from deposits from households into savings accounts. Since we have already forecasted an increase in *savings accounts of 30* as a use of funds for the household sector, we can translate this into a source of funds for the *nonbank finance sector*. The uses of this amount can be estimated on the basis of the sector's typical lending patterns. Suppose that we make an educated guess that the sector will allocate one-half the funds to bonds, one-third to mortgages, and one-sixth to demand deposits. Given these proportions, the household deposits of 30 into savings accounts at nonbank financial intermediaries will be used by the latter to acquire *bonds of 15, mortgages of 10,* and *demand deposits of 5.* (These uses along with the source from savings accounts are entered in Table 5-8.)

Unlike nonbank financial intermediaries, the source of funds for the *banking system* is not determined solely by decisions of depositors. The amount of demand deposit debt of the banking system is more a matter of monetary policy. The monetary authorities have the powers and techniques to change the amount of money in the economy. Let us suppose that these authorities wish to increase the supply of money by 50. This will show up in our forecasting matrix as an increase in *demand deposits of 50* under the source column of the banking system sector. How these funds will be used depends on the financial investment behavior of the banking system. Suppose we think that they will allocate 40 percent of funds to mortgages and 60 percent to bonds, based on past experience. With funds of 50 to allocate, the banking system can be expected to acquire *mortgages of 20* and *bonds of 30.* (These two uses along with the source from demand deposits are also shown in Table 5-8.)

We should now pause and note that the various sectors' patterns of allocating funds among alternative uses are in no way rigid. Each sector allocates on the basis of relative interest rates. The patterns indicated above are meant to hold for the existing structure of interest rates, not for the interest rates that we are attempting to forecast. It should be obvious that if we expect a change in relative interest rates, then we must also expect a change in each sector's lending pattern.

The fourth step in the forecasting process is to determine the imbalances between supply and demand in the matrix. Table 5-8 is a complete matrix containing all the first-round forecasts of the first three steps. The method employed in the first three steps ensures that desired uses of funds equals desired sources for each sector. However, the matrix does not ensure that the desires of any one sector are consistent with those of another. This means that desired uses of funds do not equal desired sources for each market (within which more than one sector participates). Such imbalances are indicated in the "all sectors" column in Table 5-8. First, the banking system wishes to increase the quantity of demand deposit money by 10 more than the amount demanded by holders of money. Second, the supply of funds to the bond market is 10 less

TABLE 5-8
First-Round Use-Source Matrix

Transaction Category	Households Use	Households Source	Business Use	Business Source	Government Use	Government Source	Banking System Use	Banking System Source	Nonbank Finance Use	Nonbank Finance Source	All Sectors Use	All Sectors Source
Saving	20	90		20		(10)					100	≈ 100
Investment	30		80									
Demand deposits			5					50	5		40	< 50
Savings accounts	30						30			30	30	= 30
Bonds	20			65		10	30		15		65	< 75
Mortgages		10					20		10		30	> 10
All categories	100 = 100		85 = 85		0 = 0		50 = 50		30 = 30		265 = 265	

than the demand for funds by business and government from this market. And third, the supply of funds to the mortgage market is 20 more than the funds demanded by households from this market. In other words, the matrix shows:

1. a surplus of money of 10
2. a shortage of loanable funds in the bond market of 10
3. a surplus of loanable funds in the mortgage market of 20

These imbalances exist despite that fact that the total of all uses by all sectors equals the total of all sources by all sectors.

The fifth and final step in the process is to determine the changes in market interest rates that will bring the matrix into complete balance. This step is facilitated by forecasting, first, what will happen to the general level of all interest rates before moving on to the question of movements in particular interest rates.

We can use either the loanable funds theory or the liquidity preference theory (both of which were presented in Chapter 3) to analyze the general level of interest rates. According to the liquidity preference theory, the level of interest rates will have to fall in order to eliminate the surplus of money and to bring the supply of money into equilibrium with demand. The same forecast is derived from loanable funds theory. With a shortage of loanable funds in the bond market of 10 and a surplus of loanable funds in the mortgage market of 20, there is an overall surplus of loanable funds in all loanable funds markets of 10. This surplus can be eliminated and equilibrium restored to the overall supply of and demand for loanable funds only if interest rates generally decrease. We can therefore forecast that market rates in general will fall.

With respect to particular interest rates, we can consider three possibilities:

1. Both the bond rate and the mortgage rate will fall.
2. The bond rate will fall and the mortgage rate will rise (but not by enough to offset the general tendency for rates to fall).
3. The mortgage rate will fall and the bond rate will rise (but, again, not by enough to offset the general tendency for rates to fall).

Of these three possibilities, the second can be eliminated. A lower bond rate and higher mortgage rate would only serve to increase the shortage of funds in the bond market and to increase the surplus of funds in the mortgage market. The third possibility would appear to be the most plausible. A lower mortgage rate would serve to reduce the surplus of funds in the mortgage market, and a higher bond rate would decrease the shortage of funds in the bond market. But the first possibility (listed above) cannot be argued away on theoretical grounds. Certainly, a lower mortgage rate would serve to clear the market for mortgage funds. But it would also serve to clear the market for bond funds. With a lower mortgage rate, some lenders would shift funds out of the mortgage market and put them into the bond market, thereby increasing the supply of loanable funds to this market. Any shift larger than 10 would turn the shortage of funds in the bond market into a surplus so that the bond rate could fall as well.

Two things are certain. The mortgage rate must fall absolutely. And the bond rate must rise relative to the mortgage rate. These things we can forecast with an air of confidence. But we are on shaky grounds when it comes to forecasting the absolute change in the bond rate. The bond rate could either rise or fall absolutely. But if it falls, it must fall by less than the mortgage rate and therefore rise relative to the mortgage rate.

Of course, an experienced forecaster would not only be able to predict the directions of change, but the magnitudes of change as well. Whatever numbers are forecasted, the forecaster would then need to check the forecasts for internal consistency. This involves redoing the whole matrix in terms of the forecasted interest rates rather than the preexisting structure of interest rates. With different interest rates, the GNP forecast itself would have to be revised, and, consequently, so would the saving and investment entries into the use-source matrix. Different sectors would now have different amounts to allocate among alternative uses. Moreover, the allocative percentages would also change to reflect the forecasted structure of relative interest rates.

It is highly unlikely that the interest rates forecasted on the basis of imbalances between supply and demand in the first round will produce balances in all markets in the second round. Furthermore, the interest rates forecasted after the second round may fail to bring the use-source matrix into balance after the third round. Every interest rate forecast implies a different set of entries into the matrix, and every set of entries suggests a different interest rate forecast. Interest rates and quantities of supply and demand are obviously interrelated. Fortunately, experienced forecasters are able to think in terms of simultaneous relationships. Two to three rounds are usually sufficient for "old hands" to bring the matrix into complete balance. Sometimes, however, it requires a fairly radical forecast of interest rates to achieve complete balance.

PROJECTS AND QUESTIONS

1. Saving is defined generally as unconsumed income. Explain precisely how this general definition fits the specific definitions for household saving, business saving, government saving, and "rest-of-the-world saving" in the flow-of-funds accounts.
2. Obtain a copy of a corporate annual report. Study the statement of the corporation's uses and sources of funds. Explain where each use and source reported fits in terms of the transaction categories included in the flow-of-funds accounts.
3. Judging from figures in the flow-of-funds accounts, would you expect interest rates in the municipal bond market to be more sensitive to supply and demand in the corporate bond market or to supply and demand in the

market for short-term credit? Would you expect the municipal bond rate to be sensitive to supply and demand in the market for corporate equities? Explain your answers.

BIBLIOGRAPHY

Board of Governors of the Federal Reserve System: *Introduction to the Flow of Funds Accounts,* Washington, D.C., 1975.
————: *Flow of Funds Accounts, 1946–1975,* Washington, D.C., December 1976.
Cohen, J.: "Copeland's Moneyflows After Twenty-Five Years: A Survey," *Journal of Economic Literature,* March 1972, pp. 1–25.
Copeland, M.A.: *A Study of Moneyflows in the United States,* National Bureau of Economic Research, New York, 1952.
Freund, W.C., and E.D. Zinbarg: "Applications of Flow-of-Funds to Interest Rate Forecasting," *Journal of Finance,* May 1963, pp. 231–248.
Goldsmith, R.W.: *Capital Market Analysis and the Financial Accounts of the Nation,* General Learning Press, Morristown, N. J., 1972.
Polakoff, M.E. et al.: *Financial Institutions and Markets,* Houghton Mifflin, Boston, 1970, chaps. 2, 23, and 24 especially.
Ritter, L.S.: "An Exposition of the Structure of the Flow of Funds Accounts," *Journal of Finance,* May 1963, pp. 219–230.
Robinson, R.I.: "The Flow-of-Funds Accounts, A New Approach to Financial Market Analysis: Comment," *Journal of Finance,* May 1963, pp. 259–263.
Taylor, S.P.: "Uses of Flow-of-Funds Accounts in the Federal Reserve System," *Journal of Finance,* May 1963, pp. 249–258.

chapter 6
Portfolio Selection and
Security Pricing

Chapters 2 through 5 have stressed the accumulation of wealth theme of this book. Wealth, either for the individual or in the aggregate, cannot grow without saving and investment. Unless everyone is financially self-sufficient, saving and investment cannot take place without lending and borrowing. And unless all external finance is direct, lending and borrowing cannot take place without financial intermediation. In a financially developed economy, the accumulation of wealth process involves elements of internal (self-) finance, direct external finance (assisted by investment bankers and security brokers), and indirect external finance. These three methods of financing are traced quantitatively in the flow-of-funds accounts. The quantities of saving, invest-ment, lending, and borrowing that appear in these accounts are determined, to a large extent, by the level of interest rates in the economy. Interest theories of saving and investment and of lending and borrowing were introduced in Chapters 2 and 3.

The determination of the equilibrium rate of interest was of primary concern in Chapter 3. There we learned that lending and borrowing and the rate of interest are mutually interdependent. Lending and borrowing decisions are guided by the rate of interest. The rate of interest is determined by the supply of and demand for loanable funds (the aggregates of individual lending and borrowing decisions). Although this looks like circular reasoning, it really is not. In equilibrium analysis, lending, borrowing, and the rate of interest are determined simultaneously.

In addition to facilitating the accumulation of new wealth, financial markets serve also to facilitate the allocation of existing wealth. Every economic entity must decide not only how much to add to total wealth, but how to allocate existing wealth, whatever its size, among alternative assets. Thus, this chapter turns from the wealth accumulation theme to the wealth allocation theme. Our concern now will be how an economic entity chooses to hold its given wealth.

For most people, the problem of choosing between alternative assets in composing one's wealth takes more time and energy than the problem of how much wealth to accumulate. The latter problem is often solved rather passively. Additions to total wealth are made when income exceeds expenditures, and wealth is drawn down when expenditures exceed income. Moreover, since one cannot add to or subtract from wealth without specifying what specific assets to add or subtract, every wealth accumulation decision implies an allocation decision. But every allocation decision does not imply an accumulation decision. Wealth can be recomposed or adjusted without changing its total size. Since, in fact, allocation decisions commonly involve asset switching, without any net addition to or subtraction from assets, the allocation process is much more a continuous process. This is one reason why allocation decisions take more time and energy.

Continuous wealth adjustment is made possible by the existence of secondary markets in securities and by the brokers and dealers who make these markets work. Without secondary markets, securities could be purchased only when newly issued by deficit units, and they could be redeemed only when they mature. Since corporate equities never mature, they could never be liquidated. With secondary markets, securities already outstanding can be purchased or sold at any time. These markets obviously facilitate the wealth adjustment process. Moreover, they enhance the process by providing continuous pricing information. Security prices are constantly changing with supply and demand. As prices change, they are disseminated instantly to prospective buyers and sellers in the market. The massive number of quotations of security prices and yields and the constant changing of these quotations tend to overwhelm the average person. This is another reason why wealth allocation decisions are so demanding.

To solve the problem of how to allocate wealth among alternative assets, the present chapter turns to the normative theory of portfolio selection, introduced by H. M. Markowitz (March 1952). The theory of portfolio selection is actually more than a theory of choosing securities. It is general enough to encompass the choosing of all kinds of assets, real as well as financial. But its introduction and its early development by Markowitz, and others, were in the context of choosing securities, particularly equity securities, and so the theory continues to go by the name of portfolio selection. The present chapter follows tradition and focuses on the choosing of securities.

One of the determinants of choosing securities is the structure of security prices. In order to explain who holds what and in what quantities, security prices must also be explained. Thus, the present chapter also covers the theory of security pricing, or "capital asset pricing model," introduced by W. F. Sharpe (September 1964). The determination of relative prices and yields in financial markets turns back, however, on the relative demand for each security outstanding in the market. Security prices are determined by, as well as being determinants of, portfolio choices. This is similar to quantity and price determination in any market. Given supply, price depends on demand, the quantity demanded depends on price, and both are determined simultaneously. The same holds for securities outstanding in the financial markets. The selection of portfolios and the pricing of securities are mutually interdependent. It will simplify matters, however, to take security prices as given when discussing the theory of portfolio selection and to take portfolio selections as given when discussing the theory of security pricing. But first, we must come to understand the key relationships, measurements, and principles that are instrumental to both theories.

RELATION BETWEEN MARKET PRICE AND RATE OF RETURN

There are three ways to perceive the value of a security. One way is to look at its current market price. Another way is to look at the future dollar returns it will bring. Still another way is to calculate the future dollar returns on the current market price as a percentage rate of return. To illustrate, if a security has a current market price of $100 and a single future dollar return of $120 one year hence, the annual rate of return is 20 percent. If, instead, the current market price is $60 and the future dollar return is unchanged at $120, then the rate of return is 100 percent. This example demonstrates a very important principle: Given future dollar returns, a security's rate of return is inversely related to its market price. This was previously demonstrated in Chapter 3.

It is easy to compute the annual rate of return when there is but a single future dollar return one year hence. But for more complex patterns of future dollar returns, the calculation of rate of return is not intuitively obvious. Fortunately, the present value formula presented in Chapter 3 is very general and will always provide a solution for the percentage rate of return:

$$\text{Current market price of a security} = \frac{\text{dollar returns in first year}}{(1+i)^1} + \frac{\text{dollar returns in second year}}{(1+i)^2} + \cdots + \frac{\text{dollar returns in }n\text{th terminal year}}{(1+i)^n}$$

The i in the equation is the annual rate of return. It can be solved after plugging in the values for market price and future dollar returns. The equation confirms the principle that rate of return is inversely related to market price. The larger market price (the left-hand side of the equation), the smaller will be the rate of return. Rate of return appears in the denominators in the right-hand side of the equation, and the smaller the denominators, the larger the sum of the terms on the right-hand side.

The equation for determining rate of return is very general and can be applied to any kind of security in any situation. When applied to a common stock, the future dollar returns are dividends and the terminal value of the stock. When applied to a bond (or other debt instrument), the future dollar returns are interest payments and the terminal value of the bond. The terminal value of a stock is its market price when sold. The terminal value of a bond is its market price if sold, its call price if called, and its face or par value if held to maturity. The rate of return on a bond held to maturity is called "yield to maturity."

Whatever the situation, rate of return can be determined from future dollar returns and the current market price. For given future dollar returns, rate of return always varies inversely with current market price. In short, rate of return and market price are two sides of the same coin.

RISK AND THE CALCULATION OF EXPECTED RATE OF RETURN

One might question how rate of return can be calculated given that no one knows the future with certainty nor the precise returns it will bring. Fortunately, there is a way around this problem. A person may not know the future but still be able to attach likelihood or probability coefficients to different possible outcomes. If so, he or she can calculate what statisticians call the "expected rate of return."

Expected rate of return is a weighted average of all possible rates of return. Each possible rate can be multiplied by its probability coefficient. The resulting products can then be totaled to get the expected rate of return. An example will illustrate how simple the procedure is. Consider a security that has a .3 probability of earning a 9 percent rate of return, a .4 probability of earning 10 percent, a .2 probability of earning 13 percent, and a .1 probability of earning 17 percent. In this case the expected rate of return is 11 percent. The calculations are shown in Table 6-1. The 11 percent expected rate of return is a statistical expectation. It is not the most likely outcome. Nor in this case is it even considered a possible outcome. Rather, it is a weighted average of all possible outcomes.

Statistically, two securities can have different possible rates of return but the same expected rate of return. Consider a second security that has a .2 probability of earning 0 percent, a .5 probability of earning 7 percent, and a .3 probability of earning 25 percent. In this case the expected rate of return is again 11 percent, as calculated in Table 6-2. Although this second security has

TABLE 6-1

Possible Rate of Return		Probability of Possible Rate of Return		
9%	×	.3	=	2.7%
10%	×	.4	=	4.0%
13%	×	.2	=	2.6%
17%	×	.1	=	1.7%
		1.0		11.0%
				(expected rate of return)

TABLE 6-2

Possible Rate of Return	Probability of Possible Rate of Return		
0%	×	.2 =	0.0%
7%	×	.5 =	3.5%
25%	×	.3 =	7.5%
		1.0	11.0%
			(expected rate of return)

the same expected rate of return as the first, most persons would not be indifferent in choosing between the two. The second security is obviously more risky than the first. Persons who like taking risks would prefer the second security to the first. Those who dislike risk would choose the first security.

An important point emerges. Portfolio choices are governed not only by expected rate of return but by risk as well. People are indifferent neither toward risk nor toward expected return. A method has been demonstrated for calculating expected return. But how is risk calculated? How can a person tell how much more risky one security is than another?

CALCULATING RISK

There are two very closely related measures of risk. One is called "the variance of return," the other "the standard deviation of return." Both measures characterize the relative spread or dispersion of possible returns from the expected return. The variance is a weighted average of the squares of the deviations of all possible rates of return from the expected rate of return. The expected rate of return is subtracted from each possible rate of return. Each difference or deviation is squared and multiplied by its probability co-efficient. The products are then totaled to get the variance of return. The standard deviation of return is then obtained by taking the square root of the variance.

This sounds a lot more complicated than it actually is. Variance and standard deviation are easily calculated for the two securities illustrated in the preceding section (see Tables 6-3 and 6-4).

The standard deviation of return for the first security is 2.45 percent, while for the second, more risky, security it is 9.54 percent. The larger the standard deviation, the greater the risk. This is because the standard deviation measures the dispersion or spread of possible returns from the expected return. Standard deviation and its square, the variance, are not the only measures of risk, but they possess certain statistical and mathematical qualities that make them specially suited for portfolio analysis.

TABLE 6-3
Risk Calculations for First Security

Possible Rate of Return	Expected Rate of Return	Deviation of Possible from Expected	Deviation Squared		Probability of Possibility	
9%	11%	−2%	4%	×	.3	= 1.2%
10%	11%	−1%	1%	×	.4	= .4%
13%	11%	+2%	4%	×	.2	= .8%
17%	11%	+6%	36%	×	.1	= 3.6%
						6.0%
						(variance
Standard deviation = $\sqrt{6\%} \cong 2.45\%$						of return)

TABLE 6-4
Risk Calculations for Second Security

Possible Rate of Return	Expected Rate of Return	Deviation of Possible from Expected	Deviation Squared		Probability of Possibility	
0%	11%	−11%	121%	×	.2	= 24.2%
7%	11%	−4%	16%	×	.5	= 8.0%
25%	11%	+14%	196%	×	.3	= 58.8%
						91.0%
						(variance
Standard deviation = $\sqrt{91\%} \cong 9.54\%$						of return)

GREATER EXPECTED RETURN FOR GREATER RISK

The two securities examined thus far have the characteristics indicated in Table 6-5: Both have the same expected return, but the spread of possible returns is greater for the second security.

If this pattern of risk-return characteristics is generally perceived in the market and if the average investor in the market is averse to risk, market forces will cause the pattern to shift in the direction of greater expected return for greater risk. People who dislike risk but are willing to take risks if the returns are high enough will not want to hold the more risky security as long as the less risky security offers the same expected return. Such people will sell but not buy the more risky security, and they will buy but not sell the less risky one. As the more risky security is sold in the market, its market price falls and its expected rate of return rises. The opposite happens with the less risky security. Buying pressure causes its market price to rise and its expected rate of return to fall. Eventually, the expected rate of return on the more risky security will be so

TABLE 6-5

	Security 1	Security 2
Expected rate of return	11%	11%
Standard deviation of return	2.45%	9.54%

much greater than on the other that each investor still holding the more risky security will feel the risk is justified. At this point the market is in equilibrium.

The equilibrium pattern of greater expected return for greater risk assumes that investors are averse to risk. If, instead, investors like risk for its own sake, they would trade return for risk. And if such behavior permeated the market, the equilibrium pattern of risk-return characteristics would be less expected return for greater risk. Some investors are known to like risk, but their influence on financial markets is overshadowed by the influence of the risk-averse majority of investors. Studies indicate that more risky securities are in fact associated with higher expected returns. The assumption of general risk aversion is thus consistent with observed market characteristics.

EFFECT OF DIVERSIFICATION ON RISK AND EXPECTED RETURN

Risk and expected return can be estimated for a portfolio of securities as well as for a single security. Most investors do diversify their holdings so that their portfolios contain more than one security. Diversification often has an interesting beneficial effect on risk and expected return. If separate returns on separate securities are not too highly and positively correlated, a combination of the securities will exhibit less risk than the risk of the securities taken separately. Thus diversification often makes it possible to reduce risk considerably with little impairment of expected return.

An example will show how this beneficial effect works. Suppose there are two securities, A and B, with the characteristics seen in Tables 6-6 and 6-7. Security B has the higher expected rate of return, but it also has the higher variance of return. This conforms to the principle of greater expected return for greater risk.

Now suppose that, instead of considering securities A and B separately, they are combined into a portfolio, with 80 percent of the portfolio invested in A and 20 percent in B. What then is the risk and expected return for the portfolio? It depends on the correlation of returns between A and B. Table 6-8 illustrates three possible probability distributions.

The probability coefficients in Table 6-8 require some explanation. Perfectly positive correlation means that security B's return is always high when security A's return is high, and that B's return is low when A's is low. If we assume A's return has an even chance of being high or low, perfectly positive correlation

TABLE 6-6
Security A

Possible Rate of Return		Probability of Possibility			Deviation of Possible from Expected	Deviation Squared		Probability of Possibility		
10%	×	.5	=	5%	−10%	100%	×	.5	=	50%
30%	×	.5	=	15%	+10%	100%	×	.5	=	50%
				20%						100%
				(expected rate of return)						(variance of return)

TABLE 6-7
Security B

Possible Rate of Return		Probability of Possibility			Deviation of Possible from Expected	Deviation Squared		Probability of Possibility		
0%	×	.5	=	0%	−25%	625%	×	.5	=	312.5%
50%	×	.5	=	25%	+25%	625%	×	.5	=	312.5%
				25%						625.0%
				(expected rate of return)						(variance of return)

TABLE 6-8

Possibility	Associated Rate of Return on Portfolio	Probability of Return When Correlation of Returns Is:		
		I Perfectly Positive	II Zero	III Perfectly Negative
High rate of return for both A and B	.8 × .3 + .2 × .5 = 34%	.50	.25	.00
Low rate of return for both A and B	.8 × .1 + .2 × .0 = 8%	.50	.25	.00
High rate of return for A but low for B	.8 × .3 + .2 × .0 = 24%	.00	.25	.50
Low rate of return for A but high for B	.8 × .1 + .2 × .5 = 18%	.00	.25	.50
		1.00	1.00	1.00

means that there is an even chance of both A and B having high returns or both having low returns. Perfectly negative correlation is just the opposite. In this case B's return is always low when A's is high, and it is always high when A's is low. If we assume, again, an even chance of high or low returns for security A, perfectly negative correlation means that there is an even chance of a high return for A but low for B or of a low return for A but high for B. Finally, zero correlation means that returns on A and B are unrelated. If both have an even chance of being high or low, there is a 25 percent probability that (1) both will be high, (2) both will be low, (3) A's will be high but B's low, or that (4) A's will be low but B's high. In this case, there is an even chance for any one of *four* possible outcomes.[1]

Given all these joint probabilities, risk and expected return can now be calculated for the portfolio of securities A and B for each of the three correlations. Tables 6-9, 6-10, and 6-11 clearly demonstrate when diversification is beneficial and when it is not. It is most beneficial when returns are most negatively correlated. In Table 6-11, the variance of return for the combination of A and B is 9 percent and the standard deviation is 3 percent. This is considerably less risk than the risk of the least risky security, A, which by itself has a variance of 100 percent and a standard deviation of 10 percent. Diversification is also beneficial, though not as much, when returns are uncorrelated. In Table 6-10 the variance of the combination of A and B is 89 percent and the standard deviation 9.4 percent, which is still less risk than the risk of the least risky security.

Diversification is least beneficial when returns are most positively correlated. In Table 6-9 the variance and standard deviation of the securities combined are 169 percent and 13 percent respectively. In this case diversification does not reduce risk below the risk of security A taken by itself. In fact, when returns are perfectly and positively correlated, as they are in this case, the standard deviation for the portfolio is a weighted average of the standard deviations for the individual securities in the portfolio, the weights being determined by the proportions of each security in the portfolio.

Rate of return for a portfolio is similarly a weighted average of the rates of return for the individual securities in the portfolio, where again the weights are given by the proportions of each security in the portfolio. This result holds for all correlations and is not dependent on the special condition of perfectly positive correlation. Thus, unlike portfolio risk, portfolio return is completely independent of the correlation of returns between the securities in the portfolio. In all three cases considered in the tables above, the expected rate of return is 21 percent. This is because the portfolio contains 80 percent of security A, whose expected return is 20 percent, and 20 percent of security B, whose expected return is 25 percent.

---

[1] The reader should be aware that these probabilities have been rigged for convenience. In the real world, securities have more than two possible rates of return, and the probabilities of possibilities are not all equal. But, since this is not a book on statistics, the exposition here is limited to the simplest possible case.

TABLE 6-9
Risk and Expected Return on the Portfolio When the Return on Security A is Perfectly and Positively Correlated with Return on Security B

Possible Rate of Return	Probability of Possibility			Deviation of Possible from Expected	Deviation Squared	Probability of Possibility		
34%	×	.5	= 17%	+13%	169%	×	.5	= 84.5%
8%	×	.5	= 4%	−13%	169%	×	.5	= 84.5%
			21%					169.0%
			(expected rate of return)					(variance of return)

TABLE 6-10
Risk and Expected Return on the Portfolio When Return on Security A Is Completely Uncorrelated with Return on Security B

Possible Rate of Return	Probability of Possibility			Deviation of Possible from Expected	Deviation Squared	Probability of Possibility		
34%	×	.25	= 8.5%	+13%	169%	×	.25	= 42.25%
8%	×	.25	= 2.0%	−13%	169%	×	.25	= 42.25%
24%	×	.25	= 6.0%	+3%	9%	×	.25	= 2.25%
18%	×	.25	= 4.5%	−3%	9%	×	.25	= 2.25%
			21.0%					89.00%
			(expected rate of return)					(variance of return)

TABLE 6-11
Risk and Expected Return on the Portfolio When Return on Security A Is Perfectly but Negatively Correlated with Return on Security B

Possible Rate of Return	Probability of Possibility			Deviation of Possible from Expected	Deviation Squared	Probability of Possibility		
24%	×	.5	= 12%	+3%	9%	×	.5	= 4.5%
18%	×	.5	= 9%	−3%	9.0%	×	.5	= 4.5%
			21%					9.0%
			(expected rate of return)					(variance of return)

In summary, it is beneficial to combine securities whose returns are not highly and positively correlated. Diversification reduces portfolio risk below the risk of the least risky security in the portfolio. At the same time it keeps portfolio return above the return on the least risky security. It thus enables the investor to reduce risk with little impairment of return.

EFFICIENT COMBINATIONS OF RISK AND EXPECTED RETURN

If time and money were unlimited, one could calculate the expected rate of return and the standard deviation of return for every potential portfolio. (The number of potential portfolios approaches infinity because there are many different securities in the market and an incredible number of ways to combine them.) One could then plot the calculated risk-return combinations on a graph in the form of a scatter diagram. The diagram would not look very scattered but rather congested. In fact the plotted points would merge into a dark or shaded area as illustrated in Figure 6-1. Figure 6-1 is obviously no more than a theoretical construct. Time and money do not permit one to make all the necessary calculations to construct a complete diagram. But, just for the time being, it will do no harm if we pretend that such a construction does exist.

Any point within or on the boundary of the area graphed in Figure 6-1 is a potential portfolio. An investor is free to select any point. Risk-averting investors would not choose just any point, however. Rather, they would select a portfolio where they get the most expected return for a given amount of risk or the least risk for a given rate of return. Such a risk-return combination is termed "an efficient combination" or "an efficient portfolio." An inefficient combination, by default, is a combination of less than maximum return for a given risk or more than minimum risk for a given return.

All points within and on the boundary of the area in Figure 6-1 (except points on the extra dark boundary from K to L) are inefficient combinations. From such a point it is possible to move upward and increase expected return without increasing risk, or to move leftward and decrease risk without decreasing expected return, or to move both upward and leftward and simultaneously increase return and decrease risk. Only the extra dark boundary from K to L contains the efficient portfolios, that is, the efficient combinations of risk and expected return. Once on this segment of the boundary, it is not possible to change portfolios without either decreasing the expected return or increasing the risk.

figure 6-1   Possible Combinations of Risk and Return.

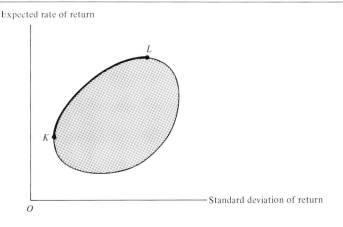

Expected rate of return

Standard deviation of return

O

Risk-averting investors can naturally rule out all the inefficient risk-return combinations in selecting a portfolio. Only the efficient combinations interest them. They know that the best or optimal portfolio for them is one of the efficient portfolios lying on *KL*.

SELECTING THE PORTFOLIO WITH THE OPTIMUM COMBINATION OF RISK AND EXPECTED RETURN

The efficient portfolios of the preceding section are all portfolios of risky securities. It is time now to bring in two other sets of efficient portfolios. One is a portfolio of riskless securities, and the other includes combinations of risky and riskless securities.

A riskless security has certain returns. Its expected rate of return is the pure rate of interest and its standard deviation of return is zero. Short-term U.S. government securities are perhaps the best known kind of riskless securities. A portfolio of U.S. Treasury bills, for example, comes as close as anything to a riskless portfolio. Such a portfolio is itself efficient inasmuch as it offers the absolute minimum in risk.

In Figure 6-2, point *P* is the zero-risk, pure return combination for riskless securities. Points on the curve from *K* to *L* are efficient risk-return combinations of risky securities. Points on the straight line connecting *P* and *Q* are combinations of the riskless portfolio *P* and the risky (but efficient) portfolio *Q*. A point lying halfway between *P* and *Q*, for example, is a fifty-fifty combination of riskless securities and the risky securities that constitute portfolio *Q*. If *P* has a certain return of 4 percent (and zero standard deviation) and *Q* has an expected return of 10 percent and a standard deviation of 6 percent, investors who put half their money into *P* and half into *Q* can expect a combined return of 7 percent and a combined standard deviation of 3 percent on their overall portfolio. When a portfolio of risky securities is combined with a riskless

figure 6-2 Efficient and Inefficient Combinations of Riskless Securities with Efficient Portfolios of Risky Securities.

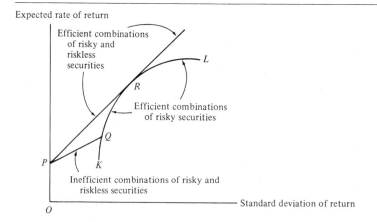

portfolio, the standard deviation of return for the combined portfolio is a proportion of the standard deviation for the risky portfolio, the proportion being the same as the proportion of risky securities in the combined portfolio.

Combining riskless securities with an efficient portfolio of risky securities does not necessarily guarantee an efficient combination of risky and riskless securities. The combinations on the line from P to Q in Figure 6-2, for example, are inefficient. The investor can get more return for the same risk, or less risk for the same return, by combining riskless securities with the efficient portfolio of risky securities represented by point R. Combinations of portfolio P and portfolio R lie on the line from P to R and beyond. These combinations are more efficient, since the line PR is positioned above (meaning more expected return) and to the left (meaning less risk) of the line PQ.

Before we can go any further, we must explain what it means to operate on the line beyond (to the right of) point R in Figure 6-2. Suppose some investors have an equity of $1 million to invest but that they would like to invest $2 million in R, which is expected to return 20 percent with a standard deviation of 12 percent. If they can borrow $1 million at the riskless rate of 4 percent, their net expected return from the $2 million of R is $360,000. This is a 36 percent expected rate of return on their $1 million of equity. It also amounts to a 24 percent standard deviation of return on their $1 million of equity. By holding a portfolio of risky securities that is double their equity, their risk on equity is twice as great. A key factor in portfolio analysis is that expected rate of return and standard deviation of return are computed for a given amount of investor's equity. Adding $1 million of risky securities to the portfolio can be accomplished by subtracting $1 million of riskless securities. Borrowing $1 million at the riskless rate has this subtracting effect. Critics of portfolio-selection theory have no argument with the use of such leverage to increase expected return and risk. Rather, they question the realism of the assumption that investors can borrow at the riskless rate.

Combinations of the riskless portfolio and portfolio R are efficient combinations. The line from P to R and beyond in Figure 6-2 is the line of efficient combinations of risky and riskless securities. This line is tangent to the curve from K to L. All other lines from P to or through points on KL are below and to the right of the tangent, PR. Combinations on these latter lines offer less than maximum return for given risk and less than minimum risk for given return. They are inefficient. Thus, except for R, no efficient portfolio of risky securities can combine with riskless securities to produce an efficient combination. Portfolio R alone is able to keep up efficiency when combined with riskless securities. For this reason it is called the optimal combination of risky securities.[2]

The optimal overall portfolio of both risky and riskless securities depends on the investor's preferences toward risk and return. If one is strongly averse to risk and weakly motivated by return, one will maximize utility by investing a

[2]In the real world, this optimal combination would be solved for mathematically through the use of quadratic programming.

small part of one's funds in the optimal combination of risky securities and a large part in riskless securities. If, on the other hand, one is only mildly averse to risk and strongly attracted to return, one may put all one's funds into the optimal combination of risky securities. One may even go beyond this and borrow other people's funds (if one can get them at close to the riskless rate) to finance additional investment in the optimal combination of risky assets. Whatever amount an investor puts into or takes out of the market for riskless securities, there is only one best combination of risky securities in which to invest. The problem of selecting a portfolio of risky securities is thus separated from the problem of selecting a portfolio of both risky and riskless securities. The former is resolved somewhat objectively through calculation of risk and expected return. The latter is resolved more subjectively by the investor's attitudes toward risk and return.

LINEAR EQUILIBRIUM RELATION BETWEEN TOTAL RISK AND EXPECTED RETURN ON EFFICIENT PORTFOLIOS

Up to now we have been looking at how an individual investor would theoretically select a portfolio given his or her estimations of and attitudes toward risk and return. We now turn to the larger issue of how security prices are determined, assuming each individual follows the rules of portfolio selection.

The theory of security pricing is a logical extension of the theory of portfolio selection. However, it operates at a higher level of abstraction. It assumes not only that each investor follows the rules of portfolio selection but that all investors have identical estimations of future prospects. This means that all investors seek the same optimal combination of risky securities.

What is in the optimal combination of risky securities that everyone seeks?

In equilibrium, the optimal combination consists of risky securities that actually exist in the market, and in proportions that actually exist. If, for example, 1 percent of the risky securities in the market are security X, each investor will (in equilibrium) want 1 percent of his or her own portfolio of risky assets to be security X. But suppose the market is not in equilibrium. Suppose each investor wants 2 percent of his or her risky securities to be security X. In such a case the desired amount of security X is twice its actual amount. Being in short supply, the price of security X must be bid up and its expected rate of return must fall. As expected return declines, each investor would decide that he or she does not want as much as 2 percent of his or her portfolio in X. At some lower expected rate of return, each investor would want only 1 percent in X. This would be an equilibrium expected rate of return, for it ensures that investors desire an amount actually in existence. The pricing mechanism thus brings demand into equilibrium with supply; it finds expected rates of return that induce investors to want what exists.

The same applies to the riskless rate of return. Recall that strongly risk-averse investors desire to invest (lend) part of their funds in riskless securities while mildly risk-averse investors prefer to borrow in this market.

The equilibrium riskless rate equates desired lending with desired borrowing. If desired borrowing exceeds desired lending, there is a shortage of riskless funds. As a result, the risk-free rate rises, decreasing the desire to borrow and increasing the desire to lend, until eventually the risk-free rate is comfortably in equilibrium.

Thus in equilibrium, different investors will have different portfolios of risky and riskless securities. Conservative investors will hold relatively small proportions of risky securities in their portfolios; less conservative investors will hold relatively large proportions. Each investor, however, will hold the same combination of risky securities, a combination including all risky securities existing in the market. Moreover, each investor will hold each risky security in the same proportion as it exists in the market. The optimal combination of risky securities for every investor is, therefore, the market portfolio of risky securities.

As mentioned before, the decision to hold risky securities is separated from the decision to own (or owe) riskless securities. The former decision is determined by objective factors of risk and return estimates. Since each investor is assumed to agree on these estimates, each investor will hold the same portfolio of risky securities, namely, the market portfolio. The latter decision is determined by subjective attitudes toward risk and return. Since attitudes vary among investors, so do positions in riskless securities. James Tobin pointed out this result (February 1958). It is called the "separation theorem."

In graphical terms, each investor selects a point from his or her line of efficient combinations of risky and riskless securities. Since each investor's line is identical to the lines of all other investors and since in equilibrium the optimal combination of risky securities is the market portfolio of risky securities, a simple linear equilibrium relation exists between risk and return on efficient portfolios of risky and riskless securities. This relation, as graphed in Figure 6-3, is called the capital market line (CML). Point P is again the

figure 6-3 The Capital Market Line.

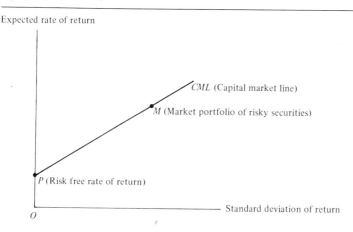

Expected rate of return

CML (Capital market line)

M (Market portfolio of risky securities)

P (Risk free rate of return)

Standard deviation of return

O

risk-free rate of return associated with a zero standard deviation of return. Point M is the expected rate of return and the standard deviation of return for the market portfolio of risky securities. The *CML* is a straight line passing through points P and M. The *CML* shows that expected rate of return on an efficient portfolio of risky and riskless securities is a positive and linear function of risk as measured by the standard deviation of return. The *CML* stipulates (1) greater expected return for greater risk and (2) linear trade-offs between risk and expected return.

The *CML* concept has implications for practical investment. It suggests that the investor should select a diversified portfolio of risky securities that has risk-return characteristics similar to those of the market portfolio. One way of approximating the market portfolio is to choose securities on the basis of a random sample, the larger the sample size the better. For most investors, however, a better way is to buy into a market-index mutual fund. These funds come as close as anything to approximating the risk-return characteristics of the market portfolio. The *CML* also indicates the effect on risk and expected return of mixing the market portfolio with riskless securities. It shows the investor how much return must be sacrificed in order to reduce risk or, alternatively, how much additional risk must be incurred to increase return.

SYSTEMATIC VERSUS UNSYSTEMATIC RISK

The linear equilibrium relation between expected rate of return and standard deviation of return does not hold for individual securities. If it did, there would be no risk-reducing benefits derived from diversification. We have seen that the standard deviation of return on a diversified portfolio of securities can be less than the standard deviation of the least variable security in the portfolio. Certainly, in terms of everyone holding the market portfolio, the standard deviation of return on each individual security overstates the "true risk" of that security in the market. We therefore need to explore the nature of this "true risk."

The standard deviation of return is a measure of total risk. Total risk is the sum of two kinds of risk: systematic risk and unsystematic risk. Systematic risk includes those variations of the rate of return on an individual security that covary with the rate of return on the market portfolio. Unsystematic risk, on the other hand, includes those variations of the rate of return on an individual security that are independent of variations of the rate of return on the market portfolio. The systematic risk and unsystematic risk of an individual security cannot be casually observed. For example, if the price of a common stock rises on a day when the whole market is up, it is impossible to say whether the stock went up because the market was up (systematic variation) or that it would have gone up even if the market had remained unchanged (unsystematic variation).

Systematic risk and unsystematic risk can be measured statistically, however. The square of the coefficient of correlation between an individual security's returns and those on the market portfolio measures the proportion of the security's variance that is systematic. If correlation is perfect, all risk is systematic. If there is no correlation, all risk is unsystematic. Since the total risk of a security can be measured by the square of its standard deviation of return, and since the proportion of total risk that is systematic can be measured by the square of its correlation of returns with the market, we can measure total risk in terms of its systematic and unsystematic components as follows:

$$\underset{\sigma_j^2}{\text{Total risk}} = \underset{r_{jm}^2\, \sigma_j^2}{\text{systematic risk}} + \underset{(1-r_{jm}^2)\, \sigma_j^2}{\text{unsystematic risk}}$$

where σ_j is the standard deviation of return on security j, and where r_{jm} is the correlation of the security's returns with those on the market portfolio.

We are now ready to discover the "true risk" of a security when all investors in the market hold the market portfolio. The market portfolio is perfectly correlated with itself. All its risk is therefore systematic. It has no unsystematic risk. This is because the market portfolio is perfectly diversified. All unsystematic risk is diversified away. The perfectly diversified investor can thus totally ignore the unsystematic risk of each security in his or her market portfolio. The only "true risk" that these securities have is systematic risk. Since perfect diversification completely eliminates unsystematic risk, the only kind of risk that enters into the risk-return trade-off in the market is systematic risk.

LINEAR EQUILIBRIUM RELATION BETWEEN SYSTEMATIC RISK AND EXPECTED RETURN

Systematic risk is usually expressed in terms of Sharpe's beta coefficient. (This is the same "beta" that you read about in *The Wall Street Journal*.) The beta coefficient is really an index of systematic risk. It measures a security's systematic risk relative to the total risk (all systematic) of the market portfolio:

$$\text{Beta}_j = \frac{r_{jm}\sigma_j}{\sigma_m}$$

Since beta is an index of systematic risk relative to the market portfolio, the beta of the market portfolio, itself, is 1. Individual securities can have betas greater than, equal to, or less than 1. A beta greater than 1 means that a security's returns are more volatile than the returns on the market portfolio. A beta less than 1 indicates that returns are less volatile than those for the market. A beta of zero indicates no systematic variation whatsoever. Riskless securities have zero betas.

In equilibrium, securities must be priced so that their expected rates of return are commensurate with their systematic risk profiles. Securities with high betas must command higher expected rates of return than securities with low betas. Such a pattern is shown in Figure 6-4. The line in Figure 6-4 is called the security market line (SML). It shows the equilibrium relation between systematic risk and the expected rate of return. Moreover, it applies to all individual securities and to all portfolios, efficient and inefficient. It is thus much more general than the capital market line (CML), in Figure 6-3, which

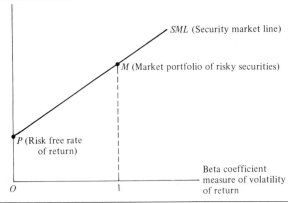

Expected rate of return

SML (Security market line)

M (Market portfolio of risky securities)

P (Risk free rate of return)

Beta coefficient measure of volatility of return

O   1

figure 6-4   The Security Market Line.

applies only to efficient portfolios. Because the *SML* is more general, it is also more interesting and useful for analyzing securities and their price movements.

Why is the security market line a straight line? The proof is too complex for this book, but we can demonstrate that a linear *SML* is consistent with the linear *CML* derived earlier. The equation of the linear *SML* is as follows:

$$\overline{R}_j = R_f + (\overline{R}_m - R_f) \left[\frac{r_{jm}\sigma_j}{\sigma_m} \right]$$

In this equation, $\overline{R}_j$ is the expected rate of return on portfolio j (or security j), R_f is the riskless rate of return, $\overline{R}_m$ is the expected rate of return on the market portfolio, and $r_{jm}\sigma_j / \sigma_m$ is the beta coefficient measure of systematic risk. Now let portfolio j be any risky but efficient portfolio of risky and riskless securities. Being efficient, its correlation of returns with the market, r_{jm}, must be perfect. Setting r_{jm} equal to 1, and rearranging terms, we get:

$$\overline{R}_j = R_f + \left[\frac{R_m - R_f}{\sigma_m} \right] \sigma_j$$

The result is the equation for the *CML*, or capital market line.

The fact that the security market line plots as a simple straight line does not mean that the *SML* is a simple-minded idea. On the contrary, the security market line is a profound concept. In equilibrium, every security and every portfolio will plot along the security market line.

IMPLICATIONS FOR ANALYSIS AND PREDICTION

The security market line graphed in Figure 6-4 can be used as a tool for analysis and prediction. It offers a straightforward procedure for analyzing securities.

The first step is to estimate the risk-free rate of return. This can be done by using the Treasury bill rate as a proxy. The rate can be plotted on the vertical axis. The second step is to estimate the expected rate of return for the market. This can be tricky, but it essentially involves looking at recent overall market performance and adjusting for future expectations. Whether one makes an educated guess or avails oneself of sophisticated computer programming, the estimated market return can be plotted against a beta coefficient of 1. The third step is to draw a straight line through the two plotted points. This is the *SML*, which shows the return-beta combinations that should exist in equilibrium. The fourth step is to estimate return-beta points for the various securities to be analyzed. These points should also be plotted and labeled. If security prices are in equilibrium, these latter points should lie on or near the *SML* because the *SML* is an equilibrium line.

Points that plot far above or far below the *SML* are the ones that interest the analyst. These points represent securities whose prices appear to be out of equilibrium. Points above the *SML* represent securities that may be under-priced, while points below the line may indicate overpriced securities. The former have returns above their equilibrium returns for their risk positions. Such securities should be in strong demand; their market prices should start advancing; their expected rates of return should fall toward equilibrium. The latter have unusually low returns for their risk. Their prices should drop and their returns increase until equilibrium is restored. The *SML* is thus a tool for identifying mispriced securities and for predicting the directions in which the prices should move to get into equilibrium.

It is far from a perfect tool, however. Remember, the *SML* is a theoretical construct. It is useful only insofar as it provides insights about the real world. We have seen that the theory is built on some artificial but necessary assumptions. This, however, does not render the theory invalid. If the implications of the theory are consistent with observed behavior, the theory is sufficiently robust to be acceptable. The theory has been gaining adherents, but adherents as well as critics recognize its limitations.

Even if the *SML* accurately depicts equilibrium, it may be difficult to estimate, as may the return-beta points of individual securities. Estimation is always a tricky business, particularly estimates of future returns. Past information can be used to calculate rates of return and beta coefficients, but unless the past is a good indicator of the future, the calculations will not tell analysts what they need to know. In this regard, studies indicate that beta coefficients are quite stable over time for efficient portfolios. However, for single securities and inefficient portfolios, beta coefficients are rather unstable.

Analysis of this kind is probably not suitable for the average person. First, there is the practical consideration of the time and expense that it takes to perform such an analysis. Second, there is the risk of coming up with poor estimates of the return-beta points, which could lead to wrong predictions. It takes a lot of training in statistics to generate good statistics. Third, there is the possibility that the analysis will not reveal any significantly mispriced securities. If professional security analysts are doing their job well, security prices should always be at or close to equilibrium. The professionals should be able to detect and correct any mispricing of securities without much delay. Of course, one might ask: If security prices are always at or near equilibrium, why should there be so many professionals doing security analysis? Indeed, there is this curious paradox. The better the job done by security analysts, the worse the rewards of doing the job. The paradox is not difficult to resolve, however. Competition, the drive to outperform others, is what keeps the game alive. Fourth and finally, the *SML* model may not be able to predict the equilibrium structure of security prices if the model itself is incomplete or incorrect. As pointed out above, the validity of a model does not rest on the realism of its assumptions but rather on its predictive power. Unless the *SML* model can withstand the scrutiny of empirical evidence, it cannot be considered a practical tool for analysis.

IS THE SECURITY MARKET LINE SUPPORTED BY THE EVIDENCE?

The theory of portfolio selection was originally constructed in the context of choosing equity securities. In this context, the market portfolio is limited to equity securities traded in the market. Most of the empirical tests of the theory of security pricing have been in this same context. Expected rates of return on equities have been regressed against beta coefficient measures of the systematic risk of equities.[3]

The statistical evidence is generally consistent with the theoretical proposition that the expected rate of return is a positively sloped, straight-line function of systematic risk. This statistical straight line, however, is not the same line as the theoretical security market line *(SML)*. The parameters of the *SML* are carefully defined by security pricing theory. In theory, the vertical intercept of the *SML* shows the rate of return on riskless securities, and the *SML's* slope is the difference between the expected rate of return on the market portfolio and the riskless rate of return. In studies, however, the statistical estimates of the parameters are not equal to their theoretical values. The statistical value of the intercept is higher, and the slope is less than theory predicts (see Figure 6-5). Apparently, the simple security pricing model provides an inadequate description of the real world.

There are several possible explanations of why the statistically estimated relation has a higher intercept and lower slope than theory predicts. One explanation is that real-world investors cannot go into debt and borrow at the riskless rate of interest. The rate of interest paid by investors for funds to finance the market portfolio is higher than the interest rate paid by the U.S. Treasury when it borrows. The higher rate paid by investors reflects the risk or probability of their defaulting on their loans. Thus, to the extent that the statistical intercept reflects a default-risk premium on debt-financed holdings of the market portfolio, we would expect it to be higher than the risk-free rate.

Another explanation derives from the fact that real-world investors seldom

[3]See Jensen (Autumn 1972) for a review and summary of some of the principal empirical studies.

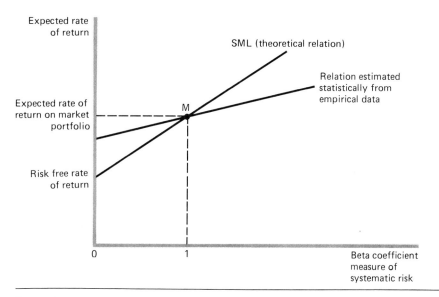

figure 6-5 Expected Rate of Return As a Function of Systematic Risk.

actually hold the market portfolio. Investors do diversify, but they do not diversify perfectly. The absence of perfect diversification means that unsystematic risk probably cannot be totally ignored. If unsystematic risk does have a price in the market, we would expect the rate of return on a zero-beta risky security to be higher than the totally riskless rate of return indicated by the theoretical intercept. The higher statistical intercept might thus reflect some element of unsystematic risk in securities having little or no systematic risk.

Still another shortcoming of the basic theory of security pricing is that it fails to account for the effect of uncertain inflation on the systematic risk of real rates of return. Because inflation is uncertain, all nominal rates of return are risky in terms of purchasing-power risk. The riskless rate of return is no exception. Although its market or nominal rate of return is perfectly certain, its real rate of return is as uncertain as inflation itself. When inflation is greater than expected, the real rate of return on nominally riskless securities is less than expected. In addition, the real rate of return on the market portfolio of risky securities is also affected. This means not only that the nominally riskless rate of return is a risky real rate, but that its risk in real terms is *systematically* related to the risk of the market portfolio. In real terms, then, even so-called riskless securities have some systematic risk. This leads to still another reason why the statistical intercept might be higher than the theoretical intercept of the basic security pricing model. The difference between the two intercepts may indicate the need to account for systematic purchasing-power risk.

The theory of security pricing has made dramatic inroads into our thinking about risk and return. However, the theory is still in the process of being more fully developed. A major area of development is to incorporate the effect of uncertain inflation on systematic risk. Another area is to reexamine the role of unsystematic risk. The fact that investors do not diversify perfectly makes it difficult to believe that unsystematic risk has no effect on the risk structure of expected rates of return. But this raises an interesting question: Why do investors expose themselves to unsystematic risk since this risk is avoidable?

PROJECTS AND QUESTIONS

1. Under what conditions is the optimal combination of risky securities for an investor independent of his or her preferences toward risk and return?
2. Under what conditions should the investor choose the market portfolio as his or her optimal combination of risky securities?
3. Security X is priced in the market to yield a 9 percent expected rate of return. New information reveals that (a) the standard deviation of return on security X is 2 percent, (b) the standard deviation of return on the market portfolio is 1 percent, (c) the correlation of security X's returns with returns on the market portfolio is .3, (d) the expected rate of return on the market portfolio is 10 percent, and (3) the riskless rate of return is 5 percent. As a financial economist, would you expect the market price of security X to change given this new information? If so, in what direction?
4. Reconstruct Figure 6-2 on the assumption that investors can borrow only a rate of interest that is higher than the rate of return on riskless securities. What are the implications of your reconstruction in terms of the separation theorem, the capital market line, and the security market line?
5. How do you account for the fact that so many investors expose themselves to unsystematic risk since this risk can be diversified away by holding the market portfolio?
6. In the real world, are there any completely riskless assets? If so, what are they? If not, what is the least risky asset that one can hold?
7. Assume that each and every risky security in the market is equilibrium priced to earn the same expected rate of return and to have the same standard deviation of return. In this case, each and every risky security will have the same systematic and unsystematic risk measurements. In addition, each and every portfolio combination of these risky securities will also have the same systematic and unsystematic risk measurements. Thus, in this case, all portfolio combinations are equally desirable, even if returns between individual securities are less than perfectly correlated. Is this reasoning correct?

BIBLIOGRAPHY

Baumol, W.J.: *Portfolio Theory: The Selection of Asset Combinations,* General Learning Press, Morristown, N. J., 1970.

Black, F.: "Capital Market Equilibrium with Restricted Borrowing," *Journal of Business,* July 1972, pp. 444–454.

Blume, M.E., and I. Friend: "A New Look at the Capital Asset Pricing Model," *Journal of Finance,* March 1973, pp. 19–33.

Francis, J.C., and S.H. Archer: *Portfolio Analysis,* Prentice-Hall, Englewood Cliffs, N. J., 1979.

————: *Investments,* McGraw-Hill, New York, 1976.

Friend, I., Y. Landskroner, and E. Losq: "The Demand for Risky Assets Under Uncertain Inflation," *Journal of Finance,* December 1976, pp. 1287–1297.

Jensen, M.C.: "Capital Markets: Theory and Evidence," *Bell Journal of Economics and Management Science,* Autumn 1972, pp. 357–398.

————, ed.: *Studies in the Theory of Capital Markets,* Praeger, New York, 1972.

Lintner, J.: "Inflation and Security Returns," *Journal of Finance,* May 1975, pp. 259–280.

Markowitz, H.M.: "Portfolio Selection," *Journal of Finance,* March 1952, pp. 77–91.

————: *Portfolio Selection: Efficient Diversification of Investments,* Wiley, New York, 1959.

Sharpe, W.F.: "A Simplified Model for Portfolio Analysis," *Management Science,* January 1963, pp. 277–293.

————: "Capital Asset Prices: A Theory of Market Equilibrium Under Conditions of Risk," *Journal of Finance,* September 1964, pp. 425–442.

————: *Portfolio Theory and Capital Markets,* McGraw-Hill, New York, 1970.

Tobin, J.: "Liquidity Preference as Behavior Towards Risk," *Review of Economic Studies,* February 1958, pp. 65–86.

chapter 7
Structure of Interest Rates

We have seen how expected rate of return varies with risk. Interest rates, the returns promised by debt instruments, are no exception. High-risk debt is priced in the market to return a higher rate of interest than low-risk debt. Interest rates on debt obligations, however, are generally lower than expected rates of return on common stocks owing to the greater riskiness of investing in stocks.

The number of market interest rates is as large as the number of outstanding debt issues traded in the market; they number in the thousands. Every market interest rate is different because every debt issue represents a unique mixture of various risk elements, tax features, and maturity dates. We obviously cannot examine the differences between all yields quoted in the market, but we will analyze yield differentials between some of the interest rate indexes kept for different classifications of debt instruments.

The *Federal Reserve Bulletin* (published monthly) includes seven pages of interest rate data. One of these pages carries interest rate indexes for thirty-six classifications of open-market instruments. We have selected, in Table 7-1, just four of the thirty-six interest rate classifications in order to introduce the major elements influencing the structure of interest rates. The bottom half of Table 7-1 shows the differences between the Aaa corporate bond rate and the other three interest rates selected.

What explains the interest rate differentials given in Table 7-1? And why do they change over time?

The spread between the corporate bond yield and the U.S. government bond yield reflects differences in risk. Holders of corporate bonds are exposed to the "risk of default" of interest and principal. The market yield is a promised yield, not a guaranteed yield. A broken promise means that the promised yield will not be realized. Treasury bonds, on the other hand, are riskless in terms of

TABLE 7-1
Selected Interest Rates and Interest Rate Differentials

	1975	1976	1977
SELECTED INTEREST RATES			
(1) Aaa corporate bonds	8.83%	8.43%	8.02%
(2) U.S. Treasury bonds	6.98	6.78	7.06
(3) Aaa municipal bonds	6.42	5.66	5.20
(4) 3-Month commercial paper	6.26	5.24	5.54
SELECTED INTEREST RATE DIFFERENTIALS			
(1 − 2) Corporate bond rate minus Treasury bond rate	1.85%	1.65%	.96%
(1 − 3) Corporate bond rate minus municipal bond rate	2.41	2.77	2.82
(1 − 4) Corporate bond rate minus commercial paper rate	2.57	3.19	2.48

SOURCE: *Federal Reserve Bulletin*, December 1978, p. A27.

default. The federal government can always keep its promises through its powers to tax and to print money. Interest rates on corporate bonds are thus higher than rates on Treasury bonds in order to compensate for the risk of default. Corporate bond yields are also higher to compensate for the fact that corporate bonds are not as marketable as Treasury bonds.

The difference between the corporate bond yield and the Treasury bond yield also includes a premium for "call risk." Most corporate bonds issued contain a call feature that gives the issuer the option to buy back the bonds at a specified call price before the bonds mature. Since bonds are usually called at the worst possible times from the point of view of those who hold them, it takes a higher market rate on callable bonds in order to compensate holders for the risk of call. Treasury bonds can also be callable, typically when they are close to maturity, but the index presented in Table 7-1 excludes all Treasury bonds callable within ten years.

The spread between the corporate bond yield and the municipal bond yield is very large. This spread cannot be explained in terms of differential risk of default because both yields are rated Aaa, which means that both are bonds of high quality (though not necessarily of the same quality). The spread does include some call risk because municipal bonds are less frequently callable. Most of the spread, however, is due to the exemption of interest on municipal bonds from taxable income. The municipal bond rates shown in Table 7-1 represent returns both before and after taxes. This does not hold for corporate bonds, however. Interest on corporate bonds is taxable. If an investor is in a 40-percent tax bracket, the after-tax return is only 60 percent of the before-tax return on corporate bonds. Market rates on corporate bonds are thus higher than they are on municipal bonds in order to compensate for the tax-exempt advantage of the latter. We will find that there are other tax features at work in the tax structure of interest rates.

Finally, the spread between the corporate bond rate and the interest rate on short-term commercial paper is the largest of the three shown in Table 7-1. This spread does not owe to differential default risk because the corporations that sell commercial paper cannot possibly be any more creditworthy than the corporations that issue the highest-quality bonds. In fact, most commercial paper is sold by corporations creditworthy enough to issue Aaa bonds. Neither does the spread owe to differential tax treatment. Interest on commercial paper is just as taxable as interest on corporate bonds. In terms of call risk, commercial paper obviously has none since maturity and face-value redemption come so quickly. The call risk of corporate bonds might explain part of the spread, but it is difficult to conceive that it would explain any more than a tiny fraction of it. Marketability factors could also account for some measure of difference between the two yields, but not a whole lot.

The primary difference between corporate bonds and commercial paper is the term (or period) to maturity. Corporate bonds are long-term debt instruments; commercial paper is short-term. Do differences in term to maturity lead to differences in yield to maturity? Definitely yes. We will find that the term structure of interest rates is frequently the dominant structure when it comes to explaining the difference between the highest interest rates and the lowest rates in the market. We will also find that the spread can go either way: Long-term yields to maturity can be higher than short-term yields (as they are in Table 7-1), or lower (as they were at times in 1974 and in 1978 and 1979). Finally we will find that there is no simple connection between maturity and risk, nor between yields to maturity and the yields expected by investors who do not plan to hold to maturity.

The four interest rates presented in Table 7-1 have thus allowed us to identify four different structures of interest rates: (1) the default risk structure, (2) the call risk structure, (3) the tax structure, and (4) the term structure. The different time periods shown in Table 7-1 indicate that these four structures vary over time. Interest rate differentials are always changing. The reasons for changes have to do with changing market conditions, changes in risk perceptions, changes in expectations, changes in tax exposure, etc. We will examine these factors as we analyze the four interest rate structures in detail in the sections to follow.

THE DEFAULT RISK STRUCTURE OF INTEREST RATES

"Default risk" refers to the possibility of not collecting interest and principal of the promised amount at the promised time. Virtually all capital market securities are subject to some degree of default risk except those issued by the federal government. The government always has the power to tax or to print money if it should get into financial difficulty. Private corporations, of course, do not have this power; they cannot guarantee that their promises will be kept. Why, then, should investors invest in privately issued securities? The answer is for the extra expected yield. A corporate bond may not be as good a promise as a Treasury bond, but it promises a higher yield—so much higher that the expected yield (after allowing for the probability that the promise will be broken) is sufficiently above the yield on the Treasury bond to compensate the investor for the extra risk.

The only objective measure of the market's assessment of default risk is the differential between the promised yield of a risky bond and the yield on a Treasury bond of equal maturity, callability, etc. This differential is called the "default risk premium." It overstates the true compensation for risk, however, because promised yield is greater than expected yield on all bonds subject to default risk. Theoretically, we would prefer to indicate risk by the difference between the expected yield (allowing for default possibilities and their probabilities) and the yield on a Treasury bond. But in the case of default risk, expected yield is an extremely subjective concept. Attempts to estimate expected yield objectively, from past default experience and yields realized in the past, have proved cumbersome and unsuccessful.

Default risk premiums observed in the market, at any point in time, vary for bonds issued by different corporations. Risk premiums also vary on the bonds of the same corporation at different points in time. This suggests that the risk of default is determined by two broad factors: (1) the internal risk position of the corporate issuer, and (2) the external environment or economic climate within which the corporate issuer operates.

A firm's risk position is conditioned by several elements. One is the ability of the firm to generate enough cash to cover interest and principal payments. A measure of this ability is the coverage ratio:

$$\frac{\text{Expected cash flow before contractual interest and principal payments}}{\text{Contractual interest and principal payments}}$$

Naturally, the higher the coverage ratio, the less the degree of default risk. We would expect, therefore, that low default risk premiums reflect, in part, high coverage ratios and related measures of financial conservatism.

Another element determining the firm's risk position is the variability of the cash flow that provides the coverage. It is not enough for expected cash flow to more than cover interest and principal payments. If the cash flow is variable, a firm may not be able to meet its promises in a bad year, even though it easily covers them in good years. The more variable earnings are, the greater the degree of default risk.

The business risk that is indicated by the variability of the firm's cash flow from operations is largely beyond the control of the firm's financial management. Business risk depends mainly on the type of business—stable or unstable—that the firm is in. The financial risk that is indicated by the firm's coverage ratio, on the other hand, can be controlled. The denominator of the coverage ratio depends on how much debt the firm uses to finance its assets. By

TABLE 7-2
Bond Rating Classifications

	Moody's	Standard and Poor's
1. Highest quality	Aaa	AAA
2. High quality	Aa	AA
3. Upper medium quality	A	A
4. Medium to lower medium quality (marginal investment grade)	Baa	BBB-BB
5. Speculative (not investment grade)	Ba-B	B
6. In default or high probability of default	Caa and below	CCC and below

going easy on the use of debt—substituting high-cost equity financing for debt—the firm can reduce financial risk and increase its coverage ratio. Thus, firms with variable operating cash flows can keep risk in check by going easy on the use of debt. Firms with stable cash flows, on the other hand, can afford to be more aggressive in the use of debt financing.

Studies indicate that the coverage ratio, earnings variability, and other accounting measures of business and financial risk are significant determinants of the default risk premium observed in the market. In his now-classic study, Hickman (1958) found close relations between market yields (and, hence, risk premiums) and a number of underlying ratios measuring internal risk. Using multiple regression analysis, Fisher (June 1959) found that the default risk premium is significantly related to earnings variability, period of solvency, and capital structure. These findings have been generally reaffirmed in subsequent studies conducted under the auspices of the National Bureau of Economic Research (NBER).

The ordinary investor does not have the resources to analyze the underlying risk elements or to estimate the overall risk position of each firm whose bonds he or she is considering investing. Instead, one is apt to rely on bond ratings prepared by professional bond rating agencies. For many years a number of agencies have assigned ratings that express their judgment as to the quality of bonds. The two major agencies in this field and the ratings they use are shown in Table 7-2.

In general, the various agencies attach about the same absolute standards to each of the rating classifications. It is significant, however, that a given security may be rated differently by various agencies. This only illustrates the fact that fundamental credit analysis cannot produce exact results and still depends ultimately on personal judgment.[1]

Still, the ratings are pretty good general indicators of default risk. As shown

[1]A number of studies, summarized in Ang and Patel (May 1975), demonstrates that about two-thirds of bond ratings can be correctly predicted by using multiple regression analysis of published accounting information.

in Figure 7-1, bonds with Aaa ratings have lower yields and carry smaller risk premiums, on the average, than Baa-rated bonds. But, remember, this is only an average relationship. The yields shown in Figure 7-1 are average yields for all bonds within the rating classification. Within each classification, individual bonds deviate from the average. Sometimes these deviations overlap with deviations from the next highest or lowest rating. For example, a bond with an Aa rating can have a higher yield than an A-rated bond. Such overlap does not necessarily mean that the rating is incorrect. It often means that the bonds are not identical in all respects other than risk of default.

In addition to the bond issuer's internal risk position, the default risk premium is determined by the firm's external environment, particularly the stage of the business cycle. Most defaults actually occur during depressions and severe recessions. A marginally rated bond may not be able to weather the storm of a depression, but it will keep from defaulting if there is no storm to weather. Some evidence on the average annual rate of default—measured by the percentage of the par amount of corporate bonds not in default at the beginning of the year that went into default during the year—was compiled by Atkinson (1967). He found that the default rate was eighty times as great in the Great Depression years of the 1930s as it was in the relatively prosperous years of the 1950s.

Figure 7-1 shows some tendency for default risk premiums to enlarge during periods of economic recession. The widening of the premium on lower-rated bonds is especially pronounced because they are more vulnerable than highly rated bonds to default during adverse economic conditions. The cyclical impact on risk premiums is tighter than one would surmise from studying Figure 7-1 because that figure reflects both cyclical and noncyclical influences. Sloane (1967) studied and measured the cyclical influence on risk premiums for the 1954–1959 period using regression analysis. His results led him to conclude that the 1957–1958 recession explained much of the widening of risk premiums and that the widening effect was greater for lower-quality bonds. More recent cyclical variations in the risk structure of interest rates have been studied by Jaffee (July 1975). He found that yield differentials between Baa grade and higher-grade bonds have varied positively with adverse economic conditions.

A remaining question is whether or not default risk premiums reflect the true risk of default. Some observers contend that risk premiums (on lower-quality bonds particularly) have been larger than warranted on the basis of actual default experience. Not all observers agree, but even if it is true, ex post default experience is not the correct basis for judging risk premiums. The risk premium is the market's assessment of ex ante default risk. By definition, it reflects a market consensus of the probability of future default. The real question is whether or not the participants in the market are informed and rational. If there is a continual one-sided discrepancy between ex ante default risk and ex post default experience, it would suggest that the market is not well informed, or not very rational, or both. In any event, the risk premium reflects only the current odds of future default; it does not categorically predict that default will or will not occur.

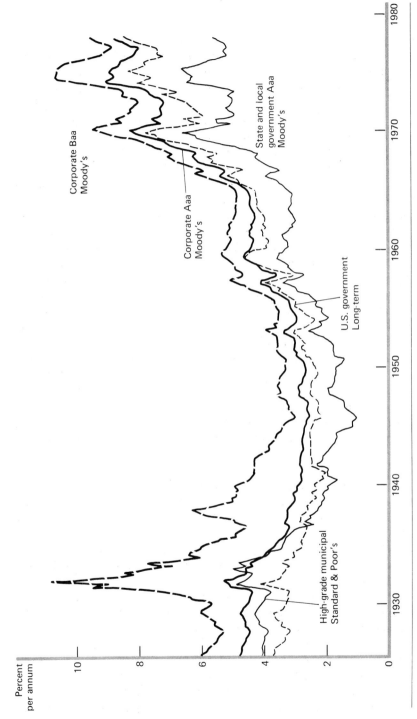

figure 7-1 Long-term Bond Yields. (*Source: Board of Governors of the Federal Reserve System.*)

DEFAULT RISK AND BANKRUPTCY PROPENSITY

One lesson from the Great Depression of the 1930s was that financial prudence does not guarantee survival in an external environment of economic adversity. Many highly rated bonds defaulted and many firms were forced into bankruptcy during this period because of conditions beyond the firm's control. A lesson from the relatively calm years of the 1950s was that prudent financial management is not necessarily required for survival in an environment of relative stability. Most marginally managed firms survived this period because the environment carried them through. By the 1960s, there was growing consensus that bankruptcy was no longer an important economic problem. President Kennedy's brain trust of "new economists" were telling the people that economic stability could be guaranteed through government action, that depression (and therefore bankruptcy) was a relic of history.

One of the lessons from the 1970s was that the difference between survival and failure is much more than a matter of external economic environment. Some of the nation's largest firms went into bankruptcy basically because of internal financial weakness. In 1970, the nation's largest railroad system—the Penn-Central—entered bankruptcy. This was followed over the next several years by other prominent defaults and failures, including the Franklin National Bank (one of banking's largest), the City of New York (obviously the largest municipality), and W.T. Grant (a very large chain of department stores). Why did these giants and scores of smaller firms get into financial difficulty? Unfavorable external environment was not the main underlying cause; rather, environment was the tip of the iceberg that influenced the timing of collapse. In every case there were signs of internal financial distress long before failure actually happened.

Can bankruptcy be confidently predicted in advance? How well do bond yields and bond ratings measure financial distress and the probability of eventual collapse?

Because bond ratings are intended to measure internal financial strength, one might expect them to be reasonably good indicators of the probability of bond default and firm bankruptcy. To some extent this is true. The incidence of eventual default on high-rated bonds is considerably less than it is on low-rated bonds. Nevertheless, the ratings are rather poor predictors on several counts. For one thing, they have little or no predictive value beyond two to four years after a bond has been rated. In general, bonds are rated before they are sold to the public. At best, the rating of a new issue indicates the risk of default and the propensity for bankruptcy for no more than four years into a bond's period to maturity. Ratings are reviewed and if necessary revised periodically, but the amount of time and energy that goes into this process is rather minor compared to the rating of a new issue of bonds. For another thing, the rating scale used by rating agencies does not match up well with the risk of default. Before 1940, the default experience of Aaa bonds was not statistically different than it was for Aa bonds. Since 1940, the default experience has been virtually indistinguishable on all bonds rated between Aaa and Baa. These bonds rarely default. Is there any reason, therefore, to have so many grades of ratings within a range where the differential risk of default is so narrow?

Bond yields are little or no better than ratings in terms of their ability to predict bankruptcy before the fact. At time of offering, yield is determined largely by rating. As a bond seasons, its yield adjusts to changing financial conditions within the firm. More often than not, however, yields adjust to actual after-the-fact conditions rather than to expected before-the-fact events. In the Penn-Central case, for example, the market yields on Penn-Central bonds provided no indication that the company was in extreme financial distress until after the collapse was already a fact. In other words, since bond yields have tended to move concurrently with financial conditions, they have not been very good leading indicators of default and bankruptcy.

Is there no way, then, to predict bankruptcy with a high level of confidence and without the benefit of hindsight? Some observers think that bankruptcy is predictable. They contend that the Penn-Central failure and others could have been predicted as early as several years in advance from then-existing accounting data available to the public. The methods advocated for predicting bankruptcy vary from old-fashioned fundamental ratio analysis to the use of statistically sophisticated multiple discriminant analysis.[2] Whether or not recent bankruptcies could have been predicted by one or more of these methods, the fact remains that they were not. Until research is directed towards advance detection of future bankruptcies, rather than exploring past bankruptcies that could have been predicted, the best method for predicting bankruptcy remains to be discovered.

The surest way for a firm to avoid bankruptcy is, of course, to keep its financial house in order. The main lessons learned by the survivors of the 1970s bankruptcy wave are (1) to go easy on debt financing when operating earnings are unstable, (2) to go easy on short-term borrowing when operating assets are illiquid, and (3) to pay much more attention to expected cash flow and bank balances than to reported earnings and assets.

THE CALL RISK STRUCTURE OF INTEREST RATES

Call risk is the opposite of default risk. Most corporate bond issues have a call option that permits the issuer to buy back the bonds at a specified call price before the bonds mature. Holders of callable bonds run the risk of having their bonds called and getting their money back before they voluntarily want it back. This is the reverse of default risk, where the holders run the risk of getting their money back later than they want it back, or, worse yet, never getting it back.

The call price of a bond usually bears a close relationship to the bond's offering price and coupon rate. For example, a bond sold at $100 par with an annual coupon of $5 will have a call price close to $105. The call price over the

---

[2] The application of multiple discriminant analysis to prediction of bankruptcy is developed in Altman (September 1968). See Murray (May 1971) for a fundamental analysis of the Penn-Central failure.

life of the bond declines toward par as the bond matures. At maturity, the call price is equal to par value.

The market price of a callable bond varies inversely with bond yields in the market except that the call price sets a ceiling on market price. As market yield falls, market price rises, but it stops rising once it reaches the call price or a price a point or two above call price. For example, investors will not pay more than a point or two above $105 for a bond that can be called at $105. No rational investor wants to invite a large and immediate capital loss.

Because call price sets a ceiling on market price, holders of callable bonds are limited in the amount of capital gains that, in the event of declining market yields, could be realized were the bonds not callable. Callability is thus a disadvantage to investors because it limits price appreciation. Moreover, there are other disadvantages. Bonds are usually called when market yields are low; issuers call when refinancing is attractive. Thus bondholders interested in long-term yields have to relinquish their bonds and reinvest at lower yields; further, they have to incur the transaction cost of reinvestment. Finally, there is the disadvantage of uncertainty. A bond may never be called, but the holder is never sure. Uncertainty as to the amount and continuity of future returns hangs over the head of every holder of a callable bond.

These disadvantages have to be offset in order for callable bonds to sell. The offset usually takes the form of a higher yield. The call risk structure of bond yields is: higher yields for callable bonds than for noncallable bonds, all other things the same. There is some question, however, whether the higher yield of callable bonds fully compensates for the risk of call. In one study, Jen and Wert (December 1967) concluded that it does not—that the extra yield on callable bonds over noncallable bonds is frequently a "yield illusion" that call risk is fully adjusted. This conclusion, although debatable, raises an interesting question: Is the degree of call risk expected before the fact low relative to that experienced after the fact?

The degree of call risk is determined largely by two features of bond instruments: (1) the length of the call deferment and (2) the level of the coupon rate. The call deferment is the period of time after a bond is issued within which the option to call cannot be exercised. This period can be as short as zero in the case of immediately callable bonds, or as long as the period to maturity in the case of noncallable bonds. Call deferment periods have varied widely depending on market conditions.

Call risk is an inverse function of a bond's remaining call-deferment period. A long deferment has a less limiting effect on price appreciation and reduces uncertainty in general. Bonds that offer protection against call during the call-deferment period do not require as high yields as bonds without this protection. The effect of call deferment on the structure of bond yields has been measured in studies by Jen and Wert (June 1968), Pye (December 1967), Frankena (1971), Ederington (December 1974), and others. These studies indicate that corporate bond yields vary inversely with the period of call-deferment protection.

The coupon rate is the contractual interest payment taken as a percentage of the face or par value of the bond. A $1000 bond that pays $50 annual interest has an annual coupon rate of 5 percent.

Call risk is a positive function of the coupon rate. There are two reasons for this. First, the temptation for the issuing corporation to call and refinance is greater the higher the coupon rate the corporation is paying. For example, if the market rate of interest is 4 percent, a bond with a 5-percent coupon rate might be called whereas one with a 3-percent coupon rate would not. Second, high coupon bonds sell at higher market prices than low coupon bonds. Market rates do not have to fall much to push the price of a high coupon bond against the call price ceiling, but they have to fall considerably before the price of a low coupon bond reaches the ceiling. High coupon bonds thus have more limited capital gains potential than low coupon bonds. Because high coupon bonds are more likely to be called, and because they are more limited in their capital gains potential, they should be priced in the market to earn higher yields. Studies by Jen and Wert (December 1967), Frankena (1971), and others indicate that this is the case for corporate bonds.

Finally, we should note that the coupon rate effect on the call risk structure of interest rates is not constant over time. What matters over time is the relation between coupon rates and market rates of interest and the direction in which market rates are expected to change. Even bonds with relatively high coupon rates stand little chance of being called when market rates are above coupon rates and rising. Such was the case in 1964 and 1965 when the spread between yields on callable bonds and those on noncallable bonds tended to vanish. On the other hand, when market interest rates reach new depths, the risk of call can reach even those bonds with relatively low coupon rates. This is especially true when the market reaches a new low and this low is thought to be the trough of an interest rate cycle. Many high coupon instruments issued during the high market rate years of 1974 and 1975 were called back in 1976 and 1977 when interest rates dropped but were not expected to drop further. Well-seasoned bonds with pre-1970s coupon rates were not called, however, since these rates remained below market rates. Indeed, without a sharp drop in the level of expected inflation, bonds issued prior to 1966 stand little chance of ever being called, regardless of coupon rate.

THE TAX STRUCTURE OF INTEREST RATES

Coupon rate differentials lead to yield differentials on noncallable bonds as well as on callable bonds. The differentials on noncallable bonds cannot be attributed to the call risk of high coupon bonds because noncallables have no call risk. Instead, they can be explained in terms of tax effects. In this section we find that there is a tax structure of interest rates. According to one source, "In a random sample of bond yields, tax factors would probably account for almost as much of the variability as default risk or maturity."[3]

High coupon bonds tend to have higher before-tax yields than low coupon

[3]Pye (November 1969).

bonds. The reason for this, apart from call risk, is the fact that capital gains are taxed at an effective tax rate that is considerably less than the tax rate applied to interest income. Investors naturally prefer to receive capital gains over interest because it increases after-tax returns. If two bonds have the same before-tax yield, the bond with the lower coupon rate will provide proportionately less interest and proportionately more capital gains than the bond with the higher coupon rate. On an after-tax basis, the lower coupon bond outperforms the higher coupon bond. Investors tend therefore to bid up the prices (and bid down the before-tax yields) of low coupon bonds relative to high coupon bonds until the after-tax returns are equivalent. Thus high coupon bonds have higher before-tax yields than low coupon bonds owing to the differential tax system.

The coupon rate effect on the tax structure of interest rates on U.S. government securities has been substantial, as reported in studies by Pye (November 1969), Robichek and Niebuhr (December 1970), and McCulloch (June 1975). Less is known about the significance of this effect as it applies to the corporate bond market, however. In one study, Frankena (1971) concluded that the effect is negligible, at least compared to the coupon rate effect on the call risk structure of corporate bond yields.

Another and very significant element of the tax structure of interest rates is the tax-exempt status of state and local government securities. Interest income from these securities is exempted from federal income taxes. As a result, yields on tax-exempt securities are considerably lower than before-tax yields on nonexempt securities. If we turn back a few pages and take another look at Figure 7-1, we can see that the yield on high-grade municipal bonds has varied in the range of 60 to 75 percent of the before-tax yield on high-grade corporate bonds. On the average, municipal bond yields have been about two-thirds of yields (before taxes) on corporate bonds. This means that municipal bonds have averaged the same after-tax yield as corporate bonds for investors whose marginal tax rate is 33 percent. (If the yield on municipals is two-thirds of the before-tax yield on corporates, taxing away one-third of the latter makes the two yields equivalent on an after-tax basis.) For investors in marginal tax brackets below 33 percent, the tax advantage is usually insufficient to induce investment in the lower-yielding tax-exempts. But for investors in higher brackets, municipal bonds usually outperform corporate bonds. The general formula for determining whether to invest in municipals is to take the percentage of the tax-exempt yield to the nonexempt yield, before taxes, and subtract it from one. If the result is less than the investor's marginal income tax rate, it pays to invest in municipal bonds rather than corporate bonds.

Because of tax exemption, the market for municipal securities is relatively segmented. Commercial banks, wealthy individuals, and casualty insurance companies dominate the market. These investors are in relatively high tax brackets and are therefore able to reap higher effective returns on municipal bonds than on corporate bonds. The corporate bond market, on the other hand, appeals to a group of institutional investors, investors who are not taxed or are taxed at very low rates. For this group, municipal bonds have no advantage.

The differential between corporate and municipal bond yields changes over time (see Figure 7-1) in response to changing supply and demand conditions in each of the relatively segmented markets. The municipal bond market is far from a totally segmented market, however. It is closely linked to the market for short-term bank credit. When short-term credit is tight, commercial banks tend to drop out of the municipal bond market and put their funds into short-term loans to their business customers. The effect of this is to depress municipal bond prices and drive up their yields. The municipal bond market is also linked to the stock market. When stock prices are advancing in a bull market, many wealthy individuals switch out of municipals and buy stocks. Again, the effect is to drive up tax-exempt yields.

The tax-exempt status of municipal bonds is very controversial. Studies indicate that for every dollar of taxes that would otherwise be paid to the federal government if these bonds were not tax-exempt, state and local governments save only about 70 cents in interest expense as a result of tax exemption.[4] The remaining 30 cents goes to high-tax-bracket investors who earn higher after-tax interest than they would if tax-exempt securities were not available. Many critics of the system think that this is unfair, that banks and wealthy individuals should not be subsidized in this way.

So why does tax exemption persist? There have been many proposals for reform, many of them recommending removal of the tax-exempt status, with the federal government returning the taxes received on interest income from municipal bonds to the states and localities that issue them. In this way, the local governments would save a dollar in interest expense for every dollar of taxes paid to the federal government. Proposals of this type have not become law, partly because of reluctance of local governments, themselves, to get involved with the federal government. Many local governments, however, do endorse in principle the option to issue either tax-exempt bonds or taxable bonds (with a proportion of the interest cost reimbursed by the federal government).

Unlike interest, capital gains on municipal securities are not exempt from federal income taxes. Investors in municipals thus prefer interest to capital gains, which means they prefer high coupons to low coupons. The coupon rate effect is therefore reversed for tax-exempt securities. In this case, low coupon securities have higher yields than high coupon securities. The higher yields compensate for tax loss on capital gains.

One other anomaly still to be discussed is the differential tax treatment of equity securities as against debt securities. The traditional view that equity securities represent ownership has led to a tax status in which dividends paid out are not a deductible expense before computation of corporate income taxes. Interest expense on debt obligations, of course, is deductible. Preferred stock, admittedly, has the legal aspects of equity but the practical role of debt. Since preferred dividends are not tax deductible, this form of corporate financing has receded in use and importance. However, since only 15 percent of preferred dividends are treated as taxable income when such securities are held by corporate investors, preferred stocks have found a good reception on the part of some corporate investors, particularly since interest income from bonds is

[4]Fortune (May 1973).

totally taxable. How, then, do yields on preferred stocks compare to corporate bond yields? The answer is not simple. Because preferred dividends are less certain than bond interest, yields on preferred stocks should be higher. But since preferred stock has a tax disadvantage to the issuer and a tax advantage to corporate investors, the market yield on preferred (which is before taxes) can go lower.

THE TERM STRUCTURE OF INTEREST RATES

"The term structure of interest rates" is the name given to the functional relation between yield to maturity and term to maturity (or period to maturity). This relation is easiest to examine when graphed in the form of a yield curve. Annual yield to maturity is measured on the vertical axis and period to maturity on the horizontal. The curve depicts yield as a function of maturity when all other factors affecting yield are held constant. Since no two securities are identical in all respects other than maturity, yield curves constructed from empirical observations can only approximate the true relation.

The slope and shape of a yield curve constantly change as market conditions change, but two general forms always appear. The most frequent form is the *ascending* yield curve, where yield to maturity is a positive function of period to maturity. The less frequent form is the *descending* yield curve. In this case yield is a negative function of maturity. Figure 7-2 shows these two general forms and the years during which they prevailed.

An examination of Figure 7-2 leads to two general observations. First, yield

figure 7-2   Yield Curves, 1930–1977.

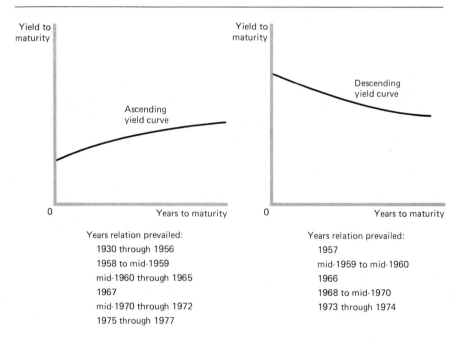

Years relation prevailed:

1930 through 1956	1957
1958 to mid-1959	mid-1959 to mid-1960
mid-1960 through 1965	1966
1967	1968 to mid-1970
mid-1970 through 1972	1973 through 1974
1975 through 1977	

curves take on different shapes at different times. And second, the ascending yield curve is the most common of all; on the average, long-term yields are higher than short-term yields. These two observations lead in turn to two questions. First, do the years in which nonascending yield curves prevail differ significantly in some important respect from the ascending years so as to explain the shifting forms? And second, why is the yield curve ascending on the average?

Let us begin by studying Figure 7-3. Observe that interest rates rose to unusually high levels in the period since 1965. During this period both short-term and long-term rates were well above what might be considered the normal interest rate level. At the same time that all rates were high, short-term rates were sometimes even higher than long-term rates. Is there a connection? Different theories of the term structure say yes, but for different reasons.

One theory, the pure expectations theory, explains the term structure in terms of what investors expect future interest rates will be. When interest rates are abnormally high, investors form expectations of lower future rates. The effect of expected lower future rates is to raise the current short-term rate above the long-term rate—hence the descending yield curve.

Why is this?

The pure expectations theory assumes that investors are out to maximize expected return over their holding periods. (A holding period is the period of time during which an investor plans to hold securities.) Their choice between short-term and long-term securities to hold is governed solely by whichever term offers the higher return. To illustrate the nature of this choice, suppose that there are only two securities to choose between: one-year "short term" securities and two-year "long-term" securities. Suppose that both pay a yearly coupon of $5, both have a face value of $100, and both currently yield 5 percent a year, so that the current price is $100 on both. Now suppose market rates are expected to fall to 4 percent next year. If investors hold the two-year security and they have a two-year holding period, their net return is $10 in interest. If, instead they hold the one-year security, they will get $5 interest the first year, reinvest their principal, and expect to get $4 the second year for a two-year total of $9 interest. Clearly, as expected return maximizers, they are better off with the long-term, two-year security. But what if their holding period is just one year? If they hold the one-year security, their net return is $5 interest. If instead they hold the two-year security, they will get $5 interest plus 97 cents in expected capital gains for a total return of $5.97. The capital gain is the difference between next year's price and this year's price of $100. Next year's price on a security that matures the following year is determined by the present value equation:

$$\frac{\text{Price}}{\substack{\text{(one year} \\ \text{before maturity)}}} = \frac{\text{interest} + \text{principal}}{1 + \text{yield}}$$

$$\$100.97 = \frac{\$5 + \$100}{1 + 4\%}$$

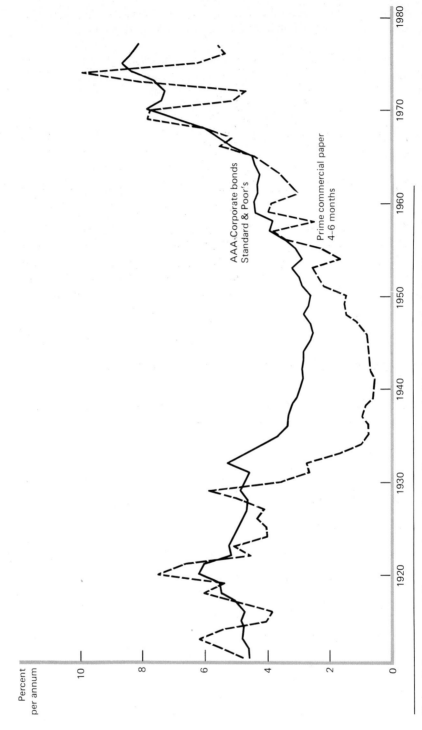

Percent
per annum

10

8

6

4

2

0

1920   1930   1940   1950   1960   1970   1980

AAA-Corporate bonds
Standard & Poor's

Prime commercial paper
4-6 months

figure 7-3   Long- and Short-term Interest Rates.   *(Source: Board of Governors of the Federal Reserve System.)*

Again, the investor is better off holding the long-term security because expected return is greater. If investors act upon their expectations, they will bid up the price of the long-term security and force its yield down from 5 percent. Similarly, they will sell off the short-term security, thereby raising its yield above 5 percent. This process will continue until equilibrium is reached and the two securities are equally profitable. The result will be a descending yield curve with short-term yields higher than long-term yields. This result occurs when the overall level of interest rates is so high that most investors expect that interest rates will fall.[5]

A rival explanation of the descending yield curve is provided by the segmented-markets theory. This theory assumes that investors are risk minimizers. The way to minimize risk is to match maturities with holding periods. If, in our example, investors have a two-year holding period, they will hold the two-year, long-term security not because they expect more return but because they are sure of getting their $10 total return. If, instead, they have a one-year holding period, they will prefer the one-year, short-term security and the sure return of $5. The two-year security has a $5.97 expected return, but if expectations fail to materialize, actual return might be less than the sure $5 return. Risk minimizers will forego possible capital gains in order to escape possible capital losses, and they will decline possible higher reinvestment rates in order to avoid possibly lower rates. The risk minimizer is interested only in those securities whose periods to maturity are equal to his or her holding period.

This behavior is assumed to operate on both sides of the market. Firms that need short-term funds will issue only short-term securities; those whose needs are long-term will issue only long-term securities. There is no substitution among securities of different lengths. As a consequence, the market for short-term securities is segmented from the long-term market and vice versa.[6] Yields in the different markets are determined solely by supply and demand conditions that operate in the separate markets. An explanation of the descending yield curve thus becomes obvious. If short-term rates are higher than long-term rates, it is because the demand for short-term funds is unusually strong, or the supply of short-term funds is very weak, or both. But why should this occur in the high interest-rate years of 1966, 1969, 1974, and the winter of 1978–1979? For one thing, these were times of very tight monetary policy; growth rates in the supply of money and short-term bank credit were exceptionally low. For another, these years tracked rising expectations of inflation. Since higher expected inflation increases the demand for funds and decreases the supply, we would expect interest rates to rise. And, to the extent that inflationary expectations are primarily short-term, we would particularly expect sharp increases in short-term rates.

Which theory is correct? Empirical studies by Meiselman (1962), Modigliani

[5]An opposite result is predicted when investors expect higher future rates. Such expectations are formed when interest rates are abnormally low. The general result of the pure expectations theory is that return is maximized in equilibrium when current long-term interest rates are equal to the average of current and expected short-term rates. See Lutz (November 1940).
[6]See Culbertson (November 1957).

and Sutch (May 1966), Malkiel (1966), and others suggest that both expectations of future interest rates and elements of market segmentation are at work, but that expectations dominate. Some empirical merging of the two theories is not surprising since the pure expectations theory looks only at return and disregards risk while the segmented market theory looks only at risk and ignores return. As we learned in the preceeding chapter, investors are generally neither return maximizers nor risk minimizers but are rather risk-return traders.

Now we turn to the question of why long-term rates are, on the average, higher than short-term rates. A generally ascending yield curve has been confirmed for high-grade corporate bonds and for U.S. government securities. Neither the pure expectations theory nor the segmented markets theory can satisfactorily explain this phenomenon. Over the long pull, investors should expect interest rates to fall just as often as they expect them to rise. If anything, the pure expectations theory should predict a generally flat yield curve. As for the segmented markets theory, one would have to assume that maturity needs are generally short for lenders and generally long for borrowers. The whole point of the segmented markets theory, however, is that different lenders and different borrowers have different maturity needs. On the lending side, banks do have short-term needs, but the needs of life insurance companies, pension funds, and individuals saving for retirement are strictly long-term. On the borrowing side, government and firms do need long-term funds, but their short-term requirements are equally substantial.

The generally ascending yield curve is consistent with a term structure theory known as "liquidity preference." This theory does not assume that investors are return maximizers, as does the pure expectations theory, nor does it assume that they are risk minimizers, as does the pure segmented-markets theory. Rather, it assumes that investors are risk-return traders. As such, they seek more than minimum risk, because that entails too little return; and they pursue less than maximum return, because that implies too much risk. The liquidity preference theory thus contains elements from both the expectations theory and the segmented markets theory. Expectations certainly matter, but so do risk preferences.

According to the liquidity preference theory, long-term securities are more risky, on balance, than short-term securities. The variance of return of capital value is greater for long-term securities than for short-term. On the other hand, the variance of return of interest income is greater for short-term securities than for long-term. If we assume that stability of capital is valued more highly than stability of interest (a preference for liquidity), long-term securities have a net risk disadvantage. Investors will accept this additional risk when long-term securities are priced to yield more. Greater return for greater risk explains the generally ascending yield curve. This view is taken in the empirical work of Kessel (1965).

A shortcoming of the liquidity preference approach to the term structure of interest rates is its assumption that investors are more averse to the risk of instability of capital value than to the risk of instability of interest income. Are investors really biased in this way? Is this assumption really necessary in order to explain the generally ascending yield curve? Perhaps not. If we follow the logic of the theory of portfolio selection and security pricing developed in Chapter 6, long-term securities should have higher expected yields than short-term securities if the systematic risk of total return (interest income plus capital gains) increases with term to maturity. In other words, it may be that long-term securities have higher expected returns than short-term securities merely because long-term securities may have greater systematic risk, and not because investors are more averse to one source of risk (variability of capital value) than to another (variability of interest income). Along these lines, Roll (March 1971) found that the systematic risk of return on Treasury securities increases with period to maturity. His analysis suggests that the yield curve ascends on the average as a result consistent with the theory of security pricing.

If it is true that long-term securities have more risk (whatever the source) than short-term securities, should not the yield curve always ascend, rather than just on the average? It would if investors always held securities to maturity, but since they do not, yield to maturity does not necessarily indicate a security's risk-adjusted rate of return. For reasons that will become apparent below, the "term structure of yields to maturity" can be interpreted as a "risk structure of holding-period yields" only under certain long-run conditions.

TERM STRUCTURE IN A WORLD OF UNCERTAIN INFLATION

None of the term structure theories discussed above considers the effect of uncertain inflation on the yield curve. We will attempt in this section to show that the generally ascending yield curve might be the result of inflation uncertainty.[7] Our analysis will require a few simplifying assumptions, but these will be relaxed as the analysis unfolds.

To start with, let us assume that investors in the market expect inflation and interest rates to stay the same in the future as they are currently. Moreover, let us assume that this expectation is held with perfect certainty. In this nonchanging world of no risk, the yield curve would be flat in accordance with the pure expectations theory. Bonds with different periods to maturity would have the same yield to maturity. Investors with different holding periods would get the same yield over their holding periods. All holding-period yields and all yields to maturity would be the same. Investors would be totally indifferent about the maturities of the bonds in their portfolios.

Such a world, of course, is so far removed from reality that it is not interesting. Let us therefore relax the assumption of perfect certainty of expectations. We will continue to assume that investors expect inflation and interest rates not to change, but that this expectation is now held with uncertainty. The presence of uncertainty means that investors have to think in terms of *expected* yields over their holding periods. Since expected future

---

[7]Alternative analyses of the term structure under conditions of inflation uncertainty can be found in Fama (June 1976), Brealey and Schaefer (May 1977), and Cornell (March 1978).

interest rates are still assumed to be the same as current interest rates, the expected yield over a holding period will be equal to the market yield to maturity of the bonds held. If long-term bonds are held, the expected yield over any given holding period will equal the yield to maturity on long-term bonds. Similarly, the expected holding-period yield on short-term bonds will be the short-term yield to maturity. The actual holding-period yield will depend, of course, on what actually happens to market interest rates and on whether the investor's holding period is longer or shorter than the maturity period of the bonds held.

The holding-period and maturity-period yields can be expressed either as nominal yields or real yields. Expected real yields are derived by subtracting the expected rate of inflation from expected nominal yields. When this is done, the expected real yield over a holding period is equal to the expected real yield to maturity. (Remember, we are still assuming that investors expect no change in inflation or market interest rates.) The expected real yield to maturity is, of course, the current market yield to maturity minus the expected rate of inflation. This yield has special importance in our analysis because it measures the expected real yield over any given holding period.

In equilibrium, the expected real yield over a holding period should be an increasing function of the risk or uncertainty of the real holding-period yield. Greater risk of real return should lead, through the pricing process, to greater expected real return. The question is: Is the risk of real return on long-term bonds greater or less than the risk of real return on short-term bonds over any given holding period? Since expected real holding-period yield is given by expected real yield to maturity, the question is, alternatively: Is the uncertainty of real yield to maturity on long-term bonds different from the uncertainty of real yield to maturity on short-term bonds? We know that yields are nominally riskless when bonds are held to maturity. Because nominal yields to maturity are given in the market, the only source of uncertainty of real yields to maturity is inflation uncertainty. The answer to the question thus depends upon what happens to inflation uncertainty as the period of time from the present into the future is extended.

Common sense tells us that uncertainty increases as we go further into the future. Short-term expectations are almost always held with more confidence than long-term expectations. If inflation uncertainty increases with period of time into the future, then the real yield to maturity on long-term bonds is more uncertain than it is on short-term bonds. Moreover, by our analysis, the expected real holding-period yield is similarly more risky when long-term bonds are held. To compensate for this greater risk, long-term bonds should be priced in the market to yield higher expected real returns in terms of both holding-period yield and yield to maturity. Thus, we provisionally conclude that the yield curve is ascending with respect to its expected real yield to maturity.

The market (or nominal) yield curve will likewise ascend given our assumption that investors expect no change in inflation or market interest rates. With no expectation of a change in inflation, the equilibrium term structure of nominal yields observed in the market will equal the equilibrium term structure of expected real yields plus a fixed expected-inflation premium. Our analysis suggests, therefore, that the generally ascending yield curve is the result of inflation uncertainty that increases with term to maturity.

This conclusion obviously rests on our assumption that investors expect no change in inflation and market interest rates. This assumption is grossly unrealistic for short-run analysis in which changes in economic variables are expected. However, for long-run analysis, the assumption of no expected change is not unreasonable. Over the long stretch of history, the rate of inflation and the rate of interest fall about as much as they rise.[8] In the long run these ups and downs tend to be offsetting so that the average change is close to zero. Thus a long-run expectation of no change is a fair assumption. Considering that the generally ascending yield curve is itself a long-run result, i.e., that the curve ascends on the average, our use of long-run analysis to explain this average tendency seems appropriate.

For the short run, however, our analysis falls to pieces. Relaxation of the assumption that investors expect no change in inflation and market interest rates means that expected holding-period yield is no longer given by current yield to maturity. Expected holding-period yield will be higher or lower than yield to maturity depending upon the direction that interest rates are expected to change and upon whether the holding period is shorter or longer than period to maturity. This means, furthermore, that the uncertainty of real yield to maturity will not measure the risk of real return over any given holding period. Without equivalency between maturity-period and holding-period risks and returns, the term structure of yields to maturity cannot be interpreted as a risk structure of expected holding-period returns. Such is the case when the yield curve is descending. Short-term yields to maturity are then higher than long-term yields. Since it is a short-run situation, however, we cannot conclude that short-term bonds are more risky in terms of expected holding-period returns. Rather, we would argue that high short-term yields to maturity reflect high short-term expected inflation.

[8] The price level rises, but not the *rate* by which it rises (on the average in the long run).

PROJECTS AND QUESTIONS

1. Select a well-known corporation that went into bankruptcy. Find out all that you can about the financial condition of the corporation two years and one year prior to the year that bankruptcy was actually declared. Write a report analyzing your findings.

2. "In 1967, 1968, and 1969 Moody's average of offering yields on new Aa public utility issues exceeded Moody's series for seasoned utility issues

with the same rating by an average of 40 basic points. In late 1970 and early 1971, the yield spread declined as interest rates fell, and in a number of instances negative yield spreads were observed." (*Journal of Finance*, December 1974, p. 1531) What are the reasons for such yield spreads and their fluctuations over time?

3. Discuss how inflation can affect the spread between the yield on corporate bonds and the yield on municipal bonds.

4. What are the spreads currently between the yields on three-month, six-month, and twelve-month Treasury bills? Write a short report interpreting the meaning and implications of these spreads.

BIBLIOGRAPHY

Altman, E.I.: "Financial Ratios, Discriminant Analysis and the Prediction of Corporate Bankruptcy," *Journal of Finance,* September 1968, pp. 589–609.

Ang, J.S., and K.A. Patel: "Bond Rating Methods: Comparison and Validation," *Journal of Finance,* May 1975, pp. 631–640.

Atkinson, T.R.: *Trends in Corporate Bond Quality,* National Bureau of Economic Research, New York, 1967.

Beaver, W.H.: "Financial Ratios as Predictors of Failure," *Empirical Research in Accounting: Selected Studies, 1966,* Supplement to vol. 4, *Journal of Accounting Research,* pp. 71–127.

Brealey, R., and S. Schaefer: "Term Structure with Uncertain Inflation," *Journal of Finance,* May 1977, pp. 277–289.

Cohan, A.B.: *The Risk Structure of Interest Rates,* General Learning Press, Morristown, N. J., 1973.

Cook, T.Q.: "Some Factors Affecting Long-term Yield Spreads in Recent Years," *Federal Reserve Bank of Richmond Monthly Review,* September 1973, pp. 2–14.

————: "Changing Yield Spreads in the U.S. Government Bond Market: Flower Bonds Bloom, Then Wilt," *Federal Reserve Bank of Richmond Economic Review,* March/April 1977, pp. 3–8.

————, and P.H. Hendershott: "The Impact of Taxes, Risk and Relative Security Supplies on Interest Rate Differentials," *Journal of Finance,* September 1978, pp. 1173–1186.

Cornell, B.: "Monetary Policy, Inflation Forecasting and the Term Structure of Interest Rates," *Journal of Finance,* March 1978, pp. 117–127.

Culbertson, J.M.: "The Term Structure of Interest Rates," *Quarterly Journal of Economics,* November 1957, pp. 485–517.

Ederington, L.H.: "The Yield Spread on New Issues of Corporate Bonds," *Journal of Finance,* December 1974, pp. 1531–1543.

Fama, E.F.: "Inflation Uncertainty and Expected Returns on Treasury Bills," *Journal of Political Economy,* June 1976, pp. 427–448.

Fisher, L.: "Determinants of Risk Premiums on Corporate Bonds," *Journal of Political Economy,* June 1959, pp. 217–237.

Fortune, P.: "Tax-Exemption of State and Local Interest Payments: An Economic Analysis of the Issues and an Alternative," *New England Economic Review,* May/June 1973, pp. 3–31.

Frankena, M.W.: "The Influence of Call Provisions and Coupon Rate on the Yields of Corporate Bonds," in *Essays on Interest Rates,* vol. II, National Bureau of Economic Research, New York, 1971.

Henning, C.N., W. Pigott, and R.H. Scott: *Financial Markets and the Economy,* Prentice-Hall, Englewood Cliffs, N. J., 1978, chaps. 13 and 14.

Hickman, W.B.: *Corporate Bond Quality and Investor Experience,* Princeton University Press, Princeton, N. J., 1958.

Jaffee, D.M.: "Cyclical Variations in the Risk Structure of Interest Rates," *Journal of Monetary Economics,* July 1975, pp. 309–325.

Jen, F.C., and J.E. Wert: "The Effect of Call Risk on Corporate Bond Yields," *Journal of Finance,* December 1967, pp. 637–651.

————, and ————: "The Deferred Call Provision and Corporate Bond Yields," *Journal of Financial and Quantitative Analysis,* June 1968, pp. 157–169.

Kessel, R.A.: *The Cyclical Behavior of the Term Structure of Interest Rates,* National Bureau of Economic Research, New York, 1965.

Kidwell, D.S.: "The Inclusion and Exercise of Call Provisions by State and Local Governments," *Journal of Money, Credit and Banking,* August 1976, pp. 391–398.

Lev, B.: *Financial Statement Analysis: A New Approach,* Prentice-Hall, Englewood Cliffs, N. J., 1974, chaps. 9–10.

Lutz, F.A.: "The Term Structure of Interest Rates," *Quarterly Journal of Economics,* November 1940, pp. 36–63.

Malkiel, B.G.: *The Term Structure of Interest Rates: Expectations and Behavior Patterns,* Princeton University Press, Princeton, N. J., 1966.

————: *The Term Structure of Interest Rates: Theory, Empirical Evidence, and Applications,* McCaleb-Seiler, New York, 1970.

McCulloch, J.H.: "The Tax-Adjusted Yield Curve," *Journal of Finance,* June 1975, pp. 811–830.

Meiselman, D.: *The Term Structure of Interest Rates,* Prentice-Hall, Englewood Cliffs, N. J., 1962.

Modigliani, F., and R. Sutch: "Innovations in Interest Rate Policy," *American Economic Review,* May 1966, pp. 178–197.

Murray, R.F.: "The Penn Central Debacle: Lessons for Financial Anaylsis," *Journal of Finance,* May 1971, pp. 327–332.

Pye, G.: "On the Tax Structure of Interest Rates," *Quarterly Journal of Economics,* November 1969, pp. 562–579.

————: "The Value of Call Deferment on a Bond: Some Empirical Results," *Journal of Finance,* December 1967, pp. 623–636.

Reilly, F.K., and M.D. Joehnk: "The Association Between Market-Determined Risk Measures for Bonds and Bond Ratings," *Journal of Finance,* December 1976, pp. 1387–1403.

Robichek, A.A., and W.D. Niebuhr: "Tax-Induced Bias in Reported Treasury Yields," *Journal of Finance,* December 1970, pp. 1081–1090.

Roll, R.: "Investment Diversification and Bond Maturity," *Journal of Finance,* March 1971, pp. 51–66.

Sloane, P.E.: "Determinants of Bond Yield Differentials, 1954–1959," in *Financial Markets and Economic Activity,* Wiley, New York, 1967.

Van Horne, J.C.: *Financial Market Rates and Flows,* Prentice-Hall, Englewood Cliffs, N. J., 1978.

part two

Money Markets

chapter 8
Money Markets: A General Introduction

The most significant function of money markets is to provide economic units with the facilities for adjusting their liquidity positions. Almost every economic unit—a corporation, a governmental body, a financial institution, even a family or an individual—has a regular and recurring problem of liquidity adjustment. If the problem is that of a cash outflow in excess of cash receipts, they go to the money market looking for funds. If the problem is that of an excess of cash inflow for which they are not yet prepared to make a long-term commitment, the money market is the place for short-term or temporary employment of these excess funds.

There are different levels of money market activity at which different economic units adjust their liquidity positions. When an individual is short of cash, he or she may withdraw funds from deposits at a bank. Or the solution may be to take a little longer in paying bills and build up more credit with local businesses. Such adjustments may seem small or trivial but when added together for a number of individuals they have the effect of extracting funds from banks, businesses, and other units so that these units become short of funds themselves. Businesses may turn to their local banks for funds, and the banks may, in turn, seek funds from their correspondent banks located in central city locations. Eventually, the demand for short-term credit will concentrate in and focus on the central money market. The same sort of concentration and focusing of funds operates on the supply side of the central money market. The funds that get "sold" in large blocks are nothing more than aggregations of small amounts of excess funds originating with many individual units. Money markets are all about us, but the summary impact of all money market activity is on the central money market.

THE CENTRAL MONEY MARKET

The central money market is a strange and mysterious territory to most persons. Unlike the bonds, stocks, and mortgages traded in the longer-term capital markets, the names of instruments traded in the central money market are not part of the ordinary household's common vocabulary. The money market instruments go by names and abbreviations such as T-bills, commercial paper, bankers' acceptances, RPs, NCDs, Eurodollars, and Fed funds. The most important thing that all these instruments have in common is a short maturity. Money market instruments are usually defined as those having an original maturity of less than one year.

The maturity characteristic is not, however, the reason why money market instruments are less well known than the instruments traded in the capital markets. Most people know little about the open money markets because these markets are open only to a select group of market participants. On the borrowing side, the issuing or selling of money market instruments is open only to governments, large banks, and large corporations of unquestioned financial strength and integrity. On the lending side, the buying of these instruments is open to everyone who can deliver the cash, but the amount of cash involved is very large. The central money market is a wholesale market dealing in transactions that usually run in multiples of $100,000. Multimillion-dollar transactions are an everyday occurrence.

Because the central money market is characterized by big wholesale transactions, some writers picture the market as physically located on the money district end of Manhattan. It is true that a physical concentration of financial firms—banks and others—is in this district, but this image gives the wrong impression of the money market. Modern communications by telephone, teletype, and computer are such that big banks all over the nation as well as some big corporations and others who can afford the rental of leased wires are participants in the central money markets. The open market is essentially a telephone market, and those who buy and sell money rarely see each other through physical contact, although they do come to be familiar with each others' voices.

While maturity does furnish the characteristic by which money markets may be distinguished from capital markets, the one-year dividing line is not always controlling. Financial markets comprehend a continuum of maturities from one-day (or within the day or overnight) money to financial instruments of theoretically infinite life. Maturity is relative, not absolute. For some lenders and borrowers, a one-day maturity differs more from a one-year maturity than the latter does from a twenty-year maturity. The line between the money markets and capital markets is therefore a line that is frequently crossed by participants in both markets.

Figure 8-1 shows the principal money market instruments with their range of original maturity and also an approximate average. This figure is logarithmic so as to show relative time relationships and demonstrate the wide range of averages in the money market.

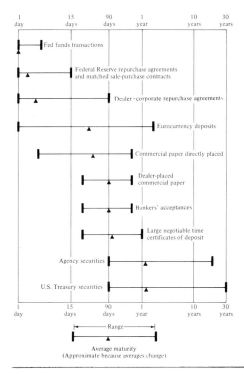

Time scale labels (top): 1 day · 15 days · 90 days · 1 year · 10 years · 30 years

Fed funds transactions

Federal Reserve repurchase agreements
and matched sale-purchase contracts

Dealer–corporate repurchase agreements

Eurocurrency deposits

Commercial paper directly placed

Dealer-placed
commercial paper

Bankers' acceptances

Large negotiable time
certificates of deposit

Agency securities

U.S. Treasury securities

Time scale labels (bottom): 1 day · 15 days · 90 days · 1 year · 10 years · 30 years

|← Range →|

Average maturity
(Approximate because averages change)

figure 8-1   Original Maturities of Money Market Credit Instruments (Time Scale Logarithmic).

CENTRAL MONEY MARKET INSTRUMENTS AND PARTICIPANTS

The money market can be viewed either in the singular or in the plural. It is a singular market in the sense that all transactions involve temporary exchanges of money. But it is also a system of markets in that different participating borrowers issue different short-term instruments in exchange for money. This latter view is taken in Table 8-1, which classifies the money market system by the different participating borrowers, the different instruments that the borrowers issue, and the primary participating lenders in each market. This table indicates that borrowers in some money markets are lenders in others. This is especially true of commercial banks, which are on one side or the other of every major money market (and on both sides of the federal funds market). To add to the confusion, every money market participant is both a supplier and a demander. Money market borrowers are the suppliers of money market instruments, but, correspondingly, they are demanders of money. Lenders demand money market instruments, but they supply money in the process. Thus, when we speak about supply and demand, we need to carefully distinguish between the money traded in the money market and the various money market instruments exchanged for money.

Of all the participating sectors in the money market, the federal government is by far the single most important net supplier of money market instruments.

TABLE 8-1
Classification of Money Market Instruments and Participants

Money Market Instruments	Primary Partici- pating Borrowers	Primary Participating Lenders
Treasury bills	U.S. Treasury	The Federal Reserve
		Commercial banks
		Foreigners
		State and local governments
		Nonbank financial intermediaries
Federal agency securities	Various U.S. Government- sponsored agencies	Commercial banks
		Nonbank financial intermediaries
		State and local governments
Commercial paper	Finance companies	Nonfinancial corporations
		Commercial banks
		Nonbank financial intermediaries
Bankers' acceptances	Businesses engaged in foreign trade	Foreigners
		Commercial banks
		The Federal Reserve
Dealer loans and repurchase agreements	Securities dealers	Commercial banks
		Nonfinancial corporations
Negotiable certificates of deposit	Commercial banks	Nonfinancial corporations
Eurodollars	Commercial banks	Foreigners
Federal funds	Commercial banks	Commercial banks

The volume outstanding of Treasury bills alone is almost equal to the volume outstanding of all other money market instruments combined. The huge supply of federal government securities is a reflection of the government's enormous demand for funds. (We shall examine the factors responsible for the massive federal debt, together with the ways in which the federal debt is managed, in the next chapter and in Chapter 13.)

After the federal government, the commercial banking system is the next leading net supplier of money market instruments. This is not apparent from Table 8-1 because that table shows commercial banks demanding more types of instruments than they supply. The very large volume outstanding of negotiable certificates of deposit (NCDs) is what tips the balance, however. This very important form of money market borrowing provides much of the funds that commercial banks need to fully accommodate the credit needs of businesses and other customers.

If the federal government is the leading money market borrower, the commercial banking system is the most pervasive money market participant.

The large money market banks (located in New York City and other important financial centers) trade in all the money markets and on both sides of the overall market. Much of this trading reflects their commitment to meeting the credit needs of their customers—corporations, financial intermediaries, well-to-do individuals, and others. For those customers reputable enough to issue their own money market instruments, the money market banks accommodate by buying their customers' instruments. Most customers, however, do not have direct access to borrowing in the money markets. For these customers, the money market banks provide credit out of funds raised from selling negotiable certificates of deposit and other bank-debt instruments. In addition to using the money markets for serving the credit needs of customers, banks use these markets for adjusting their own liquidity positions. Commercial banks rely on the money markets to the deepest and widest extent. (The pervasive involvement of commercial banks in the money markets will be covered in considerable detail in Chapter 10.)

The largest of the New York City banks are extraordinarily active in the money markets because of their additional function to serve as dealers in money market instruments. These banks, along with a few dozen independent dealers, are the intermediaries of the money market system. Instruments are bought and sold through these intermediating dealers. The dealers handle the telephone orders to buy and sell. They ensure that the market clears by selling out of their own inventories when orders to buy exceed orders to sell, and by adding to their inventories when orders to sell exceed orders to buy. As in any business, these inventories have to be financed. One method for financing dealers' inventories of money market instruments is through repurchase agreements, which is a type of money market instrument in its own right. Since the supply of repurchase agreements and other paper used to finance inventory is closely tied to the dealers' inventory demand for money market instruments, supply and demand are more evenly balanced for dealers than for other money market participants. (We shall examine the system of money market dealers and brokers and the financing of dealers' inventories in the next chapter.)

Another sector that operates on both sides of the money market is the corporate business sector. This sector supplies money market instruments in the form of commercial paper (sold primarily by large finance companies) and bankers' acceptances (arising out of foreign trade and guaranteed by large "accepting" banks). As a whole, however, the corporate business sector is a net demander of money market instruments. These instruments are especially attractive to corporate money managers who have temporarily excess cash to invest. (We shall explore the general principles of money management in a later section of this chapter, deferring the specific elements of corporate money management to the next chapter.)

The demand for money market instruments is considerably more widespread than the supply. Participants on the lending side of the money markets include all institutions (and individuals) that have substantial amounts of temporarily idle cash. State and local governments, nonbank financial intermediaries, and foreign institutions are particularly important lenders in the market. Local governments put temporarily idle tax money to work by buying money market instruments. Savings institutions and insurance companies invest in money market instruments during slack periods of demand for longer-term credit. The governments, central banks, and commercial banks of foreign countries are very extensive holders of money market instruments issued by our own government and banking system.

The reason why the foreign sector is a heavy net demander of our domestic money market instruments is easily explained by the large and recurring deficits in the U.S. balance of payments. These trade deficits have glutted the world with dollars. To a large extent, foreigners have had little choice but to put these dollars to work in our money markets. The biggest fraction of these interest-earning dollar claims is held by foreign governments directly or through their central banks. But a sizeable proportion is also held by foreign commercial banks and businesses.

By far the most important participant in the money market is the Federal Reserve System (or Fed, for short). The Fed is the largest net demander of Treasury bills. It also holds a large proportion of the volume outstanding of bankers' acceptances. The Fed adjusts its portfolio of Treasury bills and other money market instruments by buying and selling in the open market on a continuous basis. The Fed's purpose in the money market is very different, however, from that of other participants. Its open market purchases and sales are not designed to manage its own money position, but rather to manage the overall supply of money in the economy. When the Fed buys instruments in the open market, it pays for them not with money already in existence but with new "high-powered" money that it creates. This new money becomes deposited at commercial banks and adds to the latter's cash reserves. The increase in reserves, in turn, supports a multiple-expansion process of increasing the supply of demand deposit money in the economy. The Fed initiates this process with open market purchases when it wishes to pursue an expansionary monetary policy. Of course, the Fed can also initiate a process of contracting the money supply by engaging in open market sales. In addition to managing the nation's money supply, the Fed also uses open market purchases and sales to control and stabilize interest rates in the money markets. The Fed's influence in the money markets is so dominant that all other participants in the market have to keep a close watch on what the Fed is doing. (We shall analyze the policy-facilitating function of the money market system in Chapter 11, which covers the Federal Reserve.)

THE DEMAND FOR MONEY MARKET INSTRUMENTS

The demand for money market instruments is in all cases tied to money management. The Federal Reserve buys and sells Treasury bills and other instruments in the open market, adding and subtracting from its holdings, in order to manage the growth of the overall supply of money in the economy. The other participants—commercial banks, nonbank financial intermediaries, business corporations, state and local governments, and foreign institutions—hold money market instruments in managing their individual money positions.

When an individual organization has more actual cash on hand than it desires to hold, it may put the surplus cash to work by investing it in the instruments of the money markets. Money not put to work is money lost. Money is a highly perishable commodity so that even a day's lost income cannot be recovered. High interest rates dictate that excess funds be immediately and fully invested. The short-term marketable securities portfolio solves the problem. It not only earns interest but it serves as a reservoir of liquidity that can be drawn down and converted back into cash when a shortage of cash is experienced.

In the most general sense, the demand for money market instruments is a demand derived from the demand for cash. An increase in a participant's holdings of money market instruments means that the participant was holding more cash than desired. A decrease in holdings of instruments means that less cash was held than desired. The Fed, of course, has no demand for cash for itself. But its monetary policy orientation does imply a desired quantity of cash for the rest of the whole economy to hold. Thus, an increase in the Fed's holdings of money market instruments, through open market purchases, means that the rest of the economy was holding less cash than the Fed wanted it to hold. If, on the other hand, the Fed wanted the economy to hold less money, the Fed would have reacted by decreasing its own holdings of money market instruments, through open market sales.

Surpluses and shortages of cash are not necessarily corrected in the money market. A cash surplus may be used for spending or for long-term lending. These alternative uses may be preferable to lending in the money market, particularly if a cash surplus is expected to persist for a long time. Typically, however, cash surpluses and shortages run for short durations. All organizations and individuals are familiar with short-term discrepancies between inflows of cash receipts and outflows of cash disbursements. Cash holdings build up on those months of the year, weeks of the month, and days of the week during which cash receipts exceed outlays. Similarly, cash drains down during those days, weeks, and months when cash outflow outstrips cash inflow. As a result of these short-term discrepancies, the typical economic unit finds that its cash balance is highly volatile, excessive on some days, deficient on others.

Large cash surpluses and shortages of a temporary nature (due to seasonal and shorter-term discrepancies between cash inflow and outflow) are suitably corrected in the money market. The instruments of the open money market not only earn interest but they also share the common characteristic of being good liquidity vehicles or money substitutes. They can be converted back into cash quickly with very little risk. Fed funds mature virtually overnight. Repurchase agreements usually run for just a day or two. Treasury bills, NCDs, commercial paper, and bankers' acceptances are all negotiable instruments that can be sold in the open secondary market at any time.

Money market instruments are not only highly marketable, they also have highly stable market values due to their short maturities. A sharp rise in money market interest rates lowers the market values of outstanding money market instruments relatively little since these instruments can be redeemed for full face value by waiting only a few days, weeks, or months to maturity. The risk of loss of capital value (should interest rates rise) is substantially less with money market instruments than it is with bonds and stocks. Money market instruments are also relatively free of the risk of default. Unlike bonds, which vary in quality as reflected by ratings, the instruments of the money market are practically all of uniform high quality. They have to be in order to qualify for sale in the open market. Defaults are very rare, but when they do happen (as in the case of Penn-Central's commercial paper in 1970), the market works doubly hard to reestablish its integrity.

GENERAL PRINCIPLES OF CASH MANAGEMENT

Most large firms and organizations manage their money positions very carefully. Much thought is given to deciding the optimal average cash balance (above which excess cash can be invested in money market instruments, and below which money market instruments can be converted back into cash). Money managers have considerable latitude in deciding upon an appropriate working cash balance. At one extreme, cash can be held in sufficient quantity to cover all foreseen and most unforeseen net cash outflows. Holding cash to this extreme minimizes the risk of running out of cash and the attendant costs of liquidating marketable securities. It is extremely costly, however, in terms of interest foregone from holding so much cash. At the other extreme, it is possible to get by with little or no cash by liquidating marketable securities whenever funds are needed for disbursements (and by investing in marketable securities whenever the net cash flow is positive). This extreme minimizes the interest opportunity cost of holding cash, but it involves an excessive number of costly transactions into and out of the marketable securities account. For most concerns, the optimal cash balance lies between these two extremes at which the sum of the interest opportunity cost and the cost of portfolio transactions is minimized.

Although formal economic models have been developed for determining the optimal working cash balance, these models seldom fit the complex, real-world situations faced by most money managers. Money management is to a large extent an art. Nevertheless, there are certain economic principles governing the holding of cash that even the most artful manager cannot ignore. One principle is that the amount of cash held should grow with the firm's or organization's volume of transactions. Larger cash balances are required to cover larger discrepancies between cash inflows and outflows; otherwise the risks of running out of cash become too great.

A second principle of cash management is to adjust the cash balance in response to changes in interest rates. When interest rates rise, the interest opportunity cost of holding cash increases relative to the cost of running out of cash. At the margin, the cost of holding cash exceeds the cost of not holding cash. The rational money manager can therefore be expected to cut back on cash holdings and add to holdings of marketable securities. Decreases in interest rates have the opposite effect. When interest rates fall it pays to invest less in marketable securities and hold more cash.

A third principle of cash management is to consider the transaction cost of investing in (or disinvesting from) marketable securities. The more it costs (in terms of telephone calls, brokers' fees, etc.) to buy or sell instruments in the open market, the more inclined the money manager will be to keep more cash on hand (so that fewer investments and disinvestments will be required). The relative significance of the cost of transacting securities depends on the size of the firm or organization doing the transacting. The transaction cost can be virtually ignored by the major participants of the money market because they can spread the fixed element of the cost over their very large transactions. For small investors, however, the cost of transacting can make a big difference in deciding whether to invest funds or to keep them in the form of cash.

A fourth principle of cash management is to hold some extra cash as a precaution against not being able to meet unforeseen needs for cash. The greater the uncertainty of cash flows, particularly cash outflows, the larger the cash balance required to guard against this uncertainty. It is nice to end up with more money than expected, but it can be very costly to run out of cash unexpectedly. In order to reduce the risks and cut the costs of running out, most organizations (and individuals too) hold more cash than they expect they will need. This principle of holding a larger average cash balance to compensate for greater cash balance uncertainty applies even if the cost of running out involves nothing more than liquidating some marketable securities. By holding more cash, the money manager can offset the larger number of portfolio transactions that would otherwise result from greater variations in the cash balance.

The fifth (and our last) principle of cash management deals with interest rate uncertainty. Money market interest rates are the most volatile of all interest rates. The short maturities of money market instruments has the effect, however, of translating this relatively high interest rate volatility into relatively low market value volatility. Nevertheless, holders of money market instruments are exposed to the risk of capital loss, particularly to the extent that their holdings may have to be liquidated weeks before maturity. Ordinarily this risk is so minor that it has little effect on the demand for money market instruments. There are times, however, when money market rates shoot up overnight. The effect of such interest rate turbulence is to reduce the demand for the longer-term money market instruments and to increase the demand for shorter-term instruments and for cash. Cash earns no interest, but it does have the advantage of being free from the risk of capital loss.

The above principles of cash management all apply to the determination of the firm's or organization's voluntary working cash balance. Cash management is made more complicated, however, to the extent that the firm is required to keep a compensating cash balance. A compensating balance requirement is an institutional arrangement between the firm and its bank wherein the firm agrees to keep a minimum average deposit balance at the bank in return for those bank services and concessions that are not rendered on a direct fee basis. The compensating balance requirement imposes no hardship on the firm whose voluntary working balance amply covers the required compensating balance. In some instances, however, firms are required to keep larger deposit balances than otherwise needed.

While commercial banks impose an institutional demand for cash upon their customers in the form of compensating balance requirements, the banks, themselves, are institutionally required by the Federal Reserve Board of Governors and other authorities to hold legal cash reserves. Member commercial banks of the Federal Reserve System are required to keep vault cash and deposits at the Fed in amounts equal to (or greater than) prescribed percentages of their deposit liabilities. Nonmember banks are required to meet cash reserve requirements imposed by state regulatory authorities. Legal reserve requirements play a crucial role in the determination of the nation's money supply (as we shall see in Chapters 10 and 11).

PORTFOLIO SELECTION OF MONEY MARKET INSTRUMENTS

Once management has decided upon an appropriate cash balance, any substantial amount of temporarily idle cash in excess of this balance can be invested in money market instruments. The money manager's next job is to select which instrument or instruments to purchase. The instruments of the money market are not homogeneous. They differ with regard to maturity, risk, and yield. These different characteristics weigh heavily on the money manager's selections.

Maturity is a critical factor in the selection process. The money manager can minimize interest rate risk by matching period-to-maturity to expected holding period. When funds are expected to be idle for only several days, they can be suitably invested in repurchase agreements or other forms of immediately available funds. When funds are idle for several weeks, matching maturities can be obtained by investing in commercial paper. For funds idle for several months, negotiable certificates of deposit offer a good match of maturity to holding period. So do Treasury bills.

The money manager is by no means locked into a position of matching maturity with expected holding period. If a manager feels strongly that interest rates are going to rise in excess of what others are expecting, excess funds may be put to work in instruments that mature before the funds are needed, so that expected return can be maximized. On the other hand, if interest rates are expected by management to fall more sharply than expected by investors generally, funds may be invested in instruments whose maturities extend beyond the holding period. In this case, the money manager hopes to sell the instruments before they mature in order to realize capital gains and maximize total return. In either case, the money manager is betting that he or she knows better than others what interest rates are going to do. Most good money managers know when and where to draw the line, however, on using money market instruments for speculative purposes. Large deviations of maturity from the expected holding period are the exception, not the rule.

The money manager's selection process is affected not only by the term structure of money market rates (from which the investment community's expectations of future money market rates can be judged), but from the default risk structure of money market rates as well. The pattern of money market rates shown in Figure 8-2 reveals several elements, one being differential default

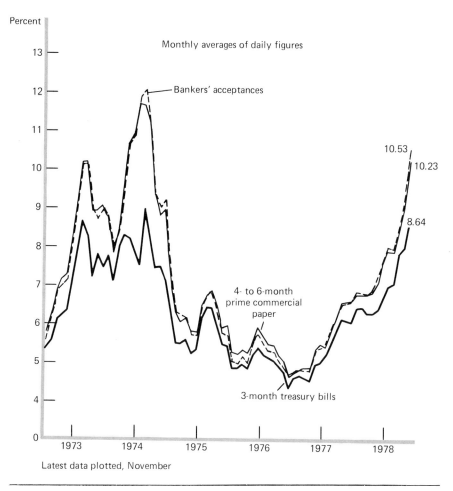

Percent

Monthly averages of daily figures

Bankers' acceptances

10.53

10.23

8.64

4- to 6-month
prime commercial
paper

3-month treasury bills

1973   1974   1975   1976   1977   1978

Latest data plotted, November

figure 8-2   Money Market Rates. *(Source:* Monetary Trends, *Federal Reserve Bank of St. Louis, Dec. 21, 1978, p. 10.)*

risk. Note that the rates on bankers' acceptances and prime commercial paper are consistently higher than the rate on three-month Treasury bills. The difference is mainly attributable to differential default risk and to the fact that Treasury bills have superior marketability. In selecting instruments from the same maturity category, the money manager must decide whether the yield differential between private open market paper—bankers' acceptances, commercial paper, negotiable certificates of deposit, etc.—and Treasury bills compensate for the differential risk of default. The tendency in recent periods for corporate money managers to invest in private paper rather than Treasury securities suggests that the extra yield on private paper more than compensates for the risk, or, more likely, that corporate money managers are less averse to risk than money market investors generally. It also suggests that corporate managers have developed efficient market mechanisms for investing excess funds.

Another element revealed by Figure 8-2 is the tendency for all money market rates to move up and down together. This high degree of covariation is significant in that it does not pay as much to have a diversified portfolio of money market instruments as it does to diversify among stocks, bonds, and other long-term instruments whose returns are less highly correlated. There is also less need for diversification simply because money market instruments are relatively riskless.

A problem facing outsiders of the money market is that quotations of interest rates or yields are often more artificial than real. An example is the persistent excess of the secondary market yields quoted on NCDs over the rates posted by banks. Are the rates that banks really offer higher than the rates posted? Or are the secondary market yields quoted artificially? A close reading of money-market-yield quotations raises other questions:

1. Published yields on agency issues often cover an irrationally wide range. Can investors, in fact, get the high-ask yields that are quoted? Conversely, are the bids at lower yields real? An outside observer cannot help but feel that the real market must be considerably more rational than the published quotes.
2. Published yields quoted for commercial paper almost always have far less maturity differential than the maturity differential of Treasury bills at the same time. However, the 90- and 180-day yields on commercial paper generally show a much more reasonable relationship to the T-bill rate than either the 30-day or the 270-day rate. Does this mean that since most of the business is done at the middle range, that the outside limits are more artificially quoted?
3. Why should the yields on NCDs lie above the commercial paper rate, and particularly the longer commercial paper rate, so persistently? It is hard to believe that the quality of bank paper is not as good as that of corporate paper. Is it possible that holders of the NCDs feel more hesitant about asking for cash at maturity than do the holders of CPs?
4. Why is the rate quoted on bankers' acceptances so stable? Is this really a sheltered market not closely arbitraged with the rest of the money market?

FEDERAL RESERVE OPERATIONS

By its constitutional nature, the Fed itself can have no liquidity "problem," since it creates money. It is a public agency, however, and, in a sense, manages the liquidity of the economy. The general objective is national economic well-being. The Fed uses its three credit market instruments—reserve requirements, the discount rate, and open-market operations—as the tools for influencing money market liquidity. Reserve requirements can be considered a structural tool. They set the rules of the game, and these rules are changed only with advance notice and rather infrequently. In a larger sense, the issue behind this instrument is who should get the earnings from the money creation process. The discount rate has an influence to the extent that some banks try to use the facility for profit-making purposes. But the number of such banks is not large, and the main influence of the rate is as a public display of the Federal Reserve's feelings about the proper level of market interest rates. The day-to-day credit instrument for Federal Reserve liquidity management is open-market operations.

Federal Reserve open-market operations are guided by an exceedingly cumbersome administrative system: the Federal Reserve Open Market Committee (FOMC). This body meets every month or oftener and gives general guidance to the day-to-day manager of the System Open Market Account (SOMA). The general guidance comes in the form of a "policy directive" to the SOMA manager to engage in open-market operations to meet money rate and monetary aggregate targets set by the FOMC. The directive sets the targets but leaves it to the SOMA manager to decide when and how much to buy and sell in the open market.

To a certain extent, the Fed's demand for money market instruments (Treasury securities primarily) varies in the opposite direction from other participant's demands for money market instruments. On days when other participants are strong buyers in the market, the Fed is apt to be a strong seller in order to keep money market rates at or near target. On days when other participants are selling, the Fed may well be adding to its portfolio, again, for the purpose of keeping interest rates within policy limits.

Over the years, the Fed has become the largest net demander of money market instruments; its open-market purchases have vastly exceeded its open-market sales. While to some extent this position has been the result of trying to keep interest rates down (as, for example, during the 1940s), it has more generally been a result of supplying more money to the economy as the economy has grown. As the monetary system adds to its holdings of securities, it pays for them with newly created money. This differs from the rest of us. When you or I demand money market instruments, or anything else, payment is made with money already outstanding.

THE SUPPLY OF MONEY MARKET INSTRUMENTS

Apart from the Federal Reserve, the demanders of money market instruments share the common characteristic of having temporarily idle cash to invest. The market is not symmetrical, however. The suppliers of money market instruments do not share a common characteristic of being temporarily short of funds. If anything, the supply side of the market is more accurately characterized by needs for long-term funds. There are, of course, important exceptions. For example, commercial bank borrowing in the federal funds market is usually very short-term. Banks borrow in this market on days when their reserve positions are deficient, but they lend on other days when reserves are in excess. The market for repurchase agreements is another example. The money market dealers and others who borrow in this market have financing needs that are generally short-term. In terms of average daily volume of transactions, these two markets are among the most active of all the money markets.

However, in terms of volume outstanding (at any point in time), the three leading money market instruments are short-term Treasury securities (Treasury bills and other Treasury instruments with one year or less remaining to maturity), negotiable certificates of deposit (issued by commercial banks), and commercial paper (placed directly by finance companies). Treasury bills lead not only in terms of volume outstanding, but they are second only to federal funds in terms of daily average trading. These three leading instruments are to some extent supplied to meet short-term needs for funds, but more often than not they are issued to finance on a long-term basis. The use of short-term instruments for financing permanently is accomplished through the technique of refunding, that is, by issuing new instruments to raise funds for paying off old issues as they come due.

The U.S. Treasury is the prime user of the refunding technique. The federal debt is huge and permanent. Yet much of it is financed with Treasury bills. New bills are sold each week and maturing bills are redeemed every week. There are weeks when sales deviate substantially from redemptions, reflecting the government's need to correct short-term discrepancies between cash (mainly tax) receipts and cash expenditures, but, over the longer run, sales and redemptions tend to go and grow together. Redemptions have to keep up with prior sales. And sales have to keep up with redemptions and additions to the national debt.

Although the money that the Treasury raises in the money market amounts to permanent borrowing, this borrowing is not used to finance real capital goods. It is used, instead, to finance the government's "consumption" in excess of its income from taxes. In other words, it is used to finance dissaving. As this dissaving has become habitual, adding each year to the national debt, the debt itself has come to be regarded as a permanent feature of the economy.

Negotiable certificates of deposit (NCDs) were introduced by commercial banks in 1961 to enable banks to attract corporate deposits and thereby compete more effectively for money market funds. Although a portion of the supply of NCDs varies in response to short-term fluctuations in the quantity of funds required by banks, most of the NCD supply has the effect of providing banks with a long-term source of financing. There are two reasons for this. One reason has to do with the law of large numbers. The typical money market bank has scores of corporate and other investors in its NCDs. When any one investor cashes in at maturity, the chances are good that some other investor will be wanting to put cash to work. From the bank's point of view, sales of NCDs to customers with cash to invest tend to cover redemptions of NCDs for customers needing cash. The other reason is that many corporate customers tend to keep invested (and reinvested) in the NCDs of their banks as long as cash is not needed. Like other time deposits, NCDs are liquid, but they do not turn over as fast as their maturities imply.

The funds that commercial banks take out of the central money market as suppliers of NCDs are loaned, for the most part, to big businesses and other borrowing customers. Some of these customers are sufficiently creditworthy and well known that they could sell their own instruments in the open market if they so elected, but apparently they prefer instead to negotiate for credit on a personal level with their banks. Most customers, however, do not have direct access to the central money market themselves, and therefore have to rely on banks to intermediate on their behalf.

The supply of commercial paper by finance companies is similar to the supply of NCDs by banks as a source of funds. Finance company paper matures quickly, but its supply is continually renewed through placement of new paper. This has the effect of making commercial paper financing more permanent than suggested by the maturities of commercial paper. The supply of commercial paper is also similar to the supply of NCDs in terms of using funds secured. The funds that finance companies take out of the central money market are turned into loans to businesses and consumers. Finance companies compete directly with commercial banks in the business and consumer credit markets. But there is one element of segmentation. Finance companies are much more willing and able than banks to assume the risks (and rewards) of lending to borrowers of marginal credit worth.

THE RETAILING OF MONEY MARKET FUNDS

The central money markets are largely open or impersonal markets. They are made homogeneous by the high quality of credit and competitive by the openness with which transactions take place. The central money markets provide an element of leadership for the financial system. The rates of interest determined in these markets are widely published and are often followed in other credit transactions. Central money markets also serve the important function of leveling out the national supplies and demands for funds. Money is fluid and moves about with agility, seeking employment on the best terms. Central money markets, however, do not embrace all segments of the financial system that might be thought of as money markets. The money traded in the central money markets is indirectly available to all comers, primarily through the network of bank loans.

A few of the large money market banks are true wholesalers of money; they do business mainly with other financial institutions and very large corporations. Most of the money market banks, however, are both wholesalers and retailers of money. Since these banks have nationwide contacts, they tend to create a national market in bank credit. This national market is closely related to the central money markets; indeed, the banks are often the money market agents of their customers. But these relationships are not impersonal open-market ones; they are customer relationships.

Most commercial bank loans are not considered open-market transactions. The borrower does not seek competitive bids. The nature of the loan agreement may contain requirements or understandings that violate the idea of homogeneity that is needed for an open market credit instrument. Nevertheless, the very large commercial banks have to be competitive with the open market for those customers of such strong credit standing that they could enter the open market with commercial paper. They have to offer credit to these customers at the so-called prime rate. The prime loan rate was at one time set largely by price leadership, although it always had to be reasonably in touch with open-market interest rates. In recent periods the prime loan rate has come to be set by a formula that explicitly links it with open-market rates.

Aside from the largest banks, which operate nationally (even internationally), many fairly large banks operate on a regional basis. Most banks, however, are wholly local in character. Those businesses (and individuals and others) that do not have the size to attract the attention of the big banks must depend on such local banking connections. In this sense, local money markets exist. The terms and arrangements that govern these local markets, however, are not detached from central money market influences. Although interest rates charged by small banks fluctuate less than the prime rate and much less than central money market rates, they are not static. The retail price of money tends to rise and fall with the wholesale price in the central market.

The retailing of money market funds extends well beyond the network of bank loans. Most large businesses use bank credit for the purpose of supplying their business customers, in turn, with trade credit. Many businesses (large and small) also filter bank credit down to individuals in the form of consumer credit. Behind every charge account transaction lurks a chain of transactions that probably began in the central money markets.

INTERREGIONAL FLOW OF FUNDS

The credit needs of some areas tend to exceed the saving done in those areas. Other areas have much more modest demands and far more liberal supplies of credit. The central money markets serve to bring about some national leveling in the availability and cost of funds. It might be asked whether there are further devices within the commercial banking system for the accomplishment of this process of redistribution. The question is particularly relevant in the United States, since this country is characterized by a unit banking system. In a few states, statewide branch banking is permitted, but that is the farthest any new banking extension can go (not nationally as in Canada or England). In most states of the United States the limits are even narrower. In some states, branch banking is prohibited altogether.

The correspondent banking system provides for some connection between areas. However, the chief funds transfer incident to correspondent banking is the movement of deposit balances from country banks to city banks. This movement is not always in the direction that would be taken if a leveling of funds were desired. Probably the more important part of the banking system that has led to some interregional movement of funds has been loan participations or the handling of "overline" parts of loans.

When a bank originates a large loan, it may offer "participations" in it to other banks. This system works in many directions. A small bank may offer a participation to its city correspondent; money flows from the city to the country. On the other hand, small banks with inadequate loan demand have sometimes been offered participations in loans by their city correspondents. Then again, a small bank with a loan application that exceeds its legal loan limit may sell the "overline" portion to a city correspondent. Participations are also shared by banks of equal size, generally in cases of very large loans. Participations are offered and accepted in both short- and longer-term credits, but they probably have been more common in the latter.

CONNECTIONS BETWEEN THE MONEY AND CAPITAL MARKETS

Any observer of the money and capital markets can testify that strong interconnections exist. Federal Reserve policy is expressed wholly in the money markets, but its influence spreads quickly to the capital markets. Strong demands for funds in the capital markets spill over into the money markets and can cause money market interest rates to increase.

Commercial banks are traditionally more money market than capital market institutions, but events have changed their operations. In the first place, the commercial banks in the United States are large and important savings institutions in that they hold large amounts of time deposits. The use of such funds tends to put them into the capital markets. In prolonged low-interest-rate periods, commercial banks are also driven into capital market investment for the sake of survival. Low short-term interest rates during the 1930s would have starved banks if they had been their sole source of income. On the other side, some of the best customers of commercial banks—corporations—have long- as well as short-term credit needs. Commercial banks have found that good customer relationships often require a willingness to extend intermediate-term credit (often just called "term" loans) to leading customers.

The shifts of commercial banks between money and capital markets are partly determined by relative interest rates. Shifts in the use or availability of funds themselves tend to tie together the two markets. However, many of the shifts back and forth are not for rate reasons but are caused by other circumstances. For example, many commercial banks would prefer to do less term lending and certainly not to do it for the small differential in interest rates. But the overriding requirements of customer-relationship solidarity force them into extending such credit.

Some borrowers prudently shift back and forth between markets. The federal government has already been mentioned as one example of an institution that can act in this way. While the federal government probably should not have too large a part of its debt in floating form, the power to create money and the prime credit of the federal government mean that it can go much further than most other borrowers in financing essentially long-term needs for funds in short-term markets.

Large corporations can also shift between markets with relative safety. Public utility concerns need mainly long-term capital. Their record of income stability, however, is such that they can safely finance new construction with short-term bank credit and even carry complete properties for a while until conditions in the capital markets are fully to their liking. Other corporations can also choose to a considerable extent. Sales finance concerns have great flexibility. Interest rates are usually at the heart of their choice, but the matter is more one of timing than of ultimate differences in financial structures. In the end, a large part of business capital needs are long-term and go to the capital markets. Well-managed corporations, however, have some latitude about just when they do their long-term borrowing.

The material on the term structures of interest rates reviewed in Chapter 7 is relevant to this matter of interconnections. When yield curves are relatively flat, there may be little choice between money and capital market rates *at that time*. But if a flat yield curve presages a general decline in interest rates, as has often been the case, then shrewd borrowers can afford to pay higher short-term rates to wait for lower long-term rates. On the other hand, yield curves with a lot of early slope may put strong pressure on investing institutions, but particularly on commercial banks, to extend maturities. If interest rates later rise, as has often happened after such a yield-curve shape, then they may regret this action. Relative interest rates are at the heart of the arbitrage between these two sectors of the markets.

PROJECTS AND QUESTIONS

1. Liquidity is a concept that is easy to talk about but hard to pin down. Write a definitive statement on the meaning and nature of liquidity. Explain in detail how the instruments traded in the central money market measure up to your definition of liquidity.
2. Most large institutions have cash management policies that call for the investment of temporarily idle funds in money market instruments. If you are a university student, find out what policies your university treasurer follows in this regard. Does your university put excess cash to work in one or more of the instruments introduced in this chapter? If so, which instruments, and why?

BIBLIOGRAPHY

Baxter, N.D.: "Marketability, Default Risk, and Yields on Money-Market Instruments," *Journal of Financial and Quantitative Analysis,* March 1968, pp. 75–85.

Budin, M., and R.J. Van Handel: "A Rule-of-Thumb Theory of Cash Holdings by Firms," *Journal of Financial and Quantitative Analysis,* March 1975, pp. 85–108.

Daellenbach, H.G.: "Are Cash Management Optimization Models Worthwhile?" *Journal of Financial and Quantitative Analysis,* September 1974, pp. 607–626.

Federal Reserve Bank of Cleveland: *Money Market Instruments,* Cleveland, 1970.

Federal Reserve Bank of Richmond: *Instruments of the Money Market,* Richmond, 1977.

Frost, P.A.: "Banking Services, Minimum Cash Balances, and the Firm's Demand for Money," *Journal of Finance,* December 1970, pp. 1029–1039.

Lindow, W.: *Inside the Money Market,* Random House, New York, 1972.

Nadler, P.S.: "Compensating Balances and the Prime at Twilight," *Harvard Business Review,* January–February 1972, pp. 112–120.

Smith, K.V., ed.: *Management of Working Capital,* West Publishing, New York, 1974, section II.

Van Horne, J.C.: *Financial Management and Policy,* Prentice-Hall, Englewood Cliffs, N. J., 1977, chap. 14.

Vogel, R.C., and G.S. Maddala: "Cross-Section Estimates of Liquid Asset Demand by Manufacturing Corporations," *Journal of Finance,* December 1967, pp. 557–575.

Woodworth, G.W.: *The Money Market and Monetary Management,* Harper and Row, New York, 1972.

collects in taxes. The difference, or deficit, has to be covered by the U.S. Treasury through borrowing in the financial markets. This recurrent borrowing accumulates over time and is responsible for our large and growing national debt. The growing size and changing composition of the national debt is indicated in Table 9-1.

Why does the government engage so persistently in deficit spending? The reason is partly economic, partly political. The economic basis for deficit spending is the pursuit of expansionary fiscal policy. The Employment Act of 1946 requires the government to promote full employment. Since actual employment is rarely as full as desired by the makers of policy, deficit spending can be viewed as the government's way of fulfilling its policy obligation. Political expediency, however, is probably the stronger factor. Spending programs are known to win votes (except from the voting minority of true conservatives). On the revenue side, almost all voters favor lower taxes.

Faced with these economic and political biases toward deficit spending, the Treasury is left with the job of managing the national debt. The Treasury has to decide on what maturities to issue as new borrowing is required and as outstanding debt comes due. Because the debt is so permanent, it would at first glance seem to make sense to finance the debt with Treasury bonds and other

TABLE 9-1
Size and Composition of the National Debt

	Size of the Federal Debt				
	1956	1966	1976	1956-66	1966-76
	(billions of dollars)			(Average annual percentage change)	
Total interest-bearing federal debt	$274.2	$325.0	$652.5	1.9%	10.1%
Nonmarketable issues	113.8	107.0	231.2	−0.6	11.6
Marketable issues	160.4	218.0	421.3	3.6	9.3
Marketable issues held by private investors	130.5	159.1	307.8	2.2	9.3

Composition of the Privately Held Marketable Interest-Bearing Federal Debt for Selected Years					
Years to Maturity	1956	1966	1976	1956-66	1966-76
				(Changes)	
Within 1 year	34.9%	42.1%	51.2%	7.2%	9.1%
1 to 5 years	30.6	30.3	33.7	0.3	3.4
5 to 10 years	12.7	15.4	10.1	2.7	−5.3
10 years and over	21.8	12.2	5.1	−9.6	−7.1
Total	100.0	100.0	100.0	0.0	0.0

SOURCE: Treasury Bulletin.

chapter 9
Business and
Government in the
Central Money Markets

In the last chapter we introduced the major money market participants and described in a general way the nature of their involvement in the market. In the course of that introduction it was necessary to mention some of the different instruments traded in the market. The instruments' common characteristics of being short in maturity and high in quality were emphasized in conjunction with their use in the general process of managing money. The specific characteristics of the different instruments, and the specific elements of supply and demand in the different markets, remain to be discussed.

In this chapter we focus attention on the participation of the U.S. government and of the business community in the money markets. We shall examine the particular credit needs of the government, the dealers in government securities, finance companies, businesses engaged in foreign trade, and businesses generally. Different money market instruments will be shown to emerge as a reflection of the particular credit needs of these different participants. The instruments that emerge include Treasury bills, federal agency securities, repurchase agreements, commercial paper, and bankers' acceptances. We shall analyze the supply of and demand for each of these instruments in this chapter.

TREASURY DEBT MANAGEMENT

The U.S. Department of the Treasury is responsible for managing the outstanding debt of the federal government, for borrowing money to meet a current deficit, for retiring debt in the unusual event of a surplus, and for managing the government's cash position. These responsibilities fall under the general heading of Treasury debt management.

The federal government, as everyone knows, tends to spend more than it long-term Treasury securities. Long-term securities certainly have the advantage of requiring fewer refundings.

The fact of the matter is, however, that the Treasury has elected to finance the largest part of the national debt with Treasury bills and other relatively short-term securities, as shown in Table 9-1. The use of short-term instruments to meet long-term needs has required constant weekly refunding of maturing securities, but this refunding has proved to be efficient, inexpensive, and reliable. Unlike refunding of corporate debt, which is risky, refunding of the national debt involves little risk. The government's credit is default-riskless; it is backed by the power to tax and, if necessary, to print money. The demand for Treasury bills is so strong and unwavering that the Treasury faces little risk of credit unavailability.

But this still does not explain why the Treasury has elected to finance the debt so heavily with Treasury bills. From the Treasury's point of view, the primary factor for shortening the maturity of the national debt has been to reduce the interest-rate cost of the debt. For every $100 billion of debt, a reduction in cost by a full percentage reduces the annual interest burden of the debt by $1 billion. Since short-term rates are on the average less than long-term rates, the Treasury has managed to reduce the average interest cost of the debt by shortening the average maturity of the debt. This is the main reason why the volume outstanding of Treasury bills is so large.[1]

Another aspect of Treasury debt management is managing its cash position. The Treasury is no different from the rest of us in terms of needing a cash balance to bridge the gap between cash inflows and outflows. Tax receipts tend to be concentrated around the scheduled tax payment dates. Federal government expenditures, however, are more evenly spaced out during the year—but not completely so.

The cash receipts of the federal government are almost all first funneled into tax and loan accounts at commercial banks. This system tends to limit the liquidity problem of commercial banks since it provides, so far as possible, that a tax check will be redeposited in the same bank on which it is drawn. However, the Treasury Department makes disbursements only from its Federal Reserve bank accounts, and so there is a regular passage of funds from tax and loan accounts at commercial banks into the Treasury accounts at the Federal Reserve banks. This passage is accomplished by "calls"—notices that on the specified date funds will be transferred. So far as is equitably possible, the Treasury calls on advance notice and tries to avoid nasty surprises to the major commercial banks.

In managing its cash position, the Treasury had been caught on the horns of a dilemma. By keeping cash in tax and loan accounts, and transferring to the Fed as needed for disbursements, the Treasury was able to assist in keeping bank reserve positions stable. (Calls cause cash reserves to fall but disbursements

---

[1]Minimizing the cost of interest is only one of the elements of debt management. Another element is to vary the maturity of the debt as a measure of countercyclical policy. The principles of debt management are discussed in several of the references listed in the bibliography to this chapter.

replenish reserves with little or no delay.) The disadvantage, however, was that the Treasury earned no interest or return on its tax and loan accounts. On the other hand, by keeping cash in its accounts at Federal Reserve banks, and as little as possible in tax and loan accounts, the Treasury could indirectly earn a return on its cash. (The interest that the Fed earns on securities financed by the Treasury's accounts at the Fed is to a large extent returned to the Treasury.) The disadvantage here, however, was that large injections of cash into Treasury accounts at the Fed, at tax time, led to sharp reductions in aggregate commercial bank reserves, thereby complicating the Fed's job of stabilizing interest rates, the money supply, and general money market conditions.

As the interest opportunity cost of maintaining tax and loan accounts rose, the Treasury opted, in 1974, to keep smaller balances in tax and loan accounts, and larger balances in accounts at the Fed. In 1971, over 80 percent of Treasury cash was in tax and loan accounts at commercial banks. By 1976, less than 20 percent of Treasury cash was so deposited. The Treasury was not able to resist the temptation to earn interest on its own money. Of course, this action left the Federal Reserve with the problem of having to stabilize commercial bank reserves.[2]

A final resolution to the dilemma came in 1978. Laws and rules were changed so that the Treasury could invest its funds in interest-bearing notes of commercial banks. In this way the Treasury could earn interest on its money without disturbing the total reserves of the commercial banking system. As for the banks, they were freed from having to keep required reserves on the new interest-bearing accounts. In a larger sense, the Treasury's new "Tax and Loan Investment Program" was in line with the general tendency toward paying interest on everyone's money.

THE MARKET FOR TREASURY BILLS

The Treasury bill is the leading debt instrument of the U.S. government. The volume of Treasury bills outstanding tends to grow with the size of the national debt. Since bills are short-term instruments, while the national debt is permanent, new bills are continually offered as old bills mature. Bills with maturities of three months, six months, and one year are offered on a regular schedule. In addition to these maturities, bills with maturities ranging from 9 to 139 days—called "cash management" bills—are offered irregularly. The maturities of these "cash management" bills are designed to coincide with tax payment dates to provide the Treasury with a smooth inflow of cash.

New offerings of three-month and six-month bills are sold at auction each week. Amounts of offerings to be auctioned are set on Thursdays. Bids are accepted up to 1:30 P.M., New York time, the following Monday. The awarding of successful bids is announced later in the day. The results of the Monday auction often set the tone of the money market week. The Federal Reserve

---

[2] The way the Fed reacted to the Treasury's shift in cash management is a very interesting part of the story that we shall resume in the section covering repurchase agreements.

itself engages in the auction and has no more explicit knowledge of bids than other participants until the bid boxes are opened for tabulation. In the last hour before 1:30, a lot of frantic telephone calls are exchanged between dealers and other bidders, which may account for the relatively close groupings of final bids.

Bids can be competitive or noncompetitive. Competitive bids are usually made by major money market participants such as dealers and large commercial banks. In competitive bids, the bidder states a price for the quantity of bills desired. Noncompetitive bids are usually submitted by individuals and small investors. In noncompetitive bids, the bidder does not state a price but is committed to pay the average price of accepted competitive bids. The awarding of bids—competitive and noncompetitive—is made by the Treasury. All noncompetitive bids ($500,000 maximum per bidder) must be awarded, so the total volume of these bids is subtracted from the total amount of the offering. The remainder is then allocated to the competitive bidders with the highest bids. The average price of the successful competitive bids is then used to charge the noncompetitive bidders. By bidding noncompetitively, the small-scale investor avoids the risk of bidding too high or unsuccessfully low. The dollar volume of noncompetitive bidding is nevertheless fairly small relative to the dollar volume of successful competitive bidding. The Treasury bill market is basically a market for large-scale investors.

Unlike three-month and six-month bills, one-year bills are auctioned only monthly. Special auctions are held for "cash management" bills. The auction procedure is similar, however.

The auction method is simple and expedient. By offering bills on an auction basis, the Treasury completely avoids the pricing problem connected with the more usual subscription methods. The Treasury avoids the risk of asking a price that is too high, resulting in undersubscription, and the risk of asking a price that is too low, resulting in oversubscription. The Treasury is therefore in the same position as the noncompetitive bidders for its bills; it merely sets an amount and lets the market do the rest. The market, of course, consists of the major money market participants who do the competitive bidding.

The auction method owes its success, however, to the nearly perfect conditions in the competitive bidding process. The competitive bidders are well informed and tend to submit bids at prices very close to the average market-clearing price. The number of competitive bidders is sufficiently large so that no one bidder can manipulate the purchase price. The demand for bills is so great among competitive bidders that the total amount of bids submitted always exceeds the total amount of bills offered.

The Treasury bill market is said to possess great "depth and breadth." Treasury bills are demanded as liquidity vehicles in large amounts by all categories of large money market investors: commercial banks, nonbank financial intermediaries, state and local governments, foreign governments and foreign banks, industrial corporations and nonprofit institutions. Bills are free from the risk of default, and they can be converted into cash at any time by selling them in the most active of all secondary financial markets.

The highly developed secondary market for Treasury bills explains to a large extent why bills are so popular. Dealers in bills operate on a high-volume basis, and the spread between their bid and ask prices is very narrow. When bills are sold before maturity to a dealer, the seller knows that the sale will be consummated immediately at the best possible price. The same applies to purchases of outstanding bills from dealers.

Of all traders with dealers, the Federal Reserve is the most active. The Fed continuously buys and sells large amounts of Treasury bills on the open market in the implementation of monetary policy. The Fed purchases bills from dealers when it wants to increase bank reserves and, ultimately, the money supply. And it sells bills to reduce reserves. It also uses open-market operations to influence open-market interest rates. Whether the secondary market in bills is highly active and highly developed because of the Fed's participation in it, or whether the Fed chooses to conduct its open-market operations in the bill market because of the market's inherent depth and breadth, the fact remains that the Fed, alone, has sufficient market power to influence money market conditions. Some people object to this power, but most realize that it goes along with the Fed's social responsibility to promote financial and economic stability.

THE MARKET FOR FEDERAL AGENCY SECURITIES

The Treasury is not the only arm of the U.S. government that borrows in the money market. Over the past fifty or so years, the federal government has created a number of agencies that extend "easy" credit to "needy" sectors in the economy, particularly farmers and home buyers. Since these federal credit agencies are in the business of lending, they, like other financial intermediaries, need their own sources of credit. The various securities that they issue to secure funds fall into the general category of federal agency securities. Most of these securities have original maturities of more than one year, but approximately 30 percent of outstanding securities have original or remaining maturities of less than one year. The latter are clearly a part of the money market.

Federal credit agencies differ from intermediaries in the private sector in that their creation and continued existence is supported by political factors rather than by purely economic ones. Much of their lending is done on a subsidized basis. Loans are often made at interest rates that are below free-market rates, with the taxpayer ultimately making up the difference. The agencies that provide subsidized credit (through low interest rates, loan guarantees, loan insurance, etc.) to the agricultural, housing, and other designated sectors, thus owe their existence to the government's felt need to provide more support to these sectors than is provided by the free market. Agencies also seem to be created by the Congress in order for the Congress to get around the debt ceiling that the Congress, itself, imposes on the Treasury.

Every federal agency (credit agency or otherwise) falls generally into one of two categories: (1) federally owned agencies, and (2) federally sponsored (but privately owned) agencies. The first category includes agencies such as the Export-Import Bank, the Farmers Home Administration, the Government National Mortgage Administration, the Tennessee Valley Authority, and the U.S. Postal Service. These and other federally owned agencies are not very important in terms of securities traded in the money market. The outstanding debts of these agencies are predominantly long-term. Moreover, since 1973, these agencies have acquired new financing from the Federal Financing Bank, which, in turn, has acquired almost all its own financing directly from the U.S. Treasury. This intragovernmental layering of claims has increasingly removed the direct securities of federally owned agencies from the open market. At the same time, it has added to the amount outstanding of Treasury securities in the market.

The securities of the major federally sponsored agencies, on the other hand, are very much part of the money market. The proportion of these securities that matures within one year is large. Moreover, these securities are bought and sold directly in the open market. Primary and secondary markets for these securities are both well developed. The demand for these securities is broadly based; in fact, they are close substitutes for Treasury securities.

Money market activity in agency securities is, for all practical purposes, confined to the securities of the "big five" federally sponsored agencies: Federal Land Banks (FLB), Federal Intermediate Credit Banks (FICB), Banks for Cooperatives (COOP), Federal Home Loan Banks (FHLB), and the Federal National Mortgage Association (FNMA). The first three of these agencies provide credit to farmers. The last two agencies supply funds in the mortgage and housing markets. A sixth agency, the Federal Home Loan Mortgage Corporation (FHLMC), also supplies funds to home buyers, but it differs from the privately owned big five in that it is a wholly owned subsidiary of the FHLB. Incidentally, the private ownership of these federal agencies does not mean that they are operated for private profit. As in the case of Federal Reserve banks, these agencies are privately owned, but, essentially, publicly controlled for the public interest.

New issues of federally sponsored agency securities are usually marketed on a subscription basis through the medium of "fiscal agents." The fiscal agent (New York based) works for the issuing agency on a contract basis, and it is the agent's job to price and place the securities in the market. For placing the securities, the fiscal agent forms a selling group of independent dealers, brokers, and dealer banks who have direct contact with market investors. The new securities are priced by the fiscal agent upon consultation with the selling group, the issuing agency, the Treasury, and the System Open Market Account manager of the Federal Reserve. Once placed in the market, the securities are then traded in the secondary market in much the same way as are Treasury securities. Most dealers in Treasury securities also make markets in the securities of the big-five federally sponsored agencies.

The demand side of the market is very broadly based, consisting of the same groups of investors that buy Treasury bills and other Treasury securities. In several respects, agency securities are nearly perfect substitutes for Treasury securities. Commercial banks can use either kind of security as collateral for securing Treasury tax and loan accounts and other public deposits. The Federal Reserve can conduct outright transactions in agency securities in its open market operations. Various nonbank financial intermediaries can substitute agency securities for Treasury securities in meeting legal reserve and investment regulations.

The securities of federally sponsored agencies do differ from Treasury securities in two important respects, however. First, interest and principal on the former are not guaranteed by the U.S. government (as in the case of Treasury securities). While the risk of default of agency securities is very low, the market does not perceive these securities as being entirely riskless. Second, agency securities are not as liquid as Treasury securities; they are traded in "thinner" markets. As a result, short-term yields on these securities tend to run, on the average, about twenty-five basis points (¼ of 1 percent) above yields on Treasury bills.

MONEY MARKET DEALERS AND BROKERS

The market for Treasury bills, Treasury notes, and federal agency securities is centered in a group of thirty-six dealers (as of 1977), located principally in New York City. Some of these dealers are specialized departments of commercial banks, but most are nonbank dealers. Several of these nonbank dealers are departments of general financial houses, but the majority are independent firms. In addition, quite a few large commercial banks *informally* conduct fairly large intermediating operations. The distinguishing mark of a dealer is that of "making a market," which means that the dealer buys or sells on either end of the bid-and-ask spread. The dealer makes a good market if this bid-and-ask spread is reasonably small in size and if the amount that the dealer is willing to both buy and sell is reasonably large. What is "reasonable" for a spread and for amounts? This is hard to pin down because this depends on the security. In the case of Treasury bills, a dealer might be considered to make a good market if its spread on, say, three-month bills were 6 percent bid and 5.95 percent ask.[3] The dealer might be expected to go $1 million either way on an individual order; and if the dealer were really substantial, it might make a market of $5 to $10 million or even more for a good customer. Since customers make counter offers, the effective spread might be smaller than the five basis points (6 to 5.95 percent). In the case of longer-term securities, a good market usually does not involve such a narrow spread nor such large amounts.

The institutional significance of the U.S. government security dealers is that they are always the link between the Federal Reserve and the money market. The Fed conducts its day-to-day open-market operations exclusively through dealers. The Fed also executes orders for various customers (foreign correspon-

---

[3] What this means is that the dealer is willing to buy at a dollar price that will yield 6 percent if held to maturity. At the same time, the dealer is willing to sell at a *higher* price that will yield the buyer only 5.95 percent.

dents mainly), but it always deals with dealers. The Fed operates rather informally and will deal with any dealer who demonstrates financial responsibility and the willingness to make what the Fed considers a good market. It is thus the dealers who get the first wind of the Fed's open-market operations.

The market in U.S. government securities is a classic over-the-counter market. It is without a central meeting place and is governed much more by tradition than by such laws and rules that are found in stock exchanges. The market is, more accurately, an "over-the-telephone" market. The willingness of dealers to make markets varies greatly with money market conditions—and with their relationship with the customer at the other end of the telephone.

The primary income of dealers is presumed to be in the spread between their bid (buying) and ask (selling) prices. While this income provides their core support, the potential for capital gains and interest income (along with the risk of capital losses in the event of adverse changes in security prices) on their inventories of securities is also important and sometimes of dominant importance. To act as both a buyer and seller, a dealer must have inventories or "positions" in individual Treasury and agency issues. The dealer's fundamental ability is that of finding willing buyers of available securities and willing sellers of needed securities—at prices that leave the dealer with a modest profit. Whether the dealer first sells the securities wanted and the replaces them in its own inventory or acts as a broker in the transaction, the dealer must service its customers to stay in business.

The amount of equity capital employed by the nonbank dealer community is relatively small. Dealer equity furnishes a very narrow margin of financing against dealer holdings of securities (varying roughly in the range of $6 to $12 billion). Dealers thus are able to carry large inventories of securities to the extent that they can find debt financing. (Their equity financing is mainly just a guarantee fund to cover capital losses.) The search by government security dealers for debt financing is one of the principal reasons why dealers, themselves, are such important demanders of funds in the money markets. The traditional source of credit to dealers has been from the large money market banks. This tradition goes back to the London money market in which the discount houses (very much like our dealers) depend on banks for credit, and in which the banks in turn depend on the discount houses as an outlet for surplus loanable funds. While commercial banks in the U.S. also lend surplus funds to dealers, the federal funds market (see next chapter) tends to give banks a somewhat better outlet for surplus funds. Loans to dealers by banks are not as favorably viewed in New York as in London. A few money market banks feel a responsibility to support dealer financing, but this is not a universal feeling. As a result, the dealers themselves have not felt content to depend solely on money market banks for financing. Their search for funds extends to the smaller commercial banks outside the central money markets, and, increasingly, to nonbank lenders. The most novel development in dealer financing has been to borrow funds from nonfinancial corporations.

Many of the giant corporations operate their financial affairs to cover their liquidity needs without bank borrowing even at the peak of such needs. This means that in slack periods they have surplus cash. Employment of this cash in the money markets was a natural consequence, particularly in the postwar period when interest rates went up to a level that made this worthwhile. This was not a new development, of course; during the 1920s many nonfinancial corporations loaned money on the call loan market.

The initial money market investment of corporations was directly in short-term Treasury securities, mainly bills. Dealers, however, found they they could offer corporations outlets for funds that were exactly tailored to the time money would be available. If a corporation has a scheduled dividend or tax payment, it may keep idle funds on hand for such purposes. If no Treasury bill matures on the payment date, this leaves a slightly untidy margin. Dealers found that they could offer to borrow the funds (secured by Treasury obligations, of course) for the exact period for which they were available. Rather than being a formal borrowing-lending transaction, these deals often took the form of a sale of Treasury securities from the dealer to the customer accompanied by an agreement to repurchase the securities at a fixed and predetermined price. These repurchase agreements or "repos," were generally negotiated at a rate that was below bank lending rates to dealers but often just slightly above the Treasury bill rate or at least the Treasury bill rate to the maturity date involved. The dealers save money in comparison with bank borrowings, but they can afford to pay a bit more than the bill rate, often because the average earnings on the portfolio they carry exceed the bill yield.

Commercial banks are the best customers of U.S. government security dealers, but the next best group of customers are the big and liquid corporations. There is, however, considerable specialization in this market. Some dealers are strong with banks, some with corporations, and few consider themselves money market specialists; they trade for other dealers.

The primary qualification for success in this market is the ability to read Federal Reserve signals and to interpret the evidence of pressures in the commercial banking system and the nature of expected business developments. The market is a tender one, and it can be swayed by rumors and random bits of news. Changes in business conditions are always very important; bearish business news is bullish news in this market—and the other way around. Steel strikes and foreign political developments have been known to move prices quite a bit. The reason for sensitivity to Federal Reserve policy is obvious, and it is notable that a fair proportion of the managers in this market are alumni of the Federal Reserve System open-market-account operations.

Many dealers in U.S. government securities deal as well in the other negotiable instruments traded in the money markets. In addition, there are about a dozen dealers that specialize in making a market in commercial paper, and there are a few dealer specialists in the market for bankers' acceptances. Most of these latter dealers are departments of investment banking firms. The sensitivity of investment banks to the financial conditions of issuing corporations makes them particularly fitted for commercial paper dealings. Dealers in bankers' acceptances are mainly those with good connections in the community of foreign banking offices and representatives in New York City. As is true of

U.S. government security dealers, these firms carry inventories of the instruments in which they trade, and they finance their inventories by borrowing from money market banks and elsewhere.

Finally, there are a number of money market brokers who specialize in making deals between money market lenders and borrowers. The money market loans arranged by these brokers sometimes involve nonnegotiable instruments. Brokers are also used for deals between dealers to conceal dealer identity and activity. Unlike dealers, who take title to securities by buying them at one price and selling them at a higher price, brokers operate purely on a commission basis. Because they carry no inventories of their own, money market brokers have extremely modest financial requirements.

THE MARKET FOR REPURCHASE AGREEMENTS

Dealers finance their inventories of securities by borrowing from commercial banks and by entering into repurchase agreements with large corporations, state and local governments, and other investors of temporarily idle funds. Loans from banks to dealers, called dealer loans, are straightforward short-term loans, secured with the securities that they help to finance. Dealer loans from New York banks tend to be one-day loans at interest rates posted daily by these banks. Large banks encourage or discourage dealer loans by varying their posted rates. Dealer loans are not among the most profitable of all loans made by banks, but the rates on them tend to be higher than the rates paid by dealers when financing with repurchase agreements.

The repurchase agreement, or RP, is a strange form of loan arrangement in which the "borrower" sells securities to the "lender" but simultaneously contracts to repurchase the same securities, either on call or at some stated date in the future, at a price that will produce the agreed effective yield. From the lender's viewpoint, it is a purchase of securities with a simultaneous contract to sell them back at an agreed price at a later date (a "reverse RP"). An illustration will demonstrate how the repurchase agreement works to finance a dealer's inventory. Suppose a dealer has an opportunity to buy twelve-month Treasury bills at a bid price to yield 6 percent. The dealer can pay for these T-bills by selling them to a corporation with a simultaneous contract to buy them back a week later at the same price plus 6.20 percent interest. Now suppose that, at the end of the week, the dealer has an opportunity to sell the original T-bills at 5.90 percent ask. The dealer can use the cash from this sale to buy back the securities from the corporation for delivery to the buyer. The dealer loses in the sense that the 6 percent interest income from carrying the T-bills is less than the 6.20 percent interest cost of funds, but this is ordinarily more than made up by the trading profit from the spread. In this particular case, the dealer's net profit is .096 percent of the value of the twelve-month T-bills (.1 percent trading profit less 1/52 of the .2 percent annualized carrying loss). Calculation of trading profit is illustrated in Table 9-2. The key to the dealer's net profit is inventory turnover. The percentage cost of borrowed funds to finance inventory is so close to the yield earned on carrying inventory that a dealer can

TABLE 9-2

Trading Profit Percentage as a Function of Bid-Ask Spread and Maturity of Issue Traded

Bid-Ask Spread	Maturity of Issue Traded	Trading Profit Percentage[*]	Trading Profit on Million Dollar Dealing[†]
2 basis points	90 days	.005%	$ 50
	180 days	.010	100
	360 days	.020	200
10 basis points	90 days	.025	250
	180 days	.050	500
	360 days	.100	1000

[*]Trading profit percentage $= \dfrac{\text{spread in basis points}}{100} \times 1\% \times \dfrac{\text{maturity in days}}{360}$

[†]$1,000,000 \times$ trading profit percentage

basically profit only by constantly turning over inventory to earn high trading profits. If our dealer firm had sold the T-bills after one day, instead of after a week, it would have made its trading profit in much less time. (The dealer might also have had to enter into a six-day reverse RP to deliver the securities and to offset the original seven-day RP.)

The extensive use of repurchase agreements by government security dealers to finance inventories reflects the pressing need of dealers to keep capital costs down. Financing through RPs tends to be less expensive than the more traditional method of dealer loans from banks. Nevertheless, most dealers borrow daily from banks. Dealer loans from New York Banks are generally at higher rates than loans from the more regional banking centers, but the New York banks are convenient for obtaining credit effortlessly at a moment's notice.

Although some regional banks are willing to lend to dealers by entering into repurchase agreements, the RP market is used much more by the banking system as one among many sources of funds. Bank borrowing in the RP market has grown because of three institutional factors. First, banks have large portfolio holdings of Treasury and agency securities with which to sell and repurchase. Second, the funds raised by banks through RPs involving these government securities are exempted by Federal Reserve Regulation D from reserve requirements. And third, banks are in a position to provide their corporate depositors with automatic conversion of excess demand deposits into RPs. This conversion from demand deposit debt to RP debt does not add to total bank funds, but it does make them more loanable since reserves are required on demand deposits but not on RPs. It also has the advantage of building customer satisfaction since RPs, unlike demand deposits, pay interest.

The corporate sector is by far the leading lending sector in the RP market. The RP is the most flexible of all money market instruments when it comes to day-to-day corporate money management. Their maturities, in units of days, are usually arranged for the corporate lender's convenience. They can even be arranged for maturity to be left open to the lender's discretion, with no loss of principal or daily interest. They are so liquid that most corporate money managers consider them as good as cash itself, even better, because RPs earn interest.

Effective interest rates on RPs are as good or better than the yields (adjusted for differentials in maturity) on the T-bills and short-term agency securities bought and resold by the lender. This is due to the possibility that the borrowing bank or dealer might break its contract to repurchase the securities. If this should happen, the lender would still be protected by the market value of the unrepurchased securities that the lender owns. The amount of residual protection depends, however, on the extent to which the market value of the securities covers the contracted repurchase price. Ordinarily, the amount of funds transacted in a repurchase agreement is kept below the value of the securities involved. With this protection, lenders in the market view RPs as virtually riskless.

After corporations, state and local governments are major lenders in the RP market. These governments are usually required to hold their financial assets in the form of bank deposits or in federal securities. The RP provides a way of meeting this requirement without sacrificing either income or liquidity.

Finally, one of the most active participants in the RP market is the Federal Reserve. The Fed uses RPs to complement its regular purchases and sales of government securities in the open market. It uses RPs (either forward or in reverse) when it wants to provide bank reserves (or, alternatively, to absorb them) for only a short period of time. As a tool for defensive day-to-day management of bank reserves, operations in RPs have certain advantages over regular open-market operations. For one thing, an RP transaction makes it unnecessary to negotiate an order to buy (or sell) securities on one day and a separate order to sell (or buy) on a later day. Instead of two transactions, only one is required. For another thing, use of RPs exerts no direct pressure on Treasury bill rates as is the case with outright purchases and sales of bills. It also exerts less indirect pressure on market interest rates in general because the dealers and other participants in the market know that reserves are being injected or absorbed only on a temporary basis. This diminished interest rate effect of the Fed's RP operations over its regular open-market operations acquired great significance during the 1974–1978 period when the U.S. Treasury was moving its tax collections quickly into its accounts at Federal Reserve banks (rather than leaving them in tax and loan accounts at commercial banks). By using RPs on tax-payment dates, the Fed found that it was able to restore the reserves absorbed by the Treasury's deposit policy, and that it could do this without causing interest rates to decline sharply.

CORPORATE MONEY MANAGEMENT

A corporation typically receives its major regular cash inflow from the collection of the accounts receivable that have been generated by sales. If a corporation, operating at several locations, sells its product nationwide or over a wide area, it collects from many customers. To speed up the conversion of these incoming checks into collected bank balances, it may use a large number of banks as lockbox collection agents around the country. Thus cash flows into a considerable number of banks.

The outflow of cash takes a wider variety of forms. Payroll payments may be at many points. Typically these payments, by check, will be from accounts at a number of banks. Indeed, the payroll checks may well have been prepared by the EDP department of the bank, which also handles the payroll account. Accounts payable must be settled, and it is possible that the verification of invoices and physical receipt of goods may require that such payments be decentralized. In addition, other miscellaneous expense items—utility bills and the like—may be paid from a variety of accounts. Thus a major corporation is likely to have a large number of bank accounts, some of which typically disburse funds.

A corporation, however, is likely to have a "lead" bank or possibly major relationships with two or three major (money market) banks, which banks will handle such accounts as dividend and interest payments and manage its pension trust. These lead banks may also make credit advances to the corporation, in which several banks participate.

Even if the total current cash flows of a corporation were in balance, considerable transferring of funds would be required: money from some banks and into other banks. The assumption of a regular balance between inflow and outflow, however, is most unlikely. Even if a corporation should have such a balance over the course of a fiscal year, seasonal differences of "money in" and "money out" would be quite likely. If a corporation finds that more money is going out than coming in, it could allow the total of its bank balances to decline. However, the relationships with cash-accumulating lockbox banks, with funds-disbursing banks, and with lead banks are usually based on a rather clear and explicit understanding of what constitutes a "satisfactory" balance with each bank. This balance is a part of the price for the performance of banking services. This understanding about the appropriate balance is not so rigid and formal that each day's balance cannot depart from this level—it can and does—but the average balance is fairly clearly specified and understood. Thus corporate treasurers can let their bank balances dwindle a bit on any one day, and even for a few days; but if they want to stay on good terms with their bankers, sooner or later these balances must be restored. Sometimes corporate treasurers may keep balances somewhat in excess of these minima, but if they do so persistently, they are wasting valuable income opportunities.

Thus a corporation can use its bank balances as a limited buffer for day-to-day unforecastable variations in net cash flows—but it needs other means for more persisting cash demands. The first line of recourse for cash is again the banks with which the corporation deals. Credit lines are maintained and can be used when needed. The use of these credit lines is also tied to the level of balances kept with these banks: so-called compensating balances. However, it must be admitted that the understandings between a corporation and its banks about which balances compensate for (used and unused) lines of credit and which compensate for services are not always as explicit and clear as indicated above.

Finance companies and certain other large corporations have found a cheaper source of short-term credit: the commercial paper market. The borrowers in this market are expected to maintain unused lines of bank credit to cover such paper outstanding. The net cost of commercial paper borrowing to a corporation with high credit standing is usually less than that of direct bank borrowing. As we shall learn in more detail in the next section, the commercial paper market provides both borrowing and lending opportunities for corporations.

Most corporations have, at least for certain seasons of the year, an excess of funds flowing into their bank accounts. First, short-term debt can be retired. After the bank's reasonable balance expectations have been met, these funds can be employed or "invested" in the money market. The nature of the use depends on how long the funds are expected to be available. This, of course, requires corporations to forecast their cash flow. The credit instruments in which corporations typically invest are the commercial paper of other corporations, negotiable certificates of deposit (perhaps issued by the banks with which they do business), and repurchase agreements (perhaps also arranged by their banks). Corporations also invest in short-term Treasury securities, securities of federal agencies, and even tax-exempt obligations of state or local government units.

Policies for obtaining money when it is needed, and for employing it when it is not needed, vary from firm to firm. Some firms manage their money by *borrowing* in the market when money is needed, and by paying off their loans from banks and retiring their other money market debts when cash flow turns around. Other firms manage their positions by *lending* in the money markets during periods of net cash inflow, and by liquidating their holdings of money market instruments when cash is needed. Which of these two basic policies is best depends, to a certain extent, on the firm's posture towards risk and cost. Liquidation of holdings of money market instruments tends to be a less risky policy for obtaining cash than is reliance upon borrowing from banks and other money market lenders. (From the point of view of the corporate money manager, holdings of short-term securities are surer money than is turning to and borrowing in the market.) But this policy also tends to be the more costly. A detailed cost comparison is too complex to go into, but it basically boils down to the fact that the firm must pay a price to reduce risk. Many large corporations can afford the price or luxury of maintaining a reserve pool of liquid assets. Most small businesses have no choice but to borrow from the local bank when cash is needed. The finance companies and other large corporations that borrow in the commercial paper market are very strong, financially, but cost considerations require them to enter the market as borrowers.

THE MARKET FOR COMMERCIAL PAPER

Commercial paper is the name given to the unsecured short-term negotiable promissory notes offered to money market investors by about 1000 highly creditworthy corporations. Commercial paper is normally (but not always) offered on a discount basis. For this reason the paper is like Treasury bills in that interest is figured on the face amount of the obligation but is then deducted, which is equivalent to collecting interest in advance.

Finance companies, such as General Motors Acceptance Corporation and C.I.T. Financial Corporation, are the primary users of commercial paper financing. They generally place their paper directly with investors by maintaining and operating their own marketing departments. These issuers offer tailored maturities of from 3 days (weekend) to 270 days. Nine months is the effective maximum maturity for commercial paper because anything longer than this would require cumbersome registration with the Securities and Exchange Commission. Although finance company paper is short-term, it is used by the companies that issue it as a permanent source of funds. Like Treasury bills, finance company paper is a floating debt. New paper is sold almost daily as old paper matures.

A number of large industrial corporations and public utilities are also users of commercial paper financing. Unlike directly placed finance company paper, the paper of nonfinancial corporations is generally placed through the ten or so dealers that specialize in the marketing of commercial paper. Dealer-placed paper is not sold in sufficient volume of individual offerings to warrant each corporate issuer to maintain its own marketing department. The maturities of dealer-placed paper are more standardized than they are for directly placed paper. Maturities run from one month to nine months, but three-month paper is the most common (probably in order to compete most effectively with ninety-one day Treasury bills). The commercial paper of nonfinancial corporations is not used as much as a permanent source of funds as it is in finance company financing. Most (but not all) offerings of dealer-placed paper expand and contract with seasonal swings in the issuers' requirements for working capital.

The finance companies, bank holding companies, industrial corporations, public utilities, and others who finance with commercial paper are almost always able to borrow in this market at interest rates slightly lower than the prime lending rate offered by commercial banks. Indeed, the prime rate charged on bank loans is often set, by formula, to be just above the commercial paper rate. New York's Citibank, for example, sets its prime rate at around one percentage above the market rate on three-month commercial paper. One reason why bank lending rates are higher than commercial paper rates is to compensate banks for catering to the specialized credit needs of their individual customers. Bank loans are negotiated on a personal level, and banks are often willing to make credit-extension and other concessions to customers that are unobtainable by financing in the open market. Thus, while commercial paper is a cheaper source of credit than bank loans, it is, at the same time, a more impersonal and, therefore, more unreliable source of credit.

The primary lenders in the commercial paper market are liquid corporations, commercial banks, and insurance companies. Since the maturities of commercial paper are comparable to those on Treasury bills, these two instruments compete with each other as investments for these lenders. Apart from maturity, however, the two instruments differ in a number of respects, including risk of default and marketability.

While commercial paper is low in risk of default, losses do occur. The collapse of the Penn-Central Railroad in 1970 was marked, if not precipitated, by the default of its $82 million of commercial paper. Like Treasury bills, commercial paper is unsecured; but, unlike bills, the credit of even the most qualified private corporation is not as good as the credit of the U.S. government. For this and other reasons, borrowers in the commercial paper market are required to carry backup lines of credit at commercial banks. These backup credit lines are supposed to serve as a form of "insurance" for the protection of both lenders and borrowers in the market. Backup credit was of little help to the holders of Penn-Central paper, however.

The other major difference between commercial paper and Treasury bills is marketability. There is no established secondary market for commercial paper as there is for government securities. If a holder of commercial paper becomes hard-pressed for cash before the paper matures, the holder can usually do no better than to sell it back to the original issuer. Finance companies often abide by a gentlemen's agreement to buy back their own paper if requested by the holder. Dealer-placed paper, also, can sometimes be sold back to the issuer, with the dealer serving as intermediary.

Owing to the lack of a well-established secondary market, along with the possibility of default, yields on commercial paper are naturally higher than yields on Treasury bills. These higher yields are attractive to corporate money managers who are able to commit funds for several months on a matching basis with maturity, for then there is no foreseen need to use a secondary market. Nevertheless, most corporate money managers are careful to scrutinize the quality of the paper that they buy. The default of the Penn-Central's paper certainly taught this lesson.

THE MARKET FOR BANKERS' ACCEPTANCES

Bankers' acceptances are, essentially, short-term IOUs of businesses engaged in foreign trade that qualify as money market instruments because they are guaranteed by large internationally known commercial banks. These instruments are almost wholly related to the financing of foreign trade. When a business imports goods from another country, it needs credit to cover the time gap between paying for the goods (as they leave the foreign exporter's hands) and selling the goods (after they arrive from shipment). Ordinary trade credit is usually unsatisfactory for financing foreign trade because (1) the seller (exporter) usually has insufficient knowledge of the buyer's (importer's) credit standing, and (2) the two parties operate with different currencies. Financing through bankers' acceptances tends to avoid these two problems. These instruments are considered to be safe because they are guaranteed by large internationally known banks. The exporting firm does not have to worry about future foreign exchange prices because it receives immediate payment for its goods. The holders of bankers' acceptances—the ones actually financing the transaction—face a foreign exchange problem only to the extent that their own currency is different from the currency in which the acceptance is denominated.

An illustration of how dollar-denominated acceptance financing works will probably better explain the nature of the market. Suppose a business (American or foreign, it does not matter) wants to import goods from Japan. It can request its New York bank (with offices all over the world) to issue a letter of credit on its behalf in favor of the Japanese exporter. If the bank has faith in the importer's credit, it will issue the letter and authorize the Japanese seller to draw a time draft in payment for the goods. (A time draft differs from an ordinary check in that it is written by the receiving party but cannot be cashed for full face value until a specified date.) Once the Japanese firm receives this authorization, it can release the goods for shipment, write the draft in favor of itself, and receive immediate payment by discounting the draft at its own bank. (It will want to make sure, however, that its negotiated sale price for the goods is inflated so that the discounted amount of the draft covers the true value of the shipment.) The Japanese bank, in turn, will send the draft, along with appropriate shipping documents and instructions regarding the disposition of the draft, to the New York bank. When the New York bank acknowledges its obligation to honor the draft—by writing "Accepted" across the face of the draft—the draft becomes a bankers' acceptance. It is at this point that birth is given to a safe, negotiable money market instrument. It is also at this point that the shipping documents are released to the accepting bank, who forwards them to the importer, who, in turn, will need them to claim the shipment of goods when it arrives. Meanwhile, the importer is still in debt. The importer's obligation is to provide the New York bank with funds on or before the maturity of the acceptance.

The accepting New York bank will not necessarily be holding the acceptance during its period to maturity. The Japanese bank may decide to keep it and hold it to maturity as an investment, earning interest in the form of the difference between the full face value received at maturity and the discounted purchase price paid previously to the exporter. Foreign banks are extremely important investors in the market for acceptances originating out of New York (and California) banks. Foreign banks have traditionally viewed acceptances as being very safe and highly liquid. This tradition goes back to the beginning of the London acceptance market and, therefore, predates the New York market by many, many years.

Alternatively, the New York bank may buy the acceptance that it originates (at a discount, of course). If the bank holds the acceptance to maturity, it will in effect be in the same position as if it had extended a loan directly to the importer. Unlike an ordinary bank loan, however, the acceptance is a negotiable instrument and need not be held to maturity. If the bank needs funds before the borrowing importer is scheduled to provide them, the bank can always sell the acceptance to a dealer in the secondary market. The secondary market is rather well developed, and acceptances sometimes change hands several times before they come due.

Among those who trade with dealers, the Federal Reserve is an important net buyer of acceptances. The Fed is empowered to buy and sell "eligible" acceptances in its open-market operations. Along with Treasury and agency securities, the Fed can trade in acceptances by buying them either outright or through repurchase agreements. The inclusion of acceptances in open-market purchases not only expands the number of markets in which the Fed can supply funds directly to the domestic economy, it also supports the growth and development of the dollar-denominated acceptance market.

Foreign banks, New York accepting banks, and the Federal Reserve Bank of New York (on behalf of all twelve Federal Reserve banks) are the most important groups of investors in the market for dollar acceptances. On the borrowing side of the market are the many businesses engaged in foreign trade. Except for the accepting banks, the link between lender and borrower is indirect. Acceptances are not redeemed at maturity by the lender going directly to the borrower. Rather, the holder receives the face value of an acceptance from the accepting bank, which, in turn, must collect from its borrowing customer. Unless the customer defaults, the accepting bank need not commit a penny of its own funds during the entire sequence of events. All it really has to do is to lend its name to the credit instrument. For this service, the accepting bank is entitled to charge the borrower a fee. This fee raises the effective interest rate cost to the borrower above the market rate on acceptances, but since the market rate is relatively low, as interest rates go, the total cost of acceptance financing is usually not prohibitive. The crucial variable is the fee that the accepting bank charges the borrower for underwriting the borrower's credit. The fee varies, of course, with the risk that the borrower might default. Generally, acceptance financing is not available to firms whose credit ratings are poor.

PROJECTS AND QUESTIONS

1. The volume outstanding of U.S. Treasury bills is a large proportion of the total national debt, but it is not a fixed or constant proportion over time. Through your own research, explain why there are seasonal, cyclical, and secular changes in the relative supply of Treasury bills.
2. Maturities of dealer-corporate repurchase agreements are usually set by the corporate lender rather than by the borrowing dealer. Speculate as to why this does or does not create a burden for dealers in financing their inventory positions.

3. Relative to their great need for short-term credit, most nonfinancial corporations do surprisingly little direct borrowing in the open money market. Why is this? You may want to look at a balance sheet in an annual report of a nonfinancial corporation to find your answer.

BIBLIOGRAPHY

Banks, L.: "The Market for Agency Securities," *Quarterly Review,* Federal Reserve Bank of New York, Summer 1978, pp. 7–21.

Brewer, E.: "Treasury to Invest Surplus Tax and Loan Balances," *Economic Perspectives,* Federal Reserve Bank of Chicago, November/December 1977, pp. 14–20.

Brockschmidt, P.: "Treasury Cash Balances," *Monthly Review,* Federal Reserve Bank of Kansas City, July/August 1975, pp. 12–20.

Cooper, R. L.: "Bankers' Acceptances," *Monthly Review,* Federal Reserve Bank of New York, June 1966, pp. 127–135.

Gaines, T. C.: *Techniques of Treasury Debt Management,* The Free Press, New York, 1962.

Garbade, K. D., and J. F. Hunt: "Risk Premiums on Federal Agency Debt," *Journal of Finance,* March 1978, pp. 105–116.

Helfrich, R. T.: "Trading in Bankers' Acceptances," *Monthly Review,* Federal Reserve Bank of New York, February 1976, pp. 51–57.

Hurley, E. M.: "The Commercial Paper Market," *Federal Reserve Bulletin,* June 1977, pp. 525–536.

Joines, J. S.: "Bankers' Acceptances," in *Instruments of the Money Market,* Federal Reserve Bank of Richmond, 1977.

Lang, R. W., and R. H. Rasche: "Debt-Management Policy and the Own Price Elasticity of Demand for U.S. Government Notes and Bonds," *Review,* Federal Reserve Bank of St. Louis, September 1977, pp. 8–22.

Lucas, C. M., M. T. Jones, and T. B. Thurston: "Federal Funds and Repurchase Agreements," *Quarterly Review,* Federal Reserve Bank of New York, Summer 1977, pp. 33–48.

McCurdy, C. J.: "The Dealer Market for United States Government Securities," *Quarterly Review,* Federal Reserve Bank of New York, Winter 1977–78, pp. 35–47.

Monhollon, J. R.: "Dealer Loans and Repurchase Agreements," in *Instruments of the Money Market,* Federal Reserve Bank of Richmond, 1977.

Prell, M.: "Managing the Debt of the 1960s," *Monthly Review,* Federal Reserve Bank of San Francisco, January 1969, pp. 11–18.

Roley, V. V.: "Federal Debt Management Policy: A Re-Examination of the Issues," *Economic Review,* Federal Reserve Bank of Kansas City, February 1978, pp. 14–23.

Schadrack, F. C.: "Demand and Supply in the Commercial Paper Market," *Journal of Finance,* September 1970, pp. 837–852.

Chapter 10
Commercial Banks in the Central Money Markets

Chapter 8, which opened the money market section, has already described the important and central role of commercial banks in the money markets. As the other sectors of the economy adjust their liquidity, the resulting impact is felt by the commercial banks in the form of changes in the supply of deposits or in the demand for loans. Commercial banks are in the business of supplying liquidity to their customers. But in the process of accommodating customers, commercial banks themselves face liquidity problems. In Chapter 9 some attention was given to the ways in which commercial banks put their own temporarily idle funds to work. The money markets that reflect the credit needs of government and business—namely, the markets for Treasury securities, agency securities, dealer loans, commercial paper, and bankers' acceptances—are all markets in which commercial banks have a strong lending position.

What was left out of these chapters was adequate recognition of the money markets that reflect the short-term credit needs of banks themselves. In making money available to others, banks have severe liquidity problems of their own. The larger, more aggressive banks are almost always short of funds, which means that they have to enter certain money markets as borrowers. We also need to show how the profit objective dominates commercial banks' operations and how it affects their money market operations. Commercial banks are profit-making institutions. Whatever else they may attempt to achieve, profits are the heart of their operations. In this regard they differ greatly from the Federal Reserve, which is not a profit-motivated institution (although it does in fact make large profits from its money creation powers). The Federal Reserve has objectives of economic and money market stability.

The central concern of commercial banks with moneymaking means that they must focus on two sets of interest rates: those that they receive as lenders or investors and those they pay (in money or implicitly) in securing money. Commercial banks are complex institutions with many sources of income—but the income from lending and investing money still dominates their revenue calculus. And while commercial banks have many costs, the most variable cost has been that of securing money.

The opportunities that banks have to employ money determines how much they are willing to pay, directly or indirectly, for money. The growing importance of this line of causation is one of the great developments of contemporary commercial banking. At one time banks were rather passive with respect to securing funds. They solicited the business of depositors and adjusted the rates paid on time deposits—but they did not "buy" money in a very aggressive sense. Since the early 1960s, however, banks have been active searchers and bidders for money. The degree of search activity and bid rates have depended on the rates available in money employment opportunities. Thus revenue rates and cost rates are interrelated.

The problem, however, is that the process of money employment involves various terms of commitment into the future. If banks are to be able to grasp money employment opportunities, they must have much of the money on hand; it is not technically feasible to go out and "buy" large amounts of money on short notice. Thus banks are forced into the activity of forecasting both demand and supply in the money markets and then planning their balance of funds so as to be able to take maximum advantage of the opportunities that they believe to be before them. Banks were among the first to employ economists for financial forecasting, and they continue to be large employers of economists relative to other types of business. Banks must engage in forecasting and planning as a necessary step in managing their sources and uses of funds. However, since forecasts can go wrong and plans can fail to materialize, banks also have to keep flexible so that they can adjust to unexpected variations in actual from forecasted funds flows. The money markets provide this flexibility. They make it possible for banks to manage their general funds more effectively and to adjust their reserve positions on a day-to-day basis.

The plan of this chapter will be to look first at the general uses and sources of bank funds to provide an overall picture of bank lending and borrowing. We will then examine the problem of managing these uses and sources and how certain money markets, notably, the market for negotiable certificates of deposit, are used by banks in this management. After that, we will give special attention to the problem of adjusting reserve positions and the role of the federal funds market in the adjustment process. The final section (which really leads in to the next chapter) will then consider bank reserves in the aggregate and how this aggregate serves to constrain the supply of money in the economy.

USES OF BANK FUNDS

Commercial banks make the largest part of their loans to businesses. A very large fraction of the dollar volume of business loans (although not so large a fraction in terms of numbers) is made at the prime loan rate. The prime loan rate was, until some years ago, set by leadership within the banking community. The identity of this leadership was clear: About half a dozen very large banks took the initiative in raising or lowering the prime loan rate. Other big (but not quite as big) banks usually went along. The prime loan rate would be raised when money was short. This might be signaled by increases in various open-market interest rates, but it would also be justified by strong customer loan demand. A decrease in the prime loan rate would come at an opposite time: when open-money-market rates were going down and customer loan demand was weak. The actual announced decrease might come after a period in which there had been some covert and not fully concealed cutting of rates to especially good customers. A change was viewed as the expressed judgment of a money market leader that such change was both needed and justified by money market conditions.

Recently the prime loan rate has lost this simple nature. More banks have gotten into the act of announcing rate changes, sometimes, apparently, only for reasons of getting some cheap and quick publicity. But a few banks, rather than basing their prime loan rates on judgment, now use a formula related to the rate on commercial paper for doing so. The prime loan rate is linked to the commercial paper rate because both rates apply to the same group of prime business borrowers. Of course, the very act of selection of the elements in a formula involves judgment. As we can see in Figure 10-1, the spread between

figure 10-1 The Prime-Paper Rate Spread. *(Source:* Economic Perspectives, *Federal Reserve Bank of Chicago, July–August 1977, p. 18.)*

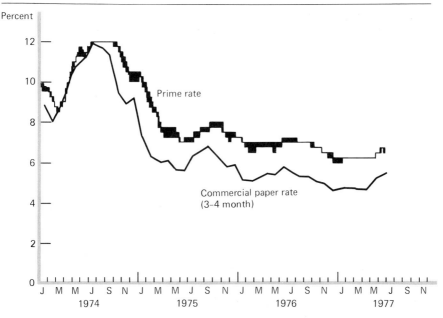

the prime rate and the commercial paper rate has not been constant; instead, it has changed with changes in the formula.

Banks away from central money markets do not adhere as closely to the prime loan rate, but most banks are influenced by it. For all banks, big and small, the rate should be viewed as one determined largely by market forces over which the individual bank has little or no control. What the individual bank can do, and what most banks do do, is to attempt to use their prime loan rate to solidify and extend their customer relationships. When money is easy, customer loans probably are the more profitable ways in which to employ money. It pays to promote loan business with customers. In times when money is tight and loan demand high, margin for negotiation remains in the level of compensating balance requirements put on customers. Even compensating balance arrangements are subject to considerable competitive pressure, and a bank cannot get far out of line with the market as a whole. But within margins, a bank can so arrange the nature of the requirement as to get the maximum balance from customers but to fit it most conveniently into customers' cash flows. Banks are increasingly offering cash management services to their customers, a part of which is that this is a way of getting the most for both sides of the bargain.

In the end, the prime loan rate should be considered closely allied to the more volatile open-market money rates, particularly the rate on commercial paper that, for many customers, represents a practical alternative as a source of funds. As mentioned already, the formulas now used by those banks that set their prime rates in this way generally put most weight on the commercial paper rates. The transmission route for influence is about this: general open-market money rates to the commercial paper rate, and from that to the prime loan rate. Two kinds of "add ons" to the prime loan rate are important: a higher rate for lower-quality customers and a higher rate for longer-term loans.

As the name indicates, this rate is for "prime" customers. Although there is no clear and unambiguous definition of what a prime customer is, many customers, and some of the most profitable, are not prime. The interest rates on business loans compiled quarterly by the Federal Reserve are always materially above the prime loan rate for the period covered by the report. For very big loans the margin is from ¼ to ½ percent, but for smaller loans the differential is much greater. There is also a regional differential that may or may not be due to differences in quality. However, even for those customers that do not rate as prime, the prime loan rate may still determine borrowing costs: Banks often classify a customer as "prime + X percent."

There are also differences for maturity. Short loans have the prime rate and longer-term loans will be made with some differential. The size of this differential cannot be quantified with available data. However, it appears that this differential is usually less than the slope of the yield curve. In other words, banks do not demand as clear a maturity differential as is demanded by the open money and capital markets.

Almost all banks make some business loans that lie outside the orbit of the prime loan rate. Loans to small businesses and to farmers usually fall in this category. The importance of such credit to money market banks is not large, but it is the main form of business credit made by small banks in remote locations.

In terms of volume, the second most important use of bank funds is mortgage lending. A mortgage is a loan secured by real estate. Mortgage loans tend to have long-term maturities and are, therefore, not as liquid as business loans. They are also not as profitable as business loans. Almost all banks make some mortgage loans to customers individually, but this is often more an accommodation than a matter of direct profit. Most banks prefer to satisfy their business loan demand first; mortgage lending is a lower priority. This means that when credit is in short supply and interest rates are high, mortgage credit tends to be rationed out to the most creditworthy customers. Some banks act as mortgage bankers and so originate a great deal of mortgage credit, but, if credit is tight, they sell the mortgages to investors located in areas of less-pressing loan demand. However, when credit is easy and interest rates are low, most banks are willing to make mortgage loans on terms that are more closely competitive with terms offered by savings and loan associations and other mortgage-credit institutions.

The third most important type of bank lending is consumer credit. Banks have become very aggressive lenders in this field. They are currently the leading institution supplying consumer installment credit in the U.S., followed by finance companies and credit unions. They compete vigorously with sales finance companies in offering credit to finance automobiles and other consumer durables. They also provide ample credit to finance nondurables and services as evidenced by the promotion and growth of the use of bank credit cards. When managed correctly, consumer lending is very profitable. The rates charged on consumer loans run much higher than they do on other loans. The differential between consumer lending rates and interest rates in the open money markets is usually so great that money for consumer loans is almost always available.

The typical bank receives, on the average, about three-quarters of its total interest income through the making of loans. The remaining one-quarter is earned by purchasing and holding securities (making "investments"). The proportion of interest from "loans" and that of interest from "investments" varies, however, as funds are shifted from the one category and into the other. The distinction of bank earning assets between "loans" and "investments" has no particular analytical significance; rather, it is simply a matter of banking convention.

The two big kinds of investments at commercial banks are both government securities: federal government securities and the securities of state and local governments. Commercial banks also hold modest amounts of corporate bonds, commercial paper, etc., but these holdings are only a small fraction of their holdings of government securities.

At one time, the main significance of U.S. Treasury and Agency securities to commercial banks was as a joint source of both liquidity and interest income. The liquidity function of federal government security holdings dwindled in importance, however, with the development of markets for "immediately available funds." The development of the "federal funds" market (which we shall discuss later in this chapter) was particularly instrumental in the decline of the Treasury securities portfolio as the principal source of liquidity.

Commercial banks now hold Treasury securities and federal agency securities for use in repurchase agreements and for the purpose of giving them collateral, which is required for tax-and-loan accounts and other public-body deposits. Under the law, all government deposits at commercial banks have to be backed, dollar for dollar, by bank ownership of government securities. Banks profit from this requirement because the interest cost of the government deposits is less than the interest income earned on the securities that serve as collateral. Few aggressively managed banks hold federal government securities much in excess of their RP and collateral needs, however, because greater returns can be earned on tax-exempt state and local government securities.

The income function of federal government security holdings dwindled in importance when commercial banks became fully exposed to the impact of the corporate federal income tax. Under present tax law, banks cannot give capital gains treatment to income from investment securities, so about the only shelter left is that of investment in tax-exempt obligations of state and local governments.

The attraction of state and local government securities is fully understandable. In recent years, the yield on Aaa municipal bonds has usually been between 5 and 7 percent. With an applicable marginal income tax rate of 48 percent facing banks, this range of yields on tax-exempt bonds is equal to a 9.6 to 13.5 percent range of taxable yields. Since the yields on banks' taxable investments have not come close to this higher range, banks have naturally chosen to concentrate their investments in tax-exempt securities. Even in 1974, when the federal funds rate averaged 10.5 percent, banks could afford to pay the price of federal funds and preferred it to foregoing the 6 percent yield on Aaa tax-exempts (equal to a 11.5 percent taxable yield).

The problem with tax-exempt securities, however, is that these high yields are available primarily on quite long-term bonds, and the marketability of these long-term bonds is not always the best. Although banks buy many short-term tax-exempts, they have tended to push out into longer maturities. If a bank commits itself to longer-term tax-exempt securities or even those of intermediate maturity, it may find some problems in trying to change its investment posture quickly.

Furthermore, the yields on tax-exempt securities are quite volatile. Since they depend very much on market demand by banks, yields are likely to be the highest when banks are pinched for funds and under the pressure of good customer loan demand. When this is not true and money markets are easier, banks tend to have excess funds with which to buy tax-exempts so that yields are driven down. Therefore, it is very difficult for commercial banks to buy tax-exempts with good timing. This difficulty is further compounded by the fact that banks do not like to report sharply fluctuating income to stockholders. Banks can reserve liquidity to wait for good buys of tax-exempts, but this accentuates the problem of income instability.

Because of the special role commercial banks play in the tax-exempt market, the market tends to be tied more closely to money market developments than almost any other capital market. Commercial banks are important underwriters in the issuance of municipal bonds as well as being the leading holders of these securities. The new-issue tax-exempt market, therefore, is more vulnerable to tight-money news and more responsive to easy-money news than almost any other type of security.

Apart from loans and investments, commercial banks hold various cash assets or reserves. These cash assets include currency in bank vaults, demand deposits at Federal Reserve banks, demand deposits at each others' commercial banks, and holdings of checks not yet collected. Just as individuals and businesses have checking accounts with commercial banks, the commercial banks, themselves, have accounts with Federal Reserve banks and with each other.

Commercial banks need these cash reserves to facilitate the process of clearing and collecting checks. The amount of cash reserves actually kept, however, goes beyond this need and is tied to legal reserve requirements imposed by bank regulating authorities. Commercial banks are legally required to keep a minimum cash reserve position equal to a specified percentage of deposit liabilities. The Federal Reserve Board of Governors sets the reserve requirements for banks that are members of the Federal Reserve System. Only certain cash assets count as legal reserves for member banks. These include deposits of member banks at Federal Reserve banks and vault cash. Reserve requirements for nonmember banks are set by state regulations. The required reserves vary from state to state but are in general lower than the Federal Reserve requirements. Moreover, since nonmember banks maintain only minimal check-clearing balances at Federal Reserve banks, state regulations generally permit the counting of deposits at each others' banks (accounts with correspondent banks) as meeting the reserve requirements. Some states even allow government securities to be counted as reserves.

Although the intent or philosophy of reserve requirements is not always very clear, the effect of these requirements is quite clear: Reserve requirements are a constraining force on the size and growth of the nation's money supply. As we shall see in the final section of this chapter, there is a close (but by no means perfectly tight) relation between the amount of money in the economy and the amount of cash reserves that commercial banks are required to hold.

This close relation has become less close over time, however, as many commercial banks have opted out of membership in the Federal Reserve System. By becoming nonmembers, banks have been able to reduce their reserve requirement burdens and thereby increase their profits. But this has left the Fed with less control over commercial bank reserves. As a result, there is much talk that Federal Reserve membership may become compulsory. The Fed will probably have to sweeten any move in this direction, however, by providing for the payment of interest on member bank reserves.

SOURCES OF BANK FUNDS

Deposits are the principal source of bank funds. Time deposits are now more important than demand deposits—and also often more volatile. In recent years, time deposits have accounted for about 70 percent of the new funds available to commercial banks; demand deposits have accounted for less than 20 percent. Banks also secure funds through retained earnings. Capital market financing in the form of common stock or notes and debentures is erratic but is seldom more than a tiny fraction of total sources of bank funds.

Most of these sources of funds are not very responsive to short-run managerial approaches. The large negotiable certificates of deposit (NCDs), as we shall see later in this chapter, are the most responsive to management, the volume being closely related to the rates offered by banks. Over a period of months a bank may press on this source of funds or retreat from it. However, NCDs are good sources of funds only for the large money market banks. Even for them, NCDs are not the largest source of funds.

The way in which liabilities are managed is central to the cost of funds secured by banks and therefore to their profitability. If a bank locks itself into a rather high average cost of funds, expecting a strong high-interest-rate loan demand for funds, but the demand fails to materialize, its profits will be considerably cut. Thus the art of liability management (which involves going into the money markets for funds) is that of securing an adequate volume of funds—but without cost commitments at a level that jeopardizes future profits.

In the early history of commercial banking in the United States, time deposits were found mainly in middle-sized and smaller banks and those which aimed at "retail" banking business. Money market banks secured most of their funds from demand deposit accounts. In 1961, however, money market banks started to use the NCD. The NCD was a path-breaking innovation in liability management. It was first aimed at getting the surplus funds of nonfinancial corporations, but it came also to be used as an investment outlet by state and local governments, foreign investors, and other investors of short-term money.

Although popular attention focused mainly on the NCD, banks also innovated in the use of other forms of time and savings accounts. Passbook savings accounts are now offered in a variety of forms. Nonnegotiable CDs are available to depositor-investors in moderate unit size. Federal Reserve Regulation Q controls the rates that banks can pay on smaller time deposits (NCDs have been exempted from such regulation since mid-1970). Within these regulatory limits, banks use many devices for the attraction of time deposits: monthly, daily, even continuous compounding of interest; various contract terms; and a variety of depository relationships that function as passbook accounts but are legally and technically much nearer to CDs.

The important feature of Regulation Q, however, is that it has made time deposits a rather undependable source of funds when funds are most demanded. The limitation on the rate of interest paid on time deposits was originally adopted in order to avoid what was feared would be ruinous competition for such deposits. In addition, the Federal Reserve appeared to view Regulation Q as a monetary instrument and welcomed the limitation that it indirectly imposed on the expansion of bank loans. However, it now appears that the Federal Reserve itself (or at least an operational majority of policy-making officials within the Federal Reserve) no longer feels the need for Regulation Q.

This monetary use of Regulation Q made time deposits a less useful source of funds. Since the ceiling rates tended to be most restrictive when interest rates were rising, it denied banks access to time deposit funds just at the very time when the most profitable opportunities were available for the employment of added funds. However, if Regulation Q should be abandoned or at least made less restrictive, which now seems probable, then time deposits would offer even more appeal to banks in their search for funds. One category of time deposits, the six-month $10,000-denomination money market certificate (MMC), has already been exempted from Regulation Q ceiling rates. MMC rates are allowed to go up and down with rates on six-month Treasury bills.

Although demand deposits have dwindled relative to time deposits as a source of funds, they are still important. The fraction of new funds coming from these accounts has been about one-fifth in recent years. What is more, demand depository services furnish one of the important elements in the customer relationships of banks.

Several background factors account for the relative decline of demand deposits. High interest rates have made depositors more conscious of the advantages of careful cash management. When interest rates were low, as in the early postwar years of the late 1940s, a depositor might leave idle funds in a demand deposit account beyond the need to compensate its bank for services because alternative employment of the funds did not yield very much income. But when short-term interest rates are high, as they have been for quite some time, then such slack management of cash is no longer defensible. The other side of the story is that the volume of payment by check has grown much more rapidly than the GNP. Rapid improvements in the technology (computer and electronic technology especially) of processing payments and collections has made it possible to get much more mileage out of each dollar's worth of demand deposits. With the dollar working harder, fewer dollars are required to do the same work. Higher interest rates and an improving technology have thus combined to change the relationship of banks to their most important customers.

The same law on which Regulation Q is based also prohibits the payment of explicit interest on demand deposits. However, banks have developed various service charge or other cost-of-service approximations that are used in figuring how much it costs banks to use various types of demand deposit accounts. Then, by use of some implicit rate of return on demand balances, it is possible to calculate how much of a demand deposit account must be maintained to make such an account profitable to the bank. This sort of cost-benefit calculus is monitored by the larger demand deposit customers by comparisons among banks, and thus there is a kind of implicit competitive rate on demand deposits even when no explicit payment is made. Customers have a fairly clear idea of just how much of a balance must be maintained and so know what are excess funds that can be employed in the money markets.

Although commercial banks are reluctant participants in this game of converting "idle" demand deposits into earning assets for their corporate customers, they know that this is the price for maintaining viable customer-depositor relations. Thus banks are more and more offering their customers cash management services. For the big nonfinancial corporations this service takes the form of planning the system of cash collection and disbursement that is most efficient. Many banks now have computer simulation programs for the estimation of such efficiency. With this planned system, they offer a full line of service for the investment of any excess funds—or a line of credit for the supplying of needed funds during periods of deficiency. Surplus-funds customers are offered a wide variety of money market investment outlets by trading departments of money market banks, including commercial paper, bankers' acceptances, repurchase agreements against Treasury or Agency securities, its own or other negotiable CDs, and short-term tax-exempt securities.

The country correspondent banks of money market banks are offered even more comprehensive services. In the first place, where physical location makes it possible and feasible, city correspondents often do all the accounting for country correspondents and handle check collections for them. The big computer installations of city banks are often able to handle this volume of work very efficiently. By this process, the city correspondent can, as mentioned above, manage the reserve position of its country correspondent. Explicit charges are made for some of these services but, in addition, balances held by the country correspondent with its city correspondent furnish a buffer for reserve position management. Funds that are in excess of reserve needs and in excess of the agreed balance held by the country correspondent with its city correspondent are bought by the city bank as Fed funds. These Fed funds purchases are really residuals and not a part of the true open market for Fed funds. However, the rate set for such purchases is the open-market Fed funds rate or close to it.

Banks also convert "idle" demand deposits into earning assets for their governmental and individual depositors. The U.S. Treasury, for example, has an arrangement with banks for its funds to be put to work in tax and loan investment notes that earn interest. An individual can arrange for funds to be kept in an interest-bearing time deposit account and transferred automatically to a demand deposit account to cover any checks written. The arrangements described in this paragraph and the two above are indicative of the trend toward paying interest on deposits generally.

The total amount outstanding of demand deposits plus time deposits (including NCDs) reflects the total amount of indebtedness of commercial banks to their depositors. Since these deposits account for approximately 90 percent of total sources of bank funds, banks have no choice but to cultivate good customer relationships with their depositors. However, when funds from deposits run short of funds required by banks, banks also have no choice but to turn to alternative sources of funds.

In addition to borrowing from their depositors, banks borrow regularly from each other in the federal funds market; they borrow from Federal Reserve banks at the Federal Reserve "discount window"; and they occasionally borrow from banks located overseas through the Eurodollar market. The extensive system of interbank lending is the primary means by which banks adjust their own liquidity. The particular markets involved in the system of interbank loans are genuine money markets in their own right. We shall examine these markets in considerable detail in later sections of this chapter. But, first, we need to come to grips with the general problem of bank funds management.

BANK FUNDS MANAGEMENT

In the ex post sense that a bank's uses and sources of funds are always equal, it might seem that commercial banks have no problem of managing their funds. In fact, however, the problem of managing funds is greater for banks than it is for almost any other enterprise. Total uses and sources have to be kept at a sufficiently high level to generate enough net interest income to cover fixed costs and turn a profit. The composition of sources of funds has to be managed so that the average cost of funds does not eat too heavily into the income earned on loans and investments. Loans have to be managed so that they do not turn sour. Investments need to be made in securities whose maturities match up reasonably well with future funds requirements caused by strong expected loan demand and/or expected deposit withdrawals. Funds must be available to meet reserve requirements. Excess reserves, if any, have to be employed if a bank is going to compete effectively. The list goes on and on. The point is that funds management is at the heart of the business of banking. The objective of funds management is to come as close as possible to the most desirable level and composition of the uses and sources of funds.

The management of bank funds is a process involving several steps. The process begins with forecasting. The demand for loans, the supply of deposits, and other leading uses and sources of funds have to be estimated in advance so that management decisions made in the present will have desirable effects in the future. After forecasting comes the step of planning. The less a bank funds manager likes what is forecast, the more inclined the manager will be to plan ways to influence loan demand and deposit supply to the bank's advantage, or, at least, to plan measures to cope with that part of an adverse forecast that lies outside the bank's control. The next step is implementation. Policies and decisions have to be made and carried out with respect to securing and employing funds in a consistent manner with planned uses and sources of funds. Rarely, however, will such implementation result in plans coming true. Banks are extremely vulnerable to unanticipated shifts in customer loan demand and deposit supply. A bank can guess what its customers are going to do, but it cannot force customers to take out loans or keep deposits. The result is that every bank faces a daily problem of having either a shortage of funds or a surplus that is totally unplanned. Since these uncontrollable losses and gains of funds impact directly on a bank's reserve position, the final element of bank funds management (and most important in terms of money market involvement) is reserve position adjustment. On days when unexpected shortfalls of funds cause reserves to be deficient, a bank must have a backup source of funds with which to quickly cover its reserve position. On other days, when unexpected cash inflows cause reserves to be in excess, a bank needs an immediate outlet with which to employ such excesses.

A simple illustration of the process of bank funds management will bring the problem into sharper focus. Suppose we look at a bank whose forecast of funds flows for the coming quarter indicates a net loan demand of $125 million and a net deposit supply of $100 million. By themselves, these two estimates indicate a $25 million gap between uses and sources of funds. Suppose, further, that the bank is required to keep 15 percent of its deposits as reserves. With deposits forecasted to increase by $100 million, $15 million of this will have to be committed to reserves, thereby increasing the gap between uses and sources to $40 million. Obviously, a great deal of planning is required, otherwise the bank will probably not have the funds to satisfy the estimated demand for loans by its customers. What can the bank do? It might raise the interest rates that it charges on loans; this would result in fewer loans, but a greater margin per dollar loaned. It might also provide more services on deposit accounts; this would increase the cost of operations, but bring in more funds from deposits. Either way, consideration would have to be given to complex interaction effects with rival banks. Suppose, after due consideration, that the bank decides that it would be profitable to close $10 million of the gap by raising rates charged on loans.

With a $30 million gap still remaining, the bank has little choice but to turn to those sources of funds over which management control can be more easily exercised. On this score, it would have a number of alternatives. It could liquidate that part of the U.S. government securities portfolio that is not needed as collateral for public deposits. This source has a relatively low cost in terms of foregone interest, but, if the bank is very aggressive, any excess above collateral needs will have already been sold off. Alternatively, it could sell off municipal bonds from its tax-exempt portfolio. Many banks do sell off tax-exempts to meet customer loan demand, but this usually comes more nearly as a last resort. Disinvestment of tax-exempts involves a very high opportunity cost in terms of both interest income and asset growth. Selling off bonds also incurs potential capital losses that may be unacceptable to a bank that does not want to show a loss. Let us suppose, therefore, that the bank is highly reluctant to obtain any part of the $30 million of needed funds through liquidation of invested assets.

If the bank is fortunate to forecast profits for the quarter, it should be able to count on some amount of internal funds from those profits retained in the business. Let us suppose that $5 million is forecasted for this source. The bank could also issue and sell new stock or debentures, but this type of financing requires considerable lead time and is usually reserved for needs that are more clearly long-term. We shall assume that sale of long-term securities is ruled out.

The bank hopes to be able to raise the remaining $25 million from borrowed sources. Since borrowing from ordinary depositors has already been accounted for, this leaves: borrowing in the federal funds market, borrowing at the Federal Reserve discount window, borrowing in the Eurodollar market, and borrowing in the market for NCDs. A few banks (predominantly the large money market banks) maintain consistent net-debtor positions in the federal funds market, but this can be a risky posture. Federal funds money is basically one-day money and the daily rates paid for this money are highly volatile. There is no guarantee that the cost of fed funds will average out below the 90-day prime lending rate. Borrowing at the discount window can be less costly than borrowing fed funds, but the Federal Reserve frowns on lending to banks for the purpose of meeting funds requirements that extend beyond a few weeks. In general, borrowing in the federal funds market and borrowing at the discount window are better suited for adjusting reserve positions than they are a part of general funds management.

This leaves the bank with NCDs and Eurodollar borrowings to bring total sources of funds into balance with *planned* uses of funds. Since the maturities of NCDs and Eurodollar borrowings can be suitably matched to the bank's need for funds on a quarterly basis, neither source can be ruled out quite so easily as we have done for the other sources discussed above. In fact, both sources (but particularly NCDs) are considered more a part of the general funds management sphere than that of reserve position adjustment. We can speculate, therefore, that our bank's first line of defense may well be to meet its expected need for funds by turning to the market for NCDs.

THE MARKET FOR NEGOTIABLE CERTIFICATES OF DEPOSIT

Around the beginning of the 1960s, commercial banks were becoming acutely aware that the supply of funds from their depositing customers was not keeping up with the demand for funds from their borrowing customers. Large banks were particularly disturbed about losses of demand deposits from corporate accounts. Corporate treasurers had become increasingly sophisticated and were moving excess funds out of nonearning demand deposits and putting them into such money market instruments as Treasury bills, commercial paper, and repurchase agreements with dealers. Since the largest corporations generally do business with the large New York City banks, the New York banks were particularly hard hit. Their share of the deposit market had fallen from more than 30 percent to less than 20 percent between 1940 and 1960. To some extent, however, every commercial bank in the system was being hit. The growth rate of aggregate bank deposits was lagging far behind the growth of aggregate savings accounts at nonbank thrift institutions.

The response of money market banks to declining corporate deposits in the face of a continued need to meet a strong loan demand was the introduction, in 1961, of the negotiable certificate of deposit (NCD). By offering their own money market obligations, the money market banks set out to restore their supply of short-term funds from corporations. Looking back now, the development of the NCD market was a huge success. The volume of NCDs outstanding grew by more than $90 billion in the period from 1961 to 1975.

As interest-bearing, maturity-dated obligations, NCDs are technically a part of commercial bank time deposits. But, unlike other time deposits, NCDs qualify as genuine money market instruments. They are issued and sold in denominations of $100,000 or greater. Prime NCDs carry the names of the largest and best-known banks. They are virtually riskless in terms of default.

They are also highly marketable. A good secondary market is made by dealers who trade actively in those prime NCDs with denominations of $1 million.

Maturities of NCDs range from one month to twelve months or longer. Banks are willing to sell NCDs to their corporate customers in whatever number of months is required by the customer. Higher interest rates are usually offered to customers who are able to commit funds to NCDs of longer maturities. This is, in part, a reflection of the term structure of interest rates, but it also has to do with differential reserve requirements on NCDs of different maturities. Since 1974, short-dated NCDs have been subject to stiffer reserve requirements than NCDs with maturities of six months or longer. As a result, banks have been able to afford to pay higher rates on the longer maturities. Nevertheless, the average maturity of NCDs has been around three months.

Corporations have been very willing investors in NCDs. Yields on NCDs are higher than yields on Treasury bills of comparable maturity. Maturities can be made to fit the period of time that funds are expected to be in excess. If funds are needed before maturity, NCDs can be sold in the secondary market. Or, if the corporate holder is also a good customer, the issuing bank may be willing to redeem its obligations before maturity. Indeed, some corporations invest in the NCDs of banks with which they do business to add a personal element to an, otherwise, impersonal activity.

NCDs play a major role in the liability management of money market banks. Basically, NCDs are used to ensure that a bank's sources of funds will be able to keep up with its uses of funds. NCD growth tends to fill the gap between growth in loans and growth in demand deposits. A bank can regulate its growth of NCDs by adjusting the interest rates that it offers on NCDs. Small changes in rates often result in appreciable changes in the corporate demand for NCDs. NCDs are easier to manage than loans and demand deposits. Rates on NCDs are easier to change and the market response to rate changes is more elastic.

Interest rates on NCDs represent somewhat an anomaly, however. Each bank posts rates for various maturities that signifies a rate that it is willing to pay all comers with money in their hands. But this posted rate is almost always a bit less than the rate prevailing in the secondary market. As a result, an investor would generally be foolish to accept posted rates; the investor could do better from a dealer. The implication of this fact is that commercial banks presumably write NCDs for their customers at rates that are a bit above posted rates. Banks are also willing to write NCDs at specific maturities that are not available in the secondary market. However, if a bank is anxious to attract money, it may move its posted rate above that of other banks and, in fact, a bit above the secondary market so as to attract money from the street. Rates also have to be adjusted for risk of default and for marketability. In general, smaller banks pay higher rates.

The growth of NCDs has been spectacular but also erratic. The greatest barrier to growth was the Federal Reserve Regulation Q that limits interest paid on time deposits. During the "credit crunch" years of 1966, 1969, and 1970, the Federal Reserve held the Regulation Q ceiling well below market-rate levels. Under these circumstances it would be expected that banks would lose their funds from NCDs as fast as the NCDs matured. As a matter of fact, well over half of NCDs outstanding were run off during the 1969 episode of market rates shooting past the Regulation Q ceiling. In addition, the secondary market virtually dried up. As a result, the Federal Reserve made Regulation Q inoperative with respect to NCDs beginning in mid-1970. However, Regulation Q still applies to certificates of deposit in smaller denominations. These CDs cannot be considered money market instruments. They are not negotiable, their denominations are too small, and their quality is far too mixed to qualify for money market trading. They are very important, however, to small banks and banks, generally, for the purpose of competing effectively with savings and loan associations and other thrift institutions for the savings of individuals.

THE MARKET FOR EURODOLLARS

In the strict sense of the word, Eurocurrencies are not traded in United States money markets. However, transatlantic communications have been perfected to the point that they are now, in reality, a steady competitor in our money markets. They furnish a vehicle by which banks can secure funds. They also furnish an outlet for investment of idle funds by our multinational corporations and others who might otherwise use domestic money market outlets. Chapter 20 will give a fuller account of how these currencies developed.

A Eurocurrency (which can also be an Asiancurrency) is simply a time deposit account in a bank denominated in a currency other than that of the host bank. A deposit account denominated in dollars in a London bank is a Eurodollar. London is, in fact, the leading center for off-country denomination of deposits, and the dollar is the leading currency for such denomination. However, Frankfurt, Zurich, Singapore, and Tokyo banks bid for deposits in nonnational currencies. Likewise German marks, French francs, British pounds, Dutch guilders, Swiss francs, and Canadian dollars are deposited in banks in countries other than their origin. The Eurocurrency market is an international money market. It is the Eurodollar segment of this market, however, that is of greatest interest to American banks in need of funds.

Eurodollar deposits generally take the form of large-denomination time deposits. A typical Eurodollar deposit is a rounded amount of $1 million to $50 million. However, some Eurodollar banks accept deposits as small as $20,000.

Eurodollar deposits come in a wide variety of maturities: from overnight or call transactions through seven-day, one-month, and various months up to one or two years and apparently longer in a few circumstances. However, the majority of Eurodollar deposits have maturities of three months or less. The one-month Eurodollar deposit is probably the most common of all. Whatever the maturity, all Eurodollar deposits pay interest.

What do the Eurodollar banks do with the funds that they secure from Eurodollar deposits? They lend them out (at higher interest) in the form of Eurodollar loans. A bank receiving a Eurodollar deposit may lend the dollars to a multinational corporation, to a currency speculator, to another foreign bank, to a bank in the United States, or to anyone able and willing to pay the price of borrowing dollars abroad. The lending of Eurodollars from one foreign bank to another, which in turn may lend the proceeds to still another foreign bank, and so on, has a pyramiding effect on the volume of Eurodollar deposits and loans outstanding. This pyramiding of Eurodollar deposits does not alter the fact, however, that it is only the last Eurodollar borrower in the chain of recipients who has any net claim against the cash reserves of United States banks. All the other Eurodollar borrowers in the chain relinquished their claims in the process of making Eurodollar loans.

Why does the Eurodollar market exist? What is the attraction of this market for those who participate in it? There are many reasons—some of them rather devious—but the basic reason is tied to the international structure of interest rates within the context of an international demand for U.S. dollars. Holders of dollars—mainly foreign holders but some domestic holders as well—naturally want to hold their dollars in those deposits, wherever located, that pay the highest interest rates. The attraction of Eurodollar deposits over the NCDs of American banks is that the Eurodollar deposits pay higher interest rates. Borrowers from banks, on the other hand, prefer to borrow from those banks offering loans at the lowest possible rates. The attraction of taking out dollar loans from Eurodollar banks is that the prime rate on Eurodollar loans is lower than the prime loan rate offered by American banks. Eurodollar banks have to pay higher rates on dollar deposits and charge lower rates on dollar loans than the rates paid and charged by U.S. banks, otherwise the Eurodollar market would tend to dry up.

But how can Eurodollar banks afford to pay such relatively high rates on dollar deposits and charge such relatively low rates on dollar loans? The basic reason is because Eurodollar banks face far fewer legal and institutional restrictions on their dollar business than do U.S. banks. For one thing, Eurodollar banks, unlike American banks, do not have to tie up cash to meet reserve requirements. (Reserve requirements do exist in foreign countries, but they apply to deposits denominated in the individual country's own currency, not to deposits denominated in dollars.) For another thing, Eurodollar banks are not subject, as are U.S. banks, to Regulation Q. Consequently, rates on Eurodollar deposits are more nearly in line with true market rates than are the frozen rates paid by U.S. banks for all deposits other than NCDs. If anything, Regulation Q tends to hurt American banks more than it helps them, with the Eurodollar banks coming out the winners. It is true that the Eurodollar loan rate charged by Eurodollar banks is only slightly higher than the Eurodollar deposit rate paid by these banks, but the margin is nevertheless sufficient to turn a good profit for those Eurodollar banks that trade dollars in large volume.

The question of greatest significance for this chapter is: How does the Eurodollar market serve as a source of funds in the liability management of our own commercial banks here at home? In answering this question, we need to separate the conditions that existed in the late 1960s from the conditions that now exist. During late 1968 and during almost all of 1969, Eurodollars were an extremely important source of funds for American banks. During this period, the Federal Reserve pursued a monetary policy that pushed money market rates above the maximum rates on deposits allowed by Regulation Q. The result was a massive runoff of deposits, including NCDs that were, at the time, still subject to Regulation Q. To offset this loss of funds, U.S. banks (mainly the large money market banks) turned to the Eurodollar banks for loans. Within a single year, total Eurodollar loans outstanding to U.S. banks more than doubled. The borrowing of Eurodollars by U.S. banks made a lot of sense. Funds from Eurodollar borrowings were not choked off by Regulation Q as were funds from NCDs. Moreover, the Eurodollar deposits at foreign branches of U.S. banks, which were in turn "loaned" by these branches to the head offices at home, were not subject to reserve requirements as are NCDs. The absence of restrictions on securing and using Eurodollars made these funds very attractive to U.S. banks despite the relatively high interest cost of these funds. To make a long story short, a lot of funds were drained out of NCDs at home and put into Eurodollar deposits abroad, only to be returned home again through Eurodollar loans to the banks whose NCD funds had been drained. It was, of course, Regulation Q's interference in the domestic money market that was responsible for this circuitous routing of funds.

The 1969 Eurodollar episode mainly proved that Regulation Q could be circumvented. Shortly thereafter, the Federal Reserve began removing Regulation Q restrictions on NCD rates. (The default of Penn-Central commercial paper also played a role in the removal of Regulation Q from NCDs.) At the same time, the Fed began imposing reserve requirements on Eurodollar borrowings by U.S. banks. Currently, the two competitive sources of funds for U.S. commercial banks now receive roughly equal treatment by the Fed.

The effect of these changes has been to place Eurodollars behind NCDs as the preferred source of funds in that part of liability management dealing with general funds management. Eurodollars almost always cost more than NCDs, even when domestic money market rates hit their peaks. However, Eurodollars can still be a useful source of funds. To illustrate, some banks have learned how to take advantage of delays in international transfers of funds to obtain, in effect, two days of reserve credit from a one-day Eurodollar loan. Used in such ingenious ways, Eurodollars can be a relatively inexpensive source of funds for adjusting reserve positions.

RESERVE POSITION ADJUSTMENT

No matter how successful a bank is in meeting its monthly, quarterly, and longer-run requirements for funds, it will invariably face the shorter-run problem of reserve position adjustment. Bank reserves fluctuate residually with loans, investments, and deposits. Deposits, especially, are unpredictable on a day-to-day basis. Being a residual, reserves follow a similar pattern. But they cannot be left alone. Reserve positions have to be adjusted, at least once a week, to keep weekly-average reserves at their legally required level.

Reserve position adjustment of small or "country" banks is usually facilitated through the correspondent banking system. Country banks use their city correspondents as a buffer in reserve management, much as do nonfinancial corporations. These banks often do not push aggressively in using surplus funds for customer loans and investments and therefore tend to have excess reserve funds that they lend to their city correspondents. When they are short on reserves, they can generally count on being able to borrow reserve funds from their city correspondents. However, they cannot enter the central money market for such funds, since their transactions tend to be too small and infrequent to be acceptable in the central market.

Major commercial banks, however, directly enter the central money market as they have deficient reserves to cover or excess reserves to put to work. Most of the big banks of New York City and the leading banks of all the other major cities are linked together in a communications network that permits rapid transfers of funds from those banks having excess reserves to those with deficient positions. Such transfers of funds are the major element of the so-called federal funds market. As we shall see in the next section to this chapter, the market for federal funds is almost exclusively a market in which the major banks can adjust their reserve positions.

There are few alternatives to federal funds for reserve position adjustment. Bank loans can be promoted or discouraged over longer periods of time, but during the reserve computation period (one week) only money market loans can be adjusted. Similarly, a bank's tax-exempt portfolio cannot be readily adjusted within the reserve computation period; it must be taken as given by the reserve position manager. Treasury bills can and have been used for reserve position adjustment. These securities can be used for fine-tuning adjustment because transactions in them involve immediate that-day settlement. However, bid-and-ask spreads are sufficiently wide that excessive in-and-out-of-the-market activity is not economical except for a dealer bank.

On the liability side, NCDs are not particularly useful for reserve position adjustment. A bank can control the amount of funds it gets from NCDs by posting higher or lower rates that it is willing to pay for NCD funds. But since the maturities of NCDs run beyond the reserve computation period of one week, NCD adjustment cannot be sufficiently fine tuned. The same goes for most Eurodollar borrowings. The maturities of most Eurodollar transactions run for periods longer than a week. However, Eurodollars can be borrowed on an "overnight" or one-day basis if needed. Short-term Eurodollar funds can and do play an important auxiliary role in reserve position management by banks with foreign branches.

When normal channels of meeting reserve requirements are not available or are too costly, the reserve position manager can borrow from the Federal Reserve at the Federal Reserve discount window. The policies of banks vary widely with respect to the use of this facility. Some banks have a policy of using this facility freely when the discount rate (the interest rate charged by the Fed) offers the opportunity for profit. The Fed itself generally discourages such use and puts direct pressure on a bank that overuses the facility. At the other extreme, some banks avoid borrowing from the Fed and make it an impermissible alternative to the reserve position manager—except in dire emergencies.

THE MARKET FOR FEDERAL FUNDS

The term "federal funds" is a rather amorphous concept. In the narrowest meaning of the term, federal funds are those deposits of member commercial banks at the Federal Reserve that are loaned usually for one day by one member bank to another. In the broadest context, however, federal funds are all loans to commercial banks that are settled in "immediately available funds" not subject to reserve requirements. Immediately available funds are, as the name implies, funds that can be converted to cash or transferred anywhere in the United States within a single day upon demand. In this larger context, federal funds still include member bank deposits at the Fed. The Fed operates a nationwide electronic communications network over which these deposits can be transferred anywhere in the country within a business day. Member bank deposits are not, however, the only source of federal funds. The deposits of nonmember banks at correspondent member banks is another source of federal funds. So also are the deposits of certain nonbank thrift institutions kept at member banks. Although not considered a part of "regular" federal funds, banks can borrow immediately available funds not subject to reserve requirements through use of repurchase agreements involving U.S. Treasury or agency securities.

The primary function of the federal funds market is to allow banks to adjust their reserve positions. Banks with excess reserves use the market by entering as lenders. They "sell" federal funds for the interest income. On the other side of the market are banks with deficient reserves. These banks "buy" federal funds to avoid legal penalties. Because the market is centered around the satisfaction of reserve requirements, it follows the rhythm of these requirements. For most money market banks the weekly averaging period starts with deposit liabilities *beginning* Thursday morning and ends with the deposit liabilities the following Wednesday morning. The balance needed to meet the requirements starts with the *close of business* Thursdays and ends with the close of business the following Wednesday, but there is a lag: The average reserves required in any given week are based on the average deposits of two weeks earlier. Saturdays, Sundays, and holidays count. Most Fed funds transactions are for one day, but weekend deals are for three days; over a holiday, two days. The right combination of a weekend and a holiday can give rise to four-day transactions.

The Fed funds market has two major sections. The wholesale section consists of transactions of unit size of $1 million or more (almost never less than $500,000). In addition, there is a kind of "flow-through" market from little banks to city correspondent banks. With the advent of the computer, many city banks now keep books for country correspondents. In doing so, they manage their reserve positions. Any excess funds of the country correspondent are purchased by the managing bank. The unit amounts are often somewhat less than common for open-market Fed funds transactions. The city correspondent, in effect, assembles these funds from its various country correspondents in its own reserve position and then resells any excess it has in the wholesale Fed funds market. Thus there is a steady trend: Small and country banks tend to be net sellers of Fed funds, and correspondent banks tend to be net buyers. A big proportion of banks tend to persist on one side of the market: to be net sellers or net buyers. While many Fed funds transactions are carried out by direct deals among banks, some banks perform a dealer function in Fed funds, both buying and selling to make a market. However, if such banks have problems settling their own reserve position, they may have to retreat from one side of the market.

Because Fed funds are so perishable, the market has certain rhythms of its own. Early in the morning, while banks are trying to figure out what check clearings have done to their reserve positions, business may be slow. Around ten o'clock business picks up. But since banks do not dare wait too long, business slacks off in the afternoon. Friday is always an exceptionally important day since that involves three-day commitments. Wednesday, which ends the reserve computation period, is the payoff. If unexpected developments have pinched reserves more than the Fed expected, the Fed may be busy putting money into the market by repurchase agreements (RPs) or other means. Any banks that miscalculated fight hard to find money. Conversely, any bank that overestimated its needs may find itself with excess funds and no buyers. Even in times of generally tight money markets, Wednesday afternoon Fed funds rates can sink backward. However, improved computer forecasting is making the market steadier over the weekly cycle than formerly was the case.

Although reserve position adjustment is the primary function of the federal funds market, it by no means tells the whole story of the market. Many major banks borrow continuously in the market, rolling over one-day debts so that they become a "permanent" source of funds. Longer-term transactions in the market are also possible. For such banks, federal funds are in a category with NCDs and Eurodollars in the big picture of liability management. Some banks continually borrow several times their required reserves in the federal funds market. Obviously, such a practice is a far cry from borrowing only to cover temporary deficiencies in reserves.

On the lending side of the market, excess reserves are still the major source of federal funds sold, but the proportion of total funds in the market from this source is diminishing. During the 1970s, banks were joined by state and local governments, savings and loan associations, business corporations, savings banks, federal government agencies, and securities dealers as important lenders in the market. Relaxation of Federal Reserve regulations made it possible for member banks to buy federal funds outright from thrift institutions and federal agencies. Although member banks are not permitted to borrow "regular" federal funds from business corporations and state and local governments, these lenders have entered the market in a big way as takers of repurchase agreements by banks. Table 10-1 indicates the extent to which various lenders entered the federal funds market in 1977.

BORROWING AT THE DISCOUNT WINDOW

One way in which member commercial banks can adjust their reserve positions is by borrowing at the discount window of the Federal Reserve. Banks with

TABLE 10-1
Report of Gross Nonreservable Borrowings in Immediately Available Funds, 7-Day Average Dollar Amounts, Millions, for Statement Week Ended December 7, 1977, (46 Banks)

Borrowed From	Type			Maturity				
	RPs on U.S. Govt. and Agency Securities	All Other*	Total	1 Day	Continuing Contract	2-7 Days	8-30 Days	Over 30 Days But Less Than 7 Years
Member commercial banks	$ 2803.5	$17,908.0	$20,711.5	$18,523.3	$ 682.3	$ 437.8	$ 571.5	$ 496.6
Nonmember domestic commercial banks	255.8	5529.2	5785.0	4873.4	582.0	46.1	188.9	94.6
Branches and agencies of foreign banks operating in U.S.	38.6	2190.3	2228.9	2180.3	1.8	14.9	4.1	27.8
Edge Act and Agreement corporations	40.6	210.0	250.6	210.9	.0	11.1	5.9	22.7
Other depository institutions	77.8	5946.9	6024.7	4106.5	364.6	96.1	372.2	1085.3
Agencies of the U.S.	403.5	2245.6	2649.1	2368.5	.5	40.9	56.9	182.3
Securities dealers	1976.1	1689.2	3665.3	2086.7	248.4	215.4	608.4	506.4
Credit unions	61.9	.0	61.9	32.4	.8	18.0	.0	10.7
Financial businesses	1701.7	.0	1701.7	1042.0	155.2	303.4	160.0	41.1
All other businesses	10,472.4	.0	10,472.4	3256.8	1198.5	2302.1	2913.0	901.0
State and local governments	3787.7	.0	3787.7	2188.8	144.5	432.2	681.2	341.0
Foreign banks and foreign official institutions	323.0	.0	323.0	225.7	.0	58.1	37.4	1.8
All others	248.4	149.3	397.7	229.8	23.2	101.1	33.6	10.0
Total	$22,191.0	$35,868.5	$58,059.5	$41,325.1	$3401.8	$3978.2	$5633.1	$3721.3

*Includes "regular" federal funds.
SOURCE: Financial Reports Section, Division of Research and Statistics, Board of Governors of the Federal Reserve System.

unexpected reserve losses can replace reserves by taking out loans, and banks with unexpected gains can use the excess reserves to pay back loans. The rate of interest that applies to such loans is called the discount rate. It is set by the Federal Reserve.

Member-bank borrowing from the Fed is governed by the Fed's Regulation A. Under this regulation, member-bank borrowing is restricted to temporary or short-term needs for funds. Permanent or long-term use of the discount window is inappropriate. The fact that member-bank borrowings are almost always for a maximum period of fifteen days is certainly in keeping with the spirit of Regulation A. However, the fifteen-day maturity is not, by itself, totally enforcing. Sometimes the Fed has to caution those borrowing members who show up at the window every two weeks to renew their loans. Legitimate use of the discount window is, to a considerable extent, a matter of judgment by Federal Reserve officials.

Reserve adjustment by borrowing at the discount window differs in a very important respect from all other forms of reserve adjustment. Trading in federal funds, Eurodollars, Treasury bills, and other instruments among commercial banks or between banks and their customers has no effect on total bank reserves. Instead, existing reserves are simply transferred from one commercial bank to another. On the other hand, borrowings and repayments at the discount window have the effect of increasing and decreasing total bank reserves. Reserves borrowed from the Fed are reserves that the Fed creates with a stroke of the pen; they are not taken away from some other bank. Since the quantity of money in the economy is tied to the quantity of commercial bank reserves, use of the discount window as a mechanism for reserve position adjustment must be recognized for having an effect on the nation's money supply.

AGGREGATE RESERVES AND THE MONEY SUPPLY

The macroeconomic significance of commercial bank deposits is that they are the major part of the nation's money supply. (There may be some question about the moneyness of time deposits, but everyone agrees that demand deposits are money.) Since the amount of money in the economy affects jobs, incomes, purchasing power, and other things that really matter to people, we need to explore how the private, profit-seeking behavior of banks affects the money supply.

When the average banker is asked to describe the effect of bank behavior on the money supply, the typical response is: no effect. From the individual banker's perspective, this is an honest answer. Each individual bank behaves on the basis that its deposit liabilities are pretty much determined by the whims of its depositors. If a customer comes in with $1000 of currency to deposit, fine, but that is the customer's decision. Now what happens to this money? A fraction of it (equal to the reserve requirement percentage, say, 20 percent) will have to be kept as required cash reserves. But the rest ($800) is excess; it can be loaned out at interest. From the bank's point of view, all that has happened is that a customer made a deposit of $1000, which the bank then allocated $200/$800 between required reserves and loans.

However, this view is rather myopic. In the larger picture of events, we need to follow the $800 that was loaned out. It will more than likely end up in some other bank, increasing the recipient bank's deposits and reserves by $800. The recipient bank, of course, will regard the increase in its deposit accounts as the depositor's decision, just as the first bank regarded the original deposit of $1000. The truth is, however, that the $800 increase in deposit money at the second bank cannot be divorced from the first bank's decision to make a loan of $800. By lending excess reserves, banks do create deposits, although not necessarily for themselves directly. To bring home the point, let us go one step further. The second bank now has $800 more in deposit liabilities and cash reserve assets. However, since it need keep only $160 of these reserves to meet legal requirements, the rest can be loaned out at interest. When the proceeds of this loan are deposited in still another (third) bank, we again have a situation where one bank's lending behavior leads to another bank's deposit expansion.

Where does it all end? New loans will continue to be made as long as there are unwanted excess reserves in the banking system. Deposits will continue to expand as long as new loans are made. Required reserves will increase as long as deposits expand. However, total reserves will not be affected by any of this. When one bank loses reserves by loaning out any excess, another bank gains them. The process of making loans and expanding deposits does not change bank reserves in the aggregate, but it does transform them from excess reserves into required reserves. The process only comes to a halt when the system is left with no unwanted excess reserves. The precise relation between total deposit money and total bank reserves can get very complicated, but the basics are quite simple. If we assume that cash reserves must at a minimum be no less than 20 percent of deposits, it follows mathematically that deposits at a maximum can be no greater than five times cash reserves. The banking system does create money, but the amount it creates is constrained by the amount of its reserves. Since the Federal Reserve controls the level of these reserves through its open-market operations, the Fed indirectly controls the supply of deposit money and bank credit in the economy.

PROJECTS AND QUESTIONS

1. Both large banks and small banks hold sizeable quantities of U.S. Treasury bills, but they may hold these securities for different reasons. Through library research and/or interviews with bankers, ascertain as fully as possible all the reasons why banks hold Treasury bills.
2. How does the nature and importance of bank liability management at the present time compare with that of ten years ago? Twenty years ago? If you

cannot find a history of liability management in a single source, refer to the literature of the period.

3. Are there any good reasons for a bank to want to keep some reserves in excess of requirements? If so, what are they?
4. When a bank is in need of funds, how does it choose where to get them? In answering this question, compare NCDs with federal funds as substitute sources of funds.
5. Do deposits determine reserves, or do reserves determine deposits?

BIBLIOGRAPHY

Brewer, E.: "Some Insights on Member Bank Borrowing," *Federal Reserve Bank of Chicago Economic Perspectives,* November/December 1978, pp. 16–21.

Crosse, H. D., and G. A. Hempel: *Management Policies for Commercial Banks,* Prentice-Hall, Englewood Cliffs, N.J., 1973.

Hodgman, D. R.: *Commercial Bank Loan and Investment Policy,* University of Illinois, Champaign, Ill., 1963.

Jessup, P. F., ed.: *Innovations in Bank Management,* Holt, Rinehart and Winston, New York, 1969.

Klopstock, F. H.: "Eurodollars in the Liquidity and Reserve Management of United States Banks," *Federal Reserve Bank of New York Monthly Review,* July 1968.

Little, J. S.: "The Impact of the Eurodollar Market on the Effectiveness of Monetary Policy in the United States and Abroad," *New England Economic Review,* Federal Reserve Bank of Boston, March/April 1975, pp. 3–19.

Lucas, C. M., M. T. Jones, and T. B. Thurston: "Federal Funds and Repurchase Agreements," *Federal Reserve Bank of New York Quarterly Review,* Summer 1977, pp. 33–48.

Melton, W. C.: "The Market for Large Negotiable CDs," *Federal Reserve Bank of New York Quarterly Review,* Winter 1977–78, pp. 22–34.

Nadler, P. S.: *Commercial Banking in the Economy,* Random House, New York, 1973.

Robinson, R. I.: *Management of Bank Funds,* McGraw-Hill, New York, 1962.

Reed, E. W. et al.: *Commercial Banking,* Prentice-Hall, Englewood Cliffs, N.J., 1976.

Smith, W. J.: "Repurchase Agreements and Federal Funds," *Federal Reserve Bulletin,* May 1978, pp. 353–360.

Wood, O. G.: *Commercial Banking,* D. Van Nostrand, New York, 1978.

Chapter 11
The Federal Reserve in the Money Markets

The Federal Reserve System is the central banking system of the United States. It is a mixture of decentralization and centralization. The Federal Reserve banks, themselves, are twelve in number. They are located in Boston, New York, Philadelphia, Cleveland, Richmond, Atlanta, Chicago, St. Louis, Minneapolis, Kansas City, Dallas, and San Francisco. These Federal Reserve banks are banks for member commercial banks in much the same way as commercial banks are banks for the public. However, the Federal Reserve Bank of New York is the only one directly involved in the money market. The Fed's open-market operations are executed at the "trading desk" of this bank. Open-market policy, however, is handed down from Washington. The Federal Open Market Committee (FOMC) meets once a month in Washington for the purpose of formulating open-market policy. The FOMC consists of twelve members. Five are presidents of Federal Reserve Banks. The other seven are the governors of the Board of Governors of the Federal Reserve System. The Federal Reserve Board of Governors, permanently housed in Washington, is the central controlling authority in the central banking system.

The Federal Reserve is an autonomous agency of the federal government, created by the U.S. Congress in 1913. As a public institution, the Fed's operations are not for the purpose of making profits. (It does, as a matter of fact, make large profits out of exercise of its operations, but these profits are promptly turned over to the U.S. Treasury.) When the Federal Reserve Act of 1913 was passed, the prime accomplishment expected of the new system was to avoid the money market panics, and accompanying hard times, that had hit the country a half dozen times after the Civil War. Although the specific goals and responsibilities of the Federal Reserve have shifted and evolved since the Fed's founding, the general goals have always been couched in terms of promoting financial and economic stability.

The Federal Reserve relies primarily on the tool of open-market operations for meeting its policy goals. Open-market operations in Treasury and federal agency securities and bankers' acceptances—either through outright purchases and sales or through repurchase agreements—have a direct effect on money market interest rates and the quantity of commercial bank reserves. An open-market purchase of Treasury bills, for example, has a direct effect of bidding up the price (and lowering the yield) on T-bills. It also increases commercial bank reserves by the amount of the purchase. The Fed pays for the purchase by drawing a check against itself. When the seller deposits the check at a commercial bank, the commercial bank then collects from the Fed through the Fed's crediting of the commercial bank's reserve account at the Fed. This increase in reserves does not take away from the reserves of any other commercial bank; rather, it comes from funds that the Fed, itself, newly creates to make its open-market purchase.

The Fed's ability to increase and decrease total bank reserves through its open-market purchases and sales has two extremely important side effects. One is to influence the supply of money in the economy. As we learned in the final section of the preceding chapter, commercial banks are able to create deposit money only up to a multiple of the amount of their reserves. The other side effect is on the federal funds rate. When the Fed increases bank reserves, the first reaction of those banks affected is to get rid of unwanted excess reserves by lending them in the federal funds market. This causes an immediate drop in the federal funds rate. The reverse happens when the Fed decreases reserves, or slows down their growth. In this case, bank scrambling for reserves causes the federal funds rate to rise. These interest-rate effects spread quickly to other money market rates and eventually to longer-term rates as funds become less scarce or more scarce throughout the entire financial market system. In the final analysis, the Fed's influence over money and interest has an ultimate effect on all markets, including the prices and quantities of real goods and services produced. This is what monetary policy is all about.

Open-market operations can be used either to change bank reserves as dictated by monetary policy, or they can be used defensively to keep reserves from changing owing to other factors affecting reserves. Factors such as Treasury deposits at the Fed, currency held by the public, and uncollected checks outstanding (called float) have an important bearing on the volume of commercial bank reserves. These factors are not controlled by the Fed, but they can be offset by the Fed by using open-market operations defensively.

In addition to open-market operations, the Fed has access to other tools for monetary management. The Fed can influence the quantity of reserves borrowed by its member banks by changing the discount rate charged on loans to member banks, or by changing its posture as to the availability of such loans. Since the discount rate is usually below market interest rates, the Fed applies moral suasion to keep down the borrowed reserves of member banks. Banks are generally reluctant to borrow too heavily at the Fed's discount window for reasons more political than economic.

The Fed also has the power to change reserve requirement percentages.

Changes in reserve requirements do not change the total reserves of banks, as do open-market operations and changes in the discount rate, but they do alter the composition of total reserves as between required and excess. Decreases in reserve requirements, for example, have a freeing-up effect on a portion of given total reserves so that commercial banks can increase their earning assets and their deposits by a larger multiple of their existing reserves. This multiplier effect was explained at the end of the last chapter. Reserve requirements can also be altered selectively to influence the volume of a specific source of funds, for example, the borrowing of Eurodollars.

The Fed uses its powers to change the discount rate and to change reserve requirement percentages at critical points in time rather than continuously. Reserve requirement changes are of a structural nature. The discount rate is changed when the Fed wishes to "announce" the direction of policy. Only open-market operations are used for continuous day-to-day implementation of policy goals and targets. Consequently, the Fed's pervasive daily influence in the money markets is felt primarily through its open-market operations.

In the sections to follow, we will take a close look at the Federal Reserve's involvement in the money markets. This will require us to examine in considerable detail the various elements of the Fed's policy framework. Special attention will be given to the goals of monetary policy, the translation of these goals into policy targets, the problem of inconsistent targets and the Fed's solution to the problem, the monthly formulation of policy targets by the FOMC, the day-to-day execution of policy at the "trading desk" of the New York Fed, and related matters of strategy and implementation. Following this, we will wind up the chapter with a few observations about the Federal Reserve's performance and operating behavior.

GOALS OF MONETARY POLICY

The Federal Reserve was created in 1913 for the purpose of providing for a more elastic supply of currency and credit in the economy. The Federal Reserve Act, under which the Fed was created, contains little guidance beyond this, however. Some reference is made to accommodating the credit needs of commerce, industry, and agriculture. Other reference is made to limiting credit for speculation in securities, real estate, and commodities. When these references are considered together, it sounds as if the founders of the Fed were seeking a more responsive supply of credit, but not too responsive. But this is just our interpretation.

Basically, the Federal Reserve was left to interpret its own goals. Clear-cut goals did not develop during the first decade of the Fed's existence; war finance dominated the early years. Instead of accommodating the credit needs of business, the Fed accommodated the government's need to finance World War I. The Fed extended credit to the Treasury (at a slight profit). A sharp economic downturn after the war still did not bring out a clear-cut policy response from the Fed.

The discovery of open-market operations, in 1923, marked the beginning of more clear-cut goal formation. Although the Federal Reserve banks had authority to buy U.S. government securities from the very beginning, open-market operations were discovered by accident. After World War I, when the volume of Federal Reserve credit to commercial banks, via the discount window, shrank, some Reserve bank presidents, accustomed to the profit calculus of commercial banking, started to put the funds released to work by buying U.S. government securities at a discount. They quickly discovered that this replenished reserves to the banking system and only hastened the decline of reserves borrowed at the discount window. They then retreated from this attempt at profit maximizing. However, the president of the New York Fed, Benjamin Strong, grasped the significance of the new tool and started to use open-market operations as a positive market instrument. At this stage the Federal Reserve passed from being a passive credit agent, as it had been before, to being an aggressive manager of the money markets. Beyond money market management, officials at the Fed envisioned that open-market operations could be used to influence general business conditions. The quest for overall economic stability was clearly a goal of the Federal Reserve in the late 1920s. However, when the Fed was faced with the demand that it stabilize commodity prices, its spokesmen denied the system's ability to accomplish this specific stabilization goal, even though they admitted to its desirability.

The severity of the Great Depression that began in 1930 caught the Federal Reserve off guard. The Fed made some feeble efforts to stem bank failures, but otherwise took no steps of a vigorous countercyclical nature. The Federal Reserve authorities lacked the knowledge and experience of how to use their policy weapons effectively. Their faith in open-market operations shattered, the Fed assumed a defeatist attitude and a passive posture in response to the drastic liquidation of bank credit and therefore of money. Ability to foster economic recovery was disclaimed.

Although the Federal Reserve did very little to cure the Great Depression of the 1930s, two important events influenced the future course of the Federal Reserve greatly. The first was the settling of a power struggle within the Federal Reserve System. During the 1920s, the real power within the system was in the Federal Reserve Bank of New York. Much of this was due to the strong leadership of Benjamin Strong who headed the New York bank during this period. Strong's success was doubtless aided by the weakness of a number of political appointments to the chairmanship of the Federal Reserve Board. However, under the pressure of Marriner Eccles, a chairman of great intuitive economic ability, the Banking Act of 1935 shifted the balance of system power from New York to Washington. This act created the Federal Open Market Committee, which became the focal point for formulating goals and the policies to achieve them.

The second event was the publication of Keynes's *The General Theory of Employment, Interest, and Money* (1936). The so-called Keynesian revolution persuaded a large fraction of the economics profession that the level of economic activity was influenced mainly by the balance of the government budget rather than by money. Keynes's role for the central bank (as many interpreted it) was to influence interest rates. These academic ideas were already part of the practical thinking at the Fed. Marriner Eccles, himself, believed that it was fiscal policy, not monetary policy, that had the major impact on the economy. He viewed the Federal Reserve's function as that of helping the Treasury Department meet its financing and interest rate goals.

World War II again required that the Federal Reserve be subservient to the Treasury Department, but this time its role was not simply to help finance the war but also to control the interest rate at which it was financed. The main concern of the Treasury was to borrow as much as the war required at low-level interest rates: ⅜ percent on ninety-day bills, ⅞ percent on one-year certificates, and up to 2 ½ percent on twenty-five-year bonds. At such low interest rates, the Treasury could not borrow all that it required from private lenders, so the Fed accommodated by lending the difference. In fact, the Fed's willingness to supply short-term credit at less than 1 percent virtually assured the banking system of ownership of most of the outstanding short-term Treasury securities. Private nonbank investors such as insurance companies and individuals quite naturally took the higher-yielding Treasury bonds.

As World War II drew to a close, the economic outlook was uncertain. Some observers thought that the end of the war would cause the economy to revert to depression. This speculation, along with the painful memory of the 1930s, and spurred by Keynesian idealism, prompted Congress to pass the Employment Act of 1946, which made full employment a goal of national policy. Other observers thought that the lifting of wartime price controls would lead to rapid price inflation. The Fed had accommodated the Treasury so extensively during the war that the money supply had more than doubled in size.

The fear of inflation was given some justifying substance by the post-price-control run-up in prices in 1946 and the sharp jump in prices at the outbreak of the Korean War episode. The feeling that the Federal Reserve System should play some anti-inflationary role grew stronger within the System. By the end of the 1940s, the Fed was anxious to use monetary policy for stabilizing the economy, but it was still supporting the Treasury by buying Treasury securities in order to keep interest rates pegged at artificially low levels. Bank reserves and the money supply continued to expand, adding to the inflationary pressures.

By a combination of superior staff work and political courage on the part of several board members, the Federal Reserve won its independence of the Treasury Department in 1951. The goal involved was simply avoidance of a monetary expansion that would lead to inflation. Very soon, however, the system developed a more complete countercyclical credit policy. The timing and strength of the Fed's actions were often criticized, but several times during the 1950s, there was a clear and sensitive response by the Fed to problems of the business cycle. Furthermore, public statements of William McChesney Martin—the new Federal Reserve chairman who took office in 1951—clearly adhered to the policies of the Employment Act of 1946. The goal of the Federal Reserve, once more, was economic stabilization.

Economic stability is still the basic goal of Federal Reserve policy. However, the meaning of economic stability is not well defined. If stability means full employment without inflation, then the goal is not clearly meaningful because these two subgoals of stability are usually in conflict with one another. Additional subgoals such as adequate economic growth and sustainable balance of payments only add to the confusion and complexity of attempting to meet all elements of stability simultaneously. Therefore, as a practical matter, stability involves a considerable amount of compromise; it means following a middle course in which the excesses of inflation and unemployment can be avoided. But even this meaning of stability is unclear. Differences of opinion about what is excessive, and what is not, exist not only within the nation but within the Federal Reserve System as well.

On top of all this, some mention must be made of the fact that the Federal Reserve has never lost sight of its mission to keep the money markets orderly, including reasonable stability of money market interest rates. Although it is doubtful that the Fed would ever return to its fixed-rates policy of the 1940s, it would come as an equally great surprise for the Fed to allow interest rates to move up and down without limit. Thus, to the general goal of economic stability we must add the particular goal of money market stability.

TRANSLATION OF POLICY GOALS INTO NUMERICALLY SPECIFIED POLICY TARGETS

Once a reasonably consistent set of policy goals is determined, the problem remains as to how to achieve these goals. The Fed does not have direct control over output, employment, and prices; all it has direct control over is the size of its government securities portfolio through the exercise of open-market operations.

The job of achieving ultimate goals would be simple if the effect of open-market operations on goal variables were instantaneous. But it is not. The chain of cause and effect relations running from open-market operations to ultimate economic activity is long and laggard. An open-market operation today may not affect output and prices for many months or more. This would present no particular problem if the Fed knew exactly when and how much open-market operations affect the economy. But knowledge is incomplete on this score. The variables representing ultimate goals are too far removed from open-market operations to get a good handle on the relationship between goal variables and open-market operations.

How, then, does the Fed operate? It breaks down the relationship into segments about which it has more knowledge. The Fed knows fairly well how open-market operations affect certain strategic variables, and how these variables in turn affect output, employment, and prices. By introducing such strategic variables as intermediate targets lying between the initiating instrument of open-market operations and the ultimate goal of economic stability, the Fed makes its job more manageable. Slippages are more easily corrected. Thus, when factors other than a strategic intermediate variable begin to show their effects on output and prices, the Fed responds by adjusting its intermediate targets and open-market operations accordingly. Also, when factors other than open-market operations affect a strategic intermediate variable, the Fed knows it is time to readjust open-market operations. The point is that the ultimate goals of monetary policy cannot be achieved with any particular set of open-market operations as long as there are a multitude of unknown and unanticipated factors, outside the Fed's influence, bearing directly or indirectly on output, employment, and prices.

Monetary policy is transmitted through a linked chain of cause-and-effect relations. Although each pair of successive links in the chain may be tightly connected in terms of cause and effect, the association between the first link and the last link—between the initiating instrument and the ultimate objective—is nevertheless quite loose. What happens to the last link, given a twist in the first, depends upon what happens to the inbetween links. In monetary policy, the inbetween links are strategic variables used by the Fed as intermediate targets of policy.

While the Fed has almost always felt the need for policy targets, or operating criteria, it has never fully resolved what the targets should be. In order to develop operating criteria, there must be some underlying economic philosophy. Unfortunately (or is it fortunate?), the Federal Reserve System has never adhered to any particular economic philosophy. The system has many people in it, both official and staff, and they are drawn from various economic philosophies. In the process of group decision making, these philosophies have become so individually compromised that it is nearly impossible to trace the Fed's chosen criteria or targets to any one single strand of economic thinking. However, there have been times in the Fed's history during which the selection of operating criteria ran parallel to the thinking of the Fed's dominant leader.

For many years the operating criterion for conducting monetary policy was mainly a "feel for the market." This criterion can be traced to Benjamin Strong's philosophy that credit should be supplied for "good" uses, but not for speculative uses. His was a "qualitative theory of bank credit," which called for qualitative criteria in the exercise of monetary policy. He trusted instinct more than statistics. He felt that those with long practical experience in the market could, virtually intuitively, guide the actions of the Federal Reserve.

Marriner Eccles did not hold to a philosophy of a close link between money and credit, on the one hand, and such real economic conditions as output and employment. He believed that monetary policy had its primary influence on interest rates, and so he chose to use interest rates as operating criteria.

William McChesney Martin was in some ways like Benjamin Strong; he had had Wall Street experience and thought in such terms. However, he had done night school work in economics. He recognized that Federal Reserve credit impact was quantitative, not qualitative. (It is true that bank reserves are homogeneous and that once created, the Fed has very little control over how banks will put them to work.) Under Martin's leadership, the Fed followed a "money market strategy." Policy was formulated by focusing on such quantifiable "money market conditions" as short-term interest rates, free reserves (the difference between excess reserves and borrowed reserves), and the inventory positions of securities dealers.

The use of selected money market variables as proximate targets for monetary policy continued through the 1950s and into the 1960s. Particular attention was given to interest rates as the link between open-market operations and the general level of economic activity, a reflection of the rudimentary ideas of Keynesian economics.

The use of "money market conditions" as the best proximate target for monetary policy was seriously questioned during the 1960s. There was growing dissatisfaction both outside and within the Federal Reserve System with the system's record of performance. Some outside critics even went so far to say that Federal Reserve policy had been largely perverse, that it had done more to amplify the ups and downs of the economy than to smooth them out. On the intellectual front, the monetarist counterrevolution (to the Keynesian revolution) was convincing, to many, that the money supply would be much superior to interest rates as a target of monetary policy. At the same time, board and staff positions at the Fed were being increasingly filled with professional economists who questioned whether the system's practices made economic sense.

In the late 1960s, the research staff of the Federal Reserve Board was instructed to study the question, with the purpose of finding appropriate policy targets. The candidate targets were various monetary aggregates and interest rates. In terms of meeting the ultimate goal of economic stability, both the supply of money and the rate of interest were well established theoretically. The money supply was the link between open-market operations and the level of economic activity in the monetarist framework. Interest rates provided the link within Keynesian economics. Thus, to maintain objectivity, the researchers sought to find which of the two targets is more closely related to the level of prices and output, empirically. The best target would be the one that, once set, results in the lowest variance of the ultimate objective around its aimed value. The research was not conclusive, but the money supply came out of the contest as the apparent winner.

Since 1970, the Federal Open Market Committee has followed a money-supply-target strategy in formulating basic policy twelve months in advance. At first, the FOMC gave the most weight to that money supply concept known as M_1 (currency plus demand deposits). However, by 1976, equal weight was given to M_2 (M_1 plus commercial bank time deposits). Increasingly, weight is also being given to M_3 (M_2 plus savings accounts at nonbank thrift institutions).

The FOMC's formulation of basic policy involves a control period that usually runs twelve months into the future. The process of formulating basic policy begins with the preparation of a consensus forecast of GNP, inflation, and unemployment, based on no change in existing monetary growth targets. Alternative forecasts involving alternative growth rates of the money supply are also prepared. This way the FOMC selects that monetary growth rate, thought to be most consistent with its ultimate goals, as its policy target over the coming year. Target values are selected for both M_1 and M_2.

The attention paid to the money supply in the formulation of basic policy does not mean that the Fed has abandoned interest rates as policy targets. Indeed, the FOMC places heavy emphasis on the federal funds rate in its policy deliberations. The federal funds rate serves a dual purpose as a policy target. For one thing, it is used by the Fed as an early indicator of the effect of open-market operations on the money supply; it serves as an operational day-to-day target on the way to hitting the money supply targets.[1] In addition, the federal funds rate is a strategic target in the Federal Reserve's quest for money market stability. The federal funds rate is very sensitive to money market activity. Control of the federal funds rate indicates that the Fed has control over the supply of funds in the money market.

One of the most important elements in the translation of policy goals into policy targets, during the 1970s, was the provision for numerical specification of targets. The expression of monetary policy now includes specific values for M_1, M_2, the federal funds rate, and other strategic variables. (This change toward greater quantification and specification was strongly supported by Arthur Burns, who was the Federal Reserve Board Chairman during the period 1970 – 1978. As Chairman, Burns was neither a Keynesian nor a doctrinaire monetarist, but he did lean on his National Bureau of Economic Research background, which was institutional and empirical.) The effect of specifying its targets numerically has been to make the Federal Reserve System more accountable. Policy directives from the FOMC to the manager of the System Open Market Account, who is in charge of the day-to-day open market operations at the New York Trading Desk, are couched in terms of specific target values to be achieved. If not achieved, the account manager must explain why not to the FOMC. In turn, the FOMC will be held accountable through the watchful eye of the public. Numerical specification, in short, has forced the Fed to keep on its toes.

PROBLEM OF INCONSISTENT TARGETS

A problem faced by the Fed in having more than one target in its policy framework is the high probability of inconsistency between its targets. Indeed, if the various targets were always consistent, they would hardly be different; any one target could stand equally well for all the others.

One area of inconsistency is between the two leading money supply targets: M_1 and M_2. These two series do not grow in lockstep fashion. The M_2 series has grown at a much higher average rate than has M_1 for some time now. Moreover, short-run changes in the growth rates of the two series have often been in opposite directions. The reason for this is tied to the behavior of commercial bank depositors. When depositors shift funds out of demand

---

[1]Although the use of the money supply as a target in formulating basic policy became a victory for monetarism, the use of the federal funds rate as a target in the control of money is strictly Keynesian, all of which points out the Fed's eclecticism. There is a pragmatic reason for this, however. The federal funds rate can be monitored continuously. Meaningful figures on reserves are available only once a week; daily reserve figures are not really reliable.

deposits and in to time deposits, M_1 goes down but M_2 goes up.[2] Shifts in the opposite direction have the reverse effect. Since the Federal Reserve has no way of controlling the behavior of depositors and has only limited success for predicting their behavior, the Fed has little chance of achieving both its target values for M_1 and M_2 simultaneously.[3]

A more serious problem of inconsistency exists between the money supply target and the target for the federal funds rate. To a certain extent, the money supply and the federal funds rate are both "controlled" by the Fed. An open-market purchase causes the federal funds rate to fall, and the quantity of reserves and, therefore, of money to rise. To this extent, there is an inverse relation between money stock growth and the federal funds rate, which suggests a pattern of consistent targeting. However, this inverse relation is not stable. Factors outside the Fed's control can cause the money supply and the federal funds rate to take on almost any combination of values. The money supply can change with no change in the federal funds rate. It does, for example, when the Fed uses open-market operations to supply and absorb reserves in response to increases and decreases in commercial bank demand for federal funds. On the other hand, when the Fed refuses to accommodate changes in commercial bank demand for funds, then the federal funds rate changes with no change in reserves. In short, the relation between the money supply and the federal funds rate is not stable.

THE FEDERAL RESERVE'S SOLUTION TO THE PROBLEM

The Fed is keenly aware of the problem of inconsistent targets, but its procedures tend to soften the problem. The two most important procedures are: (1) acceptability of on-the-average achievement of basic policy targets, rather than requiring all-the-time achievement, and (2) expression of each policy target in terms of a range of values, instead of a specific point value.

The first procedure relies on a distinction between long-run targeting and short-run targeting. The money supply targets used in the formulation of basic policy are long-run targets. They are selected for a control period running twelve months into the future. In formulating basic policy for the coming year, the FOMC may select, say, a 3 percent monetary growth rate for its M_1 target. As the year unfolds, the FOMC will be meeting monthly. An important element of each monthly meeting is the selection of a target for the federal funds rate, which will be in effect until the meeting the following month. The federal funds rate is a short-run target. The targeting of this rate is partially in response to short-run money market considerations.

---

[2] At first, the shift does not change the M_2 total because the demand deposit component falls by the same amount that the time deposit component rises. However, since reserve requirements are less for time deposits than for demand deposits, the shift creates excess reserves and an eventual increase in M_2.

[3] This problem became potentially more acute in November 1978, when banks began offering automatic transfers of funds from savings accounts to checking accounts for individual customers.

The question is: How can the series of short-run targets for the federal funds rate be made consistent with the long-run money supply target? Reasonable consistency would be next to impossible if the FOMC were to allow no deviations of the money supply from its target growth path. However, deviations are permitted. The money supply is allowed to grow faster than the target rate during some months provided that it grows at a slower rate during other times. The FOMC believes that the average rate of growth of money over a period of six months (or longer) is what counts. Stability of money in the short run is viewed as unnecessary. Whether the FOMC is correct or not in this view, its acceptance of on-the-average achievement of its long-run monetary targets provides greater flexibility for establishing achievable targets for the federal funds rate.

While the FOMC allows the monetary growth rate in the short run to deviate from the long-run target growth path, considerable control is exercised over such deviations. Indeed, the FOMC selects an appropriate short-run target for the money supply at each of its monthly meetings. The short-run money supply target is the crucial link between basic and short-run policy formulation. Its selection requires that one eye be kept on the long-run money supply target and the other eye on the short-run target for the federal funds rate; otherwise all sorts of inconsistencies begin to develop.

Inconsistency is reduced considerably by using ranges of tolerance for the expression of targets. All targets used in monetary policy are expressed as ranges. The federal funds rate is allowed to vary within a target range that is seldom wider than 150 basis points. The ranges for monetary growth rates are wider: up to as much as plus or minus 2 ½ percent growth from the midpoint of the monetary growth range. Setting the width of ranges is almost as big a problem as establishing their midpoints. (Presumably, the midpoint is the ideal target value and the width is the range of tolerable values.) If ranges are set too wide, they begin to lose their meaning as targets. On the other hand, if they are set too narrow, they can turn out to be inconsistent.

The operating procedures of the FOMC are designed to diminish the problem of inconsistent targets. However, they do not eliminate the problem completely. Apparently, the Federal Reserve is willing to tolerate a certain degree of inconsistency in its perceived need to work with multiple targets.

MONTHLY FORMULATION OF POLICY TARGETS BY THE FEDERAL OPEN MARKET COMMITTEE

The actual formulation of monetary policy takes place in the most exalted organizational element in the Federal Reserve Structure: the Federal Open Market Committee (or FOMC as we have been calling it). The FOMC formally consists of all seven members of the Board of Governors plus five Federal Reserve bank presidents. The president of the Federal Reserve Bank of New York serves continuously, but the other four are selected from among the other eleven Federal Reserve bank presidents and serve on a formal rotation.

In fact, all twelve Federal Reserve bank presidents almost always attend the meetings and enter discussions freely. In addition, a formal staff of twenty, including the manager (or managers) of the System Open Market Account (SOMA), serve the FOMC. This staff is usually supplemented by close to a dozen other staff members who are privileged to attend FOMC meetings. Thus the meetings, held in Washington at monthly intervals or oftener, consist of about fifty persons.

FOMC meetings usually get down to serious business with a review of economic and financial conditions. The economic areas covered include, among others, national income, industrial production, employment, prices, and trade—both domestic and international. Financial conditions are reviewed in even greater detail. Attention is then turned toward the future. Reports of current positions are supplemented by cautious forecasts of likely events in the immediate, near-term, and more distant future.

Armed with this information, the FOMC then enters into a lengthy discussion, debate, and deliberation over the appropriate response for monetary policy. Basic policy is examined first. Usually, economic conditions and prospects do not change sufficiently from one month to the next to warrant a significant change in the stance of basic policy. However, if conditions change sufficiently, the FOMC does not hesitate to set new one-year targets for monetary growth, thereby replacing previously existing one-year targets, even if they have been in effect for less than a year.

Having selected a long-run (one-year) monetary growth path, the FOMC then focuses attention on short-run policy formulation. The control period for short-run policy is two months. However, because the FOMC meets monthly, each two-month control period has a one-month overlap with the control period of the previous month and in the upcoming month. This overlapping of short-run policy provides an element of flexibility and continuity in the policy process.

The formulation of short-run (two-month) policy calls for the setting of target ranges for monetary growth and for the federal funds rate. The settings for these two-month targets depend primarily on money market conditions and on the current position of the money supply vis-à-vis the one-year target. If the money supply is currently below its long-run target growth path, then a relatively high target value for short-run monetary growth is in order. Similarly, a low short-run rate of monetary growth is called for when the current money supply lies above the desired long-run path. But money market conditions also enter in. If the money market is tightening up more than desired, forcing money rates sharply upward, the FOMC will then want to take the pressure off the market by setting a sufficiently low target value for the federal funds rate. If, on the other hand, the problem is one of excessive liquidity, funds can then be absorbed by setting the federal funds rate at a sufficiently high level. Before it makes a final selection, the FOMC has to consider whether the money supply target and the target for the federal funds rate are consistent. Will the upper limit of the range for the federal funds rate be high enough to accommodate a desired slowdown in the growth of money? Will the lower limit of the range for the monetary target be low enough to accommodate a desired increase in the federal funds rate? Obviously, setting targets is a difficult task.

Finally, each FOMC meeting concludes with the drafting of the FOMC's "policy directive" to the manager of the SOMA. The directive includes, among other things, specific instructions to meet the FOMC's designated targets. Consider, for example, the following excerpt from the FOMC's directive of April 19, 1977:

> The Committee . . . expects the annual growth rate over the April-May period to be within the ranges of 6 to 10 percent for M-1 and 8 to 12 percent for M-2. In the judgment of the Committee such growth rates are likely to be associated with a weekly-average federal funds rate of about 4 ¾ percent. If, giving approximately equal weight to M-1 and M-2, it appears that growth rates over the 2-month period will deviate significantly from the midpoints of the indicated ranges, the operational objective for the Federal funds rate shall be modified in an orderly fashion within a range of 4 ½ to 5 ¼ percent. If it appears during the period before the next meeting that the operating constraints specified above are proving to be significantly inconsistent, the Manager is promptly to notify the Chairman who will then decide whether the situation calls for supplementary instructions from the Committee.

This language leaves no doubt about what the FOMC expects the manager of the SOMA to accomplish.

DAY-TO-DAY EXECUTION OF POLICY AT THE OPEN MARKET TRADING DESK

The function of the manager of the System Open Market Account is to try to keep the federal funds rate and the money supply within the target ranges specified in the FOMC's current policy directive. The SOMA manager attempts to achieve the FOMC's short-run objectives through the use of open-market operations in government securities. These operations are conducted on a day-to-day basis from the Open Market Trading Desk at the Federal Reserve Bank of New York.

The influence of the Fed's open-market operations on the federal funds rate and the supply of money involves a sequence of effects. Such a sequence is roughly as follows:

1. The immediate impact of open market transactions is to increase or decrease the reserves of commercial banks. If the Fed buys securities, reserves are increased. If securities are sold, then reserves are decreased. Open-market purchases and sales may be either outright or through repurchase agreements. RPs are used when the SOMA manager wishes to supply or absorb reserves for a few days only. Regular purchases and sales are made when the purpose is to have a more enduring influence.
2. Reserves have an immediate impact on the federal funds rate. Indeed, the range of federal funds rates specified by the FOMC gives an immediate target to which the SOMA manager can respond.

3. The federal funds rate has an important impact on the profit calculus of commercial banks. Banks adjust their own operations, both in seeking funds and in the employment of funds, to their marginal cost of money—which is best reflected by the federal funds rate.

4. Bank adjustments to changes in the cost of funds and the quantity of available reserves are ultimately reflected in the amount of credit they extend—and that in turn determines the volume of bank deposits, which are the major components of the money supply. Thus, while open-market purchases have their first effect on increasing the quantity of reserves and decreasing the cost of funds—as measured by the federal funds rate—the more ultimate effect is to increase the supply of money. The reverse effects are true in response to open-market sales.

5. The transmission of effects of open-market operations on the money supply is neither exact, prompt, nor even wholly dependable. Noncontrollable elements of demand enter into the stream of influence. The amount of deposits the public is willing to hold varies with interest rates and many other economic considerations. The amount the public borrows is likewise influenced by a complex of considerations. Because the public's demand for money and credit are both important to the profit calculus of banks, the amounts of bank credit and bank deposits do not follow meekly in the path of reserves and the federal funds rate.

Knowing this, the manager of SOMA has the rather unenviable job of deciding the direction, size, and timing of open-market operations. In deciding on the direction of open-market operations—that is, deciding whether to buy or to sell in the market—considerable attention is focused on the federal funds rate. If the current federal funds rate is above the target level specified by the FOMC, open-market purchases are required; if below, then open-market sales. Unfortunately, the money supply is not a useful guide in determining the direction of current operations because of lack of knowledge of the current money supply. This lack of knowledge is caused by information lags in reporting the money supply.

Decisions about the size of open-market operations and their timing are based partly on projections of the demand for and supply of reserves. Both sides of the market are estimated in terms of the desired federal funds rate. The projected gap between demand and supply at the desired rate indicates the extent to which the account manager will have to go into the market to fill the gap. Such projections are made weekly.

The demand for reserves is projected by adding up required reserves and the demand for excess reserves. Required reserves are determined by deposits on the banks' books two weeks earlier and are, therefore, known by the account manager at the time the projection is being made. Excess reserves, on the other hand, are not known in advance. The account manager has to consider a number of factors, together with the federal funds rate, in estimating the demand for excess reserves.

The supply of reserves is projected by estimating the effects of such "market factors" as Federal Reserve float, currency in circulation, and the Treasury's cash balance held in deposit at the Fed. These factors are responsible for much of the volatility in the supply of reserves. Much careful attention is given to them because they form the basis of the need to use open-market operations defensively. Account is also taken of likely member bank borrowing at the Federal Reserve discount window inasmuch as borrowed reserves are a part of the supply of total reserves. Fortunately, the Fed has control over the volume of loans to member banks.

Given the supply and demand projections, the account manager determines the volume of reserves to be supplied or absorbed on a daily average basis if open-market operations are to clear the market for reserves at the desired federal funds rate. However, before actually entering the market, the trading desk checks the market to see whether the federal funds rate is moving in the direction that confirms the Fed's own projections. Such confirmation has an important bearing on the confidence of the Fed's open-market decisions.

The federal funds rate has an element of stickiness, however. Banks expect the Fed to keep the federal funds rate at the target level. They are willing to carry fairly large reserve deficits or excesses before taking offsetting actions in the federal funds market. In short, the demand for reserves is elastic. As a result, the federal funds rate has a tendency to stay close to the market's perception of its targeted value.

This element of stickiness in the federal funds rate poses a problem for the account manager. In seeking independent market confirmation of his reserve projections, the account manager expects the federal funds rate to be moving away from target, not gravitating toward it. Thus, the less the federal funds rate responds to independent market forces, the more the account manager has to rely on his own internal reserve projections for guiding open-market decisions. Moreover, the problem is compounded by the fact that the reserve projections, themselves, tend to be less reliable as the federal funds rate exhibits less independent market movement. The demand for excess reserves becomes especially difficult to project. The end result of all this is that a fairly narrow range for the federal funds rate may be consistent with a very wide range in reserves supplied by the Fed and, therefore, a wide range in the supply of money.

The account manager's ability to stay on target with respect to the money supply is further frustrated by the fact that the effect of open-market operations on the money supply is not known until after a considerable period of time. First, there is a lag in the actual monetary effects of open-market operations, and second, there is an information lag in reporting the monetary aggregates affected. Nevertheless, the account manager keeps a watchful eye on money supply data as it dribbles in. Having been on or off target in the recent past gives some indication of being on or off target currently. If reports indicate that the money supply has been off target, the account manager may feel a need to take some corrective action in current operations. Early-in estimates of the money supply are the most relevant indicators in this regard, but they are also the least trustworthy. When the evidence looks suspicious, the account manager cannot avoid using intuition.

As the next monthly meeting of the FOMC approaches, the SOMA manager becomes more knowledgeable about where the money supply actually is in relation to its target for the month. There is no guarantee, of course, that the money supply will be on target. In fact, the looser the connection between the federal funds rate and the money supply, the more likely the money supply will be off target if the federal funds rate is kept at the midpoint of its target range. The account manager is only too keenly aware of this, but even if he takes full advantage of letting the federal funds rate move to the upper or lower limit of its range, there is still some chance that the money supply will end up off target. When this happens, the account manager is instructed to go back to the FOMC for further instructions. Meanwhile, the participants in the federal funds market, having learned themselves that the money supply is off target, will begin forming new expectations about the federal funds rate. At this point, the federal funds rate may fluctuate considerably in response to unsettled market conditions.

ACHIEVEMENT OF TARGETS: SUCCESS OR FAILURE?

The record shows that the Federal Reserve has often missed hitting all its short-run targets simultaneously. The federal funds rate has almost always been kept within its target range, but monetary growth has frequently been off target. Sometimes it is M_1 that goes off target, sometimes M_2, and sometimes both. These results are illustrated in Figure 11-1, which compares the FOMC's target specifications with actual outcomes during 1977.

The failure of the money supply to stay within its target range raises questions about the Fed's willingness and ability to keep the money supply on target. Is the Fed simply unable to control the money supply in the short run? Are there reasons why the Fed is willing to allow the money supply to stray off target? How important is short-run monetary control relative to control of the federal funds rate?

The Fed certainly lacks the ability to exercise absolute control over the money supply. However, many observers (including some within the Fed) agree that the Fed could influence the money supply, if it wanted to, with greater short-run precision than has actually been the case. Thus, to a limited extent, the Fed has willingly allowed the money supply to stray off target. There are several reasons for this. For one thing, it may be necessary to keep one of the M_1 or M_2 measures off target in one direction in order to prevent the other measure from going too far off target in the other direction. For another thing, the Fed recognizes the fact that short-run measures of the money supply contain a certain amount of "noise" (randomness) that tends to cancel out in the long run. Some of this noise could be offset by exercising more precise short-run control of the money supply, but it would involve unacceptable fluctuations in money market interest rates. Finally, there is the excellent

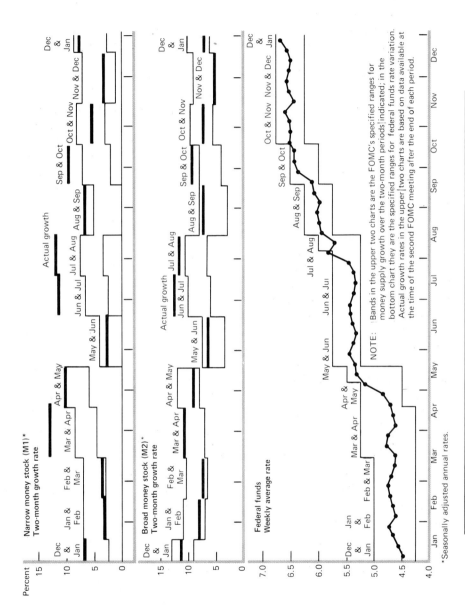

figure 11-1 FOMC Ranges for Short-run Monetary Growth and for the Federal Funds Rate, 1977. (*Source: Quarterly Review, Federal Reserve Bank of New York, Spring 1978, p. 48.*)

253

argument that the money supply is not allowed to stay off target for very long, that, as soon as the Fed has reliable information of a deviation between desired and actual monetary growth, immediate steps are taken to change the funds rate target in a direction consistent with correcting the deviation!

Figure 11-1 provides some evidence on the application of these arguments for 1977. The two money supply measures did occasionally go off target, but not in opposite directions. However, positive and negative deviations from target did tend to cancel out over the year, at least in the case of M_2. Most important, the federal funds rate target was raised in months following excessive monetary growth!

The weekly-average federal funds rate is usually held well within the upper and lower limits of the target range. This is made all the more significant by the fact that the target range for the funds rate is only about half as wide (in percentage units) as the ranges for the monetary growth targets. The facts indicate that the Fed exercises relatively tight short-run control over the federal funds rate.

DOES THE FED MANAGE RESERVES?

It is nearly impossible to read any article or listen to any speech on monetary policy without some reference being made to the Fed's management of bank reserves. Reserve management is certainly discussed at the monthly meetings of the FOMC. Indeed, the FOMC specifies two-month reserve targets along with specifying two-month targets for the money supply and the federal funds rate. Reserve management is also part of the jargon at the open-market trading desk. The account manager often refers publicly to his job as carrying out "the FOMC's instructions regarding the management of bank reserves."

However, from the point of view of the outsider, it is difficult to see that reserve management involves much actual management of reserves. Reserve targets are specified by the FOMC, but there is little explicit instruction in the FOMC's policy directive for the SOMA manager to meet such targets. There is also little evidence that the SOMA manager must live with such targets on an informal basis. The SOMA manager rarely if ever refers to the reserve management task in terms of supplying a target quantity of reserves. Instead, reference is usually made to achieving "bank reserve availability *as measured by the federal funds rate.*" To the outsider, this is similar to measuring the production of wheat by the price of wheat rather than by the number of bushels produced. In all fairness, however, the SOMA manager does not have access to reliable figures for reserve aggregates on a daily basis. The price or rate on federal funds is about all that the manager has to go on in conducting day-to-day operations.

Another problem facing the outsider is deciphering which concept of reserves the Fed is attempting to manage. The FOMC specifies its reserve targets in terms of RPDs (reserves available to support private nonbank deposits, or, total reserves less required reserves on interbank and government deposits). The SOMA manager, on the other hand, does not appear to make much use of this concept in reserve projections; rather, considerable emphasis is given to the concept of nonborrowed reserves (total reserves less borrowed reserves). Some use is also made, at various levels within the Fed, of other reserve concepts, such as net borrowed reserves (borrowed reserves less excess reserves) and free reserves (excess reserves less borrowed reserves, or, the negative of net borrowed reserves).

The question remains as to which concept of reserves is most closely related to the federal funds rate in terms of interaction of supply and demand. Other questions also remain: How does the Fed know that it is the federal funds rate rather than some other interest rate that is most closely related to the supply of and demand for reserves? If the Fed needs to use the federal funds rate as a target, why does it not shift its operations out of the government securities market and enter directly into the market for federal funds? If it did this, would the effect on the nation's money supply be any different?

FED WATCHING

Financial markets have a vital interest in the nature of current Federal Reserve policy. Although the longer-term influence of Fed actions on interest rates is disputed, everyone agrees about the very considerable short-term impact. While this impact is most immediately felt by those who hold inventories of short-term money market instruments, the short-term impact of Fed policy on longer-term financial instruments is even greater in profit-and-loss terms. Investment bankers don't want to get caught with underwriting commitments when long-term interest rates are about to go up. Investors don't want to make purchase commitments if they foresee lower prices ahead. Even the stock market is influenced by Fed policy and actions.

The profit-and-loss potential in forecasting Fed actions leads to a great deal of "Fed watching." Two quite expensive market letters are devoted solely to this subject. A great deal is written about it in the financial press. The practice of this art, however, probably reaches its peak among the professional dealers in U.S. government securities. The organization and operation of these dealers will be described in detail in Chapter 13. At this point we shall focus on the kinds of materials and evidence used by Fed watchers.

The publicly available materials used by Fed watchers include the minutes of the FOMC (released with a one-month lag), the quarterly appearance of the chairman before the Joint Economic Committee, and the weekly statement of the Federal Reserve and Treasury reserve and monetary factors. In addition to these routine materials, the market pays careful attention to any speeches or other public statements by the chairman. (Other board members and the presidents of Federal Reserve banks all make speeches, but they leave matters of Fed policy for the chairman to cover.) In addition, the economic research materials published by both Federal Reserve banks and the board are reviewed for the nature of thinking within the system.

Fed watching, however, reaches a frenzied peak in the day-to-day and even hour-to-hour trading traffic in the Treasury securities market. The principal expression of Fed policy is in its open-market operations. These operations are purchases or sales of Treasury or agency securities. All such transactions are with a group of about three dozen professional dealers. All the dealers who have a trading relationship with the Fed are tied to the Fed trading desk by a direct telephone connection. With few exceptions, the dealers do not call the Fed, the Fed calls the dealers. A call from the Fed activates a special signal light on each dealer's telephone console. The appearance of this signal light tends to attract the attention of the very top personnel in a dealer firm. Some Fed calls are just for information and market impressions. Other Fed calls are routine transactions that it conducts as agent, mainly for foreign monetary authorities. Fed transactions do not necessarily have new policy implications; they may be merely for the purpose of maintaining reserve stability in the banking community. But some Fed transactions clearly have policy importance.

How do the dealers distinguish the routine and defensively functional transactions from those with policy substance? Probably the leading signal is contained in the Fed funds rate. If the Fed engages in market transactions when the Fed funds rate is stable, it is likely that the transactions are routine or defensive. But if the Fed seems to respond to the Fed funds rate—to sell if the rate goes down or to buy if the rate goes up—then such a transaction is likely to have policy significance. The Fed treats the rate of growth of the money supply—either M_1, M_2, or M_3—as a *policy* target. But the statistics of money supply growth are both considerably delayed after the event, and are often subject to considerable revision. Fed funds rates respond quickly to differences in reserve availability and can be considered as *operational* targets. A given Fed funds operational target is judged by the FOMC to be consistent with some particular money supply growth rate, which is the policy goal. But if experience suggests that this judgment of consistency has been wrong, then the former Fed funds operational target usually gives way to a new one.

Fed watching, however, is based on a broader range of evidence. Experienced traders claim to have a "feel" of the market. This is a most unscientific, nonquantitative sort of standard, but it is an intuition on which most experienced professional traders depend. Dealers have to search for money to finance their inventories. This search for money often gives them a sense of the tightness or ease of money throughout the country. And if the Fed does—or does not—enter a tight money market with help in the form of RP money, this action—or lack of it—also has policy significance.

Perhaps the most important fact of all is that the Fed itself does not operate with perfect and complete information; it is often not sure about the nature of supply and demand in the financial markets. The Fed is therefore watching both the economy and financial markets and is often uncertain about developments in both. The Fed also watches the dealers closely. The community of watchers, therefore, is two-way; the watching goes both ways. Everyone watches the economy and both groups watch each other. The chief difference is that the Fed has more market power than any dealer (which fact it knows very well) and a mandate to use this power, not for profit, but for public good.

PROJECTS AND QUESTIONS

1. How would you define "full employment without inflation?" Is this objective, as you have defined it, achievable? Has there ever been a time in your lifetime when it was achieved?
2. Records of policy actions of the FOMC are published monthly in the *Federal Reserve Bulletin*. These records contain important information about the FOMC's economic objectives and the operating criteria for meeting them. After studying the records published in the last twelve issues of the *Bulletin*, write a brief report that describes changes in the FOMC's priorities and consequent shifts in the target values of its operating criteria. With the advantage of hindsight, explain whether or not you believe the FOMC took correct actions.
3. Be prepared to defend the use of either the federal funds rate or the quantity of bank reserves as the appropriate operating target for managing the supply of money.
4. Suppose the Fed is planning to decrease the supply of money and is deciding between using open-market operations or reserve requirement changes. Which course of action do you think a commercial banker would prefer? Which course of action do you think the Secretary of the Treasury would prefer?
5. Open-market operations are aimed at controlling the federal funds rate, but this effect is indirect. (Yields on short-term government securities are affected first.) Explain, in detail, the process by which each of the various money market interest rates is affected by the open-market operations of the Federal Reserve.

BIBLIOGRAPHY

Board of Governors of the Federal Reserve System: *Open Market Policies and Operating Procedures—Staff Studies*, 1971.
Federal Reserve Bank of Boston: *Controlling Monetary Aggregates*, 1969.
Federal Reserve Bank of Boston: *Controlling Monetary Aggregates II: The Implementation*, 1973.
Federal Reserve Bank of New York: *Monetary Aggregates and Monetary Policy*, 1974.
"Numerical Specifications of Financial Variables and Their Role in Monetary Policy," *Federal Reserve Bulletin*, May 1974, pp. 333–337.
"Record of Policy Actions of the Federal Open Market Committee," *Federal Reserve Bulletin*, Monthly.
Guttentag, J. M.: "The Strategy of Open Market Operations," *Quarterly Journal of Economics*, February 1966, pp. 1–30.
Holmes, A. R., and P. D. Sternlight: "The Implementation of Monetary Policy in 1976," *Quarterly Review*, Federal Reserve Bank of New York, Spring 1977, pp. 37–49.

————, and ————: "Monetary Policy and Open Market Operations in 1977," *Quarterly Review,* Federal Reserve Bank of New York, Spring 1978, pp. 41–53.

Lombra, R. E., and R. G. Torto: "The Strategy of Monetary Policy," *Economic Review,* Federal Reserve Bank of Richmond, September/October 1975, pp. 3–14.

Maisel, S. J.: *Managing the Dollar,* Norton, New York, 1973.

Meek, P.: *Open Market Operations,* Federal Reserve Bank of New York, 1978.

Poole, W.: "The Making of Monetary Policy: Description and Analysis," *New England Economic Review,* Federal Reserve Bank of Boston, March/April 1975, pp. 21–30.

Wrightsman, D.: *An Introduction to Monetary Theory and Policy,* The Free Press, New York, 1976.

part three

Capital Markets

chapter 12
Capital Markets: An Overview

The usual distinction made between money markets and capital markets is the maturity of the credit instruments in which they deal. By common consent, money market instruments are those with maturities of one year or less; capital market instruments lie beyond that range. This leaves a very wide range of maturities for the capital markets. Credit market instruments that are just beyond the one-year limit—often called "intermediate" maturities—frequently have characteristics that are closer to true money market instruments than to capital market instruments. No universally observed convention on the upper limit for "intermediate" maturity credit instruments is recognized: Five years might be the top, but it would almost certainly be less than ten years.

The capital markets also include those financial instruments that have no clear terminal maturity, such as common or preferred stocks. For purposes of yield mathematics, such instruments are treated as if they had an infinitely remote maturity. Again there is a sharp distinction: Any instrument having a maturity of ten years might be viewed as closer to a short-term credit instrument than to one of an infinitely remote maturity.

Nominal or legal maturity may differ materially from de facto or actual maturity. For example, passbook savings accounts in savings institutions are, by custom, payable on demand. However, the actual life of such accounts is quite long—many years on the average—and so for practical purposes passbook savings accounts can be treated as capital market financial instruments. Another example, but this of an instrument that is practically shorter than its nominal maturity, is that of the home mortgage. Almost all home mortgages start with very long terms. Twenty-five and thirty years are common. In practice, however, so many home mortgages are paid off before maturity that the average maturity is much less. Mortgage pools guaranteed by the U.S. government start with a nominal thirty-year maturity, but for yield calculation purposes they estimate an average maturity of only twelve years.

With higher interest rates older capital market financial instruments have not been retired prior to maturity as often as in the past. However, if interest rates were to go down materially, it is almost certain that there would be widespread refunding of many such instruments, giving them an effective maturity far less than contemplated when first issued.

A study of capital markets brings in still another dimension of great financial market importance: risk. The money market is not without credit or money-rate risk, but the degree of it is necessarily small. A maturity of one year or less gives little time for a default to occur, so credit risk is minimized. Money-rate risk for short-term instruments is necessarily small. In other words, the theory of portfolio and market efficiency, which was the subject of Chapter 6, is much more directly related to capital markets than to money markets. Risk varies both in its degree and character throughout the capital markets, and one of our central concerns will be with the nature of this risk and how investors deal with it.

The range of participants in capital markets is also much wider than in money markets. Some economic sectors participate in both money and capital markets, but a majority of the members of most economic sectors have far more to do with capital markets than with money markets. Furthermore, quite a few of the members of the more important economic sectors participate on both sides of both money and capital markets; both as investors and as demanders of funds. Nonfinancial corporations are often a good example of economic units that participate in both money and capital markets, and with varying conditions may appear as either demanders of, or suppliers of, funds. However, most economic units clearly fall on one side of this relationship or the other.

The nature of the financial instruments dealt with in capital markets is also somewhat more heterogeneous than is the case in money markets. Some homogeneity of financial instruments is needed for the operation of open financial markets; too much diversity would present an insuperable problem to investors. For this reason, quite a few of the financial instruments used in capital markets have been forced into a mold of reasonable homogeneity for sake of marketability; the effort to create secondary markets in mortgages is an example of this type of action. Nevertheless, diversity remains in the negotiated markets of financial instruments. In fact, some participants in financial markets make a living by their ingenuity in creating financial instruments that will fit the requirements of special cases: a kind of market in tailor-made financial instruments. Most shopping centers, for example, are financed with mortgages individually adapted to the circumstances of the developer, the nature of the basic land ownership, the speed with which economic maturity of the project is expected, and other variables. Developers call this "creative" finance.

In a number of important respects, our money and capital markets are quite similar. The lower tip of Manhattan, which is often identified as the center of the money market, is also the central location of many leading capital market institutions: the New York Stock Exchange and the offices of many investment bankers. Many financial institutions have roles in both markets. But there are great differences, and it will be a primary function of this chapter to explore some of the differences.

Chapter 8 described the basic role of the money markets as that of liquidity adjustment. The central role of capital markets is that of putting capital to work; preferably long-term, secure, and productive employment. Chapter 2 described the basic economic processes of saving and investment. As the word was used there, "investment" means direction of economic resources into real capital: machinery, factories, housing, roads, and even the intangible capital goods of education and knowledge. A nation that directs its capital into tombs for kings is not as likely to prosper and advance as one that puts its capital into schools, laboratories, irrigation ditches, and sanitary sewers.

In the money markets, there is one major type of private institution—the commercial bank. Commercial banks could be considered money market intermediaries in that they accumulate funds by deposits and then make them available in lending. The money creation process may seem to obscure this role, but it exists. The capital markets are served by a large variety of types of intermediary institutions (including commercial banks). Commercial banks are not just money market intermediaries; they are important in the capital markets. The capital markets are facilitated, in addition to true intermediaries, by a variety of institutions that are not themselves intermediaries but service institutions: investment banking firms, commission brokerage houses, and investment advisers of all sorts, sizes, and shapes—including those dealing with the problems of law, accounting, engineering, and markets.

The money markets are closely and directly tied to the Federal Reserve. The capital markets feel central bank influence, but mainly indirectly and through the money markets.

In the money markets, commercial banks are closely regulated. However, money markets themselves—for commercial paper, U.S. government securities, bankers' acceptances, negotiable certificates of deposit, and Euro-currencies—are not generally regulated beyond the ordinary influence of the law of negotiable instruments. In the capital markets the institutions are not much regulated, but the markets are. Investment bankers are not regulated as are commercial banks. Commission brokerage houses are very little regulated except by some measure of industry self-regulation. But the new issues markets and the secondary markets for outstanding securities are regulated.

MAJOR SUPPLIERS OF CAPITAL MARKET INSTRUMENTS

The major suppliers of capital market instruments could also be called the "major demanders of capital market funds": except that some of the instruments of supply do not involve any extensive and direct demand for funds. Corporate common stocks are such an example; only a small amount of new money is raised directly by new equity issues, but these issues, increased in book value by retained earnings, are a major capital market instrument. Calling the capital participants "borrowers" would also fail for the same reason: thus our section is rather awkwardly but accurately titled.

Corporations are the leading suppliers of capital market instruments, as shown in Figure 12-1. Common and preferred stocks represent the largest instrument in dollar volume, but bonds and mortgages are also relatively large.

Since corporations are also the major debtors to money markets, this reinforces their lead over all other economic sectors.

Individuals are the second leading suppliers of capital market instruments; most of this is by the mortgage route, but also to some extent through consumer credit. As we shall find later, individuals are the leading suppliers of *funds* to capital markets, but a large fraction of this supply flows through financial intermediaries. Thus individuals have a large net credit balance in capital markets. This aggregate fact is also reflected in the financial affairs of many families where holdings of financial assets are frequently combined with mortgage indebtedness.

The federal government is the third largest supplier of capital market instruments. A large part of these instruments, however, is of rather short intermediate-term maturity, so it is functionally related more to the money markets than the true capital markets. State and local governments fall in fourth place. Unincorporated business is in fifth place; farmers in last place.

Rates of growth of the various instruments vary greatly and are far from synchronous. Corporations follow business fluctuations; with new offerings

figure 12-1 Suppliers of Financial Instruments, by Sectors. *(Source: Author's estimates based on Flow-of-Funds data, Board of Governors of the Federal Reserve System, quarterly reports.)*

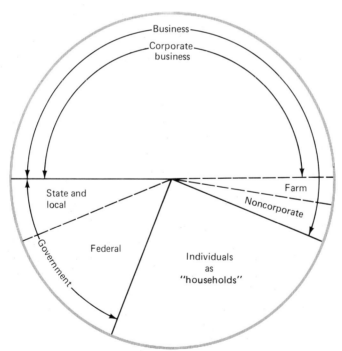

NOTE: Strictly speaking there is a conceptual inconsistency in the numbers underlying this figure. The equity of corporate business is included at market value, since most of it is a financial instrument of leading market importance. Equity accounts for other sectors are not included since they are never available for financial market transactions.

large when capital expenditures are large, which in turn depend on the state of market activity. Individuals increase mortgage borrowing for home ownership mainly. This varies widely, but the timing of the variations does not follow general business conditions very closely; the housing cycle is quite independent. The federal government follows a quite different course: budget deficits are the major cause of increases and these are more likely to be *counter*cyclical than to be synchronous with general business conditions. State and local government finance follows still another pattern. Farm financing seems to follow the pattern of the crop cycle that, in turn, does not coincide with general business conditions at all closely.

The considerable variations in growth rates and their timing give the capital markets a rather variable pattern. Lack of synchronization can be looked at as a desirable fact in that it results in less fluctuation in the totals than might be expected from an examination of the individual segments.

MAJOR CAPITAL MARKET INVESTORS

Individuals, as represented by "households" in the flow-of-funds statistics, are the major investors in the capital markets as shown in Figure 12-2. Much of this investment, however, is done through intermediaries. Financial intermediaries exist for a wide variety of reasons, some of which have already been outlined in Chapter 4. In rough terms, about one-half of the capital market assets of household investors is directly invested; the other half goes through intermediaries.

This proportion has remained reasonably stable over the long run. From year to year, however, the net additions often vary rather widely. This is particularly true of the funds passed through savings institutions; the rates paid by these institutions has tended to be rather stable even when open capital market rates of return vary. As a result, households elect to use savings institutions when interest rates are low or moderate; but when they are high, they turn to direct investment to reap the higher rate of return then available. This necessarily leads to rather disruptive circumstances in the capital markets since the investment outlets used by direct individual investors often differ materially from those followed by the savings institutions. An actual outflow of funds from savings institutions—characterized by the awkward word "disintermediation"—has happened a number of times such as in 1966, 1969, 1971 and 1974.

The mortgage market has probably been the most severely affected by these periods of disintermediation since it depends on savings institutions for so much of its funds. The gainers are rather more spread out, but the money market, such as that for Treasury bills, and the market for corporate bonds have often been leading beneficiaries.

Although commercial banks are not usually thought of as major capital market institutions, they are, in reality, probably the single most important such institutions. The various ways in which they participate include:

1. Commercial banks are major mortgage lending institutions.
2. The trust departments of commercial banks manage both large pension

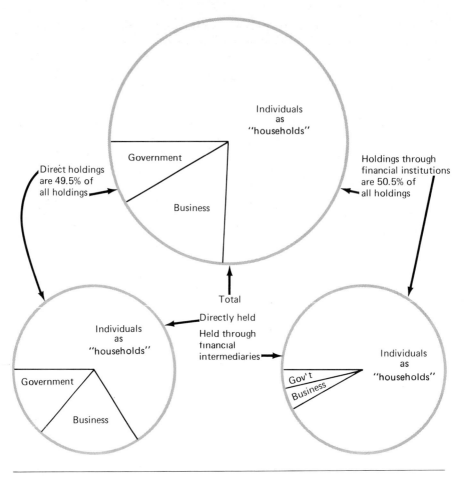

figure 12-2   Holders of Financial Instruments: Total, Directly Held, and Held through Financial Intermediaries. *(Source: Author's estimates based on Flow-of-Funds data, Board of Governors of the Federal Reserve System, quarterly reports.)*

trusts and the portfolios of individuals and estates. This role involves considerable equity and bond investment.

3. The loans of commercial banks are directly competitive with and an alternative to capital market financing. The (intermediate) term loans of commercial banks are clearly of this nature. In addition, many other loans, although nominally short-term, are so frequently renewed and extended that they are a practical alternative to capital market financing.
4. Commercial banks are major consumer lenders.
5. Commercial banks supply the working capital of brokers, dealers, and investment bankers.

What this amounts to is that the decision-making process for the investors in the capital markets is rather more concentrated than the ultimate beneficial ownership of the capital market investment assets.

INTERRELATIONSHIPS OF INVESTORS AND INSTRUMENT SUPPLIERS

At this stage it will be useful to return to the matrix of financial assets and liabilities that was presented in Chapter 5 on pages 106 – 109. The major economic sectors are spread across the top of the matrix. Corporate equities and the credit market instruments appear on lines 18 – 28. Some of the instruments are money market instruments, but the principal capital market instruments are also shown. A series of flow matrices would reveal that new money often flows in patterns that differ greatly from the patterns of the totals. In other words, investors shift the way they use funds, seeking the greatest current advantage. Several points can be learned from a restudy of this matrix:

1. Some sectors are principally suppliers of credit or capital market instruments; some are principally investors. However, many sectors are both in a rather large degree. Individual economic units within sectors are undoubtedly more unbalanced than total sectors.
2. Investment portfolios are generally diversified. However, as we shall find in later chapters, this diversification is often limited by important tax considerations.
3. The sectors that supply credit or capital market instruments also diversify their sources of funds; they finance where funds are available on the best possible terms. If we used the matrices of flows as a source, we would find that this means considerable shifting about from year to year.

The lesson this study of financial market matrices teaches is that these markets are dynamic. Long-run principles of diversification and comparative advantage prevail, but these factors change and markets are the site in which these changes are negotiated.

One of the obstacles to making meaningful measurement of the capital markets is duplication. The best example of duplication is furnished by the operation of financial intermediaries, which were reviewed in Chapter 4. These intermediaries acquire financial instruments by virtue of the financial instruments they, themselves, issue. Other kinds of duplication also exist.

The degree of duplication can be illustrated by a few simple facts. The flow-of-funds matrix for the end of 1975 counted $5 ½ *trillion* of credit claims. However, a Department of Commerce tabulation of net debt for the same date, which attempted to remove duplication, came up with a figure of only $3 trillion. In many ways, however, the analysis of financial markets requires us to look more at the gross than at the net figures. Even those financial instruments that create duplication are nevertheless important factors in markets and often explain financial developments better than any net figures One more fact, however, may help to put the matter in still a different perspective: The *real* wealth of the United States (a very rough estimate) at the end of 1975 was

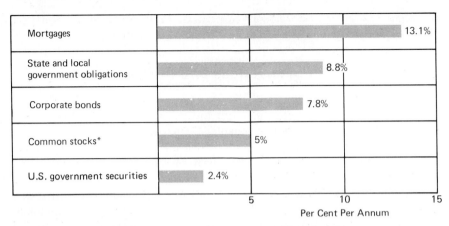

Mortgages				13.1%
State and local government obligations		8.8%		
Corporate bonds	7.8%			
Common stocks*	5%			
U.S. government securities	2.4%			
	5	10	15

Per Cent Per Annum

*The growth rate estimated for common stocks is not comparable to the other growth rates, which are based on par values of amounts outstanding. Common stocks are based on market value. Growth rates in other sectors would be slightly less (estimated to be about one-tenth) if they could be based on market value.

figure 12-3   Growth Rates of Leading Capital Market Financial Instruments, 1946-1977. *(Source: Author's estimates based on Flow-of-Funds data, Board of Governors of the Federal Reserve system, quarterly reports.)*

probably about $5 trillion. (If the intangible real wealth of human capital including health and education were included, it would add another $5 trillion.)

Growth rates for the leading financial instruments are shown in Figure 12-3. Such instruments have grown faster than GNP in current dollars: a reflection of the fact that our nation is becoming increasingly complex as a financial system. It is also significant that debt grew faster than equity in the postwar years.

INVESTMENT BANKERS AND BANKING

Just as the label "commercial" banking fails to disclose the wide range of functions performed by these banks, the label "investment" banking fails to disclose their full range of activity. The function most evidently performed by investment bankers is the distribution of securities by syndicate underwriting. These sales are generally "guaranteed," which is the functional meaning of underwriting, so the service is both selling and the guarantee of a sale. When a syndicate advertises a sale (very often after the actual selling has been virtually completed), the listing of the names of the underwriters is one of the most public revelations of the leading investment bankers. The sequence of names in listing is a form of delicate financial protocol with feelings as sensitive as in any seating plan at a state dinner.

The underwriting of newly issued securities often leads to a related function: the maintenance of a secondary market in these securities. Since an investment banker who has managed an underwriting of new securities has been forced to become intimately familiar with the financial condition and operations of the issuing corporation or body, he or she is in a superior position to continue the relationship and to make "follow-up" markets in its securities. The function is not just a service; it is expected to be a profitable operation in its own right. Bond trading and stock trading are very much central investment banking functions.

The wide range of investment banking services may be illustrated by a listing published by a leading investment banker in an ad in *The Wall Street Journal*. The firm listed twenty-one services for those *raising* money and twenty-one services for those *investing* money. They obviously stretched a bit to get such long lists, but the results are nevertheless instructive:

Services for those who are raising money

1. Corporate underwriting
2. Private placements
3. Lease financing
4. Mergers, acquisitions, and divestitures
5. Real estate mortgage financing
6. International public offerings
7. International private placements
8. Project financing
9. Industrial revenue bond financing
10. Pollution control financing
11. Commercial paper issuance
12. Corporate stock repurchasing
13. Secondary offerings
14. Underwritten redemptions
15. Sinking fund purchases
16. Investment of excess cash
17. Exchange and tender offers
18. Government agency financing
19. State and municipal financing
20. Foreign government financing
21. Financial advisory services

Services for investors

1. Investment research
2. Economic forecasting
3. Money market analysis
4. Investment strategy
5. Industry and company analysis
6. Block trading
7. Special order service
8. Equity securities
9. Foreign securities
10. Convertible securities
11. Listed option trading
12. Security arbitrage
13. Security swaps
14. Restricted brokerage
15. Commercial paper
16. Government securities
17. Bankers acceptances
18. Certificates of deposit
19. Corporate bonds
20. Tax-exempt bonds
21. Securities from managed offerings

Investment bankers vary widely in the nature of services performed and in financial strength. Some firms specialize; others offer a wide range of services. Direct placements (which will be covered in detail in Chapter 16) usually involve the actual intermediation of an "advising" investment banker. Mergers and acquisitions represent an important activity of some investment bankers. Arbitrage of the securities of the two parties to a proposed merger is a profitable, but risky, investment-banking function. Advisory activities of all kinds often earn them rather large fees.

Investment banking requires capital, but the degree of capitalization varies widely and the amount of capital is not a measure of the influence and prestige of an investment banking firm. The basic essential of investment banking is persons with talent and wide contacts. It is significant that investment banking often recruits its leading members from those who have served in high federal offices, particularly those who have served in the State Department or the Treasury Department.

Investment banking is also decidedly international. Almost all the leading investment bankers have foreign offices or maintain a kind of "correspondence" relationship with leading investment bankers abroad. Investment bankers in the United States have often been compared to the merchant bankers of Great Britain. In some Western European countries—West Germany is a leading example—investment banking and commercial banking functions are combined in single institutions, but that practice has been prohibited in the United States since 1933, Many wonder if that prohibition has not outlived its usefulness.

INVESTMENT BANKING IN TRANSITION

Investment bankers and banking will turn up in almost all the chapters that follow (except that on the mortgage market). The industry of investment banking is changing rapidly. Perhaps the greatest of all the changes is that the continuity of family control and management is being broken. In the past most firms were partnerships, and the dominant or managing partner was often in a direct succession of the family that supplied most of the capital. If direct descendants bearing the family name were not available, marriages would produce the successors to the family tradition if not name. Now many investment banking firms are shifting from partnership organization to incorporation. Along with that change, family management is less common, and the professional manager has become more frequent. Such professional managers may have no family ties and little personal capital. But the grand old names remain, and so do some of the family members. Personal relationships remain important.

The functional changes are also subtle. Investment bankers no longer have the dominant voices on boards of directors that they once had, but they remain as important and influential "advisers." They originate many of the innovative ideas for corporate mergers, but they do not have the means to push them through by sheer strength of voting power. Underwriting remains an important investment banking function, but even when it is "negotiated" rather than competitive, investment bankers have less power. The power in negotiation is sometimes more on the side of the borrowers than on the side of those who raise the funds.

The old traditional houses had strong ties with the old traditional institutional investors such as insurance companies. But the range of institutional investors has broadened to include pension funds and the trust departments of commercial banks, and here traditional ties are weaker. Institutional investment has become much more competitive and less tradition bound. The old traditional investment banking firms made sales efforts, but the efforts were so concentrated that the number of salesmen was small. The newer and more successful investment banking operations must sell to a broader market, so they must have more salesmen. The old firms might be rich in capital and tradition but have few employees; the new firms are larger and much of the increase has been in sales personnel. In fact, the change has taken this direction. Those commission brokerage firms that emphasized "retail" operations (small investors) have now become outlets so important that they have entered the traditional areas of investment banking and often dominate them.

Investment banking has adapted to competitive bidding. It has also adapted to direct placement, and some of the traditional investment bankers have become adept at the negotiation of direct placement and brag about it in newspaper advertisements; something that the truly traditional investment bankers would never have done.

Almost all investment bankers have owned a seat on the New York Stock Exchange, but it was often inactively used. Without large retail outlets around the nation, some investment bankers have promoted correspondent or clearing relationships with various smaller regional investment firms.

It is hard to summarize the influence of this change in investment banking, but it has clearly made the financial markets in which they participate more competitive. And it has made all investors and markets much better informed. Secrecy no longer shrouds the operations of these ancient giants: We now know much more about what they do and how well they fare.

INTEREST RATE RELATIONSHIPS IN CAPITAL MARKETS

At any one point in time, the interest rates or yields prevailing in the various capital markets may vary rather widely. The differences are usually explainable by factors such as taxes, risk, or by cost of investment, but other factors may also be present. Over time, however, there is an evident and considerable tendency for parallel movement of these yields. This is well illustrated by Figure 7-1 in Chapter 7. The parallel movement is a product of investor behavior. Investors seek the most favorable return, after allowance for taxes, risk, and other factors. Although some markets are limited in investor participation, there is generally enough freedom of at least a few investors to move from market to market so that the influence of broad economic developments, such as saving and investment, tend to be felt in all markets.

Nevertheless the movements are not fully parallel over time. For example, the yield curve in the market for tax-exempt securities (see Chapter 7 for a review of yield curves) often does not move in a parallel fashion with that of the yield curve for federal government securities. Theorists of yield curves have cited this as evidence supporting the segmented-market or hedging-pressure theory of yield curves. And it is clearly true that, at least in the short run, unusually heavy offerings of new securities in any one market may depress it a little relative to other markets. However, it is a testament to the efficiency of free markets that the deviations due to heavy supplies are as small as they are.

Risk factors as a cause of yield differences is most evident in the market for equities. Chapters 17 and 18 present evidence of the way in which this risk differential is expressed. In most other capital markets, risk differentials are moderate. The reason for this moderation is that, in fact, the degree of risk in most of the fixed-return capital markets is quite small. Methods of credit appraisal and of giving creditors protection have been so well developed that risk differentials are not all that large.

Tax factors are something else: They are large and significant. The most clear case is that of securities in which coupon income is tax-exempt: the so-called municipal bonds, which are really more generally "state and local government" bonds. The difference between tax rates on capital gains and on regular income has a clear influence in the market for equities. Corporate owners are tax-shielded for a portion of dividend income (85 percent). As a result, corporations that are exposed to income taxation often choose to invest in preferred stocks rather than bonds.

A very general influence of taxes is something like this: Those investors that are themselves exempt from taxation specialize in the purchase of securities, the income from which is fully exposed to taxes, while investors who are themselves fully taxed specialize in securities that offer some degree of tax shielding. For example, pension funds are themselves not taxed; as a result, they buy securities with fully taxed income such as corporate bonds and mortgages. On the other hand, high-income individuals tend to seek tax-sheltered investments, such as state and local government obligations or real estate or oil-drilling investments that offer tax shelter.

The capital markets are thus strongly influenced by tax factors and are always deeply involved whenever tax reform legislation comes before Congress.

CAPITAL MARKET MAGNITUDES

It is helpful to a student to have some idea of relative magnitudes. With this in mind, the authors of this text have attempted, wherever possible, to supply statistics and graphic devices to help the student. Single-date statistics, however, tend to get out of date rapidly when growth rates are high, as they have been during most of the postwar years. For this reason we shall depend more on *proportions* rather than absolute figures. Here are some facts in terms of proportions that have proved stable:

1. Of all financial instruments outstanding, about three-quarters have maturities of more than one year and are therefore to be counted as belonging in the capital markets.
2. Because long-term interest rates are usually somewhat higher than short-term interest rates, the amount of interest paid is about four-fifths (or a bit more) in the capital market with less than a fifth in the money markets.
3. Money market instruments, however, turn over more rapidly in the money markets so that the gross dollar volume of trading in the money markets far exceeds that in capital markets. However, the dealer margin on money market instruments is also far smaller than that on capital market instruments, so the profitability of capital marketing considerably exceeds that of money market trading.
4. Growth rates for financial instruments in general exceed that of GNP. In other words, the growing complexity of our economy demands an even faster growth rate for finance.
5. Inflation has been a factor in both growth rates, but it may also have been a factor in the more rapid growth of finance magnitudes.
6. High interest rates, one of the consequences of inflation, have made for a rapid growth of interest in national income, relatively as well as absolutely. At present, direct interest income together with imputed interest income (with duplication removed as far as possible) is about one-sixth of national income, but the share could grow. A serious consequence of high interest is the high cost of capital both for business and for housing. It is a barrier to capital expenditures in both areas.

RISK IN CAPITAL MARKETS

We started this chapter by averring that capital market credit instruments involve more risk than money market instruments. Credit risk, the risk that a debtor will not perform as promised, is generally small. Except for certain small consumer loans, the degree of credit risk is usually just a modest fraction of 1 percent per year. Defaults and bankruptcies do occur, but credit risk is not really very important.

Money-rate risk—variations in the market prices of outstanding credit instruments with fixed interest return owing to changes in yields—is much more important. This type of risk would not be very significant if most holders of capital market instruments kept possession until maturity. Then only credit risk would be significant. However, these instruments are sold in secondary markets, so realized losses occur. It is possible, of course, to have capital gains, but for the past decade long-term interest rates have gone up so much more than down that losses have been far more significant than gains. Even those holders who do not have to sell may be uneasy about unrealized capital losses.

The uptrend of long-term interest rates during the past decade suggests that the greatest source of risk in capital markets is due to inflation—the cause of these mounting interest rates. Although on a different analytical plane than the other sources of capital market risk, this is probably a correct assessment. No other factor approaches inflation in its damage to capital market stability, equity, and efficiency.

Risk in capital markets sometimes arises from the complex nature of the legal and tax rules under which investment business operates. A good example can be drawn from recent investment experience with "flower" bonds: certain long-term, low-coupon bonds of the U.S. Treasury that can be used to pay death duties at par. A rich person, about to die, could save the executors of the estate a great deal of money by buying such bonds at a discount just before death. Such persons often gave their lawyers power of attorney to make such purchases when death approached; hence the slang label "flower" bonds.

These bonds still have the right to pay death duties, but the Tax Reform Act of 1976 made capital gains taxes applicable to the securities held in estates, so this action tended to take away with one hand the benefit that was still given with the other hand. Naturally, the premium price of such flower bonds quickly diminished as the impact of this new tax rule became clear. Holders of such bonds suffered appreciable capital losses (mostly unrealized, of course) merely as the result of a change in law.

TAX FACTORS IN THE CAPITAL MARKETS

As the previous anecdote illustrates, probably no segment of the economy is as sensitive to the impact of income taxes as the capital markets. A large industry has been built up for the creation of tax shields and shelters—or tax havens outside the continental United States. Certain nations, often small and with limited economic resources, deliberately created a legal structure that attracts refugee capital: The Bahamas and the British West Indies are examples.

But at home, tax differences among various investment outlets create special market patterns and certain kinds of yield differences. The largest and most obvious example—the obligations of state and local government entities that are exempt from federal income taxation—will be covered in Chapter 14. Differential rates of capital gains taxation from the taxation of ordinary income affects several types of investment securities, but particularly common stocks (dealt with in Chapters 17 and 18). (Capital gains taxation was increased in 1976 but then reduced somewhat in 1978.) A reduced rate of taxation for dividends received by corporations that are themselves fully taxed leads to a special place for preferred stocks, as will be covered in Chapter 17.

Taxes have differing impacts also because investors are not all equally exposed to taxation. Pension funds themselves are free of tax liability, and they give their beneficiaries considerable deferment of taxation. Savings institutions are subject to special rules of taxation, but they are less heavily taxed than corporations generally. In some cases these special rules become almost unbelievably complex. Life insurance companies are taxed by a very complex set of special rules. The net effect of these rules, however, is to make them less interested in tax-exempt or tax-limited types of investments. What is more, mutual life insurance companies generally have a better tax break than stock life insurance companies.

Tax factors can also have an uneven impact on investment securities owing to interpretations of the tax regulations. Commercial banks, for example, are fully exposed to the corporate income tax. They are allowed, however, to deduct all interest paid as an expense. Individuals or nonfinancial corporations, on the other hand, if they borrow to purchase tax-exempt obligations, cannot deduct the interest paid on such borrowings. Banks don't borrow to buy any specific investment, it is argued. As a result, banks can, as a practical matter, go into the money and capital markets and "buy" money and deduct the interest they pay in computing their income taxes even if they use the funds to purchase tax-exempt obligations.

Even then, there are practical limits to the usefulness of tax exemption. If a bank builds up its tax-exempt portfolio to the point that the interest income from it equals its net income for financial reporting purposes, any further additions to the portfolio would be without tax advantage. In fact, banks like to stop a bit short of this point; they feel it would be bad public relations to pay no federal income taxes. What is more, if a bank suffers financial difficulties and losses so it has no taxable income, its tax-exempt portfolio loses its main purpose and should be sold. But the very times when this happens may be when markets are weak and losses would have to be realized. Banks do not have to expose unrealized losses in their financial reports, but realized losses must be reflected in them.

GROWTH RATES FOR CAPITAL MARKET INSTRUMENTS

During the three postwar decades, the growth rate for GNP in current dollars has been roughly 6 ½ percent. During this same period the volume of capital market instruments has grown faster; rather more than 8 percent per annum. Although we do not have facts to document it, this probably reflects a long-term trend. Primitive economies have very few financial instruments, and even if income is low, the financial magnitudes are even smaller. Growth of economies, however, usually is accompanied by more diversification, and thus finance grows faster than income.

It is hard to think of finance as a growth industry, but there is logic to the view. How much further this faster rate of growth can go is beyond our competence to forecast, but for a little while, at least, it appears to be a safe projection.

Figure 12-3 on page 268 compares growth rates for specific capital market instruments.

PROJECTS AND QUESTIONS

Although capital markets are identified with big cities, financial districts such as Wall Street, and very conservatively dressed participants, capital markets really exist in almost every part of the country. Make a rough estimate of the capital market in the area where you live or with which you are most familiar. As a starting point, capital market instruments in 1975 averaged about $10,000 per capita and were growing at the rate of about 8 percent per annum. (Many areas, of course, are considerably below the national average.) What capital market elements are probably most important in your area? If you want to undertake a really difficult but interesting project, estimate whether the area you are studying is a net *debtor* or net *creditor*. (A retirement community would probably be a net creditor; a farming area a net debtor.)

BIBLIOGRAPHY

Bankers Trust Company: *Credit and Capital Markets 1979.*

Carosso, V. P.: *Investment Banking in America,* Harvard University Press, Cambridge, Mass., 1970.

Davey, P. J.: "A Research Report from the Conference Board's Division of Research," in *Investment Banking Arrangements,* Conference Board, New York, 1976.

Jensen, M. C.: "Capital Markets: Theory and Evidence," *Bell Journal,* Autumn 1972, pp. 357–398.

Silber, W. L., and K. D. Garbade: "Technology, Communication and the Performance of Financial Markets: 1840–1975," *Journal of Finance,* June 1978, pp. 819–832.

chapter 13
The Market for U.S. Government Securities

The market for securities of our federal government developed out of the two circumstances that brought most of the great federal debt into existence. These two prime causes have been war (both hot and cold) and depressions. Management of this federal debt by the Treasury Department has proved to be one of the major problems of public affairs.

The private market mechanism that handles this debt has been shaped by the nature of the debt itself. With a large federal debt, it has been necessary for the Treasury to offer many types of securities and to appeal to several sectors of the capital market. Part of the public debt has been lodged in nonmarketable form, but the section of most interest is the share—a major one—that is in marketable form.

The one overriding characteristic of Treasury securities is that they involve no credit risk; the only risk their holders incur is associated with fluctuations of interest rates. Treasury securities thus appeal to investors interested in liquidity. In meeting this demand, the Treasury has ended up with a debt that is mainly short-term. As a result the private market mechanism is geared mainly to the provision of liquidity. The dealers in Treasury securities and the commercial banks are both suppliers and demanders of liquidity. In other words, the Treasury debt, even the longer-term portions of it, tends to belong as much in the money as in the capital segments of financial markets.

Treasury securities have no credit risk because the federal government has sovereign monetary powers. The federal government never needs to default a debt; it can create whatever money is needed to pay its debts. Treasury securities are valued according to the prevailing yields in the market. The price of these securities fluctuates in a direction opposite to movements in yields and rates.

The discussion in this chapter, and in later chapters that deal with market structure, is organized in a twofold pattern. The first part deals with the nature of demand in the market. Why has the federal government been a borrower? Several related questions also emerge. What sort of timing has characterized this demand; when has the federal government been required to borrow for its basic needs? What kinds of securities has it used to meet its needs? Maturity is usually the leading dimension of securities, and this plays an unusually important role in the federal debt.

The second part deals with the buyers of Treasury securities. What portfolio use do these buyers make of Treasury obligations? What has been the history of their market participation? If the first section could have been labeled "the demand for funds by the federal government," this section could be thought of as "the supply of funds": the investor's side of the market. This section is mostly a detailed examination of the principal investing sectors. A fraction of the Treasury debt is nonmarketable, but this chapter will deal mainly with the marketable debt: the most visible portion in the capital markets.

FEDERAL GOVERNMENT DEMANDS ON THE MARKETS

The federal government operates under a statutory budget that makes no distinction between capital expenditures and current expenditures. The budget document offers the analyst only a few shreds of evidence for the reconstruction of such a distinction. More important for the work here, federal finances are not dominated by the tradition that governs many other areas, that long-term capital expenditures are more justifiably financed by borrowing than by current expenditures.

Capital budgets for the federal government have sometimes been proposed. Since federal finance differs greatly from private and other forms of finance, however, it is not clear that such a distinction has a great deal of merit. One of the principal expenditures of the federal government has been for national defense. During peacetime some of these expenditures are for military installations or ships or other objects that could be thought of as "capital." Yet once hostilities break out, all these objects become expendable. Can one put wars fought and won on a national balance sheet as an asset? An affirmative answer would be cynical and Machiavellian; a negative answer implies that our federal government is bankrupt. Neither answer is really true.

The timing of federal government ventures into money and capital markets is not to be judged by rules that apply elsewhere. The timing that dominates such activity is the balance of the federal budget. Although much economic controversy has raged over the economic principles that should govern the balance of this budget, expediency has largely governed actual events. This is particularly true of war. Economic logic indicates that large national expenditures for war or defense should be paid for with taxes when incurred. This has never proved to be practical; a great lag in raising taxes always occurs during a war. The major share of federal government borrowing is accounted for by war.

When economic conditions turn slack, and labor and other economic resources are not fully employed, many have come to feel that the budget should not be balanced but that a deficit should be encouraged. This principle, however, does not have universal endorsement, though it is certainly true that many professional economists would support it. A downturn in business activity is, in fact, usually accompanied by a drop in federal government tax receipts, which are sensitive to corporate profits, personal income, and related factors. Federal government expenditures, however, tend to be rather fixed or at least to resist cutting, so that a downturn in business activity is automatically accompanied by a tendency toward a budgetary deficit. Thus it is said somewhat cryptically that the federal debt is a legacy of our wars, our national quarrels, and our depressions.

This might be expected to produce balance in the markets. The federal government would tend to be a larger demand factor in the money and capital markets when private economic units tend to reduce their demands. Low demand during war is due to restrictions on private capital expenditures: During depressions it is due to slack demand. To a very great extent this expectation is realized.

The federal debt, however, has become so large that even when it is not growing, the Treasury Department, as fiscal agent of the government, must constantly refund or "roll over" the existing debt. Every capital and money market analyst must be prepared for and understand the role of the Treasury in the markets. It is so large that at times it tends to swamp other financing. Treasury financing sometimes triggers sharp changes in the level of interest rates; inept Treasury financing can be, and unfortunately sometimes has been, the cause of market disturbances.

THE DEBT OF THE FEDERAL GOVERNMENT: HOW BIG?

Since numbers change so rapidly, it is hardly worth reporting a number that will certainly be out-of-date by the time students read these pages. The total debt of the federal government is quite a bit smaller than mortgage debt and is also somewhat smaller than total corporate debt. Federal government debt is between two and three times the size of state and local government debt. The rate of growth of the federal debt is more erratic than either of the two forms of private debt. This erratic rate of growth is due to the sharp shifts in the Treasury budget balance from relatively small to very large deficits. For much of the postwar period, the rate of growth of the federal debt was slower than all other major forms of debt. The recession (depression?) that got under way in 1973 and 1974 led to deficits of enormous size in 1975, which set in motion a rapid rate of growth of federal debt.

The federal debt has a far shorter average maturity than either the mortgage debt, corporate debt, or state and local government debt. As a result the volume of refunding activity is always high even when the total debt is not growing very rapidly. Later we shall note how the Treasury Department has worked to make this constant refunding process as little disruptive to the whole capital market as is possible.

TREASURY CASH BALANCE MANAGEMENT

The Treasury is very much like all other financial managers; it must keep a minimum cash balance. The Treasury makes all its expenditures from its Federal Reserve balance, but keeps only a part of its cash balance in the Federal Reserve banks; the rest is kept in commercial bank tax and loan accounts. The chief problem is the division of this cash balance between commercial banks and the Federal Reserve Treasury account. Some Treasury cash receipts are deposited directly in its Federal Reserve balance. However, to do this exclusively would complicate the reserve management problems of commercial banks since Treasury cash receipts are often both large and irregular in amount. For this reason, a portion of Treasury cash receipts are left on deposit with commercial banks in the tax and loan accounts: the proceeds of some borrowings and certain tax-withholding payments by employers.

Treasury cash balance management has gone through at least three phases. For a long period of time, the Treasury kept only a minimum Federal Reserve balance, and most of the funds were kept in the commercial bank tax and loan accounts. This eased the reserve management process for commercial banks and also the money market management process for the Federal Reserve. But this process had one flaw: It gave the earnings on these idle balances mainly to commercial banks. The second phase in Treasury cash balance management, starting in 1974, was to shift more and more of these funds to the Treasury's Federal Reserve account. Since all Federal Reserve excess earnings are paid back to the Treasury, the Treasury itself then gets the earnings advantages of its idle cash balances. And the amount is not immaterial. Because Treasury receipts both from taxes and borrowings tend to be bunched and not well coordinated with payments, the Treasury cash balance is both large and highly variable.

Although this second phase of Treasury cash balance management had earnings advantages, it also had all the reserve-balance-management difficulties that had been avoided by the earlier practice of keeping most Treasury funds at commercial banks in the tax and loan accounts. Commercial banks had to deal with more erratic deposit balances and therefore reserve requirements; the Federal Reserve, in attempting to smooth out the availability of reserves to commercial banks also had to engage in an increased amount of "defensive" open-market operations. Because the margin for error in these operations is still surprisingly large, even after years of experience, the result of this policy was frequent erratic reserve availability and also erratic movements in short-term interest rates, particularly the Fed funds rate.

The third phase of Treasury cash balance management began a few years later. In 1977 new legislation was passed that authorized the Treasury to collect interest on funds left with commercial banks. As this new latitude is used, the placement of Treasury cash may return to the pattern that prevailed during the first phase; the difference being that a major fraction of the earnings from such funds presumably will revert to the Treasury.

The 1974 change in Treasury cash management policy was based on a study of costs and benefits of the tax and loan accounts. It was found that high interest rates had made the costs to the Treasury implicit in these balances greater than the benefits of services it received. The new policy of the Treasury, expressed in the 1977 legislation, is parallel to the developments mentioned elsewhere in this text: increased emphasis on liability management by commercial banks and more aggressively managed cash balances by corporations. High interest rates have given an incentive to all cash holders for reducing balances relative to payments. In terms of monetary analysis, this means an increased velocity of money. It has been, no doubt, one of the problems in the use of monetary policy as an instrument of economic stabilization.

DEBT MANAGEMENT

Treasury debt management may be broken into two aspects: new cash borrowing and refunding. The first tends to be important when the debt is increasing but slackens when the debt is stabilized (except for short-term or seasonal borrowing). Refunding, however, is a never-ending process. The maturity structure of the federal debt, for reasons discussed below, has tended to be somewhat shorter than that of most other major debtors, so that Treasury obligations come up for refunding more frequently.

Net cash borrowing has a much greater impact on the money and capital markets than refunding: It takes a net amount of money out of the markets. The capital markets can be viewed as the focal point of a process in which the inflow from saving is taken up by borrowers. The flow of saving probably tends to be fairly steady, but borrowers queue up impatiently and irregularly. A borrower as massive as the Treasury Department can almost exhaust the current flow and leave relatively little for private borrowers and others.

This risk is one of the major conundrums of Treasury operations. Once Congress has fixed tax rates and made appropriations for expenditures, the Treasury must honor these mandates. To do so, it must offset the excess of expenditures over receipts with a schedule of demands on the markets. This schedule is never exactly fixed; even though Congress sets the tax and expenditure rules, the amounts of tax collections and the timing (mainly of expenditures) are often in doubt. This is one of the reasons why the Treasury needs to keep a healthy cash balance. The Treasury faces a hard choice; if it groups its expected borrowing operations into a small number of trips to the market, the average size of each one will be so large as to strain and possibly drain the sources of the market. On the other hand, if the Treasury reduces the average size of cash borrowings, then it "disturbs" the market more frequently.

The second element in Treasury financing is the refunding of debt that is already outstanding. Since refunding does not take "new" money from the market, several issues can be bunched into a single operation. This reduces the number of times the Treasury must come to the market. When huge amounts are refunded, however, the market mechanism may be strained.

The Treasury Department has several devices for minimizing the market pressure of refunding. In the first place, the Treasury bill, which is auctioned every week, is largely a refunding operation well known to market participants.

The new bill offerings are often of greater size than the bills maturing on the same day (less often are they less). However, this segment of the market tends to be well informed, and the huge sums involved in the bill market turn over with very little problem.

The Treasury Department has also tried to get a similar cycle going for some of its note issues. At first, this cycle was monthly and was confined mainly to the two-year notes, but recently the Treasury has started quarterly cycles for both the four-year and five-year notes. The new issues may be larger than those maturing in order to raise "new" money, but the process is so well anticipated that it involves no surprises for the market.

This is not to imply that the ownership remains constant. Some investors in both bills and the cycled notes want—and get—cash at the maturity of their obligations. Thus, new investors must be drawn into the refunding process to keep it going.

One of the most important market choices that the Treasury must make both in a cash and in an exchange financing is the maturity of the new security or securities to be offered. The market for longer-term obligations is thinner than that for short-term obligations, so fewer of them can be sold at any one time.

The average maturity of the marketable federal debt is a matter of much economic significance. Short maturity public debt is so very close to money for practical purposes that an excessively large volume of short-term public debt can thwart monetary policy. Conservative economists are inclined to prefer a debt management policy that limits the volume of short-term debt. However, populists who have a strong preference for low interest rates prefer a rather liberal monetary policy and are not as worried if the volume of short-term public debt becomes large. The postwar history of the average maturity of the public debt is instructive in how this matter is both viewed and handled.

The average maturity of the marketable federal debt at the end of World War II was a bit more than nine years. For the next three years it remained at about this level as rather large amounts of short-term marketable debt were refunded into nonmarketable debt. Starting in 1948 and until 1952 the average maturity declined rapidly from about nine years to only about 5 ½ years. Both President Truman and his Secretary of the Treasury John Snyder were populists who wanted low interest rates. They both wanted the Federal Reserve to try to force low rates on the nation's economy with monetary policy. The Federal Reserve refused, and the struggle lasted until 1951, when a settlement of sorts was patched together. Both during the struggle and even after, until the end of his term of office, in 1952, Secretary Snyder refunded all debt on a short-term basis with the Federal Reserve holding the short-term rate down but refusing to hold down long-term rates.

The matter was significant enough that it became an issue in the presidential elections of 1952, and General Eisenhower entered office with a pledge to try to reverse the slide in average maturity. His Secretary of the Treasury Humphrey, a conservative Cleveland industrialist, made valiant efforts to do so but in general was not able to stem the tide. During the eight years of the Eisenhower presidency the average maturity slid further from about 5 ½ to 4 ½ years. John Kennedy does not appear to have had a personal policy position on this matter one way or the other, but his Republican Secretary of the Treasury Douglas Dillon, together with Under Secretary Robert Roosa, did manage to make a reversal that brought the average maturity back up to almost 5 ½ years. The economic circumstances were not materially different from those that had prevailed before, so this success must be credited to technical money market skill. Secretary Dillon came from an investment banking family and Under Secretary Roosa had been an officer of the Federal Reserve Bank of New York and had been manager of the Federal Reserve Open Market Account at one time. The public debt management during that period was certainly imaginative and innovative and the results good. Lyndon Johnson, a Texan and a populist, let the downslide start once more and then, by getting involved in Vietnam, made a continuation of the slide inevitable.

Unfortunately the decline in the average maturity was continued in the administration of Richard Nixon. His first two Secretaries of the Treasury were conservatives but did not seem to be able to stem the tide. It is not clear that the second of them, John Connally, had any great desire to do so; he was a Texan and may have been infused with populist feelings even though he was a conservative otherwise. Nixon's third Secretary of the Treasury, William Simon, however, made a valiant effort that was swamped by the extraordinary large budget deficits (peacetime records) of the late Nixon and Ford administrations. William Simon brought great money market skill to the task and certainly tried, but the circumstances were against him. He left office with an average maturity under three years.

In the effort to slow down, if not halt or reverse, the shortening of the average maturity of the marketable debt, several modest steps were negotiated through Congress by various secretaries of the Treasury. First, in 1967 the allowable maturity of Treasury notes was extended from five to seven years. Considerable use of this new authority has since been made. In 1971 the Treasury sought and got an exemption of $10 billion of bond debt from the 4 ¼ percent ceiling. This authority was also used quickly and almost completely. In 1973 the $10 billion exemption was redefined so as to exclude from it debt held by the Federal Reserve or any other government agency.

In 1975 the Secretary of the Treasury sought and got a further extension of note maturities from seven to ten years and asked that the exemption from the 4¼ percent coupon ceiling be expanded to $27 billion. He also sought an increase in the yield ceiling for savings bonds to 6 percent.

In his statement seeking this liberalization, Secretary of the Treasury Simon advanced an interesting proposition that relates to Chapter 7; he suggested that Treasury debt management should seek to support the upward sweeping yield curve as the most normal and desirable state of the financial markets. Since Secretary Simon had had extensive and very successful experience as an investment banker, this suggests that the market segmentation theory discussed in Chapter 7 is the view of practiced operators in financial markets.

One of the persisting problems of Treasury debt management is the considerable seasonal variation between receipts and expenditures. Deficits are particularly great in the second half of the calendar year. July, August, October, and November are almost always deficit months. (September and December are tax collection months.) Another problem is the lag in tax collections. If times are good and income is increasing, this does not show up in better tax receipts for a period of six months to a year. In spite of long experience and sophisticated techniques, the budget estimators often are wide of the mark in forecasting budget receipts. Even more surprising, expenditures are not always well anticipated. The budget message of the President in January 1972 overestimated budget expenditures for the first six months of 1972 by almost $8 billion. During recent years, the Treasury Department has carried slightly higher cash balances than formerly, apparently because of such uncertainties.

The Treasury Department is hampered in its debt management by some basically senseless legal restrictions. (How ancient the source of these restrictions is demonstrated by the fact that they are mainly contained in a law labeled the "Liberty Loan Act of 1918," which had its origins in World War I.) In the first place, there is a coupon restriction on bonds except for an exemption that was described above. This is a coupon limit of 4¼ percent, which, of course, has long been far lower than prevailing long-term interest rates. Fortunately there is no similar limitation on the coupon rate for notes. There is also a statutory limit on the yield that may be given savings bonds.

Perhaps the silliest of all restrictions is the so-called debt limit. Congress, together with the executive office, creates the tax laws and the expenditure laws that together constitute the budget. The balance of the budget determines the size of the federal government debt. Thus, a statutory debt limit is redundant logically. This fact is well understood by Congress, but the limit is retained and, in general, kept very close to the actual debt for a political rather than an economic reason. By dragging its feet in adjusting the debt limit to the debt effects of a budget that has already been adopted, Congress can force the Secretary of the Treasury to come to it, begging for such an increase in the debt limit. It can inquire into debt management and, if it wishes, force some concessions on not very closely related matters from the administration. Sometimes it has almost become a game of "chicken" in which Congress forced the Secretary of the Treasury to take most unusual steps to avoid a literal breach of law.

INFORMAL UNDERWRITING OF TREASURY OFFERINGS

Treasury offerings are not formally underwritten except for two small issues of long-term bonds that were sold by competitive bidding in 1962 and 1963. Jay Cooke helped finance the Civil War by selling bonds—at a price. Since then the Treasury Department has been its own salesman and market manager. The Federal Reserve has sometimes assisted in Treasury financing by actual market support buying, but this has not been done for almost two decades, with a few minor exceptions.[1] In order to secure informal underwriting of Treasury offerings, pricing must be attractive to the market. When pricing is attractive, most of the underwriting support is given by dealers in government securities. The Federal Reserve Bank of New York has estimated that dealers account for about two-fifths of the marketable securities sold by the Treasury. The auctioning process, which will be described in a few paragraphs, attracts dealer participation because of their greater skill of pricing their bids close to the market. Many times dealers will have disposed of the securities they have bid for successfully even before the securities are delivered, so any profit the dealers will have made (or the occasional losses, too) will have been settled before it was necessary to put the securities in inventory.

Commercial banks were once very important in the underwriting of the sale of all securities that gave tax and loan account credits and for which an extended holding period for the cash payment was expected. As described above, new Treasury cash balance management policies have altered that profit potential so that at present commercial banks (except those with dealer departments) are somewhat less active underwriters. In addition, many commercial banks are more anxious to market their own NCDs than to market Treasury securities to customers with liquid funds to invest.

In 1970 the Treasury Department started experimenting with the sale of Treasury securities by auction rather than by announced and preset terms. Since that time the method of auctioning has been changed and extended so that at present almost all Treasury offerings are sold by auction. Auctions have the following characteristics:

1. Smaller investors are permitted to enter noncompetitive bids, which means that their purchases are priced at the average price or yield set in the bigger and competitive sector of the auction.
2. Since new issues can be paid for with simultaneously maturing issues, this means that the cyclically issued bills and notes held by "smaller" investors can be "rolled over" with a minimum of disturbance in the markets.
3. The competitive portion of the auction can be either in terms of price or yield. If it is a price auction, the Treasury Department presets the coupon rate. If it is a yield auction, no coupon rate is set in advance, but bidders compete in terms of yield. The Treasury then sets the coupon that will bring the issue to as near par as possible.

The market has become very skilled at these auctions: The range of successful bids is usually within five basis points or 1/20th of 1 percent. Since the average yield is usually fairly close to the highest accepted yield, this indicates that the majority of successful bids lies within an even closer range. It is an

---

[1]The Federal Reserve handles the mechanical details of all Treasury financing operations, but this is done as fiscal agent, not as a principal.

expert market with highly skilled specialists, of which the U.S. government security dealers are the leaders.

THE BUYERS OF TREASURY SECURITIES

The federal debt is so massive that it must be lodged in many groups of holders. Since a great part of the debt was originally issued during World War II, the original buyers were induced to buy these securities partly by patriotism. But they were also moved by more practical considerations. During the war private capital expenditures, such as those for nondefense housing and capital equipment, were curbed. Private demands for funds were thus at a low level. Old debts were also being repaid. In many ways federal borrowing supplied survival rations for the financial intermediaries. Many who would have preferred some other investment outlet bought Treasury securities as a matter of necessity and not through patriotism.

The result was a large redistribution of the federal debt during the postwar period. Because original holders were shifting out of such amounts that they felt surplus to their normal needs, the Treasury had to hunt for new buyers. Marketing of the federal debt has been a large and unsolved problem. Not the least of the reasons has been the large increase in interest rates in the postwar period.

The principal utility of Treasury securities for investors is liquidity. Short-term securities are liquid not only because maturity is near at hand but also because the secondary market in these obligations is a large one, with great absorptive capacity. An investor selling no more than $5 million worth of corporate bonds may have a bit of a marketing problem unless he or she is willing to concede an appreciable margin. The amount conceded may not be more than a fair marketing cost, but such costs are often of a magnitude to give investors pause. Investors are notoriously close figurers. For this reason they are impressed with the fact that $100 million of Treasury bills can be sold almost casually without much of a ripple in the market. The spread in bid and asked prices levies only a very small marketing cost.

The market for intermediate-maturity Treasury obligations is large enough to allow for rather sizable shifts at least for expert managers. The great commercial banks operate in this maturity area, and they often engage in rather large switching operations. The range of price movements of intermediate-term securities has proved to be somewhat larger than usually expected, but the size of the market is considerable. In light of this, the market also serves a liquidity purpose for many investors.

Long-term bonds of the Treasury admittedly have a more limited market. The amount that can be sold quickly is often small. Sometimes a skillful dealer will be able to move fairly large amounts without disturbance to the market, but this takes time. Even with this qualification, however, the market for Treasury obligations as a whole is a large one that offers considerable liquidity.

In reviewing the various buyers of Treasury obligations, no notice will be given to the government itself. The Federal Reserve is obviously in the market in a major way, but its motives are those of public policy realization and so cannot be easily considered along with a review of private investors. Its operations were covered in Chapter 11.

Commercial Banks

The commercial banking system in the United States is a rather countercyclical holder of Treasury securities; buying more when loan demand is slack and reducing holdings when loan demand is brisk. At one time, Treasury securities were regarded as liquid or "secondary" reserves by commercial banks. That function has become far less important, as recounted in Chapter 10. The use for Treasury obligations that is of importance to banks is as collateral for public deposits—for federal, state, and local government. When so used, Treasury obligations tend to be a rather frozen asset. With banks getting liquidity more by liability management, this has subtly shifted the function of the Treasury portfolio. Since agency securities serve as collateral, more of them are owned. Collateral use, of course, tends to freeze the holding of a security so used. If holdings are to be frozen, then the average maturity held might as well be longer—at least when the yield curve is favorable for this posture. As a result, average maturity of bank holdings tended to increase while the average maturity of the total Treasury debt was going down.

Foreign Monetary Authorities

Since the dollar has become the most important reserve currency, many foreign monetary authorities hold large dollar funds. Some are deposited in banks in time deposit form, but some are invested directly in our money markets. Maturities are short, but not as short as they used to be. In addition, some private foreign interests hold dollar balances in this form. Our Treasury has also issued nonmarketable bonds directly to some foreign monetary authorities.

During the past two decades, but particularly since 1968 and emphatically so in 1971, the greatest increase in holdings of Treasury securities has been by foreign monetary authorities. As explained in Chapter 19, they are somewhat unwilling holders. The dollars they have acquired originated in their support of the dollar in the foreign exchange markets. This was not altruism. When de facto convertibility of the dollar was terminated in 1968 and our balance of payments deficit continued, there were two choices open to them: to acquire the dollars or let their currency appreciate against the dollar. If their currency had appreciated against the dollar, this would have hurt their trading position vis-à-vis the United States. German and Japanese goods would have cost Americans more. So they took the dollars—reluctantly, grudgingly, but in large amounts. And since they saw little chance of getting rid of the dollars soon, they put them to work—sometimes in the Eurodollar market but often directly in our money markets.

The OPEC Nations

The foreign monetary authorities that have accumulated holdings of Treasury securities came into possession of the dollars to buy them mainly by trying to hold down their exchange rate on the U.S. dollar to a level that they felt was needed by their export industries to be competitive. They thus became investors in our Treasury debt, not because they wished to hold it, but because they had the dollars, could not dispose of them without upsetting their exchange rate policies, and did not wish to make a more risky investment of them.

The dollars in the possession of the OPEC nations, which originated in their oil exports to this country, could not be converted into the native currencies of the OPEC nations; this would have been an exchange market absurdity. The OPEC nations could convert these dollars into other leading currencies and some did. However, the magnitude of the holdings is such that investment in dollar form for a substantial part of these receipts was almost inevitable. Some portions of the funds have been invested in other forms, from real estate to common stocks. However, the big majority of the funds have been invested in government securities because of their liquidity—and possibly because the OPEC nations felt such investment gave them a bit more leverage in political negotiations for other purposes.

Individual Investors

Moderate-income individuals seldom invest in marketable Treasury obligations; the unsophisticated moderate-income buyer can meet his or her needs with nonmarketable savings bonds. Individuals, presumably those with higher incomes, have nevertheless been the beneficial owners of considerable amounts of Treasury securities in recent years.

Presumably most of these individual holdings are for investment purposes. Conservative trust accounts of which individuals are the beneficial owners often include Treasury securities. Some of these holdings have been accounted for by a special tax circumstance. Treasury bonds, selling considerably below par, could be used to pay estate taxes at par if in estate prior to death. A wealthy individual, seeing the possibility of early demise, could give his or her heirs a "tax break" by acquiring a certain number of these "flower" bonds.[2] Speculation is another factor accounting for some individual investment. From time to time individuals have bought Treasury issues (at time of offering) hoping to make a capital gain. A few may have been frozen into such holdings. The most common explanation for holding of Treasury marketable bonds by individuals, however, is simplicity. Many quite wealthy people are without a great deal of financial sophistication. Some remember the past and mistrust the stock market. If they have funds beyond their savings bond limits, they may buy marketable Treasury obligations simply because of the lack of knowledge of alternatives.

State and Local Governments

State and local government accounts are surprisingly large investors in Treasury obligations. The explanation is partly the need for liquidity to bridge

---

[2]For a person on his or her death bed the purchase of these bonds was a prelude to funeral flowers. Since the Tax Reform Act of 1976 these bonds have less tax avoidance value than before.

the gap between borrowing for a capital expenditure and the making of the expenditure. Many state and local governmental units are required to borrow before a capital expenditure project is started, sometimes before the contracts are let.

Another factor enters into the willing acceptance of this rule. Since the interest on state and local government obligations is exempt from federal income taxes, the coupons and yields on these obligations tend to be lower than those prevailing on Treasury obligations, which are subject to income taxation. As a result state and local governments have sometimes been able to make a modest profit on bridging transactions: The interest they earned on short-term liquidity funds was more than they were paying on their indebtedness. Borrowing in advance actually became profitable, and it has never been very costly. Maturities of the Treasury securities they buy and hold are, of course, quite short. Such arbitrage investment is now restricted though not prohibited by federal tax law.

Savings Institutions

The two leading savings institutions—savings and loan associations and mutual savings banks—together hold $10 billion worth of Treasury obligations. The mutual savings banks once held over $10 billion, but their holdings have dwindled to less than $5 billion. This decline, however, has not been as drastic as that of the life insurance companies.

Savings and loan associations are required to keep liquidity reserves. Treasury securities now account for about one-fifth of this liquidity reserve. The Treasury securities bought by savings and loan associations are now limited to intermediate-term obligations.

Nonfinancial Corporations

During World War II a great many nonfinancial corporations were limited in the amount of capital expenditures they could make. As a result they had very large net cash flows from depreciation charges as well as retained earnings. They were encouraged to invest these funds in Treasury securities, and many did so. In addition, the tax liabilities were large because tax payments were somewhat less current than under present law and regulations. It was considered the part of wisdom to fund these tax liabilities, and the Treasury Department encouraged this practice by offering tax-anticipation bills (TABs).

In the postwar period, corporations have gradually drawn down their excess liquidity. At the peak, nonfinancial corporations held more than $25 billion of the Treasury marketable debt—about 15 percent of the amount then outstanding. At present the amount has dwindled. Funding with TABs is still practiced by a few corporations when such bills are available, but the practice is dwindling. As mentioned in Chapters 8 and 9, some corporations supply funds to U.S. government security dealers by means of repurchase agreements that are tailored to their funds availability. Such arrangements are competitive with the tailored maturities of commercial paper directly placed, as mentioned in Chapter 9.

Insurance Companies and Pension Funds

During World War II both insurance companies and pension funds had almost no private outlets for investment of the inflow of new money. Home building was curbed so there was little demand for mortgage credit—and old mortgages were being paid off. Corporations faced curbs on their capital expenditures and so corporate borrowing was low—and such as was outstanding was being retired. As a result these institutional investors were forced into the purchase of large amounts of government securities. At one time U.S. government obligations constituted 45 percent of life insurance company assets. After the war, however, these holdings were reduced and have never since been rebuilt. Neither investor has a need for liquidity.

The only pension funds that have increased their holdings have done so because they are legally bound to do so. Both the Civil Service Retirement Fund and the Social Security Fund invest any funds available in special nonmarketable issues. The growth of both these funds was considerable for a while, but recently this has not been true of the Social Security Fund.

Dealers in Treasury Obligations

On some occasions dealers have been important investors in Treasury obligations; the total has occasionally been as high as $15 billion. Size of holdings, however, does not adequately express the function of dealers. The market for Treasury securities is the largest secondary market for debt securities in the United States (or the world). Turnover of all maturities of Treasury securities is greater than that of comparable maturities of any other securities. This is true even in the money markets. Commercial paper, bankers' acceptances, and NCDs tend to be held by the original purchaser until maturity. There is a secondary market in each of them, but it is small compared with the secondary market in Treasury bills. No other intermediate or long-term securities turn over as much as Treasuries. The reason is the "depth, breadth, and resiliency"[3] given to this market by the dealer function. Dealer portfolios turn over about every two or three days.

AGENCY SECURITIES

The market for securities for a number of agencies created by the federal government is included here for several reasons. One of the most important is that these securities are traded in very much the same channels as direct Treasury obligations. They also appear to be purchased by about the same group of investors. And since most of the agency securities can be used for the same collateral purposes of banks as direct Treasury securities, they can be considered functionally equivalent. And finally, although not guaranteed, they are widely thought to be almost a moral obligation of the federal government. The yield differentials of these securities with respect to direct Treasury

---

[3]This phrase was first used in a study commissioned by the Federal Reserve at the time of the "Accord."

obligations has been so small and so constant that the market, in fact, treats them as very good substitutes.

The largest volume of securities is issued by corporations sponsored but not owned by the federal government. They include (with acronym and date of organization):

Banks for Cooperatives (COOP), 1933
Federal Intermediate Credit Bank system (FICB), 1923
Federal Land Banks (FLB), 1917
Federal Home Loan Banks (FHLB), 1932
Federal Home Loan Mortgage Corporation (FHLMC) 1970
Federal National Mortgage Association (FNMA), 1938, 1954, 1968

The government-sponsored agencies are subject to neither the 4¼ percent interest rate limitation nor to the debt ceiling. They have enjoyed the umbrella of government sponsorship without having to suffer the penalties of governmental limitations. Each of the government-sponsored agencies has a fiscal agent who handles the marketing of its securities. These fiscal agents operate through selling groups of several hundred dealers and banks that receive modest dealer commissions. These fiscal agents keep in touch informally not only with each other but also with the Treasury Department so that, as far as possible, traffic jams in the markets for very similar securities are avoided. All fiscal agents are located in the Wall Street area even though agency headquarters are generally elsewhere.

Recently the first three of the agencies listed above, the agricultural credit agencies, have consolidated their fiscal agency in one person who, as representative of the thirty-seven underlying institutions, is marketing a single instrument to cover the market needs of all those involved.

GOVERNMENT-OWNED AGENCIES AND THE FEDERAL FINANCING BANK

The federal government also owns several agencies or guarantees the securities of agencies that it has created. The Tennessee Valley Authority (TVA), the Export-Import Bank ("Ex-im"), and the Farmers Home Administration (not to be confused with the FHA) formerly financed their needs individually, but in 1973 the Federal Financing Bank was created to handle the financing needs of these agencies together with several small ones (such as Rural Electrification Authority and New Community Development Associations). At first the Federal Financing Bank issued its own obligations and reloaned the money to the agencies. Now, however, the Federal Financing Bank borrows directly from the Treasury at one-eighth percentage point above the Treasury cost of money.

A few housing agencies still market their federal government guaranteed obligations directly: the Government National Mortgage Association (GNMA) and the Federal Home Loan Mortgage Corporation (FHLMC).

AUTOMATION OF THE U.S. TREASURY DEBT INSTRUMENT

The U.S. Treasury debt instrument has become mainly a fully automated book entry. It exists only in a computer memory bank and not on paper. The very large volume of paper work in this active market had led many years ago to centralization of much of the physical aspects of security transfer and hypothecation in one large New York City money market bank. But even that system was not adequate. There was an early pressure for as much automation as possible, one form of which was wire transfer of Treasury obligations between Reserve banks.[4] A second reason was a series of thefts of securities, including some Treasury securities, that took place in and around the Wall Street area. The large losses led the leading company insuring security safety to threaten to cancel all delivery insurance. As a result of these costs and risks, a special drive was put on to automate this market. The system is now fully tested and operational and is available for such banks as elect to open book-entry accounts. These banks can do so not only for their own Treasury securities but also those of customers. This is particularly important for the dealers who have the largest volume of transactions. At the end of 1977 four-fifths of the Treasury marketable debt was in book entry form; this proportion may have grown further since that time. The physical Treasury debt instrument, with its rococo engraving, is already obsolete and may soon disappear.

The significance for the rest of the securities market is great. If the system can work for Treasury debt, why can it not work for all other stocks and bonds? However, anyone who has struggled with repeated uncorrected errors in his or her computer-prepared brokerage account statement must hope that control of the input for the book-entry system can be improved. After all, at some stage a human action must initiate the first entry to the machine. If that entry is wrong, the whole magnificence of computer technology is wasted.

FUTURES MARKET IN U.S. TREASURY SECURITIES

In January, 1976, the Chicago Mercantile Exchange initiated a futures contract in ninety-day Treasury bills. Trading in this contract attracted such a large volume of business that in August, 1977, The Chicago Board of Trade initiated a futures contract in U.S. Treasury bonds with maturities of fifteen years or more. A contract for one-year bills was initiated in the fall of 1978.

The experience with these contracts so far suggests that they will be, like other futures contracts, mainly settled by offset and not by actual delivery of securities, although that possibility remains open to traders. The seller of these securities may elect, as the maturity of a contract approaches, to offer real delivery. After the end of trading in a contract the seller must settle by delivery. The buyer who does not close out his or her position before the end of trading must be prepared to accept delivery and to pay for the securities purchased.

So far the participants in this market have not been very accurately

---

[4]"The Program for the Automation of the Government Securities Market," *Monthly Review*, Federal Reserve Bank of New York, v. 54, no. 7, July 1972, p. 178.

identified. It is rumored that dealers in U.S. government securities have made some hedge use of this market, but most of the users appear to be speculators in the future course of interest rates.

ORGANIZATION OF THE DEALER OR SECONDARY MARKET

The opening chapter of this text referred to the distinction between primary and secondary markets. The sale of Treasury securities to investors by the U.S. Treasury is, of course, a primary market. The secondary market that has been built up by dealers is one of the most precisely described and measured markets in existence. Because the Federal Reserve Bank of New York not only collects rather extensive statistics of the market but has also written several analytical articles about the market (several of which are cited at the end of this chapter), we present below an unusually detailed account of this market.

The dealers, as has already been reported, participate in the primary market and are first buyers of about two-fifths of all new Treasury issues. However, dealers resell almost immediately, which starts the secondary market process. The remainder of this section will deal with how this dealer market is organized and will report some general quantitative measures of it.

The Number of Dealers

At the end of World War II there were about a dozen recognized dealers in Treasury securities. By 1978 this number had grown to about three dozen. Of this number, thirty-five reported statistics of their activity to the Federal Reserve. The Federal Reserve Bank of New York's published analyses of these reports furnishes the basis for all quantitative magnitudes later reported in this section.

Fewer than half a dozen of the dealers are independent firms specializing almost wholly in this market, but this half dozen includes two of the largest firms in the business. A dozen of the dealers are departments of commercial banks. The remainder are affiliates of investment banking firms. Treasury security dealers who are departments of commercial banks or affiliates of investment banking firms are expected to render some special services to the customers of these banks or firms. In all cases, however, they are also expected to be profitable operations in their own right.

Methods of Trading

Although some retail business is done, dealers are primarily wholesalers. The unit of trade has tended to increase over the years; at present the customary unit trade for bills is $5 million, for intermediate-term securities $1 million, and for long-term bonds $1/2 million. However deals are made for both larger and smaller amounts and for odd amounts that are not multiples of the basic units.

All trades are arranged by telephone. The usual organization of a dealer consists of traders who are assigned various maturity categories and salesmen who deal with customers. The traders talk (by telephone) with traders in the same types of securities at other dealers and trade with these other dealers, either directly or by intermediate brokers. About four-ninths of all trades are between dealers; the other five-ninths is with customers. A decade ago direct trading dominated these interdealer transactions, but the use of brokers has grown and now accounts for almost four-fifths of interdealer transactions. (Brokers permit a trader to conceal his or her actions from competitors.) The traders of dealers freely exchange their current bid-and-ask quotations, and the custom is that dealers will generally do business in either direction on these quotations, either with competing dealers or with customers. However, these quotations quickly become stale, and they are always subject to change. A dealer feels no obligation to honor a quotation given several minutes before. However, they will supply a fresh quotation and are presumed ready to do business on the basis of such a fresh quotation. Salesmen supply quotations to regular customers but execute a deal frequently after consultation with the appropriate trader. Any trade for more than the customary unit almost always requires consultation with the trader; any very large transaction may even require consultation with the highest executive officer available in the trading area.

Quotations become stale so quickly that keeping current with the market requires constant communication. Traders spend their lives on the telephone. This continues to be true, but the need for incessant telephoning has been reduced by widespread use of the "billboard" video screen. This service shows bid-and-ask quotations for leading issues of all contributing dealers. These quotations are "subject to change," but a dealer who backs away from the quotations too often would soon lose customers. The subscribers to the billboard service, who include institutional investors both here and abroad as well as dealers who do not contribute quotations, thus do not have to shop around in the market to get the best quote but can make comparison directly from the video screen. Changes in quotations also permit viewers to judge the course of the market.

Brokers, who act between dealers, have also adopted video-screen technology to improve their service. At present three brokers (with a fourth in the developmental stage) offer so-called execution screens. Here both offers to buy and sell are firm, at least for the first few minutes, and the identity of the prospective buyer or seller is not shown. Anyone who wants to "hit" a bid or take an offer calls the broker, and the deal can be made immediately—if it is still available. Two of the brokers operate the screens only in the offices of dealers, but one broker also has a screen in the offices of a few large institutional investors.

Early experience with the new technology suggests that, as would be expected, it has improved the quality of the market. This means, in effect, that the transaction costs for both buyers and sellers have been reduced. (And it also probably means that the profits of dealers have been squeezed a bit.)

Inventories of Dealers

Dealers buy and sell for their own accounts and therefore cannot operate without an inventory. This does not mean that they own every issue listed, and dealers may even have short positions. But a net positive inventory is natural and common. These inventories, depending on market circumstances, vary widely. When dealers are generally bearish about the market, they may become quite small; when bullish quite large. The average is not very meaningful, but it has tended to be about 1 to 2 percent of the marketable Treasury debt. Even modest price changes can produce large profits—or losses. Since inventories are usually anywhere from twenty to fifty times dealer capital, small percentage changes in the value of inventories translate into large gains or losses on equity capital.

Inventories turn over rapidly. Not counting interdealer trades, the daily sales to and purchases from nondealer customers average more than inventories; thus the turnover is more than once daily. Oddly enough, turnover of issues with a maturity of more than one year is greater than of shorter issues. Dealers, fearing losses, keep longer term holdings small and doubtless use the interdealer market to meet the needs of customers they cannot supply from their own inventory. There are, however, some positive factors for holding inventories of longer-term securities. First, there is a greater opportunity for profit in such issues—and risk of greater loss. Second, with an upsweeping yield curve, which has tended to be more common than not, the yield on an inventory of longer-term securities is more likely to equal or exceed the cost of borrowed money; thus giving the dealer a positive "carry." There is a third somewhat tenuous advantage in inventorying longer-term securities: The bid-and-ask spread tends to be wider and—to the extent dealers can keep the spread and don't have to "give it away"—they can make larger dealing profits.

Dealer Financing

Since inventories average from twenty to fifty times dealer capital, this is the same as saying that dealer capital is only 2 to 5 percent of inventories or that from 95 to 98 percent of them have to be "financed" with borrowed funds. Finding low-cost money has become a sophisticated and rather complex part of dealer management. Dealers hunt for short-term funds nationwide and almost ceaselessly. The factor that makes dealer financing such a high-pressure operation is that an increasing proportion of trades are on a "cash" basis (that is, delivery and payment is on same day as trade) and so there is less of the one-day lag that is available to arrange financing in "regular" basis trades. Corporations are dealers' customers in a double sense; they not only buy and sell securities with dealers but may also supply them with financing. In Chapter 9 the repurchase agreement has already been described; it is widely used by dealers in securing funds from corporations and even out-of-town banks. They also borrow on a secured basis from out-of-town banks. As the accounts in Chapters 9 and 11 mentioned, the Federal Reserve sometimes offers funds to dealers via repurchase agreements (and sometimes also absorbs funds from them by reverse RPs). Commercial bank dealers often depend on their own bank for a part of their financing, but they are also expected to secure outside financing. New York City bank financing is viewed as a kind of last resort. During the business day, the dealer representative who is in charge of financing may be searching the nation, but as the day draws to a close, unfilled needs may spill over into New York City money market bank financing, which is likely to be the most expensive form of all.

While dealers focus primarily on financing their own needs, they are such expert locators of available funds that they sometimes are on the other side of the deal and finance corporate customers for short-term needs.

Dealer Profits

Dealers make profits from several parts of their operations, and losses from all of them too. The basic profit is expected to be from the bid-ask spread. The spread quoted in the end-of-day quotations published in the financial press are wider than those that prevail during the trading day and are exposed, for example, on the billboard video screens described earlier. But even these quotes are always "subject" and a dealer may well decide, faced with the potential of an actual trade, to deal inside the quoted spread. This means that, in this highly competitive market, profits from the bid-ask spread can be thin.

When dealers can borrow money for less than the average yield of the inventories they finance, this positive "carry" can be a source of profit. But spreads can turn negative in tight money markets and be a source of loss.

Finally, dealers can also profit from outright deliberate speculation, which differs from unintended gains or losses due to the volatility of the market. The commonest form of speculation is so-called arbitrage. If, according to a dealer's judgment, one issue seems overpriced relative to another issue, the dealer can sell the overpriced issue and buy the underpriced issue; in effect going short on the first and long on the second. The dealer thus hedges against general price swings in the market but is speculating on a relative price movement. If right, the dealer firm can make a tidy profit when it reverses or "closes out" this arbitrage. But this may not happen quickly (or at all), and the dealer can get nervous and close out without a profit, and possibly even a loss. Outright speculation is the most dangerous of all dealer operations and generally authorized only at the highest levels of dealer management. Profits and losses can be large. The risk for dealers is illustrated by a Federal Reserve Bank of New York statistic: In the years 1967 to 1974, dealers *as a group* lost money in three of the eight years and had profits in only five of the eight!

Dealer Operations and the Efficiency of Secondary Markets

Secondary markets perform the economic function of increasing the liquidity of investors. All the scattered evidence available shows that the demanders of funds have a more prolonged need of them than the average willingness of investors to remain committed to any given security. Secondary markets resolve this problem by a constant redistribution of outstanding securities among the investor population.

When secondary markets are slow and require wide spreads between seller and buyer, they are not serving the market well. Wide price spreads are a kind of excess market friction.

The market for Treasury securities, however, is served by perhaps the most efficient of all secondary markets. The action is fast and the spreads are small. Investors are served, the Treasury Department is served, and the public is served. This service includes one added feature not yet mentioned in this section. Security markets tend to be tied together by the fact that investors can shift from market to market. The example of the Treasury security market tends to give goals to other markets. And the shifting of investor funds among markets tends to keep interest rate movements and differentials parallel—and rational.

PROJECTS AND QUESTIONS

1. Each day *The Wall Street Journal* carries a column of price and yield quotations for Treasury bonds and notes. The yields can be used to prepare a yield curve of the type described and illustrated in Chapter 7. Working directions for such a project are as follows:
   a. Use only one yield for each year of maturity. When an issue has both a call date and a final maturity, use the final maturity. The yield selected should be the highest for that year.
   b. Use no issues with a coupon of less than 5 percent.
   c. There probably will be blank dates for your series; the Treasury does not have final maturities in every future year.
   d. Maturities after the year 2000 may be bunched together.
2. Study the yield curve you have drawn. Using the analysis of both Chapters 7 and 13, deduce the type of money and capital market that apparently prevails.
3. Study the yields of the issues with coupons less than 5 percent. You will find them materially out of line with surrounding yields. Can you guess why? (Answer: They have a special privilege in the payment of estate taxes, so they tend to sell on a price-parity basis rather than on a yield-parity basis.)
4. You probably will already have noticed that the yields for nearby maturities often vary more than you might expect. Can you find any possible reasons for this fact? (Answer: Part is market randomness, but a part is the fact that the yield on issues selling at a discount can be taken as capital gains by investors (see Chapter 7).)

BIBLIOGRAPHY

The principal source for all materials on Treasury debt management, the ownership of Treasury securities, and related matters is in the annual reports of the Secretary of the

Treasury. Now that the fiscal year of the United States Government ends on September 30th, this annual report probably can be expected sometime in January of the following year. These reports contain two types of material relevant to this chapter: First, the annual chronology of financing operations together with much interesting market comment appears fairly early in the report; usually within the first fifty pages of the report. Second, in the exhibits there is a section on Treasury debt management that includes statements before Congress of the secretaries and also the relevant statements and speeches before other groups. Since pleas to raise the public debt ceilings are almost annual, the statement of the Secretary of the Treasury before Congress on that subject is often one of the most complete and philosophically revealing documents on the subject of Treasury debt management.

The weekly and/or monthly letters or bulletins of money market banks and of government security dealers review this market from a somewhat different point of view. The weekly letter of A. G. Lanston Corporation is particularly recommended for its authoritative insights into the operation of this market.

There is unfortunately almost no up-to-date academic literature on the subject. What little there is follows.

Banks, L.: "The Market for Agency Securities," *Quarterly Review,* Federal Reserve Bank of New York, Spring 1978, vol. 3, no. 1.
This article contains an excellent historical review of the rapid growth of this market and considerable analytical material on yield differentials and the nature of the secondary market.

Board of Governors of the Federal Reserve System: *Joint Treasury-Federal Reserve Study of the U.S. Government Securities Market,* Government Printing Office, Washington, D.C., 1969, 1970, 1971.

Garbade, K. D.: "Electronic Quotation Systems and the Market for Government Securities," *Quarterly Review,* Federal Reserve Bank of New York, Summer 1978, vol. 3, no. 2.

Jeffers, J. R., and J. Kwon: "A Portfolio for Government Securities," *Journal of Finance,* December 1969, pp. 905–919.

Lindow, W.: *Inside the Money Market,* Random House, New York, 1972.

Lovett, J. E.: "Tax and Loan Accounts and Federal Reserve Open Market Operations," *Quarterly Review,* Federal Reserve Bank of New York, Summer 1978, vol. 3, no. 2.

McCurdy, C. J.: "The Dealer Market for United States Government Securities," *Quarterly Review,* Federal Reserve Bank of New York, Winter 1977–78, vol. 2, no. 4.

Roll, R.: *The Behavior of Interest Rates: Application of the Efficient Market Model to U.S. Treasury Bill Rates,* Basic Books, New York, 1970.

Scott, I. O., Jr.: *The Government Securities Market,* McGraw-Hill, New York, 1965.

Snechack, A. J., Jr., and D. M. Heep: "Auction Profits in the Treasury Bill Market," *Financial Management,* Summer 1975.

Williams, R. and P. W. Bacon: "Interest Rate Futures Trading: New Tool for the Financial Manager," *Financial Management,* Spring 1976.

Yawitz, J. B., G. H. Hempel, and W. J. Marshall: "A Risk-Return Approach to the Selection of Optimal Government Bond Portfolios," *Financial Management,* Autumn 1976.

chapter 14
The Market for State and Local Government Securities

The principal characteristic of this market is that it is of securities with coupon interest income exempt from the income taxes of the federal government. This income may be taxed by states (other than the one in which the securities are issued and sometimes even by or in the issuing state). Capital gains on these securities can be taxed by the federal government. However, the basic exemption of coupon income from taxation sharply sets these securities aside from the securities issued by the federal government itself, those issued by corporations, and mortgages.

These securities are sometimes colloquially called "municipal" bonds; but, in fact, tax-exempt securities are issued by all levels of state and local government as well as by some special authorities created just for this purpose. Since more than 70,000 units of state and local government exist, the multiplicity of this market is evident. Figure 14-1 shows the principal types of issuers in a recent year. This distribution is typical of other recent years.

WHY STATE AND LOCAL GOVERNMENTS BORROW

Capital expenditures account for the largest fraction of state and local government borrowing. Such capital expenditures include the massive expansion of the physical plants for higher education in the first two decades after World War II, the very large expenditures for the building of water systems in the dry western states, the construction of bridges, tunnels, and new municipal facilities in many cities, and almost universally for many years, new elementary and secondary school buildings. These needs have now been largely met and so a different kind of capital expenditure has risen to the top: water and sewer systems for suburbs and sometimes municipally owned light and power systems. Public housing was, at one time, an important source of demand for funds.

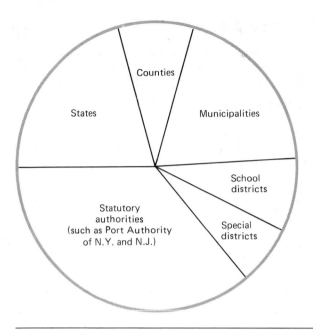

figure 14-1 Political Subdivisions Selling Tax-exempt Bonds, 1976. *(Source: Author's estimates based on Flow-of-Funds data, Board of Governors of the Federal Reserve System, quarterly reports.)*

While capital expenditures still account for the major fraction of state and local government borrowing, that fraction is diminishing. The financial problems of cities and of some other units of local government have led to more borrowing simply to meet deficits in the current account budget. Sometimes this has taken the form of increased dependence on short-term borrowing. Short-term borrowing is usually not as much exposed to public notice as long-term financing since it is usually arranged directly with banks, although tax and bond anticipation notes may be sold by public auction. Figure 14-2 shows the purpose of state and local government borrowing for a recent year.

Our comments should not imply that most state and local government capital expenditures are financed by borrowing. Capital expenditures, such as state road building, made on a regular and scheduled basis are often financed out of current receipts. This is particularly true where special earmarked taxes are used for such expenditures. However, many capital expenditures, even at state levels, are too "lumpy" (large in size relative to the regular stream of expenditures) to be financed out of current receipts. Smaller government bodies, such as school districts, find almost all capital expenditures lumpy and tend to finance them by borrowing.

For many of the postwar years, borrowing accounted for about half the total construction expenditures of state and local government, but this proportion has been increasing as state and local government struggles with increasing problems of local finance. At the same time, tax-exempt borrowing has

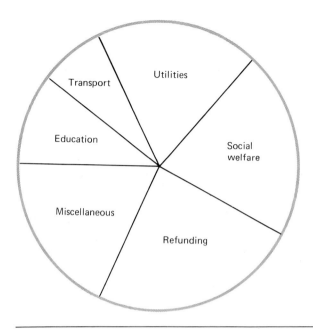

figure 14-2 Purposes for Tax-exempt Financing, 1978. *(Source: Municipal Market Developments, Public Securities Association, New York.)*

sometimes been used for purposes of capital construction that have been greatly changed from the original idea of public capital expenditures. The Port Authority of New York and New Jersey has built and operated the tunnels and bridges in the New York metropolitan area, which is quite different from operating a seaport. The operation of LaGuardia, Kennedy, and Newark airports, however, is reasonably well in keeping with the original idea of the authority. But what about the two World Trade Center towers that now dominate the skyline of lower Manhattan? They were tax-exempt financed, but they compete with the office buildings that had no such exemption for their financing. And how different is this from the industrial bonds used by cities and some states to attract industry with low-cost industrial plants based on tax-exempt financing? This practice has been curbed for larger projects, but the validity of the principle remains open to question.

A similar comparison is not available by levels of government, but it would almost certainly show that the proportion is smaller for states; for local governmental units it would be much larger. The year-to-year correspondence of borrowing and capital expenditures is not exactly constant, however. The explanation seems to be that borrowing almost always precedes construction, often by long periods. State and local government finance officers attempt to borrow when markets appear favorable, so the lead time of borrowing over expenditures varies. Bond anticipation notes can be used by some governmental bodies, but such borrowing is prohibited for others.

The basic demand for borrowing by state and local governments has a strong demographic basis; it is caused by increases in population and by movements of population. These movements may be nationwide, but they can be important even if only for short distances, as movements to the suburbs. In that respect, state and local government needs are very much like the demand for mortgage credit to finance housing purchases. The movement of population from the center of cities out into the suburbs tended to create new governmental service needs: for new roads, new schools, new sewers and other sanitary facilities, and for new fire and police protection facilities. States receiving large population inflows have tended to be heavy borrowers, and those with dwindling populations or little change have made fewer capital expenditures and borrowed less. The general prosperity of the postwar period, however, has led to some upgrading of governmental facilities; even in those areas where population is not increasing, newer school buildings were built and some roads improved.

Since state and local governments are less affected by business conditions than is true of corporations, their capital expenditures do not tend to be related to business cycle movements. On the other hand, as we shall show later, the actual borrowing process has been very much affected by changes in interest rates. In turn, interest rates are, of course, closely related to business conditions.

CREDIT RATINGS AND THEIR CONTROVERSIAL IMPACT

Sophisticated investors generally make their own evaluation of the credit quality of the securities they buy. However, the vast majority of individuals and many smaller institutional investors undoubtedly rely very heavily on agency credit ratings. Two agencies that also rate corporate obligations—Standard and Poor's and Moody's—rate a large fraction of the tax-exempt bonds sold. However, as Figure 14-3 shows, an appreciable margin of issues go unrated.

These credit ratings are controversial in two ways: First, many of the evaluations by the rating agencies are challenged; second, the issues too small to be rated may be discriminated against by the absence of ratings. A small business may be presumed to have a questionable credit rating just because smallness is a problem in a highly competitive business environment. But smallness in a local government unit is not necessarily a sign of poor credit. The sewer bonds of a small sanitary district in a high-income suburb may have very great credit strength.

The story of New York City exemplifies the problem of ratings. As long ago as 1965 both of the major rating agencies lowered the ratings of the bonds of that city from A to Baa. A raging controversy was set off, but the analysts stuck to their guns, pointing out the fiscal practices that jeopardized the ability of New York City to service its debt: the heavy welfare payments, the militant municipal unions and the reduced productivity of city workers, and finally the erosion of the tax base. In 1973 one of the agencies temporarily restored the A rating but then, only two years later in 1975, the fiscal problems of the city came to widespread national attention. Default was averted only by many improvised measures.

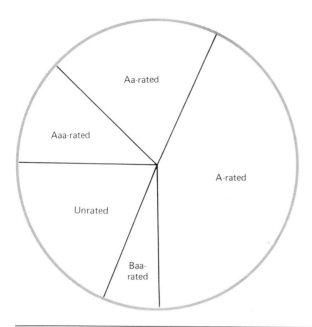

Aa-rated

Aaa-rated

A-rated

Unrated

Baa-
rated

figure 14-3 Quality-of-Credit Ratings of Tax-exempt Bonds Sold, 1978. *(Source: Municipal Market Developments, Public Securities Association, New York.)*

Although public attention was focused mainly on New York City, similar problems were present in a large number of cities and even in some smaller communities. Not widely noticed is the fact that state and local government had come to have payrolls more than twice those of the federal government (even when defense is included); and that it directly spends more than twice the money spent by the federal government. The large and recently growing items in the federal budget were transfer payments—and one of the leading transfer payments was various forms of income transfer to various levels of state and local government. The plea of New York City and other cities for federal aid is reflective of the situation at present.

These factors have pushed state and local government finances to a point at which a larger share of capital expenditures requires borrowing. When interest rates were somewhat lower, the burden of this debt was not as great. But as we shall outline in the closing section of this chapter, such rates have increased considerably. Tax exemption no longer guarantees low borrowing costs. And thus the budget burden continues to increase. The effect of this is to aggravate the problem of credit ratings. As debt and debt costs mount, any credit analyst, whether public or private, would have to conclude that the quality of the debt was no longer as good as it had been.

Nevertheless, it would be a mistake to belittle state and local government credit. As Figure 14-3 shows, more than three-quarters of the rated debt has an A rating or higher and almost two-fifths of the total is in the two top ratings.

State and local government credit has suffered still one more setback. In 1978 the voters of California adopted a constitutional amendment that is best known by its popular label "Proposition 13." This amendment limited the taxing power of both state and local government units. This "tax revolt" led to similar movements in other states. Just how this will influence the quality of state and local government credit is not yet clear. If the rate at which state and local government obligations are issued is decreased, the credit quality can be maintained. But if no such decrease takes place, a more limited taxing authority certainly will reduce credit quality.

The financial problems of state and local government have, quite naturally, tended to widen the yield spread between rating groups and also to raise the general level of yields. At least two private insurers thought this increase excessive and took action to profit thereby. One of the insurers was a consortium of four insurance companies, the other a single insurance company located in the Midwest. Both companies now offer to "insure" the payment of principal and interest of new state and local government issues. Such insured issues are automatically rated AA by the rating agencies and sell at correspondingly lower yields. The cost of insurance is estimated to be about one-third to two-fifths of the interest savings. One of the insurers will even insure the portfolios of private investors of already outstanding state and local government obligations.

INVESTORS IN TAX-EXEMPT SECURITIES

The generally strong credit of tax-exempt securities makes them a preferred outlet for conservative investors who face high marginal tax rates and who nevertheless want current income rather than capital gains. Tax-exempt securities also have an advantage over other kinds of tax shelters since the investor is almost certainly assured of this shelter over the full life of any security he or she purchases. This is not true of such tax shelters as investments induced by oil-depletion allowances or cash-flow real estate investments where a change of legislation could strip the shelter from those now holding it. Most of the proposals for tax reform of these latter areas have, in fact, been along these lines. This has not been true of tax exemption on state and local government securities. The only serious legislative effort within the past generation (since 1940) of any significance with respect to these securities came in 1969. This effort was only to give an interest differential subsidy to those state and local government issuers who would voluntarily forego the privilege of tax exemption on the new securities they issued. This would have left the outstanding issues untouched. (It probably would have also given them a premium or scarcity value and upped their price.) Thus it can be said that the state and local government bond tax shelter has superior durability.

Tax exemption has a long legal and constitutional history. In Civil War times, such interest income was taxed, but in the later part of the nineteenth century taxation of any income by the federal government was declared unconstitutional. The Sixteenth (income tax) Amendment permitted the federal government to tax income "from whatever source derived." Since there was some feeling that this exposed interest income from state obligations to federal taxation, Congress passed a law exempting such income from federal taxation, a law that has remained untouched since that time. With this statute on the books, the constitutional issue has never been tested. Opinions on this point differ and the differences generate much heat. The issue, however, is not important to the capital market analyst. Except for the relatively mild proposal described above, no serious legislative challenge has been made in the past generation. The political balance of power is such that Congress would almost certainly not repeal the existing statutory exemption (though many economists, including the authors, feel it to be inequitable). For practical purposes, the present situation can be taken as a firm basis for examination of the effects of tax exemption on the investment process.

Where tax exemption exists, it is used mainly by investors exposed to income taxation. The more they are exposed, the more likely they are to invest in tax-exempt securities. A large portion of institutional investors are tax-exempt per se: pension funds and nonprofit institutions such as university endowment funds and charitable foundations. Some intermediary institutions are technically subject to federal income taxation, but the exemption rules have been liberal until recently; the mutual savings banks and the savings and loan associations are examples of such cases. Some institutional investors, though generally taxed, are taxed at lower effective rates than apply to the unsheltered investors: life insurance companies are the principal example.

The "unsheltered" or fully exposed investors having a large stake in tax exemption of interest income are principally commercial banks, nonfinancial corporations, high-income individuals (or the trustees who manage their investment affairs), and casualty insurance companies. As might be expected, this group constitutes a somewhat narrow market. All the buyers of tax-exempt securities are important investors in other markets; they, in fact, view these other markets as more basic to their investment needs than tax exemption. This leads to an unusually complex set of crosscurrents between the tax-exempt market and other segments of the capital markets. One result of these complexities is that tax-exempt yields, while lower than other interest rates (as would be expected), are also quite variable. Market understanding of these variations requires some detailed attention to the behavior of these exposed investors.

Commercial banks are basically lenders to business and to other customers. They invest in Treasury obligations for reasons of collateral coverage and liquidity. However, the interest income from both sources is exposed to federal income taxation. Tax exemption has a powerful appeal to them. In addition, as we shall develop more fully later, some bigger commercial banks also act as underwriters and dealers in these obligations. As a result of these factors, commercial banks are large but erratic investors in tax-exempt securities. If loan demand is high, they buy very few and may even be net sellers of them. When loan demand is low they become large investors.

This erratic participation in the tax-exempt market is dramatically illustrated in Figure 14-4. In the year 1969, when money markets were relatively tight,

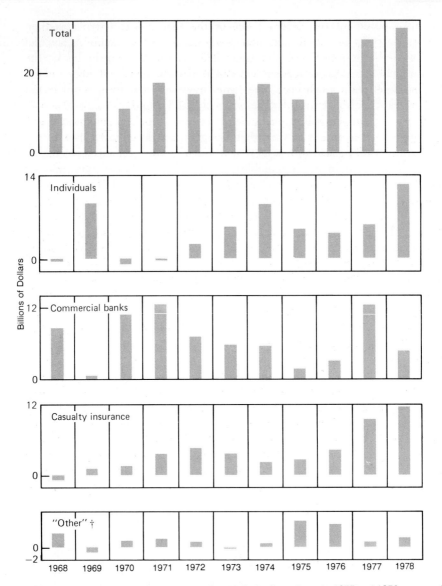

*This figure differs from figures 14-1 through 14-3 since sales and maturities are deducted from the purchases shown in the earlier figures.

†Large "other" purchases in 1975 and 1976 were made primarily by state and local retirement funds coming to the assistance of cities hard pressed to finance themselves. (New York and Cleveland are examples.) 1975 and 1976 were unusually large since S & L agencies bought their own securities those years.

figure 14-4 Net Purchases of Tax-exempt Obligations, 1968-1978.* *(Source: Municipal Bond Statistics Compiled by the Securities Industry Association.)*

commercial banks almost dropped out of the market. The withdrawal of commercial banks led state and local government issuers to delay market offerings so that the total was lower in 1969 than it would have been had commercial banks not been caught in a credit squeeze.

Commercial bank acquisitions were again relatively low in 1975, but this time the explanation was not tight money but a combination of new factors. The leading one was the highly publicized financial problems of New York City. There was a widespread fear that the already large bank holdings of state and local government obligations might be a harbinger of later credit problems. On the other hand, banks came under criticism when they did not support local government, as in this case. In that year, banks were very selective with respect to the quality of state and local government obligations acquired. The other factor was—and probably will be for some time—due to the very nature of tax exemption. An increasing number of banks have such large portfolios of tax-exempt obligations (and other tax-shielding investments) that they have relatively little taxable income. While the marginal tax rate for commercial banks remains 46 percent, the *average* taxes paid on income reported for financial reporting purposes is frequently nearer 10 percent. Many banks are reluctant, for public relation reasons, to pay no federal income taxes and thus hesitate to increase tax-exempt portfolios further. How important this will be in the future is not fully clear but worthy of continued observation.

High-income individuals have even more compelling tax reasons for investment interest in these securities. Individuals who are subject to marginal rates of income taxation above 50 percent, or even less, find that fixed income from taxable obligations has little appeal. High-income individuals concentrate their attention on corporate equities. With capital gains taxed at lower rates, this investment outlet has much appeal. However, the attractiveness of the stock market is notoriously variable. Higher-income individuals thus appear to move back and forth from equities to tax-exempt securities, depending on changes in this attractiveness. The market for tax-exempt securities is thus considerably influenced by stock market developments; more so than any other fixed-income security market. Changes in the degree of individual participation in the tax-exempt market are shown in Figure 14-4.

If it were not for inflation, even very moderate-income individuals could benefit from tax-exempt investment. Indeed, the investment bankers marketing these securities have sought to expand this market. Mutual funds of tax-exempt securities have been formed and sold. Some investment bankers now advertise in a way that is aimed at middle-income investors. Individuals continue to be the second-largest holders of tax-exempt obligations, as shown in Figure 14-5.

The mutual funds referred to above are of two types. The first type, a unit trust, is based on a practice that went back to the 1920s when similar funds were briefly popular. A unit trust is one that is put together, then sold, and is operated as a custodial trust. No changes are made in the composition of the trust; it is "fixed" and therefore without management. Aside from this lack of flexibility these trusts also suffer from impaired marketability. However, the

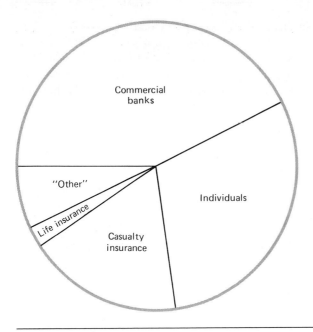

Commercial
banks

"Other"

Life insurance

Individuals

Casualty
insurance

figure 14-5 Holdings of Tax-exempt Bonds by Investor Groups, End of 1977. *(Source: Flow-of-Funds: Outstandings, Release Z-1, August 1978.)*

custodial fees are small and fixed and the investor knows when he or she buys such a trust exactly what return to expect (if there are no defaults). The Tax Reform Act of 1976 allowed the formation of managed open-end trusts. The trusts may or may not have an "entrance" or purchase fee, but all of them allow investors to liquidate at any time at net asset value. And since they are managed, there is a management fee. The realized rate of return is not known precisely in advance, but an investor knows the going rate of return on entering such a fund. So far, portfolio policies of these funds have been stable enough that the main factor changing returns is the change in net asset value—which changes the rate of return for new investors. Rate of return on a cost basis is, however, reasonably stable and predictable.

Casualty insurance companies participate in this market because of a rather special set of circumstances. These companies write a form of insurance that is less subject to precise actuarial expectation than life insurance; a hurricane, for example, can give them a nasty bunching of losses. Thus, they need far more liquidity than life insurance companies. Casualty insurance net income is also variable; these companies have little taxable income in years of unusually heavy casualty losses and a great deal of income in other years. They are also more exposed to federal income taxation than life insurance companies. For these reasons individual companies are important investors in tax-exempt securities—but also erratic investors.

Figure 14-4 showed that in the aggregate, these companies are less variable than the other investors in this market. Individual casualty insurance company experience, however, often differs from industry experience. One company may have little use for tax exemption in a year and so be selling off its portfolio of tax exempts when other companies are buying heavily—also for tax reasons. Thus the aggregate figures often conceal a lot of churning about among individual companies.

THE MARKETING PROCESS

The marketing of state and local government obligations is a good example of the way in which competition encourages efficiency in our private economic system. Bidding for these securities is usually competitive, and the process is fully exposed to public surveillance. As a result, the investment banking community has developed economizing practices that result in low-cost borrowing to state and local government bodies, even rather small ones. This result occurs even though the investment bankers face a rather volatile market. A further obstacle overcome is the fact that the number of borrowers is large and diverse and the obligations are usually serial bonds.

Competitive bidding is required as a safeguard against connivance. Fraud and graft, which have not been unknown in governmental management and financing, offer an opportunity for skullduggery if not fully exposed to public view. Most states govern the borrowing of lower levels of government by statute, and most of these statutes require public competitive bidding. State governments generally follow the same practice.

The mechanics of competitive bidding require advance notice of the intention to sell bonds and the terms attaching to these bonds. An "invitation to bid" is the signal for the formation of buying groups or syndicates among investment bankers. Large issues usually require the formation of large groups; small issues, much smaller groups. Very small issues are occasionally bought by a single buyer. Syndicate structures tend to be fairly continuous. Leading commercial banks and investment bankers assume the responsibility for the formation of the groups and their management. In this process, traditional relationships and leadership patterns develop. A large bank may traditionally lead or manage the group formed to bid on the bonds in the city in which it is located. The managing head or heads of a syndicate invite other firms and banks that were members of similar earlier groups to participate in bidding for the new bonds, and the sale of the bonds if the bidding is successful. Managers of one syndicate may turn up as nonmanaging participants in other groups, but very likely with some of the same partners in the group they managed. Traditional relationships tend to be maintained for long periods of time and reciprocity is expected. While invitations to participate are reciprocal, one of the best ways for a firm to attract invitations is to have a good record as an aggressive selling house. "Free riders" (weak sellers) get fewer repeat invitations.

New groups are seldom exactly the same as old ones. Smaller members may drop out of a group if they do not agree with the bidding proposals; they may not be asked a second time if their selling performance is poor. What is more, the relative importance of investment banking houses changes more rapidly than expected. A house that has enjoyed many years of leadership may dwindle in importance if it loses dynamic leadership; a single man has often made a great deal of difference to a firm.

A few investment banking firms specialize in state and local government obligations, but most state and local government security marketing is done by departments of firms that engage in somewhat broader financial activities. The presence of commercial banks in this underwriting process also differentiates this market from the one for corporate bonds; banking relationships tend to be long-standing and enduring, and groups formed for underwriting ventures may parallel other long-term relationships.

The widespread use of serial obligations in state and local government finance is the result of adverse experience with term bonds. In earlier days state and local governments often used term bonds in financing. Following corporate practice, they also purported to establish sinking funds for the retirement of such debt. Such sinking funds, however, were too often subject to fraud. In addition, some governments failed to meet sinking fund payments. Serial bonds were found to be a far better assurance of debt retirement; they require no sinking funds that can be plundered by sticky-fingered public servants.

The serial bond, however, imposes a somewhat more complex task on the selling groups. Commercial banks and nonfinancial corporations tend to be buyers of the short maturities. Intermediate maturities are bought by casualty insurance companies and trustees. Individuals and mutual life insurance companies tend to buy the longest bonds. These generalizations, however, have many exceptions. Since the principal buyers are all somewhat volatile in their attraction to this market, the underwriters of state and local government financing attempt to adjust the yields on the various maturities to expected market preferences as far as the underwriters can foresee these preferences. However, with all the skill and foresight applied to this market, the selling of serial obligations involves more complexities than are encountered in the corporate bond market, which is (except for rail equipment obligations) almost wholly on a "term" or one-maturity basis.

The selling process in this market is not as rapid as that in the corporate bond market. A popular state and local government issue may be sold out in one day (fifteen minutes would be a comparable record for the sale of a desirable corporate issue), but more often than not a state and local government issue of any size will require several days or even weeks for its marketing. As a result, dealers and underwriters tend to carry larger inventories of new but unsold issues. Much of this inventory is advertised in a special marketing vehicle: the *Blue List*. This daily publication lists issues alphabetically, first by state and then by city or issuing authority. The total of issues advertised in the *Blue List* is often cited as a kind of inventory figure in this market. It is generally believed, however, that dealers do not regularly advertise all the issues they own, so that this figure understates market inventories by varying amounts.

Normally dealers may prefer to show almost everything they have for sale; the *Blue List* is widely used by investors as a source of information as to where particular issues may be located. But dealers may decide to conceal some holdings for strategic reasons. They may be able to bargain better on inquiries if they show only half their holding of a given issue.

Although no systematically collected facts prove it, this market is almost certainly of smaller unit size than that of other segments of the capital market; it is more parallel to the mortgage market in this respect. Five-bond transactions are common and the odd-lot designation is applied only below this level. Big transactions take place, but many small ones are the heart of the market. With smaller unit size, it is almost inevitable that the sale of a given dollar volume of bonds requires more time.

Until very recently the predominant way in which interest cost was figured in awarding competitive bids was to sum the dollar amount of coupon interest and divide it by the amount of money received multiplied by the average number of years outstanding. This system, of course, does not satisfy the rules of annuity arithmetic in that it does not recognize *when* interest is paid. This was called the "net interest cost" or NIC method. This system led to very odd and bizarre coupon structures and, more importantly, to inefficient bid awards that were costly to borrowing units of state and local government. A system for computation of interest cost according to the rules of annuity arithmetic has been devised and is becoming used increasingly. This "true interest cost" or TIC method has been reduced to an algorithm easily performed by computer, which simplifies the job of bid awarding. Even when TIC rules are not used, methods of circumscribing NIC bids are available to avoid the old inefficient bids and coupons.[1]

The efficiency mentioned in the opening paragraph of this section is all the more remarkable in the light of the facts subsequently surveyed. The market is one of many issuers, many issues, and some degree of technical complexity. Withal, the margins taken in the underwriting process are remarkably small. These margins vary, but a high-quality borrower frequently markets its obligations with a cost of less than 1 percent of the capital sum involved. What is even more amazing is that this modest margin is often accorded quite small borrowers *if they are of very high credit standing*. Many bond issues of under $1 million have been sold for less than 1 percent of their par value. Low-quality issues and very small ones (under a quarter of a million) encounter costs materially higher, of course.

Some idea of the complexity of the market can be gained from the fact that in recent years the number of new issues annually has generally exceeded 5000 and has sometimes hit 6000. This means an *average* of twenty to thirty new issues every business day—and, of course, some days run well above the

---

[1]This anomaly was first reported in Appendix B of *Postwar Market for State and Local Government Securities* by Roland I. Robinson (1960). The work of George G. Kaufman and his Center for Capital Market Research at the University of Oregon (1977) is largely responsible for the algorithm and the promotion of the changeover. See Bibliography for more detail.

average. The average size of an issue is only a bit in excess of $5 million, and thus many of the issues are more local than national in their appeal. Because a large majority of state and local government issues are also income-tax-exempt for the income tax of the state in which issued, the market limitation of modest sized issues to the state of issue is understandable. With so many issues, the underwriters who bid on and distribute these issues have a large amount of paper work. In 1976 eight firms were managers or co-managers of over 200 issues—or an issue every business day. Because banks are such important customers for tax-exempt obligations, banks with large correspondent networks tend to be active underwriters. With revenue issues, the investment bankers who dominate the underwriting field tend to be those with good retail distribution—which means a large and active sales force. Trust departments of banks are important customers for personal trusts of well-to-do customers. By convention, a bank does not sell to its own trust department, but other banks and investment bankers compete hotly for this business—and reciprocity is generally expected.

REVENUE BOND MARKETING

The majority (but a dwindling majority) of state and local government obligations are "full faith and credit," or general credit obligations of the issuing bodies. The taxing power of their issuers protects these obligations. Some governmental authorities, however, have no taxing authority and can support their obligations only out of specific kinds of revenues. For example, sewer bonds are often of this nature; they are serviced and repaid from service charges or specified assessments on users in the areas in which they are installed. In addition, governmental authorities have sometimes been created to construct special facilities such as bridges, tunnels, or airports and have been given borrowing power to finance such construction. Payment of their obligations, however, is based only on the revenues that they can earn. The credit and value of these bonds depends on the ability of the projects they finance to earn revenues. The record is not without some failures.

The bonds issued by such authorities are "revenue" bonds; that is, they depend on the revenue they can raise, and the issuers have no power to tax. In the credit analysis of such bonds, the general wealth of the area, tax rates, the assessed value of property, and similar matters have no relevance; the one relevant factor is the ability of the authority to raise revenues from the users of the facility it provides. In the case of many sewer systems, this assurance is pretty high; unless an area is abandoned, sewers are likely to be used and paid for. However, the demand for the services of some revenue projects is elastic, even if they are a monopoly supplier of their service as in the case of a bridge. The amount of revenue is not under the exact control of the managing authority. Raising charges can discourage use, as some toll road operators have found. The price elasticity of demand may be relatively elastic; that is, raising prices can actually reduce total revenues. Of course, the elasticity is more often relatively inelastic.

With a few trivial exceptions, commercial banks are prohibited from the underwriting and marketing of new revenue bond issues. The prohibition was rather accidental. In 1933 when commercial banks were prohibited from engaging in investment banking, they were allowed an exception: they could underwrite and deal in the "full faith and credit" obligations of state and local government. At that time "full faith and credit" obligations accounted for almost all state and local government debt and revenue obligations were infrequent. The great expansion of revenue financing came after World War II and has continued right up to the present time. Commercial banks are now engaged in an active campaign to be allowed to enter this field; investment bankers are just as active in opposition to this change. At this writing the matter is before Congress. The outcome is very much in doubt, but the commercial banks probably have the odds in their favor.

Other differences in the marketing system may be found. Financial advice is more important in the initial arrangement of revenue projects. Some special agencies for handling this part of the problem have developed: Engineers and other experts are frequently consulted in planning these projects. Furthermore, the investment banking connection is more often arranged by negotiation and not quite as universally by competitive bidding; the need for an advisory relationship may account in part for this difference.

Since revenue bonds involve some credit risk, particularly when issued to finance new and untried projects, a different group of investors must be found for these obligations. In general, these issues are sold to high-income business or professional individuals who can both afford to take the risk and can use the tax shield. After a project has been tested or a series of projects carried forward successfully, then the yields can go down and original investors can also reap capital gains. An interesting example is the Port of New York Authority. It started with dock facilities but expanded into bridges, tunnels, and airports, and finally into the World Trade Center. In time it came to have a very high standing in the investment community, and its obligations became "high grade." However, the problems both of New York City and then of some of its more recent investments caused these obligations to lose a part of this gain.

Revenue obligations, in spite of their credit risk, have gained secondary markets that are, in general, larger and more active than those for general obligation bonds of the same credit standing.

POLLUTION CONTROL REVENUE BONDS

In an effort to respond to the environmental hazards of industrial pollution, the Congress authorized the use of tax-exempt revenue bonds for the financing of capital expenditures, the prime purpose of which is to reduce industrial pollution. In the first instance a private industrial corporation, faced with the need to make such expenditures, plans such a project. If the project is given approval by the federal environmental authorities, the bonds then qualify for tax exemption and are marketed as such. Most of these bonds have been sold on a negotiated basis rather than by competitive bidding. The credit basis of these bonds is the sale of the project to the sponsoring company by the local governmental unit, usually the county, in which the "project" is located. This local governmental unit is the nominal owner of the project in the first instance. Since the payments by the sponsoring company to the county or other local governmental body involved are tax deductible, this form of financing turns out to be a relatively expensive form of subsidy. For this and other reasons, the Securities Industry Association (the trade association of investment bankers) opposed the use of pollution control revenue bonds.

PUBLIC AUTHORITY HOUSING OBLIGATIONS

One other sector of the market has quite special characteristics: the market for obligations of the public housing authorities. The deficits of such authorities are guaranteed by the Department of Housing and Urban Development (HUD) under certain circumstances, and through it by the federal government. These local public housing authorities, however, are considered state and local governmental instrumentalities for purposes of taxation. As a result, their obligations combine the tax exemption of state and local governmental obligations with the credit standing of a federal governmental agency. Since a fairly large volume of these obligations has been issued in the postwar years, a fairly distinctive market in these obligations exists.

Public housing notes are both short-term and as near liquid obligations as can be found in this market. The use of these notes has represented a most interesting strategic device of the public housing authorities. When interest rates are considered high and likely to fall, they may finance on a short-term basis and then fund these short-term obligations later when the market is expected to be more receptive to tax-exempt offerings. Thus, this is one of the few tax-exempt market areas in which long-term financing is not always in advance of construction expenditures.

As irrational as it may seem, local housing authorities' bonds do not always sell on as good a basis as other Aaa state and local government obligations. This can only be explained by the large volume of local housing authorities' offerings in this postwar market. Some investors like to have a variety of good "names" in their portfolios. Aaa obligations of cities that rarely issue securities have several times sold on a better basis than local housing authorities' bonds of the same city.

SECONDARY MARKETS FOR TAX-EXEMPT SECURITIES

The secondary market for tax-exempt obligations is moderately active, particularly in periods of credit stress. Its size relationship to the secondary market for corporate bonds is not clear, but a rough guess is that the two are about equal. It is, of course, far smaller than that for securities of the federal government. The reason for the relative viability of this secondary market is that few of the principal investors tend to be "hold-until-maturity" investors. The life expectancy of individuals buying tax-exempt securities is often less than the maturity of the securities. This point is particularly relevant when one recollects that tax-exempt securities appear to be concentrated in the portfolios of fairly old and high-income investors: those beyond the age of aggressive investment. Commercial banks, as already noted, are sometimes sellers as well as buyers.

The "credit crunch" of 1966 had the unintended result of broadening temporarily the secondary market in tax-exempt securities. Many banks, under the pressure of credit demands made on them by corporate customers, sold off rather large parts of their tax-exempt portfolios to get liquidity. The tax laws allowed these losses to be charged against current income. The yields in secondary markets were so high that new investors were attracted.

Margins in the secondary market are wide at best. No public data exist, with one small exception. This study suggested that the bid-and-ask margin was about 2 ½ percent, which is almost double the selling margin on new issues.[2] Trade association standards suggest a maximum margin of 5 percent.

On the buying side, small investors often can find exactly the bonds they wish in the secondary market without waiting for a new issue that is to their taste. The secondary market is conducted by dealers most of whom are also underwriters, but some pure brokers also operate in this field.

The secondary market is one of negotiation (as is true of almost all secondary markets), but the relationship of new-issue prices to secondary market prices is probably more favorable than is true with corporate bonds and U.S. government obligations. Although the brokers are primarily secondary market institutions, they are sometimes used to sell new issues; in one famous case a small house bought a very large issue and used brokers successfully to market the issue. This was an impressive demonstration of the flexibility of financial institutions in responding to new conditions in the market.

The secondary market tends to dwindle in activity when the new issue market is active and to increase in activity when new issues are in smaller volume. This is clearly true over longer periods of time; whether or not it is true for short periods of time is not as clear.

RATES AND YIELDS

Because of tax exemption, the yields on state and local government obligations are below those of comparable maturity and risk in all other sectors of the capital markets. In addition, a number of special points appear to have at least transitory significance.

1. This differential varies a great deal. When state and local government offerings are heavy, it is likely to narrow, so that most of the advantage of tax exemption is passed on to investors and much less is retained by borrowing state and local governments. At other times, when demand for state and local government obligations is high, most of the advantage can

---

[2]*Business Review*, Federal Reserve Bank of Philadelphia, June 1968, p. 9.

be retained by state and local governments, and investors get only a modest remainder.

2. The differential between lower grade (Baa) state and local government obligations and those of the highest grade is often more than the differential between comparable grades of corporate obligations. Why? So far only conjectural explanations have been advanced.

3. Prices and yields in the tax-exempt market are subject to greater short-term fluctuations than almost any other long-term interest rate series. One hypothesis has been advanced that this market is subject to a short inventory cycle very much like the one that prevails in some merchandising fields. It is true that large holdings by underwriters have a temporarily depressing effect on this market and that a shortage of prospective offerings has a strongly bullish effect.

4. The term structure of interest rates in this market is almost always an ascending one, even when the yield curve for U.S. government obligations has become flat or humpbacked. The sole exception appears to be the last five months of 1966, when the tax-exempt yield curve was flat. The tight money of 1969 and early 1970 did not produce a return to a flat yield curve in spite of market pressure. No descending yield curve has appeared since modern yield records have been maintained.

5. The yields on bonds of untested revenue projects are often fairly high. After a project has demonstrated capacity to cover its debt service adequately, then yields tend to fall toward, but never quite fully to, those of general obligations. This results in the capital gains possibilities anticipated by some speculative buyers of new revenue bonds in this market.

PROJECTS AND QUESTIONS

1. Go to the local city (or county) treasurer and ask:
   a. for a schedule of bonded and short-term indebtedness;
   b. the interest cost for recent borrowings;
   c. if bonds of the city (or county) are rated, and, if so, what their ratings by Moody's and/or Standard and Poor's are.

   The treasurer may talk your ear off or throw you out of the office; either way you will learn quite a bit about local finance. Before you are thrown out, try to find out which functions account for most of the borrowing: education, water and sewer districts, public utility districts, etc.

2. Go to a local bank and seek out an officer in the investment department and ask:
   a. the bank's holdings of tax-exempt obligations;

b. what proportion are obligations of local or nearby public bodies;

c. what rating or quality standards they apply in the supervision of their portfolio;

d. what maturity policy they have with respect to their portfolio.

The bank officer probably will not throw you out but may be cautious. He or she might, also, offer you a job.

BIBLIOGRAPHY

Aronsen, J. R., and E. Schwartz: *Management Policies in Local Government Finance,* ICMA, Washington, D.C., 1975.

The Daily Bond Buyer, One Street Plaza, New York, New York 10004. And by the same publisher at the same address: *The Money Manager* (formerly *Weekly Bond Buyer*).

Fundamentals of Municipal Bonds, 1972, Securities Industry Association, 20 Broad Street, New York, New York 10005. Also *Municipal Market Developments,* Monthly.

Hempel, G. H.: *The Postwar Quality of State and Local Government Debt,* National Bureau of Economic Research, New York, 1971.

Kaufman, G.: *Improving Bidding Rules to Reduce Interest Costs in the Competitive Sale of Municipal Bonds,* Center for Capital Market Research, University of Oregon, Eugene, Ore., 1977. Note bibliography.

Robinson, Roland I.: *Postwar Market for State and Local Government Securities,* National Bureau of Economic Research, Princeton University Press, Princeton, N.J., 1960.

Sherwood, H. C.: *How Corporate and Municipal Debt Is Rated: An Insider Looks at Standard and Poors Rating System,* Wiley, New York, 1976.

chapter 15
The Mortgage Market

The mortgage market is based on real estate. A mortgage is a legal instrument by which a lender can keep a contingent lien on title to land and the structures attached to the land. Residential use of real estate, including both single- and multiple-family properties, accounts for about three-fourths of the volume of mortgage credit. Because of the social interest in housing and the deep conviction that a good quality of it should be made available widely, government has become very much involved in the mortgage market. However, an appreciable part of the mortgage market is devoted to leveraging the financing of real estate properties producing "cash-flow" income that is partly shielded from income taxation.

Because of this diversity, the chapter will start with a review of a few basic facts about this market. It will then turn to our analysis of the demand for mortgage credit. The demand for housing is, indirectly, a demand for mortgage credit. The demand for mortgage credit to leverage income properties is only about one-fourth of the total market, but because it is both interesting and complex, its explanation will take somewhat more than a proportionate space. The chapter will then turn to the supply of mortgage credit. Here the role of the federal government will have to be reviewed. The chapter will end with a review of the mortgage interest rate structure, which is the product of the impact of the forces of supply and demand that will have been reviewed.

MORTGAGES: PROPERTIES, BORROWERS, AND LENDERS

About the time of the vernal equinox in 1978 total mortgage debt in the United States passed the trillion dollar mark. This made mortgages the largest of all financial instruments, finally surpassing even common stocks (which were admittedly depressed on that date). The division of this huge mortgage debt by types of properties, by borrowers, and by lenders, has been reasonably stable for a number of years, so we may make these generalizations in broad form:

Types of property:
   Single-family homes account for three-fifths of all mortgage credit.
   Apartments account for about one-seventh.
   Commercial and industrial real estate accounts for less than one-fifth.
   Farms account for about one-sixteenth.
Types of borrowers:
   Individuals, as households, account for about three-fifths.
   Individuals, as farmers or small businessmen, account for between one-fifth and one-sixth.
   Corporations account for between one-fifth and one-sixth.
   Nonprofit and others account for about one-twentieth.
Types of lenders:
   Financial institutions account for over three-quarters of all mortgages outstanding. Savings and loans associations account for nearly half the financial institution total, commercial banks for a quarter, followed by insurance companies, and mutual savings banks.
   Individuals account for less than one-tenth of mortgages owned.
   The federal government itself directly owns less than one-fiftieth of mortgages outstanding, but the credit agencies it has "sponsored" together with the mortgage pools and trusts that lean on the federal government guarantee, account for about one-eighth of mortgage credit.
   The small (less than one-fortieth) proportion in the "other" category is accounted for mainly by REITs and finance companies.

Mortgages differ from other capital market instruments in one important respect: Mortgage lenders put more reliance on the value of the property on which the mortgage lien is placed for security than on the debtors. Some corporate bonds involve mortgage security, but most realistic security analysts count on the income-producing ability of the borrower more than on the liquidating value of the underlying property. A great many real estate mortgage investors, however, still depend more on the value of the property than on the creditworthiness of the borrower. Uniform mortgage terms are offered in most speculative housing developments whether the borrower be marginal or an excellent credit risk. In this respect, mortgage credit has much in common with loans on automobiles and other consumer durables. Lenders on automobile loans or home mortgages try to assure themselves that the car or home buyer is not a flagrant deadbeat, but they do not go very far beyond this point in credit checking.

Mortgages also have one other characteristic in common with consumer credit arising out of the purchase of consumer durable goods: The down payment and maturity terms are often critical factors in the merchandising process. Mass markets have required accommodation of marginal buyers who can put up only small down payments either on homes or automobiles; owner's equity thus tends to be modest. The maturities of such loans also determine the size of their monthly payments. Before the Great Depression, most mortgages were written with lump-sum maturities. In fact, they were seldom paid at maturity but were renewed often. The monthly payment amortized loan has made the final maturity a more critical matter in finding qualifying buyers. These monthly payments are often viewed as the equivalent of rent and are budgeted in much the same way.

The volume of mortgage credit extended varies widely over time. However, since 1972 this volume has exceeded $100 billion every year and at present is at a considerably higher level. The volume of credit extended considerably exceeds the net increase in mortgages outstanding since mortgages are constantly being reduced and retired. In fact, although mortgages generally have an average maturity in excess of twenty-five years, the period in which they are usually retired is about half this length of time. About two-thirds of the new mortgage credit extended for single-family homes is for existing homes, the other third being for newly constructed homes—most of which are speculatively built (that is, built without a specifically committed buyer.) Mortgages on other types of properties show about the same division between new and existing properties.

THE DEMAND FOR MORTGAGE FUNDS

For purposes of analysis, the demand for mortgage funds should be divided between those that arise out of home buying and those for funds to finance the acquisition of rental properties. Most owner-occupied dwellings are single-family homes, although a number of condominium apartments are included in this category. On the other hand, most residential rental properties operated as such continuously are multifamily dwellings.

Another classification of demand can also be used: the distinction between the demand for funds involved in the acquisition of newly constructed homes or rental properties as against the credit involved when an existing property is sold. The financing of new homes or rental projects usually must be arranged before construction can even be started. Indeed, the terms on which mortgage funds are available may have a decisive influence on the rate of housing starts. The rates on, and availability of, funds for mortgages on existing real estate properties cannot influence their basic supply; they can only influence the price at which they trade.

Mortgages on Owner-Occupied Homes

The basic source of demand for housing, of course, goes back to demographic factors such as the number of marriages, the number of children born to such marriages, and the social role of home ownership. In most families in the United States, the home is the largest single asset, the greatest cause of expenditures, and the basis of the largest personal debt. Home ownership is encouraged by our social mores and by the tax collector. During the postwar years the portion of owner-occupied homes has risen substantially to an all-time high level, slightly above 60 percent. Although an increasing proportion of persons and families are moving into apartments, this proportion appears to have stabilized at just about the 40 percent level.

Owner occupation of homes has been subject to two quite conflicting demographic and economic trends. The greater affluence has clearly encouraged home ownership, not only for sentimental and personal reasons but for very good tax reasons: The home is one of the few tax shelters available to salaried persons. However, society has also been going through a process of urbanization. Big-city dwellers more often live in rented apartments than small-town dwellers, and small towns are strongly tilted toward home ownership. However, urbanization includes not just the central parts of big cities, but also the growth of suburbs where home ownership is about as common as in more rural small towns.

A closely related development occurred during the postwar period. The construction of new homes prior to sale by "speculative" builders has been a common phenomenon for many years. The average size of speculative building firms, however, was generally small. Construction was one of the bulwarks of small business. In the postwar years, a much larger share of home building has been done by rather large operators—builders who scheduled more than a hundred homes a year rather than a dozen or a score as was true in prior periods. Merchandising devices include the prearrangement of financing for buyers. Builders found that mass selling of new homes is greatly aided by the existence of prearranged financing. To some extent commercial banks have extended short-term construction loans only where prearranged financing was available. The mortgage commitment, which will be discussed in later sections, has come to play a central role in the operations of these larger-scale builders.

Prearrangement of financing by builders usually involves the submission of building plans and estimates of construction costs. A speculative builder also needs to own or have options on enough vacant land in acceptable locations to make the merchandising of the houses feasible. After this hurdle has been passed, an institution providing the final financing may be prepared to give a firm commitment to acquire the mortgages generated or "originated" in the final sale of these homes.

The parties to this prearranged financing may include more than the builders on one side and the institutional lenders on the other; an intermediary frequently makes the arrangements. A large part of the negotiation of such prearranged financing during the postwar period has been done by so-called mortgage bankers. The role of this institution will thus have to come up for extended comment at a later point.

Several characteristics are associated with large-scale speculative building covered by committed or prearranged financing. In the first place, the formality of prearrangement increases the chance that the mortgage loan value will coincide with sales price. Since a small required down payment is frequently one of the principal attractions advertised by builders, they must be prepared to deliver at time of sale. This is, in effect, covered in the early inspection and approval of plans, sites, and the other elements by lenders to such operations. Another characteristic is that mortgage financing under these circumstances is likely to have the longest possible maturity so as to require the smallest possible monthly payments. One of the principal sales inducements is the argument that purchase of a home really costs no more than rental.[1]

One result of prearranged mass financing has been greater national mobility of mortgage funds. A one-mortgage real-estate deal is likely to be financed with local money or by the loan correspondent of a life insurance company. Mass mortgage banking operations, however, particularly when the originating and servicing functions of the mortgage banker are available, can be between remotely located lenders and local homeowners.

The market for existing houses is also dependent upon the availability of credit that will finance such purchases and sales. When existing houses are marketed, the credit arrangements are usually made by the sales agent, although buyers sometimes make their own arrangements. Since this is a smaller market, credit is usually supplied by a local financial institution. Such credit is usually in the form of a conventional mortgage.

One difference is quite likely to distinguish the mortgage credit given in the sale of an existing house as against the credit involved in the sale of a new house. Existing housing has served a part of its useful life; the maturities allowed by lenders on such housing are likely to be somewhat shorter than on new homes. Furthermore, the appraised value for loan purposes is more likely to depart from sales price than is true in the case of speculatively built new housing. For both these reasons the buyers of existing housing are more likely to find the credit terms a bit more exacting in such purchases than would be true of new housing. A larger down payment will have to be found, and the monthly payments will tend to be a bit larger relative to the capital sum involved. When down payments are onerous, there is a greater chance that some form of second or junior mortgage financing will be involved in such transactions. Junior financing has, in fact, rather more often than not, been identified with the sale of quite old, often badly depreciated and run-down property. Housing often passes through various stages of depreciation and downgrading, and terminal owners are more likely to be drawn from lower-income groups that can buy housing only with the aid of junior financing.

Income Real Estate in the Financial Markets

The federal government pervades the market for mortgages on single-family homes, as we shall explain in a later section. The participation of income-producing real estate in the financial markets is almost exactly the opposite. This sector of the market is private and unregulated. However, recent public offerings of some of the larger partnerships or syndicates have required the filing of registration statements, which action has reduced the degree of secrecy and has opened these operations to public scrutiny and evaluation. Public

[1]This matter can be debated endlessly and without conclusive results. Rental and owner-occupied residences are almost never comparable in terms of facilities, so no precise resolution can be made of this issue.

ownership of the real estate investment trusts (REITs), discussed later in this chapter, has also exposed more of this market.

The principal types of income-producing real estate include apartment houses or complexes; motels and hotels; office buildings, including those with specialized clients such as doctors, dentists, and lawyers; shopping centers; industrial parks; amusement parks; post offices; and even brand-new cities.

The principal difference in the financing of income-producing real estate is that it requires equity capital as well as debt capital. In order to give a picture of the way in which income real estate comes into being, a hypothetical illustration might help: A real estate firm becomes aware of the demand for apartments of a given type and in a given location, possibly from the inquiries it receives with respect to rentals. The firm may locate and take an option on a vacant site that would be appropriate for the type of apartment structure needed. It will then get a firm of architects and engineers to prepare preliminary plans for such a structure. The plans will then be bid by a construction firm. (Some real estate firms have affiliated construction departments.) With the plans and a price on them, it will then seek a commitment from a mortgage lender. With the option, the plans, the bid, and the mortgage commitment, the firm will then seek equity investors. It may do this by organizing a syndicate, usually in the legal form of a limited partnership, which seeks investors from upper-income groups, such as doctors of medicine, who can take advantage of the special tax-shield character of rental real estate.

The special character of income from rental real estate is directly related to two factors: (1) the provisions of tax law that allow the deduction of depreciation charges that are considerably in excess of real economic depreciation from gross income and (2) the widespread belief that inflation will continue to boost the value of real estate. An illustration of how this works is as follows:

Cost of land	$ 200,000
Cost of structure	1,000,000
Total cost	$1,200,000
Loan of 2/3 (8% interest rate)	800,000
Equity needed	$ 400,000
Rental income after real estate taxes and all other cash expenses except interest and income taxes	$ 120,000
Interest on loan	−64,000
Accelerated depreciation (first year)	−60,000
Net *loss* for tax purpose	($4000)
But after-tax cash flow ($120,000 − $64,000) of $56,000 is 14 percent on $400,000. The equity holder also has a loss charged against his or her other income.	

Of course, the accelerated depreciation declines as time goes on and more and more of the income becomes taxable. But this opens up the next step. If real estate does continue to go up in price as a result of inflation and if the accelerated depreciation is greatly in excess of real economic depreciation, the owners of this property may sell the apartment to a new set of owners, perhaps at the same price of $1,200,000. The new group can start depreciating on the new higher basis.

The selling group will pay only capital gains taxes on any gain above the base value arrived at with straight-line depreciation. Any accelerated depreciation charged after 1975, however, will be "recaptured" and subjected to taxation at regular income tax rates. The advantages of acceleration depreciation were greatly reduced by the Tax Reform Act of 1976, and at present some new income real estate projects use straight-line depreciation from the beginning in order to avoid a bunching of taxable income at a time of sale, which might push ordinary income into higher tax brackets. Nevertheless, the assumption of continued inflation in real estate values continues to make real estate investment attractive to high income investors seeking a tax shield.

Variations on the system are many. For example, the land, which is not depreciable, may be sold to an investor who does not pay income taxes, such as a pension fund or a university endowment fund. This land is then leased back to the project with a long-term contract or "ground rent" that is net of all real estate taxes or other expenses. The income from this lease would be fully subject to income taxes if held by a taxed investor. The remaining or depreciable part of the property will then be syndicated to investors who can use a tax shield. The holder of the ground rent inherits the full structure at the end of the lease, together with any renewals available and taken. Columbia University owns the ground under Rockefeller Center and, if the structures last long enough, will someday own it all.

The illustration given above can be varied to show how this would work. Suppose the land is sold to a tax-exempt pension fund for its cost of $200,000 with a leaseback at the net rate of 10 percent. The leaseback may run for thirty years, with two fifteen-year renewals available to the renters. The calculation of equity return is now as follows:

Rental income	$120,000
Less interest	−64,000
Accelerated depreciation	−60,000
Land rent	−20,000
First-year tax loss	($ 24,000)

Cash flow ($120,000 − $64,000 − $20,000 = $36,000) is 18 percent on the $200,000 equity; and the tax loss is an even bigger charge against other income! For investors in a 50 percent tax bracket, this amounts to a first-year tax-free income of 24 percent!

Junior Mortgage Demand

The inventors of the insured mortgage hoped that the higher permissible loan ratios would make junior financing unnecessary: No buyer would be forced to pile a second layer of debt on top of the first one for home purchase. In the insured and guaranteed mortgage field, this hope has been realized to a fair extent. Indeed, such additions are contrary to the rules at time of original granting of these loans. On conventional mortgage loans, however, the loan-to-assessed-value ratios often leave margins to be covered. The second mortgage is still with us.

A second mortgage is not supposed to accompany an FHA[2] loan when it is first made. VA loan values have been so high that the need for them at a time of original extension is not strong. The interest rates on many of these loans made in earlier years, however, were so low by current standards that when houses subject to such mortgages have been sold, it has often been advantageous for buyers to assume the existing mortgage. Its amount, however, may be less than the new purchaser needs to finance the transaction, so a junior mortgage may be added on the second transfer. Various kinds of junior mortgages have been developed in the financing of income properties. The rates involved are often quite high.

Such financing is usually for the purpose of facilitating the sale of property. Since the sellers often resell or "discount" second mortgages, the process involves a concealed higher interest rate and lower cash value of properties involved. Second mortgages are also used for other purposes, as to finance improvements.

The nominal contractual interest rate on junior mortgages is often limited by the usury statutes. If the mortgage is salable only at a discount, its true yield may be materially higher. Since junior mortgages are usually for shorter terms than first mortgages and are now usually amortized by monthly payments, any discount increases yield materially. For example, if a 7 percent five-year junior mortgage with equal monthly payments were sold for "90" (which means 90 percent of the par or face value), its annuity yield, if paid according to contractual terms, would be nearly 14 percent. This computation is never precise in practice. Although most junior mortgage loans are ultimately collected, default of the contractual terms is not at all uncommon.

The borrowers on second mortgages tend, as already hinted, to be lower-income buyers, often without much financial sophistication. There are exceptions, however; second mortgages are sometimes put on income or rental properties by quite sophisticated investors in order to attain a higher "leveraged" rate of return.

Second mortgages are marketed through brokers who may perform this function on a part-time basis. The full-time job of such brokers is often that of real estate salesmanship, management of a savings and loan association, or even

---

[2]FHA and VA mortgages will be explained later in this chapter. In addition, the glossary lists and explains the various acronyms used in the mortgage market. These terms may vanish as HUD (again see glossary) reorganizes its housing operations and subsidies.

management of a bank. The investors in junior mortgages are almost all individuals, usually a rather specialized kind of investor. They are frequently older people with some knowledge of real estate who are willing to keep an eye on such investments and to apply personal collection pressure if necessary. This market is completely local, but within such markets junior mortgages may be quite salable and even enjoy some liquidity. After a period of seasoning that demonstrates the payment record of the buyer, they may be resold at a lower yield or higher price. Some brokers are also investors and hold junior mortgages through a seasoning period before reselling them. In some cases they are even held with bank credit, which can produce a surprising degree of leverage.

"Wraparound Mortgages"

The considerable increase in the level of interest rates has given rise to a special form of mortgage that is similar to the junior mortgage in purpose but rather different in mechanics. The grantor of a new mortgage assumes the liability of an existing, almost always lower interest rate mortgage and usually advances an additional amount. The buyer (or existing owner) of the property assumes the liability of the new, usually higher interest rate mortgage. An example will help to clarify the mechanics. Assume the proprietor of a business had acquired a $300,000 property twenty years ago. To finance it, she had mortgaged the property for $200,000 at 5 percent interest amortized over a thirty-year period. Monthly payments would have been $1073.64. Now ten years remain on the mortgage, and it has been paid down to $101,225. The proprietor now wishes to sell the property. It has depreciated, but building costs have also gone up so she finds she can sell it for just what it had cost her—$300,000. The buyer can put up a down payment of $100,000. The old mortgage at an interest rate below the current market should not be prepaid, but it needs to be supplemented. A junior mortgage for $98,775 could be given, but the seller will find it better strategy to give the buyer a "wraparound" mortgage for the whole $200,000 and retain the liability for payments on the old mortgage. Since the property is now older, a shorter term for the mortgage is probably appropriate. If the "wraparound" mortgage is for just ten years, at 8 ½ percent, the proprietor will receive monthly payments of $2,479.71 from which she will continue to pay out the same $1,073.64. The wraparound could, however, be for twenty years in which case the monthly payments would be $1,735.65. Ten years later after the original mortgage is now paid off, this payment could be a very nice retirement annuity for the original proprietor. We should add that the down payment she received probably would be used to a considerable extent to pay her capital gains taxes on the sale of the property.

The Mortgage and Business Finance

In Chapter 16 on the corporate bond we shall point out that many bonds are secured by mortgages. However, these types of financing are not included in the mortgage market since they flow through quite different institutional channels. The mortgage, however, is used directly in business finance, particularly in small and moderate sized businesses that are not of a scale to approach the open capital markets. A farm mortgage, which we shall cover briefly in the closing pages of this chapter, is really a form of business finance: The farmer finances a major capital asset—his or her land—with a mortgage. The buildings needed for family-owned stores, automobile dealerships, small manufacturing establishments, and similar business operations may be financed with mortgages. Since the properties needed by these businesses are more special purpose than homes, such business-type mortgages usually require larger down payments and often higher interest rates than those in home mortgages. Some insurance companies have become quite expert in the granting of this type of mortgage. These mortgages may be accompanied by "equity kickers," which we shall explain later in this chapter.

One variant on this type of financing is the purchase-lease-back transaction, which usually is, but not always, accompanied by a mortgage. A business will build the type of property it needs, and then sell it to an investor (usually high income). The investor then can use depreciation as a tax shield, as already explained in reference to income properties, and he or she can leverage this investment by a mortgage. If the investor puts up the entire cost of the property, he or she is probably supplying equity capital to the seller of the property. Purchase-lease-back transactions can also be accompanied by "equity kickers."

THE SUPPLY OF MORTGAGE FUNDS

The supply of mortgage funds is more than a matter of economic analysis; the subject has become an issue of political importance. The supply of funds has been described as "erratic," although a survey of the record suggests that this description is extreme. However, in 1966, in 1969 and the greater part of 1970, and again in 1973 and 1974, funds from private sources were indeed short. As a result, federal government programs were geared up to fill this gap. Institutional participation has also changed both in character and amount. In this section of this chapter we shall examine the changed nature of the market participation: We shall note some specific factors in the participation of various institutional lenders in this market.

The mortgage market is dominated by savings and loan associations. These associations started out primarily as single-family-home lenders, but they have broadened their business coverage to include construction lending and to cover multifamily and commercial properties. They have also maintained a higher growth rate than any of the other institutional lenders, with one exception: the new mortgage pools and trusts. Even this is not wholly an exception since savings and loan associations are frequently the agencies servicing the mortgage pools and also the originators of the mortgages that are placed in the pools. Figure 15-1 shows clearly this commanding position. Commercial banks, after an earlier period of slack in mortgage lending, have become more active and are now frequent competitors of savings and loan associations. Life insurance companies remain important, but their recent rate of growth is slow and they

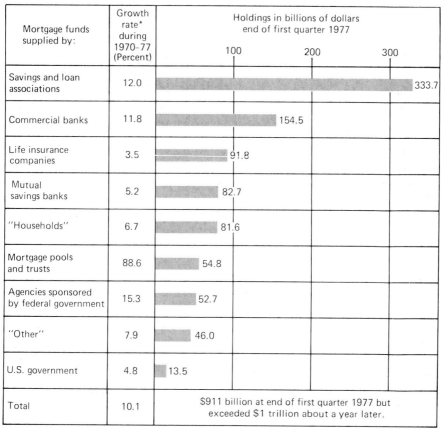

Mortgage funds supplied by:	Growth rate* during 1970–77 (Percent)	Holdings in billions of dollars end of first quarter 1977		
		100	200	300
Savings and loan associations	12.0			333.7
Commercial banks	11.8	154.5		
Life insurance companies	3.5	91.8		
Mutual savings banks	5.2	82.7		
"Households"	6.7	81.6		
Mortgage pools and trusts	88.6	54.8		
Agencies sponsored by federal government	15.3	52.7		
"Other"	7.9	46.0		
U.S. government	4.8	13.5		
Total	10.1	$911 billion at end of first quarter 1977 but exceeded $1 trillion about a year later.		

*Growth rates from logarithmic regression curves calculated by author

figure 15-1 Principal Mortgage Lenders. *(Source: Author's estimates based on* Flow-of-Funds *data, Board of Governors of the Federal Reserve System, quarterly reports.)*

will probably slowly lose place. The mutual savings banks have attempted to be strong competitors in the areas in which they operate, but their northeastern location has worked against them. Individuals are of dwindling significance as mortgage lenders except in one respect: their reluctant role as suppliers of purchase-money mortgage funds when other sources are not available. The federal government is not directly very important in the mortgage market, but the agencies it has sponsored are and have kept up a fast growth rate.

The type of mortgage preferred and the methods of acquiring mortgages vary greatly among these institutions. Since the relative tightness or ease of these various institutions do not always follow the same patterns, the market is subject to shifts in flows. Nevertheless, it is generally true that a high degree of competition prevails in this market. The great success of the savings and loan associations in the postwar period has attracted the envy of other financial institutions and forced them to modify their operating methods. Interest rates on mortgage funds have risen, but not because the competitive drive to acquire mortgages was absent. It can also be said that savers have gained because of this keen competition; the rates paid to secure the funds with which to make mortgage loans have increased more during the postwar years than the mortgage rates themselves.

Savings and Loan Associations

These associations are primarily mortgage lenders. The original form of their title—building and loan associations—emphasized this purpose. Early associations were expected to facilitate the pooling of members' savings so as to permit each member to build a home. The order in which that privilege was exercised was sometimes settled by lot. Some associations expected to disband once the objective of home building by the original members had been accomplished. Since then they have evolved into rather different institutions. More emphasis is put on the promotion of saving. Those who borrow from them are not the only ones who use them as vessels for their savings.

Until the early 1960s savings and loan associations grew more rapidly than any other major type of mortgage lender. They competed vigorously for savings and used them all for mortgage lending. However, in the mid-1960s banks become more vigorous competitors for funds and also more active mortgage lenders. In the "credit crunch" of 1966, the flow of funds into savings and loan associations dwindled and mortgage lending was brought almost to a standstill as they attempted to fulfill previous mortgage loan commitments. It was only by massive recourse to funds that the Federal Home Loan Bank System was able to raise in the capital markets that they were able to maintain a reasonable degree of current lending activity. At that time Federal Reserve Regulation Q was used to curb bank competition. A similar but somewhat less drastic pattern followed in 1969 and 1970. This led to the extension of the so-called secondary market for conventional mortgages. This rather complex arrangement will be described in a later section of this chapter.

Most savings and loan associations originate a fairly large part of the mortgages they hold for investment. However, such associations located in parts of the country with lower mortgage loan demand may buy mortgages from the secondary market, and sometimes directly from other associations that are located in areas of heavy mortgage demand. Savings and loan associations are also becoming more important as construction lenders, particularly for properties for which they intend to provide long-term financing. In the beginning the savings and loan movement concentrated almost entirely on the single-family home, but recently they have become increasingly important as lenders for multifamily (apartment) structures. A few of the more aggressive and profit-motivated associations have even gone into commercial and industrial mortgage lending.

The savings and loan association started as a mutual or nominally nonprofit institution, and four-fifths of the assets of these institutions are still of this type. However, a number are organized as profit-oriented institutions with stockholders and even holding companies. Several of these are listed on the NYSE. Two-thirds of the assets of California institutions are of this type. They also are important in Texas and in Ohio. It is a tribute to the profit motive that the most rapid and aggressive development of this industry has taken place in states with profit motivation.

Mutual Savings Banks

The basic character of mutual savings banks is quite like that of savings and loan associations. Both are "mutual" in theory but self-perpetuating bodies in practice. Both are primarily mortgage lenders. Both like to emphasize their savings promotion. They differ greatly in one respect, however: Savings and loan associations are located throughout the United States, many of them in the growing areas of the country. The mutual savings banks are mostly concentrated in the slower growing New England and North Atlantic seaboard states.

Mutual savings banks also seem to have a slight preference for conventional mortgages, but when forced to acquire their mortgages in national markets through mortgage brokers, they have turned more and more to the FHA-insured and the VA-guaranteed mortgage. Indeed, the appearance of discounts on these mortgages stimulated interest in these obligations. Some buyers of mortgages, such as life insurance companies and some large mutual savings banks, have been rather important sources of loans for rental real estate; in this market they are national factors.

Mutual savings banks do not have inflows of funds as regular as those of life insurance companies and thus have not been able to use the same mortgage acquisition techniques. Some mutual savings banks prefer to buy mortgages from mortgage bankers after the mortgages are originated rather than to give early commitments. However, commitments have been given by some of the bigger mutual savings banks. Since mutual savings banks have had fairly large liquidity reserves, they have been able to make some forward mortgage commitments and to honor them. They make local mortgage loans and invest in out-of-state mortgages, but local mortgages get preferred treatment when a pinch of funds develops. In the national mortgage market, mutual savings banks are not counted as continuous investors. The mutual savings banks in both New York State and in Massachusetts use central agencies in the acquisition of out-of-state mortgages. Most mutual savings banks make construction loans when this facilitates the acquisition of desirable mortgages, but some mutual savings banks have close ties with one or two commercial banks and prefer to channel construction loans to such banking associates.

Life Insurance Companies

Life insurance companies have relatively fewer mortgages and a much more diversified asset structure than either of the two types of savings institutions so far considered. Furthermore, since the number of life insurance companies is much smaller and since only one of the major companies operates its own agency system for acquiring mortgages, these companies are more or less forced into using intermediate agencies for acquiring mortgages. The mortgage bankers, already mentioned, furnished the principal means for doing this. Owing to the fact that they operate through intermediaries, life insurance company mortgage operations tend to be national. This circumstance has doubtlessly helped to reduce regional differentials in interest rates, since insurance companies hesitate to vary rates greatly between areas for fear of adverse publicity.

Life insurance cash inflow can be predicted with far more success than that at savings institutions. Life insurance companies receive a steady stream of premium payments. Even new sales can be forecast with fair success. With such foreknowledge and with a more diversified asset structure, the life insurance companies can commit themselves with more confidence than other mortgage lenders can. When mortgages are scarce, this assurance provides a competitive advantage in getting a supply of mortgages. On the other hand, when conditions are reversed, this factor has been used to improve yield. Some life insurance companies are reluctant to vary forward commitments to acquire higher-yielding mortgages. Some, however, have tried to extend their commitments when rates were high and to resist any softening of rates by allowing commitments to dwindle in periods of ease.

Knowledge of expected cash flow is obviously a help in complex investment operations; still, other institutional arrangements have been made to further this strategic position. At first, life insurance companies, operating through mortgage bankers, simply committed themselves to purchase mortgages when they had been processed and were ready for delivery. Since builders could not tell in advance just how long the building process would take and how fast their houses would sell after completion (and whether or not all purchasers would accept the prearranged mortgage terms), there was necessarily some ambiguity in forward commitments to buy mortgages with respect to time and amount. Some commitments were never exercised.

Rather than undertake an undated responsibility to accept delivery of blocks of mortgages when the mortgage bankers were ready to delivery them, some life insurance companies made commitments that permitted them to delay delivery of completed mortgages. This required that the mortgage bankers fall back on commercial banks for interim credit to carry the mortgages until the life insurance buyers were ready to accept delivery. This interim financing was sometimes supplied by the same commercial bank that had also provided construction loans for the builder. The mechanics of releasing the liens involved in construction loans could be coordinated with the registration of mortgages—a clear advantage if both credits are on the books of the same bank. Life insurance companies seldom advance construction loans, so this arrangement is considered a logical one. Some life insurance companies have themselves "warehoused" mortgages with commercial banks when an overcommitted position made them take delivery of mortgages beyond their current capacity to pay for them.

For many years life insurance companies have been more active in making mortgage loans for apartments, commercial properties, and farms, than for single-family homes. Since they generally do not have regional offices, they were at a disadvantage in this area. In recent years this has reached the point where life insurance portfolios of mortgages on single-family homes are being gradually liquidated. Furthermore, many life insurance companies are interested in apartment and commercial mortgages only if they give them some degree of equity participation, a practice described in the next section.

Equity Participation—"Kickers"

While the tax shield of depreciation is a principal feature back of equity investment in income-producing real estate, leverage continues to be important. Also, to the extent that equity investment in real estate is built on the assumption of continued inflation, leverage has great appeal. As a result, the bargaining by borrowers with lenders on income-producing real estate is often almost as much with respect to the loan-to-value ratio as with respect to the interest rate. Indeed, the rate applied to many large income properties is higher than the rate on a small individual family home.

As a result of more risk with larger loan-to-value ratios, many lenders on income real estate have sought and secured some form of equity participation—"kickers," as this is known. One of the earliest forms was some share in gross revenues such as a fraction of sales above some minimum level in a shopping center. For example, a principal tenant in a shopping center might be given a fairly modest basic rent but would be expected to pay 1 percent of sales above some given level. Many more complex arrangements have been worked out. The lenders that have been most aggressive in seeking equity kickers have been pension funds, life insurance companies, and those for whom the residual and long-term values were important.

Life insurance companies apparently originated this practice and are still the most active in it. It was quickly adopted by those pension funds that participate in the mortgage market. It has even been used by profit-motivated savings and loan associations and by a few banks.

Commercial Bank Mortgage Lending

Although commercial banks are not appropriate mortgage lenders according to tradition, they are in fact rather important lenders in this market. Construction loans, of course, are frequently a necessary part of the building process, and being short-term credit, are quite appropriate for commercial banks. Commercial banks, however, hold appreciable amounts of time deposits and, as savings institutions, can appropriately hold mortgages. Indeed, national banks hold mortgages according to a rule that is stated mainly in terms of the amount of time deposits held.

Commercial banks make mortgage loans of all kinds: conventional, FHA-insured and VA-guaranteed. Since national banks and some state banks are limited not only as to the total amount of mortgage credit that they can extend but also as to down payment characteristics, the conventional mortgages made by commercial banks frequently have rather more restrictive terms than the conventional mortgages made by other lenders.

Commercial banks originate more mortgages than they keep, and they sell an appreciable volume. Some commercial bank mortgage departments originate mortgages for the trust departments of their own or other banks. While unit commercial banks are somewhat limited to the area of their location, these barriers are overcome to some extent by the workings of the correspondent banking system. Big banks sometimes sell participations in large mortgages to smaller banks in need of loan outlets. On the other side, a small bank facing a larger proposition than it can handle may call on its city correspondent for participation and sometimes for technical aid. Branch banking systems, particularly those on the West Coast, usually tend to be aggressive mortgage lenders. Commercial banks also participate in this market by making short-term mortgage "warehouse" loans to mortgage bankers and to life insurance companies and even, on some occasions, to savings and loan associations.

Mortgage Pools and Trusts

A later section of this chapter will deal with the many ways in which the federal government has intervened in the mortgage market. One of the ways has been to acquire mortgages from the market through several agencies that will be enumerated in that section. Rather than financing such acquisition of mortgages by borrowing in the market, several of these agencies have been authorized to bundle up groups of these mortgages in "pools" or "trusts," to provide for the servicing of these mortgages by some experienced institution such as a mortgage banker or lender, and then to sell participation certificates or other types of instruments representing these mortgages to the investor public. These "pass-through" or participation certificates are guaranteed by the agencies and, in some cases, directly by the U.S. Treasury. Thus, investors without experience or other arrangements for mortgage lending, could indirectly participate in the mortgage market. These instruments became so popular with investors that a few private financial institutions (including the biggest commercial bank in the nation) have successfully issued such instruments *without* federal government guarantee. The total volume of such instruments now accounts for over 6 percent of the total of mortgage funds outstanding, and the growth rate of this instrument is so high further market penetration is probable.

Individuals and the Purchase Money Mortgage

Over the years, individuals have gradually become less important *relatively* as a source of mortgage funds. However, the absolute amount of funds accounted for by individuals is still almost a tenth of the total outstanding and thus of continuing importance. A large part of such funds is almost certainly accounted for by the "purchase money" mortgage. If an individual owns a property that he or she wishes to sell, and if other lenders are reluctant to supply the funds needed by a potential buyer, the owner may be forced into the position of supplying the financing; in other words, "taking a mortgage back" as part payment for the property. Such purchase money mortgages are often needed to sell properties that conventional lenders are dubious about. In times of tight money, purchase money mortgages may be required even for higher class properties. Statistics are not available to clarify the frequency of such purchase-money mortgage transactions, but common observation makes it clear that they are fairly frequent. A tax angle sometimes dictates a purchase money mortgage: A seller may prefer to lower the interest rate rather than the price of a property so as to shift as much of the gain into capital gains form as possible. Purchase money mortgages in some legal jurisdictions or states take the form of "land contracts." These obligations are sometimes sold at discounts in local and informal markets.

Real Estate Investment Trusts (REITs)

Real estate investment trusts have had an up-and-down history that illustrates the volatile nature of real estate itself. In the late 1960s and early 1970s they enjoyed popularity and for a while were the fastest-growing segment of a rather specialized segment of the market for real estate finance: development and construction. But then the depression in real estate that started in late 1973 and lasted through 1974 and into 1975 brought great distress to the REIT industry, including some bankruptcies. However, the REIT promises to be a continuing segment of this market, and so it may be instructive to follow the rise and then the fall.

REITs were of three major types: (1) those that concentrated in the extension of developmental credit for proposed shopping centers, condominiums, and the subdivision of land for single family housing, as well as other types of real estate operations; (2) those that extended long-term mortgage credit; and (3) equity investors in real estate. The last category could be further subdivided between those that were true final equity investors in real estate and those that invested in purchase-lease-back of the land lying under developed real estate. Since a lease-back is junior to any first mortgage on the developed property, these purchase-lease-back investments were very similar to junior mortgages except that they often were accompanied by "participation" rents that are similar to "equity kickers." Many REITs were combinations of these various types of operations. Commercial banks were often sponsors of the first type of REIT; life insurance companies of the second type. As experience showed, the first type was the most vulnerable to the effects of a real estate recession, but the others were not trouble-free; the purchase-lease-backs were particularly subject to problems.

The ups and downs of real estate have never coincided very well with the fluctuations in business conditions generally, and the problems of 1974 and 1975 once more illustrated this fact. Real estate started to weaken in 1973 before general business conditions had deteriorated, and it remained weak after the rest of the economy had reasonably well recovered. REITs were ill prepared for this real estate recession or the recession generally. They viewed development credit as short-term or intermediate-term credit, and construction loans as wholly short-term. As a result they used short-term financing in their own capital structures: bank loans and even commercial paper borrowing. Real estate development financing has frequently involved rather small equity contributions by promoters, and so when times turned bad, many developments quickly became insolvent. And when the inflation rate increased in spite of the depression, construction costs rose and cost overruns became very common. Then the market for the final properties weakened. As a result REITs came to have increasingly large proportions of loans, both developmental and construction, in difficulties. Thus many REITs themselves got into difficulties; they lost their commercial paper ratings, and their bank loans became frozen. The equity-type REITs survived reasonably well as did some of the long-term mortgage lenders; but the industry as a whole lost its reputation in the investment markets, and almost all REITs, even those with good survival records, found the capital markets unreceptive to their needs.

MORTGAGE BANKING

Long before World War II mortgage brokers and mortgage bankers were functioning in the arrangement of mortgage credit. The large-scale development of this system, however, was largely a product of postwar developments. When life insurance companies and later the mutual savings banks started to go outside the area of head office location to acquire mortgages, mortgage bankers became the middlemen between the new larger-scale speculative builders seeking mortgage commitments and these lenders. Mortgage bankers also played a continuing role in the servicing of the mortgages that they originated. The usual fee for servicing—½ of 1 percent—is a fairly important part of most mortgage bankers' income.

The fairly simple commitment arrangements first used became complicated when the institutional investors did not always find it convenient to acquire the mortgages originated for them at the moment when they were completed. Before the 1951 Treasury–Federal Reserve "Accord," when Treasury security prices were pegged, insurance companies in need of funds could always sell long-term U.S. government securities. When price support was dropped, the timing of such sales became a much more critical matter. Commitment arrangements were consequently revised, so that mortgage bankers were expected to be able to carry completed mortgages for at least a short period before final delivery. This, of course, required access to bank credit. Still other devices were invented, including so-called standby commitments, which were often at prices below the market but at least enough to bail out projects so protected.

Why were commitments needed? Commercial banks, as short-term lenders, hesitated to give construction loans to a project without assurance that the sale of completed homes could be financed. They might be willing to assume the risk of sale when the builder had a good record and basic demand was strong. However, a housing project without financing could become a badly frozen asset if tight money markets should arise. Some savings institutions had been embarrassed by having let themselves become overcommitted, and new commitments have not always been easy to arrange. Thus the standby could serve to hold place pending a better deal.

Mortgage bankers hesitate to commit themselves to builders unless reasonably well assured of a final buyer of the mortgages to be generated; they also know that commercial bank credit for warehousing these mortgages is usually unavailable in the absence of a final commitment. Rather than turn down otherwise attractive offers from builders when institutional investors had no funds, mortgage bankers sought standby commitments. Commercial banks have been the most frequent source of such standbys, and this function has sometimes been linked with the supplying of warehousing credit.

FHA-insured and VA-guaranteed mortgages have been the preferred vehicle for mortgage banker operations, but the development of a secondary market for conventional mortgages has increased their participation in this form of mortgage. Mortgage bankers originally handled mainly loans on individual owner-occupied homes; however, mortgages on large rental properties are an increasing part of their business. Intermediate-sized apartment house financing has often been arranged by mortgage bankers, and they often service such mortgages after originating them.

Good mortgage bankers know the preferences of institutional investors and can often help builders to tailor their plans to the known taste of these final lenders.

FEDERAL GOVERNMENT AGENCIES IN THE MORTGAGE MARKET

Federal government programs affecting real estate finance are so numerous and complex that we can only report on them in summary form. These programs may be classified under three different general categories: (1) programs of mortgage insurance that are self-supporting; (2) programs designed to even out and ensure the availability of mortgage funds; (3) programs of a social welfare nature, usually involving subsidies, which are aimed at improving the housing of lower-income groups. There is clearly some overlap of programs, and some programs have subtly changed their character through practice without legislative amendment.

Mortgage Insurance and Guarantee

During the attempted recovery from the Great Depression in the 1930s, the federal government started a system of mortgage insurance under the FHA. This system of mortgage insurance has been revised and its terms changed many times. A brief expository account of the mortgage market should not undertake to describe the prevailing terms; they are almost sure to be obsolete before the account is available to readers. However, several points about this system should be noted. In the first place, insured mortgage loans are made for amounts much nearer to 100 percent of the appraised value of the underlying properties than is true of conventional mortgages. Furthermore, the lower the price range for the property, the larger the allowable debt-to-assessed-value ratio. An insurance fee (½ of 1 percent per annum) is charged and the rate on the mortgage is nominally controlled. The principal feature of the FHA mortgage, however, is that it is always "amortized," that is, retired by regular monthly payments. Before the 1930s most mortgages (except those of savings and loan associations) were lump-sum obligations. Now almost all are amortized.

When initiated in the early 1930s, the insured mortgage system was a method of restoring order in the mortgage market demoralized by the Great Depression and of aiding economic recovery. Later it became a kind of welfare measure. Greater benefits for low-income buyers are implicit in the larger debts permitted for lower-valued houses. Furthermore, the measure has become not just a general antidepression measure but is aimed at the relief of residential construction even when other parts of the economy are not particularly depressed. Whenever home construction activity slackens just a bit, the powerful home builders' lobby starts a clamor for still easier terms.

Governmental support of mortgage credit has also been used to support the financing of veterans' housing. The VA has been authorized to "guarantee" certain portions of mortgage loans made to veterans for purposes of home buying. No fee is charged.

The maximum permissible ratio of loan-to-assessed value under both systems was set at a high level with the implied hope of eliminating the second mortgage. The FHA imposes an interest rate ceiling on its insured mortgages and the VA follows along. These ceilings have been adjusted to money and capital market conditions—but usually with some reluctance and delay, since interest rates are an issue of considerable political impact. The existence of the ceiling has given rise to the need for the so-called secondary market, described below.

Ensuring the Availability of Mortgage Funds

Programs for ensuring the availability of mortgage funds have taken three major forms: (1) creating "secondary" markets in mortgages so that primary lenders can get the needed funds to continue origination of mortgages; (2) creating a "lender of last resort" for mortgage-lending institutions; and (3) direct federal government extension of mortgage credit when all other sources fail.

The "Secondary" Market in Mortgages

When interest rate ceilings made insured and guaranteed mortgage loans unattractive to free market investors, there was political pressure for the federal government to support the market. At first this was a very simple system in which a government agency, the Federal National Mortgage Association (FNMA or "Fannie Mae") was expected to buy FHA and VA mortgages during tight money markets and then to sell off its holdings during subsequent easier money markets. This is not, of course, a true secondary market any more than the government purchase of agricultural surpluses is a true secondary market. Recently the system has been greatly changed and enlarged to cover conventional mortgages. New devices have been invented to stimulate the flow of funds into mortgages. FNMA was spun off into a private corporation listed on the NYSE. Two new agencies of government have been created. The Government National Mortgage Association (GNMA or "Ginnie

Mae") accepts bundles of mortgages from sellers—generally mortgage bankers in areas of excess demand—guarantees the package, and sells it to investors through two types of securities: "pass throughs" or serial bonds. In the first form the full cash proceeds, both interest and principal repayment, are "passed through" to investors after servicing charges are deducted by the originators. The serials do approximately the same, but at stated intervals. Investors may purchase whatever maturity they prefer. Both types have lives of about twelve years.

FNMA now conducts purchase auctions every two weeks for FHA and VA mortgages and about once a month for conventional mortgages. The sellers, mainly mortgage bankers, offer mortgages, and the FNMA accepts offers up to such rate as it decides. The FNMA both purchases and also makes commitments to purchase. Presumably the FNMA also sells mortgages, and in fact it does so occasionally. If a lower interest rate period should come, or one in which mortgage demands should decline, it might sell off much or most of its portfolio.

In essence, both the FNMA and GNMA function to absorb the flow of mortgages when the regular channels do not have enough funds. They do this by borrowing from the agency market (described in Chapter 13), which has support if not direct guarantee of the federal government.

A new agency for making secondary markets in mortgages was created in 1970: The Federal Home Loan Mortgage Corporation (FHLMC) under the general guidance of the Federal Home Loan Bank System (FHLBS). It makes a secondary market primarily for savings and loan associations. Its distinctive service appears to be to offer commitments to buy mortgages at fixed rates of interest so that it, rather than the lenders, bears the risk of interest rate changes.

The Federal Home Loan Mortgage Corporation (or *The* Mortgage Corporation, as it advertises itself) has concentrated its attention on conventional mortgages. In order to make the mechanics of a secondary market in such obligations more feasible, it developed standardized forms for such mortgages that have been widely adopted. From 1970 through 1975 The Mortgage Corporation purchased over $5 billion of mortgages for its own account, and also for the Treasury Department. At first these purchases had to be financed by loans from the Federal Home Loan Corporation, by GNMA-guaranteed bonds, and by advances from the Treasury Department. Mortgage participation certificates (PCs) of a "pass-through" variety were sold, but not in adequate volume. Starting in 1976, however, The Mortgage Corporation, by means of improved marketing techniques, has been able to meet its need fully by weekly sales of PCs and by sales of guaranteed mortgage certificates (GMCs). Now it is reducing its outstanding debt while continuing its weekly purchase of mortgages by a kind of reverse auction process (sellers bid to sell). The obligations of The Mortgage Corporation have achieved full market acceptance and themselves enjoy a good secondary market. The function of this operation is both increasing the liquidity of conventional mortgages and effecting a regional redistribution of mortgage funds.

FHLBS: Support of Savings Institutions

The FHLBS was created in 1932, in the depth of the Depression, as an agency for using its market borrowing power to give liquidity to savings and loan associations. In the beginning it was not viewed as a way of supporting mortgage lending. However, in the rapid postwar expansion of the savings and loan system, it came to support savings and loan associations more often when faced with excess mortgage demands than with share cashing. At first, the FHLBS support came in years of unusual mortgage demand, but in the 1960s the savings and loan growth rate slackened a bit, and for several successive years FHLBS support was steadily increased. In 1966 and 1969, years of credit stringency, there was special need for this support.

The greatest bulge in FHLB lending to members came in the 1973–1974 credit squeeze. In both of these years the amount advanced exceeded $10 billion, and the amount outstanding approached a tenth of the deposit footings of savings and loan associations. No direct statistics have been compiled showing the average period that such borrowing was outstanding, but an estimate based on the balance of credit extensions and repayments suggests that during the tight money period these advances were outstanding for periods averaging close to two years.

Direct Federal Government Mortgage Lending

So far, federal government direct lending has been kept to rather small proportions: between 1 and 2 percent of total mortgage credit. The principal agency for such direct loans is the Ginny Mae special assistance program. Some uses of this program have bordered on being social welfare programs for the elderly and lower income groups, but it has also been used to even out the flow of mortgage funds. The second most important direct federal government lender is the Farmers Home Administration, which has focused on rural and small town lending where mortgage lending facilities were not locally available. This program has also had a social welfare aspect. Finally, quite small amounts have been advanced as purchase money mortgages by FHA and VA in the process of selling its foreclosed properties, and even smaller amounts have been advanced by the Small Business Administration and the Federal Land Banks.

Social Welfare for Housing via Subsidies

The federal government and now forty state governments have been involved in programs of public housing for many years. However the financing of these programs, both Federal and state, has been by tax-exempt financing, so these programs were covered in Chapter 14. In 1968, however, the federal government adopted a new method for improving the housing of the poor and the elderly by subsidies. Some of these programs go far beyond the legitimate scope of this text, so they shall be only briefly mentioned. First, programs were set up for insurance of mortgages that were substandard by market standards so that losses were almost certain to emerge—and they did. Second, facilities were made for making low interest rates available (sometimes as low as 1 percent) for the needy. These programs were aimed at stimulating lower-income house ownership with the hope of instilling the social responsibility that home ownership is thought to encourage. Still other programs encouraged real estate promoters to build or rehabilitate rental properties for occupancy by lower-income groups by means of loan guarantees and interest rate subsidies for such promoters. Finally, direct rental subsidies for low-income families were attempted.

These subsidy programs led to many abuses and so most of these programs were halted in 1973. However, projects in stages of partial completion were continued, and in 1977 new pressure came for revival of these programs in forms revised so as to avoid past abuses.

PRIVATE INSURANCE OF MORTGAGES

The transformation of FHA from an agency of just mortgage insurance into one of social welfare has seemed to bog it down in enormous amounts of red tape, delay, and general inefficiency. Over the years the ½ percent mortgage insurance fee has proved to be more than adequate to insure mortgages of reasonably good quality; it is only when submarket mortgage credit is introduced that it becomes less than adequate.

Attracted by the potential profits in the insurance fee, private firms have started the insurance of mortgages. While they do not have the financial resources of the federal government, they have enough to make these insured mortgages quite acceptable in the secondary markets. The amount of business is still small, but the rate of growth is rapid. One of the private mortgage-insuring firms showed such large early profit growth that its stock became "hot" and attracted a great deal of institutional support. The traditional, though recently rather muted, opposition of the savings and loan industry to FHA will probably help the development of private insurance of mortgages.

INTEREST RATES ON MORTGAGES

At one time mortgage interest rates differed materially both in levels and in timing of movements from other interest rates. They tended to be higher than other interest rates and to move less and later than other interest rates, and there were sometimes rather material regional differences in such rates.

Much of this has changed. Regional differentials have shrunk to quite small margins. Rate movements over time have become greater, and the movements are much more prompt and synchronous with other interest rates. Thus, most of the generalizations about interest rates in Chapter 7 are applicable here. However, several characteristics of mortgage interest rates merit separate mention.

Contract rate versus yield. The true yield on a bond may vary from the coupon rate when it is sold above or below par. The same is true of a mortgage, but the words used differ slightly. Many mortgage lenders demand "points" from borrowers: Two points is really a 2 percent discount of the mortgage. The borrower gets $98 for each $100 on the face of the mortgage contract. Thus the true yield is increased over the contract interest rate. (Two points taken on a twenty-year 8½ percent mortgage makes the effective yield 8.78 percent. If the mortgage is prepaid, as is very common the increase in effective yield is much more; ten-year prepayment would make the effective yield more than 9 percent.)

Mortgage versus bond yields.   Insured mortgages and high-grade corporate bonds have recently tended to have very similar yields. Conventional mortgages for single-family homes generally yield less than Baa bonds. Conventional mortgages on income or commercial property, however, are likely to yield more than Baa bonds. Just as the spread between new issue bonds and those on the secondary market has narrowed, so has the spread between new mortgages and secondary mortgage market yields.

Insured versus conventional mortgage yields.   An insured mortgage usually yields less than a conventional one by ¼ to ½ percent, but the spread seems to have narrowed over time. Private insurance of mortgages appears to be almost as effective as government insurance in reducing interest cost to borrowers.

Inflation and the Rate of Interest on Mortgages

As argued in Chapter 3, all interest rates have been influenced by the widespread expectation of continuing inflation. In the case of real estate, however, the impact has been particularly important. In the section dealing with the financing of income-producing real estate, it was pointed out that accelerated depreciation permitted by the tax laws is widely believed to be much in excess of real economic depreciation. A large part of this excess is due to the expectation of secular inflation and the resulting increases in the price of real estate. Under such circumstances it is not surprising that the level of interest rates has such moderate impact on the demand for credit. The promoter of a tax-shielded-income real estate venture may find it more important to get a large loan and therefore more leverage than to get a lower rate of interest. Interest is, after all, a tax deduction. This is also one reason why lenders have increasingly demanded some form of equity participation: If they are to shoulder more risk, they wish a return that is not limited to the interest rate but is also geared to the income-producing potential of the property involved.

Variable Interest Rates on Mortgages as an Inflation Protection

One of the problems of savings intermediaries specializing in mortgages (savings and loan associations and mutual savings banks) is that, with fixed interest rates, they cannot afford to raise rates on their savings accounts when interest rates go up; there is too much lag in their income. Thus they not only cannot attract new money but face the risk of loss by withdrawals to other capital or money market investment outlets.

If, however, their assets had interest rates adjusted to the market, then they could do so and protect their position. The variable interest rate mortgage has been proposed as a device to accomplish this result. It was recommended by the Hunt Commission and by the Federal Reserve. Both recommendations were accompanied by careful safeguards so that mortgage borrowers would not be led into contracts that they did not understand or that involved unexpected increases in monthly payments. (Most of the proposals contemplate that monthly payments would stay the same but that mortgage principal would be retired more slowly if rates went up—in other words, an automatic maturity extension.) The principal experience with variable-rate mortgages so far has been in California. Although a fairly large volume of such mortgages have been written, it was not until 1978 that mortgage interest rates rose enough to activate the contingency provisions.

Graduated, Flexible, and Reverse Mortgage Interest Provisions

Housing prices have increased faster than the general price level. Some buyers, particularly younger families, have been unable to find homes and mortgage terms that they could afford; they were "priced out of the market." To offset this factor, it has been suggested that mortgage amortization payments, rather than being equal in amount should be graduated upwards to fit the pattern of expected increases in income. It has also been suggested that payment provisions be made more flexible so that they could be related to changes in the rate of inflation.

While the above provisions are aimed mainly at younger home buyers, a still different and novel scheme has been proposed for older homeowners who have paid off their mortgages and now have a debt-free home. It has been suggested that such owners should be able to remortgage their homes at retirement and to receive the proceeds of the mortgage as an annuity to supplement their other retirement income. If made for long periods of payout, these "reverse" mortgages would almost certainly not jeopardize final ownership of the home.

WALL STREET INTO REAL ESTATE

The widespread move of investors into tax-shielded outlets has pushed many Wall Street investment banking firms into various kinds of real estate activity. Some form limited partnership syndications (with the basic developers being the general partner or partners). These limited partnerships are registered like any other publicly offered security and then sold. Others have sponsored closely held REITs. However, the large part of this business still appears to be in small, limited partnerships that do not have to be registered. A few firms have even attempted to establish secondary markets in the limited partnerships they have formed so that individual partners can "get out" if and when they so wish.

FARM MORTGAGE MARKET

The farm mortgage debt is about 6 percent of total mortgage debt; too large to dismiss completely without notice. Nevertheless, two factors justify brief coverage: A large part of farm mortgage debt has drifted into the hands of governmental agencies and thus is outside our primary interest in private capital markets; second, the ratio of farm mortgage debt to the value of farms is so low that no material credit problems arising from this source can be imagined.

Life insurance companies were formerly large farm mortgage lenders, and a few still participate in this market. After the Great Depression, many mortgages formerly held by life insurance companies were absorbed by the Federal Land Banks, the Federal Intermediate Credit Banks, and the Farmers Home Administration. The rates of interest fixed at that time, and since raised inadequately, are so far below market rates as to leave little incentive for private lending. Individual farmers who sold off their farms (sometimes to sons or sons-in-law) often held the mortgages on their farms. An Iowa farmer retired to Florida, Arizona, or southern California may be living on a mortgage held on the old farmstead. Commercial banks in rural areas still make a modest volume of farm mortgage loans.

Farm land values enjoyed a postwar boom far beyond that justified by farm income; city investors bought farms as inflation hedges, and farmers themselves enlarged their operations as machinery made it possible for one man to handle more land. As a result, farm mortgage credit is usually well protected by a thick layer of equity ownership.

PROJECTS AND QUESTIONS

1. Examine the balance sheets savings and loan associations and commercial banks usually have in their lobbies. Look for mortgage loans. If they show comparative balance sheets, find out how much the holdings have increased over the period covered. Compare the competitors. If you have the chance to interview a mortgage loan officer, find out who supplies mortgage money locally.
2. Ask a real estate salesperson about the cost of mortgage money locally. Compare with bond yields from *The Wall Street Journal*.
3. From the same salesperson ask about downpayment requirements and mortgage maturities. Compare with the terms cited in a *Federal Reserve Bulletin*.
4. This salesperson, if he or she has an income property for sale, may be willing to show you the cash-flow projections used in trying to sell the

property. Compare with the cash-flow figures shown in the text illustrations on page 324. Calculate the loan-value ratio for this income property and compare with the same ratio taken from downpayment requirements noted in Problem 3 above. Does this comparison square with generalizations in the text?

STATISTICAL SOURCES

Federal Reserve Bulletin has one of the most compact but comprehensive statistical reports of primary and secondary mortgage markets, terms, yields, amount of activity, and amounts outstanding.

Flow of Funds Accounts, 1946–1975, also published by the Federal Reserve, is primarily useful for longer-term time series.

Fact Book of the United States League of Savings Associations, 111 E. Wacker Drive, Chicago, Ill. 60601, contains an excellent annual survey of activities of the leading thrift institutions and of mortgage market activity.

Mortgage Finance Review, issued quarterly by the Federal Home Loan Mortgage Corporation, supplies excellent regional reports on savings and loan activity and mortgage market developments.

BIBLIOGRAPHY

Bleck, E.K.: "Real Estate Investments and Rates of Return," *Appraisal Journal,* October 1973, pp. 535–547.

Boykin, J.H., and J.S. Philips: "The New Challenger: The Variable-Rate Mortgage," *Real Estate Review,* Summer 1978.

Cassidy, H.J., and J. McElhone: "The Pricing of Variable Rate Mortgages," *Financial Management,* Winter 1975.

Davidson, P.H.: "Structure of the Residential Mortgage Market," *Monthly Review,* Federal Reserve Bank of Richmond, September 1972, pp. 2–6.

Diamond, A.H.: *The Supply of Mortgage Credit,* 1970–1974, U.S. Department of Housing and Urban Development, 1975.

Ford, G.R.: *Ninth Annual Report on the National Housing Goal,* Government Printing Office, Washington, D.C., 1977, Document 82-205. Also House Document 95-53 of the 95th Congress, 1st Session, January 19, 1977.

Klaman, S.B.: *The Postwar Residential Mortgage Market,* National Bureau of Economic Research, Princeton University Press, Princeton, N. J., 1971.

———— and Jack Rubinson: "Mortgage Market: Structure and Characteristics," *Financial Analysts Handbook.* Irwin, Homewood, Ill., 1975.

McConnell, J.J.: "Price Distortion Induced by the Revenue Structure of Federally-Sponsored Mortgage Loan Programs," *Journal of Finance,* September 1977, pp. 1201–1206.

Mortgage Banker: Published by Mortgage Bankers Association of America, 1125 Fifteenth Street, Washington, D.C. 20005.

Real Estate Review: Published quarterly by Warren, Gorhan & Lamont, 210 South Street, Boston, Mass. Edited by faculty of New York University (mostly adjunct professors active in businesses).

Robinson, R.I.: "REIT's: The Risks of Financial Innovation," *MGIC Newsletter,* February 1977.

chapter 16
The Market for
Corporate Debt

The corporation is the dominant form of business organization in the United States. It accounts for about two-thirds of all business income and a somewhat larger proportion of total business capital expenditures. If farming is excluded from noncorporate business, the dominance of the corporation in business affairs is even more pronounced. Unincorporated business gets some external financing from mortgages and bank loans, but it very seldom is able to enter the national capital markets. The next three chapters, therefore, will deal with the corporations in the capital markets; this one with the market for corporate debt, and the following two with the market for corporate equities.

Corporations are of many kinds. Manufacturing corporations still top the list in terms of volume of business done, even though manufacturing is a shrinking part of the economy in relative terms. An enormous diversity characterizes other branches of corporate business. We will be unable to deal separately with all these types, but several will be singled out for separate but brief mention in this chapter—financial corporations particularly, since they make deliberate and extensive use of leverage in their capital structures and are therefore encountered more often in the capital markets than their proportion of business income would suggest.

The statistics presented in this chapter suffer from a number of limitations. For example, corporations organized solely for the owning of income-producing real estate properties, which were mentioned in Chapter 15, are unavoidably included. The flow-of-funds statistics will be used, but in spite of the great expertise in their preparation, surprisingly large and unexplained discrepancies remain.

CORPORATIONS IN THE FINANCIAL MARKETS

Corporations enter the financial markets for added funds when their internal sources of funds are not adequate to pay for the assets they feel they must add to their balance sheets. Conventional corporate finance often classifies the demand for capital into two forms: fixed capital expenditures and net increase in working capital. However, net working capital itself contains some important elements of financing, particularly short-term bank borrowing. For this reason, this chapter will use the somewhat more comprehensive form used by the flow-of-funds system.

In order to understand corporate activities in the financial markets it is necessary to start with some general analytical ideas taken from business finance. Corporations need funds mainly for the following general purposes:

1. Capital expenditures
2. Increases in inventories
3. Increases in accounts receivable
4. Increases in cash balances and other liquid assets
5. Decreases in "automatic" liabilities, mainly accounts payable

Internal financing is the first line of supply of funds. The two principal forms of internal financing are: (1) depreciation (and other noncash expense charges), and (2) retained earnings.

When internal funds are not adequate to meet total corporate needs, corporations then resort to external financing—and this is where financial markets enter the picture. The principal forms of external financing are:

1. Short-term bank loans (see Chapters 9 and 10)
2. Money market debt instruments such as commercial paper (see Chapter 9)
3. Corporate bonds (this chapter)
4. Mortgages (see Chapter 15)
5. Common or preferred stock (see Chapters 17 and 18)

In choosing the combination of the above forms of financing there is one basic guiding principle: that of minimizing the cost of capital. This goal is pursued in various ways. The costs attached to these various forms of financing do not move up and down in parallel fashion. Thus it is tempting to choose the least expensive form of financing available at the time the financing decision has to be made. However, this is not really a free option open to financial managers. A corporation, if it is to enjoy the confidence of financial markets, must meet the standards of the market. This means in the first place that the balance between debt and equity must be within the acceptable range. It also means that the balance between long-term and short-term debt must be acceptable. These are not precise standards but rather ranges. It is *within* these ranges that corporate financial managers can make the choice of the financing vehicle that, at the time of choice, appears to be the least expensive relatively. Tax considerations, of course, are central to this choice.

The demand for funds by nonfinancial corporations follows very closely the growth of GNP; it grows rapidly in good years and then slows down or even reverses itself in poorer years. The principal item in this demand is for fixed capital expenditures. As Figure 16-1 shows, this has been moderately but not excessively variable. The second most important demand factor is for net financial assets: cash, securities, accounts receivable, etc. This also has about the same pattern as fixed capital expenditures, as Figure 16-1 shows. Change in inventory tends to be third in importance in terms of gross dollars, but it is also the most variable and often accounts for much of the year-to-year changes in total demand.

Internal sources can supply only a portion of this demand, as shown in Figure 16-1. Depreciation is the major element of internal funds supply and is, as might be expected of an accounting-determined figure, quite stable. Retained earnings is the other internal supply factor and quite variable. Total profits are highly variable, but dividend distributions much more stable, and so retained earnings, a residual, reflect the full force of profits variation but on a smaller dollar base.

External sources of supply are shown in the remainder of Figure 16-1. New equity issues are both small and highly variable. Bond issues are much larger but still also variable. Mortgage financing is rather variable. Bank loans, however, are the most variable of all. This reflects the fact that banks themselves are sometimes willing and even aggressive lenders while at other times, when money is tight, they may be grudging lenders. But borrowers also shift their views about the desirability of bank loans. Demand may be high when they feel interest rates are temporarily high; demand may slacken when borrowers feel that they have too much short-term debt.

FORMS OF CORPORATE FINANCING

In this analysis of corporate debt we have elected to include both long- and short-term forms of debt. This gives us a somewhat broader scope than if we had limited our inquiry merely to the "market for corporate bonds." The reason for choosing the harder and more complicated alternative is that the two are so closely intertwined in corporate financial management.

From the side of money and capital markets it is quite easy to distinguish the instruments of finance. The corporate bond market stands apart from the market for short-term credit. But from the internal corporate point of view this is not the most important way of dividing the subject matter.

In the minds of corporate management, the important distinction in all financial judgments is between the stockholders' equity and the "outside" funds supplied by others, whether these funds be short- or long-term. Most corporate managements, even those of a professional sort and without a large ownership equity of their own, are conscious of their primary responsibilities to stockholders. Debt is an instrument to be used in such ways and to such extent

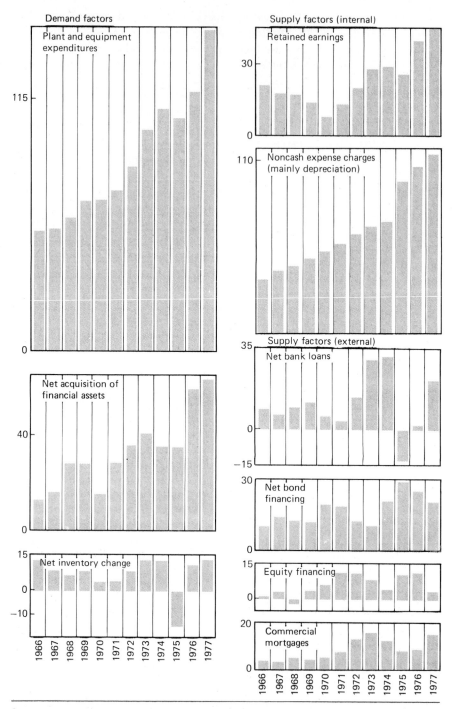

figure 16-1 Factors of Demand and Supply in Corporate Financing (Nonfinancial Corporations). *(Source:* Flow-of-Funds Accounts, *Board of Governors of the Federal Reserve System.)*

as benefit stockholders. Whether the debt be long- or short-term is often a matter of expediency. The traditional way of viewing short-term borrowing is that of covering seasonal needs. Such needs still exist and are serviced, but the prevailing management expectations of bank credit are somewhat broader. The preferred form of financing in almost all corporations is retained earnings. If profit opportunities or competitive pressures create demands for capital expenditures or require working capital expansion that cannot be met from retained earnings, then these expenditures and expansions must be financed externally. If there is no prospect that the debts can be repaid in the short run, then long-term financing is in order. Corporate managements of companies in volatile industries such as manufacturing often seem to hope that this debt can be retired before maturity from retained earnings. No long-term debt is truly long-term in the minds of corporate managements that hope to retire it quickly. In the fields of public utilities or communications (telephone), debt is used to create financial leverage, and then managements expect it to be with them for as long as human foresight runs. However, most financial managers recognize that leverage may be gained from either long- or short-term debt.

Short-term debt is used when the prospects are that the debt can be repaid fairly shortly or when the period for which it is needed is uncertain. Short-term debt is also used sometimes where the expectation of repayment is not very high but where current conditions in the long-term market make deferral of such financing desirable. Intermediate-maturity financing, such as the term loans granted by commercial banks, is frequently used by manufacturing and commercial corporations for very long-term capital expenditures, but where retirement out of retained earnings within a fairly certain intermediate period is thought to be possible. The term loan has not been much used in those industries that expect to have long-term debts for the indefinite future, such as the public utilities and telephone companies.

Short-Term Debt

Some forms of short-term debt arise more or less automatically in the conduct of a business: trade payables and tax liabilities, which have already been mentioned. These amounts have to be carefully controlled and provided for by a prudent financial management. As we have already said, however, these debts are not negotiated in the money or capital markets so will not be considered further here.

A few corporations issue commercial paper that is sold on the open money markets. Some even use bankers' acceptances when they do international business, which is the traditional way in which such financing is generated.[1]

---

[1]This fact shows the influence of tradition in finance and business. In a technical sense there is no reason why domestic transactions should not be used to generate acceptances and to secure some quite low-cost financing from the money markets. Trade credit, however, has become so general that few buying customers would tolerate the practice, and so it is not used. This appears to be no-cost financing for buyers, but in the end it may prove to be costlier for both buyers and sellers than acceptance credit.

The principal form of managed short-term business debt is bank borrowing. Most bank borrowing in the United States is based on long-standing banker-customer relationships. Even though many individual bank borrowing transactions are short-term, they have back of them a quite different and often long-standing relationship. Banks stand ready to accommodate good customers of long standing for all legitimate purposes even at considerable cost to themselves. In tight-money periods banks reduce credit lines and discourage new borrowing customers. An old customer, however, can count on a great deal of support from his or her bank.

This residual use of bank credit leads to wide fluctuations in the amount outstanding. Bank credit tends to grow most during years of high business activity and may be liquidated during slow years. Short-term corporate borrowing is sometimes secured; many ingenious devices such as field warehousing have been invented to make bank lending to marginal businesses possible. Banks prefer customers, however, with a credit standing good enough to make unsecured lending possible.

Long-Term Corporate Debt

The prinicpal form of long-term corporate debt is the corporate bond. The matter of form, however, may conceal far more important factors about the way in which such debt is generated. Bonds are often but not always generated by a public sale. The public sale may be one that is negotiated through an investment banker selected in advance or it may be arranged by holding a competitive bidding in which a number of investment banking syndicates bid for the bonds, the award being made to the highest bidder. Most public utilities are required to use competitive bidding. Most other corporations, free of this requirement, do not use it, but they "negotiate" bond sales.

For a number of years, however, much long-term corporate borrowing has been directly negotiated with the ultimate lenders: "direct placements." Most direct placements have been negotiated with a single life insurance company or a group of life insurance companies. These transactions, for reasons of convenience, are usually in the form of bonds. Thus the word "bond" is not necessarily indicative of the way in which a particular form of debt was originated.

A bond is a debt contract. It is a mortgage bond if it involves a lien on some specific property; otherwise it is a debenture or "unsecured" bond. "Unsecured" is put in quotation marks because a debenture usually has fine security, but of an intangible kind: earning power! Almost all bonds, whether based on a mortgage or on the general earning power of the issuing corporation, have their terms spelled out in a detailed contract called an indenture. This agreement spells out the rights and obligations of both parties, mainly rights of lenders and obligations of the debtor. The terms of this indenture contract are usually left to the enforcement of a trustee who acts for bondholders collectively. The terms of the agreement and the duties of the trustee were spelled out in the Trust Indenture Act of 1939, the result of some irregularities that came to light during the dismal days of the Great Depression.

Maturities of corporate bonds have gone through a number of changes in fashion. At one time very long-term bonds, such as for a hundred years, were not unknown. Most of these very long-term bonds were in the era of railroad expansion when it was expected that bonded indebtedness would be a nearly perpetual part of the capital structures of such operations. Perhaps it was the bad experience with railroad finance that led to a shortening of maturities on corporate bonds.

At present, even public utilities, which expect to continue to use bonded indebtedness for the foreseeable future, almost never sell bonds with maturities exceeding forty years. Thirty years is far more common. Industrial bond maturities almost never exceed thirty years, and twenty- or twenty-five-year terminal maturities are quite frequent. Finance companies tend to sell rather shorter average maturities, probably to give them greater control over their future cost of capital.

Almost all bonds provide for retirement in advance of final maturity by call. Premiums are paid for early calls, but later calls involve lower premiums, and finally there is no penalty.

Most corporate bond issues have only one terminal maturity. It is only in the financing of railroad rolling stock that serial issues (bonds with a sequence of maturities) have appreciable usage. Equipment financing, loans to finance the purchase of machine tools or other types of depreciable fixed assets, is also done with serial-payment or amortized types of loans.

Many term bonds have an indirect provision that may serve about the same purpose as amortization: the sinking fund for retirement of some or all bonds in advance of maturity. Sinking funds are of several complex types that may be reviewed in any good corporate finance textbook. They often provide for calls of partial lots of bonds at prices considerably less than call prices for retirement of an entire issue.

Industries needing large amounts of fixed capital usually depend on bonded indebtedness more than other industries do. Bonded indebtedness is also likely to be incurred at the time of major expansion. This can be illustrated from past railroad history and from past and present public utility history, and the gas and oil pipelines seem to be illustrating this generalization once more.

To some extent investors have changed their view of the value of mortgage security for a bond. Many railroad bankruptcies have shown that a mortgage on a property is of little value unless the property produces a good flow of income. Debentures, which are without mortgage security, have come to be quite acceptable when issued by companies with good earning power. Industrial concerns usually use debenture financing to avoid encumbering fixed property with liens.

The ways of originating bonds have varied greatly by industry. Public utilities and telephone companies are usually required to make public sale of their obligations, and many of them are required to offer them for competitive bidding. On the other hand, one public-utility type of industry, the gas and oil pipelines, has financed large amounts by private placement. Manufacturing industry has used direct placement more than public sale, but some very large corporations appear to exceed the capacity of the direct placement system; these very big ones are so large that private placement with a single buyer is not possible. Once multiple buyers are needed, it seems to be felt that a public distribution is easier to negotiate. An investment banking group handles such transactions, and the indenture terms are tailored to the preferences of the issuing corporation (within the limits of investor prudence). In public offerings of the bonds of a large manufacturing corporation, the investment bankers managing the offerings are usually selected by negotiation and not determined by public bidding. The banker-customer relationship is not as much stressed as it once was, but many corporations clearly feel that there is a great advantage in maintaining a long-standing investment banker relationship. While fear of adverse publicity has led to minimizing the evidence of these relationships, they are undoubtedly close.

Public regulation of the capital markets governs many of the sales practices, including the requirement for competitive bidding in the sale of light and power company bonds. In days gone by, investors were sometimes bilked by unscrupulous security salesmanship. "Blue sky" laws were enacted years ago in many states to counteract this possibility. They were not wholly successful, and, after the Great Depression, the marketing of large issues of debt to the general public came to be regulated by the Securities Act of 1933. The principal effect of this act is very simple: Issuers must tell the truth and the whole truth about themselves and their reasons for borrowing, first in the registration statement and then in the prospectus covering the sale. Chapter 22 will present a more complete and philosophical account of the public regulation of financial markets, but this much can be anticipated: When first adopted, regulation introduced desirable and important changes in the character of corporate financing, but many now wonder if these markets have not progressed to the point where regulation has become more hindrance than help.

In the corporate market, the practice of competitive bidding is concentrated mainly in the sale of public utility bonds. The purpose of the requirement has been to assure the public that the cost of capital was truly competitive and to avoid "banker domination" of these companies. The history of the requirement goes back to some of the abuses in public utility financing disclosed in the Crash of 1929 and dealt with in the Public Utility Holding Company Act of 1935. This is not our story, but it should be looked at by those with special interest in the capital market specializing in public utility obligations.

Competitive bidding requires investment banking firms with the capacity to form syndicates large enough to handle issues of whatever size may be offered. Since only one syndicate can win (and the sale may be called off if only one syndicate submits a bid), half the time or more a syndicate is unsuccessful. Syndication requires flexible organization—the ability to form with minimum cost when a sale is announced, to stay together to sell the bonds if their bid is successful, to complete the sale whether the offering is sold easily or meets adversity, and to reform for new sales when announced. This cycle of activity puts special demands on the flexibility of the system.

Direct placement avoids the open capital market; the whole process is one of negotiation. However, investment bankers are often parties to these negotiations as financial advisers. Direct placement has some appeal because of lower offering cost, but it may have grown because it has some strategic advantages of other sorts. The greatest is that new or unusual financings, which require technical study and might receive poor reception in the open market, may be acceptable in the more limited sphere of highly sophisticated investors.

Life insurance companies' influence on the terms involved in direct placements has been considerable. Since these insurance companies have little need for liquidity, they have offered borrowers relatively long maturities in the form of direct placements, longer than commercial banks have offered in term loans. The repayment provisions have also been influenced by the companies' policies toward call provisions. When the capital markets were easy and investors avid for good bonds, call was permitted almost immediately after issue. While call premiums were a modest barrier to early call, a substantial drop in interest rates often made it advantageous for a borrower to call and refund a higher-coupon issue soon after it had been sold. Several large bond issues sold in 1953 were called and replaced with lower-coupon and lower-yielding issues in 1954. Life insurance companies felt the call option to be unfair and unsymmetrical in its working. They started refusing to buy bonds with early call provisions. Some borrowers had to concede no-call provisions for the first five years. However, some public utility commissions refused to allow the companies they regulated to accede to such terms, and for a considerable period life insurance companies have not been active buyers of public utility bonds.

Bearing this in mind, the life insurance companies have tended to put rather restrictive provisions on the prepayment of bonds directly placed. They permit retirement out of retained earnings (although often with fairly severe penalties), but retirement for purposes of refunding at lower rates is frequently virtually impossible. On other scores, however, the indenture terms applying to direct placements have been reasonably consonant with borrowers' financial needs.

The bank term loan is really more nearly intermediate-term credit than long-term credit. Retirement for refunding purposes is generally prohibited or heavily penalized, as is true of direct placements, but prepayment out of retained earnings is usually allowed completely without penalty. As a result, the life expectancy of term loans as a whole is considerably shorter than their average contractual maturity. Furthermore, term loans are almost always in serial payment form, which makes their average maturity rather shorter than the terminal maturity. The practice with respect to direct placements is not known publicly in full detail, but the presumption is that the serial form of maturity is used less frequently.

For those kinds of business in which cash generation can be fairly rapid and where capital expenditures are limited to projects promising fairly high rates of return, the term loan has many business advantages. The tailoring of terms is useful, but perhaps the most important feature is that the borrower is able to negotiate his or her entire credit needs with a single lender: the commercial bank. This intimacy of financial relationship is highly desirable when the borrower feels the need for continuous contact with a financial adviser. Moderate-sized firms do not find continuous contact with an investment banker possible. They also find a financial relationship with a life insurance company to be rather barren with regard to help and advice. However, the commercial banking relationship has continuity and breadth in terms of financial services.

Term loans also have one material disadvantage: Bankers still have a basic preference for short-term lending. When money markets tighten, commercial banks may limit the amount of term credit they will make available. In the course of cyclical swings, commercial banks are not as dependable a source of longer-term credit as the open capital markets or the direct placement services of life insurance companies.

Leasing: A Competitor of Corporate Bond Financing

Rather than borrowing by means of bonds, a corporation can sometimes obtain the use of a capital asset by leasing it. If the lease is for a short period of time (or can be canceled on short notice), it is not a finance lease; the transaction is a rental. Also, if the lessor of the equipment also services it, the transaction is more a rental than a financial transaction. But if a lease for the full expected life of the capital equipment is involved, if it is noncancelable, and if it is "net" so that the lessee pays taxes, service charges, etc., then the transaction is a true financial lease and is competitive with alternative methods of financing—including corporate bond financing.

Computers, tankers, airplanes, and even whole factories have been leased on these financial terms. The volume of financial leases outstanding has been estimated at over $100 billion. Two reasons have accounted for the growth of leasing: taxes and the accounting treatment of leases. Investment tax credits for any one taxpayer are limited, and a corporation that has hit its limit (or has no taxable income) has no use for such an investment credit. However, other corporations such as banks or high-income individuals might need a tax shield. The lessors, as owners of the equipment, could use this shield. For example, a leasing company (a "packager") might buy a computer for a syndicate of high-income individuals and lease it to the true user. The syndicate members might never see the computer, but they 'own" it and can use the investment credits and depreciation charges in reducing their own taxes. Commercial banks have become active in the field of leasing. Commercial banks have few capital expenditures of their own, so they can use the investment credits without hitting the ceiling allowed by the IRS.

The other advantage to the lessee, formerly, was that lease obligations did not need to be shown on the balance sheet, so published statements showed more moderate debt burdens. This advantage always was less real than believed; competent security analysts could locate such leases and capitalize them and so were not fooled. However, recently the accountants, through their standards procedures, have taken the position that finance leases should be shown on financial statements. However, "operating" leases (those that involve service and are for periods of time shorter than the full life of the equipment) still do not need to be disclosed.

Leasing had great vogue for a while, but many lessees are having second thoughts. "Residual" value (the value of the equipment at the end of the lease period) has turned out to be greater than expected because of inflation—and this value is retained by lessors. Leasing of very big ticket items seems to be on the decline. Leasing of intermediate-type equipment, however, seems to be still strong. This includes such items as costly diagnostic equipment for doctors and hospitals and minicomputers for small business.

THE SUPPLIERS OF CREDIT TO CORPORATIONS

In the 1920s individuals were the most important buyers of corporate bonds: They held about two-thirds of those outstanding. During the low-interest-rate period of the 1930s, however, individuals lost interest in this market and it came to be dominated by life insurance companies and mutual savings banks. Commercial banks also bought some corporate bonds. Much of this interest, however, was expressed in the secondary market, since the amount of new issues sold by corporations during that period was small. Considerable refunding took place when lower interest rates made it profitable to call the older higher-coupon obligations and replace them with lower-coupon ones. While refunding does not take any net amount of money from the capital markets, it is likely to cause a fair amount of redistribution of ownership. This seems to have happened during the 1930s. The individuals who were holders of the high-coupon obligations might have been unwilling to accept the new rates; financial institutions, being under more pressure for current interest income, were forced to do so.

During this period, insurance companies developed the direct placement technique. At first, it was primarily a competitive tactic for ensuring priority in access to the limited supply of investment outlets. Life insurance companies also saved the costs of marketing when they were large enough to handle such transactions. To some extent the same situation prevailed in the early days after World War II, when financial institutions were trying to lighten their holdings of U.S. government obligations and to convert portfolios into higher-yielding forms.

The basic shift, from that time when there was a shortage of investment outlets to the present time of high capital demand, has led to fundamental shifts in the marketing process. Faced with a much more active demand for loans, commercial banks virtually stopped buying corporate bonds (rail equipment obligations were a slight exception) and bought only tax-exempt securities or Treasury obligations. All long-term funds made available to corporations were in the form of term loans. Mutual savings banks continued to buy a few corporate obligations, but as mortgage demand revived, their interest in them dwindled. Life insurance companies were buyers for a while, but when they came to feel that the call provisions were unfairly weighted against them, the larger ones left the open market and concentrated on direct placements. As near as can be read from public evidence, they changed the nature of direct placement in the process. Direct placements, at first, were competitive with open-market rates. Under these new circumstances, however, life insurance companies started extending credit more at the margin of creditworthiness and charging much higher rates. They were making long-term corporate credit available to a group of borrowers that might have found the open corporate bond market a little hard to crack. The life insurance companies, however, charged them a good stiff price for this credit.

With so many buyers departing from the market, where was the slack taken up? During the postwar period it was taken up mainly by the pension funds, both public and private, but particularly the former. Later, individuals returned to the corporate bond market.

Pension funds have existed for a long period; their investment policies have varied greatly. Some private pension funds have consisted mostly of the stock of the company sponsoring them, as in the case of Sears, Roebuck. Some favored the bonds of their sponsoring company, as did the pension fund of the American Telephone and Telegraph Company. Public pension funds (teachers' and other state and local government funds) were often limited wholly to governmental obligations.

The postwar emphasis on fringe benefits in the attraction of good personnel gave the pension funds a strong boost. Tax factors favored receiving a part of one's pay in such funds and security was still highly prized by persons considering changing jobs, particularly those who could remember the Great Depression.

Not only did the number of pension funds greatly increase, but for a variety of reasons the trustees of these funds came to be under greater pressure to increase the rate of return on them. Sometimes they switched from fixed-return types of investment such as bonds into common equities, a point that is noted at length elsewhere. Some funds shifted from lower-yielding bonds into better-paying bonds. One of the most dramatic changes was that of public retirement funds, some of which had been investing only in state and local government or federal government obligations. When the investment authority of many funds was broadened, they then became great buyers of corporate bonds. In this process the corporate bond market found quite a new set of customers. The salesmen of investment banking firms that had been calling on life insurance companies and mutual savings banks found themselves calling more and more on the trustees of pension funds.

As we already demonstrated in Figure 16-1, the net volume of corporate bonds is quite variable. Part of this is doubtless a funds demand factor, but it is also evident that the supply of funds by the various investor groups is even more variable, as is demonstrated in Figure 16-2. Each major investor group has its own explanation for variability. Individuals flock into the corporate bond market when yields get so high as to be considerably in excess of interest rates at savings institutions. When bond interest rates retreat, individuals leave the market almost completely. Mutual savings banks buy corporate bonds when depositors bring them more funds than mortgage money demand will absorb. Life insurance companies are reasonably stable and usually the leading investors. Private pension funds turn to corporate bonds when their view of the stock market turns negative. State and local government pension funds are the

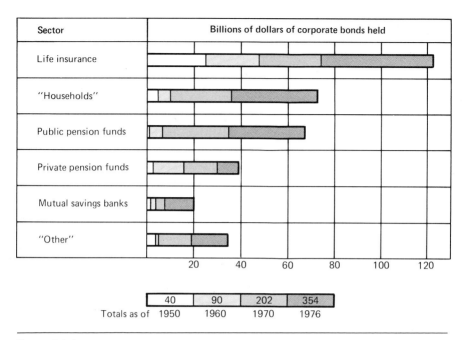

Sector	Billions of dollars of corporate bonds held
Life insurance	
"Households"	
Public pension funds	
Private pension funds	
Mutual savings banks	
"Other"	

	40	90	202	354
Totals as of	1950	1960	1970	1976

figure 16-2 Holdings of Corporate Bonds by Leading Investor Sectors. *(Source:* Flow-of-Funds Accounts; *and* Quarterly Review, *Federal Reserve Bank of New York, Autumn 1977, p. 28.)*

most stable purchasers of corporate bonds as well as the second leading among institutional investors.

MARKETING INSTITUTIONS

When corporate borrowing is arranged directly, such as with commercial banks or with life insurance companies, no separate marketing institution intervenes between borrower and lender. In most other types of arrangements, however, the investment banker facilitates the financing process.

The investment banker is, traditionally, at the very center of capital market operations. In the nineteenth century investment bankers often were the midwives of great corporations, as when the elder J. P. Morgan created U.S. Steel out of an idea and a bold deal with Andrew Carnegie. Investment bankers sat on the boards of directors of the corporations that needed money from the markets; they also sat on the boards of directors of the financial institutions that were investors, such as banks and life insurance companies. Relationships were long-term and paternalistic. Investment bankers made, and then sometimes broke, the managements of the great corporations. Finance was frequently in the saddle of corporate control.

This picture has changed. The Great Depression put investment banking on the defensive. The ties between investment bankers and life insurance companies were weakened as long ago as before World War I by a great investigation (the Armstrong investigation in which Charles Evans Hughes played a large part). Legislation in 1933 prohibited individual institutions from engaging in both commercial banking and investment banking.

Probably the greatest change was that corporations broke their bondage to finance; slack demand for money and the availability of retained earnings made them bargainers on more nearly equal terms. Investment bankers are now wise and helpful members of corporate boards of directors, but they seldom control them nor make an effort to do so. They have been reduced more nearly to their core function: marketing corporate and other debt obligations.

In performing this function, investment bankers have developed great expertise. Many corporations prefer to maintain a continuing relationship with a single investment banking house. That firm forms and manages any syndicates needed to market public offerings that the corporation may make. The investment banker is expert in many ways, two of which should be mentioned. First, markets are changeable and the expert investment banker is a good judge of timing (When should a borrower come to the market?). Second, the investment banker is adept at picking the appropriate terms to be put in the bond indenture so they are acceptable to investors under prevailing preferences but leave the borrowing corporation the freedom and flexibility it needs to meet possible future contingencies. Though less noticed than the coupon rate on new bonds, variations in indenture terms are often of considerable significance.

Even though a single investment banking house may keep such a long-term and intimate relationship with a corporation, it usually cannot wisely assume all the marketing risk of underwriting (guaranteeing the sale of) a large issue. To spread this risk, syndicates (short-term joint ventures) are formed among a group of underwriters. The firm (or firms) heading a syndicate expect reciprocity. That is, they expect to be invited to join the syndicates their invitees may form. Reciprocity is a little like the exchange of dinner invitations by couples (who keep track of who owes whom a dinner as precisely as racetrack bookies keep accounts with their customers). Investment bankers many times are partners on one venture and competitors on another at the same time. Underwriters, as contractors of the sale of an obligation, are often joined by still other financial houses who share in the selling operations but are not involved in the core underwriting process. Part of the art of being an effective leading investment banking house and of managing syndicates is choosing good associates, keeping them happy, and having the expert judgment to avoid frequent losses or slow sales that tax the patience and financial resources of smaller members of investment banking syndicates and selling groups.

When bonds are sold by competitive bidding among investment bankers, the connection of any one investment banker with an issuer is necessarily a more detached and impersonal relationship. Since investment bankers cannot know in advance whether or not they will "win" bonds in the bidding, they cannot spend a great deal of time or energy giving advice or helping the company prepare the issue. The issuing company's lawyers and financial advisers draw up the indentures. Most important of all, an issuing company must announce its intention of selling bonds some time in advance of the sale so that bidding groups can be formed. Timing cannot be precisely judged. The issuer can seek financial advice about the matter of timing, but in the end the decision is its own. Since the mechanics of competitive bidding are fairly costly and since issuers do not wish to lose the good will of possible bidders, an issuer is fairly well committed, practically if not legally, to selling bonds on the announced sale date once it has issued a firm "invitation to bid."

On the other side, competitive bidding does bring out rather close pricing. Underwriters experience difficulties in marketing competitively bought issues with enough frequency to suggest that they usually come rather close to the top price investors will pay in bidding to get bonds. No one can prove whether competitive bids or negotiated sales bring lower borrowing costs, but in either case large American corporations have little to quarrel about; they get good bargains in bond money.

Once bonds are in the hands of investment bankers, whether by negotiation or by competitive bidding, the sale process is as rapid as possible. The offering of such bonds is announced by advertisement, but the detailed information required by security analysts and investors is in a prospectus prepared according to the regulations of the Securities and Exchange Commission and also in the even more detailed registration statement filed with that commission. Since the prospectus usually has been available in "red herring" form (without a final price but with some red printing on it indicating that it is a preliminary document), investors have already studied the issue and the current position of the company as revealed by this and other evidence. The only remaining fact to be disclosed is the price itself.

As soon as a syndicate has won a bid, telephone selling starts. With good luck and planning, an issue will be sold before its formal advertisement appears in the newspapers. Ability to buy an issue after the appearance of an ad for a corporate bond issue may indicate that it is not selling any too well. (This is not true of state and local government issues, as was shown in Chapter 14.) Negotiated financings are presold to a greater extent than bonds sold through competitive bidding. The current market among pension funds and smaller life insurance companies is concentrated, so that a few telephone calls often serve to move a whole issue. A successful issue is one that achieves a small premium soon after the sale.

Although some investment banking houses are better known for their support of and skill in competitive bidding and some are better known for negotiated sales, most investment banking houses are prepared to operate in either fashion. Some houses pride themselves in taking leadership and some are mainly selling houses, but hard and fast classification of investment banking houses is not possible.

The efficiency of this system is high; it raises capital at low marketing cost. On big bond issues, the margin is often less than 1 percent. Even on moderate-sized bond issues the cost seldom exceeds 2 percent. It is only on smaller bond issues (under $5 million) that the cost is likely to exceed these levels.

SECONDARY MARKET IN CORPORATE BONDS

Nobody knows exactly how large the secondary market in corporate bonds is or ever was. The volume of transactions in corporate bonds on the NYSE has grown less rapidly than the volume outstanding. The turnover of listed bonds is very low. However, it appears (no statistics exist to prove the point) that convertible and low-grade bonds dominate the NYSE bond trading. Within this group, the rate of activity may be fairly high.

The secondary market in corporate bonds, therefore, is largely an over-the-counter (OTC) market. Relatively few firms made OTC markets in corporate bonds. All underwriters nominally made such markets for a short time after a new issue was sold, but nonconvertible bonds appear to have gone untraded most of the time. However, the high interest rates of recent years may have increased the relative as well as the absolute size of the corporate bond secondary market. Some evidence grows out of the fact that more firms are in the business of making OTC markets in corporate bonds. It also appears that the portfolio managers for pension funds are more willing to shift position. Sometimes, secondary market movement appears to be related to the new-issue market. A practice called "overtrading" is one in which an underwriting house, anxious to move its allotment of new bonds, will trade the new issue for an outstanding one and on such terms that investors get a better deal. The syndicate price is not violated in any formal sense, but the profit margin of the sellers certainly is thinned by this process.

INTEREST RATE RELATIONSHIPS

The interest rates on corporate bonds are rather closely geared to the whole interest rate structure of the market. Interest rates are one of the more volatile of prices. While long-term rates move through smaller ranges than short-term rates, their movements produce fairly large price effects in bonds, putting interest rates in a class with agricultural commodities and world-traded raw materials.

The interest received on corporate bonds is taxable income to the holders to the extent that the owners are subject to federal income taxes. In this regard corporate bonds are quite different from the tax-exempt state and local government issues, but they are like those of the federal government, which made all its debt issues taxable in 1941. Nevertheless, all these interest rates tend to move together, depending on general conditions in the money and capital markets.

Yields on Aaa or highest-grade corporate bonds move in a fashion parallel with those of the government and just slightly above them. The rate movements are slightly less volatile than those of U.S. government obligations, but most major movements are mirrored one in the other. The average maturity of the so-called long-term U.S. government obligation is actually somewhat shorter than the average maturity of Moody's Aaa corporate bonds; if maturities were comparable, the two yields would be even closer together.

The rating of corporate bonds by Moody's and Standard & Poor's has not involved controversy similar to that with respect to tax-exempt bonds. A research study by Hickman, cited in Chapter 7, showed that the ratings were reasonably well supported by relative default experience. That test, however, was of bond performance during the Great Depression. Since there has been nothing even faintly approaching the number of large business failures or episodes of financial difficulties since that time, the applicability of the ratings to present conditions is not as clear. Some portfolios of bonds are often limited to only top-rated bonds—state and local government pension funds, for example. However, more sophisticated bond investors have come to feel that the ratings exaggerate differences in credit quality and that the higher yield of the lower ratings may more than compensate for the credit risk assumed. Episodes such as the failure of the Penn-Central Railroad still shock the market into a retreat from the lower credit ratings, but some of the new bond funds aim frankly at increasing yield even at the cost of some risk.

Secondary market interest rates seem to fluctuate less than those prevailing in primary new-issue markets. The levels of new-issue yields do not differ greatly from secondary market yields in lower-rate periods. The differences become material, however, in periods of tighter money and higher rates. One technical factor explains a part of the difference. The secondary market during the 1960s handled many lower-coupon issues that gave investors part of their return in capital gains form as the discount on such lower-coupon issues was accumulated. This gave a better after-tax yield than indicated by market rates. Some tax-exposed bond investors sought out lower-coupon bonds in the secondary market for this purpose. Overall, however, it seems likely that the new-issue yields are economically more significant. Larger investors can fulfill their investment needs only in this market. If a bond is issued during a high interest rate period with an early call possible, the price of this bond will bump up against its call price in any subsequent decline in interest rates. Since investors shy away from a bond that does not protect their future income, the yield on this bond may stay above other bonds of comparable quality and maturity but with a coupon that does not bring its price near the call level. Because both low-coupon and high-coupon bonds are affected by special factors in the secondary market, the new-issue market yield appears to be more significant economically.[2]

The high interest rate period of the late 1960s and through the 1970s showed clearly the influence of callability on yield. It appears that a bond issuer, reserving to itself the right to an early call, had to pay possibly as much as half a percentage point more than on a comparable issue with call protection for five years. However, yield differences between five-year and ten-year call protection were not as evident.

Sporadic research on the subject of new versus secondary market yields has indicated that when yields were low and the corporate bond market was

[2]William H. White, "The Structure of the Bond Market and the Cyclical Variability of Interest Rates," *Staff Papers of the International Monetary Fund*, March 1962.

stagnant, new-issue yields tended to be *under* secondary market yields. However, when yields rose, the relationship would reverse. This was consistent with the logic that when yields rose, outstanding bonds with lower coupons had two advantages: (1) part of the return was taxed at capital gains and (2) such bonds were more protected against early call.

Even at high interest rate levels, the new-issue yeild can fall *under* the secondary market yeilds in spite of heavy market offerings. This circumstance prevailed during much of 1971 and throughout all 1972. The differential, however, is not large. A possible explanation, so far not tested with research, is that the excess of secondary market yields over new-issue yields both now and in earlier times is accounted for by this fact: New-issue yields are essentially "ask" prices and secondary market quotations are essentially "bid" prices. The differential may be nothing more than the normal bid-and-ask spread.

Since 1972, the differential has narrowed and has not persistently been either positive or negative. This suggests that, except for the tax factor already mentioned, the new-issue market yield and the yields on outstanding obligations tend to be almost identical except for the vagaries of measurement, which are considerable. Bonds of corporations are not homogeneous instruments, and small differences in yields can reflect nothing more than differences in the character and quality of the issuers that are too small to measure by the bond ratings.

Another difference is that these open-market yields, whether from secondary markets or new-issue markets, seem to vary somewhat from those reported to prevail in the case of direct placements. An extensive study of direct placements and the yields on them found that the credit quality of direct placements was somewhat lower than that of the bonds offered in the public market.[3] When allowance is made for this factor, yeilds on direct placements were shown to be higher than those in the public new-bond-issue market by approximately an amount equal to the greater cost of a public offering. In other words, the borrowers may not have paid materially more than they would have had to pay in the public market (assuming that they could have qualified for it at all), but the lenders increased their return by doing the work necessary for developing an effective and protective loan contract.

During the stock market boom of 1967 and 1968, the volume of convertible bonds offered the public market increased materially but in the mid-1970s declined greatly. However, the proportion has never been a large part of the total public bond market. Direct placements, on the other hand, were usually joined with some form of equity participation. In this respect direct placements were quite parallel to the mortgage loans on income-producing real estate ventures described in Chapter 15. It is also significant that the volume of direct placements did not grow materially during the upsurge of public offerings starting in the late 1960s.

[3]Avery B. Cohan, *Yields on Corporate Debt Directly Placed*, Columbia University Press, New York, 1967. A part of the financial research program of the National Bureau of Economic Research.

FINANCE COMPANY DEBT

Finance companies extend consumer loans, buy installment paper from auto and other hard-goods dealers, factor accounts receivable for corporations, and lend on inventories. Some finance companies are "captive" subsidiaries of manufacturing concerns who use them not only for profit but also as a way of supporting their sales efforts. (General Motors Acceptance Corporation or GMAC, is a captive finance subsidiary.)

Finance companies use a high degree of leverage—not as much as banks, but much more than nonfinancial corporations. They are the main direct sellers of commercial paper mentioned in Chapter 9. They also borrow directly from banks. In addition they also sell debentures to the bond market. These debentures are unsecured and may be subordinated to other debts. The volume of finance-company debt is about one-sixth of the total corporate debt. The average maturity is slightly shorter than that of nonfinancial corporations: ten to twenty years rather than twenty to forty.

Banks obtain about one-tenth of their capital funds by issuing capital notes, a form of corporate bond. The volume of bank bonds outstanding is about 1 percent of total corporate debt.

BONDS OF FOREIGN ISSUERS

Since the repeal of the interest equalization tax, there has been a substantial volume of bond issues sold in the United States market by foreign issuers. These issuers include foreign governments, foreign governmental agencies and municipalities, as well as private foreign issuers. However, for analytical purposes these issues are included with corporate bonds since the marketing facilities are much the same as those for domestic corporate bonds, and they tend to be bought by the same group of investors that buy corporate bonds since they have the same tax status as domestic corporate bonds. These foreign issues are generally handled on a negotiated basis (rather than by competitive bidding) by leading investment bankers with strong international connections and are viewed as very profitable business by these investment banking firms.

The volume of these issues is a product of two factors: comparative interest rates and the availability of funds in large amounts. In general, long-term interest rates in the United States have tended to be lower than elsewhere in the world. What is more, the amount of money that can be raised by a single issue in the United States is considerably more than in any foreign capital market, including the Eurobond market. As Chapter 20 will show, these foreign bond sales in the United States have an adverse effect on our balance of payments. Nevertheless, the interest equalization tax, which was aimed at this very problem, was felt to be a barrier to good international relations and so it was removed. Canada was exempt from this tax and for a long time has been a major borrower in our markets. Recently both Japan and the Scandinavian countries have often sold their bonds in our capital markets.

PROJECTS AND QUESTIONS

1. Using one or more current issues of *The Wall Street Journal*, locate ads relating to corporate debt financing. Try to distinguish between private placements and public offerings. Within public offerings, try to distinguish between those acquired by competitive bid and those sold to the underwriters by negotiation.
2. Business libraries often have copies of corporate annual reports. Select annual reports for several types of corporations (public utilities, manufacturing, sales, finance, etc.) with some debt in their capital structure. Try to determine how these debt issues were marketed. Also try to determine the corporate circumstances that necessitated external financing. Any ideas why debt financing was chosen?

STATISTICAL SOURCES

The *Statistical Bulletin* of the SEC contains the greatest detail on the volume of new issues, volume of trading in secondary markets (organized), and amounts outstanding. The SEC also issues a *Bulletin* dealing with regulatory actions affecting securities markets.

The *Federal Reserve Bulletin* contains somewhat more summary details of new offerings but with comparison with other types of securities.

The *Flow-of-Funds, 1946–75*, published by the Federal Reserve, contains detailed estimates of the ownership and acquisitions of corporate securities by the leading financial sectors. The sector analysis of corporations and noncorporate business units also can be used in the analysis of the causes of demand for financing.

The Wall Street Journal in news reports, ads, and sometimes in tabular form reports on new offerings and secondary market transactions.

BIBLIOGRAPHY

Cohan, A. B.: *Yields in Corporate Debt Directly Placed,* National Bureau of Economic Research Study, Columbia University Press, New York, 1967.

The Daily Bond Buyer: One State Street Plaza, New York, New York 10004. And by the same publisher at the same address: *The Money Manager* (formerly *Weekly Bond Buyer*).

Ederington, L. H.: "Negotiated versus Competitive Underwritings of Corporate Bonds," *Journal of Finance,* March 1976, pp. 17–28. Good bibliography.

Handorf, W. C.: "Flexible Debt Financing," *Financial Management,* Summer 1974.

Homer, S., and M. L. Leibowitz: *Inside the Yield Book,* Prentice-Hall, Englewood Cliffs, N. J., 1972.

Jen, F. C., and J. E. Wert: "The Deferred Call Provision and Corporate Bond Yields," *Journal of Financial and Quantitative Analysis,* June 1968, pp. 157–169.

Johnson, K. B., T. G. Morton, and M. C. Findley III: "An Analysis of the Flotation Costs of Corporate Quasi-Equity Securities," *Financial Management,* Winter 1975.

————, ————, and————: "An Empirical Analysis of the Flotation Cost of Corporate Securities 1971–1972," *Journal of Finance,* September 1975, pp. 1129–1133.

Lindvall, J. R.: "New Issue Corporate Bonds, Seasoned Market Efficiency and Yield Spreads," *Journal of Finance,* September 1977, pp. 1057–1067.

White, W. H.: "The Structure of the Bond Market and the Cyclical Variability of Interest Rates," *Staff Papers of the International Monetary Fund,* March 1962.

Zwick, B.: "The Market for Corporate Bonds," *Quarterly Review,* Federal Reserve Bank of New York, Autumn 1977, pp. 27–36.

chapter 17
The Market for
Corporate Equities

As these words are being written, the subject of this chapter—the market for corporate equities—faces the prospect of radical change. This market has changed before—it is a very old market, almost as old as our nation—but the type of change it now faces is more drastic than any changes of the past and may ultimately lead to the disappearance of the face-to-face auction market that has characterized the New York Stock Exchange. The noble old building at the corner of Broad and Wall Streets may remain, and it may even continue to serve some purpose in this industry; but its essential function, the face-to-face auction of securities, may be taken over by a new group of institutions working with the new tools of electronic communication.

Our strategy for dealing with change, the character of which we do not yet know, will be to emphasize the functional structure of the market rather than going into much detail in description of its operations. The basic trading function will remain for any new market system to perform. We will, to illustrate these functions, give some account of past and present market structure. Then, to close this chapter, we shall describe the forces that are making drastic change in this market virtually inevitable.

The market for corporate equities is divided into two organizational sectors: (1) the markets provided by organized securities exchanges and (2) the so-called over-the-counter (OTC) market (which is, of course, an "over-the-telephone" market). The bond markets, reviewed in Chapters 13, 14 and 16, are dominantly over-the-counter markets. The equities market is concentrated more on the organized exchanges than the bond markets are. The New York Stock Exchange (NYSE) dominates the organized market. The American Stock Exchange (AMEX) is much smaller, though still larger than the regional exchanges that do moderate but growing amounts of business.

CORPORATE EQUITIES: DOMINANTLY A SECONDARY MARKET

Perhaps the leading characteristic setting this market apart from other segments of the capital markets is that it is so dominantly a secondary market; most trading is in securities that are already outstanding. New equity capital is raised by established corporations rather rarely, but ownership of their outstanding equities is transferred at a brisk clip.

This characteristic goes back to the way in which corporation finance is conducted. Corporate equity capital largely originates in retained earnings. This fact is even more true in an economist's sense than it is in an organizational sense. Most corporations start very small, with only the funds of the founders, their friends and families, and sometimes other backers. In terms of number, though not dollar size, most corporations continue throughout their lives to be so closely held. If they grow, they grow by virtue of retained earnings. After such growth, these companies may "go public" in the sense that some portion of the original owners' shares is sold on the impersonal public market. Such transactions dominate the statistics of so-called new equity issues. In an economic sense, however, these are not new issues; new capital is not being raised—rather, the small group of original owners is selling out some portion of its ownership to the public. This is why it was said above that the equities market is even more a secondary market in an economic sense than in an organizational sense.

The volume of trading on the organized securities exchanges far exceeds that in any other segment of the capital market. In the year 1968 this volume approached $200 billion, and in 1972 it went over this level. If the volume of trading in the OTC were included, the total is more than $250 billion. Since then, except for a brief period in 1978, the volume of trading has not approached that level.

Although the volume of trading in this secondary market is larger than in any other capital market, it is not particularly large relative to the value of securities outstanding. A comparison of the volume of trading with total market value suggests that the average holding period for equity investors appears to be about five years. However, this trading volume includes that of members of the NYSE who have much shorter holding periods. If the trading volume of members and other short-term speculators is removed from the figures, the average public investor probably tends to have a holding period that is much longer; possibly near ten years. As we shall see later, the gradual growth of institutions as holders of equities has led to some increase in trading activity; their average holding period is shorter than that of the individual investor.

An exception to the general rule that the organized stock exchanges are secondary markets should be noted. Preemptive rights of existing stockholders in some corporations give them a first chance at buying any new voting stock offered by such companies. In addition, existing shareholders may have the "right" to purchase any debentures that are convertible into equities. Even though not required to do so by law, some corporations employ rights financing as an economical means of raising new equity capital. The volume of rights financing varies directly with the strength of the equity market. When stock prices are booming, rights financing becomes more frequent; when the market weakens, the volume drops off. Even so, the volume is never very great when compared with the larger magnitudes of financing for corporations.

When the stock market is looked at as a source of new capital, it is far less important than several other capital markets. The $14 billion raised in the new-issue equity market in 1971 was far higher than in any other year of record. In the other years of the preceding decade, the volume of new capital raised was between $3 billion and $9 billion and averaged only about $5 billion. Mortgages, corporate bonds, state and local government securities, issues of the federal government, and even consumer credit drew more on saving than equity financing.[1]

It is entirely possible that future years will see a renewed volume of equity financing. Corporations came out of World War II with high liquidity and little debt. For the first two postwar decades, new equity financing was modest relative to capital expenditures. Such new financing as was needed could easily be done with debt. Furthermore, debt financing had clear tax advantages since interest, but not dividends, is a tax-deductible expense. While the tax advantage of debt financing remains, the capital structures of many corporations have now been expanded with about as much debt as is prudent, and thus further external financing requires some injection of new equity capital.

The positive economic contribution of secondary equity markets is frequently misunderstood. Many look upon these equity markets primarily as speculative outlets. The volume of trading tends to increase whenever prices are rising; it falls off greatly when prices stabilize, even at high levels, and increases again on declines. Excess emphasis on speculation, however, tends to conceal the economic function of equity trading. In effect, corporate equities are perpetuities. An individual owner, limited to the natural life-span of a person, can realize on a market investment only by giving the equity to an heir or selling it in the market. Sale permits the individual to adjust his or her portfolio to changing needs, tastes, and expectations. The much-abused word "liquidity" reflects the purpose served by equity markets; they allow owners to liquidate their holdings quickly. Prices fluctuate (and some feel that equity prices fluctuate irrationally and excessively), but the existence of the equity markets makes equities more liquid—at a price.

The owners of shares in closely held corporations have a hard time liquidating such investments. Some of them are able to sell out to colleagues or friends, but they cannot all be certain of being able to do so. This shortcoming often explains why prosperous, closely held companies go public. Principal owners often have no need of cash but foresee the time in their personal affairs

---

[1]Professor Roger Murray, in the first Buttonwood lecture (published as an undated pamphlet by Columbia University and NYSE), suggested that retained earnings should be considered as capital "raised" by the stock market, since it is this market that gives investors the chance both to use new funds and to liquidate holdings increased by retained earnings. The idea is not without merit, but it strains the concept of markets beyond its normal boundaries.

when they will need a market for their shares. In such sales, owners frequently sell only a portion of their holdings, but enough to create a fairly active trading market. This market serves to evaluate the remaining shares they own and to give them financial maneuverability.

THE OWNERSHIP OF CORPORATE EQUITIES

As we have seen, the majority of other capital market instruments are owned directly by intermediary financial institutions with individuals on the other side of the balance sheets of these intermediaries. In the case of equities, the dominant ownership is, and will be for many years, directly in individuals. Table 17-1 gives estimates taken from the *Flow-of-Funds* statistics.

The principal message of Table 17-1 is that while households continue to dominate the ownership of corporate equities, their proportion is steadily diminishing while that of institutions is increasing. Foreign holdings are also increasing slightly. The expansion of institutional ownership is mainly by pension funds. Pension funds, as long-term investors, are able to accept the short-term swings in price and return that characterize common stocks, in return for the higher return in the long run that has generally characterized our financial history.

Although the proportion of corporate equities owned by households has shown a long-term decline, the *number* of persons greatly increased in the postwar period. Such ownership went from 6.5 million in 1952 to a peak of about 32 million persons in 1972. Since that time, however, the number of individuals owning corporate equities has diminished more than 5 million. This decline was presumably accounted for by relatively small holders of stocks, many of whom had entered the market through the vehicle of mutual funds or investment companies that had encouraged expectations of high returns that never materialized. In fact, the returns during the decade covered by Table 17-1 was in general a disappointing one to investors in corporate equities even though the all-time high in the stock market was scored during the middle of

TABLE 17-1
Ownership of Corporate Equities: Market Value

Sector	Amounts in Billions of Dollars					
	1967		1972		1977 (est.)	
	Amount	Percent of total	Amount	Percent of total	Amount	Percent of total
Households	$686	83.3	$ 876	76.7	$610	70.2
Institutions	122	14.8	238	20.8	230	26.4
Foreign	16	1.9	28	2.5	30	3.4
Total	$824	100.0	$1142	100.0	$870	100.0

SOURCE: *Flow of Funds Accounts 1946–1975*, Board of Governors of the Federal Reserve System, 1976, p. 145.

this decade in 1972. In the first half of this decade the overall return of corporate equity investors was about 10 percent per annum. During the second half of the decade, however, such investors suffered a net loss of about 2 percent per annum. For the decade as a whole the average annual return was only about 4 percent; considerably less than was available by bond investment or even investment in ordinary savings accounts. It was a poor return on the average, combined with the great variability of return for shorter periods of time.

Share ownership exists in all fifty states. It is clear, however, that the incidence of such ownership is relatively more common in the northeastern states than in the agricultural states; also that the share ownership is more common in cities than in rural areas. Ownership of small blocks of shares doubtless imposes a considerable cost on corporations, but it is a burden they bear willingly for the sake of its public relations value.

The institutions in the stock market are of several different types. Some are virtually pure intermediaries; some are far more complex both in purpose and operation. The closest to a pure intermediary in the equity market is the mutual fund or investment company. This type of institution interposes professional investment analysis and portfolio selection between the ultimate investor and the equity market, and it charges a fee for the service. Most of these investment companies are "open-end," which means that investors can be added and can also withdraw. Some open-end investment companies have sales loading charges in addition to management fees; others are "no-load" in form. A small number of closed-end investment companies, most of whom were organized many years ago, are listed on the NYSE. Open-end companies cannot be listed; they are directly sold and redeemed.

Life insurance companies and pension funds have come to be very large equity investors. The reason is fear of inflation. Both life insurance and pensions involve very long-term liabilities. Since the value of both life insurance and pensions is eroded by inflation, there has been an effort to offset this influence by investment in common stock. In fact, some pensions are now partly annuities that are related to the level of equity prices.

In the statistics of trading volume, the NYSE treats commercial banks as institutional investors. They are, in fact, the most important of such institutional investors in terms of trading volume. However, the basis for this is that commercial bank trust departments manage or operate many trusts. Total trust assets are over $300 billion, of which common stocks are over $200 billion—half in pension trusts and the rest in personal trusts. Legally this is not an intermediary relationship; the commercial bank does not interpose its balance sheet between the investor and the market. Individuals are the direct beneficial owners of the trusteed shares. However, for all operational purposes, the investment activities of the trust departments of commercial banks are so similar to those of true intermediary investors that this is the more realistic view of the equity market. Treating equity securities in trust accounts as "institutional" raises such ownership to about a third of total equities. Since the volume statistics of the NYSE show that institutional trading exceeds that of individuals, this means that the turnover of institutional equity portfolios is materially higher than that of individual or "household" equity portfolios.

THE ORGANIZED EXCHANGES

The principal characteristic of an organized exchange is that it provides a physical place for trading and enforces rules of trading that govern all transactions on the trading floor as well as the relationship of brokers to their public customers. The physical trading area involves a kind of face-to-face double auction. The spot at which a specific security is to be traded is designated. At this "post" records of past prices and trades are kept, and from it reports can be quickly dispatched both with respect to price (to the public) and execution (to the buyer and seller). All trades involve public "crying out" of bids and offers. A broker does well to have a strong and durable voice.

The trading rules not only require the public calling of bids and offers; they also require that the best price prevail, the highest available for sellers and lowest for buyers. No playing of favorites is allowed; a bidding broker must buy from the quoting broker who offers the lowest price. Furthermore, the rules forbid sham transactions used only to bull up prices or to bear them down. Any sort of rigging of the market or collusion between brokers is forbidden. While these are hard rules to enforce and violations probably occur from time to time, trading almost certainly has become far more honest than was true in earlier and wilder days.

Among organized exchanges, the NYSE dominates. In terms of dollar volume, a far better measure than number of shares, the NYSE has accounted for close to 80 percent of all trading on organized exchanges. American Stock Exchange volume fluctuates, but it has averaged around 10 percent of the total. The remainder is accounted for mainly by several regional exchanges of which the Midwest, the Pacific Coast, and the Philadelphia-Baltimore-Washington stock exchanges have been the three most important.

On organized exchanges, trading takes place among members, who have the privilege of trading on the floor of the exchange. Some members act as specialists, a few trade solely for their own account, some trade for other members, but the great bulk of them trade for, and generally are partners in, commission brokerage firms. The major business of most commission broker-age firms is offering buying-and-selling service to the public. These members may trade for their own account, but they usually consider commission brokerage to be their principal activity. Commission brokerage houses may be linked with investment banking firms or departments of them, but some specialize in providing just this service. Commission brokerage business in securities may also be allied with commission brokerage in commodity markets or even other types of markets such as financial futures.

The members of an organized exchange are subject to its rules, including the rules of conduct governing their relationships with customers. Most of the exchanges now have extensive procedures for the policing of their members and the disciplining of those who violate their rules. This zeal is doubtlessly reinforced by the fact that the Securities and Exchange Commission stands ready to take over should their own zeal slacken. The principal purpose of trading rules and policing is to avoid the bilking of customers and the rigging of prices, practices that unfortunately were once rather more common than not. Violations may occur now, but they are the exception and not the rule in modern equity markets, particularly in the organized sector.

All the securities traded on the New York Stock Exchange are listed on that exchange. Listing is allowed only for the securities of companies that comply with the rules of the exchange, principally with respect to publication of pertinent financial data and the disclosure of all facts of relevance for investors, such as the trading in a corporation's securities done by its principal owners and officers. In order to qualify for listing, the volume of shares available for public trading must also meet certain minimum standards. For example, the shares of a big but closely held corporation would not be listed. A minimum number of public shareholders as well as shares is required to assure reasonably continuous and viable markets. Listing requirements will be specified later in this chapter.

The American Stock Exchange (AMEX), with somewhat less stringent listing requirements, tends to be the market for smaller and often younger companies. Some companies have viewed an AMEX listing as an intermediate step between OTC trading and a NYSE listing. Many other companies have attempted to leapfrog AMEX listing and to go directly from OTC trading to NYSE listing. This differentiation did not extend just to companies; it also went to types of securities. For example, for many years the NYSE would not list warrants, so that a NYSE-listed company might have its warrants AMEX-listed. However, the NYSE has opened its doors to warrants of *some* companies.

Some companies have dual listings, on the NYSE as well as on one of the regional exchanges. Indeed, some of the regional exchanges get most of their trading volume from such dual listings. Transfer taxes, which are steep in New York, often account for the preference for a trade on a regional exchange. Where such dual listing exists, prices on the regional exchange are kept parallel with those on the NYSE by constant arbitrage. Arbitrage is the buying of a security or commodity in one market and selling the identical security or commodity in another market whenever a price differential appears. Arbitragers tend to equalize prices among markets. This arbitraging is mostly done by specialists.

The role of the specialist on an organized exchange is one of considerable responsibility but also opportunity. Brokers representing commission broker- age firms have to move around the trading floor of the exchange and cannot keep in constant touch with the individual stocks, which are traded at fixed points or "posts." Specialists are more than brokers; they are dealers in specific stocks. A "dealer" in a security deals for himself and therefore has an inventory in that security. The inventory, however, may be "short" or negative as well as "long" or positive. These specialist-dealers take orders from other brokers for both buying and selling, and when prices justify, they execute such orders. The rules of the exchange require specialists to give priority to customer orders, and they are charged with maintaining some continuity to the market for the security in which they specialize. Specialists are expected to buy when no other buyers appear or to sell when no other sellers can be found. Specialists often take losses in discharging this role. However, profits are not forbidden, and a specialist can serve as a buffer against irrational price movements and make a profit at the same time.

The information in the specialist's book of unfilled orders is of great strategic importance. If disposed to try to rig the market in their own favor, they have a strategic advantage in launching such an operation. For this reason, specialists are constantly under the surveillance of the governors of an exchange; their order books and the records of their transactions are subject to scrutiny at all times. If they perform their duty conscientiously, they serve an important role in the market, but the margin between conscience and cupidity is not always a clear one.

The role of the specialist is very much like that of the dealer in the U.S. government security market already discussed in Chapter 13.

THE OVER-THE-COUNTER (OTC) MARKET

About half a million corporations in the United States are active enough to file a tax return. About nine-tenths of these corporations are so closely held that their stocks never "trade" in any public sense. Thus there are about 50,000 corporations with possible public trades. Most of them, however, do not trade regularly and so are not really within the framework of the OTC or any other securities market.

The NYSE and the AMEX between them list 3300 corporations. A few more are listed on regional exchanges. There are 1500 OTC stocks with enough activity to justify daily quotation in *The Wall Street Journal* and *The New York Times*. However, another 1000 stocks trade actively enough to justify inclusion in the automatic quotation system of the National Association of Security Dealers (NASD). In addition, a number of other stocks get quoted weekly in the pink sheets of the National Quotation Service. Thus it can be said that about 10,000 stocks are "publicly traded." Of these, the OTC concentrates on about 2500 and can give service to the securities of about 4000 other companies.

The OTC market is made by dealers. A dealer differs from a broker in that the dealer acts as a principal to a trade. The dealer is similar to the specialist who has already been described or the dealers in other security markets that have already been described. The NASD has 4600 members but not all of them act as dealers. A small securities firm may be nothing more than a sales agent. However, if they have sponsored the public sale of stock of a local company, they will very likely "make a market" in it. The number of true market makers is not clear, but the bulk of the business is done by a few hundred firms.

Some very big companies still have their stocks traded in the OTC market. Traditionally both banks and insurance companies avoided listing and so were traded in these markets. However, the development of one-bank holding companies and the financial conglomerates that owned insurance companies led to the listing of many leading banks and insurance companies. A big company may attract as many as twenty or more market makers. The NASD likes to have at least two market makers for any company that it includes in its automatic quotation system (NASDAQ).

The new NASDAQ system has given rise to the first volume figures for the OTC market. On some days the OTC has had twice the share volume of the AMEX and half the share volume of the NYSE.

The NASDAQ system now lists and quotes about fifty listed third market stocks. It is possible that if the service of this market proves more efficient than block trading on the NYSE, the reversal of volume, elsewhere described in this chapter, will be rereversed at some later time.

A further change has been a broadening of the stock price quotation system. Thus the quotation tape now includes a consolidation of transactions in listed stocks not merely on the NYSE, but also on all regional exchanges where there is dual listing, and also the NASDAQ transactions plus those on a special network for block trading: Instinet.

Perhaps the greatest accomplishment of the NASDAQ system has been a demonstration of the fact that the face-to-face auction market is no longer necessary and is probably obsolete. The telephone and the cathode-ray-tube quotation and other informational systems are now adequate to handle the mechanics of trading. A body of adequately financed dealers could replace the function now performed by the floor specialists.

BLOCK TRADING AND ODD-LOT TRANSACTIONS

The increased importance of institutions in the stock market has led to an increase in the number of large transactions. (The NYSE defines a large block as one of 10,000 shares or more.) These large block transactions have taken two forms: transactions on the NYSE and transactions of listed stocks in a special OTC market called the "third market." Block trading on the NYSE has grown faster than third market trading. Since 1967 the growth has been particularly rapid, and big block trading now accounts for about one-fifth of NYSE volume. The combination of these two forms of trading now accounts for about one-fourth of total stock market activity. Some institutional trading, of course, does not involve large blocks. Commercial banks, as was noted above, are the most important of the institutional traders, mainly for their trust accounts. In the case of individual trusts, the size of transaction is not necessarily large and so, although the number of trades originated by commercial banks is substantial, the average size is less than that for other institutions. The allowance for negotiated commissions on large trades doubtless accounts for the fact that the NYSE retained this type of business, which otherwise might have gone to the third market.

The NYSE developed an information system to facilitate big block trading. The Block Automation System (BAS) has computer terminals in twenty-two metropolitan areas with over 180 subscribers. Each subscriber can enter offers or bids for blocks of a thousand or more shares in any listed stock with protection of anonymity. Brokerage firms use this information to bring together buyers and sellers.

Although the NYSE and other exchanges are primarily geared to transactions in units of 100 shares, they also provide for transactions of lesser amounts or "odd lots." Some of the regional exchanges have this odd-lot dealership function performed by the specialists assigned to given stocks. OTC dealers will also handle odd lots. On the NYSE, however, the business evolved into a specialty of certain firms. For many years two such firms did almost all this business, but finally the number was reduced to a single firm. Two leading brokerage firms, however, created in-house facilities for such business. If an electronic market is evolved, there would be every reason to have this function performed by the dealer-specialist; it presents no difficulties that cannot be easily solved by the computer.

THE COMMISSION BROKERAGE BUSINESS

The link between the organized exchanges, the OTC market, and the ultimate investor is provided by commission brokers. These brokers are sometimes small firms with a specialized or local market; some are large firms with many branches and highly developed merchandising programs to attract investors. Some are independent; some are affiliated with investment banking firms. Some specialize in common stocks, but most also cover bond investment as well. A few also offer commodity brokerage. The number of these firms was greatly reduced within the past decade when financial difficulties forced weaker firms into mergers, but recently the emergence of competitive commissions has lead to the creation of several new firms making this their specialization.

Competitive Commissions

Until 1971 all commission rates on the NYSE were set by its board of governors, and no member could depart from this schedule of rates. This schedule of rates was based on 100 shares as the unit of sale and no "quantity discount" was allowed. In other words, large transactions of many hundreds of shares paid the same brokerage commission per 100 shares as a single 100-share transaction. Naturally because costs of operating a brokerage concern were fairly fixed, large orders were much more profitable. Institutional business tended to be in this category. The principal attraction brokerage firms could hold out to such institutional (and other large) investors was investment research. In the booming 1960s and early 1970s the NYSE raised its fixed schedule of commissions several times, which aggravated the problem, particularly for large investors and led to the "third market" that is described above.

The SEC, backed by strong Congressional sentiment, pressed the NYSE into a partial relaxation of this rule in 1971. Commissions on quite large single orders were "competitive" and could be negotiated. By 1975 the NYSE had repealed the rule for orders of all sizes and allowed its members to set their own schedules of brokerage charges. This freedom led to two developments. Small or even moderate-sized investors did not get any benefit; indeed in some cases they faced increased brokerage charges. However, a specialized group of "discount" brokers started to lower brokerage fees for "no research" accounts and often made these lower rates available to rather moderate-sized investors.

Competitive commissions are undoubtedly better in principle and probably in practice. However, the considerable increase in the level of commissions that took place both before 1971 and since 1975 may have had something to do with the retreat of the small investor from the corporate equity market described earlier in this chapter. At one time brokerage commissions were small enough so that investors could shift about in their holdings without too much regard to the brokerage cost. In the early 1960s these costs were generally less than 2 percent and on fair-sized transactions nearer 1 percent. At present, however, the rate on transactions of about $5000 charged by the leading commission brokerage firms is about 3 percent. Commissions on smaller amounts are even higher; for 500 shares of a stock selling at 2, the commission cost for both buyer and seller is about 7 percent or 14 percent in total since brokerage commission is paid by both buyer and seller. Small investors may have been discouraged not only by the disappointing returns to stock investment in recent years but also by the turnover cost of this market.

Brokerage Account Insurance

Brokerage accounts are now insured very much as deposit accounts. The circumstances that led to the adoption of this insurance are an instructive illustration of the way in which most reforms are adopted: *after* the most severe need for them has passed.

During the 1960s the volume of trading in corporate equities increased greatly on all exchanges and OTC. This led to what was then called the "paper-work crisis." Many brokerage firms did not have adequate back-office facilities to process the paper work created by this upsurge in trading. Delays were frequent, and many firms failed to meet required deadlines for the delivery of securities. Even more vexing, the new help hired to handle the increased volume of work often made many errors of a variety of kinds. Dividends were not credited to the right accounts, transactions were not reported correctly, and deposits or withdrawals of cash in margin accounts were improperly handled. The problem of inadequately trained help was compounded by the fact that many brokerage firms were just starting to use computers at that time, and they had not yet debugged the programs and the operating procedures adequately. The problems were so severe that the NYSE and other exchanges several times shortened trading days to reduce the volume of transactions to manageable proportions. The worst of the crisis came in 1967 and 1968. The 1969 decline in the stock market gave the brokerage industry time to catch up and by 1970 the paper-work crisis could be said to have ended.

However, the problems were not yet all solved. This very drop in the market brought to the surface the fact that many brokerage firms had themselves been suffering losses, and a number of spectacular failures of brokerage firms followed. In addition, many more firms, when approaching insolvency, liquidated and went out of business without having to go through bankruptcy.

Many customers suffered varying kinds and degrees of losses as a result of both these events. The NYSE, and to a lesser extent other exchanges, had customer protection funds and tried to offset some of the losses. The major means used by the NYSE was to attempt to transfer the business of failed or liquidating firms to still viable brokerage firms so that there could be a continuity of service for as many customers as possible. As a result of the losses Congress passed the Securities Investor Protection Act of 1970 (SPIC), which created a quasi-public/private nonprofit corporation financed by the securities industry. This provides $50,000 of protection to a single brokerage account and provides rather complex procedures for the handling of brokerage firms that are in financial difficulties. Seven brokerage firms were placed in liquidation by the SPIC in 1975, the most recent year for which complete data are available. Some commission brokerage firms provide insurance in excess of the $50,000 amount by resort to private insurers.

SPECULATION IN EQUITY CAPITAL MARKETS

The popular image of the stock market as a speculative arena needs brief examination. Speculation in securities in contrast with investment is often thought of as an effort to realize capital gains quickly. The element of "quickness" is a legitimate distinction, since investment is clearly a long-range process. But capital gains are common to both types of operations; indeed, capital gains rather than current income have become the goal of a great deal of equity investment.

Even the time distinction is not altogether relevant. It is true that investors may hold what they buy for long periods of time, but prudence may sometimes require them to sell rather quickly if new circumstances arise. The common canons of investment urge the readjustment of portfolios whenever new conditions would seem to favor the move.

The fact that trading in equities becomes brisk whenever price movements are wide and falls off when prices are lethargic (even at fairly high levels) suggests that there is a fair amount of speculative volume in the market. Speculation, of course, should be viewed as a constructive force in the equity market *if it is based on good information*. The capital markets allocate capital, as we said in Chapter 1. If the bidding for equity securities is based on valid projections of the future, this can encourage the flow of capital into productive uses and discourage it from those that are of flagging value. Since equity returns are based on hope and expectations rather than promises, as is true of debt securities, the art of security selection is based on accuracy of anticipation. If security investors anticipate where future growth will be, they make capital available for the productive segments of the economy. The computer industry has been able to tap the capital markets on good terms because security investors foresaw the growth and were willing to put up the money for the expansion of this vast industry. On the other hand, a declining industry cannot raise new capital, and therefore new capital is not wasted on it by investors. Speculation discriminates not only among industries but also among companies. A good management will be rewarded by good stock prices; a poor one will be disciplined by the retreat of investors.

The National Bureau of Economic Research found that stock prices were a leading indicator, to a fair degree of accuracy, of general economic activity. Thus the stock market speculation also has the merit of giving some guidance to general public economy policy.

If speculation is based on false information, the process tends to be destructive. Much of the speculation of the bad old days was so based. As later segments of this chapter will make clear, the leading regulatory effort with respect to the equity markets has been to assure the honesty and, as far as possible, the accuracy of information available to investors.

A sober view of the facts, moreover, demonstrates that the speculative content of equity markets is much reduced from former days. The enforced reduction due to the limitation of credit in equity purchases will later be mentioned. Perhaps the most important point, however, is that the securities exchanges and many other elements in this market, including the leading commission brokerage houses, have attempted to discourage uninformed speculation. Professional speculation is still practiced and stock exchange members engage in it themselves. But the stock market gambler, characterized more by cupidity and stupidity than by acuity, is not given much encouragement except by marginal members of the securities business.

One statistical measure of the great reduction in speculation is afforded by the rate of turnover of corporate equities. This is shown in Table 17-2.

A 21 percent ratio for the most recent decade suggests that the amount of speculative froth in the equities market is fairly low. If there were none, the

TABLE 17-2
Turnover Ratio for Shares* Listed on the NYSE

Period	Percent per Annum
1900–1909	202
1910–1919	97
1920–1929	89
1930–1939	35
1940–1949	16
1950–1959	16
1960–1969	19
1970–1979	21 (estimate)

*A better measure would be provided if turnover were measured in terms of dollar volume, but unfortunately such data are not available.

rate of turnover of legitimate investors would suggest average holdings of about five years. If half the volume of market trading, which appears to be a generous estimate, is purely speculative and the average holding is just over nine months (to put capital gains on a long-term basis), the average holding period of investors appears to be about ten years.

Speculators operating no more actively than this cannot dominate the stock market nor throw it badly off the course indicated by real economic factors. The large amount of true investment funds keeps the market from deviating disastrously from course.

Short selling is sometimes criticized as a form of destructive speculation. Short selling is selling what the seller does not then own and making delivery on this sale by borrowing the security. The completion or the closing of a short position requires that the security borrowed be replaced by a later purchase. The short seller's hope is that he or she can make this later purchase materially under the price at which he or she initially sold.

The rules of all organized exchanges regulate short selling rather closely, and short selling on the over-the-counter market is very risky—except for insiders. On the NYSE, the size of the short interest has averaged less than 1/10 of 1 percent of listed shares, and it has almost never gone much above this level since 1934. If short sellers anticipate economic developments correctly, they hasten but do not amplify inevitable price movements. If they are wrong, they lose their capital.

OPTION TRADING: PUTS AND CALLS (PURE SPECULATION)

For many years there was a small OTC market in options for the purchase or sale of equities. An option to "call" or purchase shares is a contract fixed both in terms of price (the "striking" price) and the period for which it is valid. The seller of a "call" option contracts to sell the shares at the striking price within the set period, if called upon to do so by the purchaser of the option; that is, if the call option is "exercised" by its buyer and holder. An option to "put" or sell shares is a similar contract in reverse: the seller of a "put" option contracts to buy the shares from the purchaser at the "striking" price if the buyer exercises his or her "put" option. The motivation of each of the four parties might be described as follows:

The buyer of a call option expects (or at least hopes for) a higher price for the equity involved, *within the set period of the option*.

The seller of a call option does not share those expectations: The seller expects stable or declining prices. If the seller owns the equity involved, he or she is a "covered" seller; otherwise he or she is a "naked" option seller.

The buyer of a put option expects falling prices within the set period of the option. If this happens, he or she can purchase the equity in the open market for the lower price and present the shares ("exercise") to the seller of the put option for purchase at the set price. That is the option. The buyer may already own the shares but, fearing a price drop, purchases in advance the right to sell at the fixed put option price.

The seller of a put option presumably does not expect falling prices but may also be an investor who is willing to acquire the equity at the fixed option price, if the option is exercised against him or her.

Option trading is pure speculation. It is always short-term in its nature: the option period with the heaviest volume of trading is three months or less; no options are available for a period longer than nine months. Investors may combine option trading with portfolio investment but the option, taken by itself, is a zero-sum game (without allowance for brokerage commissions; with such allowance it is a net losing game for all participants combined).

After many years of relatively small OTC activity, the Chicago Board of Trade (beating the organized exchanges at the starting gun) instituted listed option trading by a face-to-face auction. Later the AMEX and still later several of the regional exchanges also added option trading in a certain number of shares. The Chicago Board reaped the advantages of an early start: it listed the speculative favorites, and the AMEX and other exchanges had to pick from among the remainder. As a result, the Chicago Board leads in terms of activity. There is a certain amount of duplicate listing but not a great deal.

INFORMAL EQUITIES MARKET

If one wishes to stretch the concept of markets just a bit further, still one more equities market should be mentioned: a purely local, informal, and rather confidential market.

All across the United States local businessmen, doctors, dentists, bankers, and others own small interests in local enterprises. Sometimes these enterprises are operated as partnerships, but more often they are incorporated. These owners sometimes must sell their shares in such small local corporations. They may sell because health or nature requires them to do so, for capital gains, or because even newer ventures have become more attractive. The local "capitalist" still exists, even if somewhat less conspicuous in recent years.

The buying and selling of equities in such local enterprises is sometimes done through business brokers and therefore handled rather impersonally as a market process. These business brokers may even act as financial agents, hunting up capital loans for buyers as well as buyers for sellers. Motels, stores, laundromats, gas stations, frequently pass through their hands, but less well-standardized businesses are also bought and sold. This market is one in which some measure of uniformity exists by virtue of the valuation process. Motels may tend to sell for certain multiples of gross or net earnings. No one knows how large this market really is or how well it fits into the other capital markets. But if one has faith in the process of market leveling, it would seem reasonable to think that some sort of tie probably exists.

The market for small, locally owned banks is also very much like this. Local bank presidents often operate a market in the shares of their banks as a service to shareholders. These presidents keep track of those who have expressed an interest in buying some bank shares; when some shares become available, they call up to find out if the inquiries are backed by money. Often the price is largely set by the president with very little haggling—unless the amounts be large. (Many bank-share deals regularly take place at book value.) There is some evidence that prices in this bank-share market are loosely tied to the more open and urban markets for bank shares.

REGULATION OF THE STOCK MARKET

Capital markets in the United States are regulated, but the character of the regulation differs materially from that applied in other areas. A majority of capital market institutions are not monopolies, and therefore the regulation in force is not similar to that governing public utility enterprises that are given an exclusive franchise but then limited in prices and earnings. Nevertheless, there are some near monopolies: for example, the NYSE dominates the organized equity market by accounting for four-fifths of such activity. Furthermore, the stock market lives with a blend of public and self-regulation for which parallels are hard to find except possibly in professions such as law and medicine. Stock market regulation of a limited kind has existed for a long time, but the most important (and controversial) elements of it date back to the mid-1930s. Much of this regulation was a product of vast disillusionment produced by the Great Depression.

Because regulation of the stock market is marked by a number of intents and guided by several laws and agencies, the following sections will use fairly rigid expository devices to avoid confusion. The first section will discuss the basic objectives of this regulation. The second section will outline the specific problems that have led to regulation. Then, and only then, will the legal basis of regulation be introduced. With this background, it will then be possible to enumerate and describe the agencies involved in the regulatory process.

OBJECTIVES OF REGULATION

The story of public regulation has usually been a simple one: Some catastrophic event discloses a problem and public pressure forces the lawmakers to "do something about it." Post hoc analysis with hearings, investigations, and debates among the various parties at interest follow, and then compromises, which always accompany the legislative process, are made. No one is fully satisfied but "something has been done." One of the strange parts of the process is that the objectives of such regulation are often not very much discussed. Lawyers, in drafting these acts, put some lofty language in the preambles, but as often as not it is more windy than meaningful. But with the advantage of hindsight, what were the basic objectives that capital market regulation was expected to accomplish?

Fair and Equitable Treatment of Investors

Prosperity and a more egalitarian distribution of income has created a large number of persons who have the means to be security investors. A large proportion of them have little skill or background for such a function; thus a prevailing ethic is that such persons should be protected. This ethic is similar to the ideas back of pure food and drug laws or laws requiring weights and measures to be shown on packages.

Security selling in the past was sometimes very close to outright fraud. At one time in this country, securities were sold for enterprises that did not exist and for purposes that are describable only as fantastic. But the major problems were of a kind more at the margin of ethics. Railroads were legitimate and important business enterprises, but in the nineteenth century the stocks of railroads were often grossly manipulated on the NYSE. Investors were not given adequate information by many corporations, so that they were unable to estimate the true value of the securities to be purchased or which they already owned; they were at a disadvantage relative to the better informed "insiders."

It is notable that emphasis was put on the protection of the investor and not on the borrower or raiser of capital. It was thought that corporations were presumably able to protect their interest without help. One possible exception is a small business, where special kinds of financial aid have received a great deal of political support. However, this is not really a part of stock market regulation; it is, rather, a form of special interest legislation.

While the protection of investors was originally considered mainly a matter of equity and ethics, the whole movement probably has had far more sweeping consequences. Participation in the stock markets is now very widespread. While this may not have raised much new capital for corporations, it certainly has created a very large body of support for the corporate system that would not have existed with narrower common stock ownership.[2]

Promotion of Market Efficiency

Better information has been one of the chief means used to promote market efficiency. The publicity that has been required for the process of raising capital has exposed the margins or "markups" taken by the securities industry both in new-issue sales and in secondary market transactions. Both sides of the market—investors and borrowers—have become more aware of these margins and more disposed to bargain for narrower spreads. Better information in the OTC market has probably reduced the bid-and-ask spreads and improved executions for investors on both sides of the market. But most important of all, the improved information about the operations of business that have been required for security selling and listing on exchanges has clearly given investors

[2]A very interesting and readable account of regulation of equity trading markets may be found in Sidney Robbins, *The Security Markets*, Free Press, New York, 1966. In spite of its very broad title, this book deals almost solely with the equity market and particularly the NYSE. Robbins was chief economist for the 1963 special study of securities markets sponsored by the Securities Exchange Commission (SEC).

a more accurate view of prospective rewards. By making more correct investment decisions, the whole process of capital allocation is thereby improved.

One of the important feedbacks has been from the more aggressive investors to the management of corporations. In times past, many giant corporations doubtless became complacent and self-satisfied and did not press as aggressively as might have been possible. However, the exposure of such policies in the actions of aggressive investors who dump the shares of such companies if they do not perform has doubtless been a spur to more active search for growth and efficiency.

PROBLEM AREAS THAT HAVE RECEIVED REGULATORY ATTENTION

Public regulation tends to be pragmatic; it concentrates on problems exposed in past distressful episodes. The objectives we have just finished enumerating may have a general philosophical consistency, but actual regulatory law and action tends to be more specific. This section gets down to specifics; it enumerates the itches that regulatory legislation tried to scratch.

New-Issue Market: "Telling the Truth"

One of the earliest forms of public regulation of security markets was the requirement that those selling securities should tell buyers the truth. State "blue sky" laws preceded federal government entry to this field. (One exception was the application of postal regulations to prosecute security sale frauds that made use of the mails.) The Securities Act of 1933 was the major federal effort in this area. The major impact of this act was to require those selling new issues of securities to provide enough information to permit investors to make a valid investment judgment. The law did not prohibit highly speculative ventures as long as they were honestly and forthrightly described. Not only must the truth be told, material facts could not be withheld; the story had to be the "whole" truth.

The intent is valid; the result less certain. With certain exceptions, whenever a concern sells securities publicly (that is, a large number of buyers), it must issue a prospectus with detailed relevant information. Except for a few students—dragooned in the academic processes—and a few security analysts, these long and dull documents have become among the most unread compilations in an age when the printing press is inundating us all. However, at least a few points have been read and widely understood. Underwriters were required to tell the size of their own margins; this exposure has undoubtedly led to smaller margins (although other forces have helped in this process too).

Security Markets: Organized Exchanges

The central focus of financial market regulation has been on the organized exchanges, which are primarily, as we have seen, secondary markets. Even more specifically, the focus has been on the stock market and particularly the NYSE. The Securities Exchange Act of 1934 was concerned mainly with this central issue (although it did deal with other problems). After a period of preliminary struggle, the major impact of this regulation was to change the NYSE from what amounted to a private club into a public institution with acknowledged public responsibilities. Later in this chapter we shall deal at more length with the double harness of public regulation and self-regulation, but we must immediately recognize that the NYSE has now become a leading regulatory agency.

Stock market regulation dealt with a rather wide range of specific problems. The NYSE had always had trading rules to govern the conduct of its members. After NYSE reorganization in 1938, the trading rules were revised to provide more protection for investors who used the facilities of commission brokerage houses. Financial requirements for membership were beefed up. The practice of floor trading by members was subject to greater limitation. Trading practices that tended to manipulate or artificially influence prices were prohibited. One of the most significant areas of regulation has been an increase in the amount of information that companies listed on the NYSE must supply to investors. This protection was extended, in a measure, to over-the-counter markets in 1964. The whole art (some new-wave security analysts might want to say "science") of security analysis has been vastly supported by prompter access to information of a more extensive and more accurate nature.

One area in which markets have been greatly changed has been in the nature and intent of trading rules. In the days before the Crash of 1929, but even more in the nineteenth century, the NYSE was often more like a gambling enterprise than a true economic instrument of development. Prices of stocks would be bulled up by excessive activity until a speculative following had been attracted. Then the pool pushing the price up would drop out and let the bubble burst. Sometimes corners would be established; sometimes prices would be driven down by vast short selling. Price manipulation was so common that conservative investors often felt it unsafe to include publicly traded common stocks in their portfolios. The pre-1938 trading rules were mainly for the purpose of settling differences among members. Protection of the outside public investor using commission brokerage access was not very extensive. However, the exchanges added trading rules that changed this situation materially. In the first place, the practice of floor trading (when a member buys and sells for his or her own account) was greatly restricted, which made outside investors more nearly on a par with floor traders. Most members on the exchanges now operate solely as agency traders or specialists. The power both of the NYSE and of the SEC to suspend trading in an individual stock was used far more effectively to avoid unsound speculative bursts in the price of an individual stock. Short selling was restricted. Unusual activity in an individual stock has been given much closer scrutiny both by the NYSE and the SEC. Credit sales were greatly restricted. Most of these changes have been aimed one way or another at making the market a safer one for the ordinary outside security investor.

The Specialist

One of the most interesting developments has been the increased role of the specialist and the consequent regulation of that function. Even though a large number of buy and sell orders flow into the floor of the NYSE, matching buy and sell orders may fail to appear within the very few seconds in which a floor broker may try to execute an order. The goal of a floor broker is to do as much business as possible. Some floor members assumed the role of taking the other side of these orders for their own account: They would buy at a price somewhat below the one at which they would sell. They became, in effect, dealers. Soon, they began to "specialize" in this function. Specialists also kept limit orders on their books that were to be executed at preset prices that were at various intervals away from the prevailing market. With the course of time, the specialists' operations became much more formalized—and at the same time more regulated. At the present time specialists are expected to "make markets" in the stock or stocks assigned to them. They are encouraged to quote a narrow bid-and-ask spread and are expected, under some circumstances, to absorb a flow of selling or to accommodate a surge of buying from their own positions. So far as possible, they attempt to make price changes continuous; that is, by steps of one-eighth. This matter becomes of the greatest significance when some momentous news suddenly becomes known. For example, a company unexpectedly announces reduced earnings or cuts its dividend; a surge of selling may develop. The specialist is expected to preside over an orderly retreat in price. (Economists may legitimately ask if an important change in investment information may not justify price discontinuity.) The question that really hurts is this: How much of the selling wave should specialists be required to take into their own position in the process of presiding over the "orderly" retreat? The specialist's book with its sequence of limit orders presumably gives him or her privileged knowledge, but where should the primary responsibility be: to the continuity of the market or to his or her own capital gains and losses?

Listing

For the market in a listed stock to be "reasonably good," enough stock must be in the hands of enough shareholders to generate a fair volume of trading. If too few buy and sell orders enter the market, it is too "thin" and trades are too infrequent. Therefore, exchanges have generally enforced listing requirements based on both number of shares outstanding and number of shareholders. The requirements for initial listing tend to be rather more exacting than those for continued listing. The initial listing requirements adopted by the NYSE are:

1. Demonstrated earning power under competitive conditions of $2.5 million before federal income taxes for the most recent year and $2 million pretax for the preceding two years
2. Net tangible assets of $16 million, but greater emphasis will be placed on the aggregate market value of the common stock
3. A total of $16 million in market value of publicly held common stock

4. A total of 1,000,000 common shares publicly held
5. Round-lot shareholders numbering 2000

To allow for the fact that a company may experience a period of adversity but still recover from it, the requirements for continued listing are not quite as great as those for initial listing. The NYSE says:

> . . . The Exchange may at any time suspend or delist a security where the Board considers that continued dealings in the security are not advisable, even though a security meets or fails to meet any specified criteria. For example, the Exchange would normally give consideration to suspending or removing from the list a common stock of a company when there are:
>
> 1. 1200 round-lot holders or less
> 2. 600,000 shares or less in public hands
> 3. $5,000,000 or less aggregate market value of publicly held shares
> 4. $8,000,000 or less in aggregate market value of all outstanding common stock or net tangible assets applicable thereto, combined with an earnings record of less than an average of $600,000 after taxes for the past three years

Information

One of the interesting by-products of listing requirements has been the agreement by listed corporations that they will supply shareholders with such information as may be required for intelligent evaluation of share prices. Specifically:

> The listing agreement between the company and the Exchange is designed to provide timely disclosure to the public of earnings statements, dividend notices, and other information which may affect security values or influence investment decisions. The Exchange requires actively operating companies to agree to solicit proxies for all meetings of stockholders.

Although the initial requirement came from the NYSE, the SEC has taken continued interest in the matter of public information. Among other things, the SEC has conducted a continuous inquiry into the accounting methods used by listed corporations in reporting to shareholders. They have also pressed for early disclosure of relevant information.

Insider Trading

The managers and directors of publicly owned corporations constantly face a serious ethical dilemma: Their position gives them far better knowledge of the future prospects of a firm than outside investors can possibly have. To what extent are they entitled to make use of this superior knowledge in stock market trading? For incentive reasons these managers are usually urged to be substantial stockholders; stock option plans for promoting this are widespread.

In the "bad old days" there was undoubtedly a lot of rather unscrupulous insider trading. Insiders bought on good news before the news became widely known or understood. If unfavorable developments were pending, insiders might sell the stocks of their companies. In a few extreme cases, unscrupulous traders would get control of a corporation with no goal other than manipulation. These pirates would sell short the stocks of their own companies and then issue *false* bad news. They would then cover their short sales at lower prices and subsequently correct the false news report so as to allow them to cover their short sales at a profit. The opposite ploy was also practiced. Misinformation was used as a kind of market strategy. However, this picture of past horrors could be overstated. Many publicly owned corporations conducted their affairs with scrupulous regard for the rights of shareholders and did not allow insiders to engage in any such shenanigans.

The Securities Exchange Act (Sec. 16) provides the following limitations on insider trading:

1. Each officer, director, and beneficial owner of more than 10 percent of any listed class of stock (the legal definition of an "insider") must file with the SEC and the exchange on which it is listed an initial statement of holdings and thereafter monthly reports that reflect changes in holdings.
2. Profits obtained by insiders (as defined above) from purchases and sales of the company's stock with less than a six-month holding period may be recovered by the company or by any security holder on its behalf.
3. Insiders (as defined above) cannot sell short.

It should be noted that long-term capital gains derived from insider purchases are not prohibited by these rules. The impact of the SEC pressure tends to shorten the period that such information is considered insider information. Court decisions have tended to broaden the statutory definition of "insider." Families of the persons named or their agents to whom confidential disclosure might be made (such as brokers) have been found to be covered by the law.

In spite of the limitation on insider trading, there is a feeling that insiders still have some trading advantage. A number of stock market advisory services are avid readers of the SEC monthly reports of insider transactions. Insider buying is taken as a good omen for investment in a company and insider selling as a bad omen or a reason for retreat. However, the research studies that have attempted to correlate subsequent price movements with insider trading have failed to prove conclusively that any such relationship exists.

Stock Market Credit

Some aggressive investors attempt to increase their market profits by the use of leverage: They finance a portion of their market purchases with borrowed money. Such "margin trading" has a very long history. Perhaps the most dramatic episode in this history, however, came in the stock market collapse of 1929. In the two years preceding September 1929, brokers' loans grew from $4 billion to $9 billion. Since some direct loans by banks to individuals for stock market purposes are not included in these figures, the total growth of stock market credit is unknown. However, in the last three months of 1929, brokers' loans were reduced from the $9 billion back to $4 billion. In the next 2 ½ years, brokers' loans all but disappeared.

Exactly what part this rapid and unpremediated liquidation of stock market credit had to do with the ensuing depression is unclear. The relationship of stock prices and business activity, as we have already noted in this chapter, is not wholly clear. But it is clear that the rapid liquidation of that amount of credit was a serious depressant on stock market prices. Many security purchases were margined very thinly; some by as little as 10 percent. Thus a modest drop in prices reduced the coverage of other margined positions. If margin owners were unable to raise more margin, they were then sold out. The selling out of margined positions of owners who could not come up with more margin thus put added pressure on the market. The whole process became self-reinforcing. When regulation of the securities markets was adopted, regulation of stock market credit was one of its principal features.

The Federal Reserve rather than the SEC was directed to regulate stock market credit. The regulation imposed by the Federal Reserve covers listed and some unlisted stocks. Other unlisted stocks are on an "all cash" basis. Federal Reserve Regulations T and U require the buyer to supply a specified part of the purchase price at time of purchase.

In practice the Federal Reserve has varied the minimum margin to be supplied by purchasers at time of purchase fairly frequently: It was changed eighteen times in the thirty-four years during which stock market credit has been regulated. Since 1945 the required margin has never been less than 50 percent, and for one brief period it was 100 percent.

Since the margin requirement applies to the time of purchase, requests for added margin if security prices go down are a private and not a regulatory matter. Brokers ask for added margin only to protect the security of a credit and not for regulatory reasons. However, if security prices go up, then the security profits, whether realized or not, supply added margin for further trading. The purchase of stock as the result of a rights offerings is subject to a lower (25 percent) margin, and security brokers in their normal operations (but not for personal speculation) are also subject to lower margins.

The amount of stock market credit outstanding has drifted around a level of $10 billion for nearly a decade. However, this is only a little more than 1 percent of total stock market value, whereas in 1929 the $9 billion was closer to 10 percent of the total value of stock. In terms of floating supplies of stock, the contrast between margined holdings and outright holdings is even more striking.

AGENCIES OF SECURITIES MARKET REGULATION

Before undertaking to review the specific agencies involved in securities market regulation, it will be helpful to review briefly the unique principle of regulation widely described as that of "self-regulation." This phrase, by itself, fails to convey the rather subtle combination of forces at work. Self-regulation, as practiced in the securities markets, means that a large part of the day-to-day rules and standards by which the markets operate are those adopted by private agencies organized by the firms and individuals doing business in these markets—but always subject to the overview of a government agency with strong powers of intervention. The NYSE makes the rules and, strictly speaking, does not have to get approval of the SEC before putting them into effect. But the SEC has large reserve powers granted by the Securities Exchange Act of 1934, and if the NYSE adopted rules that it considered against the public interest or *failed* to adopt rules it considered necessary in the public interest, the SEC could then intervene with its own requirements. The SEC can also initiate civil or criminal suits against firms or individuals. All legal actions of the SEC, of course, are utlimately subject to full judicial review. So far, the courts have tended to support the SEC. The NYSE thus knows that, in the end, it probably would lose if there were a test of wills. For this reason, the degree of public interest self-regulation the NYSE undertakes is probably greater than it would be without prodding. At the same time, the character of regulation is probably better adapted and shaped to the operational problems of business firms operating in the market than if the regulatory harness were one imposed directly by the SEC or any other government agency.

The Self-Regulators: the NYSE and the NASD

Since we have already described the functional organization of the NYSE and other organized exchanges, at this point we need only recount the circumstances in which self-regulation arose and to outline some of its subsequent developments. The original Securities Exchange Act of 1934 gave the SEC broad powers but not very explicit mandates as to how they were to be carried out. Badly shocked by the Great Depression, the securities industry in general and the NYSE specifically were not able to thwart the passage of the legislation. They attempted, however, to resist the implementation of the law. This tactic was dropped in 1938, when the NYSE suffered a devastating publicity blow: Richard Whitney, its president, who had led the fight against the SEC, was found to have been embezzling trust funds. Under the shock of this disclosure, internal NYSE opposition to reform collapsed, and a reform administration was put in office. William McChesney Martin, later to achieve even greater fame as the chairman of the Federal Reserve Board, was made president of the NYSE at thirty years of age. Change was prompt and drastic.

Since that time the NYSE has become very conscious of its public role (and of its public image). The membership of the NYSE is subject to disciplining, and the number of publicly exposed cases of discipline underindicates the degree of quiet pressure for living by the rules. The relationship of the NYSE and the SEC has not been exactly friendly, but they have learned to work together in this rather unusual relationship.

Perhaps the long-time description of the NYSE as a "private club" was a bit exaggerated, but it was not far from the truth. The NYSE was organized as a nonprofit association, just like a club. Social pressures were very much like those in any similar group. Moreover, William McChesney Martin, the first paid full-time president, came from inside the exchange. As to organization power, however, the chairman of the exchange was more powerful, and the chairmanship was, until 1972, a part-time job held by an active exchange member. Now that post has also been made a full-time one, and the first person to hold it comes from outside the NYSE. Not only that, but the first public members of the Board of Governors of the Exchange included a female economist.

The regional exchanges faced problems of survival as well as regulation. Most of them had to be reorganized after being registered to effect the changes needed. Full-time professional presidents with considerable regulatory power were often brought in to replace part-time officers drawn from the member firms and individuals. The American Stock Exchange was rather considerably reformed as the result of a series of misdealings exposed and prosecuted by the SEC.

Before 1938, the over-the-counter market was almost wholly unregulated. In 1933 the Investment Bankers Association had been formed, and later it created a "code" for industry operation under the aegis of the National Industrial Recovery Act (which was declared unconstitutional in 1935). After some negotiation, the Maloney Amendment to the Securities Exchange Act was passed in 1938, and under this act the National Association of Securities Dealers (NASD) was formed. This organization was given powers of self-regulation but—even more important—it was given a power that made it necessary for virtually every securities firm to be an NASD member. Cooperative selling of securities is traditional, and the actual seller is customarily given a "concession" by the underwriters. The NASD was given power to require its members to give such concessions *only to other NASD members*. This made membership virtually mandatory for any firm wishing to join the community of security salesmanship.

The NASD has functioned in a variety of ways, but its effects on the over-the-counter market were most notable. It has narrowed the bid-and-ask spread, generally to not exceed 5 percent. Disclosure of the role of the seller as a dealer or broker has also been required. In general, trading standards have been improved to the point where ordinary private investors can venture into this market without losing too much fleece.

The Governmental Regulators: Mainly the SEC

It has been necessary to mention the Securities and Exchange Commission (SEC) at many previous points. The SEC is an independent federal agency headed by a commission of five members, each serving for a five-year term. They are appointed (and the chairman is also designated) by the President subject to Senate confirmation. The SEC staff has been small as federal agencies go: it has averaged less than 1500 persons. Every one of the laws mentioned at earlier points in this chapter in some way affects the work of the SEC. (In addition, the SEC has some marginal duties imposed by laws *not* mentioned here, such as those dealing with bankruptcy and corporation reorganization.) As already indicated, a central part of the SEC's work is regulatory. The chairmen of the SEC have usually been lawyers; law school professors have been frequent appointees. The SEC collects and publishes a number of leading statistical series; but apart from this activity, its work in economic analysis has been sporadic, and Congress has tended to starve this segment of the SEC's function.

The regulatory powers of the SEC are great, but an almost equally powerful impact has resulted from its investigative powers. This power has shown itself in two ways. First, the SEC has often been more diligent than the NYSE or the NASD in digging up cases of market shenanigans; the resulting exposure has sometimes left these agencies with rather red faces. Second, the SEC has several times undertaken detailed investigations of various market practices without the objective of civil or criminal prosecution but to open up industry practices to public scrutiny. Such inquiries have covered commission charges, floor trading, the specialists' function, odd-lot dealing, the influence of institutional investment on the markets, management of investment companies, and other subjects. The publicity resulting from these studies has often resulted in legislation; but even without legislation it has often had marked impact on market practices and on the standards of self-regulation.

Several other government agencies have, in various ways, been involved with the regulation of the financial markets. The Anti-Trust Division of the Department of Justice brought a monopoly suit against a number of investment bankers at one time. The suit was lost, but the decision of the presiding judge has become a classic description of the underwriting process. The Federal Reserve, as already noted, has control of margins required for security purchases. In addition, the Federal Reserve takes a paternal if not regulatory view of the money markets, particularly the market for Treasury securities. The open-market function of the Federal Reserve gives it great power of moral suasion. Trading rules and standards of professional performance in this market have certainly been strongly influenced even if not directly regulated by the Federal Reserve.

Finally, it should not be forgotten that regulation of outright securities frauds was undertaken by most state governments, long before the federal government got into this business, by so-called blue sky regulation. In most states this regulatory function still exists, even if it is overshadowed by federal operations.

HOW COMPETITIVE IS THE SECURITIES BUSINESS?

If the securities markets were limited to institutional investors who had the same degree of financial sophistication as the financial managements of corporations, it is possible that no regulation at all would be needed. With an equivalence of market power and knowledge, they could fend for themselves without protection. However, if a large number of investors with little market power and less knowledge are involved, they could be fleeced unless protected. Under the shelter of regulatory protection, 25 million citizens have become corporate shareholders. Could it have happened without regulation, or would this growth have been desirable? It is possible that for reasons of long-run interests in business promotion, commission brokerage houses would have supplied some such protection even without public regulation. But can we be sure? In fact, the nature of competition in the securities business deserves some very concentrated attention.

The NYSE is not an inherent monopoly, but by long standing it is in a de facto position of monopoly in the organized trading of the shares of the great nonfinancial corporations. Thus its trading rules can have the effect of limiting market participation. An interesting example can be found in the matter of Rule 394. This rule provides that a member of the NYSE may not trade a listed stock in the OTC market. When the disclosure requirements imposed by the 1964 SEC amendments persuaded the Chase Manhattan Bank to seek NYSE listing, this put a gap in the business of the OTC bank stock trading firms. Later, when the one-bank holding companies were listed, this increased the transfer of business to the NYSE. This development raises an important question of market efficiency; it can be argued that in this largely institutional market the OTC is more efficient than the listed market. Should the NYSE be able to bar its members from doing business with firms that are not members of the NYSE?

For small but publicly held corporations, a still different problem exists. The presence of a large number of firms in the OTC market suggests strong competition. And to a considerable extent this is true; in the marketing of securities having a broad regional or national appeal, the number of firms ensures competition. But in the markets for securities having a rather limited appeal, this will not be true. Only one OTC firm may make markets in the stock of a moderate-sized, publicly owned, but not well-known company. Can competition work in a case such as this? One bit of evidence suggests that it can: The number of bidders for small issues of state and local government obligations is often quite large, suggesting a high level of competition.

The growth of the third market is also an illustration that where a need of any great size exists, financial innovation will increase the amount of competition. At the same time, efforts of the NYSE to keep business from going to the third market may have imposed limitations on its members that some would not view as consistent with the existence of free competition.

CONGRESSIONAL MANDATE FOR A NATIONAL MARKET

In the early 1970s there was considerable dissatisfaction with the functioning of the corporate equity market. The paper-work crisis in the late 1960s and then the failure of so many brokerage firms were events somewhat antecedent to, but clearly contributing to, this dissatisfaction. In addition brokerage commission rates were considerably increased but without any evidence of more satisfactory service and order execution. Brokers were criticized particularly for the quality of their executions. (Buyers felt brokers did not get as low a price as possible; sellers felt brokers did not get as high a price as possible.) The inadequate functioning of the specialist system was thought to be part of the cause: lazy brokers turned orders over to specialists rather than trying for a better price. But perhaps the deepest cause of the dissatisfaction was that the equity market went through (and is still going through at this writing) a period in which the expectations of investors for return were not being met.

During this period Congress as well as the SEC concerned itself with the question of market organization. Finally Congress in 1975 mandated the elimination of all barriers to competition in the corporate equity market and instructed the SEC to supervise the establishment of a national market. The first step taken by the SEC was to eliminate a part of Rule 390 that prohibited members of the NYSE from executing orders to customers "off the board." The eliminated part covered circumstances when member brokers were acting as agents for customers. This action took effect at the end of 1975. The SEC later proposed that Rule 390 be completely eliminated effective the first day of 1978. This proposal created strong controversy since it would have allowed brokers to become dealers in listed stocks (in-house specialists so to speak) and to execute orders for customers themselves and without use of NYSE facilities. But by December 1977, elimination of Rule 390 had been indefinitely postponed.

Elimination of Rule 390 would not by itself create a national market. What form that market will take cannot be forecast. Old institutions often tend to linger on long after their functional usefulness has shriveled or ended completely. An outside observer cannot help but note that the example of the NASDAQ may give guidance. There is really no need for the organized exchanges as such. The securities industry might have its own private central association such as NASD has been for the OTC market, but it would be mainly a body for self-regulation and not one to provide physical facilities. Private securities firms with adequate capital could set up as dealers in such stocks as they chose to cover and thus bring competition to the specialists' function. An expanded NASDAQ quotation system could put a broker in touch with all dealers whereby the broker could pick the best trade price at any one moment. Brokerage firms already have a centralized depository facility so that shares can be transferred simply by book entries. A connection of transfer agents to the centralized depository makes it possible to deliver shares to customers with a minimum of paper work. Settlements between all parties could be effected with the greatest of ease. The heart of the matter, of course, would be an information system so that news of corporate developments can be spread to investors as well as market professionals with speed and accuracy.

The existence of a smoothly functioning corporate equities market is of the greatest importance to everyone whether or not they be investors in this market. The need for increased equity capital beyond the amount that can be provided by retained earnings probably will grow. But investors are not likely to provide such capital unless they have confidence in the corporate equity market to work efficiently and equitably. The mechanics of the market are at the heart of efficiency, and the quality of the information system is at the heart of equity.

Perhaps the greatest unsolved problem in the way of establishing a truly national market in corporate equities is how to manage the transition from the present market to the new system. Every new program needs debugging and a national market system would necessarily be complicated in many ways and prone to early error and failure. The old system probably should not be disbanded until the new one has been proved in experimental runs.

One of the most interesting and complex problems would be that of providing ways of handling contingency or limit orders for corporate equities. At present, an investor (speculator?) can place limits on both buy and sell orders. A simple contingency or limit order is to buy at some price below the present market or to sell at some price above the present market. A more complex type of contingency order is that of so-called stop-loss orders. The owner of shares, often held on margin when this type of order is used, may order that if the price of the stock goes down to or below a fixed price to sell (in order to limit loss or to ensure a profit that is still unrealized). Short sellers can also use stop-loss orders at prices fixed above the present market and for the same reasons.

At present such orders are placed with the specialist or specialists in a stock. With only one specialist, which is true of most stocks, all these contingency orders are recorded in the specialist's "book," which gives a comprehensive picture of the results of either an increase or a decrease in the price of that stock. Even when there is more than one specialist on the NYSE, they are physically located at the same post, and a consolidation of their books can be made quickly by the governors of the NYSE whenever there is a question about how the market should respond to unusual news or other special developments.

If OTC dealers replaced the specialist, they could accept contingency orders, but a consolidation of their respective books would no longer be such a simple matter; it would require some kind of electronic system. Such a system would be possible but costly. Furthermore, there is a policy question as to whether or not this consolidated "book" should be available only to the dealers (plus, of course, some sort of regulatory body) or whether it should be publicly available. If such information were given wide currency, the results probably would be to increase speculation against the book; an activity which the NYSE tries to restrain in the operation of the specialist function. Such speculation might tend to make a more "perfect" market as economists understand the term, but it might also tend to make a more erratic market—which upsets the confidence of long-term investors who count on the liquidity of the market as a protection.

The uncertain view that members of the NYSE have of the future of their institution is indicated by a trivial but interesting fact: the price they pay for "seats" (privileges of membership) on the NYSE. In the boom year 1929 a half century ago the price of a seat went as high as $625,000. In the late 1960s the price again rose, this time to $515,000. In the damp autumn of 1977, the price of seats on the NYSE went under $40,000; the lowest they had been since the period before World War I.

As an institution the NYSE will try to find a role in the new system of markets as it evolves. It may succeed, but the hard-boiled brokers of Wall Street see only a dim future; one in which they are not inclined to invest much of their own money.

FULLY AUTOMATED STOCK TRADING?

The NASDAQ system for trading OTC and a limited number of listed stocks depends on highly sophisticated communications equipment. By means of this equipment, the need for the face-to-face auction system is eliminated. However, this is not a fully automated system; it still depends on human beings who act as dealers and stand ready to buy and sell at their bid-and-ask prices. An experiment is now being conducted with a system that carries the degree of automation even further. The Cincinnati Stock Exchange is experimenting with a fully computerized system that matches buy-and-sell orders for thirty-eight listed stocks. Merrill Lynch, Pierce, Fenner & Smith are using the Cincinnati system to transact most of their customers' business in five selected stocks.

The Cincinnati system may be vulnerable to manipulation, and flaws, not yet detected, may emerge. However, the experience so far suggests that such a system might function effectively. One of the amusing ironies of this experiment is that tne two minicomputers used by Cincinnnati are, in fact, located in Jersey City!

PROJECTS AND QUESTIONS

1. Obtain the most recent NYSE composite index from a current issue of *The Wall Street Journal* (or *The New York Times*). Using this index estimate the market value of all outstanding corporate equities. As a base, the NYSE composite index at the end of 1975 was 48 and the *Flow-of-Funds* estimated that corporate equities had a market value of $854.7 billion on that date.
2. Again using *The Wall Street Journal* as a source, compare the volume of transactions on the OTC with those on the NYSE. Use the year-to-date summary for each. As a basis of comparison, the OTC equaled 29 percent of NYSE volume in 1975 and 36 percent in 1977. Has the gain continued?
3. This text was revised while the date for the abolition of NYSE rule 390 was still in doubt. If it has since been abolished, can you find any evidence of its effects on markets? Any changes from the situation described in the text?
4. This text reports a peak of the number of equity owners at about 1973 and a decline from then till the time of revision of this text in 1978. Do you have any evidence of a continued decline, or has it been reversed once more?

STATISTICAL SOURCES

Statistical sources are the same as for Chapter 16, with the addition of the *Fact Book* issued annually by the NYSE: 11 Wall Street, New York, New York, 10005.

BIBLIOGRAPHY

Baumol, W. J.: *The Stock Market and Economic Efficiency,* Fordham University Press, New York, 1965.

Branch, B., and W. Freed: "Bid-Asked Spreads on the Amex and the Big Board," *Journal of Finance,* March 1977, pp. 159–164.

Farrar, D. E.: "Toward a Central Market System: Wall Street's Slow Retreat into the Future," *Journal of Financial and Quantitative Analysis,* November 1974, pp. 815–828.

Fisher, L., and J. H. Lorie: "Rates of Return on Investments in Common Stock: the Year by Year Record 1926–1965," *Journal of Business,* July 1968, pp. 291–316.

Goldsmith, R. W., ed.: *Institutional Investor and Corporate Stock—A Background Study,* National Bureau of Economic Research, Columbia University Press, New York, 1973.

Hamilton, J. L.: "Marketplace Organization and Marketability: NASDAQ, the Stock Exchange, and the National Market System," *Journal of Finance,* May 1978, pp. 487–504.

Keran, M. W.: "Expectations, Money and the Stock Market," Federal Reserve Bank of St. Louis *Review,* January 1971, pp. 16–31.

Malkiel, B., and R. E. Quandt: *Strategies and Rational Decisions in the Securities Option Market,* MIT Press, Cambridge, Mass., 1969.

chapter 18
The Stock Market: Myth versus Research

The market for corporate equities has attracted more attention, generated more myths, but at the same time stimulated more solid economic research than any other segment of the financial markets. The purpose of this chapter will be to compare the myths with the research. Unfortunately, much of the research is still rather inconclusive. However, the situation is such that practical investment policy is coming more and more to follow the guides suggested by this research, rather than the myths that have pervaded the market in the past.

Much of the attention attracted to the market was doubtless due to the popular belief that the stock market was an opportunity by which one could "get rich" quickly. Some have done just that. But some have also suffered sharp losses and even financial reverses, so this had led to still another type of myth: that the market was a dangerous place for the average investor. This chapter should dispel the extremes of both of these quite opposite myths.

This chapter also serves the purpose of indicating how the research that has focused on the stock market might be applied to some other financial markets. An illustration would be helpful: The market for the financial instruments covering real estate, and equity investment in real estate itself, represents an important economic and investment area. It is possible that research into real estate risk and return and its relationship with risk and return in other economic sectors might yield important results. Intuition suggests both parallels and differences, but we should not stop with intuition if research is possible. Another illustration is the capital market in state and local government securities. This used to be considered an almost riskless market, but no longer. Portfolio theory might be tested in this market with great utility, particularly since the appearance of managed investment funds concentrating in these securities.

STOCK MARKET RETURNS

Fortunately, this is one area in which the research of historical stock market returns is remarkably definitive and complete. Two University of Chicago economists, Fisher and Lorie (July 1968) have measured the returns on an average of all the shares listed on the New York Stock Exchange for the period 1926–1965. This forty-year period covered the greatest stock market collapse of all time, as well as what probably was its greatest boom period. They computed returns with dividends reinvested, and also without. They computed returns before and after taxes on income. They computed returns for portfolios that ended in cash and those that ended in securities (both started with cash) so that the effects of commissions were allowed for.

Although this research yielded a mass of calculated rates of return, the one that has been cited most often is 9.3 percent per annum that represents the forty-year cash-to-portfolio return without allowance for taxes. This return was unquestionably higher than the return on either bonds or savings accounts during the same interval and so became a powerful argument for long-term stock market investment.

However, several other features disclosed by this research deserve comment:

1. The return for the first twenty-year half of the period was 6.3 percent; it was 14.1 for the second twenty-year interval. Not only that, but there is great variation in the returns for ten-year intervals and even more for five-year intervals. Just what is "long-term" is more a subjective investor concept than one that has objective scientific content. Thus there is considerable risk depending on when an investor gets started in the stock market.

2. The 9.3 percent return was for the whole market. Research that we shall report later in this chapter has shown that portfolios with less coverage or diversification than the whole market would tend to have an even greater variability of return; in some cases, considerably greater.

3. Slightly more than half the 9.3 percent return was provided by dividends, less than half by capital gains.

4. The time period covered by the study ended in 1965. Since that time more than a decade of further experience has accumulated. This decade has been far less happy for stock market investors. During this decade the return on stock market investment, estimated in the same way, probably would have been less than 5 percent. Thus the average for the fifty-year period would be only slightly above 8 percent. During considerable periods of this decade, high-grade bonds with yields of above 8 percent have been available. The stock market looks less attractive now when compared with bond yields.

5. The fact that a 9.3 percent return was received in the past is *not* a valid argument that such a return can be expected in the future. Although no formal research on the point was conducted, it is intuitively almost certain that no combination of periods in the study covered could have been used as a reliable forecaster of returns in the following periods. Indeed, as reported above in paragraph 4, such was clearly not the case for recent experience.

IS THERE A DEPENDABLE ROUTE TO STOCK MARKET PROFITS?

Myth has it that some stock market investors have done much better than others—and this probably is not an unfounded myth, even if it does not have full support by research. If so, what accounted for the differences? Was it pure luck or was some skill and knowledge the source of superior performance?

The oldest of the formulas for stock market profits was simply: "Buy cheap and sell dear" (which has sometimes been turned into a kind of pun). In more sober terms, this rule is "timing" one's purchases so as to run counter to the thrust of popular opinion. This is a fine intuitive rule, but it was never given any degree of precision, and therefore could not be evaluated critically. For many years Alex Dow, the publisher of *The Wall Street Journal* and originator of the Dow-Jones stock price indices, popularized a theory of stock market prices according to which certain sequences of price movements were thought to forecast future stock prices. The "Dow theory" had many true believers and for a while was influential. Recently very little has been heard of it. Since the Dow theory was best illustrated by use of a chart of stock prices, he was the first of many stock market astrologists who based their forecasts on charts of stock market prices. Such "chartists" or "technical analysts" have gone out of fashion, but a few are still employed by commission brokerage firms or operate independent advisory services.

Very early it was noted that stock prices moved with general economic conditions. It was reasoned that the forecasting of general business conditions could then also supply a stock market forecast as a by-product. The obvious problem was that no one ever devised a very successful method of forecasting general business conditions. One of the most recent versions of this general family of stock market forecasting has focused on money as a determinant of general economic activity and therefore of stock prices. This version continues to enjoy considerable support, and so the formation of monetary policy by the Federal Reserve has become a central feature of stock market price analysis. Purported changes in such policy, or in its indicators such as M_1 or M_2 or the Fed funds rate (see Chapter 11) now are thought to have a substantial bearing on short-term movements in stock prices.

Research results. In the late 1950s and early 1960s a lot of research effort focused on the question of whether or not the past record of stock price movements contained evidence or clues as to later stock market price movements. This was lumped together under the general title of testing of the "random walk" hypothesis (Cootner, 1964). At first the results did not yield any clear single-valued answer but in time it became evident that the practical results, at least after the allowance for payment of stock market commissions, did not give any formulas by which an investor could use the past record of the market to forecast future price movements profitably. The sequence of movements of stock market prices is largely a random walk.

For many years the National Bureau of Economic Research (NBER), in its massive studies of the business cycle, has collected and classified various economic time series according to changes in general economic activity

(Moore, 1961). Some specific indicators moved just about with changes in general economic activity; some lagged behind such activity, but a few led it. Among the slightly more than a dozen (the exact number has been changed from time to time) such leading economic indicators, stock market prices were one. Thus the conclusion emerged that while stock prices could be used to judge future economic activity, a reversal of roles was not possible. The role of money remains unsettled. A large body of research from monetary economists, most of whom had their training at the University of Chicago under Milton Friedman, find money a decisive causative factor in general economic activity. Sprinkel (1971) has applied this conviction to the search for stock market "timing," but so far the results are inconclusive.

Since Beryl Sprinkel is the principal advocate of this relationship, it may be a good idea to follow his line of reasoning. Sprinkel is clearly a monetarist in the full sense of the word. He believes that the relationship of money to general economic activity is clear and causal. An increase in the stock of money stimulates business; if it persists when resources are nearing full employment, it creates inflation. Decreases in the money stock dampen business activity. But since stock prices are or have been found to be a leading indicator by the NBER, how can money be a causal influence on stock prices? Sprinkel takes two lines of approach. First, he argues that since stock prices depend basically on the flow of profits, money influences stock prices through its influence on profits. However, the profits effect of money is often lagged. Sprinkel then adds another factor that can create a more direct result: liquidity. If money supply increases, investors involuntarily find themselves with more funds than they plan. When they adjust their total portfolio of all assets, including money and stocks, they will tend to purchase more stocks, increasing their prices since the supply of stocks is relatively fixed.

However, the influence of money on stock prices is constructive only so long as it expands economic activity, but not if it spills over into inflation. An increasing rate of inflation is an adverse factor in the stock market, and so too much money is bad for the stock market. Sprinkel is not doctrinaire. He recognizes that other factors influence the stock market, and he uses money as a *leading* but not the sole factor in his forecast of likely stock price movements. Furthermore, forecasting monetary policy may be just as futile as attempting to forecast stock prices directly.

The general but far from unanimous conclusion is that the effort to profit by timing stock market purchases and sales by some objective system is not yet fully proved. Obviously many believe that they can "time" their purchases and sales, but we know very little about the results of such activity. Mutual funds, whose portfolios are exposed to public scrutiny, do increase and decrease the proportion of uninvested funds, so they reveal a belief in an ability to "time" transactions. There is no scientific evidence, however, that mutual funds have been successful in this effort on the average and over the long pull.

One strange version of this "timing" belief is in a stock market myth that odd-lot stock buyers almost always time their transactions wrong: buy when prices are high and sell when they are low. Some investors have used the balance of odd-lot transactions to time purchases and sales in the opposite direction. To the best of our knowledge this has not been studied in a formal, scientific way.

DOES SECURITY SELECTION BY ANALYSIS WORK?

The second general line of approach to stock market profits was to pick the "right" stock; one that was "undervalued" or that would "outperform" the market. Obviously this approach could be combined with an effort at "timing" the whole market. An even simpler and cruder version of this approach was the rule to "buy high-quality stocks and hold them a long time." It was hypothesized that in the long run such stocks would always go up in price.

This approach had a far more respectable air than the first one. More than a generation of college students who took investments courses were trained in the art (some courses seemed to imply "science") of security analysis. Graham and Dodd had the leading text (Cottle was added later [1964]). While the canopy of security analysis covered many factors, its principal coverage was the growth and stability of earnings and dividends. For a while there was a debate between the relative emphasis on earnings as against dividends. Regression studies that included both as independent variables generally seemed to find dividends much more important determinants of stock prices than earnings. Durand's study of bank stocks (1957) was representative of such research efforts. However, there were serious methodological questions (the independent variables were not really "independent"), and so the question was not quickly settled. However, in a landmark pair of articles Modigliani and Miller (June 1958, October 1961) argued that the two really were identical sources of information. If earnings were not paid out as dividends but retained, this allowed for a more rapid rate of growth of earnings—and later dividends. The implication was that, if one assumed a profitable use of retained earnings, the dividend decision was immaterial. The focus was on growth.

Even before the Modigliani and Miller articles, stock market practitioners of security analysis had put major emphasis on growth. The cult of growth stocks was the central feature of the stock market of the 1960s. Long-term growth of earnings per share is an undeniable advantage for a company and its shareholders. The question is: Can it be forecast, particularly the period that such growth can be sustained? A stock valuation model with academic origins (Gordon and Shapiro, October 1956) gave a central role to growth, but its arithmetic form made an assumption that was absurd on the face of it—growth to infinity.

Research results. If those equities with a more promising future can be identified by some before the knowledge becomes general, then there should be investment managers who do better than average. In the world of competition, some are always more skillful than others. Because the data were available, the investment performance of mutual funds was one of the first studied (Friend, 1970; Sharpe, 1970; Jensen, Autumn 1972). Some funds did, indeed, do better than others, but if time periods were broken down, consistently superior performance was rare. And such differences as did emerge could, as was found in the more mature research, be accounted for by differences in risk taking. Later research probed into such other areas as pension funds and similar institutional investment funds. In general, these funds did not reveal any capacity to do better than the average of the whole market. Randomly selected portfolios seemed to be able to perform just as well as those picked by the elite of portfolio managers who depended on the best security analysis that money (or commissions) could buy.

The results of this research tend, of course, to be discouraging to the professional practitioners of security analysis. Their livelihood and earnings depend on being able to pick winners better than the average of the market. The profession is still practiced, even if its effectiveness is in doubt. (Racetrack handicappers still make a good living: better than that of bettors.)

The research, however, can be used to comfort and encourage the average investor. The long-run average return from common-stock investment has been good. The theory suggested only that portfolio diversification is needed. This can be achieved by an investment fund or company. Already a few "index" funds are being organized: funds that should approximate the movement of the market as a whole. No-load and listed closed-end investment companies can give the amateur investor a fair approximation of the market. The uninformed and busy investor can venture into common-stock investment with these vehicles—and he or she may do just as well as the average of the professionals.

Whether the research is right or not, we do know that in one area, practice is quite different from that which is indicated by theory. The Capital Asset Pricing Model (CAPM) suggests that all security buyers should have the same market portfolio but vary the degree of risk they assume by differing degrees of positive or negative leveraging. But investors do hold vastly different portfolios; some "conservative" and some "aggressive." The same is true of mutual funds. Furthermore, we know that investment advisors and the trust departments of commercial banks charge investors for services that theory, and some supporting research, suggest cannot be performed, i.e., delivery of superior investment performance. Unfortunately, there is evidence that these professionals of the market do not regularly deliver these services with much success.

The question remains unresolved. Rather than declare the whole profession of security analysis and portfolio management obsolete and irrelevant, Lorie and Hamilton suggest that they might change the services they offer to emphasize advice on risk assumption (1973). Investors are often poor judges of how much risk they should assume; very often they do not even fully realize how much they *are* assuming. Advice on this can be given; both theory and research suggest that risk differentials can be measured to some extent and that this can then be applied to the issue of investor risk assumption.

RISK: WHAT IS ITS PRICE?

Chapter 6 has already presented one of the major formulations of investment strategy of this generation. In the early 1950s Markowitz presented the novel but eminently sensible idea that diversification could be best accomplished by combining assets whose variability of return had low—or if possible, negative—correlations. Diversification was a very old idea in portfolio construction. What is more, intuitive wisdom had held that diversification should be accomplished by combining unlike securities such as those in differing industries. The Markowitz idea was nearer the truth since the stocks of companies, even if in differing industries, might still be highly correlated in return and price movement and therefore not give very much protection. But while the Markowitz idea was simple, the mathematics for giving it expression was cumbersome since it involved calculation of correlations representing the factorial of the number of stocks from which choices could be made. Sharpe simplified the required calculations. But even more to the point, he created the Capital Asset Pricing Model (CAPM), which could be used as a security valuation model.

A simple but profoundly important idea that grew out of the Markowitz/ Sharpe (March 1952, 1959, 1970) concept (and which has already been developed in Chapter 6) was that the bearing of systematic risk had a market-determined price but that nonsystematic risk should have no measurable price since it could be avoided by the selection of an efficient portfolio. It was this idea that became the basis for researching and testing the CAPM (Jensen, Autumn 1972).

Research results Risk bearing has a measurable price. Much of the difference between the returns from portfolios can be attributed to different degrees of risk assumed. A further finding was that the relationship of this risk-return price was reasonably linear with respect to risk (as measured by beta, of course). The only exception was that the portfolios having the highest risk, appeared to have less than the expected return. In other words, the returns of high-risk stocks did not fall on the regression line but below it. This may be explained, so the major researchers hypothesized, by the "lottery ticket principle": Extreme risk takers will accept a smaller *expected* return in exchange for the possibility of a higher *possible* return.

One negative result of the research was a failure to demonstrate with assurance that nonsystematic risk does not have a price. That point remains moot.

One further point remains for note: As was shown in Figures 6-1 and 6-2, the most efficient portfolios lie along the upper left-hand edge of the envelope. An investor might most usefully pick the portfolio at the point of tangency (Figure 6-2) of the ray connecting the risk-free rate to the envelope. The investor could reduce risk by going to the left of this point by partial investment in the risk-free asset; the assumption of greater risk could be done by borrowing at the risk-free rate and carrying a leveraged portfolio. If all investors followed this rule, they would all carry identical market portfolios, but, as we noted above, this is not done.

IS UNSYSTEMATIC RISK WHOLLY UNREWARDED?

CAPM theory tells us that expected returns include a premium for the bearing of systematic risk, but that a rational or efficient market would not give any reward for bearing *un*systematic risk. To put the point bluntly, it says that a security with a highly variable return but with zero correlation with the market return would have no risk premium and would yield only the risk-free rate of return. The question of whether or not unsystematic risk is without reward has not gone unnoticed by researchers. Unfortunately only inconclusive results have been found. The problem is that most stocks have returns that are positively correlated with the market return and so the very few exceptions do not furnish adequate data for conclusive testing. The question remains moot.

Another issue of importance is the stability of the covariances and correlations of the individual securities (betas). The research on this point is far from unanimous in its results. The betas of individual stocks do not appear to have very much stability. The betas of portfolios, however, do appear to have reasonable stability—though this is not really fully proved. The true believers in the CAPM find the evidence convincing enough to be willing to base investment policy on it: to create portfolios by randomizing techniques and to control total risk by positive or negative leveraging. Those who are not yet true believers (and they are many, including many academic economists who have worked in this area) still elect to use the investment method of security analysis (Malkiel, 1973).

The use of variance and covariance and correlation with the market portfolio as risk measures is far from fully accepted. At the fringe of this research, quite a few have tried other measures drawn from the arsenal of statistics. (Markowitz himself experimented with semivariance). Some nonacademic but experienced investors resist complete conversion by the feeling that risk eludes all these measures. Risk, to them, is more of the nature of random shocks, like earthquakes or the disasters of nature, that do not fit neatly into the arms of statistical technology. Life for a middle-aged or elderly investor is not "long-term" and he or she can't wait for the averages that are the very foundation of statistical significance. These questions of methodology are yet to be resolved.

ARE COMMON STOCKS AN INFLATION HEDGE?

Until less than a decade ago, the conventional wisdom was that common stocks were an effective hedge for investors against the ravages of inflation. But when the United States suffered an inflationary interval that started in 1967 and at first seemed to pause in 1970, stocks did not seem to counter loss of purchasing power; but the point was moot. However, when even more rapid price inflation came in 1974 and 1975 amidst a recession, stock prices retreated and loss of investor purchasing power was thus doubly compounded.

Research has been addressed to the point. Nelson (May 1976) finds that at least over the short run, stock prices and inflation are negatively correlated. However, Cagan (March 1974) in work for the NBER based on experience in other countries where hyperinflation had been experienced, as well as the United States, concluded that there was some positive value in common stocks as inflation hedges.

This research must be treated as preliminary and nonconclusive. There has not been enough experience with the more secular kind of inflation that now seems to be our problem to give us the foundation for dependable findings.

One problem with evaluating the effect of inflation on the stock market is that the market should, theoretically, become depressed when the rate of inflation is *rising*, but that stocks should be inflation hedges when the rate of inflation is *stable* (even if high). Since we have not had enough experience with stable inflation, it is too soon to say whether common stocks are a hedge against *stable* inflation as theory suggests. Our guess is that they are.

HAVE OUR GROWTH PROSPECTS FUNDAMENTALLY CHANGED?

Since capital gains for the stock market as a whole depend mainly on economic growth, it is important to focus more directly on both the record and prospects for growth. As we indicated near the beginning of this chapter, over the forty-year period of 1926 to 1965 a little less than half the 9.3 percent return on common stocks was due to capital gains (about 4.5 percent). This is not too far from the rate of economic growth over the period covered if a moderate allowance is made for secular price increases over the same period. The price increase for the period (using the price index implicit in the GNP deflator) was less than 2 percent per annum. The real economic growth rate during the same period was not far from 3 percent.

How likely is it that this growth rate will continue on into the future? We already know from the example of energy that world resources are limited. To what extent the growth rate of the past two or three generations has been due to a one-time exploitation of resources that can never be replaced is hard to say—but it is a sobering reason for not taking growth continuation for granted. We already know that the rate of population growth has started to slow down. We also know that through recorded history, until the industrial revolution of the nineteenth century, economic growth was never very long sustained by any nation, and always then only at rates far below those of recent history.

IS THE STOCK MARKET EFFICIENT?

The concept of efficiency has several meanings; here we shall deal with three: First, does the market incorporate information about both general economic conditions and about specific companies promptly and precisely? Second, is the allocation of capital at an optimum in terms of economic efficiency? Third, is the stock market operationally or technologically efficient?

The research, already reported, that the stock market is a leading economic indicator can be cited as evidence that the market promptly incorporates all known information about general business conditions and economic activity. But what about the affairs of specific companies? The research, already reported, about the inability of professional mutual fund managers to outperform the market suggests considerable efficiency in the incorporation of market information. Even more severe tests have been made by studying the investment timing of insiders who must report their transactions to the SEC. These studies are not conclusive (Samuelson, Spring 1965). They suggest, however, that insiders can profit from early access to information but most of these advantages disappear very rapidly: usually between the time insiders trade and the reports of the trades are published by the SEC. This is fragmentary support for the efficiency of the stock market as a reflector of information.

Efficiency in the sense of an optimum capital allocation is a much harder subject to deal with (Nielson, May 1976). The starting point is some basis for the determination of an optimum that requires recourse to the arcane reaches of utility analysis. Some interesting efforts have been made (Gordon, May 1976; Rubinstein, May 1976). The results so far: inconclusive!

Still a third kind of efficiency might be mentioned briefly: Is the stock market "efficient" in the sense of requiring of corporations, which raise money in the stock market, a return that is only reasonably above the return expected and demanded by investors? This can be viewed as parallel to the concept of engineering efficiency: An engine is efficient if the energy output is a reasonably large fraction of the potential energy input available in the fuel used. The cost of flotation has been studied, and the stock market does demand a fairly high price for new equity capital. However, financing by rights has become quite cheap (in terms of transaction costs) and financing by retained earnings virtually costless (also in terms of transaction costs). Compared with the open equity markets of all other developed nations, the United States almost certainly has an unusually efficient equity market.

One recent development suggests evidence leading in a slightly different direction. In May 1975 brokerage commission rates were made fully competitive. Brokers could charge what they wished to charge; investors could shop around for cheap rates. For the big institutional investors, this undoubtedly yielded an increase in market efficiency. Since they dominate the market in a quantitative sense, this can be counted a clear increase in efficiency in this sense. For small investors, however, commission rates have tended to increase during the past decade. Competitive rates have not appeared to help any but the very active traders who can offer a brokerage house considerable volume. The "buy-and-hold" investor has a few new options but on the average is not as well off. This raises a question: Was it ever really efficient (in the operational sense) to invite and encourage stock market investment by the small investor? Is it possible that the market would become more efficient by exclusion of the uneconomic small investor from the stock market?

THE STOCK MARKET MAY BE EFFICIENT BUT IS IT RATIONAL?

Any retrospective examination of the stock market shows that it has almost always "overdone" it. When economic difficulties arise, the market overdiscounts the problems; when things are going well, the market lets its optimistic expectations get out of hand. The amplitudes of swings in market prices are far greater than are the amplitudes of swings in the discounted value of dividends and capital gains—if we make the computations after the event.

Another observation of fact is worth recording here: Almost always the rate of *decline* of the stock market is slower than the rate of advance when it turns up.

Apparently the perceptions of investors about bad news is rather slower than it is about good news. However, the NBER research on leading economic indicators suggests that the stock market is an equally effective (or ineffective) forecaster of both ups and downs.

Do these observations mean that the market is inefficient? Not necessarily. The market may have efficiently reflected the information *and its interpretation* available at the time. That subsequent events differ from earlier expectations only reflects the inability of all of us to forecast the future.

All the above observations refer to the stock market as a whole. What about individual securities? Prices of individual securities also often seem to move excessively relative to the good news or bad news that affect them. CAPM theory tells us that the price of a security reflects its portfolio value as well as its individual value. There is, however, no research evidence, as far as we know, that suggests individual security prices move excessively because their portfolio values change apart from their individual values as investments. A reasonable interpretation of the fact, observed in retrospect, that security prices seem to fluctuate excessively is that markets efficiently reflect the interpretations that nervous and timid investors put on current information—but that investors themselves are the irrational elements in the market.

PROJECTS AND QUESTIONS

1. Inflation was cooling down as this chapter was being written (Winter 1977). What has been happening with inflation since that time? Can you detect any relationship of recent inflationary developments and stock market developments?
2. After reading this chapter do you still think you can beat the stock market by picking winners? If so, pick five, put the names away for a year and then compare with the changes in *average* market prices. (If you pick very risky issues, what results would you expect—if the CAPM is right?)
3. Check recent issues of the *Journal of Finance* and report on any new additions to research on the stock market that have been made since this text was published.

BIBLIOGRAPHY

Cagan, P.: "Common Stock Values and Inflation—The Historical Record of Many Countries," National Bureau of Economic Research, *Supplementary Report #13*, March 1974.

Cootner, P. ed.: *The Random Character of Stock Market Prices,* MIT Press, Cambridge, Mass., 1964.

This volume of essays contains most of the early articles including those of Roberts, Osborne, Alexander, and others.

Durand, D.: "Bank Stock Prices and the Bank Capital Problem," National Bureau of Economic Research, *Occasional Paper #54,* 1957.

Fama, E.: "Efficient Capital Markets: A Review of Theory and Empirical Work," *Journal of Finance,* May 1970, pp. 383–417.

A summary of more recent work on the random walk.

Fisher, L., and J. H. Lorie: "Rates on Return on Investments in Common Stocks: the Year-by-Year Record 1926–1965," *Journal of Business,* July 1968, pp. 291–316.

Friend, I., M. Blume, and J. Crockett: *Mutual Funds and Other Institutional Investors,* McGraw-Hill, New York, 1970.

Gordon, M. J.: "A Portfolio Theory of the Social Discount Rate and the Public Debt," *Journal of Finance,* May 1976, pp. 199–214.

————, and E. Shapiro: "Capital Equipment Analysis: the Required Rate of Profit," *Management Science,* October 1956.

Graham, Dodd, and Cottle: *Security Analysis,* 4th ed, McGraw-Hill, New York, 1964.

Jensen, M. C.: "Capital Markets: Theory and Evidence," *Bell Journal,* Autumn 1972, pp. 357–398.

An excellent review article covering the work of almost all those who have worked in this field.

Lorie, J. H., and M. Hamilton: *The Stock Market: Theory & Evidence,* Irwin, Homewood, Ill., 1973.

Malkiel, B. G.: *A Random Walk Down Wall Street,* Norton, 1973.

Markowitz, H. M.: "Portfolio Selection," *Journal of Finance,* March 1952, pp. 77–91.

————: *Portfolio Selection: Efficient Diversification of Investments,* Cowles Series, Wiley, New York, 1959.

Miller, M. H., and F. Modigliani: "Dividend Policy, Growth, and the Valuation of Shares," *Journal of Business,* October 1961.

Modigliani, F., and M. H. Miller: "The Cost of Capital, Corporate Finance, and the Theory of Investment," *American Economic Review,* June 1958.

Moore, G. H., ed.: *Business Cycle Indicators,* 2 vol. National Bureau of Economic Research, 1961.

The current data are available in the *Business Conditions Digest* published monthly by the Department of Commerce.

Nelson, C. R.: "Inflation and Rates of Return on Common Stocks," *Journal of Finance,* May 1976, pp. 471–482.

Nielson, N. C.: "The Investment Decision of the Firm Under Uncertainty and the Allocational Efficiency of the Capital Markets," *Journal of Finance,* May 1976, pp. 587–601.

Rubinstein, M.: "The Strong Case for the Generalized Logarithmic Utility Model, etc." *Journal of Finance,* May 1976, pp. 551–572.

Samuelson, P. A.: "Proof that Properly Anticipated Prices Fluctuate Randomly," *Industrial Management Review,* Spring 1965.

See also Samuelson's statement before the Committee on Banking and Currency of the Senate, August 2, 1967 on mutual fund legislation.

Sharpe, W. F.: *Portfolio Theory and Capital Markets,* McGraw-Hill, New York, 1970.

Sprinkel, B. W.: *Money and Markets: A Monetarist View,* Irwin, Homewood, Ill., 1971.

Part Four

The International Environment of Financial Markets

chapter 19
International Dimensions of Financial Markets: The Exchange Rate Barrier

The wealth accumulated in a country is not always committed to financial institutions within that country, nor is it necessarily allocated to demanders of capital within the country of accumulation. Financial markets extend beyond national boundaries. Almost all large banks, both commercial and investment, look to international business as a source of considerable profit. Profit is not the only gain from international business; the world is more likely to remain at peace if there is large economic intercourse between nations—which inevitably involves financial markets.

Superimposed on the monetary systems of individual nations is a kind of international monetary system. It tends to be rather fragile because international relationships are not subject to the specific sanctions of domestic law. The bridge between monetary systems—exchange rates—is always a central feature of money markets. Governmental economic policy must be aimed not merely at domestic problems but also at the international financial situation of a country; small but developed nations are more conscious of this than we are in the United States. International finance is seldom far removed from international politics and ultimately from the forces that determine the relationships of nations. Good international finance cannot cure the hatreds and traditional enmities that separate nations, but bad finance can exacerbate these feelings beyond endurance.

This chapter will deal with the basic barrier faced whenever a financial market crosses a national boundary: the need to convert its native money into the money of the foreign market being entered. This barrier has become complicated, and it is not at all clear that present arrangements will continue unchanged. We shall present, therefore, more of a progress report than a definitive description. The following chapter will deal with the problems of the financial relationships of countries as expressed in their balance of payments.

Public policy is expressed in foreign exchange systems; it is even more pervasively expressed in the policies countries follow with respect to public influence on balances of payments. These two chapters, therefore, are concerned not only with private financial institutions and markets but also with the roles of government and intergovernmental relationships.

WHY FINANCIAL MARKETS HAVE AN INTERNATIONAL DIMENSION

International economic intercourse is almost as old as history. When early explorers ventured beyond their native lands, they found attractive commodities not available at home. Spices were one of the first of the commodities that generated trade with far-off lands. Columbus was able to persuade a queen to finance his west-sailing venture with the hope (false, as it turned out) of finding a shorter and cheaper route to the sources of spices in the Indies. Such voyages required financing, so financial markets of those days were early involved in foreign business. When the Americas turned out to lack spices, the temporary disappointment that followed was quickly replaced by much zeal in exploiting the new Americas as sources of gold and silver. The (then) grossly underdeveloped Americas were quickly explored and developed by both private venturers as well as governments, with finance being central to the process of exploration and exploitation.

Once the Americas reached a moderate degree of development, they, in turn, became international explorers and developers. Whale oil and natural dyes were early commodities of trade. Raw materials have always been an early item in international development. Copper, tin, petroleum, and bauxite are only a few of the many materials that have stimulated foreign exploration. And in every case, finance has followed the explorer.

Raw materials do not exhaust the potentials of foreign business. When a country develops a superior technology, it may reap the profits not only of its sale at home, but also abroad. At one time the United States was a very large exporter of automobiles. Subsequently other countries developed their own automotive industries, and they have been able to penetrate our markets to some extent. We sell a great deal of aircraft to foreign countries. The greater efficiency of the airplane as a transporter of people across oceans has in turn made a great increase in still another form of international economic activity: travel. Tourism has now become a major source of revenue for many countries, and by the same token, has created a major demand for foreign currencies in those countries whose citizens travel more than they entertain foreign visitors.

The participation of financial markets in these processes is widely varied. A corporation that goes abroad in search of raw materials will need a banking connection that can serve it in a variety of ways. The simplest service, though fundamentally important, is that of supplying such foreign money as the corporation will need. The commercial bank serving such a customer will find it useful to establish a correspondent relationship with a foreign bank that has offices in the area where its customer is seeking to exploit and develop the new raw material source. The bank may even locate a branch in this foreign country. It will need to be able to advise the customer about laws and regulations that apply to the type of business it is going to conduct. Even more important, though much more intangible, it needs to be able to advise its customers whether it will encounter a hospitable or a hostile political and bureaucratic climate.

A corporation going abroad to sell its products will need to have knowledge not only of laws and regulations but also of the creditworthiness of its potential customers. Because doing business abroad usually means keeping balances in foreign currencies, a bank will need to advise its foreign-operating clients as to risks of loss in such holdings and ways of minimizing the risks. While our corporations doing business abroad will usually establish banking relationships in the countries in which they do business (particularly if their United States banks do not have branches conveniently located in such areas), there is a general feeling that the selection of such foreign banking relationships should be compatible with their domestic bankers.

Our financial institutions and markets also have foreign customers. Foreign companies entering our market usually have a United States banking relationship. When interest rate relationships are favorable, they may prefer to borrow in the United States rather than at home. Many of the less developed nations have customer relationships with our big money market banks and borrow from them as well as from the public agencies, which will be described in Chapter 20. Foreign banks also establish branches in the United States, with major concentrations in port cities such as New York and San Francisco, but also, because of the St. Lawrence Seaway, as far inland as Chicago.

Our stock market has attracted investment by foreigners. At the present time, the newly oil-rich Arab states are the most conspicuous example. However, Switzerland has long been an important customer of the New York Stock Exchange. The Zurich financial district is often quite busy into late evening hours until the NYSE closes.

It is also sometimes more convenient to borrow in a foreign market than at home. For years, Canadian businesses and provinces have come to the New York capital market where they can borrow larger amounts, and usually at lower interest rates, than at home. We shall find that the somewhat erratic bunching of such borrowing activities sometimes leads to interesting results in the related markets for foreign exchange. These examples anticipate the subject matter of our next chapter to some extent.

These examples also serve to make one central point: The advantages of international economic relationships are so great that they push participation across national boundaries even though there are both problems and risks in venturing into other currencies. The purpose of the following section will be to develop the economic rationale for international economic relationships before we turn to the real barriers there are to such relationships.

WHY TRADE? ABSOLUTE ADVANTAGE AND COMPARATIVE ADVANTAGE

The advantages of trade seem so obvious to any sensible person that one must ask: Why argue the point? It is because the history of nations shows that this simple lesson is easily forgotten, usually to the disadvantage of all involved. If the world never changed, perhaps the lesson could stay learned. However, new technology or new development sometimes causes a change that in turn produces public policy inimical to international trade.

When an absolute advantage exists, the pressure to trade is very strong. Brazil and several African states can produce coffee; we can't do it at all efficiently. But we can produce farm machinery efficiently; so trade is obviously advantageous to both sides. We also produce soy beans more efficiently than Japan, which lacks suitable soil and climate. However, Japan has a body of experienced camera designers and a productive work force to assemble them; so we sell them soy beans and buy their cameras. However, this last example can be used to illustrate the working of *comparative* advantage. We have excellent lens designers and camera producers. If there were a need, we probably could assemble a labor force just as productive. During World War II we were able to do so. Before the war was over our optical industry was very efficient; maybe the best in the world. It is quite likely that the United States has an *absolute* advantage in soy beans and could have one in camera production, if there were any reason for having it. But if our absolute advantage is greater in soy beans than in cameras, it will still be to our advantage to buy cameras and sell soy beans. Arithmetic illustrations of comparative advantage can be found in most elementary economics textbooks.

One aspect of comparative advantage, however, deserves special attention from the student of financial markets. Efficiency is a very general term covering a wide variety of circumstances. Many subtle differences in circumstances may account for differences in efficiency. Differences in climate and soil are obvious causes of absolute advantage. Differences in educational levels, cultural traditions, and work skills can also create absolute advantages, but ones that are not necessarily as enduring. Differences in the amount of capital can also create absolute differences in efficiency. A rich country with an educated population, cultural traditions that encourage hard work, and ample capital is likely to have absolute advantages in a wide variety of products. Their external needs are confined mainly to raw materials and a few products that require exotic climates or soils.

Financial markets come to play an important role in determining comparative advantages. If financial markets are international in character and distribute capital through wide areas of the world, they may change the balance of advantages. The export of capital to underdeveloped countries may change the terms of comparative advantage. But this process often takes on political as well as economic dimensions. Proud nations do not like to see the control of important industries in the hands of foreigners. We do not need to look far afield for illustrations of this feeling. It is evident in the feelings of our neighbor to the north, Canada. But the canons of finance come into play: Why export capital without retaining control of it? The conflict between political sensibilities and financial considerations is almost inherent in the process.

What this means is that absolute advantage and comparative advantage are not enduring, stable elements of international relationships. Both can be changed and do change. While the rate of change is usually not fast, victims are almost always left in the path of change. These victims may have a claim on the political sympathies of their countrymen, and political interposition to modify the natural economic flow of trade is a natural and common phenomenon.

Another force sometimes obliterates the influence of both an absolute and comparative advantage: cyclical swings in prices and costs. At one level of prices the balance of advantage may be in one direction, but if prices change unequally, the balance may go in the other direction. Cycles in both economic activity and prices are widespread in the world of international trade. As a result, short-run balance of comparative advantage may shift considerably, which seems to give a considerable instability to international trade, particularly in some raw materials.

Fixed costs also are a factor in the determination of comparative advantage. When countries develop considerable plant capacity, they may want to sell in international markets even if they cover only variable costs with a moderate margin for profit. This is called "dumping" and is understandably resented in the receiving countries.

All these factors illustrate the proposition that comparative advantage, which looks like a simple matter of logic in the economics textbook, may prove complicated and even controversial in the world of affairs. It leads to the fact that artificial "protectionist" barriers to trade still exist even in our more rational world.

BARRIERS TO INTERNATIONAL TRADE

Before launching on an examination of some of the barriers to trade between nations, we have a happy fact to report: World trade has shown a strong tendency to increase during the post-World War II years. Even after correction for inflation of prices, the volume of "real" world trade appears to have increased about 6 percent a year during these post-World War II years. However, the year-to-year increase has often been erratic. In some boom years, such as the year 1973, the increase was about 12 percent, while just two years later, in the recession year of 1975, world trade fell by about 5 percent.

Another interesting factor is that the already well-developed industrial nations of Western Europe and the United States seem to have had larger increases in world trade than the less developed nations. This has varied widely, however, and the vast and almost catastrophic problems of the sudden large increase in world petroleum prices in late 1973 and in 1974 show how drastically trade can change in its character as well as its total volume.

However, these happy tidings of large increases in world trade should not cover up the real and continuing barriers to such trade. The first and still probably the most important is the cost of transport. Even in domestic trade, transport is often an important part of total costs of delivered goods. But in world trade it generally turns out to be an even more important factor. Goods with high value for weight and size (cameras) do not present much of a problem. Also, in a highly industrialized and compact area, such as Western Europe, transport cannot be too important an element and is usually very little different for domestic and foreign trade. A north German manufacturer can deliver just about as easily to Brussels, or to Paris, as to Munich or Vienna. Nevertheless, large and bulky commodities are greatly affected by cost of transport. Coal is an important commodity in international trade; with energy problems it could become even greater. But the cost of transport is always a large element in its price.

Another barrier to trade is simply differences in legal systems and regulations. Domestic trade regulations, such as for consumer protection or for environmental protection, exist in many other countries than our own, but their nature varies from country to country. Gearing up to sell in a number of markets may create problems both with respect to labeling as well as quality of products.

Trade customs and habits may not have the force of law, but they can also present problems and barriers to trade. Products socially acceptable in one society may be strongly proscribed in another.

Perhaps the oldest if not the greatest barrier of all, however, is the natural chauvinism of persons. While some people with hypersophisticated tastes may prefer foreign goods, many of us have a natural preference for home products.

Another barrier is differences in political systems. Totalitarian countries generally centralize foreign trade in government agencies so they engage in a kind of "state" trading. Free countries generally leave trade to private businessmen. The interface of these two systems may lead to serious problems and certainly tend to restrict trade. Russian purchases of our wheat, its effects on wheat prices and on our domestic cost of living, and the bitter internal political controversy it generated, illustrates this "interface" problem.

A related barrier is that of international cartels, such as the Organization of Petroleum Exporting Countries (OPEC), which form near monopolies to increase price. They may increase the monetary value of trade by such actions, but the actual physical volume is certainly decreased; worse, the willingness to depend on foreign sources is certainly weakened. Who can depend on the reliability of supply from an international cartel?

Perhaps the most widespread barrier, however, is that which is introduced by differences in money systems, which necessitates the exchange of one money into another. We shall turn to that barrier in the next section.

THE FINANCIAL ASPECTS OF INTERNATIONAL TRADE

Now that we have examined the basic economic logic of international trade, as well as some of the barriers to it, the time has come to look at the financial aspects of such trade. The principal one is that trade gives rise to purchases and sales of one currency for another: foreign exchange. This is just about the oldest of all banking transactions; money changers were mentioned (not very flatteringly) in the Bible! This would appear to be a very simple market, but it is not. Some of the most interesting and sophisticated of trading practices have arisen in this market.[1]

The need for passage from one currency into another is a further barrier to trade; sometimes it is only a trivial barrier, but other times it proves to be one of considerable importance. Minimizing this barrier is a legitimate goal of public financial policy—but often it remains only a goal.

The Money Barrier: Multiple Monetary Systems and Foreign Exchange

The principal barrier to the completely free international passage of financial influences is the multiplicity of monetary and legal systems. As we emphasized in the very first chapter of this book, money is the vehicle through which both short-term credit and longer-term investment operations proceed. Money is the universal solvent to the financial system. Within the borders of a nation with a unified money system, financial transactions can take place over wide areas without encountering any barrier. A dollar in New York is virtually the same as a dollar in San Francisco.

National borders, however, give rise to monetary barriers. Each nation has adopted its own monetary system. Most financial transactions in each nation take place with that nation's own money. There are some exceptions to the rule: Anyone who travels with dollars can usually buy goods and pay bills with dollars. This only means, however, that the exchange of moneys will be done by the vendor of goods and services (and probably at a little extra profit). We have already been introduced to a money market in our dollars that developed outside our borders. However, this is an exception. Passing over a national boundary usually requires some kind of exchange of money.

Just how much of a barrier this proves to be varies with time and circumstances. In the nineteenth century a large proportion of the leading nations made their currencies convertible into gold. As long as this was true and gold could be freely imported and exported, the rates of exchange between currencies were set by the ratios of the physical definition of monetary units. Variations from this parity were limited to the cost of physically transporting gold. Thus reasonable stability prevailed, so that business planning could take place on the assumption of such rates.

The system, however, broke down from time to time. The usual reason was that monetary expansion in some countries would proceed to the point where convertibility into gold could not be maintained in the face of loss of confidence. Only when confidence was restored would convertibility become possible. It was a system that worked well as long as money holders had confidence that they could exercise the right and thus did not feel compelled to do so.

---

[1]Kubarych, cited in the Bibliography, is strongly recommended as a supplementary reading.

Some countries maintained the effect of such convertibility by holding stocks not of gold but rather of leading currencies that were convertible into gold. This gold *exchange* standard is important, since it furnished the example on which most of our present world monetary arrangements have been based.

The nineteenth century was an era of internationalism. Its critics also call it an era of colonialism (although this system had started much earlier), but the net effect was the development of many areas rather more rapidly than would have been possible without colonialism. The network of reasonably stable monetary relationships permitted not only a growth in world trade but also the movement of capital from country to country. Much of the rapid development of the United States was due to the inflow of foreign capital that built our railroads and cities and aided the rapid push from an agrarian economy to an industrialized one.

But the system of gold convertibility always carried with it the risk of collapse. When money expanded faster than gold reserves, this exposure was increased. World War I was accompanied by a general suspension of gold convertibility of currencies, but at the time it was widely assumed that the system would be restored after the war. Efforts at restoration were made, but most of them collapsed in the Great Depression or even before. The Great Depression was followed by a period of nationalism, and the currency systems of the great nations were generally separated by systems of exchange control. And then came World War II.

For many, the principal political and economic lesson of World War II and of the events that had preceded it was that internationalism had to be restored. The political aspects of this restoration were to be found in the United Nations and the financial aspects in the Bretton Woods agreements that led to the establishment of the International Monetary Fund (IMF) and the International Bank for Reconstruction and Development (the "World Bank"). Our interest is mainly in the system of monetary relationships created by the IMF.

The great stability of the United States during an era in which many foreign nations had suffered great instability had led to the accumulation of a great gold stock. At the peak, the United States had two-thirds of the world's visible gold supply (an uncounted but large amount was in private hoards or unreported Russian reserves). In the negotiation of the Bretton Woods agreements for the IMF, gold was kept as a basic part of the international monetary system. But its part was a new and somewhat reduced one. In the panics of the 1930s, the private ownership of gold had been outlawed in the United States and in some other countries. Gold was made an asset of official monetary agencies. Its significance became more international than national. The United States, to its later embarrassment, insisted on the retention of gold in this international role. Each IMF nation was required by the agreements to denominate its currency in terms either of gold or of a currency convertible into gold. The United States was the only one to denominate its currency in gold; the others denominated their currencies in dollars! This restored the system of fixed exchange rates that many felt was so essential to world trade and capital movements, but it left the United States and its dollar with a special role; the dollar came to be a kind of international as well as national money. As long as the United States preserved a monetary and fiscal balance that commanded the confidence of the world by being strong so that the dollar would be in demand, the system could work.

The Dollar as a Reserve Currency

In the early post–World War II years when the dollar was the strongest currency in the world, it was natural that it should be treated as a reserve asset by other countries. The Bretton Woods agreement and practice both solidified this arrangement. But when the dollar was no longer the strongest currency, the stronger ones resisted assuming this role. The West Germans (deutschemark), the Swiss (franc), and the Japanese (yen) did not wish to have their currencies used as reserve currencies and they placed obstacles in the road of such use. Foreign holders of these currencies were taxed, forbidden to have certain kinds of holdings, or discouraged by even more direct means. The two nations whose currencies had been reserve currencies—Great Britain and the United States—had ultimately found that role more troublesome than profitable. In the short run it seems like a great advantage; in the long run it can threaten domestic stability excessively.

The dollar has been weak against the three major currencies listed in the preceding paragraph. The prestige of the dollar has greatly diminished; some would say that it has vanished completely. Nevertheless, the dollar continues to be a reserve currency. It might have been expected that the dollar devaluations in 1971 and 1973 would have choked off the dollar as a Eurocurrency—but it has not. In fact, the Eurodollar market has continued to expand, as we shall see in the next chapter.

Decline of Bretton Woods System

The IMF continues as an institution, but the Bretton Woods agreement that created it is dead. What did the Bretton Woods agreement aim to do? It was an effort to retain much of the classical kind of international monetary system while making it workable in the post–World War II environment. Even though the Bretton Woods system failed, its principles seem to many to still be the most desirable goal, with present variable exchange rates a less desirable alternative forced on the world by unfortunate circumstances. The Bretton Woods agreement aimed at:

1. Preserving the classical gold standard, but limiting the circuit of gold dealings to the member governments and/or their central banks. It also contained elements of the classical gold-exchange system since it made the U.S. dollar a reserve currency, which put the implied responsibility on the United States of preserving the gold convertibility of the dollar with all other central banks and governments. The Bretton Woods agreement did supplement gold with drawing rights in the IMF, so the classical monetary expansion system could be said to have been used to give some flexibility to the volume of international reserves.
2. The Bretton Woods agreements also preserved, along with gold, the

concept of fixed exchange rates. However, the agreement did not contemplate fixity to perpetuity but for periods as long as was practical or possible. It allowed for devaluation under specified circumstances, which was viewed as a kind of safety valve.

3. The third element in the Bretton Woods agreement was not spelled out but was implied: It was that each member would use domestic monetary and fiscal policy in some measure to make its internal economic affairs consonant with those of world economic conditions. It implied an acceptance of what might be called monetary "internationalism."

The Bretton Woods system has not been formally disbanded by the member countries. The IMF continues to operate much as before, and many of the formal trappings, even if rather meaningless, still are kept and observed. What is more, the system did not fall apart with any one single blow; it disintegrated bit by bit, which may explain why the institutions it created continue (and why they argue that they serve useful and important purposes) even though the basis of the agreement is largely disintegrated. An account of how Bretton Woods disintegrated may be useful in understanding where we are now and what the problems are of creating a new system.

The first element of disintegration came when the U.S. dollar lost some of its scarcity value. A dollar shortage that prevailed in the first decade and a half after World War II was quickly replaced by a dollar glut. Our gold stock, which had been very large during the war, was depleted by conversions of the central banks of other countries having more dollars than they needed or wanted. Some countries, West Germany most notably, refrained from such conversion but just accumulated dollars; if they had not, the loss of gold by the United States might have disrupted the Bretton Woods system even earlier than it happened. About the only factor that kept the system functioning was that the growth of world trade was more rapid than the growth of the gold stock from mining, so more monetary reserves were needed, and the accumulation of dollars by other countries went on for a long time after gold conversion was theoretically possible only so long as it was not fully exercised in practice. In fact, during the mid-1960s other countries joined West Germany in refraining from gold conversion to the full extent of their legal rights, which shored up the system. Another shoring action was by the IMF itself in supplementing its drawing rights with *supplementary* drawing rights (SDRs).

Another step in the disintegration of the Bretton Woods system was the emergence of a fairly large and active private gold market. For some years there had been a small private gold market in which prices for gold were above the official conversion price of the dollar, then $35. Gold-producing countries channeled some of their output into this market, but it did not absorb their full output at first, and so they were forced to sell some of their output at official prices. But the market grew and soon absorbed most of the new output. First the leading Western nations tried to control the price of gold in this private market. When this failed, they then tried a two-tier pricing system, which also soon failed. Finally the gold pool was disbanded and for a while did nothing. All gold went into the private market, of course, and so the IMF system came to have a smaller proportion of gold and a larger proportion of drawing rights, whether regular or special, in the system of monetary reserves.

The Post–Bretton Woods Situation

The United States took the lead in retreating from fixed exchange rates and from convertibility into gold. This was generally contrary to the wishes of most Western European countries, but they really had no other choice. Fortunately the rather abrasive negotiations of 1971 that the United States forced on its western allies and later unilateral pressure in 1973 did not lead to a rupture of trade or economic relationships. The wounds inflicted at that time, however, have not yet fully healed.

The United States now views exchange rates as floating or subject to market forces. Many other nations resist this view. The Japanese, for example, are anxious to continue large exports to the United States, so they intervene so as not to let the dollar get too cheap with respect to the yen. (This is called a "dirty" float since it does not accept the natural forces of the exchange market without interference or intervention.) On the other hand, they do not attempt to maintain a fixed relationship, so that market speculators cannot pin them to any particular price. They choose the time, amount, and character of their intervention. The United States, however, "dirties" the markets very little with intervention. The Federal Reserve foreign exchange managers try to promote continuous markets without sharp or irrational breaks but do not "defend" any particular level of exchange rates. Other countries take rather different courses.

The Western European countries, for example, have tried to maintain a fixed relationship between their currencies but have not been very successful. Both Britain and Italy have been forced to let their currencies float, mostly downward. On the other hand the West German deutschemark has been strong and has been revalued, but only by a small amount, which other countries consider inadequate. France has been in and out of the "narrow margins" arrangement (for exchange rates fixed within "narrow margins") but out more than in.

Considerable sentiment for fixed exchange rates remains in many countries. The issue is not dead. However, official sentiment in the United States appears to be for flexible exchange rates and—at least at this writing—it also appears to be a bipartisan matter. Without the concurrence of the United States, fixed rates would be hard to revive. Even regional arrangements probably will tend to erode. On the other hand, almost everyone agrees that violent shifts in exchange rates are economically disruptive. Most nations would prefer to conduct domestic economic policy with natural economic forces tending to keep exchange rate fluctuations within reasonable margins.

The fear that flexible exchange rates would dampen world trade and discourage movements of capital does not appear to have been well founded. Trade, while still strongly cyclical, has continued to grow, and the interdependence of the world in economic terms is greater than ever before. Capital movements still take place in response to interest-rate differentials and differential profit opportunities.

Almost all, but not all nations, have accepted the formal withdrawal from gold convertibility. Before 1971 it had been officially in force but kept alive only by the forebearance of leading nations, such as West Germany, in the use of their formal legal right. Now even the IMF has dropped gold convertibility. Furthermore, both the IMF and the member nations have some authority to sell their gold on the open markets. This makes gold more a commodity than a monetary metal. Both the IMF and the United States have, in fact, conducted gold auctions. Gold hoarders still absorb the newly mined gold and the gold taken out of official reserves—but as a commodity. A few believe that gold will be revived as a monetary metal, but not the majority of market observers.

The Trade-Weighted Dollar

When exchange rates were very generally fixed, the relative *de*valuation or *re*valuation of any one currency could be rather easily measured against the average of the unchanged fixed-exchange rate currencies. However, when the major currencies are floating, there is no longer a standard against which such a measurement can be made. If the dollar goes down against half a dozen currencies but up against another half dozen, what does that mean? No change because of the numerical offset? Obviously it does not. The Morgan Guaranty Trust Company makes available daily an interesting and useful way in which to judge the value of the dollar. It is a "trade-weighted" value of the dollar figured against the values of fifteen other currencies, weighted, as the name indicates, by the volume of trade, with three base dates for comparison: The first, May 29, 1970, which was Bretton Woods–based (and before the Canadian dollar float); the second, December 18, 1971, which marks the first dollar devaluation (Smithsonian Agreement central rates); and February 15, 1973, which was the second dollar devaluation and the start of its formal "float." This is computed daily and is published most days by *The Wall Street Journal* along with its quotations of exchange rates.

DETERMINANTS OF FOREIGN EXCHANGE RATES: PRELIMINARY VIEW[2]

As is true in almost every economic sector of a free society, prices are determined by supply and demand. But as is also true whenever this simplistic statement is made, it fails to say much about the reality of supply and demand. The supply of foreign currencies in the United States results from our exports of goods, supply of services to foreigners, the foreign tourists entertained here, the amounts our nationals borrow abroad, repayments of debts to us, the sale of the securities of our corporations and of our government to foreigners, and their direct investment in productive facilities in this country. The demand for

---

[2]The Appendix to this chapter presents a full balance of payments table as the economic foundation of exchange rate determination. For a more detailed account, see Kubarych, cited in the Bibliography.

foreign currencies is the obverse of each of these items: our imports of goods, our use of foreign services, foreign travel of our citizens, borrowing by foreigners in our money and capital markets, the sale of securities of our corporations or government by foreigners, direct investment abroad of our corporations or citizens in the land or productive facilities in other countries. One proviso must be added: This list of demand elements assumes that the dollar proceeds of the transactions listed are repatriated by the foreign holders. If they are not, then these proceeds can enter into the Eurocurrency market, which we have already encountered in Chapter 10 and shall examine in greater detail in the next chapter.

An illustration of the way in which a catastrophic event can change the trade position without an effect on exchange rates is the sudden, near quadrupling of petroleum prices by OPEC in late 1973. This change in price produced a drastic and frightening change in the payments balances of every petroleum-importing country. It was wondered if the economies of these nations could stand such an abrupt and drastic blow. Nevertheless, the whole event took place without any material effects on exchange rates. How could this happen? It was because the OPEC countries were at pains not to convert the much larger monetary proceeds in a way that would disrupt these markets. They did not try to convert the proceeds into the currencies of their native countries; this would have been absurd. Instead, they accepted dollars and pounds and other leading currencies and started to use these funds either for purchases for domestic development or to make investments in the countries whose currencies they held. In other words, they immediately offset the receipts by a corresponding trade or capital transaction.

Since supply and demand do not necessarily tend to be equal, the balancing item is the monetary reserves of the nation. If demand for foreign currencies exceeds supply and the government resists the natural fall in the value of the dollar, our monetary reserves tend to diminish, or foreign holdings of dollars tend to go up. If supply exceeds demand, then the opposite happens. The policy of the government with respect to rates has already been implied in the description of various international monetary systems, but the subject—really public policy on the balance of payments—will also come up for consideration in the next chapter.

Principal Participants in the Foreign Exchange Market

The private market in foreign exchange is almost completely centered in the commercial banking system. The major money market commercial banks of New York City and two or three dozen big commercial banks outside New York City act as wholesalers and are prepared to either buy or sell almost all the currencies of the world in relatively large amounts: relative, that is, to the total volume of transactions for such currencies. Some other banks wholesale selected currencies.

The comparative importance of currencies in our foreign exchange market has shifted greatly in recent years. At one time the British pound was the leading currency, but its relative (not its absolute) importance has diminished. The great strength of the West German deutschemark has brought it to the top of the list of currencies traded in our foreign exchange markets. The Swiss franc, although the nation is small and its money supply modest, is also a very actively traded currency. We have more trade with Italy and travel there extensively, but trade in the Swiss franc is twelve times as great as in the Italian lira. We trade more with the Japanese than the Dutch but transactions in the Netherlands guilder is greater than in the Japanese yen. Volume of transactions at forty-four leading United States banks in April 1977 is shown in percentage terms in Table 19-1.

To some extent location may influence the relative importance of currencies. West Coast banks, not surprisingly, do a large business in Japanese yen and also Mexican pesos. Large banks in Gulf of Mexico ports do a great deal of business in South American currencies. Detroit does a specially large volume of business in Canadian currencies.

Almost all banks offer their customers service both in buying and selling foreign currencies. The banks other than those that are principal wholesalers do not deal for their own account (except for trivial amounts in coins and paper currency) but through their city correspondents. Thus, the impact of supply and demand from the whole nation tends to be quickly funneled into the central foreign exchange markets.

The major wholesalers in New York City have policies guiding their foreign exchange traders as to the extent to which they can be net owners or borrowers of the various foreign currencies. Although the tradition is that banks generally should keep rather balanced positions, the recent financial difficulties of some large banks have disclosed that banks do sometimes have net speculative positions—and that they are not always right about future rate movements.

TABLE 19-1
Volume of Foreign Exchange Transactions by Countries (44 leading U.S. banks, April 1977)

German mark	27.3%
Canadian dollar	19.2
Pound sterling	17.0
Swiss franc	13.8
French franc	6.3
Netherlands guilder	5.7
Japanese yen	5.3
Belgium franc	1.5
Italian lira	1.1
All other	2.8
	100.0%

SOURCE: R. M. Kubarych: *Foreign Exchange Markets in the United States,* Federal Reserve Bank of New York, 1978, p. 20.

Large foreign exchange losses have been disclosed, and it is suspected that other losses have been suffered by banks that otherwise remained solvent. And, of course, some gains probably have been earned.

The major speculators in foreign exchange, however, are undoubtedly the large multinational corporations, of which the international integrated petroleum companies are a leading example. They sometimes make large profits in this way—and as the recently adopted rules of the public accounting profession have disclosed—sometimes they suffer large losses. The exact extent to which these gains and losses were the product of currency positions for business reasons that could not be hedged, as against deliberate speculation, is not known. A reasonable assumption would be that most of them are the first type: unavoidable because they are related to necessary foreign exchange transactions and holdings.

The remaining major participant in foreign exchange markets is the federal government, as represented by the U.S. Treasury Department and more specifically by its agent in the markets: the Foreign Exchange Trading Department of the Federal Reserve Bank of New York. In the next chapter we shall have more to say about public policy with respect to these markets. The Federal Reserve, however, has a relationship to the wholesale foreign exchange market that is not unlike that of the Federal Reserve Open Market operations described in Chapter 11.

This list of participants is not meant to exclude the great body of those who travel, who import or export goods, perform services for foreigners, or send remittances to relatives abroad. They are the ultimate factors that influence the structure of the banking system's foreign exchange dealings.

Exchange Rates in the Analysis of Financial Markets

Many readers of the financial press in the United States will spend time on stock market quotations, glance at bond yields and markets, but pay very little attention to foreign exchange rates. (This does not apply to money market bankers or executives of multinational corporations, of course.) Foreign exchange rates and the whole panoply of international news behind them, however, are an important part of financial analysis. Many times movements of our exchange rates reflect how other countries view our economic progress. They often show, through this mirror, how inflation problems are being met, how economic developments are going, what is happening in the capital markets. Because the United States is so large and, in many ways, so self-sufficient, this indifference to international views of our nation is understandable, even if not farsighted.

Businessmen of other nations are generally much more sensitive to world economic developments and the rates at which their currencies are traded against other currencies. The benefits of open economies with considerable economic intercourse are well understood—but foreign trade and finance are still often subject to fits of destructive nationalism. Economics and politics go hand in hand, and the failures of one often turn out to be the failures of the other.

PROJECTS AND QUESTIONS

1. Look up the most recent trade statistics from the *Federal Reserve Bulletin* or the *Survey of Current Business*. What are the trends in both imports and exports for the past few years? What is happening to the *balance* of trade?

2. From data in the *Federal Reserve Bulletin*, draw some conclusions about current holdings of dollars by foreign central banks and others. Have these holdings continued to increase since the text was written or have they stabilized? (As we write this, we wish we knew!)

3. From a recent *Wall Street Journal*, hunt up the "Trade-Weighted Dollar" values. (They will be with the foreign exchange quotations.) From these data decide whether or not the dollar has recently been "strong" or "weak."

4. Has the United States policy with respect to foreign exchange rates changed since the text was written? (We also wish we knew this!)

5. As this is written (July 6, 1979), the current quotations are as follows: Canadian dollar, $.8623; West German deutschemark, $.5442; Swiss franc, $.5997; British pound, $2.2080; Mexican peso, $.04379. What has happened since then?

STATISTICAL SOURCES

Euromoney: a London monthly magazine rich in the gossip of the Eurobond market, together with many revealing interviews with both highly placed bankers and economists. Written in the clear and lively style of British financial journalists. Not often found in United States libraries; it is $65 a year and very slow in delivery.

Federal Reserve Bulletin: useful particularly for data on short-term capital movements. Well organized and documented.

International Financial Statistics (IMF): useful for general economic data of its member countries; also on world trade.

IMF Annual Reports: useful for analysis of international liquidity and exchange rate developments. Also useful on relative monetary policies of leading nations.

Survey of Current Business (Commerce Department): runs annual articles on direct investment; usually during the summer or early fall issues. Articles on portfolio investment appear less regularly. Many statistics, but less well organized than those in the *Federal Reserve Bulletin* (see above).

World Bank Annual Reports: excellent verbal analysis of world economic affairs but with fewer statistics than most of the above. These reports contain, hidden away in its operational report on "Borrowings and Finance," just about the best annual analysis of the international bond and credit market. The World Bank is the compiler of the basic statistics in this area.

BIBLIOGRAPHY FOR CHAPTERS 19 AND 20

Holtrop, M. W.: *Money in an Open Economy,* Stenfert Kroese N.V., Leiden, the Netherlands, 1972.

Explains how domestic monetary policy is related to international monetary relations.

Kareken, J., and N. Wallace: "International Monetary Reform: The Feasible Alternatives," *Quarterly Review,* Federal Reserve Bank of Minneapolis, Summer 1978.

A point of view based on the new theory of "rational expectations."

Kindleberger, C. P.: *Foreign Trade and the National Economy,* Yale University Press, New Haven, 1962.

Still a fine exposition of "real" international relationships.

Kreinin, M. E.: *International Economics: A Policy Approach,* 2d ed., Harcourt, Brace and Jovanovich, New York, 1975.

Excellent textbook; clear and authoritative.

Kubarych, R. M.: *Foreign Exchange Markets in the United States,* Federal Reserve Bank of New York, 1978.

Excellent combination of "real world" arrangements with a strong foundation in theory. Recommended.

Lee, W. Y., and K. S. Sachdeva: "The Role of the Multinational Firm in the Integration of Segmented Capital Markets," *Journal of Finance,* May 1977, pp. 479–492.

An application of the CAPM to multinational risk-reducing diversification.

Makin, J. H.: "Portfolio Theory and the Problem of Foreign Exchange Risk," *Journal of Finance,* May 1978, pp. 517–534.

Hard to read but original.

Root, F. R.: *International Trade and Investments,* Southwestern, Cincinnati, 1973.

Textbook treatment of direct investment. Managerial rather than analytical point of view. Useful publication.

APPENDIX

A BALANCE-OF-PAYMENTS EXPOSITION OF EXCHANGE RATE DETERMINATION

A foreign exchange transaction is almost always a simple purchase of one currency with another currency. Either a buyer or a seller may initiate a transaction. It would seem, at first glance, that the economists' favorite tool, supply and demand, could be brought to bear in explaining the "price" or exchange rate involved. Complications start, however, with the fact that such transactions take place simultaneously all over the globe and among many parties. For the foreign exchange market to be a "good" market, the price must be almost exactly the same for all transactions at any one point in time. This is solved primarily by a very complex system of communications that connects all major market participants. A further complication is that although there are relatively few major currencies, the number of rate pairs between individual currencies goes up by the mathematical rule of combinations. Fewer than a dozen leading currencies can still result in a hundred paired or "cross" rates. This complication is solved by an extensive use of a single "reserve" currency—which is still the dollar, badly beaten as it has recently been in foreign exchange markets.

Perhaps the greatest complication, however, is that the economic circumstances that lie back of each transaction are of a wide variety of transactions with many different reasons for buying and selling. The transactor may be a businessman, a traveler, a borrower or a lender, a speculator, or even a central bank acting as a monetary authority for its nation. To get at the root causes of why transactors want to transact business, the best expository device is the balance of payments of an individual country. In turning to this device, we start with one simplifying assumption: We list the supply and demand factors for the currency of that country against *all other currencies*. Table 19-2 gives a schematic pattern of the balance of payments of the United States, but without dollar amounts. A balance of payments is a "flow" statement and therefore for a period of time.

TABLE 19-2

Tableau of the Supply of and Demand for Foreign Currencies (and its inverse: the demand for and supply of U.S. dollars)

	Supply of Foreign Currencies (demand for dollars) (credit item in U.S. balance of payments)	Demand for Foreign Currencies (supply of dollars) (debit item in U.S. balance of payments)
Current Account	U.S. exports (incl. gold) Services we do for foreigners Foreign travel in U.S. Investment income returned to U.S.	U.S. imports (incl. gold) Services we hire from foreigners U.S. travel abroad Investment income sent abroad U.S. economic and military aid: Remittances to foreign countries

Capital Account	Foreign investment in U.S.:
	   Direct
	   In securities
	 U.S. nationals borrow abroad
	
	 Foreigners repay debts to U.S.
	 Holders of foreign currencies invested
	   in U.S. market
		U.S. investment abroad:
		   Direct
		   In securities
		 Foreigners borrow in our financial
		   markets
		 We repay debts to foreigners
		 Holders of dollars invested in foreign
		   money market

Monetary Authorities	*Fixed exchange rates:* The U.S. monetary authorities (Treasury and Federal Reserve) support the dollar by buying it with foreign currencies (1) on hand, or (2) borrowed from IMF or foreign monetary authorities. Foreign monetary authorities can also support the dollar by buying and holding them. (Reverse also possible.) *"Dirty" float:* Same as above but the exchange rates at which U.S. or foreign monetary authorities intervene shift. *True float:* At some price, but possibly a sharply changed and rapidly fluctuating one, the capital and current account supply and demand would balance.	

A balance of payments, by theoretical definition, always balances. In practice, the statistics used to compile it are imperfect, and large discrepancies usually exist. In addition, the balance of payments only balances against *all other countries,* not just any one country. If they could be perfectly compiled (they cannot), the balance of payments of all nations would balance, though those of pairs of countries would not. But with all these imperfections, balance of payment statistics give us the best clues as to how exchange rates are determined and what the forces are that move them about.

Several points from Table 19-2 should be noted. Supply and demand factors are often interrelated. Much of our economic and military foreign aid is tied to exports of our goods. Direct investment abroad may be linked to the availability of credit to finance the operation. Finally, we expect debts to be repaid at some later date.

An observing student might ask: If the balance of payments balances, why are there deficits or surpluses? By convention, the net slack taken up by the monetary authorities is the deficit or surplus. If foreign monetary authorities end up holding more dollars, and/or our monetary authorities hold less foreign currencies (or have incurred debts to secure foreign currencies used in support operations), the sum of changes is the deficit in our balance of payments. The reverse would be a surplus.

chapter 20

Impact of International Finance on Financial Markets: Capital Flows, Balance of Payments, and Public Policy

In the previous chapter trade and travel were stressed as important elements in the foreign exchange market. However, in enumerating the factors of supply and demand for foreign exchange it was necessary to enumerate a full balance of payments. Beyond the trade, travel, and service items, the biggest addition was that of capital flows.

As earlier chapters have made clear, almost all capital transactions involve some degree of risk. In general, the longer the term of the transaction the greater the risk. Capital that flows over national boundaries, however, faces two added kinds of risk. The first is that of changes in exchange rates. As we shall see, this can be offset in very short-term capital transactions but not in longer-term ones. An investor may have to convert back into a lower-valued currency when he or she reverses an investment transaction. A borrower may have to pay back in a higher-valued currency. The second kind of risk is of a legal and political nature. When one invests in a foreign country, the investment is subject to the laws and politics of the host nation. The investment may be subject to discriminatory taxation. It may be hampered by regulations aimed at it selectively. And in more extreme cases, a foreign investment may be subject to nationalization or to expropriation. There may be some formalities of nominal compensation (although even this is not always done); but the whole valuation process is controlled by the host country, and the investor may get a very raw deal. United States foreign investment in copper and oil has been nationalized or expropriated (as have other kinds of industry), and almost any impartial judge would have found the compensation to be skimpy to nominal. But the rewards of foreign investment can be great, and so the risks are accepted and capital does flow internationally.

The organization of this chapter gives first and most prominent attention to various kinds of capital flows. Because the subject is complex, these descriptions will tend to be compressed, but we hope comprehensible. The chapter will then examine balance of payments problems related to capital flows. Finally a more general view of public policy in the international financial area will be examined rather briefly.

CAPITAL FLOWS

Our financial markets often entertain foreign guests. Canada is a frequent visitor. This includes Canadian provinces, public authorities such as great hydroelectric enterprises, and private corporations. It is a tribute to the efficiency of our capital markets that they come here rather than borrowing at home, since borrowing here involves a material exchange-rate risk because of the floating rates. When Canadians borrow in our markets, the debts are almost always denominated in U.S. dollars. If a Canadian borrower faces repayment at a lower exchange rate (in U.S. dollars, which means a higher cost of U.S. dollars in terms of Canadian dollars) the cost of borrowing will have been increased, possibly materially. Furthermore the U.S./Canadian exchange rate is often more influenced by these capital transactions than it is by current transactions. A period of heavy Canadian borrowing is likely to be accompanied by a strong Canadian dollar.

Other countries borrow in our markets: Australia, New Zealand, and the Scandinavian countries, all of which have good credit records so that sale of their securities in our market is feasible. It is significant that two countries have gone unmentioned: West Germany and Japan. Both countries have private savings rates that are almost twice as high as those of the United States. Since they do not encourage foreign borrowing in their markets, they have ample domestic funds for their capital needs. An added reason for the low rate of foreign borrowing in West Germany and Japan is that both of their currencies are strong, and borrowers think it likely that they would have to repay at a higher exchange rate; something they think less likely with the U.S. dollar.

Short-term borrowing in our money markets by foreign business and government is also often quite large, although also rather erratic. Short-term interest rates do not always hold parallel courses between countries so that the attractiveness of such borrowing, both to lender and borrower, depends on relative exchange and interest rate levels. However, in general our money market rates tend to be lower than elsewhere except for a few strong currency countries, i.e., West Germany, Japan, and Switzerland, and so our money market is usually attractive. Furthermore, the strong currency countries often present the risk of currency appreciation—unless this can be hedged by forward exchange.

Forward Exchange Protection for Foreign Lending

The forward exchange market provides a kind of round trip or two-way ticket for passage into a foreign currency, and then, return to the base currency. A simultaneous cash purchase of a foreign currency together with a forward sale of the same currency is, in effect, such a guaranteed round-trip ticket. With such a "covered" arrangement, funds can move temporarily and safely into our markets. With allowance for this factor, there is some relationship between these four factors: the interest rates in two markets and the spot and forward exchange rates between these two markets. This four-way relationship is shown in the chart in Figure 20-1, which was originated by the Federal Reserve Bank of New York.

This chart is essentially a comparison of the premium or discount of the forward exchange rate (converted to an annual basis) with the interest-rate differential. Along the declining diagonal, any gain or loss on forward exchange is exactly offset by a loss or gain on the interest-rate differential. When actual market rates give a relationship that is not on the diagonal, then an arbitrage opportunity exists. For example, if London exchange had a forward discount of 2 percent (annualized) but London Treasury bill rates were 8 percent when ours were 5 percent, then the gain on London investment would more than

figure 20-1 How Forward Exchange-rate Premiums and Discounts Can Push Money into Lower Interest-rate Markets. *(Adapted From A. R. Holmes and F. H. Schott,* The New York Foreign Exchange Market, *Federal Reserve Bank of New York, 1965, p. 54.)*

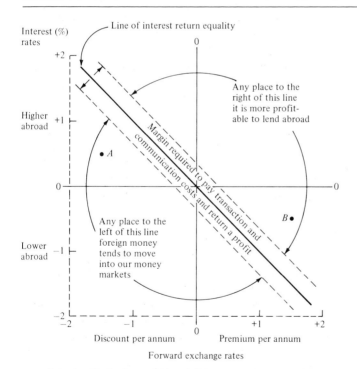

Point A: The foreigner could get 1/2% more at home but the forward exchange rate discount (premium to him) of 1 1/2% gives him a full percent point advantage in our money markets!

Point B: Money rates are 1/2% lower abroad but the forward exchange premium makes it profitable for U.S. money market investors to go abroad for a net 1 percent advantage.

offset the forward exchange loss. In a frictionless market, money would move to London. If forward rates have a premium, it is possible that funds can flow to a lower rate market. For example, suppose the premium on forward Swiss francs was ½ percent for ninety days, which is the same as 2 percent per annum. Even if Swiss bill rates were 1 percent below New York rates, money could flow to Switzerland. And if the differential were the other way around, money would flow into our market. For example, if there were a market premium on forward Canadian exchange of 1 percent but our Treasury bill rate were 2 percent above the comparable Canadian rate, we would expect an inflow of Canadian funds.

Arbitrage does not bring all exchange-interest relationships as close to the diagonal as theory suggests it should. The principal reason is that the market for forward exchange is not large enough to absorb the full burden of arbitrage transactions, so that enough funds to erase the rate differential cannot flow. While the forward market is used by the monetary authorities for support purposes, there is a tendency to attempt some discrimination in purchase so that "foreign exchange speculators" are not accommodated. In other words, the market forces of arbitrage are not allowed to work freely.

Another force, though one not always fully recognized, is that the assumption of freedom from credit risk is never quite absent from these transactions. While the solvency of the great financial institutions that deal in the international money market is widely assumed, in times of crisis it is not thought prudent to lean on this assumption with too much weight. An instantaneous or "spot" transaction in foreign exchange involves virtually no credit risk. A forward transaction, however, is tinged with just a small shade of such risk. While the risk is small, older traders' memories of the hectic days of the 1930s still remain.

Figure 20-1, although a useful expository device, suffers from two defects: one analytical and one institutional. The analytical defect is that it is a static situation, but it is not in equilibrium. If equilibrium had been reached, points A and B would then have moved to within the declining diagonal. But since it is a static diagram, we cannot show the process by which equilibrium would be reached. In fact that process is indeterminate unless we should introduce added assumptions. Any one of the three factors could change: the spot exchange rate, the forward exchange rate, or relative interest rates. The institutional defect is that it leaves an impression of simplicity that is very unrealistic. Rather than simple forward contracts, the forward foreign exchange market is more often than not conducted in the form of "swaps." These contracts, mainly in the interbank market, are really two contracts: one a spot deal and one a forward deal. What is more, the customs by which forward transactions are dated differs between the interbank market and the bank/customer market. For those who wish to pursue this interesting but complex market, Kubarych, who is cited in the Bibliography at the end of Chapter 19, is highly recommended.

Although forward exchange markets theoretically appear to be an excellent vehicle for hedging of foreign exchange situations by both banks and multinational corporations, they are not used as much as might be expected. In the first place these markets are not always of such size that they can absorb large transactions without some slippage of quotations. In addition, forward premiums or discounts often tend to be costly. Weak currencies generally have discounts, strong ones premiums. Although hedging seems to remove risk from foreign exchange transactions, it may also cost so much that it is more of a burden than the assumption of foreign exchange risk. In addition, professionals in the markets often feel that their own judgment is better than that of the market, so they are willing to accept the risk. In effect this says that such professionals do *not* accept the efficient market hypothesis.

In practice forward exchange markets of adequate depth for substantial trading exist for only a few currencies: the Canadian dollar, the British pound, the West German deutschemark, and the Japanese yen.

Eurocurrency Loans

The Eurocurrency market (see Chapter 10) also furnishes a channel by which there is, in effect, international movement of both long- and short-term funds. The Eurocurrency market provides a market by which there can be international movement of ownership of currencies without going through the foreign exchange market. Both lenders (holders) and borrowers of Eurocurrencies may assume some exchange risk, but others may actually avoid it. When our money market banks have excess funds that they place (probably through their foreign branches) in the Eurodollar market, they avoid exchange risk without having to resort to the forward market with all its costs and inconveniences. This is also equally true of our multinational corporations, if we assume that dollars are their basic currency. (We need to be reminded now and then that some multinational corporations are foreign-based and use some other currency than dollars as their base currency: Royal Dutch Petroleum, for example.)

The Eurocurrency market provides another linkage between markets so that interest rates tend to be equalized among the open economies. However, the barriers to complete equalization are still rather important. While the Eurocurrency markets are mainly for top quality credit risks, there is not a complete absence of credit risk. And there is, for all users of this market with other currency bases, some degree of exchange rate risk.

The Eurocurrency market furnishes a special and interesting example of a term structure of interest rates. Since quotations exist for the whole range of credit transactions from one day up to about fifteen years with many intermediate quotations, it is possible to construct a full yield curve from these data. (Yield curves are treated in Chapter 7.)

In recent years the growth rate of assets and liabilities of the foreign branches of our banks have grown at a rate of almost 20 percent annually. At the same time, commercial bank domestic assets and liabilities of foreign branches now are about $200 billion compared with a total for all domestic commercial banks of about a trillion. However, this one-fifth ratio becomes even larger if one compares the assets and liabilities of foreign branches with assets and liabilities of United States banks that maintain such branches. The statistics for an exact comparison are not available, but a rough estimate suggests that for banks maintaining such branches, the branches have balance sheet footings close to two-fifths of the parent banks' balance sheet footings. Published statistics show that about half the New York City banks make more from their foreign operations than they do from domestic operations.

However, a comparison of earnings does not furnish a full picture of the significance of these branches. The Eurocurrency market is large, growing, and unregulated. So far, it has shown great adaptability to changing international conditions. A foreign branch opens a direct window in this market so that a domestic bank can either draw money from this market in times of tightness or invest surplus money in times of money market slack. Branches offer a degree of flexibility unknown a few years ago, a management advantage not directly reflected in earnings.

Eurobond Market

The Eurobond market is somewhat less used by citizens of the United States than the Eurocurrency market. Eurobonds have mainly "intermediate" maturities from seven to fifteen years; they are seldom for more than twenty years. When in the 1960s there were restrictions on capital export for direct investment, United States multinational corporations borrowed in this market extensively. Since these restrictions have now been lifted, this borrowing has tapered off. The major borrowers in the Eurobond market are foreign: often foreign governments of smaller countries that do not have strong or sizeable internal capital markets. While dollars are still the principal currency in which Eurobonds are denominated, the West German deutschemark (DM) has been increasingly used. Investors have more confidence in its long-term value than in the dollar. However, borrowers also face the possible foreign exchange risk of having to repay in revalued DM.

It must be admitted that one of the principal appeals of the Eurobond market is to those investors seeking to evade the taxes of the country in which they reside. A Swiss Eurobond underwriter was quoted in a press interview (*Euromoney*, July 1976) as saying that his picture of the typical Eurobond investor was a dentist in Lyons, France, who collected his bills in cash, bundled the franc notes up in a suitcase and carried them to Switzerland where he bought a coupon (nonregistered) Eurobond denominated in DM. It is significant that almost all Eurobonds are in coupon form (bearer bonds that can be transferred simply by delivery and without a record of the owner's name). It is for this reason that we cannot say with any confidence (as we tried to avoid doing above) that there is not a large United States participation. For all we know, United States citizens may have gotten money into Switzerland and are doing just as the Lyons dentist was reported to have been doing.

The Eurobond market, although efficient in terms of the standards of most of the investing countries, is still not as efficient as the bond market in the United States. The underwriting margin for high-grade bonds in the United States, as we disclosed in Chapter 16, is generally not far from one percentage point. For issues of equal quality and shorter maturity, the Eurobond underwriters take a gross spread of nearer to two-and-a-half percentage points. There is a modest secondary market in Eurobonds, but exactly how large it is, is not known; nor can we say anything useful about the bid-ask spreads in this market. The presumption is that the market is much thinner and the spreads much wider than in the United States—another presumption of lower market efficiency.

Foreign Ownership of U.S. Treasury Securities

Motivation for the foreign ownership of U.S. Treasury securities differs greatly from that of almost all other capital transactions. In the first place, most of this ownership is by foreign governments or their central banks, not by private investors. And these foreign governments and central banks were, in general, reluctant buyers.

In the preceding chapter we outlined the story of changes in exchange rate policy. During the decade preceding 1971 the United States remained formally bound to gold and without unilateral power to change its exchange relationship with other currencies. Foreign governments resisted a devaluation of the dollar but assisted in maintenance of the Bretton Woods system by abstaining from gold conversion—and by absorbing large amounts of dollars. The use they generally made of these dollars was to invest in U.S. Treasury securities.

The period of 1971 to 1973 could be considered one in which there was a struggle to maintain the formalities, if not the reality, of the former Bretton Woods system—with again the burden on foreign governments of maintaining the fixed exchange rate with the dollar, now moderately devalued. Again, funds left the United States and these foreign governments were forced to absorb dollars to keep the fixed exchange rate. The United States made only rather lukewarm efforts to help in achieving this goal. Again, more investment by foreigners in U.S. Treasury securities took place.

When in 1973 the United States, almost unilaterally, abandoned fixed exchange rates it might have been expected that foreign governments would have abandoned support and would have stopped absorbing dollars. However, the export industries of such nations as West Germany and Japan were reluctant to see further dollar decline, which would have hurt their markets in the United States. When the United States stopped making more than token efforts at support of its dollar, the whole burden fell on foreign governments, mainly the two countries mentioned above, so dollar absorption has continued to the present time.

The continued dollar absorption has meant further investment in U.S. Treasury securities. In the late 1960s foreign ownership of these securities was only about 3 percent of the total. Now it is in excess of 12 percent. Since 1969 foreigners have absorbed about three-eighths of the increase in privately held Treasury debt of the United States.

Portfolio Investment

Foreigners borrow in the United States when they can find a lower cost for such borrowings. Foreigners invest in the United States when they can get, or expect to get, a higher rate of interest or return. The two processes would seem to be contradictory, but they are not. The United States has been an important market in which foreigners borrow; the amounts are far more than the amounts by which our citizens have borrowed abroad. The opening paragraphs of this chapter gave several illustrations of such transactions. But at the same time portfolio investment in United States equity securities has greatly exceeded our portfolio investment in equity securities of corporations in other countries. Portfolio investment is without control over the economic entity in which investment is made. *Direct* investment involves control, and when it comes to direct investment, our multinational corporations have invested far more abroad then foreigners have directly invested in the United States. A chauvinistic observer—and maybe even a less biased one—might think that this says something about the quality of business enterprise in the United States.

Most of the portfolio investment in the United States has been in corporate equities. This investment has been quite volatile, but foreign ownership of our equities has generally been between 5 and 10 percent of the total. Until recently, the major part of such investment was made from Switzerland, from London, or from Amsterdam. However, this only tells us the site of the financial institutions acting as agents. The principals to such investment are well hidden by the traditional secrecy of the process, and so we know little about their nature, except that rumors tell us the rich Arabs have always been important. For all we know, such investors may include many citizens of our own country possibly living as expatriates; but on that point we can only speculate.

In the past few years the Arabs have appeared more openly and directly as portfolio investors in the United States. The huge income produced by high petroleum prices could not, as we pointed out in the last chapter, be converted into their native currencies; so one form of investing it is in our equities. It is also worth noting that the Arabs have invested in high-grade bonds, including the bonds of the United States government itself; something that was far less common with the more traditional portfolio investors of Western Europe.

Our citizens do some portfolio investment abroad. We have invested in French, German, British, and even Japanese publicly held corporations. In a few cases it was not necessary to take the exchange risk directly because foreign securities were sometimes, by a trust arrangement, made available as American Depositary Receipts (ADRs), which were traded in U.S. dollars. However, although the passage through foreign exchange was thus directly avoided, the risk was not eliminated. Presumably the price of the ADRs was influenced by conversion risk as well as by business risk.

While portfolio investment in both directions is fairly moderate, there are times when it has considerable influence on our financial markets. Foreigners usually seem to show about the same cycle of enthusiasm and disinterest as our native investors; a bull market brings in foreign participation. However, there is an added factor: When economic conditions in foreign countries deteriorate but remain fairly good in our country, we are likely to find an unusually large inflow of foreign funds. A few years ago it worked in the opposite direction: Japanese securities became suddenly quite popular in our markets (a mutual fund was formed to exploit the popularity) when our equity market was not doing well.

Direct Investment

Direct investment is the acquisition of control of a foreign business operation or "affiliate." The acquisition may be by purchase of an existing company, or it may be by organizing a new operation with plant and equipment expenditures, training of a work force, acquisition of working capital, and all the other steps involved in starting a new enterprise. Direct investment is usually associated with the so-called multinational corporations. When International Harvester made arrangements to manufacture farm machinery in South America, it was by means of direct investment. When Sears & Roebuck established branches in South America, it was direct investment. When Volkswagen established a manufacturing facility in the United States, it was direct investment.

Direct investment, over the long term, is the most significant form of capital import or export. United States direct investment abroad now exceeds $150 billion. Direct investment of other nations in the United States is now over $30 billion. In spite of the larger size of our direct investment abroad, it is growing only about half as fast as direct investment in the United States.

In days gone by, direct investment tended to be closely related to colonialism. England made large investments in India, in the gold and diamond mines of South Africa, and in rubber and tea plantations in Southeastern Asia. France invested heavily in her African colonies, such as Algeria. The United States invested in the Philippines and more recently in Puerto Rico. This protected against the risk of expropriation mentioned at the beginning of this chapter. However, now that colonialism is largely dead, this kind of protection is no longer available.

Direct investment has relatively little direct impact on financial markets. Many of the multinational companies have been able to finance such investments out of their own retained earnings so that the demand does not appear directly in the capital markets. However, many of these companies make it a policy to borrow in the host countries where they have invested so as to minimize the risks in the event of some later political pressure for nationalization or expropriation. Unfortunately, direct investment seems to be a love affair that cools rapidly all too often. Host countries at first may welcome outside investment, particularly underdeveloped countries. They welcome the creation of jobs, the importation of new technology with its education of the native work force, and the import of capital. After time, however, this ardor cools. When the new industry is fully established, no further jobs are being created, little new technology is being added; and now, instead of capital import, the remittance home of profits by the established affiliates of foreign companies is a burden on the balance of payments.

Direct investment does have a cycle in its impact on the balance of payments. At first a new direct investment is a net outflow of funds for the investing country. Even after the foreign affiliates become profitable, profits may be used for further capital expenditures and additions to working capital so that at this intermediate stage a direct investment is not yet a drag on the balance of payments of the host country. But when maturity of the investment project is reached, so that further expansion is not needed and profits can be remitted home to the parent company, then a direct investment is a drag on the balance of payments of the host country and a positive item in the balance of payments of the country in which the parent company is sited.

The location of foreign affiliates depends on the nature of their operations. An international petroleum company naturally goes where oil can be found—and then where it can be sold. The search for copper, iron ore, bauxite, and uranium is governed by the same need. Raw material sources, more often than not, are in underdeveloped countries. However, when an affiliate is located where there is a market for a product, it is more likely to be in a developed country where income is high enough to furnish a market. Raw material affiliates, therefore, tend to be more exposed to the political demands for nationalization and expropriation. The appeal to foreign multinational companies for investment in the United States is doubtless increased by the wealth, political stability, and reputation for fairness in treatment of foreign interests of our nation.

A recent example of a late comer to direct investment in the United States will help to clarify some of the considerations that go into such decisions. France has not been, until recently, very active in direct investment in the United States (or elsewhere except in its former colonies). However, in the past few years the amount of such investment has increased materially. Why? Although it is hard to pin down motives, it would appear that a number of large French companies had two fears: that the political climate at home was becoming increasingly hostile to free enterprise and that French labor was becoming increasingly uncooperative and more sympathetic to communistic ideas. They also saw the United States as perhaps the one remaining nation where free enterprise was assured. It was reported that some French companies not only wanted to shift production to the United States, but would consider moving their headquarters to this country if the political climate at home became too hostile.

One might ask: Why did they not consider West Germany where economic freedom remains, where inflation is low, and where workers are still very productive? Firm answers cannot be given; the question is all the more provocative since the idealism of the Common Market suggests that capital should move just as freely as goods. One answer may be (but this is far from certain) that there are still French memories of three German invasions of France within a century. Another explanation may simply be that the United States is a bit further away from the Russians than any site in Europe.

The rate of earnings on direct investment tends to be fairly high. This follows of necessity since the risks are greater than in domestic investment. This is what gives rise to some of the friction involved in investment in underdeveloped countries. No matter how warmly they may welcome such investment initially, when, in a later stage, they observe the relatively high profits being made (and possibly being remitted home), they then have a feeling of being exploited. That is when such enterprises become targets for political pressure for nationalization and/or expropriation. In a following section in which we deal with capital export to underdeveloped countries by the World Bank and IDA, we shall note that the earnings from these operations have often been relatively low—a fact that aggravates even further the high profits of privately financed, direct foreign investment.

"Hot Money"

"Hot money" is not really a new category of capital movement, but it has similarities to some of the types of short-term international capital transactions treated before in this and the preceding chapter. A hot money movement is any transfer of funds in anticipation of a change in exchange value. Money will be moved *out* of a country when holders of the money expect (under fixed exchange rates) a devaluation, or (under variable exchange rates) a decline in its value. Money will be moved *into* a country when *re*valuation of its currency or any other upward movement of its exchange value is expected. Hot money movement often tends to be a wish-fulfilling action: The sudden sharp outmovement may force devaluation or a decline in exchange value when it would not have occurred without the hot money outpouring. An inflow of hot money may force revaluation or an upward movement in exchange value that might not have happened without this hot money movement.

Who are the movers of hot money? They are all holders of short-term funds seeking to profit from such changes. Banks are large holders of such funds, and so are multinational corporations. In addition, rich individuals with international interests (Arab oil billionaires and Greek shipping magnates are most frequently gossiped about) may be involved. In addition it must be admitted that foreign governments sometimes are involved, at least unfriendly ones. At one time General De Gaulle used French public funds to embarrass the United States in the foreign exchange markets. Unfriendly foreign governments have done the same. Rumors of a Russian sally against the dollar turn up now and then. It has also been rumored (but never proved) that our CIA has moved against the currencies of countries whose governments it wished to push out of office.

The amounts of potentially hot money are very large. An agency of our government once estimated that the amount was in excess of a quarter of a trillion dollars. Exact figures, however, are impossible to assemble since an acceptable definition of hot money would be almost impossible to frame. The undisputed fact, however, is that the amounts are clearly very large—large enough to swamp the resistance of almost any single government.

An analogy between the hot money risk of governments and the deposit-shift risks of any commerical bank may be drawn. Any commercial bank could be pushed into insolvency by its depositors if it were not aided by some arm of government. Runs are no longer common because there is general expectation that government would not let failures happen. However, in the international field, the agencies of relief such as the IMF simply are not powerful enough to ensure against devaluation. For this reason, a generally weak economy may be "run" by the holders of its currency and pushed into devaluation or exchange rate deterioration.

BALANCE OF PAYMENTS PROBLEMS

A free society implies an open economy: one in which each citizen and business interest can pursue its own self-interest and make choices between purchases and investments inside or outside the economy. I can buy an imported car rather than a domestic one. I can travel to Italy or to California. I can invest my money in a domestic corporation, or I can invest abroad. All these choices (plus some technical ones) can add up to a chaotic total, that total being our balance of payments.

In the view of some, a balance of payments problem is viewed as a reflection of a kind of economic sin: that we have indulged ourselves too much and have not kept out economic affairs in good order. There is something to this view, although it is far from the whole story. It is true that if a nation allows inflation to push up its price level faster than that of its trading partners, it is likely to be unable to sell abroad, while its citizens buy more and more from abroad. If a nation becomes unproductive owing to a deficiency of capital expenditures, to inefficient management, or to a labor force that is sloppy and engages in many disruptive strikes, balance of payments problems can result. Poor quality goods lose out in international markets, and delays and disruptions in deliveries do not encourage foreign buyers to repeat orders.

On top of these problems is that of hot money—already noted above. Since balance of payments problems are likely to lead to devaluation of a currency or to a lower value on a floating exchange market, those with short-term capital funds are likely to rush for the exit when they detect evidence of the above conditions. They try to get out of the local currency and into a stronger one. Speculators can even sell the currency short in the foward exchange market. This tends to make the forecast self-fulfilling.

However, a nation can suffer balance of payments problems even if it has been conducting its economic affairs with prudence and productive vigor. From the early 1950s to the mid-1960s the United States had an overall balance of payments deficit even though its domestic economic affairs were in relatively good shape. The basic reason was the large volume of direct investment abroad. Our vigorous multinational corporations were pushing into new markets and new sources of raw materials. The long-run results also proved to be generally good for us: The income generated by foreign investments has been one of the strong features of our balance of payments in recent years. The short-run effects, however, were adverse and precipitated direct control measures in the early 1960s.

Random events can also have a sharp impact on our balance of payments. The Vietnam war was not only a tragedy on moral and political grounds, it was also a heavy drain on our balance of payments. Fighting a foreign war means foreign expenditures by government. Another, and even sharper, event was the drastic increase in petroleum prices at the end of 1973 and in early 1974. The balance of payments of almost every petroleum-importing country was thrown into reverse by this event. As we have already noted, it did not have any strong exchange rate effect because the Arabs did not convert the currencies received, but employed them abroad, to some extent in the same countries from which they came (though there is no evidence that this distributional effect was deliberate).

Low interest rates due to a high rate of saving, usually considered a desirable economic condition, can have the effect of tending to push capital out of a country into markets where a higher rate of return can be earned.

In other words, balance of payments problems can arise for economically virtuous nations as well as for economic sinners.

The gold standard or the gold exchange standard was traditionally thought to have a self-regulating characteristic. If a nation's balance of payments was in deficit on current and capital account, it would lose gold or foreign exchange holdings. This would force monetary contraction, which would lower prices and stimulate exports and discourage imports. In modern times this solution has become wholly unacceptable on political grounds. The accompanying unemployment is too high a price to pay for balance in the payments account.

The Bretton Woods system did not expect a country to try to right its payments balance by any such spartan self-denial; it allowed for devaluation, but in limited circumstances. However, it was flawed since it provided no real cure when the problem was that of the United States, with its dollar acting as a reserve currency. The two dollar devaluations of 1971 and 1973, while formally within the Bretton Woods boundaries, were large ruptures of the system. The quick passage to a floating dollar in 1973 was the formal end of the system.

The question now is whether a floating exchange rate will solve the balance of payments problem. A floating rate with a nonconvertible dollar does solve the problem in formal terms. But can a truly international economic order with trade and capital movements survive, prosper, and grow under these new circumstances? This will not be answered maturely or fully for many years. So far the results suggest a positive answer, but it is a tentative one at best.

FOREIGN POLICY AND FINANCIAL MARKETS

Much of what has been said before has probably exposed the authors' strong predilection for internationalism. This is not inadvertent; it is based on the conviction that the best financial markets are free markets, and that this freedom must go beyond national boundaries. However, it would be less than candid not to recognize that there are still very strong forces in the world working in the opposite direction; that is, toward extreme nationalism. When they succeed, they put limits on the freedom of financial markets.

The most extreme examples of nationalism are found in the policies of both fascist and communist governments. The extreme forms of such nationalism include: control of foreign exchange, state buying or rigid control of imports, control of tourism, and usually an almost complete prohibition to the movement of capital. Exchange control is a system in which the government expropriates any foreign currencies that its citizens may acquire and then rations or doles out such currency only for approved uses. Nazi Germany sharply limited imports *except* as they were used for military purposes or food needs; it limited the foreign travel of its citizens but subsidized foreign travel within Germany by a cheap exchange rate; and it largely prohibited capital transactions. If a list were to be made for Russia currently, it would be very similar except that Russia does not encourage tourism. These are the extreme forms, but various degrees can be found in many nations that are otherwise internationalistic in policy and sentiment.

As we have already noted, West Germany has resisted revaluation so as to encourage exports. Japan has done very much the same. The United States uses tax incentives to encourage exports. An example is tax deferral for so-called domestic international sales corporations (DISCs). Both Canada and Japan discourage the import of capital if it results in an equity control of a business by a foreign investor. They are glad to have the capital but don't want to give up control. Europeans sell us rail passes at rates cheaper than those available to their own citizens so as to encourage tourism. We do very much the same thing though much less successfully. Two-tier foreign exchange systems are still used from time to time, with one rate abnormally low so as to discourage capital export. Health and safety regulations may be selectively enforced so as to discourage imports.

Financial markets follow the flag, and they tend to be impeded when there are barriers to the movement of the flag.

Foreign Aid

The portrayal of governments as completely selfish in their foreign policy is neither true nor fair. Starting with the Marshall Plan after World War II, the United States has had a long history of giving foreign aid. When the Western European nations returned to productivity and prosperity, they joined in these efforts. While such aid averages much less than 1 percent of national income, it is still a material force. It could also be a material balance of payments problem, but increasingly the nations giving aid try to tie it to expenditure at home so it does not have such an effect. The newly rich Arab nations are being encouraged, so far without great success, to assume the "responsibilities of the rich."

The World Bank and IDA

The Bretton Woods conference produced not only the IMF but also an agency for supplying long-term capital to countries that might not be able to secure it in the ordinary financial channels. The institution was given the clumsy title International Bank for Reconstruction and Redevelopment

(IBRD), which was quickly shortened by common usage to the World Bank. The rules governing lending by this institution required that there be a reasonable prospect for repayment of such loans. Since some poor nations could not offer this assurance, another agency, the International Development Corporation (IDA), was created in 1960. Its rules for lending were somewhat easier, or "softer" as its critics would like to call them. The World Bank has about $35 billion of credits outstanding and the IDA about $12 billion. Under the aggressive leadership of Robert McNamara the pace of activity has been increased and these totals are mounting rapidly.

The World Bank secures its funds from world capital markets. The capital subscription of the member governments amount to loan guarantees, so the securities of the World Bank command high credit ratings. At first most of the World Bank's issues were sold in the United States, but in recent years West Germany, the Netherlands, Switzerland, and Japan have been the sites of offerings. The World Bank also makes direct placements with some central banks and other governmental agencies of countries such as Kuwait, Qator, and Yugoslavia. The World Bank borrows for itself and IDA.

The World Bank has clearly led to capital movements that would not have taken place with only private institutions in the market. So far it has had a fairly good record in the collection of its loans, and its impact seems to have been constructive. Nevertheless, some potentials for disaster remain. For example, over half the IDA credits are concentrated in the area of India, Pakistan, and Bangladesh. As long as the spirit of internationalism is stronger than the forces of nationalism, this good record may be continued, but if the world should revert to nationalism as it did in the 1930s, the World Bank and IDA probably could not survive.

The logic of World Bank lending is a sophisticated exercise in the economics of development. Many of the World Bank loans are for highways, electric power, education, agricultural development such as irrigation dams and canals, and related purposes. The IDA loans are even more clearly for infrastructure purposes. The logic is that if the economic development of the borrowing country is improved by such infrastructure, the credit is profitable even if the specific project does not produce a profit. The rules of accounting for such public projects are not parallel to those followed by private corporations, so a comparison of profitability cannot be made in any precise terms. It is very likely, however, that many of the projects financed by the World Bank and by IDA were "vanity" projects (public monuments or uneconomic dams) that had dubious merit. This may, however, slander the credit evaluators who work for these institutions. It is significant that the World Bank is one of the largest supporters of theoretical research into economic development.

The critics of the system say that it promotes governments with political philosophies antithetical to our own. This may well be true, but the World Bank is an international institution, not a United States institution. Its policies present one of the dilemmas of foreign policy that our country will continue to face for a long time.

PROJECTS AND QUESTIONS

1. Hunt through several issues of *The Wall Street Journal* and you are likely to find an offering of a foreign issue. Compare its terms with those of recent or current domestic bond issues.
2. Look up direct investment in a recent issue of the *Survey of Current Business*. What has happened since the text was written?
3. If a World Bank annual report is available, look up the most recent survey of foreign and international bond markets. Report on current and recent developments.
4. From the *Federal Reserve Bulletin* (or other sources) look up comparative interest rates and inflation rates in a number of leading nations. Is there any relationship between the two items?

BIBLIOGRAPHY

The bibliography for this chapter is the same as that for Chapter 19.

part five

The Influence of Government on Financial Markets

chapter 21
Government Efforts at Economic and Financial Stabilization

The federal government has become a large factor in the working of the economic system. Whether this influence has been a beneficial or detrimental one is hotly disputed, but the fact that there *is* an influence, and that the influence has been *consciously and deliberately exercised*, is not disputed. In many ways the structure and operations of financial markets have been particularly subject to this influence. The announced policy of the federal government since World War II, fully expressed in legislation, has been to stabilize economic activity. The effects of such a policy on financial markets will be the subject of the first chapter in this concluding part. Government has also regulated the institutions of financial markets through many acts of legislation and administrative action. The concluding chapter of this part will deal with such regulation and with ways in which government has had an impact both on competition and on the rate of innovation and evolution in the financial structure. We can describe but shall not attempt to make a conclusive evaluation of this impact. We shall, however, in the concluding paragraphs, supply the student with some standards that may be used in making such an evaluation.

BACKGROUND ON ECONOMIC INSTABILITY AND FINANCIAL MARKETS

Economic instability has had a long history in the United States. Although the Great Depression of the early 1930s is the best known of such episodes, there were at least half a dozen instances in which the economy of the nation had been convulsed by sharp depressions of economic activity. The beginnings of these depressions were usually marked by bank solvency panics in which financial markets ceased to operate normally. These depressions had a number of influences on financial markets: Among the most important were declines in the quality of credit and contractions in the quantity of credit. Commercial bank failures in large numbers accompanied many of the panics. Other types of financial institutions also failed or at least ceased operation for a period of time. Financial markets would be first chaotic, with both bond and stock prices falling rapidly, and then would become quite inactive. The decline in bond prices was often much more a reflection of fear about credit quality rather than a reflection of changes in interest rates. Long-term economic growth not only stopped during such depressions but was replaced with economic contraction. Even after the early bank panic stages had passed, economic growth was seldom renewed for several years. This general reversal of economic growth had its counterpart in the financial system and financial markets: Often the contraction of financial markets was even greater in relative terms than for the economy as a whole.

It would be wrong to assume that these early episodes of economic distress went wholly without attention from government. While the general economic policy prevailing was one of laissez faire or automatic self-adjustment by the economy, the human distress was such that a variety of stop-gap measures were often used. But once the depression period was passed, further measures of public economic assistance were no longer applied to the problem. The economic system was again expected to be self-regulating. However, the Great Depression of the early 1930s was different and the variety of economic measures adopted at that time were much more than temporary. Many of the measures of financial regulation that will be reviewed in the next chapter were adopted at that time; they were expected to be long-term elements of the system of financial markets. At the depth of the depression about one-quarter of the population was unemployed, and many others were underemployed. Although there was some measure of recovery after 1933, complete recovery did not occur until World War II when defense spending rapidly shifted the economy from one of a labor surplus to that of a labor shortage. This experience had another aspect that was most impressive for economic observers: Although war is normally expected to be accompanied by considerable deprivation of the civilian economy, this was not really true in the United States. Except for a few specific items, civilian standards of living were remarkably well maintained, and for many families, improved. One crude lesson was learned: If the government spent enough money, there need not be widespread unemployment and economic misery.

An intellectual factor was also at work. Lord Keynes, a celebrated British economist, had made much the same point in a much more refined and less crude way. He called the wounds of a depression "self-inflicted." Although not well known to the public, his ideas spread rapidly among economists. He was one of the leading figures in shaping the Bretton Woods agreements, reviewed in Chapter 19, and his ideas were expressed in many postwar plans for full employment. In the United States, a full employment act was drafted.

Business cycles have been less pronounced since the passage of the Employment Act of 1946 than they were before. The economy has had its ups and downs, but the peaks and troughs have been less severe in duration and magnitude. The recessions of 1949, 1954, 1958, 1961, 1967, and 1970 were minor compared to the Great Depression of the 1930s. The recession (or depression?) of 1974 and 1975 was something else. The recession of 1970 had shown that prices could continue to rise during a recession. This naturally posed a dilemma for the governmental stabilization authorities because actions to relieve the unemployment could further exacerbate the price inflation. But this came to be an even sharper dilemma in 1974. The energy crisis and the sudden and sharp increase in petroleum prices in late 1973 were parts of the problem. However, the underlying causes probably were more general and pervasive. Unemployment increased rapidly, but the *rate* of price advance also increased so that stabilization policy was faced with an almost impossible task. Compounding the difficulty was the further fact that the inflation led to very sharp increases in interest rates that would have occurred regardless of the nature of monetary policy.

The major conclusion to be drawn from this experience is that the optimism of the early post–World War II years about the potentials for economic stabilization was excessive. There are limits to the power of government policy. The problem can be put in summary but possibly not wholly accurate terms by suggesting that the constructive potentials of governmental economic policy are more limited than had been expected, but the destructive potentials for bad governmental economic policy are greater than had even before been surmised. Government has become too deeply involved in the economic processes of expenditure and income to withdraw to any very great extent, but its exercise of power remains fraught with danger.

ARE FINANCIAL MARKETS INHERENTLY UNSTABLE?

First, it should be noted that the Employment Act of 1946 does not contain the word "full" in its title. The word had been in the titles of most of the draft legislation first submitted, but in the process of political compromise it was dropped. Many feared, and probably correctly, that an effort to push employment to very high levels would be inflationary and possibly self-defeating. Another characteristic of the Act was that it focused mainly on fiscal policy but did not seem to give much of a direct role to monetary policy. Furthermore, the Act paid little or no attention to the system of finance or financial markets; it seemed to assume that if employment were to be stabilized, then all other elements of the economy, including financial markets, would be automatically stabilized. But that did not prove to be the case. Although the stability of the financial system has been improved, large elements of instability remain. The question then has to be asked: Is the financial system inherently unstable?

At one time it was thought that financial markets were the major cause of economic instability. Much of the early regulation of finance, the subject of our next chapter, was based on the implicit belief that reducing financial instability would cure general economic instability. We now know that this was an overly simplistic diagnosis of the problem. However, it is not at all clear that causation runs solely in the opposite direction. In truth, it is almost certain that causation goes in both directions. This still leaves unsettled, however, the question of *which* direction is more important. We cannot settle that issue, but we shall try to shed some light on it.

To a large extent, financial movements are the effects of fluctuations in general economic activity. Financial markets are unusually sensitive to the health of the economy. An excellent example may be found in business capital expenditures, which are important factors in the level of business activity. The timing of such expenditures can be adjusted to meet the needs and expectations of business management. The markets for the raising of business capital are early reflectors of variations in the demands for such funds.

A closely related variable is business profits. In the long run, the return on capital as well as the existence of capital itself depends on the level of business profits. Business profits, in turn, influence capital expenditure decisions. Financial markets are swayed by the actions of those in a strategic position to know something about future profits. If the promise of future profits and business prosperity looks bright, stock market trading often leads to rising stock prices well in advance of an actual upturn in economic activity.

While financial markets are affected by economic events originating in other sectors of the economy, reverse causality also exists. Developments in the financial markets influence business, government, and consumer expenditure to a considerable extent. Fluctuations in the cost and availability of credit usually lead to fluctuations in the demand for real goods and services. So do movements in the money supply. Sometimes these effects are merely feedback effects from movements originating in the real side of the economy. Other times these effects originate in the financial markets themselves.

In general equilibrium analysis, everything depends upon everything else. This principle applies to the interrelations between the financial markets and the markets for real goods and services. Fluctuations in financial market activity are both cause and effect of fluctuations in general economic activity. Cyclical impulses can originate anywhere in the economy, including the financial markets. First-round effects and feedback effects can work in any direction.

This leaves us with the question of whether the real side of the economy would be more stable or less so if financial markets did not exist. One might argue that the economy would be more stable in the absence of financial markets because it is these markets that make it possible to separate the acts of saving and investment. Discoordination of investment decisions from saving decisions is a source of instability. If investors want to invest more than savers want to save, an economic expansion is set in motion. On the other hand, if savers want to save more than investors want to invest, the economy contracts. Without financial markets, desired saving and desired investment would always be equal. The economy might still fluctuate, but it would not be due to disparity between ex ante saving and investment. However, such an economy would be characterized by permanent stagnation. Without financial markets, resources would be grossly misallocated; consumer welfare would drop and economic growth would be stifled.

One can also make the opposite case: that is, that the economy is more stable because of financial markets. One line of argument in this case is that the financial markets absorb pressures from other markets in the economy. In this view, swings in financial market activity provide relief from swings that might otherwise occur in the markets for real goods and services. For example, many businesses extend credit to customers in the face of declining income in order to stabilize sales. Such credit often runs countercyclically to general economic activity, thereby dampening the general business cycle. Another argument in this case is that the financial markets play an originating causal role in the economy, and that by controlling financial market activity through official monetary and credit policies, one can indirectly control the overall business cycle.

This chapter does not take the position that financial markets are, on balance, either inherently stabilizing or destabilizing in terms of the overall economy. Rather, it recognizes that both the real and financial sides of the economy do in fact fluctuate and that these fluctuations are interconnected, with cause and effect patterns working in both directions.

One problem with discussing fluctuations in financial market activity is that there is no single aggregate measure of the volume of this activity. Unlike the concept of GNP, aggregate measures of credit involve considerable double-counting because of the layering of credit by financial intermediaries. Thus, in the sections to follow, we shall be looking at movements in specific quantities such as the supply of money. But quantities do not tell the whole story. Interest rates—the prices in financial markets—are logical indicators of economic instability, financial and real. We must pay attention to interest rates and also to stock market prices, since it has long been fashionable for observers to tie the stock market and the business cycle together.

CYCLICAL MOVEMENTS IN MONEY, INTEREST RATES, AND GENERAL ECONOMIC ACTIVITY

The historical record shows that money, interest rates, and general economic activity tend to move together in the same direction. Economic upswings are generally characterized by rising rates of interest and inflation as well as rising rates of growth in money and production. During downswings, rates of interest and inflation as well as growth rates in money and production tend to drop.

These parallel movements are usually but not always visible to the naked eye. Some variables lead while others lag, so at any given point in time a movement in one variable may be nearing completion while another is still picking up steam. The 1970 to 1971 recession was a good example of this. The decline in the rate of growth of the money supply actually began in 1969, several months before production, employment, and interest rates started their downward course. When production hit bottom, the rate of inflation had yet to show any sign of subsiding. The same pattern was repeated in the mid-1970s.

The discussion thus far raises two important questions: Why do money, interest rates, and general economic activity tend to move in parallel fashion? Why do the parallel movements fail to correspond exactly at any point in time? To answer these questions we must analyze the interrelations between the principal variables.

The foundation for a positive relation between the money supply and nominal income (GNP measured at current prices) can be traced to the "quantity theory of money," now commonly called monetarism. This theory holds that the growth rate of nominal income is tied to the growth rate of the money supply. According to this theory an increase in the growth rate of money will bring about an increase in the growth rate of production after a lag averaging some six to nine months, and it will also bring about an increase in the rate of inflation after an additional lag again averaging about six to nine months. Thus money grows first, then production, and finally prices. Lag time is thought to be long and variable, but apart from this, nominal income cannot expand appreciably without an expansion of the money supply, nor can nominal income fail to contract if the money supply is appreciably contracted.

Economists in the neo-Keynesian camp agree that there is a positive relation between money and income, but they do not see a necessary relation. In their view, the level of production and prices can expand or contract without a corresponding expansion or contraction of the money supply. Neo-Keynesians consider "autonomous demand" to be a prime mover of change in general economic activity. An increase in autonomous demand is thought to lead to an increase in production and prices. With nominal income rising, the demand for money also rises, which creates a shortage of money. This shortage may be eliminated by increasing the money supply, so that money rises with production and prices. Alternatively, the shortage may be corrected by a rising level of interest rates that reduces the demand for money. In this alternative case, an expansion in production and prices is accompanied by higher interest rates rather than a growing money supply. The money supply may grow, but it does not have to grow.

Those who hold to the monetarist position admit that interest rates do tend to rise and fall with general economic expansion and contraction, but not necessarily for the reasons given by the neo-Keynesians. According to the monetarists, observed interest rates largely reflect expectations regarding inflation. Lenders who want a 4 percent constant-dollar return on their investment and expect a 3 percent rate of inflation must charge a nominal interest rate of 7 percent to obtain a "real" return of 4 percent. If lenders expect inflation to be at a 5 percent rate, they must then charge a nominal interest rate of 9 percent to get a 4 percent "real" return. Thus interest rates vary positively with the rate of inflation, which in turn varies positively with the growth rate of the money supply.

This book is not the appropriate place to go deeply into the various nuances of rival monetary theories, but one key difference between the quantity theory (monetarism) and neo-Keynesianism is worth pointing out, and that has to do with the effect of changes in interest rates. In the quantity theory view, interest rates affect spending decisions more than they do decisions about holding money. If "autonomous demand" but not the money supply is increased, interest rates will rise; but this increase will do more to discourage spending than to directly decrease the demand for money. Reduced spending due to higher interest rates thus works to offset the increase in autonomous demand. On balance, nominal income and the supply of and demand for money are very nearly restored to their original levels. A change in autonomous demand may initiate a change in nominal income, but only a change in the money supply can sustain a change in nominal income.

In the neo-Keynesian view, interest rates affect decisions about holding money more than they do spending decisions. In this view, a change in autonomous demand is sufficient to sustain a change in nominal income. Monetary change is not a necessary condition. If autonomous demand but not the money supply is increased, income and interest rates will rise. The increase in income will increase the demand for money. But the increase in interest rates will decrease the demand for money. On balance, the demand for money will be little affected and will therefore remain in equilibrium with the unchanging money supply.

A synthesis of monetarism and neo-Keynesianism recognizes that interest rates affect both spending decisions and decisions about holding money. Whether one effect is stronger than the other is an empirical question. The facts do reveal that money, interest, and income move up and down together in a systematic fashion. These facts are consistent with a synthetic approach to monetary theory.

The Federal Reserve has generally taken a synthetic or eclectic approach in conducting its monetary policies. Unbound by economic ideology, it has gauged the thrust of its actions by keeping one eye on the money supply and the other on interest rates. However, as we saw in Chapter 11, the Fed began in the early 1970s to give more weight to monetary aggregates than to interest rates in conducting and monitoring its operations. Although this fundamental shift in the guidance of monetary policy has now been tested in both recessionary and inflationary circumstances, the verdict on its success is not yet clear. In 1972 monetary policy was clearly too expansionary; that has been admitted by the Fed. Possibly as a reaction to the excess on one side, during 1974 monetary policy was quite tight, in spite of a high and increasing level of unemployment. As a result of this tightness, interest rates went to very high, almost unprecedented levels. Even so, the rate of price inflation was also very high.

Fiscal policy also seems to have had less impact than was formerly assumed and expected. Very high levels of budget deficits in 1975 and 1976 did not seem to have a great deal of impact on unemployment. Consumer expenditures started expanding in 1976 and on into 1977, but business capital expenditures lagged. Housing was stimulated in 1977, but this expansionary development may have been due more to pent-up demand than to fiscal or monetary stimulation—although the availability of mortgage money was doubtless a strong positive factor.

CYCLICAL EFFECT OF NONBANK FINANCIAL INTERMEDIATION

We have seen that monetary policy works through Federal Reserve management of bank reserves and the money supply. Most of the money supply is in the form of deposit debt of commercial banks. The commercial banking system, however, is but one part of a larger system of financial intermediaries that borrows from ultimate savers and lends to ultimate investors. Monetary policy therefore works through controlling the liabilities (deposits) of one type of financial intermediary (commercial banks). When the economy is overheated, the Fed may attempt to cool it off by contracting the growth of the liabilities of commercial banks. When the economy is depressed, the Fed may try to promote recovery by expanding the liabilities of commercial banks. The idea of discretionary monetary policy is to get the growth rate of these liabilities to move somewhat countercyclically to the growth rate of general economic activity.

One might reasonably ask what happens to the liabilities of financial intermediaries other than commercial banks. Do these uncontrolled liabilities follow a cyclical pattern? If so, do they move pro- or countercyclically? If pro-cyclically, do they undermine the intent and effect of monetary policy? If countercyclically, do they have a general effect on interest rates and capital expenditures, or do they affect certain markets and sectors more than others? These issues have puzzled economists and policy makers for a number of years.

The idea that the liabilities of nonbank financial intermediaries move pro-cyclically with the economy, offsetting the effect of monetary policy in the process, was promoted some years ago by Professors Gurley and Shaw. The reasoning went something like this: Suppose the Fed decreases the money supply with the intent of raising open-market interest rates and lowering capital expenditures. In the face of higher open-market rates, nonbank intermediaries will be induced to raise the interest rates that they pay on savings accounts and other liabilities in order to attract more funds. The higher rates paid on these liabilities will increase the demand for them and decrease the demand for money. The decreased demand for money, in turn, will decrease open-market interest rates, thereby offsetting the attempt of the contractionary policy to raise open-market rates. In other words, if the monetary contraction is initially successful in increasing open-market rates, it is probable that nonbank intermediaries will raise their rates in order to attract funds for investment. When the intermediaries use these attracted funds to purchase open-market instruments, the effect is to decrease open-market rates. In the end, the open-market rates may fall back nearly to where they began, thereby undermining the intent of the policy.

In a similar vein, an increase in the liabilities of nonbank intermediaries at a time when the liabilities of banks are decreasing will leave the total supply of liquid assets largely unaffected. For those who believe that the economy is related more to "stores of value" than it is to "means of payment," control of only one store of value—bank deposits—is insufficient to control the economy. In this view, monetary control should be extended to the liabilities of all financial intermediaries, not just the liabilities of commercial banks.

These ideas have been criticized both on theoretical and empirical grounds. Even if one accepts the theory, the evidence shows that nonbank financial intermediation has had only a minor pro-cyclical effect at worst. In fact, during the tight credit period of 1974, the liabilities of nonbank intermediaries not only failed to expand but actually shrank.

Several reasons account for the disintermediation during this period. Open-market interest rates climbed dramatically, reaching near-historic highs. Rates paid by intermediaries on savings accounts did not increase relatively. They were held back by legal ceilings and by the fact that savings and loan associations and mutual savings banks were carrying a large volume of low-yielding and slow-moving mortgages and therefore could not have raised the rates that they pay by very much, even if they had been allowed to. The demand for money did decrease, but not because people wanted to put it into savings accounts. In fact, the demand for savings accounts also decreased. Many people switched out of demand deposits, savings accounts, and life insurance policy reserves and put their funds directly into the open market to take advantage of extra-good yields. Others liquidated their accounts to finance consumption and other expenditures.

HOUSING CYCLES AND THE MORTGAGE MARKET

As we said in Chapter 2, one of the more striking features of the postwar period has been the tendency for housing starts to move countercyclically with general business conditions. Residential construction has typically risen sharply when general activity was reaching a trough. Declines in building activity have tended to take hold well in advance of peaks in the general business cycle.

Most housing market economists have linked this countercyclical behavior to countercyclical movements in the supply of mortgage credit. In an expanding economy, the total demand for credit tends to run ahead of the total supply of credit. Credit becomes "tight" and interest rates rise. The feedback effects of tight credit conditions on general expenditures is to dampen economic activity somewhat, but not by enough to reverse its generally upward course. Housing, however, is an exception. The supply of mortgage credit has typically become so short during general expansion that housing starts have actually fallen while other kinds of production have continued to rise. For various reasons, tight credit has a tendency to become concentrated and compounded in the mortgage market.

One reason for this is the "disintermediation" process described in the preceding section. The inability of savings institutions to raise their rates on savings deposits when open-market interest rates are rising serves to facilitate a flow of funds out of these intermediaries and into the open market. This would have little effect on the mortgage market were it not for the fact that savings and loan associations and mutual savings banks, and to a lesser extent life insurance companies and commercial banks, invest heavily and disproportionately in the mortgage market. Consequently, a dollar of savings taken out of one of these intermediaries is apt to be a dollar taken out of the mortgage market. When it is reinvested in the open market, it is unlikely to go back into the mortgage market. The supply of mortgage credit is therefore reduced.

But this is not the end of the story. Financial intermediaries are apt to reduce their investments in mortgages by more than the funds lost through disintermediation. Mortgage rates of interest do not rise or fall as far or as fast as other rates of interest. When interest rates are rising, mortgage rates tend to lag behind. Profit-motivated commerical banks and other intermediaries can therefore increase return by switching out of mortgages and into other forms of investment. The supply of mortgage credit is thus further reduced.

Why do mortgage rates lag behind other interest rates? There are two views. One explains "sticky" mortgage rates as the result of market interferences such as legal rate ceilings on insured and guaranteed mortgage loans. The other view argues that mortgage borrowers are more responsive and sensitive to mortgage rates than other borrowers are to other rates. With an "elastic" demand curve for mortgage funds, mortgage rates may change little even if there is a large shift in the supply of funds. There is probably some truth to both of these views.

A different approach to explaining the countercyclical behavior of housing starts emphasizes the effect of credit conditions on the supply side of the housing market. In this approach, home building is seen as an inventory problem. Tight credit conditions are thought to reduce the demand for builders' inventories of houses under construction and therefore to reduce the supply of new housing starts. Easy credit is thought to increase the willingness of builders to expand their inventories under construction.

FLUCTUATIONS IN THE BOND MARKET

Movements in business activity clearly have an influence on the bond market. This influence is effective both upon yields and upon the volume of business. The significant point, however, seems to be that although the influence on yields is an early and prompt reflection of movements in business activity, changes in the volume of bonds issued and sold seem to lag. An important question arises: How much is the volume of business influenced by yield changes?

Bond yields show a clear cyclical pattern. They go up as business activity advances; they recede as business activity slackens. The timing of this movement is roughly synchronous, although the yields may have some element of lead in them. If a lead exists, it is probably due to the strong link between the money markets and the bond markets. If the money markets show any tendency to lead, then it is quite natural that the bond markets should reflect a similar pattern.

Within bond yields, the movements are so nearly parallel that one can almost use any one of the yield series as reflective of events in the market as a whole; but some deviations do occur. For example, the yields on tax-exempt state and local government obligations sometimes depart from other yield series by material amounts. A large part of the reason for this is that the demand for state and local government bonds is tied more closely to stock market prices and money market rates than it is to yields on corporate and Treasury bonds. During economic expansion, when stock market prices and money market yields are on the rise, wealthy individuals tend to switch out of state and local obligations and into stocks while commercial banks tend to switch into short-term loans and investments. Often this behavior lowers the prices and raises the yields on state and local government bonds much more dramatically than is the case in other parts of the bond market.

The movements of yields on corporate bonds and on bonds of the U.S. Treasury are parallel. Interest on both types of bonds is fully exposed to income taxation. The quality of corporate bonds has also become so good that the differential between these yields is deservedly small.

Movements in the volume of bond financing are clearly rather laggard of general business conditions. One of the probable reasons is that bond financing takes a lot of time to put into effect after the decision to finance has been made. This lag is equally true of other business cycle series, such as capital expenditures. Bond financing may lag during the later phases of an upturn since profits are high and because of hope for a slightly better market. When the market does start to change and yields decline, volume picks up while borrowers are taking advantage of the situation. But if lower borrowing costs persist for long enough to indicate a general weakening in business conditions, then overall financing plans are changed.

One interesting but unexplained fact is that the yields on lower-grade bonds seem to lag behind changes in the yields on higher-grade bonds. The volume of financing is not classified on a quality basis by months, so the length of this lag cannot be measured. It seems likely, however, that the lower-grade market may be subordinate to the market for top-grade issues and follows it.

One of the problems involved in using bond market data in financial analysis is that both yields and volume are subject to short-term variability. Differences in the behavior of new-issue and secondary markets may account for some of this randomness. The new-issue market for both corporate and U.S. government bonds is so sporadic that one cannot secure wholly satisfactory new-issue yields from these markets. For this reason much of the judgment of these markets is drawn from yields taken from secondary markets. These markets produce a steady stream of bid-and-ask quotations from which the published and most widely used statistical series are drawn. Some business is done at these levels, but secondary market yields often depart materially from new-issue market yields, particularly under conditions of stress. It even appears that this differential has a business-cycle character that as yet is not fully understood.

Conditions in the bond markets appear to have a feedback effect on capital expenditure decisions; but aside from this one influence, it seems unlikely that they have any profound effects on business conditions. The market is not very well publicized and its practitioners are skilled professionals, not given to panicking. Most markets produce some feedback influence since that is the very nature of a price system. Prices serve the function of influencing market supplies and demands in an economizing way. Nevertheless, the feedback effect of bond yields on capital expenditure is apt to be small to the extent that decision makers are able to untie their capital expenditure plans from the cost and availability of long-term debt. One such method of "time financing" is to borrow short-term when interest rates are high and long-term when rates are low. However, if interest rates are high over a long period of time, this strategy may not work and decision makers may be forced to abandon certain capital expenditure plans. Studies show that the tight credit conditions of the latter years of the 1960s did in fact lead to cutbacks in planned capital expenditures.

High interest rates in the mid-1970s increased the cost of capital to business and capital expenditures seldom showed the strength they had had in the 1960s. Furthermore, business first responded to high interest rates by avoiding the bond market with short-term bank borrowing. However, the mid-1970s had the sobering effect of showing that short-term debt for long-term purposes could be embarrassing and even dangerous. After the soaring short-term interest rates of 1974, there was a general retreat from such financing. Bond financing increased in late 1975, 1976, and early 1977 but much of the proceeds were used, not for capital expenditures, but to retire short-term debt. In the recovery of 1976 the demand for short-term debt lagged. The continued high level of long-term interest rates was an inhibitor, though to just what extent cannot be said. The relative sluggishness of long-term business capital expenditures can be said to have been caused, at least in part, by the high interest rates, but they also had the effect of being a cause of a less than complete recovery of business activity. Again, this is an illustration of the way in which the dilemma of inflationary expectations and unemployment can thwart the public and private economic policies that might stimulate economic expansion.

BUSINESS CYCLES AND THE STOCK MARKET

Even the most casual observer of the stock market is aware of the great extent to which the prices of common stocks fluctuate. The conclusion that these fluctuations are related to the ups and downs in general business conditions seems almost equally evident. The purpose of this section is to examine a little more closely the nature of this relationship and to consider the matter of causality.

Stock market prices are used as one of the leading indicators of changes in business conditions by the National Bureau of Economic Research and by other business-cycle analysts. This selection is supported by very widespread popular interest in the stock market. Many businessmen believe it to be a reliable guide as to future economic events and follow the market closely even if they are not themselves much involved in it as investors or speculators. Millions of ordinary citizens are given the impression that stock prices are important economic indicators as the averages are quoted every evening in television news programs.

There is undoubtedly a widespread impression that the stock market has some kind of causal effect on general economic activity. This notion was fostered by the Crash of October 1929, which preceded the 1932 to 1933 trough of the Great Depression. But most people do not know that the decline of general economic activity actually began in the summer of 1929, several months before the crash of October. Economic historians now regard the Crash as more of an effect of the deepening Depression than as its cause.

Most of the time the stock market does turn in advance of turns in general economic activity. Figures from the National Bureau of Economic Research show that cycles in stock prices tend to lead general business cycles by an average of four months. Upturns in stock prices are frequently followed by upturns in business conditions, and market downturns are often followed by business downturns. But this is only a general tendency. Sometimes the lead and lag positions are reversed, as they were in 1929. What is more important, sometimes the stock market moves at crosscurrents with general business conditions. Bull markets have occasionally emerged during recessions and bear markets during economic recovery. In 1962, the stock market declined even though the economy was on the road to recovery. In the late 1960s and into the 1970s, there seemed to be little relation between stock market movements and movements in general economic activity.

In general the stock market of the 1970s has been far less ebullient than in the 1960s. Many of the enthusiastic speculators of the 1960s have dropped out of the stock market and turned to other outlets such as stock options, or to commodities, particularly gold and silver. In 1972 the stock market, stimulated by easy money and a business recovery, did manage barely to exceed the highs of 1968. However, this level was held only briefly, and since that time there has been more bad news for stock investors than good news. The depression of stock prices in 1974 was excessive and was recovered in several spurts in 1975 and 1976. Nevertheless, the market has never approached its 1972 peak. The market seems to be sensitive to bad news, as in 1974, but it does not respond positively to good news, as for example, in 1976 and 1977. The use of stock market prices as a leading business-cycle indicator by the NBER continues to have some validity, but it can also be said that the stock market often departs from the trend of general business. As one economist wit is reputed to have said: "The stock market forecasted seven of the five postwar recessions."

The discussion to this point raises two questions: Why do the stock market and general economic activity sometimes move in opposite directions? Is the stock market a cause or an effect of the business cycle?

There are at least three ways in which a turn in the stock market might cause economic activity to change. One way is through a wealth effect. A sharp fall of stock prices reduces the market value of investors' financial wealth. Feeling poorer, investors may feel compelled to reduce their consumption expenditures for such luxury items as eating out, fancy automobiles, extended vacations, and luxury housing.

Another way is through a financing effect. Business corporations are prone to issue new stock when stock prices are high and terms are favorable. Selling stock when prices are abnormally depressed can have an adverse dilutive effect on existing stockholders. To the extent that corporations rely on external equity to finance capital expenditures, an unfavorable stock market can lead to a postponement of business investment and initiate a downturn in economic activity. The fact is, however, that most corporations raise considerably more new capital through retained earnings and by borrowing in the credit markets than by selling new stock. Thus a stock market decline cannot be said to make funds much less available for business capital expenditures.

Still another way is through an expectations effect. A declining stock market may cause businessmen to develop pessimistic expectations of future business conditions. It may make them more cautious and conservative. The thing about expectations is that they have a way of becoming self-fulfilling: Business expects an economic downturn, so it does not invest and a downturn materializes. The Great Depression of the 1930s would have happened anyway, but it probably would not have been as severe as it was had there not been a shattering of business confidence following the Crash.

The fact that declining stock prices are not always followed by declining business conditions lends credence to the idea that the stock market is not the primary mover of economic activity. Even when stock prices and economic activity do move together, stock market causation is questionable. Other, more fundamental causes may be at work. These causes include such factors as changes in the quantity and quality of natural and human resources, innovations and technological changes, monetary and fiscal policies, changes in tastes and preferences, war and peace, the weather, etc. The stock market may have some vague effect on general economic activity, but no serious economist would put it at the top of the list of causal factors.

Most economists view stock prices as being more reflective than effective. The main channel of causation is thought to flow from general business conditions to stock market conditions. There is ample theoretical reason to accept this view. Theoretically, stock prices are the capitalized values of future profits. If business conditions and profits improve, so should stock prices.

If stock prices reflect business conditions, why then does the stock price cycle tend to lead the general business cycle? The answer rests in the future profits that investors capitalize. Investors do not know in advance what actual future profits will be, but they can (and do) form expectations of future profits. Current stock prices are, therefore, capitalized values of *expected* future profits. If these expectations come close to the mark, future business conditions will bear a close relation to current stock prices. For this reason stock prices are considered a leading indicator of the course of the economy.

When the stock market runs counter to the general business cycle, incorrect profit expectations are not always the reason. As important as expected profits are in determining stock prices, they are not the only factors affecting the market. Other factors are also important. One such factor is the discount rate by which investors capitalize expected profits. The discount rate has a time value of money component plus a premium for risk and uncertainty. The time value of money is indicated by the level of interest rates. If individuals prefer to trade future consumption for present consumption, they will save less and interest rates will rise. In terms of the stock market, expected profits will be discounted at a higher rate and stock prices will fall. An increase in the uncertainty of the future also raises the rate of discount, thereby lowering stock prices. When interest rates and uncertainty are both increasing, the stock market is apt to be depressed. Such was the case in 1969 and 1970. Interest rates were higher than most people could remember. Vietnam, pollution, student revolt, and general social unrest were dividing the nation and increasing the uncertainty of its future. And the stock market? It was in a terribly depressed condition. Since then the problems have changed (Watergate, oil shortages, food shortages, inflation, recession) but the stock market has stayed generally depressed.

IS MANAGED ECONOMIC STABILIZATION INHERENTLY INFLATIONARY?

The evidence of thirty years' experience both in the United States and in almost all the free nations of Western Europe suggests a positive answer to this question. The issue is larger, more complex, and in some ways more controversial than appropriate for a textbook devoted to financial markets. However, several corollary issues are closely related to the operation of financial markets.

High Interest Rates

As Chapter 3 has already shown, inflation has a powerful impact on interest rates. Investors insist on higher rates to offset the loss of real value in invested funds. Most studies, however, suggest that investors are not able to accomplish this goal fully; their real rate of return after allowing for the impact of inflation is less than it would have been without inflation.

High interest rates so far have not ruined financial markets or institutions. Some financial institutions have suffered "disintermediation," as we have noted above. Most financial institutions, however, have been able to balance interest costs and interest revenues reasonably well. High interest rates have also been one of the most important factors in the sluggish equity markets of the 1970s. When higher rates of interest were available on bonds, common stock investors naturally expected higher returns on common stock, which meant a drastic downward adjustment of basic price-earnings ratios.

Higher interest rates have probably reduced the quality of credit because debtors face higher debt service charges. With a given earnings stream the ratio of such earnings to debt service is lower, which is conventionally viewed as a reduction in the quality of credit. This has certainly been true of much public utility debt and also that of state and local governments.

An Increase in Debt Preference

The increase in interest rates does not appear to have reduced the demand for borrowed funds. Some even appear eager to assume debts. The argument is that "with inflation debts can ultimately be paid off with cheaper dollars!" The simplest but most dramatic illustration of this tendency has been in housing. Many younger couples have been violating traditional rules of prudence in the amount of housing debt that can be safely assumed, buying more expensive homes with a higher ratio of debt service to income. Even if current earnings make debt service a relatively heavy burden, they are confident that earnings will increase with inflation so that debt service will later be relatively easy to cover.

In corporate finance, equity financing has almost always been mainly by retained earnings. As a result external equity financing has always tended to be small, and so a clear-cut change in corporate financial policy is harder to detect. Nevertheless, it is not without some significance that a number of giant corporations that had formerly avoided debt financing have recently changed policies and have undertaken external debt financing: General Motors and du Pont are two leading examples of such actions.

Expectation of Inflation as a Blight on Economic Health

At several junctures in this chapter reference has been made to the damaging effect of inflation on public economic policy and the dilemma it poses to economic policy makers, as well as to those in the private economy who try to operate in financial markets. In truth, it is not just current recorded inflationary increases in prices that are to blame, it is the sustained *expectation* of continued inflation. Even a brief interlude of less pressing inflationary price increases does not seem to have much impact either on interest rates or on general business activity. The reason is that the interlude is expected to be temporary; inflation is expected to be the recurring force at some later—and probably not much delayed—date.

Financial markets in general, but particularly the capital markets, are blighted by the persistence of that conviction of expected inflation. Thus, the public authorities who form policies aimed at economic stabilization suffer from frustration. They are inhibited by the dilemma of inflation and unemployment. Even when they try to cut through the dilemma with clear pressure on one side or the other, their actions are less effective than they would be if the blight of inflationary expectations were absent.

A new idea has been filtering through the academic scene. It is now at a point of tentative consideration at the level of national policy formation but is not yet at a level of acceptance. The idea, in drastically simplified form, is that if the critical economic decision makers hold rational expectations as to the ultimate impact of monetary expansion, (1) its employment goal will be frustrated, and (2) a higher rate of inflation will result. This can be illustrated in the workings of monetary policy through financial markets. The basic thrust of Keynesian monetary policy was that monetary expansion would lower interest rates and thereby encourage increased borrowing for business investment, which was expected to produce a higher level of employment. The "rational expectation-ists" point out that if past experience has shown that such stimulative policies had also led to more inflation, investors would commit their funds to the financial markets only if they could get higher interest rates to offset the expected rate of inflation. Thus monetary expansion would produce *higher* nominal interest rates rather than lower real rates, and would frustrate monetary policy by providing no real investment incentives. At the same time, the monetary expansion *would* increase prices and cause the expectation of inflation to be fulfilled. As we have noted above, financial markets have been afflicted with some of these dire results in recent years.

This new theory of rational expectations is parallel to another new theory of public social policy as illustrated by the "war on poverty." The welfare programs of this war on poverty were initially expected to be temporary and transitional in the effort to improve the lot of the poorest members of society. However, in many cases welfare programs seem to have embedded the poor even deeper in their poverty. The expectation of welfare has frustrated accomplishment of social reform. Other illustrations of the unexpected results of public policy could be marshaled.

These new ideas have not yet achieved general acceptance; indeed they may not yet claim adherence by even a majority of professional economists specializing in public economic policy. However, these ideas have reached the attention of public policy makers. Since the old policies have not been working very well, some change in the structure of public economic policy is almost certain. Equally important is the fact that financial markets will be one of the major arenas in which the new policies will be tried. The only suggestion we can make at the present time, therefore, is that change is likely and that the student should be prepared to study and understand such changes when they come.

PROJECTS AND QUESTIONS

1. Since the revised draft of this text left the hands of the authors, there have doubtless been further ups and downs of economic activity and of prices and yields in financial markets. Review these more recent developments. Compare government economic stabilization actions with developments in the financial markets. Do the generalizations about causation of this chapter still seem valid? Do you think governmental stabilization actions were helpful to financial markets?

2. The authors of this text usually avoid the risk of forecasting, but we greatly fear that price inflation, continuing at the time of the text publication, will still be in motion as you study it. However, whether it has abated, gotten worse, or remained the same, summarize recent effects of prevailing

inflationary developments on financial markets and on interest rate levels particularly.

3. Not all financial markets are equally affected by economic fluctuations and inflation. Can you detect material differences in such effects among markets?

BIBLIOGRAPHY

The literature on general economic stabilization is large; references to it can be found in almost any textbook on macroeconomics. The literature on the special role of financial institutions and markets in economic stabilization is much smaller and fragmented. After the President has submitted his annual economic report to Congress, the Joint Economic Committee (JEC) holds hearings for presentations of other points of view. Almost every year several economists representing money market commercial banks and other financial institutions are included among the witnesses appearing before the JEC. Whereas these witnesses usually address themselves to the general problems of stabilization, they often include a few comments relative to the role of the institutions they represent in the stabilization process. Trade association representatives sometimes are among the witnesses, and the publications of trade associations occasionally contain relevant material. The *Monthly Economic Letter* issued by Citibank, which has a distinct monetarist cast, often includes brief articles on stabilization policy. The *Morgan Guaranty Survey* is somewhat less committed to the monetarist point of view, but is also a less frequent commentator on stabilization policy.

Brookings Papers: This publication, issued three times a year, often contains articles on stabilization policy. While Brookings Institution has often been identified with the liberal point of view on economic policy, the articles are wholly the products of their authors and reflect a considerable diversity in point of view.

Federal Reserve Banks of Minneapolis and St. Louis: The annual reports and current economic publications of these two banks often present a conservative point of view quite at variance with that of the other elements in the Federal Reserve System.

Modigliani, F.: "The Monetarist Controversy, or Should We Foresake Stabilization Policy?": *American Economic Review,* March 1977: A defense of stabilization policy.

Poole, W.: "The Relationship of Monetary Deceleration to Business Cycle Peaks: Another Look at the Evidence," *Journal of Finance,* June 1975.

————: *Money and the Economy: A Monetarist View,* Addison-Wesley, Reading, Mass., 1978.

Rogalski, R. J., and J. D. Vinso: "Stock Returns, Money Supply, and the Direction of Causality," *Journal of Finance,* September 1977.

chapter 22
Governmental Regulation of Financial Institutions and Practices

Next to the public utilities, finance is probably the most regulated segment of the economy. Unlike public utilities, the regulation of finance is not based on a unified and consistent body of economic logic; it has usually been ad hoc in origin and inconsistent in results. Many, both inside and outside government, have urged a drastic overhaul of the regulatory harness to which finance is subject, but it will be slow in coming if it comes at all. Because of the scattered and fragmentary nature of much of financial regulation, this chapter will be somewhat episodic. It will not be comprehensive; an adequate treatment of financial regulation would require many times more space than is available to us. However, some examination of financial regulation is required if the student is to get a full picture of the working of financial markets.

The ad hoc nature of financial regulation is explained by the fact that most of it was adopted at the time when an emergency arose. Each new regulatory action or system was fitted to the current problems as they were then understood, but each regulation has usually remained in place long after the originating conditions changed. Very early in the history of this nation, waves of bank failures caused great hardship and economic distress. As a result, the chartering of banks was curbed by legislation, and in a few states banking was even, for a while, prohibited. The methods of chartering were controlled by the states until the Civil War, so they varied greatly. Further waves of bank failures in the late nineteenth century and again early in this century led to further bank regulation, generally in the form of specific legislation covering bank practices and of bank examinations that tested the adherence of banks to this legislation. In the course of time bank examiners were given considerable discretionary power on points not explicitly covered in banking legislation.

Another example of the ad hoc origin of much financial regulation occurred in the Great Depression. Many blamed speculation on the stock exchanges, particularly the New York Stock Exchange, for this depression. In addition many persons lost money by investing in securities sold by the investment banking community in the preceding period. Based on this experience, a great deal of legislation was adopted in the 1930s: The Securities Act of 1933, the Exchanges Act of 1934, the Public Utility Holding Company Act of 1935, the Investment Company Act of 1940, and the Investment Advisers Act also of 1940. The Securities and Exchange Commission (SEC) was created by the first of these acts and was given administrative authority in connection with all of them. Other bits of regulatory legislation were included in these acts: the prohibition of commercial banks from engaging in investment banking, the prohibition of payment of interest on demand deposits and the regulation of interest paid on time deposits. This later regulation is known as "Regulation Q" and is administered by the Federal Reserve. Later this authority was expanded, and some of it was lodged in other government agencies.

The creation of the Federal Deposit Insurance Agency in 1934 was another illustration of ad hoc adoption of a regulatory system; likewise the adoption of the Securities Investors Protection Corporation (SIPC) in 1970, following a period during which many brokerage firms had fallen into financial difficulties and some customers had lost control or possession of their securities. The creation of SIPC was covered in Chapter 17, but it has a characteristic difference from that of the FDIC, in that this is an agency in the twilight zone of self-regulation and governmental control.

Some financial regulation is basically inconsistent with other segments of such regulation. For example, restrictions on bank and branch chartering, prohibition of investment banking activities by commercial banks, and limiting interest paid on time deposits by Regulation Q all minimize competition. On the other hand, much of the efforts of the SEC in the regulation of securities markets has been an effort to *increase* competition: The rules covering the activities of specialists and the requirement for competitive brokerage commissions are examples. Some regulatory agencies seem to limit or curb the potential for profit of those regulated: This is thought to be true of commercial bank regulation. On the other hand, the regulators of savings institutions generally have been supportive of the activities and profitability of the agencies over which they preside. Some describe this difference by saying that in certain circumstances the regulatory "climate" is disciplining (maybe even hostile); in other cases it is cooperative, friendly, and supportive.

With the diffusion of characteristics of financial regulation it is inevitable that no single point of view or position is possible. Our effort in this chapter, therefore, will be to present a stratified sample of leading examples of regulation.

REGULATION OF FINANCIAL MARKET PRACTICES

The collapse of financial market prices in the Great Depression brought to light a great many practices that were then believed to have accounted for the difficulties experienced. The regulation that resulted was a direct response to what were then accepted as the reasons for the debacle. The following discussions are illustrative and not comprehensive.

Security Selling

Before the Great Depression frauds in the sales of securities occurred rather frequently. Many states had adopted "blue sky" laws in attempts to protect naive investors. Many of these frauds were rather simple in nature: selling mining shares for mines that had no geological hope of reward, selling worthless company shares, or even selling claims to little more than a bit of blue sky. However, in the late 1920s, the upsurge in stock market profits led to a number of security sales of very involved and complex corporate structures. Even fairly sophisticated security investors were deluded and ultimately lost money in the subsequent collapse of security prices. The Securities Act of 1933 is a complex law, but its essence is a requirement that sellers of securities "tell the truth, the whole truth, and nothing but the truth." This kind of summary statement may seem biased in favor of this legislation, and it is a bit on the extreme side. Still, the law did take the wise course of not trying to take risk out of security investment but to give investors access to the kind of information that would enable them to evaluate the risks and the potential rewards fairly. Security sales to the public had to be registered with a statement that disclosed great detail, and the securities themselves had to be accompanied by prospectuses that met minimum standards of disclosure. Some exceptions were made for short-term securities, small companies, private sales, and sales of municipal bonds.

Operation of Securities Exchanges

The stock market had long been subject to varying degrees of rigging and manipulation. Such practices were common in the nineteenth century; they were rather prevalent in the 1920s. Because the organized securities exchanges were very much like private clubs, they tended to be protective of their members and their practices and to resist regulatory efforts. However, the public image of the stock exchange was deeply blemished, and after fairly long and complex struggles, a great many measures of regulation were adopted, the main thrust of which was to reform trading practices such that investment by outside individuals was safe from the depredation of inside manipulation. The system of market rules was and is complex and far beyond the scope of this text, but the purpose of the reforms was simple: they give priority to the interests of long-term outside investors and they limit the potential for manipulation by insiders or members.

The system of regulation was also extended beyond the organized stock exchanges to the previously unorganized over-the-counter markets by creation of a new quasi-public–quasi-private organization: the National Association of Security Dealers (NASD). Both the NASD and the governing bodies of the NYSE and other stock exchanges then engaged in a kind of *self*-regulation, but with a guiding hand from the SEC. This combination was thought to be necessary because of the technical complexities of trading rules. These rules are subject to the review and revision of the SEC, but they are enforced by the agencies themselves, often with day-to-day or even hour-by-hour adjudication by the officers of the exchanges or the NASD. All actions, however, are subject to later review by the SEC.

One of the very long standing rules of the stock exchanges had been to set the commission rates at which orders were to be executed for nonmember customers. This was really a form of monopoly pricing and was aimed at avoiding cut-throat competition. The SEC put pressure on the exchanges to drop such fixed exchange rates and to allow the setting of competitive exchange rates. As already mentioned in Chapter 17 this was done in two steps. Since 1975 all commission rates have been subject to negotiation.

Unfinished business in this area of regulation remains: the full application of electronic technology to security trading. As recounted in Chapter 17 the automated quotation system of the NASD (the NASDAQ) has proved to make the over-the-counter market far more efficient. It raises questions as to whether the actual physical exchanges as now constituted are necessary; whether a greatly expanded NASDAQ could not do the job more efficiently, cheaply, and accurately. Odd-lot trading, once a monopoly of a couple of NYSE firms, has now been automated and individual commission brokerage houses are handling the business by means of automation. With this as a precedent, the pressure is slowly building for what may prove to be a vast structural reorganization of securities trading.

Margin Trading in Securities

Another illustration of the ad hoc origin of much regulation is that which applies to so-called margin trading: that is, the use of borrowed money to purchase securities, presumably for the purpose of short-term profits. It was thought to have been an evil that helped bring on the market collapse of 1929. This practice has now been regulated for more than four decades. The administration of it was delegated to the Federal Reserve rather than to the SEC.

REGULATION AIMED AT INCREASING SAFETY OF FINANCIAL INSTITUTIONS

In a perfectly competitive economy it is assumed that the owners of businesses try to preserve the safety of their businesses, both in order to attract customers and to protect their own investment. In the case of financial institutions, however, it has come to be accepted (though not by all) that good public policy requires some intervention to protect ill-informed and helpless customers against loss. This kind of public intervention has taken many forms: legislation controlling the kind and quality of assets financial institutions may acquire, regulation of the interest paid on time and savings deposits, regulation of management practices, examination procedures to ensure that the legislation and administrative regulations are followed, and the insurance of the liabilities of financial institutions by public agencies created for that purpose.

Thus, not only are financial markets themselves regulated as we saw in the previous section, but the financial institutions that are such central figures in these markets are likewise covered by a complex web of regulatory restrictions.

Kind and Quality of Assets

Whereas the kind and quality of assets of financial institutions is almost universally regulated, a very recent example of an area newly regulated will illustrate the burden that has been borne by other financial institutions for long periods of time. Our example has to do with the private pension plans that were described in Chapter 4. In 1974 the Congress passed the Employee Retirement Income Security Act (ERISA). A similar measure for public pension plans has been introduced into Congress and is under consideration (PERISA).

Although the law has not yet been clarified, its central theme is to use an old rule of law—the "prudent person" rule—that requires professional portfolio managers to exercise the prudence that an informed person would use in the management of his or her own financial affairs. The rule seems simple, but in practice it appears to have worried professional portfolio managers considerably. The administration of this law has been placed primarily with the Department of Labor rather than a branch of government with more financial background. One of the results of this legislation has been that some companies have closed out their pension plans rather than assume the legal risks that they felt were inherent in operating under this law. The other side, however, is that several private pension plans—notably those administered by unions—had engaged in investment practices that clearly would have met no standards of prudence.

This is only an illustration. Banks, both commercial and savings, credit unions, insurance companies, and investment companies all operate under legal regulatory systems of varying degrees of complexity and with potentials for both good and bad.

Regulation of Interest Paid on Savings and Time Deposits

This is commonly identified as Regulation Q, but in fact it covers several regulations applying to nonmember as well as member banks and to savings institutions in general. Originally the idea was that unrestrained competition for deposits led to banking difficulties and failures. But it has now become a different kind of regulation. Although official language has avoided admitting the present purposes, they can be stated as two: (1) to protect savings and loan associations from overvigorous competition by commercial banks, and (2) to give the Federal Reserve an indirect way to keep all banks, but particularly big money market banks, from expanding credit by an overvigorous "buying" of money in the money markets. It is, to use the terms of Chapter 11, a way of holding the growth of M_2 in check.

This illustrates the way in which regulations evolve over time into creatures quite different from the ones envisaged by the writers of the original laws. Perhaps this is not always bad; it can be argued that if the administrators of regulations flout legislative intent, Congress can always cure such practices easily and simply by passing a new law (or, better, repealing an old one).

Bank Examination to Enforce Banking Regulation

Bank examiners are now employed in rather large numbers by three federal agencies and most of the fifty states. In practice, these various agencies coordinate their activities and attempt to avoid duplication of effort and excessive inconvenience for the subject banks. With all this effort, however, the size of the burden is not inconsiderable and its usefulness is not beyond dispute.

In both theory and practice, bank examiners are meant to detect deviations of banks from the rules and standards set by law and regulation; they are presumed not to be capricious or unreasonable. The laws and regulations, however, often have areas of generality that allow for large margins of interpretive differences. Since many of these matters pass along in the enforcement process to the courts, a considerably body of judicial interpretation of these matters exists. In practice, however, it is probably true that smaller banks are less willing and able to challenge the authority of examiners than are big banks. Research studies of the bank examination process are few in number and thin in content since the basic materials needed for such studies are so fully concealed by rules of confidentiality.

Insurance of Deposits and Brokerage Accounts

Insurance of deposits or other liabilities of financial institutions has led, in practice, to accompanying forms of regulation. Institutions must "qualify" for insurance, and regulation is to ensure the continued qualification.

Such insurance has a long history; state insurance of bank deposits was tried early in the twentieth century. However, the first federal intervention in the field came in 1934 and was consolidated in its present form in 1935. The insurance of small bank deposits was soon followed by the insurance of savings accounts in savings and loan associations. Within the past few years it has been extended to the insurance of small brokerage accounts. The size limits for such insurance have been increased a number of times, and if inflation continues, will almost certainly be increased further.

This kind of insurance has the effect of not only protecting small depositors, but of increasing the safety of the insured institution. Since it is presumed that small and ill-informed depositors are more likely to "run" or withdraw deposits in a kind of panic, this protection gives institutions security against such irrational losses of funds. To make the protection significant, however, it would probably be necessary to extend coverage of insurance to deposits of all sizes. Large depositors may "run" a bank more silently and cleverly, but they can do so just as well as and maybe more quickly than small holders.

Because banking runs are not independent events but may be the products of contagions of fear, such insurance is not subject to actuarial evaluation. It thus cannot be offered by private insurance companies but must be handled by public agencies created for that purpose. Such public agencies may not have the explicit guarantee of the U.S. government, but they certainly have implied support.

COMPETITION: AIDED OR THWARTED BY REGULATION?

Although financial markets are subject to various forms of regulation, we depend mainly on competition to spur efficiency and equity. However, competition in the financial markets differs in a variety of ways from that in other sectors of the economy. Perhaps the most significant difference is that quality of financial service is very important; so important that price competition is often muted. In order to appreciate fully the nature of financial competition, the next part of this chapter will deal with qualitative elements in competition.

The nature of competition has been changing. Chapters 14 and 16 described the competition between negotiated underwriting, competitive bidding, and direct placement as an innovative response to regulation. Progress and innovation in the financial markets have shifted the focus of financial competition. Another example came to attention in Chapter 17, where it was shown that NASDAQ terminals have made the OTC market competitive with the organized exchanges—and might ultimately displace them by virtue of superior efficiency.

In finance, information has both cost and value. One of the major thrusts of financial regulation has been to require the publication of a greater amount of more dependable information.

Qualitative Nature of Competition in Financial Markets

Competition among financial businesses is a somewhat more complex economic phenomenon than competition among ordinary industrial or commercial enterprises. Public interest in the level of competition is more complex and characterized by more seeming contradiction than is true of public policy with respect to most other types of business. In the first place, a great many financial institutions cannot start business unless they secure a charter or license: "Free entry" is not present. The granting of charters is restricted to those applicants that have adequate capital and have arranged a location in a market area adequate to earn a fair income. When charters are granted in such a restrictive way, the quality of newly formed institutions is improved, but competitive pressures are less than they would be with free entry. The trouble is that the public interest is involved in the solvency as well as the competitiveness of financial institutions. We allow restaurants and grocery stores to fail freely, believing that free entry ensures competition. The burden of their failure falls mainly on the owners of such enterprises. But the losses that result from the insolvency of financial institutions, particularly those that handle the money of the relatively unsophisticated public, are thought to be socially if not economically intolerable.

Do Enduring Customer Relationships Minimize Competition?

One of the problems of determining the degree and character of competition in financial markets is that some of the customer-institution relationships in these markets tend to be of a long-standing nature. Just as people cling to a known and trusted doctor, so the relationship of businesses and individuals to commercial and investment banks tends to be personal and enduring. This tendency is common among financial institutions but particularly among commercial banks and investment banks. The financial aid and support together with advice and related aid make the relationship one that considerably transcends matters of price.

This does not mean that price is an unimportant element in such relationships. The financial institution that consistently charged prices that exceeded those prevailing elsewhere would lose business. The concept of the fair price seems to prevail and be accepted widely. Customers bargain with financial institutions about price under some circumstances; under others, they accept the prices quoted without haggling.

The unmeasurable quality, however, is that of service. A financial institution does more than lend money or act as an intermediary in its employment. Particularly in the lending of money, the certain availability of funds may be much more important to borrowers than price. The advisory role is often important. Furthermore, in the reciprocity of favors in the business community, the support of a strong banker who has widespread contacts may be far more important than can be demonstrated by quantitative means.

Competitive Tactics

Financial institutions use many of the devices employed by other businesses in the competitive struggle. Advertising was once frowned on in the financial community and institutions ran only chilly little "tombstone" ads that announced their continued existence. This feeling has changed greatly. The advertising of banks and other financial institutions has become informal, breezy, and often revealing. Many financial institutions have also established public relations departments and concern themselves about their corporate image.

Much of this, however, is applicable mainly to the retail or mass marketing sector of finance. The business of attracting funds from many small savers is a valid use of such mass media devices. Those institutions making small personal or business loans are also inclined to employ such devices. Commission brokerage houses that solicit small accounts and those selling investment company shares are mass merchandisers.

At the same time an important group of businesses—the really large accounts—probably are more successfully approached by other means. It is significant that the few banks that are mainly money wholesalers and a large part of the investment banking community still have not resorted very much to informal advertising.

The answer seems to be that in this sector of finance, close working relationships are achieved by rather different means. As was discussed in the preceding section, the customer relationship in many cases is close and enduring. Furthermore, the matter of the choice of a financial connection is probably made at the very top level of business management. Many purchasing and marketing decisions are made at intermediate levels of management. But the banking connection is changed (or made) only at the top, usually in full consultation with the board of directors.

Thus the quality of top personnel in financial institutions and their acceptability and personability in dealing with the top levels of business management are of the greatest importance. At one time the personnel of investment banking was drawn to a considerable extent from the great moneyed families; this ensured entry into many places denied those of more humble birth. Business management of all types has probably become more fluid in recent years. Most posts are now accessible to the ambitious person with ability and personal charm. But at the same time it cannot be denied that the person fully at home at the city or country club has some advantage over the person who has risen to the top by the Horatio Alger path of the paper route and the night class.

Competitive tactics include a variety of elements. In the first place, financial institutions are still much concerned with projecting an image of wisdom, sagacity, and integrity as well as one of dignity. But they encourage the belief that they are active and aggressive in business. They also try to convey this image to much wider audiences. Another change in practice that reflects the new emphasis on aggressiveness is the willingness to visit customers. At one time, most banks waited for business to come in the front door; they did not go out and solicit it. This was particularly true of investment bankers. They did not hesitate to use intermediaries or "finders" to encourage business to come to them, but they felt it beneath their dignity to go out soliciting business. This has changed; the old inhibitions are virtually dead. Both commercial and investment banks have new-business development persons constantly traveling and visiting potential customers.

Still another change is in the matter of business size. Leading bankers once rather discouraged the business of small concerns; they had an attitude of polite snobbery about size. Some of this feeling persists, but too many bankers have found that the small firm becomes big and the big may become old and financially feeble. The small business with growth potential is often surprised at the welcome it gets from the giants of the financial community.

Competition within Homogeneous Types of Financial Institutions

The usual concept of competition has to do with business concerns that offer similar or identical goods or services to the markets. Among similar financial institutions such competition is the normal order of business. Examples would be competition of commercial banks with other commerical banks, of savings and loan associations with other savings and loan associations, or of investment banking houses with other investment banking houses. Different types of financial institutions, of course, offer similar services, so that the range of competition is somewhat broader than it would be if it were merely within homogeneous types of financial institutions. This broader concept will be considered in a later section of this chapter.

Competition between similar institutions is partly a matter of the quality of the services they offer, but differences in quality may be hard to demonstrate, particularly for rather simple financial services such as those of handling savings accounts. The widespread presence of deposit insurance, for example, has tended to make all savings accounts under the insured limit of $40,000 similar to other savings accounts. The principal variable in such relationships subject to competitive differentiation is price.

Price competition in lending rates is less openly displayed by financial institutions, but such competition undoubtedly exists. Among big commercial banks, the prime loan rate (discussed in Chapter 11) applies to a large part of the lending. Usually, the prime loan rate is adhered to. It can be considered a form of price leadership that is generally viewed by economists as involving some restraint on true competition. The significant question, however, is whether other dimensions of credit arrangement are used to express competitive activity. At least one such outlet probably exists. Most customer loans are accompanied by a general understanding that the borrower will also maintain a "satisfactory" depository relationship. The size and character of a satisfactory deposit balance is sometimes left to informal and even vague understandings. Quite often, however, it is formalized in a specific compensating balance agreement. These arrangements are not uniform, and the sizes of these balances can be and are bargained.

Among commercial banks outside the money market center, loan rates are less uniform. While a given area is usually fairly homogeneous with respect to rates, variations exist and these differences are used competitively. Variations exist even within a given institution, so that good and desirable customers may be given fairly good rates and less desirable customers are charged higher rates. The competition is for good customers, not for a particular bit of business, and good customers are rewarded with more favorable treatment than they can probably expect if they should switch their banking connections.

Competition among life insurance companies as lenders does not appear to take the form of rates as much as of credit selectivity. For administrative reasons a life insurance company may post a uniform rate for mortgage lending. The rate has to be in line with general market conditions, but variations from this rate tend to be infrequent. The significant differences, then, are in the character and quality of credit tolerated within this announced rate. Mortgage bankers, in negotiating sales of mortgages to life insurance companies, know the standards and rules of the various companies and try to tailor the mortgages offered to the requirements of the companies that have funds.

When life insurance companies lend to business in the form of direct placements, rates are not uniform. On all large contracts, the rates are individually negotiated and are influenced mostly be prevailing yields in the corporate bond market. On the smaller placements, rates are likely to be somewhat more uniform and to be changed less frequently. Even in such cases, however, these rates are usually subject to some margin of negotiation. In the end, these rates have to be "competitive."

Investment bankers compete almost solely on the basis of service and not price except in competitive bidding financing. The borrower has a large interest in financing in an acceptable way and of getting good timing in such financing. The fees or margins taken by investment bankers are small in comparison with the savings in cost that can be effected by expert management or the increases in cost due to clumsy handling. Even so, the margins taken by investment bankers have been greatly influenced by examples of narrow margins displayed publicly in competitive bidding. The margins now prevailing are far less than those that used to be charged, and the example of public bidding doubtlessly helped borrowers who have used negotiated financing.

Market Areas

One of the problems of judging the degree and range of competition is the size of the normal market area. The normal market area for a grocery store is bounded by the distance that buyers will drive (or walk) to buy their groceries. The physical representation of market areas might be thought of as a map with a dot shown for each customer's location with respect to the store or financial institution he or she patronizes.

Market areas vary widely in types of business. The market area of investment bankers tends to be nationwide and even worldwide. Large borrowers are not deterred by distance in going to the investment banker who promises the best service. Most of them are located in the central capital markets anyway, so location is not a critical factor in choice of an investment banker. A saver, in choosing the institution at which to keep his or her account, however, may be considerably influenced by convenience and location. A few institutions have successfully attracted funds from great distances by advertising, but these examples are exceptions.

Market area is also influenced by the modes of transporation. In Manhattan, where few residents use automobiles for city travel, the market areas of savings institutions tend to be bounded by modes of travel; an important subway stop may be a locational factor. The distances between savings institutions can be smaller without an overlap of market areas. On the other hand, in thinly populated areas where automobile travel for longer distances is quite common, the market area of a savings institution may be rather large. The number of persons and the wealth in such a large physical area may not be very great, but the distance spread will be considerable.

It seems likely, although no facts are available to support the view, that the sizes of market areas have changed greatly and may be subject to even more change in the future. For example, the greater use of "bank-by-mail" service has been promoted as a modest convenience to customers. With time, however, it could produce very large changes. If one can bank by mail with an institution inconveniently located for a visit by car, why cannot one bank by mail with an institution clear across the country? It is true that one cannot cash a check by mail, but chain stores have developed simple systems of check cashing for established customers; therefore why should a customer visit his or her bank at all? One of the reasons that financial institutions might smile on such developments is that, as personal service institutions, they find personnel costs one of their greatest drains on earnings. Any sort of mechanization that will reduce personnel costs would be a great boon to financial institutions.

The concept of market area has been most important in the decisions of the supervisory authorities for the establishment and merger of financial institutions. The crowding together of too many institutions within a natural market area is considered unwise for reasons of solvency protection. The reduction of the number of competing institutions within a market area by merger, however, may reach proportions that are thought to be contrary to the public interest. Unfortunately very little is known about the size of areas served by various financial institutions. The circumstances described above are based on casual observation and intuition rather than on formal and dependable information.

Competition among Various Types of Financial Institutions

The day-to-day competition of financial institutions tends to go beyond the homogeneous types. There is intense competition, particularly among savings institutions, in seeking funds. Each type of financial institution tends to evolve as it tries to improve its market position, and this effort generally leads to competition with other types of financial institutions. In the beginning, a bold or innovating institution may devise a way in which it can increase its business by seeking out a type of business not done before or done by some other type of financial institution. If the early innovators are successful, others soon copy them.

Counterinvasions of each other's traditional type of business can also occur. At one time, investment bankers maintained a depository relationship with some customers and so ran what were really private commercial banks. This was forbidden by the Banking Act of 1933, but before this prohibition commercial banks had invaded investment banking territory by going into the securities merchandising business, directly or through affiliates. This counter-competition was likewise outlawed by the same act, but these excursions into each other's type of business still exist in the competition between commercial banks and investment bankers for marketing state and local government obligations.

A more current illustration of interindustry competition is that between self-administered or trusteed pension funds and life insurance pension plans. Life insurance companies have developed pension plans that furnish all technical and financial services and also guarantee the payment of pensions according to the contractual terms. However, some companies believe themselves able to better the terms offered and so have organized do-it-yourself pension plans. Owing to the willingness to engage in somewhat more aggressive investment policies than the life insurance companies like (or can legally undertake), they have generally succeeded in bettering the terms (or at least they did as long as equity prices were rising briskly).

This competition led to some very interesting financial innovations. The increases in the price level and talk of secular inflation had led many savers and investors to seek protection against loss of purchasing power. One such form of protection (devised first for college teachers) was a pension annuity invested in common stocks and payable not in fixed dollar terms but in units that varied in price with the prices of equities. This was initiated just before the great boom in the stock market. The success of this variable annuity plan (CREF) led to efforts to copy it on a commercial scale. This effort was resisted by various segments of the financial community: the investment companies, because they foresaw a threat from this new invention, and the more conservative insurance companies. Of the two largest life insurance companies, one opposed the idea while the other favored it. Initiation of the new ventures was delayed by legal actions, but they were ultimately allowed to get started, mainly after the larger part of the stock market boom had taken place. This story illustrates the way in which competition sometimes arises—and also the way in which it is often resisted.

A Tentative Conclusion

While regulation may have reduced competitive activity within financial markets, the degree of reduction is not large. Financial institutions have been innovative and aggressive too. Customers have enjoyed good service at fair prices. In fact, financial institutions have sometimes been able to surmount the barriers created by regulation in order to improve customer service. The record shows more positive than negative results.

MULTIBANK HOLDING COMPANIES

Branch banking is prohibited in some states. At one time the number of states prohibiting branching was even greater than now, but the barriers have been dropping. Where branching was prohibited, the bank holding company was developed, mainly during the 1920s, as a substitute. The first legislation for control of bank holding companies came in the 1930s, and the administration of this regulation was placed in the Federal Reserve System. This legislation was revised considerably in 1956 and 1969.

Although financial soundness was the excuse for some of the regulation, its primary impact was felt on competition. Did the multibank holding company increase or decrease competition? Either case could be made. If a community was served by only two banks, one of which was smaller and weaker, the acquisition of the weaker bank by an outside holding company could increase competition. On the other hand, the acquisition of the dominant bank in a community could effectively reduce competition. In time federal interest in this matter was extended so that not only the Federal Reserve and other federal banking regulators but also the Justice Department became involved. What is more, this multiple-headed administration of bank holding company regulation disclosed clearly how much the judgments of regulators could differ: The federal agencies were often at odds with one another in their judgment of the effects of bank acquisitions on competitive situations. When judges differ, there obviously cannot be a single and certain truth.

Multibank holding companies originally crossed state lines, but such systems are now no more than statewide systems.

ONE-BANK HOLDING COMPANIES

In areas where branch restrictions inhibited multiple bank office operations, bank holding companies and banking chains were a device for avoiding these restrictions. However, bank holding companies were involved in some bank failures in the early 1930s (most notably in Detroit). As a result, bank holding companies were put under regulation at the federal level. However, a holding company, usually mainly in some other type of business, which owned only one bank was exempted from such regulation. In the 1960s a majority of the big money market commerical banks, and a great many others as well, took advantage of this exception and formed holding companies that, in the beginning, owned almost nothing but the bank itself. Shareholders exchanged their bank stock for stock in the holding company. This move could be considered a competitive action to escape regulatory restraint.

The purpose of these one-bank holding companies was to engage in a wider variety of business than permitted by their basic bank charters. As they expanded, one-bank holding companies bought mortgage banking firms, leasing firms, and other types of financial services. As would be expected, this loophole in the law was closed, and they were put under regulation. However, even under regulation, they have more and broader powers than they had as unit banks.

MUTUAL FUNDS AND PENSION FUNDS

These two classes of financial institutions offer an interesting contrast. Mutual funds are a closely regulated type of financial institution. Pension funds, until recently, were virtually free of regulation. It appears, however, that both have been about equally effective in serving the needs of their respective customers. Research on the performance of mutual funds is far more extensive than that on pension funds. From such evidence as exists, however, they appear to have achieved about the same level of investment performance. Neither one has been able to do much better than the market as a whole, but the two have run about an even race.

Although regulation sets the standards by which mutual funds must operate, they face intense competition in the sale of their shares to the public. Most private pension funds are managed by investment advisers, of which the trust departments of commercial banks are leading competitors. Thus there is also a great deal of competition for this business. In fact, some corporations divide their pension funds among several banks and then reward the banks with the best investment performance with more business, and penalize those who trail by less business or none at all.

LESS REGULATION AND MORE COMPETITION FOR SAVINGS INTERMEDIARIES

The Hunt Commission (HC) report recommended that savings intermediaries be given a much broader opportunity both in attracting funds and in investing them. At the same time the HC recommended changes that would have more nearly equalized the competitive scales—such changes as in tax laws and reserve requirements.

At one time, most savings intermediaries really offered only one type of investment vehicle to savers: a savings account usually evidenced by a passbook. Commercial banks varied this offering slightly by also offering nonnegotiable certificates of deposit maturing at fixed dates. Recently both types of institutions have innovated by expanding the types of deposit accounts considerably. Some are aimed at small savers; others at substantial investors. Savings intermediaries are being allowed to invade the area formerly available only to commercial banks and to offer the equivalent of checking accounts—"third-party payment services"—to their customers. Savings intermediaries are becoming full-service financial institutions for individuals, just as commercial banks are full-service institutions for corporations as well as individuals.

INFORMATION AS A GUIDE TO COMPETITION

One of the assumptions of perfect competition is the complete and instantaneous availability of pertinent market information to all participants. Obviously, this assumption can never be more than partly true. However, the amount of information in financial markets has been greatly expanded and the quality improved. To the extent that regulation has caused the greater and better information, it can be said that regulation here was tending to make competition more nearly perfect.

Examples of greater information are legion. For a long time the NYSE has required listed corporations to make public their financial statements. They also require the statements to be audited periodically. The quality of this information has been improved, partly by the action of the SEC but also by self-imposed standards of the accounting profession. The regulation of new security issues has required the release of detailed financial information (called "10-K" reports) to the public via the SEC. "Insiders" (managers, directors) are required to report buy or sell transactions in the stock of their companies.

Banks very seldom published any earnings figures. After World War II a few banks started publishing such figures, but the number was not large. However, in 1964 larger banks and other companies with OTC-traded stocks were required to publish financial information much like listed companies. Banks now publish reports with full disclosure of earnings. The quality of these earnings has also been more fully disclosed as a result of an opinion of the accounting principles board.

Information, however, is not without cost. As was related in Chapter 16, many corporations have chosen to seek new money via direct placements, with its slightly higher costs, rather than prepare the required 10-K (and bear other expenses involved in a public offering). Legal and accounting costs involved in complying with the public information requirements are material.

More important, questions have been raised as to the extent to which this great information explosion has been of real benefit to investors. Research on this subject is not uniform in its finding, but it cannot be assumed any longer that more information necessarily increases net social benefits.

NO EVALUATION BUT A MODEST PROPOSAL

The body of this chapter has been an abbreviated recital of the range of regulatory structures that affect financial institutions and financial markets. It was intended to make clear the great diversity in the form and philosophy of such regulation. With such diversity, it would be almost impossible to attempt an abbreviated evaluation of regulation. Only a very few would favor junking the entire regulatory system. On the other hand, almost everyone would agree that it contains a great deal of inconsistent and outdated requirements. The usual proposal is that the regulatory system should be "reviewed." Indeed, the Hunt Commission and agencies before that commission have already made such reviews. Reports have been written, but virtually no action has been taken to implement them. A wholesale review by Congress is an impractical suggestion; it would never be done.

A more modest but possibly practical suggestion would be that every *new* regulatory law or agency should be adopted with a built-in terminal date. All regulatory legislation and the resulting administrative structures should be presumed to be temporary. In this way, they would pass out of existence unless they had demonstrated need and value during their lives. Existing regulatory laws and agencies could also be given a schedule of termination dates. The mere act of scheduling would be a difficult, negotiated process, but it would impose on the legislative system of the nation the obligation for piecemeal and scheduled review rather than a kind of aggregated or lump-sum review. This proposal can be considered a kind of zero-based regulatory budget.

A CHECK LIST FOR STUDENT EVALUATION OF FINANCIAL MARKETS

Even though the authors of this text have felt it inappropriate that they should evaluate the regulatory influence of government, the student may wish to make his or her own evaluation. Such an evaluation should start with some kind of standard for testing. We suggest these standards: efficiency, equity, and safety. The influence of government should be to promote efficiency rather than to thwart it. Certainly governmental regulation fails if it does not make the financial system and the markets that serve it more fair and equitable. Safety, however, is not necessarily a prime factor. We want to be safe, but the effort to legislate safety can be carried too far. If an exaggerated emphasis on safety reduces innovation and the kind of risk taking that is needed in a dynamic society, then it is a net detriment. Governmental roles in furthering safety require a balance between avoiding excessive risk, while still allowing latitude for constructive, innovative, imaginative, and private managerial policies.

Efficient and equitable financial markets are vital. Nations that do not have such markets tend to be retarded in their economic development. While our proposition is so axiomatic as to be beyond dispute, it suffers from two ambiguities: First, how are efficiency and equity measured? Second, what type of public policy is most effective in attaining efficiency and equity?

The concept of efficiency is usually broken into two types: operational and allocational. Operational efficiency is measured by the costs involved in the financial process relative to results. If the going rate on mortgages is 7 percent, the rate that a financial intermediary could return to savers after covering its costs would be a measure of operational efficiency. If one institution could return 5 percent and still make a satisfactory profit but another only 4 percent, the first is obviously more efficient. Transaction costs in the stock market or in the foreign exchange market can also be considered tests of operational efficiency. A low-friction financial machine is an efficient one.

"Allocational efficiency" means effectiveness in channeling the flow of saving into productive uses. A capital market that invested funds in low-return companies and industries or uses of capital that had little social utility would be allocationally inefficient. One that channeled funds into highly productive uses would be efficient. But how is this to be measured?

The concept of equity seems to be simple and easily grasped on an intuitive level, but in fact it turns out to be highly elusive. The ethical norms of society give us a starting point, but this can lead to conflicting judgments. For example, the principle of egalitarian wealth and income distribution has gained a great deal of support. This principle could be interpreted to mean that all persons should have equal access to financial markets. But if this were the case, the financial markets might not concentrate resources in the hands of those who could make the most efficient use of them. The goals of efficiency and equity might, under an egalitarian system of ethical behavior, come into serious conflict.

Safety differs from the concept of stability developed in Chapter 21 in that it focuses on the losses that usually result from credit defaults. These defaults tend to shake confidence and impede the investment process. Some economic risk is unavoidable. It would be unwise to try excessively to avoid risk. But if episodes of random credit losses occur too often, the whole process of financial investment tends to be inhibited.

It is true, of course, that the more dramatic episodes of unsafe financial investment have been concentrated in periods of downside instability. Furthermore, unsafe financial investment has an aspect of equity, since those damaged by such events have tended to be the less well-informed investors and often those with smaller means. As a result, the insurance devices that have been devised to make the financial system safer have tended to concentrate their protection on smaller investors.

As old problems are solved, new ones emerge. For many years the problem of safety in financial markets was viewed mainly as a matter of contract performance. A "safe" credit instrument was one that would be paid as promised in the contract by the debtor. A "safe" broker and dealer in a financial market was one who performed his or her function according to the terms of the implied or explicit contracts that govern such relationships. Safety was something that could be comprehended within our existing legal and judicial system.

New risks—new at least to the United States—have become more important. The gravest of emerging hazards has been the threat of unending secular inflation. Changes in the value of money tilt greatly the safety of financial contracts that are expressed in terms of money. This risk is one for which our financial markets are not well prepared. Other countries with longer and more severe experience with inflation have invented practical and sometimes legal systems for dealing with the problem. Some countries, particularly those in South America, have adopted systems for the revaluation of financial contracts when the value of money changes drastically. So far, that has not been done in this country. However, financial markets have been greatly influenced by the individual efforts of investors to protect themselves against this form of risk.

Inflation, of course, is an enemy of efficiency, equity, and safety. Inflation creates false incentives and reduces the efficiency with which resources are used. It is certainly inequitable. Finally, it is one of the greatest risks this nation faces, internally or externally.

PROJECTS AND QUESTIONS

1. Old governmental regulatory activities "never die," and they seldom fade away even after their prime usefulness has past. But this seldom discourages the adoption of new regulatory policies. Have any regulatory activities affecting financial markets been discontinued since this text was published? Have any new financial market regulatory programs been instituted?
2. Test the new programs by the standards suggested in this chapter. Try to adopt a "public policy" attitude and not that of any special interest group.
3. Do you find evidences of competition among financial institutions in the area where you live or in an area about which you have some knowledge? Do you think this competition is an adequate protector of the "public interest?"
4. Select one financial institution about which you have some knowledge. Could you marshall any evidence about the efficiency of this institution (in both senses of the word)? Do you think its operations are equitable?

BIBLIOGRAPHY

Bell, F. W., and N. B. Murphy: "Costs in Commercial Banking: A Quantitative Analysis of Bank Behavior and its Relation to Bank Regulation," *Research Report No. 41,* Federal Reserve Bank of Boston, 1968.

Benston, G. J.: "Bank Examination," *The Bulletin,* New York University Institute of Finance, Nos. 89–90, May 1973.

———, and C. J. Smith: "A Transactions Cost Approach to the Theory of Financial Intermediation," *Journal of Finance,* May 1976.

Concludes that government regulation increases transaction costs and thereby reduces benefits of financial intermediation.

———: "Rate Ceiling Implication of the Cost Structure of Consumer Finance Companies," *Journal of Finance,* September 1977, pp. 1169–1194.

Compendium of Major Issues in Bank Regulation: Government Printing Office, Washington, D.C., May 1975.

Franklin National Bank failure was stimulant for this review.

Crosse, H. O.: "Bank Supervisor—Quality and Quantity," *Bankers Magazine,* Autumn 1975.

Fand, D.: "Financial Regulation and the Allocative Efficiency of Our Capital Markets," *National Banking Review,* September 1965.

Hunt Commission: *Report of the President's Commission on Financial Structure and Regulation,* Government Printing Office, Washington, D.C., 1971.

Miller, R. B.: "F.D.I.C.: Savior or Sinner?", *Bankers Magazine,* Winter 1976.

Mingo, J. J.: "Regulatory Influence on Bank Capital Investment," *Journal of Finance,* September 1975.

Murphy, N. B.: "Removing Deposit Interest Ceilings: An Analysis of Deposit Flows, Portfolio Response and Income Effects in Boston Cooperative Banks," *Journal of Bank Research,* Winter 1977.

Concludes more competitive without regulation.

Pettway, R. H.: "Market Tests of Capital Adequacy of Large Commercial Banks," *Journal of Finance,* June 1976.

Robinson, R. I.: "The Hunt Commission Report: A Search for Politically Feasible Solutions," *Journal of Finance,* September 1972.

Treynor, J. L.: "The Principles of Corporate Pension Finance," *Journal of Finance,* May 1977, pp. 627–638.

Glossarial Index

Glossarial Index

A Glossary of definitions and a Glossary of acronyms have been incorporated into this index. Glossary terms appear in **boldface** and are followed by their definitions and any page references, subentries, and/or cross-references.

Absolute advantage (*see* Foreign trade)
Accelerator principle, 24
Accumulation of wealth, 4
Actuarial liabilities, life insurance, 78
ADRs American depository receipts, 442
Agency securities Obligations of credit agencies sponsored by the Federal government such as FHLB, FHLMC, GNMA, FCA, and FICB. Most of these securities are not directly guaranteed by the federal government but the implied support of the sponsorship causes them to sell at yields only moderately above those of Treasury obligations of the same maturity. 290, 291
Alberts, W. W., 30
Allocation of wealth, 10
Allocational efficiency, 487
Altman, E. I., 155n.
AMEX American Stock Exchange, 369, 374–376
Ang, J. S., 151n.
Arbitrage of foreign exchange rates and interest rates, 438
Atkinson, T. R., 152
ATS Automated transfer service (between savings and demand deposit accounts), 89

Auctions of Treasury securities, 285
Automation:
  of stock market, 398
  of U.S. Treasury securities, 292
Availability of mortgage credit, 29

Balance of payments The social accounting system embracing all of the financial transactions of a nation with the rest of the world for a designated period of time. 431–433
public policy, 446
Bankers' acceptance A credit instrument initiated by a creditor with payment guaranteed by the debtor's bank (i.e., it is "accepted"). Most bankers' acceptances originate in foreign trade but a few are solely for the purpose of borrowing money in this market. Bankers buy their own acceptances sometimes. 209–211
Bankruptcy propensity, 154
Basis points A basis point is 1/100 of a percent. An interest rate of 6.85 percent is ten basis points above a rate of 6.75 percent.

493

Beta coefficient A measure of the volatility of the rate of return on a security or portfolio of securities relative to the rate of return on the market portfolio. If the beta coefficient is less than one, the security or portfolio of securities is less risky than the market; if beta is greater than one, the security or portfolio is more risky than the market. The beta coefficient of the market portfolio itself is equal to one. 139

Birch, E. M., 24

Block trading, 377

Blue sky laws, 354

Boczar, G. E., 86*n.*

Bond market:

   cyclical pattern, 462 – 464

   ratings, 151

Boskin, M. J., 35*n.*

Brealey, R., 165*n.*

Bretton Woods system, 423 – 426

   permission for devaluation, 447

Broker One who acts as an intermediary between buyers and sellers but does not himself take a position in the securities for which he acts as broker. (Customers' representatives of commission brokerage firms are not, strictly speaking, themselves brokers, but are sales representatives who transmit orders to the professional brokers or traders within the firm who perform the brokerage function.)

Burns, Arthur, 245

Cagan, Philip, 408

Call feature An option which permits the issuer of corporate bonds to buy back the bonds at a specified call price before the bonds mature.

   risk, 155 – 157

Calls (stock option), 382

Capital Cumulated employment of funds in the form of assets, both real and financial. Economists usually use it to mean only real assets, such as housing, plant and equipment, inventories, and the present value of the flow of human services. Accountants use it to mean the sources of funds cumulating in the form of liabilities (debt capital) and net worth (equity capital). Still other meanings of this much overused word may be found.

Capital budgets for government, 278

Capital flows (international), 436

Capital market line (*CML*) Equilibrium relationship between the expected rate of return and the standard deviation of return for efficient portfolios of risky and riskless securities. In graphical terms the CML shows that expected rate of return on an efficient portfolio of risky and riskless securities as a positive and straightline function of risk, as measured by the standard deviation of return. The slope of the line is the extra expected return per unit of risk; the intercept is the risk-free rate of return. 137

Capital markets Financial markets where securities with maturities of more than one year are bought and sold. The principal capital markets are the corporate stock and bond markets, the mortgage market, and the markets for municipal and Treasury securities.

   versus money markets, 9

CAPM Capital Asset Pricing Model, 406, 411

Cash management, 180

   corporations, 205 – 207

   U.S. Treasury, 280

Cash surrender values, life insurance, 78

Central money market City with a major concentration of large commercial banks which engage in wholesale banking. 174–175

Closed-end mutual funds, 86, 373

CML Capital market line, 137

Coincidence of wants, 3

Commercial banks, 71–74

Commercial paper Negotiable note sold by corporations in the open money market. They may be "directly" sold by the issuer or "dealer-placed." Maturity ranges from 3 to 270 days, but most transactions are from 90 to 180 days. 207–209

Commission brokerage firms Partnerships or corporations organized to handle brokerage business for customers. They usually not only execute sales and purchases but also arrange credit for margin transactions and hold securities in custody. Commission brokerage business may be combined with investment banking, money management, commodity as well as securities brokerage, and other financial functions. 378–380

Commitments, mortgage, 332

Comparative advantage (*see* Foreign trade)

Compensatory balance Part of a loan agreement, of varying degrees of explicitness, by which a borrowing customer agrees to maintain some minimum balance. The amount is usually computed as a proportion of the maximum loan outstanding.

Competitive bidding:
  for state and local government securities, 309
  for U.S. Treasury securities, 196–197

Competition aided by regulation?, 477–483

Competitive commissions, 378

Consumer durables, 31–32

Convergence (of deposit-type intermediaries), 87–89

Cornell, B., 165n.

Corporation as supplier of financial instruments, 264

Correlation of expected returns, effect on risk, 129–132

Cost of capital, 26

Coupon bond, yield, 58–60

Coupon rate Ratio of annual interest, in dollars, to the par value of the bond. Since the number of dollars of interest promised and the par value of the bond are fixed at the time of sale, the coupon rate is fixed for the life of the bond. When a bond is first sold by its issuer, its coupon rate is usually close to then prevailing current market yields.

Coverage ratio, 150

Credit, 267
  stock market, 390

Credit line Loan limit given by a commercial bank to regular customers. The amount is reviewed annually or oftener and is considered an informal but not legal obligation by the bank for the accommodation of its customers.

Credit rating, state and local government securities, 302–304

Credit risk Possibility that the borrower will not pay as promised. 262

Credit unions, 77–78

Culbertson, John M., 163n.

Cyclical movements of money, interest rates, and general economic activity, 457–460

Dealer A man, woman, or firm which makes both bids and offers for a designated security or securities. Dealers usually accumulate a "position" or inventory in such security or securities which may be "long" or "short." A dealer risks his own money in contrast with a broker who acts only as an

intermediary in trying to match
buyers and sellers, taking a
commission "in the middle."
money market instruments, 200
U.S. Treasury securities, 293–297
Deaton, A., 35
Debenture, 352
Debt management, U.S. Treasury,
281–284
Default risk, 149–155
Deficit sectors, 42
Desired stock of capital, 24
Determinants:
of investment, 22–32
of saving, 32–36
Direct external finance, 7
Direct investment   Investment by
U.S. corporations in plant and
equipment and other business
properties in foreign countries.
443
Direct placement   Negotiation of a
credit between a corporate
borrower and an institutional
investor. An alternative to an open
market sale. 354–355
yields, 364
"Dirty" float, 425
Discount function of Federal Reserve,
232
rates, 239
Disequilibrium of mortgage market, 29
Disintermediation, 30, 461, 467
Diversification, 12
effect on risk and expected return,
129–132
of investments, 84
for risk reduction, 66
Dow, Alex, 403
Durand, David, 405

Eccles, Marriner, 241
Ederington, L. H., 156
Efficiency:
allocational, 487
operational, 487
of stock market, 385–386, 409
Efficient market   Market in which the
prices reflect fully and

immediately all available and
pertinent information. It would be
impossible to "beat" an efficient
market, if such existed, since no
one would know anything that is
not already known and therefore
reflected in market prices.
136–138
Efficient portfolio   Portfolio that
offers maximum expected return
for given risk or minimum risk for
given expected return. An
efficient portfolio is fully
diversified to eliminate
unsystematic risk. 133–136
EFTS   Electronic funds transfer
systems, 89
Eisner, Robert, 26
Empirical tests:
of *SML*, 142–144
of theory, 93
Employment, role of money in, 15
Employment Act of 1946, 454
Equilibrium:
funds market, 45
general, 41
partial, 41
Equilibrium analysis by use of flow of
funds, 112–114
**Equity "kickers" or participa-
tion**   Contractual arrangements
by which an institutional
lender exacts, as the price of
making a loan, some added
return of an equity nature. The
amount of this return is
dependent on the income earned
by the project or company for
which the loan is made. It may be
a percentage of sales or rentals or a
warrant to purchase shares of
common stock. 333
ERISA   Employment Retirement
Income Security Act, 475
Eurobond   Bonds denominated in a
currency other than that of the
country in which it is marketed.
The currency denomination may
be, but does not necessarily have
to be, that of the issuer. U.S.

corporations have sold bonds denominated in dollars in Europe. Swedish cities have sold bonds denominated in D-marks in Switzerland. 440

Eurocurrency Deposit account denominated in a currency other than that of the host country. A dollar, Deutschemark, or Swiss franc deposit in a London-based bank would be a Eurocurrency. 439

Eurodollar A Eurocurrency denominated in U.S. dollars. 227–229

Exchange rate determination, 426–427, 429, 431–433

Exchanges Act of 1934, 472, 473

Exchanges between currencies (*see* Foreign exchange)

Expectation theory of term structure of interest rates, 162–164

Expected rate of inflation, 51

Expected rate of return Weighted average of all possible rates of return on a security or portfolio of securities, the weights being probabilities. 12, 126–134

linear relationship to risk, 136–138

External cost of capital, 26

finance, 7

direct and indirect, 63

Fair, R. C., 30

Fama, E. F., 55*n.*, 165*n.*

FDIC Federal Deposit Insurance Corporation, 70, 472

"Fed" Informal abbreviation of Federal Reserve; sometimes applied to the whole system, sometimes to the Board of Governors of the Federal Reserve System, sometimes to an individual Federal Reserve bank such as the Federal Reserve Bank of New York.

Fed funds A collected or available reserve balance at a Federal Reserve bank which is loaned ("sold") by a bank with excess reserves to a borrowing ("purchasing") bank which is in need of reserves. Most transactions are between member banks but a few other financial institutions, mainly dealers in Treasury securities, buy and sell Fed funds. 222, 231–233, 244, 252–253

Federal agency securities, market for, 198

Federal Reserve, 70–71, 178, 237–254

criticism of reserve management, 254–256

eclectic monetary policy, 459

Ferber, R., 35*n.*

FHA Federal Housing Administration. May disappear by merger into HUD by the time this index is in print. Also used to indicate the Farmers Home Administration. 337, 340

FHLB Federal Home Loan Board. Sometimes used to apply to the whole system of Board and banks. 339

FHLBS Federal Home Loan Bank System, 340

FHLMC Federal Home Loan Mortgage Corporation. Under the supervision of the FHLB and for creation of a secondary market in conventional mortgages. 339

FICB Federal Intermediate Credit Bank. Federal agency for financing the Production Credit Associations.

Finance companies, 86, 365

Financial assets A claim in money terms on some other economic unit which thus is a liability of the other unit. Since every financial asset is matched by a liability, financial assets net out to zero when all balance sheets are consolidated, leaving only real assets as the basis for wealth. Financial assets are the outgrowth of the separation of the acts of saving and real investment. Savers who do not wish to acquire real assets have the alternative of acquiring financial assets issued by investors who wish to acquire real assets without having to save. Financial assets are traded in financial markets.

Financial Institution Act of 1976, 88

Financial institutions Composite of intermediating and marketing institutions operating in the financial markets. Financial intermediaries borrow from savers and lend to ultimate investors at terms which are attractive to all parties. Financial marketing institutions offer facilities by which buyers and sellers of securities can effect purchases and sales.

Financial intermediaries Institutions which transfer funds from ultimate lenders (savers) to ultimate borrowers (investors in real assets). They include commercial banks, mutual savings banks, savings and loan associations, credit unions, insurance companies, pension funds, finance companies, and investment companies. The process of intermediation is carried out by borrowing from ultimate lenders and lending to ultimate borrowers at terms attractive to all parties.

Financial investment Acquisition of financial assets over a period of time. Making loans and purchasing securities are acts of financial investment. These acts take place in financial markets.

Financial markets The institutional facilities that link saving and real investment. Individuals who want to save but not invest (in a real sense) can do so only if there are financial markets in which to lend. Anyone who wants to invest, but lacks the savings, can do so only if there is a source of external financing via the financial markets. The instruments traded in financial markets are called financial assets, including loans and securities of all types.

international dimensions of, 416

Fisher, Irving, 20, 53

Fisher, Lawrence, 151, 402

Fixed business investment, 23−27

Fixed exchange rates, 421−425

Flexible mortgages, 343

Floating exchange rates, 425

Flow of funds, 93−114

accounts for 1978, 100−103

asset liability matrix, 104−108

forecasting interest rates, 115−120

interregional, 188

sectors, 96

transactions, 95

use: in equilibrium analysis, 112−114

and sources matrix, 98, 267

FNMA Federal National Mortgage Association. Also often known as "Fanny Mae." Now a private corporation listed on the NYSE and making a secondary market in mortgages of all types. 338

FOMC Federal Open Market Committee. Part of the "Fed." 184−185, 237

Forecasting interest rates, 115−120

Foreign aid, 448

Foreign exchange:

as barrier, 421

as link between monetary systems, 415

Foreign issuer bonds, 365

Foreign monetary authorities as buyers of Treasury securities, 287

Foreign trade:

absolute and comparative advantage of, 418

barriers to, 419

Forward exchange A contract to sell or buy a specified foreign currency at a rate fixed at time of transaction but with delivery at the specified future time. 436–439

Frankena, M. W., 156–158

Friedman, Milton, 404

Friend, Irwin, 405

Futures market in U.S. Treasury securities, 292

Gearing assets to liabilities, 70, 80

General equilibrium, 48

Gibson, W. E., 55n.

GMC Guaranteed mortgage certificate, 339

GNMA Government National Mortgage Association. A Federal government agency to improve the marketability of conventional mortgages; usually by packaging such mortgages into more attractive market securities, some of which "pass through" all cash receipts. 338

Gold exchange standard, 422

Gold standard, 421

Goldsmith, Raymond, 33

Gordon, Myron, 405, 410

Graduated mortgages, 343

Gramlich, E. M., 30

Great Depression, 453, 455, 466

Ground rent, 325

Growth prospects, 409

Growth rates, financial instruments, 268, 273

Guttentag, Jack, 30

Hamburger, M. J., 32

Harberger, A. C., 32

Heller Report, 88

Hess, A. C., 32

Hickman, W. B., 151

Holding period Period of time an investor plans to hold securities. If holding period is longer than the maturity period of the securities, the investor must reinvest. If shorter, he must liquidate before maturity.

"Hot money," 445

Housing bonds, 314

Housing cycles, 461

Hunt Commission, 88, 485

IDA International Development Corporation, 448

Identities, financial, 5–7

IMF International Monetary Fund, 423–426, 445

Income, role of money, 15

Income real estate, 323–325

Incremental time value of money, 22
rate of return, 22

"Indirect" credit instruments, 8

Indirect external finance, 7, 63–64

Inflation:
damage to financial markets, 488
expectation of, 468
expected rate of, 51–52
hedge, 408
common stocks, 81–82, 408
term structure of interest rates, 165–167

"Insider" buying and selling, 389–391, 485

Insurance, private: brokerage accounts, 379
mortgages, 341
state and local government securities, 304

Intended consumption and saving, 36

Interest, mathematics of, 56–60
price for borrowing and lending, 4, 42

Interest rates:
cyclical pattern, 457–460
econometric studies, 55
effect on saving, 35
nominal versus real, 52
structure, 147

Intermediaries, financial, 7

Intermediation:
cyclical pattern, 460
financial, 63–69
marginal cost and revenue analysis, 64–65

Internal finance, 7, 63

Internal Rate of Return (IRR) The rate of discount which makes the present value of the stream of future dollar returns plus the terminal value of the asset equal to the current market price of the asset. If the asset is a security held to maturity, IRR is called yield to maturity. The internal rate of return varies inversely with the current market price of the asset. 26, 51, 125

International monetary system, 415

Inventory investment, 27–28

Investment Conversion of money to assets. In economics, the word usually means the acquisition of real assets such as plant and equipment, etc. In finance, the word is often used more broadly to also include the acquisition of financial assets. 22–32

Investment Advisors Act of 1940, 472

Investment banker An individual or firm of individuals (traditionally in partnership form but now increasingly often as corporations) which arranges long-term financial transactions for customers. The traditional transaction is raising capital, which may involve underwriting such sales, but the negotiation of mergers, planning reorganizations, investing pension funds, and financial advising are frequent services. Investment bankers also may bid for securities in open competitive sales, 268–271, 359–361

Investment companies, 84–86, 484

Investment Company Act of 1940, 472

"Invisible hand" (interest), 7

Jackson, W. D., 55n.

Jaffee, D. M., 30, 152

Jen, F. C., 156, 157

Jensen, Michael, 405

Jorgenson, D. W., 25n., 27n.

Joyce, J. M., 28

Junior mortgages, 326

Juster, F. T., 34

Karnosky, D. S., 55n.

Keynes, J. M., 33, 53–54, 240
  discrediting of interest rate theory, 458

Keynesian liquidity preference, 47

Kubarych, R. M., 421n., 426n., 428n., 438

Kuznets, P. W., 28

Leading indicators, stock market, 465

Leads and lags, 457

Leasing, 356

LeRoy, S. F., 54n.

Liability management of commercial banks, 213–214

Life insurance companies, 78–80
  bond investment, 358

Linear equilibrium between risk and expected return, 136–138
  between systematic risk and expected return, 139–140

Liquidity management, 173

Liquidity preference theory, 47
  as explanation of ascending yield curves, 164
  for interest rate forecasting, 119

Listing on NYSE, 388–389

Loanable funds theory, 44–46
  as basis for interest rate forecasting, 119

Lorie, James, 402

Lovell, M. C., 28n.

"Lumpy" (consumer) expenditures, 32

M_1, M_2, M_3 Definitions of money supply of increasing comprehension:
  M_1 Demand deposits and currency owned by nonbanks.
  M_2 M_1+ commercial bank time deposits less large NCDs.
  M_3 M_2+ deposits of other savings intermediaries.
  stock market influence, 403
  as targets, 244, 252–253

McCulloch, J. H., 158
Margin buying of securities, 390, 474
Market area, 481
Market portfolio All risky securities
that actually exist in the market
and in proportions that actually
exist. An individual holds the
market portfolio when the
percentage composition of his
portfolio is identical to the
percentage composition of all
risky securities in the market. In
security pricing theory, the market
portfolio is the optimum portfolio
of risky securities for all investors.
139
Markowitz, H. M., 124
Martin, William McChesney, 241
Matrix, flow of funds, 98
asset-liability, 104 – 108
for 1978, 100 – 103
Maturity The data when repayment
of the principal of a debt
instrument is due; also refers to
the span of time between issue or
purchase and ultimate maturity.
Original maturity is the period of
time between the issuing date and
the maturity date. Term or period
to maturity is the period of time
remaining before an instrument
matures. Maturities can range
from as short as one day to as long
as several decades, depending on
the type of instrument.
Meltzer, A. H., 30
Miller, M. H., 405
Modigliani, Franco, 405
Monetary identities, 45
Monetary policy, 15
day-to-day execution, 249 – 252
goals, 239 – 242
Money Broadly defined, money is
any liquid store of value. Narrowly
defined, money is a medium of
exchange (or means of payment).
Financial assets which satisfy both
definitions include currency and
demand deposits. Instruments
traded in the so-called money

markets, while highly liquid, do
not satisfy the medium of
exchange definition of money. 3
cyclical pattern, 457 – 460
(*See also* M_1, M_2, and M_3)
Money-market certificates (MMC), 221
market for, 225 – 227
Money-market mutual funds, 85
Money markets Financial markets
where credit instruments, with
maturities of less than one year,
are traded. The principal money
market instruments are Treasury
bills, securities of U.S.
Government agencies, repurchase
agreements, federal funds,
commercial paper, negotiable
certificates of deposit,
Eurodollars, and bankers'
acceptances.
Money-rate risk Possibility that an
investor will realize a lower yield
than indicated when a credit
instrument was purchased due to
interest rate changes. An investor
may receive a smaller return from
a sale of a credit instrument before
final maturity in the secondary
markets than he had originally
expected, even if the borrower
pays exactly as he promised.
Money supply, 15, 234 – 235
Moore, B. J., 65n.
Moore, Geoffrey, 404
Morgan Guaranty Trust Co., 426
Mortgage banking, 336
Mortgage debt distribution, 320
Mortgage insurance, 337 – 338
Mortgage market disequilibrium, 29
Mortgage pools, 329 – 334
Mortgages:
in commercial banks, 217
flexible, 343
graduated, 343
reverse, 343
variable interest, 342
Multibank holding companies, 483
Multiple expansion (of deposits)
Process by which the
commercial banking system is

able to expand its loans, securities, and deposits by a multiple of any increase in reserves supplied to it by the central bank. The process of multiple expansion is based on the fractional reserve system. Since the commercial banking system is required to keep only a fraction of its deposits in the form of reserves, the corollary is that deposits will be a multiple of reserves.

Municipal bonds, 158–160
   (*See also* State and local government securities)
Murray, Roger, 155*n.*
Mutual funds, regulation of, 484
Mutual savings banks, 74–75

NASD   National Association of Security Dealers. Includes most investment bankers and other security houses active in the OTC market. 473
NASDAQ   NASD automated quotation system; the computerized system of quotation of OTC securities (and also selected listed securities) sponsored by the NASD. 474
National debt, 194
National Market (stocks), 395–397
NBER   National Bureau of Economic Research, 151, 403, 411
NCD   Negotiable certificate of deposit, 88, 220, 230
Nelson, C. R., 408
Neoclassical loanable funds theory, 44
Neo-Keynesianism (*see* Keynes, J.M.)
Net present value, 26
New issue yields corporate bonds versus secondary market yields, 362–364
NIC   Net interest cost. A nonactuarial and therefore crude method of calculating interest cost associated with a state and local government securities bid to purchase. In contrast to "true" or actuarial

interest cost. 311
   (*See also* **TIC**)
Niebuhr, W. D., 158
Nielson, N. C., 410
Nominal interest rate, 52
NOW accounts, 75, 88–89
NYSE   New York Stock Exchange, 369, 370, 374–376, 472, 485

Odd-lot transaction in stocks, 377, 474
   theory of market timing, 404
One-bank holding companies, 484
OPEC   Organization of Petroleum Exporting Countries, 427, 442
   as buyers of U.S. Treasury securities, 287–288
Open-end mutual funds, 84, 373
Open markets   A market open to all qualified participants. The number of buyers and sellers is large enough that prices are determined impersonally by the forces of supply and demand. The open market involves audible and/or visible price quotations so that uniform securities tend to be traded at uniform prices. Open-market prices and rates are quoted daily in the financial press. 8
Operational efficiency, 487
Optimum combination of risk and expected return, 134–136
Option trading, 382
Organized exchanges, 369, 374–376, 386–391
Ostas, J. R., 31
OTC   "Over-the-counter" market for securities which is really over the telephone or teletype. 370, 376–377, 395, 397
Ownership of corporate equities, 372–373

Par value   The stated or face value of a security; usually also the final principal payment of a debt instrument at maturity. It differs from market value as the market rate of interest differs from the coupon rate of interest. Bonds sell below par (at a discount) when the market rate is above the coupon rate, and they sell above par (at a premium) when the market rate is below the coupon rate. Variations of market value from par value are larger the longer the period to maturity. As a bond approaches maturity, market value approaches par value.

Present value   Current worth of future returns computed by discounting future returns at an appropriate rate of interest. A dollar today is worth more than a dollar in the future; the present value of a dollar in the future is therefore less than a full dollar. The more distant the future return, and the higher the appropriate rate of discount, the less the present value of the return. 57

Primary markets   Financial markets in which financial assets and liabilities are created; also called "new issue" markets. A primary market is a market for newly issued securities as opposed to a secondary market which is a market for securities already outstanding. When a corporation goes into debt by issuing bonds it sells them in the primary market. Primary markets, or new-issue markets, add to the flow of saving and investment. 11

Prime loan rate   The rate publicly announced or "posted" by a bank as the one charged to its best customers for short-term credit. 215–216

Real assets   The stocks of houses, factories, machines, inventories, etc., which exist at a point in time and which yield real productive services over time. Real assets constitute the wealth of society.

Real income   Nominal income, or income in current monetary terms, deflated by a measure of price change such as a consumer price index. 35

Real interest rates The nominal interest rate prevailing in the market less an adjustment for inflationary expectations. 52

Real investment The acquisition of real assets over a period of time. Real investment includes expenditures for housing, plant and equipment, inventories, and human capital. These expenditures do not take place in financial markets but are often financed with funds secured from financial markets.

Rediscount A further discounting of a credit obligation that has already been discounted one or more times. Its most common usage referred to transactions in which a Federal Reserve bank rediscounted a loan that had already been discounted by a member bank. Such transactions have become uncommon but the term is still used (loosely) to refer to member bank borrowings from a Federal Reserve bank.

Refunding, U.S. debt, 186

Regulation:
  ad hoc origins, 471
  aid to competition? 477−483
  of financial intermediaries, 70
  of investment, 70
  self-regulation, 392−393
  of stock market, 384−394

Regulation Q, 221, 229, 472, 475

REIT Real estate investment trust, 85, 335

Repurchase agreements ("Repos" or RPs), 203

Research, stock market, 401

Reserve currency, 423

Reserve requirements, 238−239

Residential construction, 28−31

"Rest of the World" Used in flow-of-funds accounting to lump into one sector all financial sectors outside continental United States. "Rest of the World" embraces more than just "other nations" since it also includes international financial institutions such as the IMF and the World Bank.

Retail banking Transactions with customers of smaller means: small checking accounts, consumer credit, the holding of savings deposits, or the sale of certificates of deposit in small amounts to individuals.

Revaluation An increase in the command of a currency either on gold or, more recently, on SDRs.

Revenue bonds, 312−313

Reverse mortgages, 343

Risk The possibility of an adverse outcome to an event. Its application in this text is mainly adverse outcomes to investment activities.
  in capital markets, 273−274
  caused by inflation, 488
  credit, 262, 277
  of default, 149−155
  linear relationship to expected return, 136−138
  money rate, 277
  price of, 406
  relation to expected return, 126−128
  versus return, 71
  systematic and unsystematic, 138

Risk aversion Attitude that most investors have toward risk, which is: less risk is preferred to more risk, all other things being the same. A risk-averse investor will assume more risk only if other things are not the same, such as if he expects to earn a sufficiently higher rate of return on his investment.

Risk-free rate of return The IRR of a security having what is believed to be a certain or invariate outcome. The best example of a risk-free rate of return is the yield on short-term Treasury securities such as Treasury bills.

Risk premium The difference between the rate of return on a risky security and the risk-free rate of return. The risk premium is the reward for incurring risk. The greater the risk, the greater the risk premium. 152

Robins, P. K., 31

RP Repurchase agreement. A simultaneous sale of securities together with a contract to repurchase them at a fixed date and at a price which provides an agreed rate of interest. "Reverse" RPs or "matched sale and purchase" agreements are the same type of transaction; the initial seller (usually the "Fed") originates the transaction. 203

Rubenstein, M., 410

Saving, determinants of, 32–36

Savings and loan associations, 75–76

Schaefer, S., 165*n.*

SDRs Supplementary drawing rights, 424

SEC Securities and Exchange Commission, 390, 393–394, 472, 473, 485

Second-stage intermediaries, 86

Secondary market yields, corporate bonds versus new issue yields, 362–364

Secondary markets Those financial markets in which existing financial assets are sold by one owner to another. A secondary market is a market for securities already outstanding as opposed to a primary market which is a market for newly issued securities. Secondary markets are the "used car lots" of the financial world. Their purpose is to enable portfolio adjustments. The best known secondary market is the New York Stock Exchange. 11, 59

corporate bonds, 362

corporate equities, 370–371

economic function, 371

state and local government securities, 314–315

Securities Market Line (*SML*), 139–140

empirical test, 142–144

Security Act of 1933, 354, 472, 473

Security analysis for stock market profits, 405

Security pricing, 123, 136–144

Security valuation with SML, 140–142

Segmented markets theory of term structure of interest rates, 163

Self-regulation, 392–393

Separation theorem, 137

Serial bonds, state and local government, 310

Shapiro, Eli, 405

Sharpe, William, 124, 405

Short position One in which an investor (more often thought of as a speculator) has sold an asset he does not own, has borrowed the asset to make delivery of it, and therefore is obligated to repurchase or otherwise reacquire the asset for ultimate return to the owner from whom he borrowed the asset.

Short-term interest rates, 50

Siebert, C. D., 24, 27*n.*

SIPC Security Investors Protection Corporation, 472

Size of capital markets, 272–273

Smith, Paul F., 65*n.*

SML Security Market Line, 139–140

SOMA System Open Market Account, 249–252

Specialist, 375, 388

Sprinkel, Beryl, 404

State and local government capital expenditures, 300–302

State and local government securities Debt instruments issued by states, cities, school districts, or any of the 70,000 governmental units below the federal level. The distinctive feature of these securities is that their coupon income is exempt from the income taxation of the Federal government and usually of the state in which issued. They are not exempt from capital gains taxation. These securities have sometimes been rather too narrowly described as "municipal" bonds. 218, 304–313

Stock market:
  cyclical pattern, 464–467
  leading indicator (of cycles), 465
Strong, Benjamin, 240
Structure of interest rates, 147
Substitution effect, 35
Supply and demand in money and capital markets, 110–112
Supply of loanable funds, 46
Supply of money, 15
Surplus sectors, 42
"Swaps" of foreign exchange, 438
Syndicate A group of investment bankers organized to share in the risk of selling a security to the public. The leader of a syndicate is its manager; most, but not necessarily all, of the members are involved in the selling effort.
System Open Market Account (SOMA), 185, 249–252
Systematic risk Deviation of realized from expected return on an efficient portfolio due to the tendency for rates of return on individual securities and portfolios to move with the rate of return on the market as a whole. A measure of systematic risk is given by the beta coefficient. Movements in rates of return which cannot be explained by movements in the market as a whole fall into the category of unsystematic risk. 138–140

Target expected return, 12

Target level of risk, 13
Targets used in Federal Reserve policy implementation:
  Fed funds, 244, 252–253
  inconsistency of Fed Funds and M_1 and M_2 targets, 245–246
  M_1 and M_2, 244, 252–253
  monthly choice and revision, 247–249
  numerical specification, 242–249
Tax-exempt securities (*see* State and local government securities)
Tax exemption, influence on investment policies of financial intermediaries, 70
Tax factors in capital markets, 274–275
Tax structure of interest rates, 157–160
Taylor, L. D., 34
10-Ks Detailed corporate annual reports structured by a form required by the SEC. 485
Term bonds, 353
Term loan A loan of intermediate maturity, mainly made by commercial banks and generally to corporate borrowers.
Term to maturity (or period to maturity) The remaining period of time before a debt instrument comes due. A ten-year bond issued four years ago has a remaining period to maturity of six years.
Term structure of interest rates The functional relation between yield to maturity and term to maturity. Graphically this relation is called the yield curve. 160–165
TIC True interest cost. An actuarially accurate method of calculating the interest cost associated with a bid to purchase state and local government securities. Requires an algorithm which depends on computer calculating power. Improvement on former "net interest cost." 311
(*See also* **NIC**)

Time preference, 20
Tobin, James, 34, 137
Trade-weighted dollar (price), 426
Transformation effect, assets and
liabilities, 65–67, 84
Transmutation effect (*see*
Transformation effect)
Treasury debt management, 193
(*See also* U.S. Treasury debt)
Turnover of equities, 381

Ultimate lenders and borrowers, 63
Underwriting   Guarantee of the sale
of a financial obligation. Formal
contracts by investment bankers to
corporations selling securities
provide that the investment
bankers will themselves buy the
securities at the selected date of
issue if they fail to sell them to
others by that time. Informal
underwriting also takes place
when U.S. government security
dealers, by informal
understanding but not by contract,
bid for large enough a volume of
new issues to assure the sale of all
of an issue offered by the Treasury
Department.
U.S. Government securities, foreign
ownership, 441
U.S. Treasury debt:
automation of instruments and
transfer, 292
debt management, 193
futures market in, 292
U.S. Treasury security sales,
284–286
Unintended disinvestment and saving,
36
Unit trusts of state and local
government securities, 307
Unsystematic risk   The tendency for
rates of return on individual
securities and portfolios to move
independently of general price
movements in the market.
Unsystematic risk can be reduced
through diversification. The

market portfolio is a fully
diversified portfolio and therefore
contains no elements of
unsystematic risk. 138, 143, 407
Uses of funds   Real or financial
investment. In accounting terms, a
use of funds is any increase in
assets or any decrease in liabilities
and net worth.

Variable annuities, 80
Veterans Administration guarantee of
mortgages, 337
VRM   Variable rate mortgage, 342

Wealth   The assets of an economic
unit, real and financial, minus its
liabilities. Wealth is synonymous
with net worth. The wealth of the
world consists of real assets only;
financial assets are cancelled out
by an equal amount of liabilities.
Any smaller economic unit,
including a nation, may have a
portion of its wealth in net
holdings of financial assets.
wealth effect, 34
Weber, W. E., 35n.
Wert, J. N., 156, 157
World Bank, 448
Wraparound mortgages, 327
Wright, C., 35n.

Yield   The rate of discount which
makes the present value of the
stream of future dollar returns plus
the terminal value of the asset
equal to the current market price
of the asset. 58–60
(*See also* **Internal Rate of Return**)
Yield curve   Describes graphically
the relationship between yield to
maturity and term to maturity (or
period to maturity). The curve
depicts yields as a function of
maturity for otherwise
homogeneous securities. The

slope and shape of a yield curve change as market conditions and expectations about market conditions change. 160

Yield to maturity   The rate of discount which makes the present value of the stream of future interest payments, plus the return of principal at maturity, equal to the current market price of the debt instrument. It is the internal rate of return (IRR) on a debt instrument held to maturity.

Yohe, W. P., 55n.